NINTH EDITION

SECRETARIAL PROCEDURES AND ADMINISTRATION

Rita Sloan Tilton, Ph.D.
Consultant, Business and Office Education

J. Howard Jackson, Ph.D., CPS
Professor, Department of Management
Virginia Commonwealth University

Estelle L. Popham, Ph.D.
Professor of Business Education Emerita
Hunter College of the City University of New York

Published by

K79 **SOUTH-WESTERN PUBLISHING CO.**

CINCINNATI   WEST CHICAGO, IL   DALLAS   LIVERMORE, CA

Preface

Whether you are using this book to prepare for a secretarial career, to advance to a management position, as a reference in your present job, or to get ready for the Certified Professional Secretary examination, you will be made aware of the secretarial skills and abilities needed to perform at both the operational and managerial levels required in today's office. You will learn that technical literacy is an important competitive edge for the top-level secretary. Your study of *Secretarial Procedures and Administration*, ninth edition, will help you develop an understanding of computer functions, word processing, telecommunications, electronic mail, and a host of other automated devices that allow management to cope with the avalanche of paperwork.

In your operational role as a secretary, you must demonstrate in-depth knowledge of office and secretarial procedures: making appointments, managing records, processing words, handling travel arrangements, coordinating conferences, and directing the flow of information in the organization that employs you. At the managerial level, you will supervise the work of others, make decisions, and provide feedback to your employer on personnel, law, payroll, insurance, and financial matters.

The ninth edition of *Secretarial Procedures and Administration* is designed for use by both the secretarial student and the working secretary. Basic keyboarding skills are assumed. Other skills are presented as if they were new to you. Emphasis is placed on the development and exercise of decision-making ability and human relations skill. Without a pleasant personality and the ability to work with others, it will be difficult for you, no matter how technically qualified, to be successful in business.

A quick look at the Table of Contents will introduce you to the subjects you will cover. Notice that the text is divided into eight parts and 25 chapters. Part One discusses the secretarial profession in general, secretarial responsibilities, the characteristics of a successful secretary, and office environment. Part Two covers document preparation and mail processing. Technological advancements, including data processing, word processing, reprographics, and telecommunications, are discussed in Part Three. Travel, meetings, and large-scale conferences and conventions are the subjects of Part Four. In Part Five you will learn how to research business topics and techniques for preparing business reports. A secretary to an executive may be asked to handle financial and legal documents. These topics are covered in Part Six. Part Seven deals with seeking employment and planning your future in business.

Part Eight is a reference and communications guide. It identifies accepted practices for abbreviating and capitalizing words, writing and using numbers, and dealing with plurals, possessives, and other punctuation. Some basic arithmetic is also reviewed. You will use the Reference Guide throughout your study of this book.

At the end of each chapter is a list of carefully selected suggested readings. You will find many uses for these lists. Each chapter also has discussion questions and special problems which will allow you to apply what you read.

Several case problems, close adaptations of actual office situations, are included at the end of each part. These cases bring realism to this course. As you solve these cases, try to develop a set of principles you can use to cope with similar situations you may encounter on the job.

The authors and the publisher wish to thank the educators who reviewed many chapters of the first-draft manuscript and contributed their expertise in the development of this text: Dr. Carol Henson, Clayton Junior College, Morrow, Georgia, and Dr. Patsy Nichols, Murray State University, Murray, Kentucky, in particular. We also want to give special thanks to Dr. Sue Rigby, Northern Michigan University, for writing Chapters 4, 5, 6, and 8 of this text.

The authors hope that this textbook will help you adopt high standards of performance. We hope, too, that you will experience some of the excitement that can be found in the business office by those who are prepared to perform competently and who bring with them a zest for learning new things. We believe, too, that you are entering a field that has great potential for career-minded individuals. We sincerely wish you a happy and prosperous secretarial career.

Rita Sloan Tilton
J. Howard Jackson
Estelle L. Popham

iv

Contents

Chapter 1

The Role of the Secretary

In this age of automation in which office equipment and procedures are changing dramatically, the secretarial position continues to provide employment and promotional opportunities for entry-level and experienced secretaries. In 1982 the Department of Labor estimated a 2.4 million secretarial work force. By 1995 that figure should be 3.1 million, a 29 percent increase.[1] Although secretarial work has no gender, women continue to dominate this area of office employment (still approximately 99 percent female.)[2] While it is believed that automation has the potential for increasing the number of male secretaries, thus far it has had little or no effect on male employment. Women continue to gravitate toward the secretarial profession, and, as in the past, few men choose to do so. The attractiveness of the secretarial position for women is especially noteworthy in view of the increased opportunities for them in other fields once open exclusively to men.

Of general interest is the increasing number of women entering and remaining in the labor market. In 1984 the United States Census Bureau reported that women represented 44 percent of the total labor force or 54 percent of the total female adult population. Projections are that in the 1990s 63 percent of the total female adult population will be on the job.

The demand for secretaries exceeds supply in every geographical area and in every type of business, government, or philanthropic organization. Even in times of economic recession, secretarial positions are available and go begging. In fact, it is currently estimated that approximately 20 percent of all secretarial openings are not filled.[3] It is no surprise, then, that secretarial salaries are on the rise. All these facts

---

[1]U.S. Department of Labor, Bureau of Labor Statistics, "The Job Outlook in Brief," *Occupational Outlook Quarterly*, (Washington: U.S. Government Printing Office, Spring, 1984), p. 18.

[2]"Secretary Facts 80s," *The Secretary* (October, 1983), p. 17.

[3]Thomas B. Duff and Patricia A. Merrier, "Secretaries: Caught in the Past?," *Management World* (October, 1984), p. 10.

lead to the conclusion that the secretarial field continues to be a stable and good source of employment.

This chapter presents various definitions of the secretarial position and discusses secretarial responsibilities, job opportunities, salaries, the effect of automation, and the personal characteristics of the successful secretary. It serves as an introduction to the secretarial profession and sets the stage for your study of *the* profession for this decade.

DEFINITION OF A SECRETARY

In this text, the words *employer, principal, manager,* and *executive* will be used interchangeably to denote the individual to whom the secretary reports.

The secretarial classification is perhaps one of the least understood in office occupations. Many employers are unclear as to what a professional secretary is expected to do on the job; thus employers tend to use the title *secretary* generally to describe clerical positions. To attract applicants, an employer will advertise for a secretary when a study of the position's requirements indicates that the position is actually of a clerical nature.

The individual performing secretarial responsibilities in today's office may have any of the following titles: secretary, administrative secretary, administrative assistant, executive secretary, or private secretary. The most popular title is *secretary*.

One common definition of *secretary* is that adopted by Professional Secretaries International (PSI), an organization representing more than 42,000 secretaries in the United States and other countries:

> A *secretary* shall be defined as an executive assistant who possesses a mastery of office skills, demonstrates the ability to assume responsibility without direction or supervision, exercises initiative and judgment, and makes decisions within the scope of assigned authority.

According to this definition, a secretary is a highly qualified person who has not only mastered office skills but possesses personality requisites of the highest order. A secretary must know the scope of his or her authority and discharge the responsibilities within that sphere. The secretary must judge correctly when to follow through alone and when to consult the employer about how to handle a job. Here is a person capable of making many decisions, of composing routine correspondence independently, and, perhaps, of supervising other office workers and keeping their personnel records.

The person who fits the PSI definition is frequently secretary to a chief executive officer (CEO) or to a managing official in a large organization. This secretary is often referred to as an *executive secretary* or an *administrative assistant* (see Illus. 1-1).

The executive secretary enjoys informal rank within the company according to the formal rank of the executive. The executive secretary has access to privileged information and knowledge of official power in an organization; thus, the executive secretary occupies a unique position of influence and power in the office.

Illus. 1-1
An executive secretary performs duties of a highly confidential nature requiring initiative, judgment, and knowledge of company practice.

The Administrative Management Society classifies secretaries into three categories (Secretary B, Secretary A, and Executive Secretary/Administrative Assistant). These classifications are defined here.

Secretary—Level B

Performs a limited range of secretarial duties in a small company or for a supervisor in a larger firm. May take dictation and transcribe from notes or dictating equipment with speed and accuracy. Screens calls, makes appointments, handles travel arrangements, answers routine correspondence, and maintains filing systems.

Secretary—Level A

Peforms an unlimited range of secretarial duties for middle management personnel or more than one individual. Composes and/or takes and transcribes correspondence of a complex and confidential nature. Position requires a knowledge of company policy, procedure, and above-average secretarial and administrative skills.

Executive Secretary/Administrative Assistant

Performs a full range of secretarial and administrative duties for a high-level member of executive staff. Handles project-oriented duties and may be held accountable for the timely completion of these tasks. Relieves executive of routine administrative detail. Position requires an in-depth knowledge of company practice, structure, and a high degree of secretarial/administrative skillls.

These groupings are of special interest because they were adopted by people who usually administer salaries and supervise job evaluations. Obviously they are advantageous to secretaries in clarifying job functions.[4]

It is likely that in a first secretarial position an employee will be classified as a Secretary B. With experience and knowledge, the employee should eventually rise to the Secretary A level and ultimately to Executive Secretary/Administrative Assistant. It is also possible that as the secretary gains experience, a shift may be made to a supervisory level.

THE SCOPE OF SECRETARIAL WORK

The specific responsibilities of the secretary will depend on at least three factors: the experience level of the secretary, the nature of the employer's work, and the electronic equipment available. There are, however, certain basic functions inherent to the secretarial position. They are

> Typing/keyboarding
> Transcribing (from shorthand or machine dictation)
> Processing mail
> Telephoning
> Scheduling appointments
> Greeting visitors
> Composing and editing
> Research and abstracting information

---

[4]*1985-86 Office Salaries Directory* (Willow Grove, PA: Administrative Management Society, 1985).

Organizing time and work
Maintaining special records
Completing various administrative duties
Coordinating meetings
Making travel arrangements
Selecting appropriate copying/duplicating methods
Exercising effective human relations

The secretary performing all these functions operates in the established or traditional role and will be referred to as a *multifunctional secretary*. The multifunctional secretary may work in any of a number of environments. A physician or owner of a small business may have only one secretary on the staff. The office may be a small one, and the secretary may have access to limited equipment. Or the secretary may hold a position in a large corporation with a variety of electronic equipment and sophisticated organizational patterns. In this situation, the higher the secretarial level, the greater the number of functions to be performed.

THE EFFECT OF OFFICE AUTOMATION ON THE SECRETARY

The secretary, even in the smallest office, will be increasingly involved with office automation. The automated office environment will broaden the scope of office functions performed by the secretary and provide more options for career opportunities. Every secretary, therefore, needs to be familiar with the concept and the technology of office automation.

In a broad sense, *office automation* is concerned with the accomplishment of office functions through the application of technology to the processing and communicating of information. Today, office automation provides the basis for the *integrated office* (also called the office of the future). In the integrated office, previously separate office functions (dictating, typing or keyboarding, storing and retrieving information, communicating, and distributing information) are interdependent functions. More will be said about the integrated electronic office later in this text.

Word Processing

Although words have been processed ever since man put chisel to stone, the term *word processing* has been adopted to describe a new method of improving the efficiency of business communication. With the introduction of IBM's (International Business Machines Corporation) Magnetic Tape Selectric Typewriter (MT/ST), automation entered the secretarial work place. This breakthrough made possible the mechanization of much of the secretary's production of typed material. Since this new equipment was too expensive to place at every secretary's desk, a new organizational pattern was introduced to maximize its use. Secretarial functions were reorganized and were divided into two parts—typing activities and nontyping activities.

One group of employees, identified as *word processing specialists* or *word processing operators*, was trained to operate the expensive equipment. This group was located in a central *word processing center*. The center was responsible for most, if not all, of the typing activities formerly accomplished by individual secretaries. Nontyping secretarial activities were performed by *administrative secretaries*. These secretaries were clustered in a central location and served several employers.

Many large companies found it advantageous to decentralize the word processing function by dispersing the clusters of secretaries and placing them near or in the departments they served. The advantages of departmental centers are that (1) operators can master the specialized vocabularies of the departments involved; (2) there is better communication between the originator of a document and the transcriber; and (3) the operator has a stronger sense of identity with the originator and, as a result, a more personal relationship.

Many large corporations continue to use the word processing center/administrative support organizational pattern. For this reason, this system is described in detail in the next section.

The Word Processing Center/Administrative Support System

Word processing centers are organized according to a company's needs. One large center may serve all departments, or there may be a center for each heavy volume department or a center for several related departments. The flowchart in Illus. 1-2 shows one possible organizational pattern. It shows the interrelationships of the word processing center and the secretary in an administrative support center. In this plan the administrative secretary gets materials ready for dictation and the principal (originator) dictates. The administrative secretary may

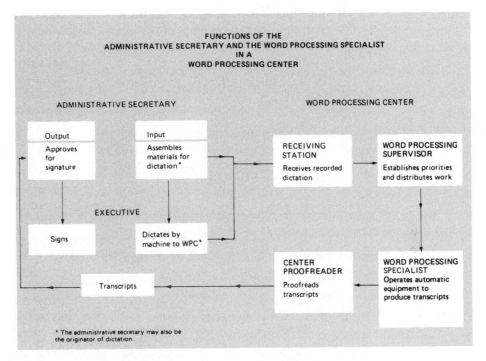

Illus. 1-2 Interrelationships of the word processing center and the administrative secretary.

dictate the material if it is routine. In this word processing unit there are four components:

1. The receiving station, which logs in the received dictation
2. The word processing supervisor, who decides the order in which work is to be done and assigns the work to individual specialists
3. The word processing specialist, who operates the equipment
4. The center proofreader, who proofreads the transcripts

The approved transcripts are then sent back to the administrative secretary, who attaches the necessary enclosures and approves the document for signing. The principal signs and the administrative secretary distributes the output.

Group needs determine the number of administrative secretaries in a center; for example, six administrative secretaries may serve as many as twenty principals. Administrative secretaries may have general functions for all other-than-typewriting tasks, or they may be assigned special functions in which they excel. For instance, an administrative secretary may handle all records management or travel arrangements or library research for all the principals served by a unit. Although in theory the administrative secretary performs only nontyping functions, many administrative secretaries have access to typewriters for small typing jobs.

Word Processing/Administrative Support Job Titles

From the inception of word processing/administrative support centers, a number of job titles have emerged, particularly in the word processing center category. Illus. 1-3 provides a list of typical job titles and brief job descriptions.

WORD PROCESSING/ADMINISTRATIVE SUPPORT JOB DESCRIPTIONS

Word Processing

Title	Description
Manager	Overall responsibility for word processing center; budgets, reports, forecasts.
Supervisor	Schedules and coordinates work, institutes work measurements, analyzes production.
Proofreader	Proofreads all work; may be responsible for training programs.
Senior Specialist	Acts as assistant word processing supervisor; knowledgeable in all equipment.
Specialist	Experienced operator; capable of revising and formatting complicated documents including lengthy, technical, and statistical work.
Trainee	Entry-level position.

Administrative Support

Title	Description
Manager	Responsible for all services in the administrative support area.
Supervisor	Schedules and administers work flow; responsible for staffing requirements, budgets, etc.
Senior Adm. Secretary	Acts as assistant to supervisor, composes documents for principals (employers), researches information; other semiprofessional duties vary.
Administrative Secretary	Works for a number of principals under the direction of a supervisor; duties vary.

Illus. 1-3
Typical job titles and brief job descriptions for word processing and administrative support personnel.

Source: Adapted from "Job Descriptions," *Words* (February-March, 1986), pp. 37-39. Copyright 1986 AISP; reprinted with permission from the Association of Information Systems Professionals, 1015 N. York Road, Willow Grove, PA 19090; (215) 657-6300.

As Illus. 1-3 indicates, there is a career ladder for word processing and administrative support personnel. The various positions represent promotions and salary increases for those persons working in a word processing center environment. Since the administrative secretary works with several principals and can demonstrate special capabilities that attract more management attention than a secretary to only one person can hope for, opportunities for promotion may be enhanced.

Personal Computers and Microcomputers

The presence of *personal computers* (also called *microcomputers*, see page 243) in the office has accelerated the decentralization of word processing. As the number of personal computers able to handle word processing applications increases, the centralized word processing center in many organizations will disappear or get smaller. Departments that could not justify expensive word processing systems can now justify a personal computer for their word processing needs.

Employers as well as secretaries are taking advantage of the capabilities of the personal computer to handle their word processing work load. Employers (managers and other professionals) who have personal computers are beginning to create text in first-draft form. Their secretaries, therefore, have more time to do other tasks. As secretaries become proficient in the use of personal computers and begin to develop applications for their use, the secretarial role will change from a predominately clerical function to a problem-solving and an information-analysis function.

In summary, personal computers offer employers the opportunity to do some of their own word processing, resulting in better turn-around for documents that are finalized by the secretary or in the word processing center. Personal computers have also given multifunctional secretaries a tool that enables them to build valuable skills, enhance their careers, and become more valuable to their employers and the company. In many cases, the secretary's access to and use of personal computers has, in fact, reinforced the secretary/employer team concept.

The Electronic Workstation

Many secretaries that now have word processing equipment or a personal computer at their desks will eventually work at electronic workstations. An *electronic workstation* (a work area with a video display terminal connected to a computer, a printer, and other electronic equipment) has the capabilities of filing and retrieving information, performing financial analysis, handling correspondence, scheduling, preparing graphics, taking/sending electronic messages, and, perhaps, accessing vital company information. With the electronic workstation, many important office functions can be accomplished at one location on a single piece of equipment. Also, electronic workstations are expected to provide benefits to both employers and secretaries in the areas of work organization, time management, and information management.

The Secretary's Attitude Toward Automation

The secretary is not intimidated by automation because most secretaries are equipment-oriented. They believe that automated equipment will make them more productive and efficient. In addition, automation frees the secretary to assume more administrative responsibilities.

In a survey conducted by Minolta in cooperation with Professional Secretaries International (PSI),[5] close to 90 percent of the secretaries surveyed stated that automation has had a positive effect on the secretarial position, and 99 percent do not perceive automation as a threat to their employment. Instead, participating secretaries strongly believed that automation would open up new career opportunities.

The secretary on the job and the secretary entering office employment must, of necessity, be experienced in using word processing equipment and have a background in computer operations and capabilities. It is estimated that in a few short years every office worker will be using electronic equipment. Computer literacy will, therefore, be a built-in requirement for most "knowledge workers," an office group which includes secretaries.

JOB SATISFACTION OF SECRETARIES

At a time when technological advancements in the office are changing the way in which secretaries perform their responsibilities, it is well to consider whether secretaries are satisfied with their jobs. The

---

[5]"The Evolving Role of the Secretary in the Information Age," *The Secretary* (April, 1983), pp. 6-17.

Minolta survey mentioned earlier asked secretaries about job satisfaction. An overwhelming majority (87 percent) indicated that they were satisfied with their positions overall. This outcome certainly speaks well for the secretarial position. Factors included in the job satisfaction analysis were nature and variety of the work itself, level of responsibility, opportunity for advancement, working conditions, and salary and benefits. Two of these factors, nature of the work and salary, are discussed here. The other factors are covered in later chapters.

Nature of the Work

The Minolta survey indicated that variety of work is very important to the multifunctional secretary. Secretaries rated receiving visitors, preparing correspondence, arranging meetings, and scheduling appointments very high on their list of favorite tasks. As for tasks disliked, photocopying and filing were mentioned. One can only speculate as to the reasons why: Both photocopying and filing take the secretary away from the desk and can, therefore, be a source of interruption. Also, filing has always been perceived as secretarial drudgery; however, with the use of automated equipment for storage and retrieval of information, this particular secretarial responsibility should begin to be viewed differently.

Secretarial Salaries

Salary is one very important aspect of job satisfaction. In recent years there has been a shortage of qualified secretaries entering the labor force. This shortage has been compounded by business expansions in certain industries and in certain geographical areas. Highly qualified secretaries are in great demand throughout the country. The help wanted section of any Sunday newspaper confirms this shortage. The Department of Labor projects that there will be an average of 55,000 new secretarial jobs each year until 1995. This figure does not include natural replacement needs such as those created by resignations and/or retirements.[6] Facing this kind of job market, secretarial salaries will continue to rise.

The Administrative Management Society's *1985-86 Office Salaries Directory* indicates that the median salary for the beginning secretary (Level B) is approximately $14,700, while the median salary for the

---

[6]"BLS Projects 29 Percent Increase in Secretarial Jobs by 1995," *The Secretary* (August/September, 1984), page 8.

executive secretary is over $19,000. The Bureau of Labor Statistics 1985 salary survey reported the range of average salaries of five secretarial levels to be $15,870 (Level 1) to $26,210 (Level 5).[7] In addition to needed qualifications, the job requirements, and the employer's position, several other factors play a role in determining secretarial salaries: region of the country, size of the company, and type of business.

In this age of mechanization it may come as a surprise to learn that personnel managers continue to value shorthand skill. In a recent survey of help wanted advertisements for secretaries, 17 percent required shorthand or fast note-taking skills. One estimate by a placement agency valued employees with shorthand skill at approximately $1,800 more a year.

It is estimated that secretaries holding the Certified Professional Secretary (CPS) rating (see Chapter 24), earn an additional $2,250 a year. Secretaries with experience on word processing equipment command $2,000 to $3,000 more per year, according to one placement counselor at a prominent New York secretarial school.

In summarizing the employment outlook for secretaries, it is clear that the demand for qualified secretaries is great and is expected to continue in the foreseeable future. The yearly salary surveys conducted by the Administrative Management Society and by Professional Secretaries International indicate that average secretarial salaries are rising steadily—a most-welcomed trend.

PERSONAL SECRETARIAL CHARACTERISTICS

Displaying a positive attitude fosters a healthy work climate (Illus. 1-4). Working in harmony with others requires diligent application of the three C's of effective human relations: courtesy, cooperation, and cheerfulness.

A good secretary is a staff assistant and the executive's office memory. As a public relations expert, the secretary must represent the company and the employer effectively to the public. Of equal importance is the ability to work cooperatively with all employees inside the

---

[7]"1986 Newspaper Help Wanted Ad Survey," *The Secretary* (January, 1986), page 8.

organization: with executives on a high level, with co-workers on the same level, and with those to be supervised. Strangely enough, research tells us that human relations problems occur infrequently between workers of higher and lower levels. Rather, most personality problems occur in contacts with employees at the same level, in this case, with other secretaries.

The enormous problem of ethics in business is attracting a great deal of attention, so much so that PSI has adopted a secretary's code of ethics. This code, described in Chapter 24, is available for class use in solving some of the problems the secretary encounters in relations with employers and peers. A secretary's code of ethics can serve as a guide to behavior on the job. In addition, a person's good judgment should suggest the importance of loyalty to the employer, respect for the employer's materials and property, and adherence to company policies and rules.

Illus. 1-4
Working in
harmony with
others requires
courtesy,
cooperation, and
cheerfulness.

Review the self-evaluation in Illus. 1-5. It can form a basis for determining your set of professional ethics.

THE PROFESSIONAL SECRETARY

A Self-Evaluation

The secretary's behavior in an office sets the stage for the employer-secretary relationship.

	Yes	No
When I work, I work.	____	____
I dress appropriately for the office.	____	____
I address my employer or employers in a formal manner.	____	____
I leave my personal life at home.	____	____
I respect my employer.	____	____
I am punctual.	____	____
I mind my own business.	____	____
I execute my duties with dispatch and with accuracy.	____	____
I keep confidential work confidential.	____	____
I do not contribute or listen to office gossip about my employer.	____	____
I owe allegiance to the company first, then to my immediate employer (if in controversy).	____	____
I recognize that materials and equipment with which I work belong to my employer.	____	____
I criticize in private and compliment publicly.	____	____
I continue to educate myself to enhance my value to my employer.	____	____
I am committed to create and encourage a pleasant working atmosphere.	____	____
I recognize that my position is a supportive one.	____	____
I attempt to maintain good health to better execute my duties.	____	____
I am dependable.	____	____
I adhere to company policy.	____	____
I display a positive attitude toward my work.	____	____
I have confidence in my dealings with peers, management, and clients.	____	____
I accept and handle responsibility without supervision.	____	____

Illus. 1-5
Can you answer
yes to each of these
statements?

Because secretaries work closely with management and aspire to be a part of the management team, they should look and act like management. They should take pride in their profession and work toward a positive self-image. Proper business attire is expected. As professionals, secretaries must also speak, behave, and think in those terms. Study the qualities of an ideal secretary on page 17. Many employers expect these characteristics in their secretaries.

QUALITIES OF AN IDEAL SECRETARY

Accurate, alert
Neat, nicely groomed

Industrious, intelligent, interested in job
Dependable, diligent
Efficient, exercises poise
Ambitious, agreeable
Loyal, logical

Sincere, systematic
Enthusiastic
Cheerful, courteous, cooperative, confident
Reliable, resourceful
Eager to please, exercises good judgment
Tactful, thorough, trustworthy, truthful
Attentive, adaptable
Responsible, refined
Your attitude (thoughtfulness and helpfulness toward others)

Anonymous

Most college students try to conform to the standards of dress and hairstyling that will win the acceptance of their peers. When they move into a new environment, that of the office, they must try equally hard to meet new standards—those of business.

Some employees, especially at the entry level, do not realize that good grooming and appropriate business dress are important to their business success. Observing the appearance of secretaries to the executives in an office will provide insights on what is considered proper business attire for that office.

Two excellent references on business attire are John Molloy's *The Woman's Dress for Success Book* and *Dress for Success*. Suits, coordinated jackets and skirts, and jacketed dresses are recommended for women; for men, the traditional business suit or, perhaps, a sport coat and slack combination. Certain colors project the proper business look: navy blue, tones of gray, tan, beige, taupe, and burgundy. When selecting business outfits, buy quality. Choose clothing for its durability and dependability. Resist fads. Use your working attire to reflect your good taste and a positive image of yourself and your employer.

Good grooming requires efficient scheduling of grooming activities and clean, pressed garments. If you are overweight, you may have to consider body training exercises, jogging, tennis, and/or calorie counting.

Equally important are good posture and good health habits. The secretary to an executive must be in top physical condition. As pressures on the executive increase, so do they on the secretary. To meet capably all the demands of the day, the secretary must begin the day well rested and well nourished.

College students usually take a speech course—but not very seriously! Yet the personnel officer in charge of work assignments for 20 college students who were on an internship program between their junior and senior years reported that the one universal complaint of the executives with whom the students worked was *speech*. Students should analyze their speech patterns and, with faculty help, embark on a speech improvement campaign.

ADVANTAGES OF THE COLLEGE-TRAINED SECRETARY

Most of you reading this chapter have made the secretarial profession your vocational choice, and wisely so. You are obtaining your secretarial training at the college level and are about to embark on your business career. You will bring to your new employer the background of business knowledge studied in your college program. You are well grounded in the functional areas of business—accounting, marketing, management, and so forth. At the end of your college study, you will be well qualified to act as a partner in the employer/secretary team. As a multifunctional secretary, you will be part of the management team and will associate with executives at the exciting core of the company's activities. Often you may find yourself as a decision maker, perhaps in a position to recommend change in procedures and/or equipment.

A Manager of Change

You undoubtedly have heard the adage, nothing is more certain than change. Accept that challenge. Because of the rapid expansion of office technology, secretaries can expect to work in an ever-changing automated office. Many offices operate through shared technology and technical service centers. In later chapters of this book you will see interrelationships among such office activities as data processing, word processing, reprographics (reproduction of copies), telecommunications (electronic communicating), and records storage and retrieval.

How changes affect the office you join is difficult to say. Changes do not happen overnight. Generally, when changes in the office are implemented, office employees do not meet them gracefully. You, as a college-educated secretary, have the advantage of a strong background in office technology; thus, you have the flexibility to assume different office functions.[8] In addition, you should be in a position to make recommendations whereby you and your office *work smarter, not harder*. You certainly must welcome the challenges that increase office efficiency.

Promotion Possibilities

For the qualified, ambitious secretary, a secretarial position is not a dead-end job, as some would have us believe. It can be a stepping-stone to another career. Ask any successful secretary what characteristics lead to success in the profession, and you will find that working hard, assuming responsibility, continuing education, and learning every aspect of every position held are high on the list. Further, if the secretarial shortage continues, those who do enter the field will have a decided advantage in moving into management positions. Since the implementation of affirmative action programs, secretaries, probably more than any other group, have benefited. Many an executive has looked within the firm for possible candidates for promotion. Often the executive's choice has been a secretary whose quality of performance is known. Secretaries who have a college background and/or hold the coveted Certified Professional Secretary designation increase their chances for promotion.

What about promotional opportunities for the word processing specialist and the administrative secretary? The word processing specialist was probably attracted to word processing because of the ability to produce larger volumes of higher quality documents in a given period than the multifunctional secretary. The word processing specialist who demonstrates competency in English and in decision making related to equipment capabilities will probably advance through the job titles within the word processing center as illustrated on page 10.

Administrative secretaries realize that they may have to adjust to the whims of several principals rather than just one. Still, they see their opportunities for promotion increasing in direct proportion to the number of principals served.

---

[8]In a survey conducted by Manpower, Inc., over 53 percent of the secretaries questioned indicated that flexibility and adapting to changing situations were the keys to their success.

TRENDS IN SECRETARIAL WORK

One of the attractive features of the secretarial profession is the relative ease with which one can become employed after years away from the field. In fact, recruitment of former secretaries has become a necessity in some areas of the country. Some former secretaries, anticipating reentry into business, enroll in a college course to learn new office technology and to revitalize their knowledge and skills. Those of you in this situation will find this text valuable in bringing you up to date on office technology and procedures.

Some employers are willing to adjust workday hours to accommodate secretaries with small children in school. Some of these employers have adopted a *flexitime work schedule*; i.e., a schedule requiring employees to be on the job during specified "core hours," but providing employees flexibility in their arrival and departure times. The flexitime work schedule is approved by the employer and must total the number of hours in the company workweek. Permanent part-time work and job sharing are also possibilities. With job sharing, two people work at the same position, but at different times or on different shifts.

In some industries *telecommuting* offers employees an alternative to being physically present in the office. With this arrangement, automated equipment is installed in the employee's home and linked to computers in a main or branch office of a firm. The employee's workday is spent at home working on the automated equipment. Telecommuting is particularly attractive to secretaries who need to be home during the day, who may not have transportation to the office, or who may be physically disabled.

SUMMARY

This chapter described the role of the secretary in today's office. The Professional Secretaries International's definition of a secretary, the secretarial job classification system, and job descriptions used by the Administrative Management Society all illustrate what secretaries and managers believe the secretarial position includes. Specifically, secretarial work involves a range of responsibilities from typing/keyboarding to exercising effective human relations.

Even in the smallest office, automation is having an effect upon how the secretary performs certain tasks. Word processing equipment, a forerunner of automation, has mechanized typing production. As a result, many large companies have separated the typing and nontyping functions of the secretarial position into a word processing center/

administrative support organizational pattern. This plan offers viable career paths for word processing specialists and administrative secretaries.

The trend today, however, is toward the integrated office. Previously separate office functions, such as dictating, typing, storing, retrieving, communicating, and distributing information, are now interdependent. Rather than being a threat to the secretarial position, technological advancements have had a positive effect upon the profession. Using automated equipment to perform routine tasks gives the secretary more time to devote to more challenging, decision-making duties. A recent survey revealed that an overwhelming majority of secretaries were satisfied with their jobs. As the need for well-qualified secretaries continues to grow, salaries are expected to remain attractive.

A successful secretary works in harmony with others, has pride in the profession, and demonstrates a positive self-image in behavior and appearance. The college-trained secretary has a distinct advantage when entering the field. With a solid background of business coursework, the college-trained secretary has the qualifications to be a partner in the employer/secretary team and can look forward to career advancement.

The secretarial field continues to offer opportunities for employment to secretaries reentering the working world. In addition, employers are offering secretaries alternative work hours or work-at-home arrangements.

The secretary of tomorrow must be flexible. Because of the rapid expansion of office technology, secretaries can expect to work in an ever-changing, automated office. Anyone now in secretarial work or preparing for it must accept change and adjust to it. In fact, the areas where changes are occurring most rapidly may be the areas of greatest opportunity.

SUGGESTED READINGS

Jackson, Carole. *Color Me Beautiful*, Discover Your Natural Beauty through Color. Washington, D.C.: Acropolis Books, Ltd., 1984.

Murphy, Elizabeth R. *The Assistant*, New Tasks, New Opportunities. New York: Amacom, American Management Association, 1982.

Code of Ethics for the Professional Secretary. Kansas City, MO: Professional Secretaries International. (Abbreviated version appears in *The Secretary* (April, 1981), p. 20.

Yerys, Arlene. *The Professional Secretary at Work*, Strategies and Skills for Success. Englewood Cliffs, NJ: Prentice-Hall, Inc., 1984.

PERIODICALS AND SUBSCRIPTION SERVICES

Administrative Management. Monthly. The Automated Office, Ltd., a Dalton Communications Company, 1123 Broadway, New York, NY 10010.

From Nine to Five. Semimonthly. Dartnell Corp., 4660 Ravenswood Ave., Chicago, IL 60640.

Information and Word Processing Report. Semimonthly. Geyer-McAllister Publications, 51 Madison Ave., New York, NY 10010.

Information Management. 10/year. PTN Publishing Corp., 101 Crossways Park West, Woodbury, NY 11797.

Management World. Monthly. Administrative Management Society, 2360 Maryland Rd., Willow Grove, PA 19090.

Modern Office Procedures. Monthly. Industrial Publishing Co., a Division of Pittway Corp., 614 Superior Avenue West, Cleveland, OH 44113.

Office Guide. Semimonthly. Bureau of Business Practice, 24 Rope Ferry Rd., Waterford, CT 06385.

The Office Professional. Monthly. Professional Training Associates, Inc., 1316 Sam Bass Circle, Round Rock, TX 78664.

The Office. Monthly. Office Publications, Inc., 1200 Summer St., Stamford, CT 06904.

Personal Report for the Professional Secretary. Research Institute of America, Inc., 589 Fifth Ave., New York, NY 10017.

The Professional Secretary's Development Program. A monthly self-training course. Bureau of Business Practice, 24 Rope Ferry Rd., Waterford, CT 06385.

The Secretary. 10/year. Professional Secretaries International, 301 East Armour Blvd., Kansas City, MO 64111.

Today's Office. Monthly. Hearst Business Communications, Inc., 645 Stewart Ave., Garden City, NY 11530.

Word Processing and Information Services. Monthly. Geyer-McAllister Publications, 51 Madison Avenue, New York, NY 10010.

Words. Bimonthly. Association of Information Systems Professionals, 1015 North York Rd., Willow Grove, PA 19090.

Working Woman. Monthly. Hal Publications, Inc., 342 Madison Ave., New York, NY 10173.

QUESTIONS FOR DISCUSSION

1. In what ways has this chapter changed your concept of the secretary's role?

2. Do you think that PSI's definition of a secretary is valid? Why or why not?

3. If there appears to be no gender gap in technology, why is it that relatively few men are entering the secretarial field?

4. What are the distinctions between the duties of an administrative secretary, as defined in this chapter, and those of the multifunctional secretary?

5. In this chapter the comment is made that a secretarial position may be a stepping-stone to another career. In what ways do you think this is true? How do you plan to use your secretarial career?

6. Of the number of personal attributes of a successful secretary, which ones would you consider the most important?

7. Why is professional business attire linked with a successful secretary?

8. Often secretaries are asked to run personal errands for the employer, serve refreshments to office visitors, and do other tasks unrelated to the technical skills of the position. What is your opinion about doing these nontechnical tasks?

9. Why would Professional Secretaries International decide to adopt a code of ethics?

10. What advice would you give a secretary to update business knowledge and skills after being out of the work force for the past ten years?

11. In the following sentences select the correct verb to agree with the subject. Check the Reference Guide at the end of this book to correct your work.

    a. Neither the chairman nor the committee members (is, are) present.

    b. The number of votes (was, were) insufficient to elect a president.

    c. Your pair of scissors (is, are) being sharpened; my scissors (needs, need) sharpening, too.

    d. Not only the speaker but also the members of the panel (were, was) late.

    e. No prices or delivery date (was, were) quoted.

    f. Ten pieces of fine jewelry, as well as the ancient bronze statue, (was, were) sold.

PROBLEMS

1. Interview a secretary employed in your community to determine how office automation has changed the way in which secretarial tasks are performed. Mention specifically the secretarial responsi-

bilities listed on pages 6-7 of this text. In your discussion ask if office automation is opening up opportunities for advancement for the secretary. Report results to the class.

2. You are about to begin your secretarial career and are in the process of completing your professional wardrobe. Your budget allows you to purchase five basic outfits. From newspaper advertisements and catalogs, prepare a display board of these outfits. Identify the style, color, and fabrics chosen. Be prepared to defend your choices.

3. From the Sunday edition of your newspaper, cut out the want ads for secretaries. Compile a list of all personal requisites mentioned. How would you evaluate your personal characteristics in light of these requisites?

Chapter 2

The Secretary in the Office Environment

A secretary seeking employment learns quickly that secretarial opportunities exist in all types of businesses, in urban and suburban areas, and in all parts of the country. Some basic decisions regarding career, therefore, must be made. A secretary must decide what particular area of interest to pursue: law; government; medicine; banking; manufacturing; a service industry; or a division of a large corporation, finance or marketing, for example. The size of the office should also be a consideration. The secretary may prefer to work in a one-secretary office or in a company with a large secretarial support team. Environment and office arrangement may enter into the decision as well. Some offices are very modern and colorful while others are conservative in architecture and decoration.

Finding a suitable position—one with advancement and salary potential—is important to every secretary. The reputation of the company in the community in addition to its financial strength should influence the secretary's decision.

After careful consideration of all options, the secretary makes a decision and a secretarial career—let's say your secretarial career—is launched. This chapter classifies your duties, discusses the organization of your work, and investigates the management of your time. It provides guidelines in the event you are assigned to more than one principal. It concludes with suggestions for securing outside assistance for periodic overloads and for supervising other office employees.

UNDERSTANDING THE ORGANIZATIONAL STRUCTURE

As a newly hired secretary, one of the first things you should do is acquaint yourself with the organizational structure of the office. You need to know the chain of command and where your employer fits into the management team. If you join a one-secretary office or a small company, the hierarchy will be readily apparent. If you are in a large company, however, the situation will be quite different. There you must learn the names of persons to whom your employer reports. You must also know the names of those who report to your employer and of those of equal status with your employer. An organizational chart, like the one pictured in Illus. 2-1, can give you this information.

The simplest form of organizational structure is the *line organization*, where authority and responsibility flow vertically from the top executive down. A variation of the line organization, known as *line and staff*, includes individuals in staff positions who serve as advisors or provide services to all line managers. Whatever the structure, the organizational chart is restricted to officers, management, and/or supervisory staff. If an organizational chart is not available, ask your employer questions and research the files to determine the chain of command.

The discussion that follows describes the line organization of a large manufacturing firm, the duties of its officers, and the functions of its major divisions.

Company Officers

The administration of a company usually consists of a president, an executive vice-president, one or more vice-presidents, a secretary, and a treasurer. Each of these officers has a support staff.

President. In most corporations the president is the *chief executive officer* (CEO) who is responsible to the board of directors for the profitable operation of the business. This position is one of liaison between the board of directors, on which the president usually serves, and management personnel. Thus, the president interprets the board's actions to management and management's plans to the board. The office of the president puts board resolutions into effect.

The duties of the president are as varied as the activities of the firm. To many people, the president is a company symbol. What this executive does has a bearing on the reputation of the firm and possibly on the community in general. The leadership ability of the holder of this office often determines the type and caliber of management personnel in the organization.

Executive Vice-President, Vice-Presidents, Secretary, and Treasurer. The executive vice-president (or senior vice-president) is second in command in the organization. This officer serves in place of the president and may be selected to succeed the president. Generally it is the responsibility of the executive vice-president to suggest changes in policy and to coordinate the efforts of the other vice-presidents in carrying out their specific programs and functions. This executive also coordinates the work of various departments.

Often there are one or more vice-presidents. Each is a general officer of the company and, with the president and executive vice-president, is involved in achieving the goals of the firm. Each vice-president is responsible for a special phase of administration, such as production or marketing, and strives to reach the objectives set for that division.

The secretary of the company, often an attorney, is responsible for the legal actions of the business. Typical activities of this office include scheduling stockholders' meetings, drafting resolutions, recording the proceedings of meetings, executing proxies or powers of attorney, and preparing contracts.

The treasurer known in some organizations as the vice-president of finance, directs all monetary, budget, and accounting activities.

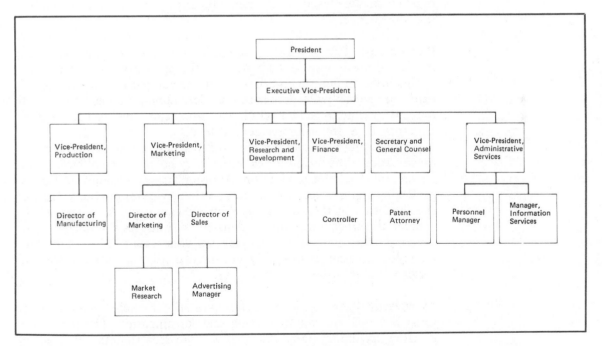

Illus. 2-1
The organizational chart for the company described on these pages might look like this. Positions will, of course, vary among companies. This chart clearly identifies the levels of administrative authority in a line structure. Note that secretarial support positions are not included on this chart.

Divisions of a Company

A large company is usually organized into departments or divisions. The functions and titles of these divisions vary depending on the type of business in which the company is engaged. For example, a manufacturing firm may have such operational divisions as production, purchasing, marketing, finance, research and development, and administrative services. A retail chain may have the same divisions with the exception of a production, or manufacturing, department.

Production. The executive in charge of the production division is the vice-president of production. In some companies this executive's title may be director of manufacturing, director of engineering, or factory manager.

The production division controls and is responsible for all matters pertaining to the manufacture of the company's products. The objective of this division is to manufacture the product to its specifications in the proper quantity, and at the lowest possible cost. This division must cooperate closely with other company divisions, such as marketing and finance.

Purchasing. The purchasing division is responsible for procuring materials, machinery, and supplies for the company. The complexity of this division depends on the size of the company. In a small company, one person (with perhaps some clerical help) can accomplish all purchasing functions. In a very large corporation, the head of the division may be at the vice-presidential level.

Purchasing functions are specialized according to the needs of the organization. One buyer, for example, may be in charge of purchasing all raw materials for production. Another may be responsible for the packaging requirements for the corporation's various products. Further specialization in the purchasing division may occur as necessary. In general, the procedure is this: A department initiates a purchase requisition, providing as many specifications as necessary. The appropriate buyer locates a source of supply; considers quality, quantity, price, and service; and negotiates the purchase.

Marketing. Because a business survives only if it sells its products, it must have an effective marketing/sales organization. The marketing division may be separated into two or more departments, the heads of which report to the vice-president of marketing.

Sales Department. The sales director (or sales manager) usually directs a staff of salespeople. The department may hire the members of the sales staff, give them special training, and assign them to territories. It may supply samples and literature, introduce new products, and perform myriad other activities through the sales staff. In addition to managing the sales department, the sales director may be responsible for developing product policy, approving credit extensions, and preparing a sales budget.

The selling function, of course, is one of the most important activities of the company. How well this function is performed often determines the company's profit.

Advertising Department. The advertising department is also concerned with selling. It is responsible for devising a broad advertising plan appropriate to the overall marketing program of the company. This department coordinates its advertising with the selling effort. In some instances a company turns over its advertising entirely or partly to an outside agency which, in turn, plans and executes promotional programs. In this event the advertising department acts as a liaison. It supplies information to the agency about the company's products and marketing goals and approves the agency's proposals.

Market Research Department. The work of a market research department is statistical and interpretive in nature. This department gathers useful data to guide the business in marketing current products or in launching new ones. Its scope is extensive. It continuously reexamines and estimates the market for the company's products. Market research also evaluates the new products of other manufacturers and provides management with the information necessary to make sound decisions regarding the competition.

Finance Division. The finance division handles a company's monies and its accounting procedures. It records, analyzes, summarizes, and interprets the financial affairs of the company. Thus, the financial division provides a continuous record of company financial transactions. It is responsible for devising systems, forms, and procedures to summarize financial activities. This division is also involved in formulating company policy.

The financial vice-president is in charge of the finance division. This officer directs the work of the treasurer and the controller. The controller (sometimes spelled comptroller but always pronounced controller) usually directs all phases of accounting.

Research and Development Division. Recognizing that their survival depends upon success in developing better products, large companies are increasing their budget allotments for research. Scientists and engineers work to develop new and improved products and production methods. These specialists occupy a position of high status in the company.

Administrative Services Division. Departments that serve other departments are presented here as administrative services departments. These departments generally report to the vice-president of administrative services.

Human Resources Department. One function of this department is interviewing and hiring employees. This responsibility involves exploring labor sources, processing and filing application forms, organizing and conducting interviews, administering tests, and adhering to government standards regarding fair employment practices. Some human resources departments also conduct training programs for new employees (usually excluding sales trainees) and in-service training for present employees. It is the function of the human resources department to administer employee services and fringe benefits; establish health and safety programs; and accomplish the work of transferring, promoting, and discharging employees. The department also develops job descriptions and job analyses. In some corporations this department is known as the personnel department.

Information Services. Some companies centralize such office functions as records management, reprographic services, mailing, and word processing by maintaining a specialized staff to perform these activities. The offices of this staff are located where the services are provided. The company with a specialized services staff relieves individual employees of some routine office jobs.

In a company without centralized office services, each functional division or department operates as a complete, self-sufficient unit. It handles all office duties that would otherwise be turned over to a centralized department.

OFFICE LAYOUT

The early 70s marked the beginning of a new look in business offices. Instead of the conventional office with its enclosed floor plan and heavy, traditional furniture, many companies began to convert their offices to the *open plan design* and use compact, modular furniture known as *systems furniture*. Companies viewed the open plan as a solution to the costly problems of space utilization, office relocations, and expansion. In addition, the open plan promised to facilitate communication between employees and their supervisors. Today the open plan is very popular with office tenants, architects, and interior designers. In fact, the open office design is fast becoming the rule, rather than the exception, in new and renovated facilities. The location of the secretary's work place in both conventional and open floor plans is discussed in this section.

The Conventional Office Layout

The traditional office is characterized by floor-to-ceiling walls, solid doors, ceiling light fixtures, and heavy wood or metal office furniture. The secretary's workstation in this office is referred to as the secretary's desk. A wood or metal desk, chair, and credenza are standard equipment. Lighting, file storage, and shelving are separate components and sometimes are not easily accessible to the secretary.

In a conventional office the secretary's desk is usually located in any one of four places. Rare in these times of cost consciousness and space and energy conservation is the secretary who has the luxury of a private office. Still, the secretary to an executive may enjoy this privilege. The secretary's desk may also be either immediately inside or outside the employer's office or in a nearby location with several other secretaries. Whatever the arrangement, the employer and the secretary should be accessible to each other.

The Open Plan Design

The modern approach to office design is popularly known as *open plan* or *open landscape*. Instead of floor-to-ceiling walls, the open office uses movable partitions and acoustical screens as dividers. Rather than standard office furniture, colorful systems furniture with panels and panel-related components is used extensively. Individual workstations are self-contained movable units, which are far less expensive than traditional office furniture. Each station is adaptable to the particular needs of the employee and is furnished with lighting, tools, and equipment. Paintings, thick carpets, and live or artificial plants also typify the open office. Because of its flexibility in changing the location of personnel and furniture, the reduction in square footage required by each employee, and its lower original cost outlay, substantial savings are possible.

Besides visible changes in the office, the open plan facilitates work flow and communication. Employees are positioned according to the flow of work and are readily visible to their supervisor. This office plan emphasizes the fact that employees are a part of a process and, thus, integral parts of the company team. An example of an open plan office appears in Illus. 2-2.

One problem with the open plan is the loss of audio and visual privacy. Conversations, ringing telephones, and the humming and clicking of such electronic equipment as printers and/or word processors contribute to the noise level within an area. The installation of noise-masking devices (equipment hoods and other scientific aids) and conference rooms for meetings can overcome this problem.

In the open office, employees work in close proximity to each other. Because the square footage available to each worker is approximately 20 percent less than in the traditional office, distractions increase. Using only established traffic patterns is one remedy. The most effective solution, however, is for each employee to show consideration toward co-workers at all times.

Another disadvantage of the open office is the need for increased personal and equipment security. The greater accessibility of open spaces may force an office to maintain a staff of security personnel 24 hours a day.

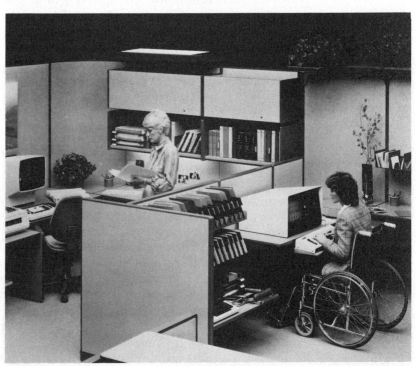

Illus. 2-2
Open Plan Office
Design

Photo courtesy of Haworth, Inc., Holland, Michigan

HEALTH AND SAFETY CONSIDERATIONS

As office automation affects a rapidly growing number of workers, issues of health, safety, and comfort are being discussed by business people, manufacturers, and legislators alike. *Ergonomics* (from the Greek words "ergon" for work and "nomos" for natural laws of) is the science of adapting equipment, work routines, and work environments to meet workers' physical and psychological needs. It is concerned with equipment and furniture design, office layout, acoustics, color, heating and cooling systems, and so forth (see Illus. 2-3). In short, ergonomics is the science that deals with issues raised by office automation. These issues include health and environmental factors.

Health Concerns of Video Display Terminal Users

Over the past several years, people in labor, industry, government, and science have debated the physical and psychological hazards of video display terminals (VDTs). Currently, over seven million Americans use video display terminals during the workday. By 1990 it is estimated that forty million workers will use VDTs. Research studies

Illus. 2-3
Ergonomic
Workstation

Duffy Incorporated, Interior Designers

conducted by the National Institute for Occupational Safety and Health (NIOSH) have found a number of health complaints among video display terminal operators. These complaints fall into two health categories (physical and mental) and are discussed below.

Physical Concerns. A universal complaint of video display terminal operators is eye fatigue, which is often caused by improper lighting and screen glare. The lighting required to read paper copy is five times brighter than that required for using a VDT keyboard and screen. This unnecessary brightness produces screen glare and causes eye fatigue, burning eyelids, and headaches. The solution to this problem is through the use of indirect lighting, anti-glare panels for display screens, and softer colors on walls and partitions. A 15-minute break every two hours to give operators a chance to rest their eyes is recommended. Many companies insist on a 15-minute break every hour, and some companies require eye examinations prior to employment.

The second major physical complaint of operators is skeletal and muscular distress, such as backaches and neckaches. In fact, backaches are second only to colds as the nation's leading cause of time lost from work. Since several operators may use the same workstation, adjustable display screens, tables, and chairs, detachable keyboards, and foot rests are recommended.

Noise ranks as the third physical concern of workers in the automated office. Although word processing equipment and telephones contribute to the noise level in an office, the worst offenders are computer printers. Each printer is responsible for 60 to 70 decibels of noise. With several printers operating at once, the noise can cause headaches and earaches. In fact, long exposure to noise levels over 70 decibels can permanently impair hearing. As discussed earlier, acoustical hoods on equipment can reduce noise levels considerably.

Mental (Psychological) Concerns. Besides physiological complaints, video display operators often suffer from depression and job stress. They offer these reasons: (1) lack of job control, (2) little or no opportunity for socialization, and (3) entire days spent with a terminal that never gets tired. Many VDT operators must also work under a quota system, which eventually creates a great deal of strain. To make matters worse, the complexity of some equipment increases the working time involved in getting projects done. These situations contribute to psychological stress.

To resolve these complaints, supervisors are giving operators the chance to make decisions which affect their work, are setting goals for the group rather than for individuals, and are assigning a variety of projects. In order to reduce absenteeism and increase worker productivity, supervisors should encourage employees to be comfortable at their work.

Other Common Job-Related Health Concerns

The physical work environment is a problem in some offices. To conserve energy and cut building costs, office buildings today are typically constructed with few windows or with windows that do not open. People in these offices, therefore, must rely on ventilation systems to safeguard air quality. Without such systems, indoor air pollution, especially from employees who smoke, may become a problem. Air quality can also be impaired by the use of office machines that produce heat and/or emit odors and certain building insulation materials.

Employees who do not operate video display terminals may also complain of job stress. Job stress is attributed to a number of causes, but the main culprit is reported to be lack of control regarding the job itself. Strong emotional support from family and friends and a daily exercise regimen can help an employee cope with stressful situations. On-the-job techniques to alleviate stress include resting the eyes by looking off at a distance, changing the sitting position, moving the head clockwise and then counterclockwise, and doing deep breathing exercises.

As a final note, a fairly recent survey of 500 secretaries found that over 63 percent believe that automated equipment has made their jobs less stressful.[1] One interpretation of these results indicates that automated equipment contributes to a healthful environment for the secretary.

Office Mishaps

In addition to expressing concern about the effects of the work environment upon the health of employees, most companies take precautions to prevent accidents in the work place. Yet accidents can and do happen. Accidents can be caused by employee carelessness, or the company can be at fault. To allay accidents, the Occupational Safety and Health Administration (OSHA) was established in 1970 to regulate

---

[1]"The End of an Era," *Financial World* (March 21-April 3, 1984), p. 46.

safety and health standards for businesses dealing in interstate commerce. Most office accidents are falls, and most can be avoided. Falls can occur when

1. A desk drawer or a file drawer is left open.
2. A tear in a carpet goes unnoticed.
3. An employee walks or runs on a highly waxed floor.
4. Obstructions, such as extension cords or wastebaskets, are left in the aisle.
5. Equipment is not in its regular place.
6. Hallways and stairways are poorly lighted.
7. Insecure filing ladders are used.
8. An employee rushes through a swinging door, and someone is on the other side.

Accidents involving fire can result from careless smoking habits: leaving a burning cigarette unattended or emptying an ashtray containing smoldering ashes into a paper-filled wastebasket. With the addition of computers and computer-related equipment to the work place, it is quite possible that electrical fires may occur if electrical circuits are overloaded. Every office should be equipped with a sprinkler system, smoke alarms, or fire extinguishers. In the office where only a fire extinguisher is available, every employee should know where it is located and how to use it.

Large organizations have established written procedures to follow in case of accidents. Bulletins outlining these procedures are posted where employees have access to them. Every employee should be aware of these procedures and, if necessary, follow them explicitly.

Office Security

It is not uncommon for some employees to arrive at the office very early or to stay late in order to finish a rush job, to work without interruption, or to adhere to a commuter train or car pool schedule. Working overtime (hours in addition to the regular 35- or 40-hour schedule) is standard in many offices. An hourly wage employee who is willing to work overtime is rewarded with increased income, the appreciation of management, and frequently, a promotion to a better position.

Security guards who monitor the entrances and exits of a building are quite common in metropolitan areas and in businesses whose operation is of a classified nature. They control visitors by issuing passes;

sometimes they conduct office visitors to their destinations. Security guards are on duty longer than other employees to ensure the safety of employees and property. Although the building may be monitored by television screens or by security guards, employees should not take a lax attitude about their personal property. Valuables should be kept out of sight in a safe place. Furthermore, any suspicious stranger in the office should be intercepted and questioned with "May I help you locate the proper office?".

If you are accustomed to arriving very early or expect to work late, you should inquire about the company's security measures. If there are no established procedures, you should set your own and abide by them. You may suggest to your employer the merits of an alarm system that can be activated at strategic positions in the office. Secretaries who often work after hours recommend these practices:

1. Notify the guard or personnel department that you are working late and when you expect to leave.
2. Situate yourself near others who are working late or near the alarm system.
3. Work next to a telephone and have emergency numbers handy.
4. Lock all doors leading to your work area.
5. Know when to expect custodial help and establish a cordial relationship with them.
6. Call the self-service elevator before locking your office door. Enter the elevator only after you are sure it is unoccupied. Stand next to the panel buttons.
7. Travel home in a group or have the guard escort you to your car or the source of your transportation.

If your office or building is small, it is not likely to have a security force. If you work in such an office, avoid being the only person in the office before and after working hours and during lunch. If you must work in an unprotected office alone, particularly after hours, notify someone at your home that you are working late and call again just as you are leaving for home. While working, keep all doors locked and admit no one to your office. If you are typing, be aware that the sound carries, making it obvious that you are in the office. If you hear any strange noises, call for help. Do not investigate on your own. Another suggestion is to avoid using the restroom if it is located off a hallway. It is not safe to enter even a locked restroom if you are the only person working late.

As you leave the building look around the parking lot before locking the door and have your keys ready to unlock your car. It is a safe practice always to lock your car after entering or when leaving it.

Office Emergencies

Office emergencies are sudden and unexpected; they require immediate attention. Delays in responding to an emergency can result in chaos, destruction of property, and/or loss of life. Offices should have plans for emergencies posted at conspicuous spots.

In case of fire or bomb scare, employees must evacuate the building. Use stairways, not elevators. If you are at your desk when the alarm sounds, take your valuables with you. If you are away from your desk, do not add to the congestion by returning to your desk. Go to the nearest exit.

If you are in charge of valuable company records, put them in a safe place as quickly as possible. Supervisors leave the office last, only after they are sure all employees have vacated.

For illnesses or severe accidents, such as heart attacks, burns, or choking, an office's emergency procedures should include a list of employees who can administer first aid. Phone numbers for the emergency squad, ambulances, physicians, the nearest hospital, and similar information should also be included. Oxygen kits and first aid kits are standard equipment in most offices.

If there is no established procedure for emergencies, take it upon yourself to (1) post emergency numbers at your desk, (2) suggest purchasing a first aid kit, and (3) take a first aid course.

AREAS OF SECRETARIAL RESPONSIBILITY

Secretarial work can be divided into three areas: (1) routine duties, (2) assigned tasks, and (3) original work.

All secretarial positions involve some *routine duties*, although automation has reduced the amount of routine work performed by secretaries. Examples of routine work include filing, answering the telephone, operating the copy machine, sorting the mail, replenishing supplies, and locking up confidential materials at the end of the day.

Assigned tasks are given to the secretary by the employer. They can be simple, complex, or a mixture of both. In any event, it is work that must be done, usually in a limited amount of time. Making travel reservations, making a bank deposit, or getting technical material from the library are examples of assigned tasks. A secretary may have to make adjustments in the work schedule to accommodate these assignments.

Original work is defined here as that area of responsibility in which the secretary displays initiative and creativity in assisting the employer. Work that demonstrates forethought or requires the secretary to follow through an activity to its conclusion is typical of this category.

The secretary's contribution in the area of original work is especially appreciated by the employer. At the same time, it is most gratifying to the secretary. The more efficiently the secretary handles assigned and routine tasks, the more time remains for service of an original nature. Such service earns attention that may lead to promotion.

The opportunities for original work on the part of the secretary depend largely on the executive's willingness to delegate responsibility. Delegating responsibility is an indication of progressive leadership. The secretary can, however, increase her/his scope of responsibility by demonstrating competence in initiating supportive activities. For example, a secretary who wants to perform work of an original nature should anticipate requests for data that would support a business report and supply it before the employer requests it. Initiating an instant reference system to increase the employer's effectiveness is also an example of original work. In addition, the creative secretary who notices an important article in a magazine would call it to the employer's attention.

Creativity is not a trait one inherits. Creativity can be nurtured, and there are several ways this can be done. First, gather ideas and develop an "idea bank" for yourself, then brainstorm with these ideas. Second, learn to be independent in your thinking and in your impressions about office problems. Third, continue to expand your thinking by reading about secretarial work, office technology, and the office environment. Always be curious about new developments.

ORGANIZATION OF TIME AND WORK

Time theft, the deliberate waste and misuse of on-the-job time, cost American business over $150 billion in 1984.[2] A cost-conscious and work-conscious secretary, therefore, makes every minute in the workday count. Punctuality is expected in reporting for work, in completing material for the employer, in submitting periodic reports, in relaying messages, and so on. A lackadaisical attitude about time is a source of irritation to employers. It can also directly affect the atti-

---

[2]"A Huge Time Theft," *Office Administration and Automation* (January, 1985), page 19.

tudes of other office workers. An effective secretary maintains an efficient work area and keeps supplies, tools, and equipment within easy reach.

The Working Day

Secretaries may work from 8 to 5, from 9 to 5, or any other variation of an employer-specified workday. They may follow a flexitime schedule or work part-time, perhaps 15 to 20 hours a week. Flexitime divides the day into two parts: core hours, during which all employees work, and discretionary hours, which fall on both sides of the core. With their supervisor's approval, employees may individually set their arrival and departure times so long as they work a certain number of hours each day. This plan is especially attractive to employees with responsibilities at home. The person holding a secretarial position may have a schedule that is different from that of other employees in the same office. The secretary's schedule is set to suit the employer's convenience, but it must, at the same time, cover a full workweek in terms of hours. Any comments of co-workers are irrelevant, since the secretary is accountable only to the employer. Vacations may also be irregular, because a secretary must defer to the employer's schedule by remaining on the job when the work load is heaviest. A secretary to several principals, though, must be available to all of them during regular office hours.

The Secretary's Workstation

To work efficiently, using the least amount of time, effort, and frustration, a well-organized and well-equipped workstation is necessary. The objective is to have all that is needed to accomplish daily tasks either on the desk, in the desk, or within easy reach.

A flat, uncluttered surface is the best work area. A secretary should find the following recommendations helpful (if the secretary is left-handed, the reverse of some of the statements is true):

1. Place an in/out basket for mail on the right-hand side of the desk or work surface.
2. Keep a message pad and pencil beside the telephone. Place the telephone within reach to the left of your chair. Answer the telephone with your left hand, so the right hand is free to take messages.
3. Place reference manuals at the front of the work surface.

4. Keep a stapler and a tape dispenser next to your reference books.
5. Keep a desk calendar at the front of the work area.
6. Keep a bulletin board for posting messages.
7. Place your typewriter or word processor on a separate table, on an extension of the desk, or, if systems furniture is used, on the work surface.
8. Keep electric cords to equipment out of sight.

Drawer space should also be organized. Keep pencils, pens, and paper clips in special compartments in a top drawer. Keep stationery in a deep drawer in an organizer that has slats for different types of paper. For instance, you might store company letterhead in the first bin, carbons in the second, second sheets or lightweight paper in the third, memorandums in the fourth, and so on. A place for envelopes is often provided in front of stationery organizers. Position envelopes with their flaps down and facing the front of the drawer so that they are in the proper position for placement in a typewriter, printer, or word processor. Use a deeper desk drawer, or in the case of modular systems furniture, a storage compartment, for files that are referred to daily. These files include mailing lists, work in process, and other types of reference files.

Before leaving for the day, you should remove all papers from your work surface and lock your desk. A clean drawer at the bottom of the desk is a good place to put unfinished work at the end of the day. In addition to locking the desk at the end of the day, the secretary should lock the desk during lunch hours and coffee breaks to safeguard any material of a confidential nature.

Today, many executives have offices equipped with computers and related equipment. As such, these offices are often referred to as "executive workstations." The secretary may work intermittently in the employer's office or in an area equipped with computers to keyboard data, retrieve information, receive or send electronic mail (see page 330), plan schedules, or perform other tasks requiring the use of a computer. When working in another area, take all necessary materials and supplies with you so that work can be done as quickly as possible. You should also make arrangements to have the telephone answered in your absence.

The Secretary's Work Plan—Managing Time

Planning each workday is a necessity for any secretary because work does not come in an even flow. There are periods when the employer, and accordingly the secretary, must turn out important work in a limited time. The secretary's analysis of the time and motion spent on routine tasks may free additional time in anticipation of high priority work. A thorough analysis of all activities performed by the secretary may provide clues to where time can be conserved. If the secretary anticipates periodic jams and distributes part of the rush work to slack days, it may be possible to reduce the pressures of peak loads.

Work Analysis. Every secretary should strive to perform such repetitive tasks as typing and filing as efficiently as possible by using a minimum of motion, effort, time, and labor.

The first step in organizing time and work is to make an analysis of your duties. Illus. 2-4 is an example of a work analysis sheet. For at least two weeks keep a record of each duty you perform and the amount of time given to it, or you may record only those duties performed at predetermined time intervals. Establish a coding system to streamline your work analysis. Use "IM" for incoming mail, "T" for transcription, etc. A careful study of this sheet will show you where time is not being used to your best advantage. For instance, you may

EFFICIENCY is doing a task RIGHT. EFFECTIVENESS is doing the RIGHT task.

Peter Drucker

WORK ANALYSIS SHEET

Date October 15   Position Secretary to V-P

TIME		TASK	CLASSIFICATION					TOTAL TIME	EVALUATION
Start	Complete		Outside Contact	Intraco. Contact	Subordinates	Adm. Matters	Routine		
8:00	8:10	Housekeeping duties					✓	10	Total time necessary to maintain standards
8:10	8:15	Telephone confirmation of meeting	✓					5	
8:15	9:05	Open, sort, distribute mail		✓	✓		✓	50	Train Susan to distribute
9:05	9:52	Daily Briefing		✓		✓		47	Suggest holding of telephone calls
9:53	11:30	Transcription of memos, letters					✓	97	
12:30	1:00	Explanation of monthly report preparation			✓			30	No need to replicate

Illus. 2-4
A work analysis classifies tasks and indicates starting and completion times. The amount of time and the type of work involved should suggest which tasks can be delegated to others in the office.

see that you spend too much time searching for information, keyboarding rough drafts, or performing other routine tasks that could be delegated to someone else.

Time Wasters. The work analysis sheet will identify weaknesses in the use of your time and indicate changes that can be made. You may find that one of the biggest robbers of time is the telephone. The trend today is for employers to answer their phones directly. This trend should reduce the time secretaries spend answering phones, taking messages, transferring calls, and the like.

Any interruption between the employer and the secretary wastes time. You can reduce interruptions by communicating with your employer via memorandums and by consulting each other only at convenient times during the day.

Socializing with co-workers is another time thief. Certainly some employee socialization is acceptable and even encouraged in offices, but it should never occur at the expense of getting work done. In open plan offices this problem is more acute than in offices of conventional design. Other wasters of time include working with incomplete information, failure to delegate, lack of a daily plan, equipment breakdowns, unclear deadlines, and procrastination.

Be mindful, too, of such subtle time wasters as filing papers that could be thrown away, duplicating information on several company forms, or recording information that is no longer valid or necessary. Concentrate your energy and your time on those activities that lead to increased efficiency and work productivity, activities that are most valuable to your employer and to yourself.

You can implement timesaving practices on your own. Certain major changes, though, require the cooperation and approval of your employer. For instance, if you answer all phone calls, perhaps you should discuss with your employer the possibility of changing this procedure.

Daily Work Plan. The real key in managing time is to manage yourself. Every secretary should make and follow a daily work plan. Prepare this plan the night before or first thing in the morning. A daily work plan requires setting objectives for the day, listing the work to be done based on the objectives, and assigning priorities to the work. A sample priority rating is "A" or "1" for work to be done immediately; "B" or "2" for work to be done today; and "C" or "3" for work to be done when convenient. Ascertain priorities according to your employer's requests or according to built-in schedules which state when weekly reports are due. Illus. 2-5 is an example of a daily work plan. In preparing your daily work plan, you should follow these principles on the proper use of time:

1. Plan each project thoroughly; have complete instructions before beginning.
2. Avoid handling several projects at once.
3. Make the easy decisions quickly.
4. Initiate a plan to control interruptions.
5. Set deadlines; allow yourself a cushion of 20 percent more time than you think will be necessary.
6. Allow some time, perhaps on a weekly basis, to clear out clutter.
7. Jot down notes of business conversations that are essential for recall.
8. Delegate nonessential tasks, if possible.
9. Get unpleasant tasks out of the way.
10. Do the most complex tasks during your best working time.
11. Do routine work when your momentum is low.
12. Do the hardest tasks in uninterrupted blocks of time, if possible.
13. Group similar tasks, such as making copies or telephone calls.
14. Stay with a task until it is completed.
15. Pick up paperwork only once and finish the task immediately. (Time managers estimate that over 50 percent of daily paperwork can be disposed of in the first handling.)
16. Divide tremendously long tasks into manageable parts and complete one part at a time.
17. Do tasks right the first time.
18. Put spare moments to work for you.
19. Coordinate your daily plan with your employer's work plan.

Most secretaries and employers complete a daily work plan. Most employer/secretary teams go over their respective plans at the beginning of the day and make adjustments as necessary. Generally if the plans do not agree, the employer's plan is followed. If your employer has no such plan, you can suggest a plan by example. For instance, the first thing in the morning you can submit your plan and by give-and-take discussion, a daily plan for the employer/secretary team is made. Then follow this practice on a daily basis.

If you work for more than one person, you should check with each individual daily to determine his/her work priorities. Sometimes it is difficult to decide which job to do first, second, and so forth. There are guidelines, however. If one employer holds a higher position than another, generally the higher-ranked employer's work takes prece-

DAILY WORK PLAN

Date _October 16_____

Goals: 1. _Complete research for report_   Priority Code

2. _Select meeting time/place_   1 — Urgent
                                       2 — Do today
3. _Compose notification letters_   3 — Do when convenient
                                       4 — Do when all other duties
4. _____   are accomplished

Time	Task	Priority	Evaluation
8:00	Open, sort, distribute mail	2	Delegate to Susan
8:30	Library research	1	
9:00	" "	1	
9:30	Compiling data	1	

Illus. 2-5
Sample of a daily work plan that incorporates a list of objectives for the day, a time analysis, and the priority of work.

dence, unless a matter is of such urgency that it must take priority. If your employers are at the same management level, or if you are in doubt about which work takes precedence, ask your employers to assign priorities as a matter of routine. Some secretaries use a system whereby employers complete a priority slip when assigning work so that there is no question about the order in which work is to be completed. If there appears to be a conflict, you may have to rely on your own judgement to determine priorities. If you work swiftly and are able to do work within reasonable time limits, the question of priorities is often academic.

Some office forms, such as the work analysis sheet and the daily work plan, are handwritten. To ensure that your handwriting is legible, place both elbows on the desk surface and use proper writing tools: a sharp pencil or ball-point pen. Write uniformly: allow proper spacing between letters and words, make lowercase letters one third the height of capital letters, and cross the t's and dot the i's. Be sure to distinguish between 1's and 7's and 3's, 5's, and 8's.

In an automated office, some entry data are handwritten; therefore, you should begin a program now to develop handwriting skill. Be a good judge of your penmanship. If you cannot read your own handwriting when it is cold (24 hours old), you can be sure that others will have a difficult time reading it.

Periodic Peak Loads. A study of a month's flow of work may indicate patterns of fluctuation. For instance, Mondays traditionally bring heavier mail and, subsequently, heavier dictation. Thus, other Monday plans should be light. A secretary who must issue first-of-the-month statements of account should spread their preparation throughout the month in an organized pattern. Slack periods are ideal for transferring files, preparing new record cards, bringing address files up to date, and duplicating sets of frequently requested materials. Always be on the lookout for ways to simplify work.

To help meet the demands of periodic peak loads, a secretary should think ahead by making weekly or even monthly "to do" lists. Addressing envelopes, partially completing forms, preparing enclosures, and requisitioning supplies in advance of need are all ways that the secretary can be sure that the office will run smoothly even during the busiest times.

Real Emergencies. Even with the best planning, unavoidable emergencies will occur. An unexpected illness, for example, may upset the normal functioning of the office force. All at once you may be faced with a difficult job and insufficient time in which to perform it.

With experience you will know which jobs are critical and how and when each is to be accomplished. If subordinates are available, some of the work may be delegated to them. Other secretaries in the office may also be approached to assist you. Office employees should cooperate with each other to accomplish what must be done. However, if the work load is far more than the office force can handle, you may suggest employing temporary help.

Office Memory Devices

A secretary needs a good memory to maintain office efficiency. The secretary who has access to a computer should use it as an office memory device. Secretaries should also rely on their daily work plan to complete pending assignments and to follow through on assignments with specific due dates. Several other manual types of memory aids are described here.

Secretarial Desk Manual. Every secretary should compile a loose-leaf desk manual and keep it up to date. It should cover each duty, responsibility, and procedure that the secretary performs. It is also a useful place in which to keep often-needed company information. Chapter 24 of this book explains the contents and organization of such a manual.

Secretarial Desk Calendar. Employer and secretary should have individual desk calendars for notes and reminders, business as well as personal. To supplement the employer's calendar, a secretary usually maintains an appointment book. The secretary consults this appointment book daily and reviews future appointments regularly in the event advance preparation is necessary—travel arrangements, for example. Paper and electronic appointment schedules are covered in detail in Chapter 3.

At the end of the year prepare next year's desk calendar. Using your present calendar as a guide, mark important dates, meeting times, and other similar information on the new calendar. If deadlines for projects are known or vacations set, note these on the calendar as well. Keep your employer's old calendar for several months into the new year until you are sure its notations are of no further use.

The Tickler. The most widely used paper reminder system, filed according to dates, is the tickler. This efficient office aid derives its name from the accounting term *tick*, meaning to *check off*. A tickler is an accumulating record, by days, of items of work to be done on future days. Items are ticked off when completed. Illus. 2-6 is an example of a tickler file.

The daily calendar can also be used as a tickler. Calendar page space is limited, however, so a separate tickler is usually set up and maintained. The most flexible tickler is a file box with five- by three-inch colored guide cards. The file box has cards for each month, one to three sets of date guides (numbered from 1 to 31), and one card labeled "Future Years." The guide for the current month is placed in the front of the file, and the set of cards for each day in that month is placed behind it. Additional date guides may be placed behind the next one or two months. An item of future concern is written on an individual card, and the card is filed behind the guides for the proper month and date. If the item is to be followed up several months later, it is dropped behind the month guide. It will be filed according to date when the month comes to the front.

Illus. 2-6
The secretary
enters a tickler
item concerning an
express shipment
due before the end
of the week. Notice
the abbreviated
form of writing
memorandums.

Since an item is often forwarded and reforwarded, write the follow-up date in pencil so that it can be erased and changed when necessary. In fact, since the tickler is a memorandum type of record, the entire item is usually written in pencil. Annual events, such as due dates for taxes and insurance premiums, are refiled for next year as soon as they are ticked off.

It is the secretary's responsibility to remind the employer of tickler items. An oversight can be very embarrassing and costly to the firm. You should use the tickler as a memory aid in these ways:

1. To remind yourself of work to be done.
2. To tick off items accomplished.
3. To record work for a future date.

As a matter of routine, the secretary checks the tickler file when making the next day's work plan. After this check, the secretary places that day's guide in the file at the end of the numbered guides for that month, leaving the following day's numbered guide at the front of the file. Near the end of the month, the secretary arranges tickler items for the next month behind the appropriate numbered guides.

Pending File. The pending file is another memory aid. It is a file folder in which the secretary temporarily holds mail concerning matters that are in the offing. It is kept in the secretary's desk, in the employer's desk, or in some other place near at hand. If the secretary's desk has a deep file drawer, the pending file can be kept conveniently there. It is not satisfactory to keep the folder in a flat position because the folder and its contents often become dog-eared. The secretary must be careful not to isolate letters in the pending file that should be available in the regular files. This can be avoided by making extra copies of incoming and outgoing letters and filing the originals in their respective files. If a matter that is pending does not involve a letter, type a special note about the matter and place it in the pending file. A regular check of the pending file should be made to determine which matters to call to the employer's attention. A notation regarding pending matters should be made on the daily work plan. Any letters that have been answered should be released to the regular files and extra copies should be discarded.

Desk Reference Files. The secretary can organize office work more efficiently by keeping desk reference files. Such files should include the names of important clients, telephone numbers frequently called, addresses of regular correspondents, items that must be followed through before they are placed in the central files, stock identifications and descriptions, and work in process. The secretary keeps these reference files in a deep desk drawer. They save time that would otherwise be lost hunting for information. Desk reference files are frequently needed files; they can be planned only after the secretary is thoroughly familiar with the job.

The Chronological File. Some secretaries make an extra copy of everything they type in order to maintain a complete chronological file of their work. This file is kept in the secretary's desk. Copies for this file are sometimes made on colored paper. Many a day has been saved by this ready reference file. If you are also in charge of the employer's files, it is a good practice to note the location of the employer's file copy on the chronological copy.

How long you keep copies in the chronological file is a matter of preference. Some secretaries keep copies in the chronological file for three months and copies of older correspondence in a separate file drawer. (See page 352 for additional information.)

Outside Assistance

When there is not sufficient time to complete a sizable office job, the secretary should ask for additional workers. The secretary exhibits good judgment by requesting assistance if a situation warrants such action. If help is not available, a secretary may obtain a supervisor's permission to contact an agency that supplies experienced temporary help. Among such agencies are Manpower, Inc., Kelly Services, Inc., and Olsten Corp. A secretary who supervises temporary workers should acquaint them with company hours, facilities, office procedures, and other office employees. An office temporary should be given a copy of the company's procedures manual and forms guide. The work for the temporary person should also be well organized so that time is not wasted waiting for information.

Sometimes work requires professional skills or abilities beyond those of the secretary, or perhaps the job is of such size that it can be done more quickly and less expensively outside the office. In such cases, with the employer's permission, the secretary turns to a special service agency. These agencies prepare multiple copies of original letters and mail them, obtain hotel and travel reservations, take full recordings of meetings and prepare transcripts, reproduce materials, furnish and maintain mailing lists, or provide competent help for other jobs of a specialized or technical nature.

On completion of the work, the secretary writes a note in the desk manual identifying the agency or the individuals employed. Also, a record of the total cost and a brief evaluation of the service should be kept for future guidance.

Supervision of Subordinates

The secretary may be assigned one or more full-time assistants or temporary helpers. With relatively inexperienced assistants, the supervisor assumes the role of *teacher*. In this capacity, the secretary provides the assistant with opportunities to develop efficient work habits. In addition, the secretary teaches the proper use of equipment and physical facilities.

When assigning work, the secretary gives thorough directions to subordinates. There should be no doubt as to what is to be done. If the work is complicated, written instructions should supplement oral directions. Periodically the secretary should check on the progress of the work so that mistakes are avoided. Assignments of varying difficulty give subordinates the opportunity to display exactly what they can do.

In addition to being a teacher, the secretary is also a student—a student of human behavior. The secretary studies the abilities of office assistants. It is the secretary's responsibility to motivate subordinates so that they work to their full potential and take pride in their work. A supervisor gives credit and praise when due. If criticism becomes necessary, however, a supervisor discusses the *work* not the *worker*. It may be useful to read literature concerning supervision.

At specified intervals the secretary may formally evaluate subordinates' performance, perhaps using an evaluation instrument similar to the one shown in Illus. 2-7. Note that such an instrument lets the evaluator comment on each factor being rated. This is an advantage both to the evaluator and to the subordinate. The secretary has a responsibility to evaluate a subordinate objectively.

EMPLOYEE EVALUATION

Name of Employee _Joe A. Morgan_   Department _Human Resources_

Directions: Read over each section carefully. Appraise employee performance by placing a check mark in the box below the comment that applies to the employee. Check only one box in each section. Appraisers are encouraged to use the remarks section for additional comments pertinent to the employee's evaluation.

KNOWLEDGE OF THE JOB — Technical job information and practical know-how	Proficient on job; makes the most of experiences--a "self-starter" ✓	Rarely needs assistance but asks for it to save time ☐	Knows job fairly well; regularly requires supervision and instruction ☐	Job knowledge limited; shows little desire or ability to improve ☐

Remarks: _has thorough understanding of machines_

QUALITY OF WORK	Consistently does an excellent job; errors very rare ☐	Usually does a good job; seldom makes errors ✓	Work is usually passable; regularly requires reminder to do a better job ☐	Doesn't care; work is inferior in many respects ☐

Remarks: _proofreads thoroughly_

QUANTITY OF WORK	Exceptionally fast; efficiency unusually high ☐	Fast; usually does more than is expected ✓	Turns out the required amount of work--seldom more ☐	Slow; output below minimum requirements ☐

Remarks: _____

ADAPTABILITY — Mental alertness; ability to meet changed conditions	Learns new duties easily; meets changed conditions quickly ✓	Grasps new ideas if given a little time; adjusts to new conditions ☐	Routine worker; requires detailed instructions on new duties and procedures ☐	Slow to learn; requires repeated instructions; unable to adjust to changes ☐

Remarks: _____

RELIABILITY — Confidence in employee to carry out all instructions conscientiously and completely	Dependable; on time, does what you want, when you want it ☐	Conscientious; follows instructions with little need for follow-up ☐	Generally follows directions, but needs occasional follow-up ✓	Requires frequent follow-up, even on routine duties; apt to put things off ☐

Remarks: _Capable of formatting documents without instructions_

Summary Statement: _Mr. Morgan is highly productive and extremely creative in his work._

Signature and Position of Evaluator _P.B. Schultz, Supervisor_

Illus. 2-7
A sample employee evaluation.

SUMMARY

A secretary may work for a small or large firm, in an urban or suburban area, in any type of industry, and in any geographical location. One of the first things a newly hired secretary should do is become acquainted with the organizational structure of the office. This can be done by studying an organizational chart and learning the names of the officers and managers of the various divisions of the firm.

Where the secretary works in today's office may differ from where secretaries worked in the conventional office layout of the past. The *open plan* design places the secretary at a workstation that has modular-type furniture and panels, rather than ceiling-to-floor walls that afford total privacy. In the open plan design the secretary must be considerate of other office workers with respect to noise, interruptions, and the like.

As office automation becomes widely implemented, issues of the health, safety and comfort of employees have been raised. The Greek word *ergonomics* is the term used to describe the science of adapting equipment, work routines, and the work environment to meet workers' physical and psychological needs. One of the main health concerns of video display operators is eye fatigue. Another physical complaint of VDT operators is skeletal or muscular distress. Still another is the noise generated by automated equipment. A psychological concern of video display operators is job stress. A health concern for all employees in any office is the need for proper ventilation.

Most offices have established safety procedures to safeguard the health of its employees, yet office accidents do happen. In the event of an emergency, the secretary should know exactly what to do and have emergency phone numbers available.

Efficient secretaries know the importance of time and, therefore, plan their work daily. They set priorities and plan ahead with weekly (and sometimes monthly) schedules. They anticipate their employers' requirements and observe the time management principles set forth in this chapter.

In addition to a daily work plan, the secretary has a desk manual which outlines the various duties of the position. A desk calendar and a daily work plan remind the secretary of unfinished and new tasks to be done. Other office memory devices utilized by the efficient secretary are the tickler, the pending file, and the chronological file.

It is not unusual for a secretary to supervise clerical workers. As a supervisor the secretary becomes a teacher, a student of human behavior, and an evaluator.

SUGGESTED READINGS

Cook, Fred S., and Lenore S. Forti. *Professional Secretary's Handbook.* Chicago: Dartnell Corp., 1984.

Ferner, Jack D. *Successful Time Management.* New York: John Wiley & Sons, Inc., 1980.

Finn, Nancy B. *The Electronic Office.* Englewood Cliffs, NJ: Prentice-Hall, Inc., 1983.

Green, James H. *Automating Your Office,* How to Do It, How to Justify It. New York: McGraw-Hill, Inc., 1984.

Mackenzie, R. Alec, and Billie Sorensen. "It's About Time. . . ." *The Secretary* (January, 1980), pp. 12-13.

Galitz, Wilbert O. *The Office Environment,* Automation's Impact on Tomorrow's Workplace. Willow Grove, PA: Administrative Management Society, 1984.

QUESTIONS FOR DISCUSSION

1. Considering your interests, abilities, and aptitudes, in which department of a business organization (production, purchasing, market research, sales, advertising, accounting, human resources, etc.) would you prefer to work? Give reasons for your choice.
2. You work in an open plan office. What is your responsibility concerning the workers in your immediate area? concerning the security of equipment and confidential files?
3. In view of the fact that you most likely will operate a video display terminal during your working career, how do you plan to insulate yourself from the health complaints discussed in this chapter?
4. Some secretaries believe that automated equipment has made their jobs less stressful. Give specific instances why this would be true.
5. What efforts should you make to guard against accidents in your work area?
6. What measures should you take to protect your personal valuables in an open plan office?
7. Determine whether each of the office duties given below is a routine, an assigned, or an original task. Describe the working

situation in each case (working with an employer, other company employees, things, or outsiders).

a. Filing a piece of correspondence
b. Answering the telephone
c. Looking up a word in the dictionary
d. Answering an employer's buzz
e. Typing a letter from dictation
f. Setting up your own chronological file
g. Proofreading a document with another person
h. Compiling information from periodic reports

8. Your employer frequently gives you rush assignments at the end of the day resulting in your working overtime. What steps would you suggest to your employer to increase efficiency and reduce overtime?

9. What plan would you suggest to control interruptions which disrupt your work?

10. What would you do first if all the following happened at the same time while you were composing an urgent communication: your employer, who was talking long-distance, buzzed you to enter the office; the secretary to the company president walked by your desk into your employer's office; and a subordinate was at your desk who wanted to borrow a file from your desk drawer? Explain your reasoning.

11. In your opinion which factors should be considered in an employee's evaluation? Which person in the organization should be responsible for an employee's evaluation?

12. Capitalize the appropriate words in the following sentences. Refer to the Reference Guide to correct your sentences.

a. Tonight's meeting will be held in the college of education building.
b. The contents of hague towers will be auctioned at the hanover courthouse.
c. All students must take american history.
d. Prices are slightly higher west of the mississippi river; customers on the east coast should take advantage of this sale.
e. When spring comes to georgia, all the sights and sounds of nature delight the tourists.

PROBLEMS

1. Before leaving work at 5 p.m., you must prepare tomorrow's daily work plan. On a plain sheet of paper, type the order in which you would perform the following tasks:

Call about airline schedule for next week's proposed trip.

Verify employer's 1 p.m. crosstown appointment.

Prepare agenda for 10 a.m. staff meeting.

Obtain sales figures from marketing for the second page of a four-page report. The report is urgent.

Order flowers to be sent to an employee in the hospital.

Transcribe three letters still on transcription equipment.

Purchase get-well card to send to an employee in the hospital.

Obtain agenda items from your employer for the staff meeting.

2. The following items are on your desk on March 2 to be marked for the tickler file. Before filing these items in the regular files, type a card for each one for the tickler file. Indicate on each card the date under which the card would be filed. Note on the card where the original material is filed.

   a. Notes for an article to be written for the September issue of the *Journal of Accountancy*. The deadline for an article is April 1.

   b. A note about setting up a conference with a bank official about a short-term loan to pay an invoice due April 1.

   c. A letter accepting an invitation to speak at a meeting of seniors from the School of Business Administration on May 8.

   d. The program of the annual convention of the International Controllers Institute to be held on April 6 in Brussels. Your employer plans to attend.

   e. A notice of a March 8 meeting of the Administrative Committee. Your employer is a member.

3. It is late Friday afternoon and you are 15 minutes away from your two-week vacation. Your employer is out of town until Monday. You have a number of pending matters on your desk. Decide which of the following tasks you should handle yourself in the time remaining, which to leave locked in your employer's desk, and which to leave for your replacement to handle. On a sheet of paper, type your decisions and give the rationale behind them.

   a. Your employer's insurance premium is due the following Wednesday. You are authorized to make payment.

   b. Notification of meeting scheduled for Thursday of the following week.

   c. Shorthand notes of a letter dictated by a staff member.

   d. Confidential promotion papers concerning a staff member.

   e. Interoffice memorandum requesting technical data from your employer.

   f. A letter from your employer's daughter at college.

4. In order to determine how you can better utilize your free time, keep a record of your at-home activities for one week. Prepare a form with the following headings, duplicate it, and use one copy for each day: Time of Day (in half-hour increments), Type of

Activity, and Personal Evaluation. Every half hour, record your activities. Analyze how you spend your time. Use the Personal Evaluation column to note where time could be used to better advantage, i.e., to accomplish a personal goal, to study, to exercise, and so forth. Be prepared to discuss your findings in class.

Chapter 3

Office Visitors and Employer's Appointments

When over 2,000 professional secretaries were asked to identify the job functions they particularly like, an overwhelming 98 percent said they like receiving office visitors most.[1] This result should be of no surprise, because secretaries, by the very nature of their work, must enjoy working with people.

The secretary is often the first contact a visitor has with the company or with the employer. In this public contact role, the secretary creates the first impression of the company. Needless to say, the impression must be a good one. Creating and maintaining a favorable company image requires courtesy, patience, persistence, sensitivity, tact, and the ability to get along with others.

Skill in dealing with people can be worth uncountable dollars in goodwill to the company. Some of this skill is innate to certain individuals, but for most people it comes with on-the-job experience. Being gracious to every office caller is the hallmark of an experienced secretary. The secretary's personal contribution to the maintenance of a hospitable atmosphere is the foundation for a businesslike office.

A responsibility associated with receiving office visitors is scheduling the employer's appointments. The secretary quickly learns the personal preferences of the employer and follows these guidelines to set appointment times. This responsibility is compounded when the secretary reports to more than one employer.

This chapter discusses one of the very important public relations duties of the secretary: receiving office visitors. Appropriate behavior in meeting the public is described. In addition, procedures for making appointments and maintaining records associated with the scheduling of appointments are given in detail.

---

[1] "The Evolving Role of the Secretary in the Information Age," *The Secretary* (April, 1983), page 12.

RECEIVING VISITORS

Methods of receiving visitors vary among companies. Large organizations generally have a reception area near the main entrance. Here a trained receptionist assists callers in determining which department or person to see and then calls the appropriate secretary for instructions as to the availability of the employer. If the visitor is known, the receptionist telephones the secretary without delay. If the caller has an appointment, the receptionist gives the visitor directions to the office. In some offices, the receptionist asks the visitor to wait until a secretary can personally escort the caller to the correct location. In offices requiring security clearance, the receptionist notifies the secretary after security procedures are completed, then the secretary meets the visitor in the reception area. When a secretary shows a visitor the way to the office, he or she walks slightly ahead, opens any doors, pushes elevator buttons, and talks about generalities.

In small companies, visitors may use a telephone in the lobby to announce their arrival. Assuming the caller has an appointment, the secretary may give directions or personally escort the visitor to the office.

Secretaries in very small offices are a visitor's initial contact with the company. Callers may or may not have appointments. These secretaries must decide immediately whether the visitor is at the right place, whether to admit the visitor, whether to schedule an appointment for a later time, or whether to refuse an appointment.

Whatever the office organization, the secretary has a twofold obligation: first, to adhere to the employer's preferences in admitting visitors and, second, to be courteous to all visitors.

The Employer's Preferences

Office visitors with or without appointments can be from outside the company, employees of the company, or personal friends. Members of the employer's family usually arrive without appointments. As a new secretary or as a secretary with a new employer, you need guidelines for handling office visitors. Your predecessor, if available, can give you this information. If the former secretary is unavailable or if your employer is new, ask your employer general questions about how to handle office visitors or learn through experience. If you report to several employers, you need to determine each one's preferences. Here are some questions about employer preferences and comments regarding them:

Questions	*Comments*
1. Does your employer want to see everyone who calls?	Many employers pride themselves on their open-door policy, meaning they will see any caller during office hours. You should ask this question.
2. Does your employer prefer to see certain callers (salespersons, for instance) at specified times only?	Some employers find this policy useful in making the best use of their time. Learn the answer to this question.
3. Which personal friends and relatives are likely to call? Which of these should be sent in without announcement? Who else should be admitted without appointments?	Do not ask these questions directly. You will soon sense the answer. Certain persons can always enter the employer's office without first obtaining your permission: top executives to whom your employer is responsible and their secretaries; co-executives and their secretaries; and the employer's immediate staff. Special privilege callers come in with confidence. They know they are welcome and usually introduce themselves to a new secretary.
4. How should callers be announced?	You may use the telephone or go directly into the office to announce a caller. Procedure may differ depending on the caller or the work the employer is presently doing. You may have to learn how to announce visitors from experience. Watch your employer's reactions to the way you approach different circumstances.

5. When should you attempt to terminate visits?

For some appointments, your employer will instruct you when and how to initiate a termination. When an appointment is running overtime and another caller is waiting, you should inform your employer that the next appointment is waiting. You can do so with a note or by using the telephone.

6. Are there callers that your employer prefers to avoid?

Feel free to ask this question. Often an employer is plagued with zealous salespersons.

Office Etiquette

Some secretaries are very adept at greeting visitors. They have personal characteristics which make them feel comfortable meeting strangers, and they have a knack for recognizing visitors who have been in the office previously. Their courteous manner makes the visitor feel welcome. Experience teaches this very important public relations function. As a new secretary, you should learn to be gracious and to follow proper office etiquette.

Attitude plays an important role in developing good office manners. Visitors to your office should be considered office guests, not interruptions. In other words, when a visitor comes to your desk, courtesy requires that you stop what you are doing, look directly at the person, smile, and speak immediately. Your greeting should be friendly and cheerful. A simple, pleasant "good morning" or "good afternoon" sets the stage for effective communication. To finish typing a line, to file another three letters, or to continue chatting with another employee is rude. If you are on the telephone, acknowledge the caller with a nod or a smile, indicating that you will be free momentarily.

When addressing the visitor, use Mr., Miss, Mrs., Ms., or a professional title and the last name. Although the use of first names is common in many of today's offices, you should use last names when addressing one of your superiors. In conversations with visitors, always refer to your employer by his or her last name, for instance, Mrs. Alexander. The same is true when addressing your employer in the presence of guests.

If the caller has an appointment, greeting the person by name adds a personal touch to the welcome. After the usual pleasantries, the secretary escorts the visitor to the executive's office and makes any necessary introductions in a courteous manner.

If an *unscheduled caller* wishes to see your employer, you should identify yourself and ask the caller's name, the company the caller represents, and the purpose of the visit. A greeting such as the following is appropriate: "Good morning. May I help you? I am Alice Brown, Mrs. Alexander's secretary. May I tell her who is calling?" The caller's business card provides some of this information and may give a clue to the reason for the visit. However, actually questioning the caller about the purpose of the visit may be necessary. In this case, tact and patience often are important. An experienced secretary handles the situation graciously and obtains the information for the employer.

The visitor on legitimate business is accustomed to making office calls. She or he will approach you, provide identification, state the purpose of the visit, and ask to see your employer. Occasionally, however, it may be necessary for you to ask: "May I tell Mrs. Alexander what you wish to see her about?" or "I am Alice Brown, Mrs. Alexander's secretary. May I help you?" If you need clarification from the visitor, ask questions. The easiest way to be sure that you have the information correct is to repeat what has been said. State it as you understand it.

Clients and customers are always given cordial and gracious treatment. Marketing representatives from businesses that supply materials and services related to the employer's work are treated with courtesy and attentiveness.

Deciding Whom to Admit

Scheduled appointments generally do not pose a problem. These visitors are admitted readily. For unscheduled appointments or in making appointments, some secretaries are inclined to become too protective of their employer's time. Often they turn away visitors the employer should see. Engage in a conversation with the caller long enough to determine if he or she should be admitted. When in doubt, ask if your employer wants to see the visitor.

A caller's business may involve a matter *outside the scope of your employer's duties.* You will save everyone's time by determining the nature of the visit first and, if necessary, referring the caller to the proper person. If you do not know the department or person the visitor should see, make every effort to find out before dismissing the visitor. The transfer should be made immediately by telephoning the proper office and explaining the situation. If an appointment is made at once, direct the caller to the correct office. If an appointment must be made for another day, confer with the visitor and set a mutually convenient time. In most cases your helpfulness in arranging this appointment will more than offset any inconvenience which the visitor may experience.

If your desk is placed inside the executive's office, callers will be inclined to bypass you and go directly to your employer. But if your desk is just outside the office, you will probably be fully responsible for determining who may enter. Although certain co-workers, friends, and family may enter your employer's office without your permission, they usually ask courteously if it is convenient to go in. When a visit is concluded, you may usher an infrequent caller to the exit, particularly if you work in an open plan office where traffic patterns may not be obvious.

Remembering Names and Faces

One extremely valuable secretarial technique is remembering names and faces so that you may greet callers in a sincere and natural manner. To remember names requires the following:

1. *Listening skill.* The key to good listening is paying attention to the speaker. Listen carefully without interruption when the name is pronounced. If in doubt, ask the person how to pronounce it or spell it. Writing the name phonetically in shorthand or in longhand will prevent mispronunciation. Being called by name is pleasant, but having one's name mispronounced is very annoying.
2. *A forceful effort to remember the name.* You can train yourself to remember a person's name by repeating it when you first hear it; using it when addressing the person; recording it, perhaps in a reference notebook or in a card file; and associating the person's name and face with the business represented or with sound alike words or phrases.

The ability to remember faces is another attribute of the superior secretary. Several devices may be used to develop this skill. The secretary may keep a card file of frequent callers, or when filing a business card, the secretary may associate the name on the card with the face of the caller. Illus. 3-1 contains two examples of how you may use business cards (or file cards) to remember names and faces. To recognize the employer's colleagues, the secretary should watch carefully for their pictures in company publications, newspapers, or magazines.

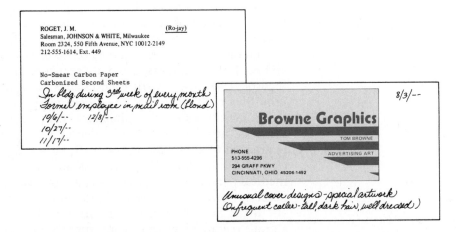

Illus. 3-1
These cards are
examples of
efficient memory
aids. Prepare a card
for each caller or
make notations
directly on the
caller's business
card.

Several companies whose success depends on effective public relations have developed techniques for improving internal relations. To help personnel recognize other members of the organization, one advertising agency publishes an organizational chart with the picture, title, and name of each executive in its company induction manual. Secretaries should learn the organization of the company early so that they know where the power in the company lies and can instantly address executives by name.

Keeping a Record of Visitors

Some offices maintain a register of office visitors as a matter of record or for security reasons. In a large company this register may be kept at a receptionist's desk; in a small office the secretary may keep this information. A register includes names, dates of visits, business affiliations, purposes of visits, and other pertinent information (see Illus. 3-2).

Illus. 3-2
With this ruled
register of visitors,
the secretary (or
the receptionist)
keeps a daily record
of helpful
information about
callers.

REGISTER OF OFFICE VISITORS						
Date	Time	Name and Affiliation	Person Asked For	Person Seen	Purpose of Call	
6/8/--	9:30	H. Horton, Cove Lighting Fix.	S.G.	✓	Sales rep	
"	10:30	L. Alton, Standard Printing	R.B.	✓	"	
"	11:45	R. Krause, luncheon appt.	R.B.	✓	Merrill cont.	
"	1:40	J. Keller, Flexwood Consultant	S.G.	✓	" "	
"	3:50	Flexwood delivery driver	—	—	Brought samp.	

To keep a record of visitors, offices ask callers to complete a printed registration form. In some cases the secretary may secure information from the caller and add it to the register at a later time.

Professional offices, such as those of lawyers, doctors, engineers, and public accountants, use daily registers in preparing periodic time reports. Time spent with each client, as recorded on the register, is used to compute the cost of services rendered.

Some offices keep an alphabetic card file of visitors, recording all visits as they occur. A card is filed by the caller's name and is cross-referenced to show the business affiliation. Doctors use the card system as a basis for billing patients and as a record of each patient's medical data. Purchasing agents can more easily remember the correct names of products and sales representatives by using such a file.

If the flow of visitors is small, the efficient secretary can keep a simple record of visitors conveniently and permanently on a desk calendar.

THE SECRETARY'S CONTRIBUTIONS

The individual secretary's personality, maturity, and knowledge of office etiquette set the stage for the employer to develop a positive rapport with the office visitor. A receptive climate includes making the visitor comfortable, making introductions, and using good judgment in interrupting the visitor's conference with the employer.

Preparing for Visitors

If the office has a receptionist (or a security officer), the secretary gives that person the caller's name, the time of the appointment, and any special instructions in anticipation of the caller's arrival. If several visitors will be meeting with the employer at the same time, the secretary arranges for extra seating and places notepads and pencils at convenient locations in the office. If you are aware that a caller is disabled, make preparations for special service.

Prior to an appointment, place all applicable files and documents on your employer's desk. Make your desk and your employer's office presentable by removing extra papers, folders, and newspapers. Empty ashtrays; remove used cups, soft drink bottles, and the like.

Discuss with your employer guidelines for handling interruptions and any other matters you think might come up during the appointment. Ask whether you should remain at your desk during the conference. Do not hesitate to pose these questions. You should have a clear understanding of your employer's preferences.

When an important out-of-town client or executive is expected, the secretary may be asked to make hotel reservations, order a rental car, and arrange for the visitor to be met at the airport. If the visitor is to see several members in the firm, notify each of the visitor's expected arrival time and, if appropriate, provide a brief description of the purpose of the visit. Some secretaries make a practice of sending visitors a city map with the office location and major travel routes marked on it.

A special situation arises when a visitor will be in the office for an extended period. You may be asked to find desk space and a temporary secretary, or you may assume additional responsibilities. Look upon this additional duty as an opportunity to learn more about your employer's work and the company.

Pleasant Waiting

In your role as a public relations representative for your employer, you should make a visitor's wait comfortable and pleasant. In order to accomplish this objective, attend to the visitor's hat and coat; offer coffee, tea, or an ashtray; provide current magazines or the morning newspaper.

Always check with your employer before ushering a visitor into the office. If a visitor is early for an appointment, ask your employer for instructions. Perhaps the appointment time can be changed. If it is not convenient to move up the time of the appointment, and the visitor must wait, give some indication of how long the wait will be.

After an unduly long wait, you may remind your employer that the caller is still waiting. If the employer indicates that it will be only a few more minutes, you may report this to the caller.

You are not expected to entertain office visitors. After exchanging pleasantries about the weather, travel time, and so forth, return to your duties. If the visitor persists in talking, avoid any discussion about company business or your employer.

If several visitors are waiting, admit each in proper turn. You are under no obligation to introduce them to each other unless all are attending the same conference.

Admitting the Visitor

If this is the visitor's first call, you should lead the way to the employer's office. Before leaving your desk, cover your work or unobtrusively slip it into a folder. If the employer's door is closed, knock. After a slight pause, enter the office with the visitor. When the proper introductions have been made, leave and close the door quietly.

In some instances you will not be able to leave your desk to escort the visitor to your employer's office. If this is the case, a simple gesture will indicate that the visitor may enter.

Sometimes the employer walks out to greet the caller. Should there be two callers waiting, indicate who is first.

Should voices carry from your employer's office, type or turn on soft music. If your employer has a speakerphone (see Chapter 12), be sure that it is off.

Introductions

Self-introductions are common in business, but occasionally the secretary is responsible for making introductions. Remember this rule when making introductions: The person given the greater courtesy is named first. In business introductions, the name of the person of higher position is given first. Include titles, such as Doctor, Captain, and Bishop, if known. For instance, a secretary to Harold Jenkins would introduce a new secretary, Mrs. Mary Elkins, to Mr. Jenkins in this fashion: "Mr. Jenkins, this is Mrs. Elkins, secretary to Ms. Elsworth." In introducing Bishop Manning to Mr. Jenkins, the secretary would say: "Bishop Manning, this is Mr. Jenkins." If a person has a hard-to-pronounce last name, practice saying the name several times before making the actual introduction.

When your employer introduces you to a client, business position takes precedence; therefore, the client is addressed first. Respond to introductions in a natural way. Say "I am glad to meet you" or simply "Hello." Never say "How do you do?" because it sounds too stilted. You should stand when greeting visitors or when being introduced to show respect, particularly if the visitor is considerably older than you or of great importance.

You should be aware of the following situations where sex, age, and rank, rather than strict business position, are factors in making an introduction:

Introduction	Factor in Presentation	First Named
1. woman to man (in a social setting)	sex (usually)	woman
2. woman to man (in a business setting)	rank	person with higher rank
3. dignitary (head of state or church dignitary) to your employer	rank	person with higher rank
4. young person to mature person	age	mature person
5. member of the armed forces or a college faculty to your employer	rank	person with higher rank
6. distinguished visitor to your employer	rank	distinguished visitor
7. an individual to a group	convenience	the individual then each person in the group

Handshaking

The practice of shaking hands reduces barriers between people. It is said that the way a person shakes hands reveals a great deal about that person. An enthusiastic handshake, for example, can signify that the person is sincere in offering the greeting.

Handshaking is customary and almost automatic between men. However, when a man and a woman shake hands, usually the woman offers her hand first. In a business office, the position of the other person may preclude the secretary from taking the initiative. One always accepts an extended hand. To do otherwise is a slight and will probably cause embarrassment.

The Difficult Visitor

Being courteous to certain visitors may require considerable discipline and restraint. Some callers are gruff; some are condescending; some are self-important or aggressive; some are even rude. To be gracious to these persons requires strong willpower.

A nuisance visitor can resort to all sorts of ruses to get past the secretary's desk. In such cases the secretary must exercise tact and firmness. Be wary of a person who, without giving a name, says, "I'm a personal friend" or "I have a personal matter to discuss with Miss Jones." The caller with legitimate, important business has everything to gain by providing a name and stating the purpose of the visit. You may explain to the caller that you are not permitted to admit visitors unannounced. You may also suggest that the caller write to your employer to request an appointment at a later date. If that fails, and the caller still refuses to give you a name or to state the purpose of the visit, offer a piece of paper and request that a short note be written. Enclose this note in an envelope and take it to your employer who can then decide whether to admit the caller.

Some callers try to obtain information from the secretary either about the executive, other employees, or the company. Be wary of prying questions. Do not answer them, except in generalities. A remark such as "I really don't know" will ordinarily stop such inquiries.

Interrupting a Conference

Most employers do not like to be interrupted during a conference. Interruptions are distracting and waste the time of all participants. For certain conferences you will be told that there are to be absolutely no interruptions. Most of the time, however, employers realize that an interruption is sometimes necessary. You and your employer should come to an understanding as to what matters warrant an interruption and also the best method to handle them—with a written note or a telephone call, for instance.

An unobtrusive way to handle an interruption is to type the message on a slip of paper and take it into the office, usually without knocking. Give the message directly to the conferees. If it requires a reply, wait for the answer. Two examples of written messages appear in Illus. 3-3. As a general rule, however, keep interruptions to a minimum. Try to handle matters that arise yourself.

```
Mrs. Judkins

Your secretary just called and asked that you
call back within 20 minutes for a very important
message. There is a telephone which you can use
just outside the conference room, (Dial 9 for an
outside line.)

A. A.



Mr. Zants

The secretary of Dr. Joseph Chou is on the line
at my desk and asks that you come to the
telephone for an important message from the
doctor. I'll wait outside my office while you talk.
Will you please let me know when you are ready to
leave my office?

A.A.
```

Illus. 3-3
Shown here are
two acceptable
ways in which to
handle typical
interruptions of
business
conferences. Before
acting, the
secretary decides
which procedure
will make the
interruption as
unobtrusive as
possible.

When there is a telephone call for the visitor, ask if you can take the message. If so, type it along with the caller's name, the date, and the time of the call; give the message to the visitor after the conference. If the one calling insists on speaking to the visitor, go into the conference room and say something like this: "Mr. Lawrence, Mrs. Rowett is on the telephone and wants to speak with you. Would you like to take the call here *(indicating which telephone he is to use)* or would you prefer using the telephone on my desk?" If the latter is chosen, the secretary takes care of other business away from the desk to afford the visitor privacy.

Some inconsiderate visitors do not know when to leave. Usually the employer rises as an indication that the conference is over, but occasionally a caller will not take the hint. You may help by taking a note in to the executive. This provides an opportunity for your employer to announce apologetically that it is time for another meeting. In order to free your employer, you may telephone from another person's desk to ask if an interruption is required. Often answering the telephone affords a sufficient break in the conversation to make the caller realize that the visit is over. You can also reduce overlong visits by informing the visitor upon entering that your employer has another scheduled appointment in ten minutes.

THE EMPLOYER'S APPOINTMENT RECORDS

A busy employer may see a number of visitors in the course of each day; therefore, in order to keep the office running smoothly, you must keep a manual (paper) or electronic record of daily appointments. It is also a good practice to keep appointment records from year to year as a general reference of important dates, names, meetings, etc. The effective secretary follows the employer's personal preferences in scheduling appointments, keeps a close watch on the employer's time, and uses good judgment in maintaining the appointment schedule.

Scheduling Appointments

Appointments are arranged in different ways. For example:

1. Appointments may be scheduled on a recurring basis. Using a calendar from the previous year, the secretary records regularly scheduled conferences of boards or corporation committees at which the employer's presence is necessary on the calendar at the beginning of the year. Additional recurring appointments are scheduled as new commitments are made.
2. The employer or the secretary may schedule an appointment over the telephone.
3. The executive or the secretary may schedule an appointment by mail.
4. The executive may ask the secretary to schedule a follow-up conference with someone who is currently in the office.
5. The secretary may schedule a definite appointment with a caller who happens to come in when the employer is out.
6. The secretary may arrange an appointment for the executive away from the office with individuals from outside the company.

If the office computer permits *electronic calendaring* (schedule planning), the secretary or the employer enters all appointments into a computer terminal. On a daily basis or a weekly basis, the secretary depresses the appropriate keys to print a record of a specific day's or week's appointments. The secretary may also view the schedule on a video display terminal. If electronic calendaring is not available, the secretary handles appointments manually as described below.

In most offices, an appointment book is used to record the employer's appointments (see Illus. 3-4). Note that appointments are for half-hour intervals. Calendars are also available in fifteen-minute segments. In maintaining this book, the secretary follows the four W's of scheduling appointments:

> WHO the person is—the name, business affiliation, and telephone number
>
> WHAT the person wants—an interview for a position, an opportunity to sell a product or to discuss business, etc. (Indicate any materials that will be needed for the appointment.)
>
> WHEN the person wants an appointment and how much time it will take.
>
> WHERE an appointment is to be held, if other than in the executive's office (Be sure to include the address and room number.)

If the individual making the appointment is in the office at the time of scheduling, the secretary gives that person a written reminder.

APPOINTMENTS
FRIDAY, APRIL 9, 19--

Time	Engagements	Memorandums
9:00	Mr. Smith, ext. 245	H R- Call DC Mohr re contract
9:30		
10:00	Meeting with sales personnel in third floor conference room	See Jane Kumar for annual sales graph
10:30		
11:00		
11:30	Mrs. Alice Carter of ABC Systems, 555-8297	Annex blueprints
12:00	Dr. Pardi, ext. 131	Hampton specifications

Illus. 3-4
An example of an appointment book.

The secretary's first duty each morning is to remind the employer of appointment commitments for the day. Pertinent information and files are placed on the employer's desk. Some employers prefer a typed list of the day's appointments that also includes a list of other matters that need attention. This list can be placed on the employer's desk the day before or the first thing in the morning. The list may be on 8½-by-11-inch paper or on a 5-by-3-inch card (see Illus. 3-5). If your employer prefers a 5-by-3-inch card, place it in a plastic sleeve so that it will not become dirty or dog-eared.

Some employers prefer a separate typed list of matters to be handled that day. The appropriate files are then attached to this list. Any matters not completed that day are carried over to the next day's list.

Illus. 3-5
The secretary types the employer's appointments in an appropriate format and places the list on the employer's desk the day before or the first thing in the morning.

```
                APPOINTMENTS AND REMINDERS FOR

                    Monday, April 7, 19--

     10:00    Staff Meeting

     11:00    James F. Syzek, Chamber of Commerce, 829-2300,
              Ext. 509, concerning the center development

     11:30    Sally Bennington, Mutual Life, 829-4502,
              renewal of policy

     12:00    Luncheon Meeting with Frank Snyder, University Club

      2:00    Budget Meeting


              Today's Reminders:

                 Call Frances Prouloz, 425-0034
                 Follow up on Emerson contract
                 License No. 533-429-3001 expires end of month
                 Review Inundo's proposal
```

Another successful practice is to include any questions you may have on the list of reminders that you type for your employer. The executive can write the answers directly on the sheet and leave it on the desk. In this way you can get answers without disturbing your employer.

The executive generally keeps a pocket diary or calendar as a convenient reference when attending meetings or visiting outside offices.

In addition to the official appointment book you maintain and the pocket calendar retained by your employer, there may also be an informal calendar on your employer's desk. To avoid conflicts in scheduling appointments, check all calendars on a daily basis.

The secretary who works for several executives maintains a separate list of appointments either on a computer or in a record book for each (see Illus. 3-6). The procedure for scheduling appointments for several executives is the same as that described in the foregoing paragraphs.

Keep appointment books, calendars, and/or computer printouts of your employer's appointment schedules for at least one year. They provide an excellent record of names, dates, and activities. The assistance they can provide in preparing activity reports, locating addresses and phone numbers, and settling possible business differences is immeasurable.

Date and Time Preferences. In selecting the date and time for an appointment, consider the personal preferences of the employer. Some guidelines to be considered are:

1. Schedule few, if any, appointments on Monday mornings, because the weekend accumulation of mail requires attention.
2. Provide unscheduled time between appointments so that they will not overlap.
3. Allow ample time in the schedule each day to take care of the mail.
4. Avoid late afternoon appointments.
5. Avoid appointments just before a trip.
6. Avoid appointments on the first day the executive returns to work after an absence of several days.
7. Suggest two alternate times for the appointment rather than ask the caller when it would be convenient for an appointment.
8. Make appointments to be held away from the office at convenient times for your employer; for example, the first thing in the morning on the way to the office, before or after lunch, or just before the end of the day are convenient times for these appointments.

Unless advised to the contrary, you must seek the approval of the employer in granting appointments. Tentatively record appointments in the appointment book or enter them into the computer terminal until they are explained and approved.

JANUARY 14

	Altman	Cross	McNutt	Haynes	Froehlich
8:00		In Miami 305 989-1011			
8:30					
9:00	R. Bender 821-4211		L. Timmons 356-8254	C. Basil 789-9339	Courthouse 9 – 5
9:30					
10:00			V. Skim 215-6129	Mrs. Rodder 981-7991	
10:30	L. Samuels 203 420-1481				
11:00				T. Benjamin 201-421-0219	
11:30					
12:00	T. Bandino Lunch 873-1891		Lunch	Lunch	
12:30				R. Braun 239-7969	
1:00			F. Perez 888-6239	S. Solomon 914-6199	
1:30					
2:00	D. Amos 739-4989		J. Silver 219-4569	Leave for Chicago 3 p.m. flight	
2:30					
3:00			J. Taylor 819-1699		
3:30					
4:00	Out from here		B. Matthews 819-8393		
4:30					
5:00			L. Nelson 766-7916		
5:30					
6:00					
6:30					

Illus. 3-6
An example of an appointment book kept by a secretary for five principals.

Avoiding Unkept Appointments. Nothing destroys good relations faster than an appointment not kept. Preventing conflicting appointments is one of the secretary's most difficult problems. Sometimes the executive forgets to tell the secretary about appointments made outside the office. Three suggestions from experienced secretaries may prove helpful:

1. Each morning try setting aside some time to review the day's appointment schedule with the executive. This may bring to mind an unrecorded appointment.
2. Provide the executive with a pocket diary to carry at all times.

Each day ask to see this book until the executive becomes accustomed to giving it to you for checking.

3.   At the end of the day, remind the executive of any unusual appointments. These may include a very early morning appointment or a night meeting.

Sometimes an employer may be unavoidably prevented from keeping an appointment. If so, you should notify the appropriate person(s) by telephone and, after checking calendars, suggest a later meeting time. Occasionally your employer may forget an appointment. You can be helpful by quickly locating your employer and seeing that the appointment is kept as scheduled. If the employer is suddenly called out of town, you may have to cancel an appointment or arrange for another person to see the visitor. If you must cancel an appointment, you should contact the visitor and report the cancellation without going into great detail. Be discreet and noncommittal. Comments such as "Mr. Sloan has been unavoidably detained" or "something unexpected has come up requiring a cancellation" are all that are required.

Saying No Tactfully. Obviously appointments should be refused as tactfully as possible. Refusals should be prefaced by a sincere "I'm very sorry, but. . . ." A logical reason for the refusal should always be given. Use your employer's name rather than the impersonal pronoun when explaining the situation to the caller. Other tactful ways to refuse appointments are to explain that the executive is in conference, must attend a meeting on that day, has a heavy schedule for the next two weeks, or is preparing to leave town. If a caller seems very disappointed over a refusal, you might offer to relay a message to the executive or take other appropriate, helpful action.

The Actual Appointment

Appointment records tell the secretary when to expect a person's arrival. If an individual within the company is late for an appointment, it is entirely proper for you to telephone that person's office to see if there has been a delay.

Often more than one person is involved in a meeting. When the first conferee arrives, should you tell the executive of the arrival or wait until the entire group has assembled? There is no hard and fast rule. The decision depends on the visitor's status, the employer's activity at the time, and individual preference. If the first visitor is very important, you may not only inform the employer of the arrival, but you may also notify other conferees to assemble at once. Otherwise, it is appropriate to wait until the whole group is assembled before informing the executive.

When your employer is going to another office for a meeting, anticipate the papers and files that will be required and place them in her or his briefcase.

Scheduling Appointments by Letter

Appointments with persons out of the city are frequently made by letter. A request for an appointment should be answered promptly and completely. A typical letter granting an appointment follows:

Dear Mr. Graham

Mrs. Andrews will be pleased to interview you on
Friday, April 3, at 11 a.m. If you can't be here
at that time, please let me know. I shall be glad
to reschedule the appointment.

Sincerely yours

When refusing a request for an appointment, include a tactfully phrased explanation. Note the following example:

Mrs. Andrews will be out of town the week of May
8; therefore, she will not be able to meet with
you on that date. She has asked me to express her
regrets and has suggested that you contact her
during the third week in May.

Canceling Appointments

If an appointment must be canceled, the secretary calls and notifies the visitor of the cancellation. The executive often asks the secretary to write a letter to an out-of-town visitor to confirm a cancellation to prevent embarrassment in case the telephone message was not received. If possible, the secretary schedules a new appointment immediately to take the place of the canceled one. The following is a typical cancellation notice:

Because Mrs. Andrews has been called out of town
unexpectedly, she cannot keep her appointment

with you at 3 p.m. on July 19. I shall let you
know when she returns so that we can arrange
another appointment at a mutually convenient
time.

SUMMARY

One of the most enjoyable secretarial responsibilities is receiving
office visitors. Recognizing frequent callers—their faces and names—is
an important aspect of this responsibility. Welcoming office callers
gives the secretary the opportunity to be a public relations representative for the employer and for the company. It also provides variety in
the office routine and a chance for the secretary to exercise social
skills.

If the company has a reception area, a register of office visitors
may be kept by a receptionist. Sometimes, however, such a register is
completed by the secretary.

Every employer has a set of preferences which the secretary must
consider when scheduling appointments. The secretary must know
these preferences and follow the employer's instructions.

The secretary schedules appointments using a paper appointment
record or a computer terminal. In many offices, the secretary gives the
employer a typed list of daily appointments, either on a five-by-three-
inch card or on standard-size paper. Prior to appointments, pertinent
files and other information are put on the employer's desk. During the
appointment, interruptions are kept to a minimum. If appointments
must be canceled, the secretary does so by telephone, often confirming
cancellations by letter.

SUGGESTED READINGS

Baber, Lina G. *Office Practices and Procedures.* Columbus, OH:
Charles E. Merrill Publishing Company, 1982.

DeVries, Mary A. *Private Secretary's Encyclopedic Dictionary*, 3d ed.
Englewood Cliffs, NJ: Prentice Hall, Inc., 1984.

Post, Elizabeth L. *Emily Post's Etiquette.* New York: Harper & Row
Publishers, Inc., 1984.

QUESTIONS FOR DISCUSSION _____

1. Why is the secretary often considered a public relations representative for the company?
2. Why is a secretary's attitude a contributing factor to office etiquette?
3. Describe the uses of a card file for frequent callers, the register of visitors, and the appointment book. Which of these three office tools do you regard as most important and why? Do most offices need all three of these records? Explain your answer fully.
4. Given a choice, which would you prefer to use exclusively, paper appointment records or electronic calendaring? Give the reasons for your choice.
5. When greeting office visitors, how can a secretary show *active* listening?
6. In the following situations, you are asked to introduce the two persons specified. Which person would you afford the greater courtesy by naming first?
   a. Your employer's 14-year-old daughter and a secretary in the office
   b. A well-known politician and your employer, president of the company
   c. Your elderly mother and your employer, Carl Samson
   d. Miss Alvarez, a business product sales representative, and your employer, Ralph Hazelton
   e. Rabbi Harold Silverman and your employer, Ms. Fishburg
   f. Professor James Ford and Alfred Bostick, Dean, College of Business
7. In discussing an employer's absence from the office or in canceling an appointment, why should a secretary guard against giving specific reasons to a person outside the organization?
8. Describe specific situations where you would request employer guidelines in handling interruptions.
9. Generally employers do not like to be interrupted during a conference. Yet, as a secretary, you may have to talk with your employer. How would you proceed to do this?
10. Circle the proper word in the parentheses. Refer to the Reference Guide to correct your answers.
    a. There were (less, fewer) people at the concert this year.
    b. I can (cite, sight, site) the regulations from memory.
    c. The (eminent, imminent) author has written so many best-sellers that the literary prize seemed (eminent, imminent).
    d. Because I will be moving (farther, further) away from the city, I have no (farther, further) interest in the position.

e. As a member of the (consul, council, counsel) on banking, I am in a position to give the president wise financial (consul, council, counsel).

f. The legislative committee will meet in the east wing of the (capital, capitol).

PROBLEMS

1. Analyze the following situations. How would you handle each of them? If the solution requires a conversation or note, indicate exactly what you would say. On a piece of paper, type your answer to each situation.

a. A visitor on crutches is expected in ten minutes. You think the visitor will be bringing a carton of materials for your employer.

b. A visitor is in your employer's office, and it is closing time.

c. A visitor, while waiting for a scheduled appointment, makes the following statement: "I understand your employer was in New York last week."

d. Your employer's daughter has called the office three times within the last hour. Your employer is in a meeting with other officers of the company.

e. Your employer has called an important meeting in the office for 10:30 a.m. The company's most important customer arrives fifteen minutes early for this meeting.

f. A visitor whose appointment you forgot to cancel arrives as scheduled. Your employer is working under pressure to complete an important contract.

g. An unscheduled visitor comes into the office to talk with your employer.

h. Two important visitors are in the office with your employer. It is time for your coffee break.

i. A caller who has failed to keep two appointments telephones for a third one.

2. As secretary to Russell Sabin of Universal Interiors, one of your responsibilities is to maintain his appointment book. The following appointments and activities have been scheduled for October 30. Type a list in an attractive style to give to Mr. Sabin before the office closes on the 29th. Note any reminders at the bottom of the page.

a. Mr. Sabin has an appointment with the president of Universal Interiors, Charles Mackey, at 9 a.m., in Mr. Mackey's office.

b. A letter from S. T. White of San Francisco requested a 10 a.m. appointment, which was granted by return mail.

c. Mr. Sabin is to attend an Administrative Management Society meeting at 7:30 p.m. at the Hyde Hotel.

d. Mrs. Unger, a marketing manager with Universal, has an appointment at 2 p.m. to show samples of home decorations.

e. Mr. Sabin must appoint a committee by November 1 to handle an outing for the Advertisers' Club.

f. Luncheon at 12:30 with Sara Miller, controller of Universal, at Sullivan's on 10th Street. Mr. Sabin is to meet Ms. Miller downstairs at 12:15 for the short walk to the restaurant.

g. Mr. White wrote that he is unable to keep his scheduled appointment for 10 a.m.

h. Mr. Sabin is to interview an applicant, Miss Ellen Crane, at 11 a.m.

i. Mr. Sabin requested that you make a morning appointment with Mr. Andrews, a loan officer, at the bank. You made the appointment for 10 a.m.

Part One   Case Problems _____

Ruth Freed was in her first week as secretary to Howard Gerard, sales manager for Consumer Products. She had been selected from a dozen applicants and was enthusiastic about her new position until she heard Mr. Gerard on the telephone: "Yes, I will get the figures to you immediately. In fact, I'll have my girl hand-deliver them to you within fifteen minutes."

Ruth was annoyed by her designation as "my girl" and by the tactless "I'll have her. . . ." Her immediate reaction was that perhaps she had made a mistake in accepting this position. Mr. Gerard's comments suggested that he did not view her as a professional.

She delivered the figures, however, and said nothing. After thinking over the situation, she realized that she liked everything about the new position except Mr. Gerard's attitude. She decided to plan a course of action that would change his feelings about secretarial employees and came to you for advice.

What would you tell her? Why?

Robert Slocum is secretary to Bertram Wine, manager of administrative services for Advance Advertising Company. In addition to Mr. Wine, Robert works for three other individuals, all of whom have different demands and schedules. Robert's job duties include general tasks, such as sorting the mail, answering the telephone, and greeting the public. Within the last month, Robert has felt increasing stress in trying to complete all of his work during the regular workday. Coming to work a half hour early and leaving later in the day has not helped the situation. When he mentioned the work overload to Mr. Wine, Mr. Wine told Robert to discuss the problem with his other three employers because his (Mr. Wine's) work takes priority. Feeling caught in the middle further increased the amount of stress Robert associated with his work. Being company-minded, Robert realized that the work of all his employers must get done, and he decided not to bring up the matter with them.

How can Robert convince Mr. Wine that additional staff is needed?

81

**Case 1-3
ENFORCING
SAFETY
REGULATIONS**

Janet Simms works as a secretary in the research and development department of a large corporation, an area that is vulnerable to accidents. She is a member of the company's safety committee, which has just issued a safety manual for all employees. As a member of the committee, she is safety inspector for her division.

Dr. Fred Larrimore, a research chemist, is one of the worst violators of safety measures. As Janet walked into his office to pick up a report on her way to lunch, he was reading a statistical report while smoking and leaning back in his chair with his feet on his desk. She tripped on an electrical cord connecting Dr. Larrimore's computer to the printer on a side table. Exasperated and shaken Janet exclaimed, "Dr. Larrimore, haven't you read our safety manual? I could have injured myself by your carelessness. Why do you suppose we have a safety committee if the executives themselves are going to ignore the regulations?"

Dr. Larrimore apologized, but made no effort to place the cord behind his desk, out of the way of visitor traffic. He gave her the report and then returned to his former position. Janet apologized too, for speaking rudely and left.

What management principle should Janet follow to secure compliance with regulations?

PART TWO

INFORMATION PROCESSING: BASIC TASKS/RESPONSIBILITIES

Information is the orderly and useful arrangement of ideas or facts. The office is the place where information is gathered and put into written form. The way an office is organized to handle information, from origination to final distribution, is called *information processing*. Your responsibilities as a secretary will put you at the center of your company's information processing activities.

Preparing high quality written communications is a primary information processing responsibility for the secretary. The secretary who applies good written communication skills and adapts to and uses available equipment, such as electronic typewriters, word processors, and microcomputers, will be an asset to the executive.

Another major information processing responsibility of the secretary is handling mail effectively. This involves recording its receipt, organizing it, assembling data for an answer, and finally transmitting the reply. In addition, the secretary is frequently responsible for handling postal and shipping services in the least expensive and most expeditious way.

Chapter 4

Preparing Final Documents

Businesses process and distribute many kinds of written communication. Letters are received and sent, memos are dictated, and reports are analyzed. All these types of communication involve the preparation of documents. A *document*, as referred to in this chapter, is any written or printed business communication that conveys information. The most common type of written business communication is correspondence: letters and memos. Other kinds of documents include reports, forms, statistical tables, envelopes, labels, and index or file cards.

The ability to produce error-free, attractive documents is a basic requirement of the secretarial position. This chapter focuses on the various kinds of equipment used to produce documents, the supplies associated with document preparation, and the most effective procedures for producing superior documents. Familiarity with different kinds of keyboarding equipment, supplies, and procedures will help make your job easier and the documents you produce more attractive.

TYPES OF EQUIPMENT

At the core of document preparation is the equipment used by the secretary to produce documents. In preparing documents, secretaries may operate one or more types of equipment: single element electric typewriters, electronic typewriters, word processors, or microcomputers. This section will briefly explain the features of equipment used to prepare documents.

Single Element Electric Typewriters

The single element electric typewriter has a stationary carriage. An *element*, a sphere the size of a golf ball, moves on its own carrier from left to right across the paper. Alphabetic and special symbols are embossed on the surface of the sphere. Striking a key positions the element to type that letter or symbol.

The first single element typewriter to receive wide acceptance was the IBM Selectric. Many other manufacturers have single element machines on the market today.

A distinctive feature of the single element machine is that it permits the use of a wide variety of type styles and special symbols. Over 75 interchangeable elements are available, each with a different type style or with different symbols. To change the type style, the operator removes the element and inserts one with the desired type style. Furthermore, some single element machines enable the typist to switch from pica type (ten characters per inch) to elite type (twelve characters per inch) simply by releasing a lever and changing the element.

One single element machine that has gained wide acceptance among secretaries is the self-correcting typewriter introduced by IBM. Through the use of lift-off tape and a single button on the keyboard, errors are lifted off the page. The correction key makes erasures unnecessary; therefore, typing is faster, neater, and easier.

Electronic Typewriters

An example of an electronic typewriter that is widely used in today's offices appears in Illus. 4-1. Unlike an electric typewriter which has roughly 1,000 levers, springs, gears, and screws inside the case, the electronic typewriter has almost no works; only a printing element glides across the paper. When the keys are depressed, a handful of tiny silicon chips, about one-fourth inch square, tell the machine what to do. The distinguishing feature of this typewriter is its memory. Material once keyboarded can be stored internally and retrieved automatically.

Most major typewriter manufacturers have introduced electronic typewriters with a wide range of special features. Illus. 4-2 identifies some of the common features of electronic typewriters.

Word Processors/Microcomputers

The use of word processors and microcomputers allows documents to be revised and reorganized without complete retyping. The introduction of word processors and microcomputers into the office has, therefore, improved the secretary's ability to produce superior final documents in a relatively short period of time.

Word processors and microcomputers operate electronically and have a number of common components including a keyboard for entering information, a memory for storing information, and a device for printing stored information. Most word processors and microcomputers have video display screens that enable the operator to see information being produced. The functions of word processors and microcomputers will be covered in detail in Chapter 9, "Data and Word Processing."

Illus. 4-1
The electronic typewriter makes work easier for the secretary because functions that were performed manually by the typist are done automatically. This typewriter stores in memory information that is typed on the keyboard.

Brother International Corporation

FEATURES OF ELECTRONIC TYPEWRITERS

Automatic Centering and Underscoring	Copy can be centered between margins and between tab settings automatically.
Electronic Margins and Tabs	Frequently used margins and tabs can be stored and recalled.
Error Correction	Errors can be corrected by backspacing and striking over. A word or a full line can be erased with one stroke.

Decimal Tab	Statistical columns can be automatically aligned at the decimal point. This feature is especially useful in typing financial and other statistical reports.
Automatic Carrier Return	A hot zone consisting of five to seven characters before the right margin is established. The carrier automatically returns when the word ending a line comes within the hot zone. Some systems do not hyphenate; rather, any word that will not fit entirely on a line is automatically dropped to the next line.
	Some systems provide a feature called *Scan.* This feature stops at any place where a hyphenation decision is required to allow the operator to examine the material.
	The automatic carrier return allows the operator to type text at a uniform pace without having to pause at the end of each line to return the carrier.
Dual Pitch	Ten and twelve characters can be typed to the inch and a wide variety of type styles is available.
Proportional Spacing	Right margins can be justified.
Automatic Indentation	By depressing the carrier return key, the carrier returns to the desired place in the copy automatically. Once the operator decides where indentations are needed, the typewriter remembers where to indent.
Automatic Relocate	When it is necessary to go into the body of a document to make a correction, the relocate key returns the carrier to the point where typing is to be resumed.
Phrase Dictionary Storage	A self-contained dictionary stores 7,000 to 8,000 characters on an electronic chip. (This is equivalent to storing five one-page letters of average length.) Frequently used words, phrases, sentences, and paragraphs can also be stored and played back without retyping.

Illus. 4-2
Special features of
some electronic
typewriters.

RIBBONS, STATIONERY, AND CARBON PAPER

Most supplies with which a secretary works are available in a wide range of quality. Many factors, particularly use and quality, must be considered in the selection of supplies. Illus. 4-3 summarizes the features of some of the paper supplies secretaries use.

Typewriter Ribbons

Typewriter ribbons are of three types: one-time film, multiuse film, and fabric. Each type has certain properties to recommend it for producing the specific kind or quality of work desired.

The sharpness of final documents depends upon the thinness of the ribbon used: the thinner the ribbon, the sharper the imprint. Also, the thinner the ribbon is, the more yardage on a spool. More yardage means less frequent ribbon changes. Ribbons range from cotton (the thickest) to nylon, to coated Mylar, to polyethylene film (the thinnest).

One-Use Film Ribbon	Also called carbon ribbon. Continuous, narrow, coated strip advances at the rate of one stroke per space on the ribbon. Used once and discarded. Produces uniformly even type on page. Preferred for high quality work.
Multiuse Film Ribbon	Similar to one-use film ribbon except the same spot can be struck from six to nine times. No variation in print density. Designed to travel very slowly from spool to spool. Does not reverse and is discarded when it comes to the end. Provides security of information, since the imprinted ribbon on the spent spool cannot be read as it can on one-use film ribbon. Has longer life than one-use film ribbon.
	Because it prints very sharply, does not fill letters, is clean to handle, and erases easily, film-base ribbon is preferred for high quality work.
Fabric Ribbons	Nylon is the longest wearing and the thinnest. Economical and appropriate for most in-house communications. Available in several colors and concentrations of ink.
Special Purpose Ribbons	Choices vary according to typing purpose: offset ribbon for typing offset masters; photostat ribbon for preparing copy for photostating; opaque ribbons for photocopy work.
Colored Ribbons	Available in various colors to complement company letterheads and add distinction to correspondence. Available with lift-off tape for the IBM Correcting Selectric typewriter.

Bond Paper

Bond paper is so called because originally it was used for printing bonds, which had to be long lasting. It can be made of all-cotton fiber (sometimes called *rag*), of sulfite (a wood pulp), or of any proportion of the two. High cotton fiber bond suggests quality and prestige, and it ages without deterioration or chemical breakdown. It has a good, crisp crackle. It is hard to the pencil touch and is difficult to tear. High sulfite bond is limp, soft to the pencil touch, and easy to tear.

There are excellent all-sulfite papers in crepelike, ripple, or pebble finishes that many companies use exclusively. Letterhead is usually made of 25 percent or more cotton fiber. Forms for business records are usually made entirely of sulfite or a high percentage of sulfite.

Watermarks. Hold a piece of paper up to the light. See the design or words? That is the *watermark*. It can be the name or trademark of the company using the paper or the brand name of the paper. Since only better bond paper is watermarked, the mark is a hallmark of quality.

There is a right side and a top edge to plain watermarked sheets. Always have the watermark read across the sheet in the same direction as the typing. Put watermarked sheets in your stationery drawer in such a manner that they will be in the right position when they are inserted in the typewriter.

Substance. The weight of paper is described by a substance number. The number is based on the weight of a ream consisting of 500 sheets of 17-by-22-inch paper. If the ream weighs 20 pounds, the paper is said to be of substance 20 or 20-pound weight. One thousand sheets of 8½-by-11-inch paper can be cut from one ream. Paper is produced in a wide range of weights. Letterhead and envelopes are usually of substance 16, 20, or 24. Airmail stationery, now used primarily for overseas correspondence, is usually of substance 9 or 11.

Erasability. You can erase typing from some bond papers very easily. This feature is usually indicated by the paper's brand name, such as *Ezerase* or *Corrasable*. Ribbon ink or carbon rests lightly on the surface of the paper and is only gradually absorbed into the paper; thus, you can quickly and neatly remove fresh typing with a pencil eraser. But you can also easily smear or smudge the surrounding typing.

The most difficult papers on which to make neat erasures and corrections are the inexpensive all-sulfite ones like those you probably use in your typing courses. A neat erasure can be made without too much difficulty on a 16-pound high cotton fiber bond.

Second Sheets

Thin sheets of paper used for file copies of letters and for multicopy typing are described as *onionskin, manifold,* or simply *second*

sheets. They are lightweight papers of substances 7 to 13 with smooth, glazed, or cockle (rippled) finishes. A stack of these sheets can be difficult to control, because they tend to slither and slide—mostly onto the floor. Sheets with cockle finish slip less than others and give the appearance of being of better quality, but they create more bulk in the files than do smooth finish papers.

Copy sheets are used in many offices. They are second sheets with the word "COPY" printed on them. They are used for material that should be so identified. When necessary, indicate that a plain sheet is a copy by typing the word "COPY" conspicuously in all capital letters on the sheet, letterspaced and centered from seven to nine lines from the top.

Letterheads

Letterheads vary widely, depending on individual taste and the nature of the company's business. Most large companies have a standard company letterhead that includes the company's name, address, telephone number (including area code), and sometimes the name and title of an individual. The letterhead may contain information about the company's product or display the company's trademark. All letterheads may be ordered with matching envelopes and blank sheets for two-page letters.

Top management usually has prestige letterheads that differ from the standard company letterhead in style, printing process, weight, and cotton fiber content. The letterhead of top management usually shows only the company name, address (no phone number), and the executive's name and title. In addition, the executive may have a personal letterhead that is used mainly for outside work with foundations or charity organizations. Personal letterheads may show only the executive's name and address or only the name. In general, as an individual is elevated in the company, his or her letterhead acquires simplicity and dignity befitting the position. The trend in all letterheads is toward simplicity.

Carbon Paper

Traditional typewriter carbon paper is thin, dark-colored tissue, coated on one side with carbon. It is available in a great variety of sizes, colors, weights, finishes, and qualities. It can be obtained in special purpose packs as well as in single sheets. Following is a brief description of the various kinds of carbon paper:

Topcoated	The top side is coated with finish that prevents curling. Reduces wrinkling which causes "trees"

	or "veins" on the copy. A good grade is usually smudge-free and long lasting.
Conventional	Basically the same as topcoated but comes in different finishes, such as soft and hard. The finish preferred depends on the typewriter (manual or electric), size of the typeface, hardness of the cylinder, and the number of copies to be made.
Plastic Base	Similar in appearance to carbon paper but more accurately described as a copying film. It employs ink, not carbon. Made of film, not paper. Curl-free, easily handled, difficult to tear, smudge-free, and long wearing. Used for high quality work.
Special Features	*Extended uncoated side or bottom edge* permits easy, smudge-free handling. *Micrometric edge* contains a numbered guide on an extended right edge which shows unused lines on the page. Preassembled *carbon sets* are convenient to use, but can only be used once.

LETTERHEADS, ENVELOPES, AND OTHER PAPER SUPPLIES

Letterheads	*Standard Company Use.* Business size (8 1/2" × 11"); usually 16, 20, or 24 pound with 25 percent cotton fiber content (rag).
	Top Executive Use. Business size and Monarch size (7 1/4" × 10"); usually 24 pound bond with 100 percent cotton fiber content.
Matching Envelopes	*Standard Company Use.* No. 10 (9 1/2" × 4 1/8") of same weight and cotton fiber content as letterhead.
	Top Executive Use. No. 10 and No. 7 (7 1/2" × 3 3/8") of same weight and cotton fiber content as letterhead.
Color	Usually white, however tinted pastel shades are increasing in popularity.
Plain Sheets to Match Letterheads	Same weight, cotton fiber content, color, and size as letterhead. (Never use a letterhead for the second page or subsequent pages of a letter.)

Interoffice Letterheads	Business size or half size (8 1/2″ × 5 1/2″); usually 16 or 18 pound bond with high sulphite content.
Interoffice Envelopes	Oversized, strong, perforated reusable envelopes with many ruled lines for the names of successive addressees.
Oversize Envelopes	Strong white or manila envelopes with gummed flaps and/or metal clasps (9 1/2″ × 12″ or 10″ × 13″) that allow letters and reports to be mailed unfolded.
Second Sheets or Carbon Copy Sheets	Thin sheets; business size or legal size (8 1/2″ × 13″ or 14″); various colors and finishes; usually 7 to 13 pound. Also called onionskin or manifold. Used for rough drafts and carbons.
Carbon Paper	For description and use, see page 91.
Forms	Usually in pads to prevent waste. Multicopy forms may be continuous, accordion-folded, and perforated. After the "chain" is inserted in the typewriter to type the first set, the rest feed through automatically. To eliminate handling interleaved carbons, accordion-folded forms often have spot carbon coating on the back of each copy only where the typing is to appear on the copy underneath.
Labels and Return Addresses	Usually gummed on the back; packaged in sheets or strips; printed with the company's return address.
Legal Paper	Top quality bond; legal size (8 1/2″ × 13″ or 14″); plain or with ruled margins.
Plain Sheets	Business size; usually 13 to 16 pound; possibly made of easy-to-erase bond. Most often used for reports and general typing. Also used for copying machines.
Reprographics Paper	Business and legal size; various colors and substances.
Writing Pads	*Ruled Paper.* Business or legal size; usually yellow. *Scratch.* Assorted sizes; usually sold by the pound.

Illus. 4-3
Summary of paper
office supplies.

OFFICE FORMS

American business *runs* on paper forms. In fact, every business function involves some type of business form at some point in its operation. A function is either initiated by a form, authorized by one, recorded on one, or summarized on one. Everyone in a business organization is involved with paperwork, and the secretary is no exception. A significant portion of the secretary's time is spent completing forms, copying information onto forms, reading forms, interpreting forms, routing forms, filing forms, using forms for reference, and handling and transmitting forms. Furthermore, the secretary is not only a user of forms but may be a designer of them as well.

Types of Forms

Modern technology and business ingenuity have provided multiple copy business forms in different configurations that encompass many timesaving features.

Unit Sets and Snap-Out Forms	Also called carbon sets or carbon packs. Preassembled with interleaved one-time carbons. Each unit is self-contained. Permits easy one-motion removal of carbons; timesaving; convenient.
Carbonless Forms	Permits impressions from copy to copy through dyes and chemicals built into the paper; timesaving; smudge-free. Less bulk increases the number of copies that can be made.
Continuous Forms	Forms are joined together in a series of accordion-pleated folds. Used for quantity work, such as processing invoices, statements, purchase orders, payroll checks, and the like; timesaving.
Spot Carbon Coated Forms	Carbon is applied at designated spots on back of each form in pack. Permits production of a number of different forms at one sitting. For example, packing slips, shipping orders, address labels, inventory withdrawal slips, and invoices—each containing only the appropriate data—can be processed at the same time.

Forms Control and Design

As a business expands, the number of forms that it needs seems to multiply at an astonishing rate. Consequently, most large business and government organizations have established systems for forms control. Such systems periodically review forms and discontinue those that have become useless or obsolete. Provision is also made for the establishment of definite procedures to prepare and approve new forms.

The secretary may be expected to exercise similar control over forms originating in the executive's office. This would include a systematic review of all forms for their possible improvement, the elimination of unneeded forms, and the design of new forms that will expedite the work of the office. In designing new forms, consider the following factors:

Necessity. Is a separate form really needed? Could it be combined with an existing form? In what ways will a new form save time?

Wording. Does the title clearly indicate the purpose of the form? Does it contain a code number for filing reference? Does the form contain all necessary information? Does it provide *only* necessary information? (Example: The company name is not needed on intra-company forms.) Does the form mechanize the writing of repetitive data? Are code numbers and check boxes used to eliminate unnecessary typing?

Disposition. Does each copy of the form clearly indicate its disposition? Is color coding or other appropriate means used to facilitate distribution?

Arrangement. Is the form compatible with the equipment on which it is to be used? (Example: If it is to be filled in on a typewriter; do the type lines conform to typewriter vertical line spacing and require a minimum of tabulator stops?) Does the sequence in which the data are to be inserted follow the sequence of information on the data source? Is there the right amount of fill-in space? Will the arrangement of the form speed operations?

Retention. If the form is to be retained, how and where? Does the form size fit the filing system?

Before designing a form, answer these questions:

What is the purpose of the form?
How does it affect other procedures? other forms?
Can it be combined with another form?
Where does the information originate? Where does it go?
Where do parts go?
How is the form filed?

Will additional copies ever be needed?

What types of data will appear on the form? words? figures? check mark responses?

Does the form present information in a logical sequence?

Can the form be easily identified by title, number, or color?

Is the form a standard size that can be processed on existing equipment?

OFFICE SUPPLIES

The executive usually delegates to the secretary the responsibility of procuring office supplies. Unless the executive has a special need or unless high costs are involved, the secretary uses personal judgment to make selections. The procedures for obtaining office supplies differ for the secretary in a large office and the secretary in a small office; however, both must have a knowledge of supplies in order to choose those that best fill executive and secretarial needs.

The secretary in a small office is a direct buyer. In a large office, however, the secretary may either request forms and supplies from a central stock or requisition them from a purchasing department. The secretary who has supervisory responsibilities may select and purchase supplies for an entire department or company. In this case, the secretary must use sources of product information to compare supplies and find dependable vendors. Businesslike purchasing procedures, of course, must be followed.

Quality of Supplies

Some business people believe it important to use only the highest quality stationery, forms, and office supplies; others find medium quality adequate. Every office uses a pride factor and an economic factor to determine the level of quality it pursues. You will not find this quality level precisely stated or written out for you, nor is there a question you can tactfully ask to determine it. You can deduce it, though, by observing the characteristics of supplies currently being used in your office and by examing cost records.

Local Sources of Supply

Local office supply stores cannot carry all varieties of all brands of all office supplies. Each store carries one or two brands of an item in varieties most commonly sold, none of which may exactly fill your needs. Therefore, your selection is limited and often you cannot buy as discriminatingly as you would like.

Sales Representatives. Representatives of office supply agencies may call on you with samples and price catalogs. They, too, limit themselves in brands and varieties; so choice is again restricted. Since you cannot possibly know everything about all supplies that a particular sales representative carries, it is helpful to have a dependable sales representative of whom you can ask advice. When you are in the market for an item, explain your exact needs. Sales representatives are trained to help you make a wise selection. After you have made a selection, you will probably order your supplies directly from a sales office over the telephone.

Brand Name Supplies. Sometimes you want a *specific variety of a specific brand*. If the variety is not sold locally, you can order it from the manufacturer, or you may ask your local office supply store to order it for you.

Some pieces of equipment, you may decide, produce better results if you use supplies that are sold by the manufacturer. If no local source is listed in the telephone book, ask the manufacturer to send your dealer information on the availability of their products.

Collecting Information

Collect specific information about each kind of office supply you use. Suppliers often furnish helpful literature. Sales representatives can also provide you with information. Often descriptive, informative brochures are given away at exhibits of office equipment and supplies. Frequently advertisements in professional magazines offer to send more detailed information about specific products.

Choosing Supplies

Choose supplies that are in the quality range of your office. There is no economy in cheap supplies. Unknown brands may contain inferior materials or may be off-sized. Consequently, they may be more expensive in the long run than the better grades. For example, a carbon paper of good quality gives many more writings than an inferior brand. *Usually you get just about what you pay for.*

There is no reason for shifting from one brand of supply to another as long as the one in use is satisfactory and fair in price. On the other hand, supplies are constantly being changed. A product may be greatly improved since the last time you examined it.

When contemplating a change in brand, get samples of competing products and test them all under the same circumstances. Compare prices and quality. Analyze claims made regarding extra service or added efficiency. If the price is higher, you should decide whether the difference is justified.

Overbuying

Some office supplies deteriorate when they are held in stock too long. For example, carbon paper dries and hardens, typewriter ribbons dry out, some paper yellows, liquids evaporate, and erasers harden. New products may be preferable to those you have stocked. It is better, then, to err on the side of underbuying than to overbuy. Repeat orders can always be placed shortly before supplies are needed.

You may tend to overbuy because of quantity prices. An item that costs 50 cents a unit in small quantities usually costs appreciably less when bought in large quantities. Consequently, it may seem to be economical to order in large amounts. The monetary savings is not always the prime consideration, however.

Some paper suppliers have arrangements whereby a year's supply may be purchased at one time. Thus, while you obtain the price advantage of a bulk purchase, the paper is delivered in specific lots at designated intervals through the year. Such a plan provides a price advantage without the problem of storing the paper until it is needed.

Requisitions and Invoices

In a large company, most supplies are kept in stock and are obtained by submitting either a supply requisition or a written request. Items not carried in stock must be requested by submitting a purchase requisition to the purchasing department. This form should provide as detailed a description of the needed item as you can provide.

'A secretary or supervisor who has the authority to purchase supplies has added responsibilities. These include making a careful record of each item purchased, checking deliveries, and verifying the accuracy of the items and extensions on the invoice or bill that accompanies or follows delivery.

When an item is invoiced (included and charged on an invoice) but is omitted from the shipment or is substituted or defective, the secretary notes that fact on the invoice and requests an adjustment.

Storage of Supplies

If you wish to determine how neat and orderly a secretary really is, examine the supply storage cabinet. A storage cabinet that presents an array of boxes, packages, and articles in complete disorder is no recommendation for efficiency.

The well-arranged storage cabinet has several characteristics. Similar materials are placed together. Materials used more frequently are placed at the front of the cabinet at the most convenient level for reaching. Small items are placed at eye level; bulk supplies and reserve stock are placed on the lower shelves. Shelf depths should be adjustable to fit supplies and conserve space.

All packages are identified by oversize lettering made with a marking pen or by a sample of the contents affixed to the front. Unpadded stationery is kept in flip-up, open-end boxes. (There are no carelessly opened paper-wrapped packages.) Loose supplies, such as paper clips, are kept separately in open marked boxes. A list of all supplies by shelves is often posted on the inside of the door.

YOU AND YOUR EQUIPMENT

Typing competence is more than speed with accuracy. It is economy in using time and supplies and knowing how to organize your work. It is also discovering ways to increase your output and efficiency. Competence comes only with experience. Become comfortable with your equipment by exploring its features and learning its capabilities, then give it the care it requires.

Instruction Booklets

Every piece of equipment has a helpful, reassuring booklet of instructions on its use. The booklet accompanies the machine on delivery but often disappears before the machine does. If your predecessor has not left an instruction booklet for you, request one from the manufacturer. It will save you time and give you confident know-how. There is nothing worse than struggling with a strange machine.

Learn the capacities of your equipment. It may have features of which you are not aware, such as aids for the accurate realignment of typing, scales to determine center positions, fractional spacing devices, and tabulation time-savers. The special features of your equipment are illustrated and explained in the instruction booklet.

Machine Care

Even though most equipment is sturdy and almost self-sufficient, it does require attention from you. Read the machine care section of your instruction booklet. No amount of skill is going to produce good copy if the equipment is not kept in excellent working condition.

CARBON COPIES

The number of carbon copies that secretaries prepare is decreasing because of the accessibility of copying machines. Making corrections on multiple carbons is a slow, costly, and boring process. Consequently, secretaries love copying machines, but in all too many cases the copier is overused to produce a very costly substitute for the carbon copy. The cost of operating and maintaining a copying machine and the cost of time lost going to and from the copier results in a very high per copy cost. Therefore, management consultants are emphasizing that the carbon copy is still the least expensive method of producing copies of outgoing correspondence and short reports.

The techniques concerning carbon copies given here may seem commonplace; but these procedures are used by master secretaries. They will allow you to produce quality documents and to save motion, time, and material.

Carbon Sheets—Copying Film

You will find the following practices in using carbon film sheets to save paper and time:

1. Keep your desk supply of carbon film sheets flat with the carbon ink side down to prevent curling. Keep the sheets inside a folder or box away from heat and dampness.
2. Reverse carbon film sheets end-for-end each time you use

them. The carbon quickly wears off on spots where the dateline and other letter-part positions fall.

3.   Discard a sheet at once if it becomes wrinkled or treed.

4.   Do not discard a sheet just because it looks worn or because the shine is off the carbon side. Instead, check the clarity of the last copy typed. Discard the carbon film sheet only when the copy is faint.

5.   Use extended bottom edge carbon paper with cutoff corners for the most efficient removal and reuse. If carbon film sheets are square cornered, lay them carbon ink side down and cut one-inch triangles from the top left and bottom right corners. This space provides room to hold the set of typed sheets and to remove the set of carbons intact in one quick , clean pull.

6.   Use carbon sheets with cutoff corners to check for the proper insertion of carbons into the carbon pack. With the carbon pack in typing position, the cutoff should be visible in the top left corner. If the cutoff shows at the right, you have inserted the carbon ink side up.

Making Up a Carbon Pack

Two methods of making up and inserting a carbon pack are the *desk method* and the *machine method.*

Desk Method. Using the following procedure, assemble the carbon pack and insert it directly into the typewriter. Refer to Illus. 4-4A.

1.   Place a sheet of paper on the desk; on top of that sheet, place a sheet of carbon film, *glossy side down.* Add one set (a second sheet and a carbon) for each extra copy desired. Place a letterhead or a plain sheet of heavier paper on top of the pack for the original copy.

2.   Turn the pack around so that the glossy sides of the carbon sheets face you.

3.   To keep the sheets straight when feeding, use a *leader*—place the pack in the fold of an envelope or in the fold of a narrow folded piece of paper.

4.   Straighten the pack by tapping the sheets on the desk.

5.   Insert the leadered pack with a quick turn of the cylinder; roll it up; remove the leader.

Machine Method. Using the following procedure, build the carbon pack right in the machine. Refer to Illus 4-4B.

1.   Arrange the required number and kinds of paper for insertion in the typewriter.

Illus. 4-4A
An efficient secretary folds an evelope or a
slip of paper over a carbon pack as a leader
for inserting the pack in the typewriter
rapidy and evenly.

Illus. 4-4B
Correct positioning of the cutoffs at the
upper left and lower right corners of the
carbon paper permits easy removal of the
carbons from the pack.

2. Insert the sheets normally, turning the cylinder until the sheets are gripped slightly by the feed rolls; then bring all but the last sheet forward over the cylinder.

3. Place the carbon film sheets between the sheets of paper, with the carbonized surface (glossy side) toward you. Flip each sheet back as you add each carbon.

4. Roll the pack into typing position.

5. When the typing is completed, roll the pack nearly to the bottom of the sheets. Operate the paper release lever and remove the copy sheets by pulling them out with one hand. The paper fingers will automatically hold the carbon film sheets in the machine. Remove these sheets with the other hand.

Adjusting the Impression Regulator

Most electric typewriters are equipped with an impression regulator to adjust the pressure with which keys strike the paper. This regulator should be adjusted to the thickness of the carbon pack. In general, it should be set at the lowest pressure that will produce the required number of copies. Pressure set too high will emboss the letterhead or front sheet, and the carbon impressions will be heavy and lack sharpness.

Avoiding Bottom Line Slippage

To control bottom line slippage, roll the pack back to about mid-page. From the back, drop a sheet of paper between the original and the first carbon. Roll the pack forward. As you type near the bottom, the extra sheet will hold the pack securely in place. Steady the top sheet with one forefinger if necessary.

CORRECTIONS

Keyboarding is a term often used to refer to typewriting on electronic typewriters, word processors, or microcomputers. Keyboarding differs from typewriting in that the words and numbers entered into the equipment are saved or stored; thus, the stored information can be reused and changed.

Secretaries who use electronic typewriters, word processors, or microcomputers to produce documents can easily correct keyboarding errors before producing a document. However, many secretaries continue to use electric typewriters. They must know how to correct errors so that the final document is top quality. On pages 848-853 of the Reference Guide, suggestions for erasing and making undetectable corrections can be found.

Corrections that defy detection are evidence of the top-notch secretary. Good corrections are an absolute necessity for high quality final documents. In fact, if any correction is evident in an otherwise perfect document, the typescript is not quality level.

SPECIALIZED TYPING

Specialized typing can expedite, control, and add visual appeal to completed documents. Such specialties as display typing, justified typing, decorative typing, preparing labels, high-speed envelope and card routines, and fill-ins are discussed in this section.

Display Typing

Very often a secretary must design a layout for a special document (see Illus. 4-5). The document may be a notice, an invitation, a program, or the like. The finished piece requires that the units of copy, the decorations, and the white space be pleasingly arranged and that the headings stand out. To achieve this effect, the secretary prepares blocks of copy and headings in various line lengths, spacings, and styles, then experiments with their placement on a dummy layout.

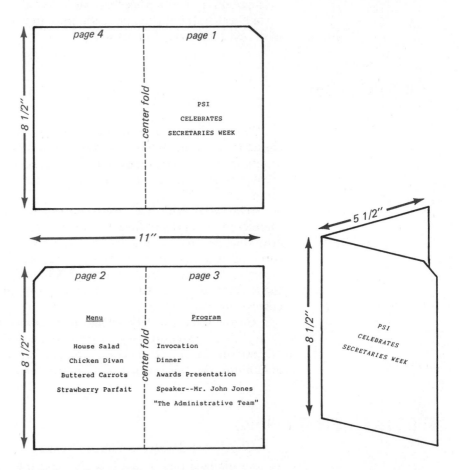

Illus. 4-5
This is a layout for a program to be duplicated on both sides of a single-folded 8 1/2-×-11-inch piece of paper. The finished program should be 5 1/2 × 8 1/2 inches. Although the original copy is prepared on two separate sheets of paper the final copy is printed on both sides of a single sheet.

Sample Blocks of Copy. To find the most pleasing size and shape for blocks of copy, prepare one paragraph or a short unit of copy in different spacings and line lengths. Experiment with this set of samples on the dummy layout. You can vary sizes and shapes by:

1. Single-spacing or double-spacing
2. Using different line lengths: full width, three-fourths width, etc.
3. Preparing copy in columnar arrangements
4. Preparing copy or columns with even right margins

Sample Headings. To make sample headings with which to experiment, take the longest heading and prepare it in different styles by:

1. Using uppercase and/or lowercase letters
2. Using different spacings between letters; using conventional spacing between letters
3. Underlining with continous or broken lines, single or double lines, hyphens, or periods
4. Framing headings with periods, small *o's*, asterisks, diagonals, hyphens, or apostrophes

Justified Typing. Unless you have an electronic typewriter or a word processor that automatically justifies the right margin, you will need to use the following technique to perform this specialized typing function. Even right-margin or *justified* copy is illustrated below. To justify copy on a typewriter with standard spacing:

1. Set the margins for the exact column width desired. Type each line of copy in double-spaced form the full column width, filling in each unused space at the end with a diagonal.
2. Pencil in a check mark to indicate where you will insert each extra space within the line. Try not to use an extra space after the first word in a line or to isolate a short word with an extra space on each side.
3. Retype the copy, inserting the extra spaces.

```
First, set up the column width;///
then type each line of copy the///
full width of the column filling//
in each unused space at the end///
with a diagonal.
```

```
First, set  up  the  column  width;
then type  each line  of copy  the
full width  of  the column  filling
in each  unused space  at the  end
with a diagonal.
```

To bring an address book up to date, type the new address on a gummed label and paste the label over the old address.

Preparing Labels. Most labels are packaged in sheets or strips. To prevent slippage, they should be typed before they are separated from these sheets or strips. When it is necessary to type a single label, make a carrier by folding a sheet of paper in the middle; then fold it again to make a pleat. Make the pleat so that enough of the label appears above the pleat to expose all but a slight bottom margin. Insert the label in the pleat and position it for typing.

If you use the same mailing list frequently, perforated carbon sets of labels are available that contain 33 labels per sheet. By using these carbon sets, you can type four sets of labels at once—a big time-saver in mailing such items as monthly statements and recurring announcements.

Decorative Typing. Distinctively typed words, designs, and patterns may be used occasionally as eye-catchers on the cover page of a notice, an announcement of a meeting, or an item to be posted on the office bulletin board. The illustrations at left are a few samples of decorative typing that can be done by straight typing and spacing. Such decorative typing is rarely used in business work. It requires more time than the results justify, and frequently it is out of place on a formal business document.

High-Speed Envelope and Card Routines

You will occasionally have small typing production jobs to do or to supervise. These jobs might include addressing a hundred or so envelopes or making up a 5-by-3-inch card index. Master the following high-speed routine used in these specialized assignments.

Back Feeding Envelopes. When you have a number of envelopes to address, you can save time by back feeding them.

1. Stack the plain envelopes at the left of the typewriter flap down with the bottom edge of the envelopes toward you.
2. Feed the first envelope into the typewriter until only about one half of the bottom of the envelope is free.
3. Place the top of the second envelope between the platen and the bottom of the first envelope. Turn the platen to the address position for the first envelope and type the address.
4. With the left hand pick up the next envelope and drop it into feed position as you turn the platen with the right hand to remove the addressed envelope.
5. With the left hand remove the addressed envelope and stack it face down at the left of your machine.

Front Feeding Envelopes. To front feed envelopes, roll a just-addressed envelope *back* until about one inch of the top edge is free. Have a stack of envelopes at the side of the typewriter flap up with the flap edge toward you. Drop one of these faceup between the cylinder and the top edge of the addressed envelope. Roll the cylinder back until the blank envelope is in typing position, then address it. The addressed envelopes stack themselves in sequence against the paper table on the typewriter.

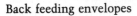

Back feeding envelopes   Front feeding envelopes   Front feeding small cards

Front Feeding Small Cards. To front feed small cards, make a pleat a half inch or less deep straight across the middle of a sheet of paper to form a pocket. The depth of the pleat controls how far down you can type on the cards. Paste or tape the pleat down at the sides to hold it in place. Roll the pleated sheet into the typewriter and align the fold of the pleat with the alignment scale. Place the first card in the pleat and position it for typing. Draw a line on the paper along the left edge of the card to serve as a continuing guide for consistent margins. Specially designed platens are available for typing cards.

Government Postal Cards. Government postal cards can be purchased in sheets four cards wide and ten cards long. These sheets can be cut into strips and addressed. Postal cards are 5 1/2-by-3 1/4 inches and should be typed lengthwise using a 4 1/2-inch writing line.

Fill-ins

The term *fill-in* refers to the insertion of typed material in a space provided on duplicated or printed letters, bulletins, or business papers. The fill-in may be an address, a salutation, a word, a phrase, or numbers. On interoffice correspondence no attempt is made to disguise fill-ins, but on outgoing mail fill-ins should match the body of the message. The procedure is as follows:

1. Use a ribbon that matches the body of the message in darkness of color.
2. Set the carriage in position to insert the fill-in. Test the position by striking over a period or a comma in the text.
3. When the position has been determined, set the paper guide and margins for use in succeeding fill-ins.
4. Unless a pinpoint placement dot shows where to begin the

first line, salutations and addresses are placed more accurately if the lines are typed from bottom to top.

SUMMARY

The preparation of error-free, attractive documents continues to be an important requirement for the secretary. The equipment and supplies available to assist with this task are continually improving.

One of the most widely used pieces of equipment with which the secretary prepares documents is the single element electric typewriter; however, the electronic typewriter, with its automated functions, is increasing in popularity. Word processors and microcomputers, which have even more sophisticated automated capabilities, are further improving the secretary's ability to produce superior documents.

Because the secretary frequently has the responsibility for ordering office supplies, a secretary must be knowledgeable about the type and quality of supplies available, from typewriter ribbons to letterheads. A good working relationship with the local office supply store and a collection of information from various vendors about each kind of office supply used will enable a secretary to make wise purchases for an employer.

Business forms are used in most business transactions. The secretary must be able to utilize these forms efficiently. Forms control, which includes a review of forms for possible improvement, elimination of unnecessary forms, and the design of new forms, expedites the work of the office and may be the responsibility of the secretary.

If equipment is to be used to its maximum efficiency, the secretary must know how to operate all its features and how to care for it properly. Instructional booklets that accompany a machine upon delivery should be used to become knowledgeable about the equipment's capabilities and its care.

Carbon copies are still the least expensive method of producing copies of outgoing correspondence and short reports; therefore, the secretary must handle carbon paper and produce carbon copies skillfully. This includes using the desk method or the machine method to make up and insert carbon packs into the machine.

Often the secretary must do specialized typing. By using various line lengths, different spacing, and type styles, and by justifying the right margin, certain desired effects for some documents can be achieved. Practicing various techniques for processing labels, envelopes and cards, and fill-in forms will enable a secretary to produce work more quickly and efficiently.

SUGGESTED READINGS

Doris, Lillian, and Bessemay Miller. *Complete Secretary's Handbook*, 5th ed. Englewood Cliffs, NJ: Prentice-Hall, Inc., 1983.

House, Clifford R., and Kathie Sigler. *Reference Manual for Office Personnel*, 6th ed. Cincinnati: South-Western Publishing Co., 1981.

Wanous, S.J., *et al. College Typewriting*, 11th ed. Cincinnati: South-Western Publishing Co., 1985.

QUESTIONS FOR DISCUSSION

1. If your employer offered to let you select your own equipment for producing final documents, what are some of the features you would want on a machine and how would you determine this?

2. You are employed as secretary to the manager of the R & D (Research and Development) Division. This is a highly sensitive area and thus under strict control for security leaks. A major security leak was traced to your wastebasket and to the snap-out carbon forms you have been using.
    a. Explain how this could happen.
    b. Is there any solution other than discontinuing the use of these forms?

3. Office costs used to be 20 to 30 percent of a company's total costs; now they have grown to 40 to 90 percent (e.g., in service-oriented businesses, such as insurance companies) of all costs. The cost of producing a business letter is 40 percent more than it was five years ago. List the things a secretary can do to help curb the spiraling costs of a business letter.

4. Faulty handling of carbon copies can mar superior workmanship. What precautions should you observe in handling carbon copies?

5. Correct the following sentences that have numbers expressed incorrectly. Refer to the Reference Guide to check your answers.
    a. 14 men worked on the project.
    b. Enclose 5 22-cent stamps.
    c. Margaret was eight and one-half when she played in her first recital.
    d. He ran the twenty-six mile marathon.
    e. His car is two years old.
    f. John's letter dated the tenth of July did not arrive until the twenty-ninth.

PROBLEMS

1. The electronic typewriter is growing in popularity with secretaries because it provides many automatic features at an affordable price. There are several brands on the market but IBM, Olympia, Olivetti, and Xerox were among the first to market this machine. Assume that your employer is interested in purchasing an electronic typewriter for your use. Prepare a report comparing two of these brands and indicate those features available on the basic model at no extra cost.

2. A secretary must know how to change a typewriter ribbon. As a supervisor, the secretary may need to demonstrate the ribbon-changing process for both film and fabric ribbons. Practice changing the ribbon on your typewriter and also on typewriters of other makes until you believe you are qualified to demonstrate the technique.

3. A study shows that it takes the following time to correct *one* typing error:

Original only	8 sec.
Original and 1 carbon	17 sec.
Original and 2 carbons	25 sec.
Original and 3 carbons	35 sec.

   For the following questions, assume an average of *five* correctable errors per letter. Also assume that the total cost for the secretary is $12.05 an hour. (This includes hourly rate, fringe benefits, employer payroll taxes, supplies, equipment costs, and overhead.)

   a. What is the cost per letter for correcting errors on the original only? original and 1 carbon? original and 2 carbons? original and 3 carbons?

   b. If an original and 2 carbons are made of each letter, how much would be saved per letter if the policy were to correct errors on originals only. Do you see any disadvantage to this?

   c. One business has a policy that all copies are made on a copying machine. The original is corrected before copies are made. On the average it takes the secretary five minutes to go to the copying machine, make two copies, and return to the workstation. What is the cost of an original and two copies using this process?

   d. What is the differene in cost between using the copying machine process for an original and two copies and correcting the original and two carbons? What are the advantages and disadvantages of using the copying machine?

4. You are employed as the secretary to an architect whose office is located in a small community. Because of the location, all office supplies are ordered via letter from Midwest Office Supply, 23 East Town Street, St. Louis, Missouri 63130-1235. Prepare a letter ordering the following supplies. Design the letterhead (create the name and location), and use the current date.

> 2,000 letterheads (These are for general use and should be of good quality, but not the very highest grade.)
> 2,000 envelopes to match the letterheads
> 1 dozen typewriter ribbons for your IBM Correcting Selectric typewriter
> 2 boxes of carbon paper

Chapter 5

Processing Incoming Communications

Preparing mail for effective handling is a primary secretarial responsibility. Handling incoming mail is a visible means of demonstrating efficiency and decision-making ability. Usually the major portion of the mail arrives from the mail room early in the morning. Many secretaries plan to *process* it (prepare it for the employer's attention) before the employer arrives so that action can be taken on it immediately. Additional mail may arrive throughout the day and must be acted on in terms of its importance.

This chapter describes techniques for processing mail: sorting it, opening it, recording it both upon receipt and when it is passed along to others, accumulating supporting information required for its handling, reading and annotating its contents, and arranging it for presentation. It also discusses disposition of mail when the executive is absent from the office and when the secretary works for several persons.

MAIL-PROCESSING PERSONNEL

The first step in processing mail is sorting envelopes into groups for expeditious handling. The personnel involved in this function differ according to the way the mail is addressed and according to the size of the company.

The Mail Room

Mail room personnel receive mail from the post office, from a company mail service, or from a private mail service. It is not unusual for an organization to develop a mail service among its branches and its most frequent correspondents. This service can speed up delivery by at least a day. The secretary should become familiar with such services and their schedules.

If a letter is addressed to the company and not to an individual in the company, the envelope is opened in the mail room. The mail clerk follows established procedures for assigning the mail to the appropriate department. The mail clerk also makes a record of the receipt of the mail and the routing assigned to it.

The mail room is prepared for quantity handling of mail and contains equipment more elaborate than that in individual offices. For instance, it may include a mail opener (like the one pictured in Illus. 5-1) that feeds, transports, removes envelope edges, disposes of waste, and stacks and counts opened envelopes all in a single operation. Another mail opener automatically processes mail of mixed sizes. Still another opens envelopes on two sides, the long end and one side; thus, contents of the envelopes are completely exposed, making their removal effortless.

In larger companies, mail is distributed by a messenger from the mail room who has an established route through the office. The messenger normally follows a fixed schedule for deliveries and pickup.

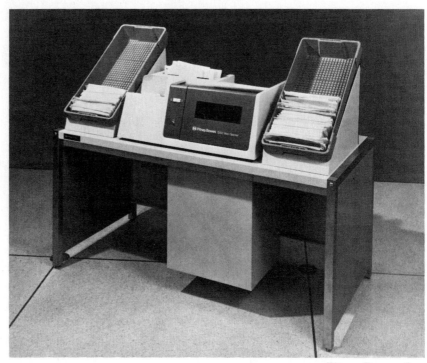

Illus. 5-1
This automatic mail opener, suitable for large companies with mail room operations, quickly opens mail of almost any size without presorting.

Pitney Bowes, Inc.

Many newer office buildings are equipped with automated delivery systems that bring mail to the secretary's desk. These self-powered, unattended, robot-like carts move through the office on tracks or on an invisible path. They are programmed to make stops for mail pickup and delivery at specific locations in the office. An example of an automated delivery cart appears in Illus. 5-2.

Illus. 5-2
This automatic delivery cart is programmed to make stops for mail delivery and pickup.

Photo courtesy of Bell & Howell,
Automated Systems Division

The Secretary

If letters are addressed to specific employees or departments, the mail room delivers the envelopes unopened. The secretary usually gives the unopened envelopes to the addressees, with the exception of the employer's mail. The employers mail is sorted, opened, and processed in ways that will expedite its handling when it is presented to the employer for action.

In a small office, the secretary opens all mail that is not addressed to a specific employee, gives it to the appropriate person for answering, and prepares the employer's mail for action.

PROCEDURES FOR PROCESSING MAIL

The secretary's role in processing the mail is a very sensitive one. Offices are inundated with mail; however, the secretary's desire to reduce unnecessary burdens on the employer may annoy an employer who wants to see everything. On the other hand, the executive who wants to give attention to only the most important communications will appreciate the secretary who enables her or him to devote less time to mail that can be handled by someone else. Study your employer's preferences and work style. Then demonstrate that you can assume responsibility for routine matters, but be careful not to assume unassigned authority.

Steps to follow in sorting, opening, reading, and expediting the handling of incoming mail are discussed here. The processing of outgoing mail is described in later chapters. Electronic communications are fully covered in Chapter 12 and special delivery, certified, and registered mail in Chapter 8.

Classifying and Sorting the Mail

Mail falls into eight categories:

1. Electronically delivered communications: telegrams, Mailgrams, Telex or TWX messages, and hard copy printouts of computer sent material (only in organizations with terminals)
2. Special delivery, certified mail, express mail, and registered letters and packages
3. Airmail and first-class letters, including bills and statements
4. Interoffice communications
5. Personal mail
6. Newspapers and periodicals
7. Booklets, catalogs and advertising material
8. Packages

The first four groups, except Mailgrams, are delivered throughout the day and should usually receive first attention. However, some first-class mail may be put aside until all other priority communications have been processed. Telegrams and other electronic communications are delivered directly to you as soon as they are received. Someone, possibly you, has to sign for special delivery, certified, registered, and express mail. Special delivery mail has additional postage attached to it to pay for delivery by a special letter carrier at an earlier time than the regular mail. Certified mail is so designated on the envelope and is signed for on a form that is returned to the sender as proof of delivery. Registered mail contains valuables, either papers or small articles, and involves special security measures to ensure safe delivery. Express mail, a service provided by the post office, guarantees next-day delivery. It must be signed for to verify the date and time of delivery.

Mailgrams are sent by Western Union to local post offices and are delivered with the regular mail the morning after they are filed. The word *Mailgram* is printed on the envelope in large letters.

You can recognize first-class letters in regular envelopes by the amount of postage they carry and the dated postmark. Oversize first-class mail is sent in large manila envelopes with distinctive borders or the sender labels it *First Class* in a conspicuous way . As you become familiar with the employer's business activities and personal associations, noting the sender's return address and the postmark, will help you identify business and personal correspondents of high interest. Keep these points in mind when sorting the mail:

1. Bills can be identified by the window envelopes in which they are frequently sent; however, window envelopes are being used more and more for all mail, since they save addressing time and reduce the chance of error in addressing.
2. First-class letters are sometimes attached to packages or enclosed in packages labeled *First-Class Mail Inside*. Be alert for these letters.
3. Interoffice mail is always treated as important.
4. The mail may be sorted three times, if it is received in considerable volume.

First Sorting. On the first sorting pull out all electronically delivered communications, special class mail, important looking first-class and interoffice mail, and personal mail for immediate processing. Put a large *X* on the back of any incorrectly addressed or odd looking envelopes for the executive's attention. Unless you are authorized to open personal mail, leave these letters unopened (even though they are not marked *PERSONAL* or *CONFIDENTIAL*) and submit them with the processed mail. While you scan the mail, distinguish between urgent and routine items, putting the important ones in the first group to be processed.

After completing the first sorting, stop and process the important mail according to the steps on pages 118-119. Keep in mind that including something unimportant is preferable to missing something important.

Second and Third Sortings. Lay out the mail by kind in a second sorting. First process routine first-class mail. Sort it into like kinds— mail from branch offices, from the home office, from customers or clients, from traveling associates, from suppliers, and so on. Group first-class window envelopes; they usually contain invoices or statements. If instructed to do so, accumulate bills and statements for a specific bill-paying day. Otherwise they are submitted each day.

The sorting of personal mail follows a pattern. If there is enough volume, sort it according to the executive's outside activities and financial interests. You may maintain special files relating to these activities and interests. (This type of file is discussed in Chapter 20.) Separate personal financial mail into like kinds—bills, bank letters, investment-house letters, and stock-ownership letters.

The third sorting involves advertising mail. To get attention, *advertising mail* comes in envelopes of all sizes, shapes, and colors. You can easily spot it, although advertisers try hard to mislead you. The envelopes rarely, if ever, carry first-class postage. They almost always have open ends with sealed flaps. They have precanceled stamps or printed permit numbers and are not postmarked. Open advertising mail when you have time, after other mail has been processed and handed to the executive. Organize the contents of advertising mail (always full of floating, loose pieces, it seems) and give it to the executive at your convenience sometime during the day. Do not destroy it. Executives like to keep up with *direct mail*—as it is called in the advertising profession—to know what is being advertised and whether to return the enclosed postcards. You can, though, reduce volume by consigning to the wastebasket duplicate copies of advertising that may be received.

Because of their bulkiness, put aside publications; later on, open, scan, and stamp or initial them as your employer's copies.

Opening the Mail

You need special supplies for opening mail. Place them on your desk before you start to work, arranging them within convenient reach.

You need:
An envelope opener
A stapler or clips
Pencils (several colors)
The tickler
Mail-expected list
A memo pad for *to-do*
   items

You may also need:
A date or time stamp
A routing stamp or slips
An action stamp or slips
Transparent tape for mending

You can save two-thirds of your envelope-opening time if you use either a hand operated or an electrically driven machine, like the one pictured in Illus. 5-3. You can also reduce the possibility of cutting an envelope's contents if you use a machine. In either case, tap the lower edges of envelopes on the desk before opening them so that the contents fall to the bottom; then cut along the top edge. Keep the mail in the order in which it was sorted. Open all envelopes before removing the contents.

Removing the Contents. Remove the contents, flatten them, and stack them *facedown* at your right. If necessary, mend any cuts with transparent tape.

Hold the envelopes to the light to double-check for enclosures. Stack the opened envelopes to your left with open edges to the right and flap side up, in the same order as the contents to your right.

Illus. 5-3
An electrically
driven mail opener
can save two-thirds
of your envelope-
opening time.

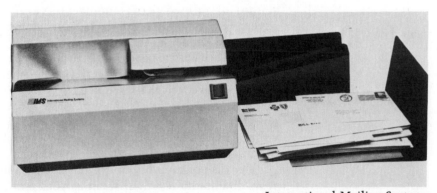

International Mailing Systems

Use both hands to unfold and flatten letters; attach enclosures with staples or paper clips. Scan the letter to see if it contains the sender's address; if not, retrieve the envelope and attach it to the letter. Scan also to see if the letter mentions enclosures and whether those you found agree with the letter. If not, after checking inside the envelope again, underline the enclosure notation or the mention of the enclosure in the body of the letter; write *No* nearby. Attach any envelopes with missing enclosures to the letter.

Save the envelope if

1. It is incorrectly addressed. In this case, the executive may want to mention the correct address in the return letter for the future guidance of the correspondent or as an explanation of why the letter was not answered promptly.
2. A letter was missent by the post office and had to be forwarded. The envelope is needed to explain the reason for a delayed answer to the missent letter.
3. A letter does not contain a return address.
4. The return address in the letter differs from that on the envelope. Sometimes an individual uses business, hotel, or club stationery and does not indicate a return address. Therefore, the reply should not be sent to the address given on the letterhead, so the return address on the envelope is needed.
5. The date of the letter differs too much from the date of its receipt. A comparison of the letter date with the postmark date will reveal whether the fault lies with the sender or with the postal service.
6. Neither a handwritten nor a typewritten signature appears in the letter. The name of the sender may appear as a part of the return address on the envelope.
7. A letter specifies an enclosure that was not attached to the letter nor found in the envelope.
8. A letter contains a bid, an offer, or an acceptance of a contract. The postmark date may be needed as legal evidence.

Another envelope that is always saved is the interoffice chain envelope. Draw a line through your principal's name on the envelope and reuse it. You will notice that these envelopes are usually perforated with holes so that all enclosures can be easily detected.

Registering, Dating, and Time-Stamping. It is often desirable for the secretary to keep a *mail register* of important mail for follow-up or tracing purposes. The mail register is used to record special incoming mail (such as registered, certified, special delivery, express, or insured mail), expected (separate cover) mail, and mail that is circulated to the executive's associates. For expected bulk mail, it may be necessary to use a memorandum to inform the mail clerk or the receiving clerk that a package is coming. Telegrams and cables are also logged in the mail register.

Secretaries say that a mail register is worth its weight in gold. It is a protective record that verifies the receipt and disposition of mail. Only a few minutes are needed to record entries since abbreviations are freely used. A ruled form similar to Illus. 5-4 may be used. The blank space in the "Sep. Cov. Received" column, for example, indicates that the executive's banquet tickets have not yet arrived. As an aid in tracing lost mail, the secretary usually indicates on the face of the item the number assigned to that item in the mail register. The date on which each piece of mail is received is important for several reasons:

1. It furnishes a record of the date of receipt.
2. It furnishes an impetus to answer the mail promptly. (Each reply should be regarded as a builder of goodwill, but no reply

MAIL REGISTER

Name _Arlene Dylan_

Dates this page _3/14 –_

	RECEIVED Date | Time	FROM Name/Address	DATED	ADDRESSED TO Dept. | Person	DESCRIPTION Kind of mail/enc/sep cov	SEP. COV. RECEIVED	REFERRED To | Date	WHERE FILED	FOLLOW UP DATED
1	3/14 9:15 a.m.	F. Dapinsky New York	3/12	Adv.	Ad. pamphlet – layout	—	Adv. 3/14	Adv.	
2	3/18 9 a.m.	Steel Equipment Co. Chicago	3/11	MLA	Expected catalogs– file cabinets	3/21	Q 3/22	Purch	
3	3/20 1 p.m.	H. H. Sims New York	3/19	MLA	ACA Banquet tickets				3/24
4	3/22 3 p.m.	L. Cox Lima, Ohio	3/18	Adv.	Book – typefaces	4/10	Adv. 4/11	Adv.	
5	3/23 2 p.m.	D. Schmidt Chicago	3/22	MLA	Special delivery – rush order	—	3/23		
6	3/24 9 a.m.	IRS – local	3/23	K. Logan	Quarterly taxes – forms enclosed	—	3/24		4/1
7	3/26 2 p.m.	Jones, Inc. local	3/26	Auto	Registered Ch. #345	—	3/26		
8	3/28 9:20 a.m.	R. Fugazzi Denver	3/26	O. Miller	Insured package	—	3/28		

Illus. 5-4
Secretaries rely on the mail register to verify the receipt and disposition of mail.

that is unduly delayed—no matter how courteous or affable it may be—will promote good public relations.)

3. A letter may arrive too late to take care of the matter to which it refers. The date of receipt authenticates that inability.

4. The letter itself may be undated. The only clue to its date is the date of receipt. (You may find it hard to believe, but undated letters are frequently mailed—even letters typewritten by secretaries.)

If the mail has not been date- and time-stamped in the mail room, do it now, either by hand or with a stamp. Show both the date and the time of day if the hour of receipt is important. Some secretaries use a mechanical date-time recorder to stamp the mail. An example appears in Illus. 5-5. The date stamp is especially important if a letter is undated. It is also necessary because of the legal implications for some mail, such as bids. Occasionally mail may be delayed in transit so long that the addressee needs the protection of the stamped date to determine where the time lag occurred. Stamping may also speed up action on correspondence, especially in organizations that target replies for a same day or a next day response. Stamps are made in upper left corners.

Illus. 5-5
The secretary uses a date-time recorder to indicate the time a letter is received. Time and date stamping may speed action on correspondence.

Cincinnati Time

Reading, Underlining, and Annotating

After opening envelopes and dating the contents, you begin the interesting part of handling the mail. Follow these steps:

1. Read each letter through once, scanning for important facts. Make notes on your calendar and notes to yourself about getting needed information.
2. Underline words and phrases that tell the story as you read the letter again. Be thrifty with underlining. Call attention only to what is necessary.
3. Annotate letters by writing any necessary or helpful notes in the margin. Refer to Illus. 5-6.
4. Color code your markings (if your employer approves this procedure) for those letters the employer must handle, those you can answer, and those to be referred to someone else.

Marginal annotations come under two headings:

1. *Suggested disposition of routine letters.* The secretary anticipates the executive's decision regarding the disposition of a letter by writing *File, Ack.* (for acknowledge) or *Give to Sales Department*, for example, in the letter's margin. However, the executive may overrule the secretary's suggestion.
2. *Special notes.* These notes are usually reminders of some type. For example, the secretary might write *When Mr. B was here, you agreed to give this talk* to remind the executive of a commitment. If a letter is a follow-up, the secretary might remove an item of correspondence from the files, attach it to the letter, and note *See our last letter attached* in the letter's margin. The secretary may also annotate a letter by providing a brief who's who of the sender.

You may ask, "Should I, as a new secretary, read, underline, and annotate my employer's mail if my predecessor did not?" The answer is yes. Act as if it is a part of your understanding of a professional secretary's service. If the employer questions the routine, abide by the decision. The employer is more likely to praise the practice, however, than to question it. If underlining and annotating are intelligently done, they save time.

Notations for Filing. As you open the mail, add filing notations on letters that do not require replies. For example, if a reply to your letter can be filed without further correspondence, put the filing notation on the letter during processing. (Methods of determining where to file letters and when and how to make filing notations are presented in Chapter 13.)

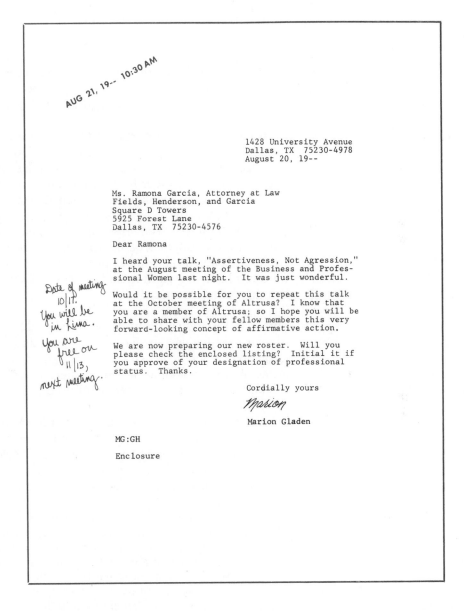

AUG 21, 19-- 10:30 AM

1428 University Avenue
Dallas, TX 75230-4978
August 20, 19--

Ms. Ramona Garcia, Attorney at Law
Fields, Henderson, and Garcia
Square D Towers
5925 Forest Lane
Dallas, TX 75230-4576

Dear Ramona

I heard your talk, "Assertiveness, Not Agression,"
at the August meeting of the Business and Professional Women last night. It was just wonderful.

Would it be possible for you to repeat this talk
at the October meeting of Altrusa? I know that
you are a member of Altrusa; so I hope you will be
able to share with your fellow members this very
forward-looking concept of affirmative action.

We are now preparing our new roster. Will you
please check the enclosed listing? Initial it if
you approve of your designation of professional
status. Thanks.

Cordially yours

Marion

Marion Gladen

MG:GH

Enclosure

Date of meeting
10/17.
You will be
in Lima.

You are
free on
11/13,
next meeting.

Illus. 5-6
The annotations
and the date-time
stamp indicate that
this letter is ready
for presentation to
the executive.

Limiting Annotations. Since original letters are sometimes copied
on machines and sent outside the organization, an executive may ask
you to avoid writing on the face of letters and to add annotations only
on the back of them. Removable adhesive paper slips are available in a
variety of sizes and colors for annotating correspondence. These can be
removed prior to copying. On the other hand, many executives want
notations copied to achieve compact yet comprehensive records.

Expediting the Executive's Handling of Mail

You can expedite the executive's handling of specific letters by anticipating and preparing for certain procedural steps that will be taken. You can be of help by adopting the suggestions described below.

Letter Requiring Background Information. In many cases a letter cannot be answered unless additional information is at hand. For instance, suppose you are a secretary to a sales manager who receives a letter canceling an order because the customer is tired of waiting for delivery. You would look up and attach all pertinent information about the order (its date of receipt, its present whereabouts, and the cause for delay) to the letter. You may have to judge how much background information to supply. If certain information *might* only prove marginally useful, weigh the amount of time required to get it, the amount of time you have to give to it, and the executive's probable attitude concerning the information.

Letter Referring to Previous Correspondence. When there is need to refer to previous correspondence, get it and attach it to the current letter. Write *See attached* in the margin. If the previous correspondence involves a bound file, put the letter on the file and insert paper markers in the file at the pertinent points.

Letter Requiring Follow-Up. Often a letter may refer to mail that will follow in a separate mailing, or it may contain a request that requires additional action besides a routine answer. Sometimes a letter must be answered within a certain time. Other time factors may also be involved. In such cases, follow these steps:

1. Select the earliest date when action should be taken.
2. Write the date on the face of the letter with a key (like *T* for *tickler*, or *FD* for *follow-up date*) so that the executive and you know that a reminder has been recorded.
3. Make a tickler entry under the selected date and write the follow-up date in the mail register.
4. If material is expected in a separate mailing, write a note on your calendar and send a memo to the mail room describing the expected mail. Indicate separate mailing notifications in the margin of the letter. (See also mail register, page 119.)

Letter to Be Referred to an Associate. Often an executive passes along to an associate a piece of mail either for action or information. For instance, perhaps the communication is to be acknowledged, answered, or followed up by the associate. It may require the associate to prepare a report, or it may provide information for the associate's attention. If you can anticipate your employer's preferences, you might fill out a routing slip (Illus. 5-7) or an action slip (Illus. 5-8), lightly penciling in both the associate's name and the action needed. Give the letter and the slip to your employer. If the suggested routing is approved, attach the slip to the letter and circulate it. However, if there is any possibility that you may need to refer to the letter later, photocopy it and indicate on the copy the names of the persons to whom you sent the original, the action taken, and your own follow-up date.

The trend in modern offices, however, is away from circulating originals via routing slips in favor of circulating photo-copies. Because you can send photocopies to the attention of several persons at one time, it speeds up the dissemination of information.

Please read the attached material and pass it on to the persons indicated.

Seq.	Refer to	Date Received	Date Forwarded
	Mr. Adams		
	Mr. Berger		
4	Miss Bessler		
	Mr. Caldwell		
	Ms. Carmen		
	Mr. Davis		
	Mrs. Goodman		
	Ms. Hessler		
	Mr. Holmes		
2	Miss Kerr		
	Mr. Perot		
	Mr. Robinson		
	Mrs. Rodriquez		
	Ms. Smith		
1	Mr. Stretch		
	Ms. Swillinger		
3	Mr. VanDerbeck		
	Ms. Zimmerman		

Return to: *M. J. Davis*

Illus. 5-7
One of these slips is attached to mail that is to be distributed to others. The secretary or executive indicates the order in which associates should receive it. Since routing slips must conform with changes in personnel, they are often duplicated in the office rather than printed.

DATE_____

TO _____

Refer to the attached material and
☐ Please note.
☐ Please note and file.
☐ Please note and return to me.
☐ Please mail to _____
☐ Please note and talk with me
    this a.m._____; p.m._____

☐ Please answer, sending me a copy.
☐ Please write a reply for my signature.
☐ Please handle.
☐ Please have_____ photocopies made
    for_____
☐ Please sign.
☐ Please let me have your comments.
☐ Please RUSH — immediate action desired.
☐ Please make follow-up for _____
_____

REMARKS:

Signed _____

Illus. 5-8
A secretary devised this check-off slip to save the executive's time in distributing information to and requesting action from associates. There is room for a signature at the bottom of the slip because an initialed or signed request is more personal than a printed name.

Misaddressed Letter. If a letter addressed to the executive should actually have been sent to another person, note the correct name in the top margin and put the letter with the employer's other mail. Although you will probably be asked to forward the letter to someone else, you should give the addressee the right to see the letter first.

Personal Letter Opened Inadvertently. If you should inadvertently open a personal letter addressed to your employer, stop reading the letter as soon as you discover that it is not business. Refold the letter, replace it in its envelope, and attach a short note bearing your initials to the face of the envelope: Sorry, opened by mistake.

Enclosed Bill or Invoice. When an envelope contains a bill or an invoice, if possible compare the prices and the terms with those quoted. Always check the mathematical accuracy of the extensions and the total. Write *OK* on the face of the bill or the invoice if it is correct, or note any discrepancy. Any computations in a letter should be checked for accuracy as well.

Enclosed Check or Money Order. Compare the amount of an enclosed check or money order with the amount mentioned in the letter of transmittal or on the statement or invoice. If mailed alone examine the check or money order against the file copy of the bill to verify the correctness of the amount. Handle the remittance according to the procedure of your office. If it is to be turned over immediately to a cashier, indicate the amount in the margin of the letter or invoice, or prepare a memorandum for the executive, reporting the amount and the date of receipt.

Packages. Packages should be processed before newspapers, periodicals, and advertisements; certain packages should be opened before others. In some cases your mail register will alert you to watch for a package's arrival. If you are handling a package marked *Letter Enclosed*, or if a first-class letter is attached, check the package contents before separating the letter from the package. Always examine the contents of a package at the time it is opened. If the contents are bulky and represent a quantity of like items, put a sample on the employer's desk and store the rest.

Publications. Permanently identify each publication with the executive's name or initials. Scan the table of contents and indicate any item that might be of interest to the executive. If an article is of special interest, underline its salient points and paper clip all the preceding pages together so that the publication opens to the article; or attach a note to the front cover calling attention to the article.

Final Arrangement of the Mail

Arrangement of processed and personal mail for presentation to the executive depends on preferences, daily schedule, or even mood. In general, though, the mail is separated into these five categories:

1. *For immediate action.* Possible order of precedence: electronic communications, important business letters, unopened personal letters, letters containing remittances, pleasant letters, unpleasant letters.
2. *To be answered.* Routine letter having no great priority.
3. *To be answered by secretary.* Letters that are usually turned over to you for handling. (Don't preempt the executive's right to make this decision.)
4. *Letters to be answered by someone else.*
5. *To read for information.* Advertisements, publications, routine announcements.

One successful secretary recommends the use of a five-pocket organizer for submitting mail, with each pocket clearly identified as to contents. This organizer keeps the mail confidential. In any case, the mail should be covered if the executive is not at the desk when you present the processed mail. Another possibility is to separate the mail into color-coded folders, with a different colored folder for each of the above categories.

On a day when the employer has only limited time for the mail, you may submit items from Category 1 only. On a day when working with the mail seems to have high priority, send in the first half as soon as it is ready, and take in the rest when it has been processed. If you know that a specific piece of mail is expected, take it in as soon as it arrives.

HANDLING MAIL DURING THE EMPLOYER'S ABSENCE

Some executives spend a great deal of their time in travel. When they are away from the office, crises occur in handling the mail. Simply forwarding personal mail or sending photocopies of incoming business mail will not always meet the situations that arise. The secretary is in a decision-making role and *must* evaluate each piece of mail before giving it routine treatment.

For instance, an employer may be out of the country when the quarterly income tax falls due. Before the due date, the secretary mailed the required checks and forms, which had been signed before the executive's departure. If the trip is an extended one, the secretary may be asked to take care of rent, telephone, or utility bills and pay them with checks on which only the amounts are to be filled in. (These bills should not be forwarded to an executive in a foreign country.) However, before the executive leaves on an overseas trip, the secretary should get explicit instructions for similar contingencies.

The same caution holds for business mail. The employer should not receive a photocopy, forwarded and reforwarded, of a letter about a major reorganization that may have personal ramifications. This kind of information should be transmitted by express mail. The secretary must assume full responsibility for making the right decisions about handling mail in the employer's absence.

If the executive is traveling abroad, make copies of incoming mail and forward them overseas in packets. Number the packets. Overseas mail is not always dependable. If a packet goes astray, the numbering system helps the executive know whether all mail has been received. If 1 and 3 are the only packets received, 2 is obviously missing.

The Executive's Business Mail

When the executive is out of the office, you will be expected to do the following with the mail:

1. Maintain the mail register meticulously.
2. Communicate with the executive immediately when mail of vital importance arrives that no one else can handle. Executives on business trips may telephone their secretaries regularly, but occasions arise when the secretary must initiate a call.
3. Set aside letters that can await the executive's return, but acknowledge their receipt if the answer may be delayed for several days.
4. Give associates or superiors letters which must have immediate executive action. Make a photocopy of each one for the executive's information, noting to whom you gave it and stating the action taken.
5. Send copies (not originals) of letters that contain information of interest or importance or that require the executive's personal attention, if they will arrive in time.
6. Answer or take personal action on letters that fall within your province.
7. Prepare a digest of mail and either send it to the executive or keep it in the office, depending on circumstances (see Illus. 5-9).

8. Collect in a mail-received folder (a) all original letters await-
    ing attention, (b) copies of all letters given to others for action,
    and (c) both the originals and answers of letters you have
    answered. Before giving the file to the executive, sort the let-
    ters into logical sequence, with the most important on top.

The Executive's Personal Mail

Before the executive leaves, ask what personal mail you are to
open and attend to. Do not, however, open personal mail unless
expressly asked to do so. Hold it in the mail-received folder. If forwarded mail will have time to arrive before the executive leaves a
destination, forward it. It is usually better to forward a letter in a fresh
envelope with your business return address than to add the forwarding
address on the original envelope. Keep a running record of all letters
forwarded to the executive at an out-of-town address in the mail-
received folder. Identify each forwarded letter by its postmark date and
sender's name or by the postmark city, if that is all that is shown.

Illus. 5-9
When handling
mail during the
employer's absence,
prepare a digest and
either send it to
the executive or
keep it in the
office.

DIGEST OF INCOMING MAIL

Date Rec'd	From	Description	Disposition
8/16	Clark Oil	Notice of Board of Directors meeting 9/4 in Chicago at 9.	Marked calendar.
8/16	Syracuse U.	Request to give telephone interview to School of Business students 11/13 at 10. Conflicts with staff meeting.	I wrote declining request.
8/16	J. K. Smith	Wants conference on proposed budget cuts.	Confirmed date and time; marked calendar.
8/16	Forbes	Wants more info on overseas operations.	Referred to MJB.
8/16	M. Mason	Wants conference on patent application for Project 117.	Confirmed date and time; marked calendar.

The Executive's Advertising Mail

Hold the advertising mail in a separate large envelope. Sort it and
give it to the executive after the trip is over and the press of accumulated work has lessened.

WORKING FOR MORE THAN ONE EXECUTIVE

When the secretary works for more than one executive, the mail-processing routine is basically the same. Probably a higher level of decision making is required, because several employers' preferences and spheres of responsibility must be kept in mind and materials must be kept flowing to each one.

The secretary will, of course, keep mail in separate piles for each executive. If one of them is obviously waiting for the mail, that executive gets the first delivery of processed mail.

The value of the mail register increases when the secretary is responsible for mail to several addressees. The register supplies proof of receipt for many different items of mail.

When one executive is more demanding than the others, the secretary must exercise tact to maintain a peaceful environment. Because several executives are sharing the secretary's services, many situations arise that require impartial decisions.

SUMMARY

Processing incoming mail efficiently and effectively is a primary responsibility of the secretary. The personnel involved in sending and delivering mail will vary according to the size of the company and the way mail is addressed. In large organizations, the mail is delivered to the mail room. The personnel in the mail room follow established procedures for processing mail and for delivering it to appropriate departments. In smaller offices, the secretary opens all mail that is not addressed to a specific employee and distributes it to the appropriate people.

The amount of responsibility the secretary assumes in processing mail depends on the executive's preferences. Most employers appreciate a secretary who can effectively expedite incoming mail.

Classifying and sorting is the first step in processing mail. Incoming mail is classified into eight categories: electronic communications, special-class mail, airmail and first-class mail, interoffice communications, personal mail, newspapers and periodicals, catalogs and advertising materials, and packages. During the first sorting, electronic communications and special-class, first-class, and interoffice mail is identified. The important mail in these categories is then processed. After the second sorting, routine mail is processed. The third sorting involves processing advertising mail.

Before opening the mail, the secretary should arrange special mail-processing supplies on the desk. After all envelopes are opened, the contents should be removed and placed facedown at the secretary's right. After checking for enclosures, the envelopes should be placed facedown on the left. Envelopes should be attached to correspondence if they are needed to help identify addresses, missing enclosures, etc. Always save interoffice chain envelopes for later use.

A mail register, which is used to record special incoming mail, should be maintained for follow-up and tracing purposes. Stamping incoming correspondence with the date and time received provides an important record should problems arise relating to the processing of mail.

Unless it is personal, the secretary should read each letter for important facts, make necessary calendar notations, underline important words or phrases, and annotate helpful information for the executive. Filing notations may also be added at this time to correspondence that does not require replies.

The secretary can expedite the executive's handling of specific letters by anticipating steps that should be taken and preparing for them. These steps include gathering background information, attaching previous correspondence to the current letter, making notations to follow-up correspondence, preparing routing slips for correspondence that will be shared with associates, and noting misaddressed correspondence. In addition, the secretary can check the mathematical accuracy of bills or invoices; handle checks or money orders according to established office procedures; open packages; and scan publications, marking articles that may interest the executive.

After the mail has been processed, it should be presented to the executive in order of priority. Mail that needs immediate action should be presented first. It should be followed by mail to be answered by the executive, mail to be answered by the secretary, mail to be answered by an associate, and mail to be read for information only.

When an executive travels a great deal, the secretary must accept greater decision-making responsibility for the mail. The secretary must decide which correspondence requires immediate communication with the executive, which should wait for the executive's return, which should be handled by associates, which should be forwarded to the executive, and which should be handled by the secretary. If the travel is for an extended period, the secretary can forward packets of mail to the executive periodically.

The secretary who works for more than one executive must balance the preferences of various executives. Careful attention must be given to keeping the mail separate for each executive.

SUGGESTED READINGS

The Periodicals and subscription services listed at the end of Chapter 1 would be helpful. Especially recommended are current issues of *From Nine to Five* and *The Professional Secretary's Development Program.*

House, Clifford R. and Kathie Sigler. *Reference Manual for Office Personnel*, 6th ed. Cincinnati: South-Western Publishing Company, 1981.

Rubin, Ann Elise and Lamont Wood. "Conventional and Electronic Mail," *The Professional Secretary's Handbook* (Chapter 9). Boston: Houghton Mifflin Company, 1984.

QUESTIONS FOR DISCUSSION

1. If you were secretary to an executive who did not utilize your services in processing mail as suggested in this chapter, what would you do?
2. In processing a morning's mail for the president of a corporation, decide what you would do if
   a. A letter refers to a letter the executive wrote nine months ago.
   b. A customer's letter complains about the actions of a sales representative who was discourteous.
   c. A letter asks that certain material be prepared and sent before the first of the month.
   d. A letter requests a photograph, the responsibility for which is in the public relations department.
   e. A letter contains important information for three department heads.
   f. An envelope obviously contains a bill from an engraver who recently supplied personal stationery for the executive.
3. The executive, Miss Alva Miller, is away on a two-week trip. Decide what you would do with a letter that
   a. Asks her to give a talk five months from now
   b. Requires immediate management action
   c. Is from her mother, whose handwriting you recognize
4. What steps could you take to obtain the address of a person who typed a request for product information and prices on a plain sheet of paper? No address was given on either the letter or the envelope.
5. If the executive is out of town but expects to return tomorrow, what action would you take to record receipt of the following communications? How should you handle each situation?
   a. A special-delivery letter requesting an estimate on a large quantity of coated paper

b. A Telex from one of your branch sales representatives sending in a rush order for a customer

c. A letter about a shipment of card stock complaining that one fourth of the blue is two shades lighter than the rest (samples are enclosed as proof)

d. A letter asking for the length of time a Mr. Edwards was employed as a sales representative by your company, his reason for leaving, and a reference

6. Fill in the correct spelling in the following sentences. Check your answers in the Reference Guide.

a. The department has _____ the procedures to comply with new company policy. (adopted, adapted)

b. He did a _____ job in publishing the school yearbook. (credible, creditable, credulous)

c. The _____ budget for the next two years will include additional funds for office salaries. (biannual, biennial, semiannual)

d. Please _____ your employees of the cost of this project. (appraise, apprise)

e. We have _____ assembled the booklets, and they are _____ to be shipped. (already, all ready)

PROBLEMS

1. Mari Rodriguez is a secretary with responsibility for processing incoming mail. Type your comments and suggestions for improving the steps she follows in performing this task.

a. The secretary arranges all the mail in a stack and proceeds to open it and to remove the contents of each envelope in regular sequence.

b. She flattens out the letters and enclosures and discards the envelopes as useless items.

c. After all the letters have been removed, she checks them for stated enclosures. Pertinent enclosures she separates from the letters and sends to those concerned (such as orders for the order department). She discards the advertising.

d. She then time-stamps, reads, underlines, and annotates all letters. She prepares a routing slip for letters requiring the attention of more than one person, and she fastens each routing slip to the proper letter with a paper clip.

e. She then places the letters, in the order in which they were processed, on the executive's desk faceup for immediate attention.

2. While your employer is on an extended business trip abroad, you make copies of incoming mail and forward the mail overseas in numbered packets. Your employer has received Packets 1 and 3 but has not received Packet 2. What would you do?

3. What action would you take to prepare the following four letters for your employer, Ms. Mary Jane Schmidt? Where would you locate the necessary information? Exactly what underlines and annotations would you make in each of the four cases?

Continental Industries, Inc.
204 West Madison Street
Chicago, IL 60606-3313
(312) 555-5600

March 15, 19--

M. J. Schmidt, Attorney
Anderson, Sakyo and Harmon
Bank of Utah Plaza
2651 Washington Boulevard
Ogden, UT 84401-4320

Dear Ms. Schmidt

At the suggestion of Alger Holmes, I am writing to inquire whether you would be willing to represent my interests in a uranium mine near Provo that has now been closed and is being liquidated. I understand that a hearing is scheduled for May 4 and 5.

If you agree to accept this case, I will plan to come to Ogden on March 28 and would like an appointment with you then. What information would you like me to bring to such an appointment?

I will telephone you at 10 a.m. on March 18 to discuss this letter.

Sincerely yours

W. W. Kim
President

711 State Street
Madison, WI 54303-2619
March 16, 19--

Ms. Mary Jane Schmidt
Anderson, Sakyo and Harmon, Attorneys
Bank of Utah Plaza
2651 Washington Boulevard
Ogden, UT 84401-4320

Dear Ms. Schmidt

In your talk before the Business and Professional Women's Club in Eau Claire, you mentioned a book about problems confronting men and women in management, especially women. All I can remember is that both the words "men" and "women" appear in the book's title and that it was written by a woman. It may have the word "corporation," "company," or "management" in the title.

I have just been promoted to a position in middle management and need all the help that I can get. If you think that this book would be beneficial, will you please tell me the correct title, the publisher, and the price?

Thank you again for bringing us not only facts but inspiration in your presentation.

Cordially yours

Regina Yoko

340 Ocean Drive
Key Biscayne, FL 33149-1439
March 15, 19--

Ms. Mary Jane Schmidt
Anderson, Sakyo and Harmon, Attorneys
Bank of Utah Plaza
Ogden, UT 84401-4320

My dear Ms. Schmidt

We want to invite you to be the keynote speaker at this year's annual convention of Professional Secretaries International at the Brown Palace Hotel on Thursday, May 4, at 10 a.m.

We understand that you began your business career as a secretary. Now that you have become one of our country's most distinguished lawyers, it would be an inspiration to our members to hear from someone who came up through the ranks.

Choice of topic is left to you. We know that you understand secretarial problems and will have something to say that will help us raise our sights whether in our present jobs or in advancing to other levels.

Will you please indicate the fee you would expect in addition to travel expenses. Also, please tell us by March 30 whether it will be possible for you to accept our invitation.

Cordially yours

Dolores Menotti
Chairperson, Program Committee

Howard Enterprises

940 OAK BOULEVARD   OGDEN, UT 84401-1150

March 15, 19--

Ms. Mary Jane Schmidt
Anderson, Sakyo and Harmon, Attorneys
Bank of Utah Plaza
2651 Washington Boulevard
Ogden, UT 84401-4320

Dear Ms. Schmidt

Will you please start collection proceedings against Jerry Youngman for $354.82. This amount represents two invoices, January 14 for $102.96 and February 8 for $231.86, copies of which are enclosed.

Mr. Youngman's last known address was 436 Maple Street, Ogden, but we have received no answers to our telephone calls to that address. Our letters, however, have been delivered.

Thank you for your very efficient handling of the overdue account of the Sports Shop. We received full payment of this account, which we did not expect to collect.

Sincerely yours

HOWARD ENTERPRISES

K. H. Howard, Credit Department

KHH:AD

Enclosures (2)

Chapter 6

Taking, Giving, and Transcribing Dictation

The secretary is involved in the processing of practically all written documents. As a result, it is highly likely that the secretary will transcribe either from shorthand notes or from machine dictation on a regular basis. The secretary may use shorthand while doing research, taking instructions, or recording telephone conversations. Producing a quality transcript will be the ultimate test of your ability to complete the dictation/transcription process.

This chapter first discusses the secretary's responsibilities for handling dictation. Various methods and types of dictation are presented. Since many secretaries are beginning to dictate for their employers, instructions for giving easily transcribed dictation are included. Techniques that good transcribers use to produce quality documents are also described.

As you read this chapter, keep in mind that the concern for cost reduction is changing the way business communications are produced. In whatever situation you expect to function as a secretary, your dictation/transcription techniques should be systematized so that your output is of the highest quality and quantity. In this way you will contribute to a reduction in the spiraling costs involved in the preparation of business documents.

PREDICTATION RESPONSIBILITIES

The secretary has several predictation responsibilities to perform regardless of how dictation is given. Among them are preparing a list of items for the day's attention, replenishing the executive's supplies, and assembling materials from the files that will be needed for the dictation.

Attention-Today Items

The first preliminary to dictation is the collection of *attention-today* items. The secretary prepares a list of items that should receive *attention today* for the executive early each morning. Some of the items will require dictation, while others may consume part of the executive's available dictation time. Overdue letters, reports, and shipments or letters and reports that must meet deadlines all require dictating attention. The day's appointments, conferences, and meetings will affect the time available for dictation.

Type in brief form, in duplicate, a list of attention-today items. Or, if you prefer, type a separate note for each attention-today item. Retain a copy and use it to carry over unfinished work to tomorrow's list. Clip the list (or separate notes for each item) to the edge of a portfolio or file folder, as shown in Illus. 6-1. When an item has been attended to, the dictator can either check it off the list or discard its note. Take the collection of items to the dictator's desk as early in the day as possible, before dictation begins.

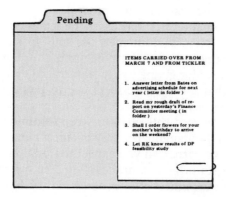

Illus. 6-1
Folder containing carry-over correspondence and attached list of carry-over items in folder requiring attention.

The Executive's Dictation Supplies

Another predictation responsibility is the daily checking and replenishing of the executive's supplies. The following items must be available in sufficient quantity:

Sharpened pencils. An executive often dictates with pencil in hand, jotting down reminders on the letter being answered or entering items on a calendar.

A scratch pad. An executive often writes auxiliary notes and general outlines, while dictating.

A filled stapler, paper clips, and pins.

If the dictation will be given to a dictation machine, also include the following:

A supply of disks, cassettes, or tapes, as appropriate.
An empty file folder or portfolio in which the dictator can insert materials related to the dictation.
A wax pencil with which to date and identify dictated units.
A supply of printed forms for listing the material dictated on a unit, for special instructions regarding transcription, or for indicating any changes to be made.
A supply of special envelopes required for mailing dictation. (This applies when the executive dictates while out of town.)

If the executive dictates directly to the word processing center, also provide a number of folders for material related to the dictation. These folders of material do not go to the word processing center. Retain them in your files for reference by you and the executive. Finally, provide the executive with a supply of the appropriate printed forms for giving special instructions to the center.

The Secretary's Dictation Supplies

If you take shorthand dictation, keep your supplies ready and waiting for instant availability. To avoid unnecessary clutter at the executive's desk, only take an adequate amount of the following supplies with you:

A notebook. Choose one designed specifically for taking shorthand notes.
Several pens. Notes written in ink are easier on your eyes at transcription time.
Pointed pencils. Choose your favorite kind for size, shape, softness, or hardness. Some secretaries prefer automatic thin-lead pencils.
A colored pencil. The secretary most often uses red or blue.
Possibly a folder or portfolio with pockets on each side. The executive may wish to put each piece of correspondence in a folder or a portfolio when the response has been dictated.

Enlarging Your Dictation Vocabulary

A secretary has to experience only once the embarrassment of using *iniquity* for *integrity, impetuous* for *impervious,* or *ambitious* for *ambiguous* to learn the meaning, spelling, and pronunciation of words that sound alike in dictation and look alike in shorthand. To learn the executive's vocabulary quickly, read file copies of recent letters and appropriate technical and trade publications. From these sources make a list of words new to you. If shorthand is your primary method of taking dictation, write the shorthand equivalent along side each word. Learn the meanings of the words, their spellings, and their pronunciations. In other words, compile your own glossary.

Several secretarial handbooks in special fields such as law, accounting, medicine, and real estate, have word lists that can increase your vocabulary.

METHODS OF DICTATION

To initiate the written communication process, the executive or word originator must provide dictation for the secretary. Dictation often takes one of the following forms: machine dictation, manual shorthand, or electronic shorthand.

Machine Dictation

As greater emphasis is being placed on increasing office productivity, machine dictation is being used more frequently than shorthand. This method assists the executive and the secretary in processing communications in the fastest, most economical way.

Portable and Desk Models. The hand-sized, battery-operated portable dictation unit was and is a boon to the traveling salesperson or executive. It allows the word originator to mail recorded material to the secretary for transcription. A portable unit can be used in a car or in an airplane, wherever it is convenient for the word originator. Many executives who like to work at home find this dictation unit indispensable.

A desktop dictation unit is often located at the dictator's desk. The unit saves time because the originator dictates to a desktop machine while the secretary is free to perform other tasks. Some desktop units may also be used for transcribing. However, only one operation can be performed at a time—either transcribing or dictating—on a combination unit.

Centralized Dictation. Central systems are distinguished from other types of dictation machines by the fact that recorders are grouped in a central place. Several recorders are located in a word processing center; and with the most sophisticated systems, a recorder not in use is automatically selected and put into operation to process incoming dictation. The medium on which dictation is recorded varies. Cassettes, continuous loops of magnetic tape, and magnetically-coated disks may all be used in a centralized dictation system. An example appears in Illus. 6-2.

Dictation to a word processing specialist or operator in a word processing center is transmitted to the center by the word originator via public or private telephone connections. Connection to a dictation system by public telephone lines enables any telephone on or off premises to serve as a dictation unit; thus, dictation may take place from an executive's office, home, hotel room, or even from a telephone booth. The advantage of a private wire is that the dictation system does not tie up the dictator's or the word processing center's public telephone lines. Also, once installed, the expense of a private telephone line is diminished.

Illus. 6-2
The centralized system groups all recorders in one location so that a number of dictators and transcribers can have access to the system.

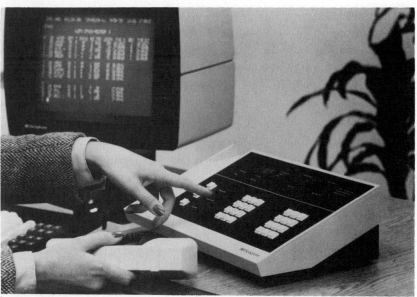

Dictaphone Corporation

Endless Loop or Continuous Flow Systems. All of the dictation machines described up to this point have used a specific receiving medium, such as a disk or a cassette. These types of receiving mediums are called *discrete media*. Discrete media can be stored, mailed, or switched from dictation machines to transcription machines. Most portable and desktop dictation units use discrete media that allow the dictator to play back the dictation and make changes and corrections by dictating over it.

The endless loop-based system is an alternative to cassettes or disks. Loops of magnetic tape, which are sealed inside a case or tank, go round and round for hours of use and reuse. Dictation is recorded on one head while another head plays out the dictation for the secretary to transcribe. Since the magnetic media does not have to be removed from the machine for transcription, it is possible for the secretary to start transcribing while the dictator continues recording. This feature proves invaluable when processing rush work. Another advantage of the endless loop system is that the encased tape requires no reloading.

In a centralized system, monitoring panels with visible dials show the word processing supervisor at a glance which machines are in use, which are idle, and how much untranscribed dictation has yet to be assigned to a specialist. Some endless loop systems automatically send priority items to the front of the line to be transcribed first. Others indicate the length of items to be transcribed.

Manual Shorthand

Shorthand dictation, dictation by the executive to the secretary in a face-to-face situation, will continue to be used in the office for several important reasons. Many executives prefer to work with one person on a regular basis who is familiar with their routines and can assist them when they are dictating. In addition to traditional dictated correspondence, such as letters and memos, shorthand dictation is often used for complex documents which need extensive explanation. Shorthand is also the preferred method for recording instructions, telephone messages, minutes of meetings, and ideas exchanged during informal meetings.

While shorthand may not be widely used for extended face-to-face dictation in the future, it will remain an extremely useful skill for the secretary, and many employers will continue to require shorthand skill for employment.

Answering the Call to Dictation. If the executive tries to dictate at approximately the same time each day, stay at your desk during this time. If you must leave your desk, tell a co-worker or roll a note into your typewriter explaining your errand and the expected time of your return so that you can be located if necessary.

Before leaving your desk to take dictation, or if you will be away from your desk for an extended time, cover, put away, or lock up all confidential papers. Ask someone nearby to take care of your telephone calls and visitors.

You may resent being called to dictation when you are engrossed in other work; but, when the call comes, do not act annoyed. Go to the executive's desk with an attitude of willingness and helpfulness.

At the Executive's Desk. During the actual dictation, the secretary should adopt certain accepted practices. Seemingly unimportant details that often affect the success of the session are the secretary's location and attitude.

In the give-and-take of dictation, the executive and the secretary work together at very close range. Your chair should be conveniently close to the executive; but, if you have a choice, sit where you have a generous-sized writing area.

As a thoughtful, considerate secretary, you need to be as unobtrusive as possible during dictation: only then can the dictator concentrate on content and search for the most effective phrasing. Take dictation without interrupting; manage your supplies and papers with few motions; refrain from unnecessary movements, such as tapping on the desk; and avoid any indication of a critical reaction to the dictation.

Machine Shorthand

The standard shorthand machine, which enables a person to take notes in excess of 300 words per minute, has been used for years primarily by court reporters. The operator can achieve such rapid speeds because words are recorded by depressing one or more keys at a time.

A new process using shorthand machines is called *electronic shorthand*. This technology enables machines to record keystrokes on both paper tape and magnetic tape simultaneously. The paper tape can be used to read back notes, immediately if necessary. The magnetic tape is read into a computer and transcribed into words. The transcript is displayed on a screen for editing and revising. The final copy can then be printed or stored for retrieval at a later date. With this tehnology, material that would formerly have taken weeks to transcribe can be transcribed immediately at extremely high speeds—over 500 pages per hour.

Voice Recognition Systems

The use of voice recognition systems for office dictation is still in the experimental stage. These systems recognize human speech patterns and translate them into printed words onto a computer screen.

Voice recognition systems are either speaker-dependent or speaker-independent. The speaker-dependent system requires a sample of how the speaker pronounces each vocabulary word before it can recognize that speaker. A speaker-independent system can recognize the vocabulary within its memory without having a sample of each speaker's voice. These systems currently are being used by word processing specialists to perform function commands such as center, delete, search, and replace. Trained operators are required for these systems to be effective.

When voice recognition systems are perfected, a dictator's words will be keyboarded as they are spoken, thus eliminating the need for a typist to input the dictation. Direct input by the dictator will greatly speed production time.

TYPES OF DICTATION

In addition to business communications, dictation transcribed by the secretary may include instructions, reminders, and requests. Various types of dictation may be intermingled depending on the executive's preferences. Whether taking dictation by shorthand or transcribing from machine, the secretary should record instructions on paper rather than relying on memory to carry them out. Dictation falls into several categories.

Communications

The bulk of dictation falls into the category of communications. It includes letters, memos, reports, outlines, drafts, and electronic communications such as telegrams, Mailgrams, Telex messages, and computer-sent material. Electronic messages are first transcribed and then sent via automated equipment. Usually, this automated equipment is operated by an employee other than the secretary. The equipment used to send these messages is fully discussed in Chapter 12.

Instructions

The executive will frequently dictate instructions for a variety of tasks while dictating regular communications. *All instructions should be written down.* If using shorthand, take down the instructions in your notebook as they are given. If transcribing from a machine, jot down the instructions on a note pad.

Directions for Transcribing. The dictator will often give directions for transcribing a communication after it has been dictated. If taking dictation in shorthand, this information should be placed at the beginning of the communication because certain actions must take place prior to transcribing. Directions for transcribing a communication include instructions for handling rush communications, for complying with unique stationery requests, for supplying the number of copies needed, or for gathering additional information from special resources.

An electronic or manual index is located on the front of the dictation machine so the secretary can identify the beginning and end of documents as well as the location of specific instructions. The secretary can scan the tape for instructions before beginning the transcription process.

Directions for Composing. The executive often delegates the composing of a letter to the secretary. The secretary may be asked to compose a letter in response to one at hand or to originate an item of correspondence. Complete directions for composing a letter must be taken in writing to be sure that all points are covered. Often the secretary can use almost verbatim the information provided by the executive in composing a reply.

Specific/General Work Instructions. Any specific instructions, such as canceling one of the executive's appointments, planning an itinerary, or writing and cashing a check, should be written down. Highlight these instructions with colored pencil or draw a box around them.

When the executive explains office routines or his/her preferences concerning procedure, write them down. As time permits, transcribe them and insert them in your desk manual for reference use.

Highly Confidential Material

Transcribe highly confidential dictation when there is little likelihood of anyone being around. Give the original and any copies to the executive as soon as possible. Destroy the dictated notes or erase the machine dictation immediately. If carbon copies were made, destroy the carbon paper if it retains a clear imprint of the typescript.

Telephone Dictation

Keep a separate notebook near the telephone for dictation purposes. In taking telephone dictation, you may have to ask for phrases to be repeated, because you only have the use of one hand. Since the dictator cannot see how fast you are taking notes, it helps if you say yes after you have completed each phrase. To avoid errors, read the entire set of notes back to the dictator.

Occasionally the executive may request you to monitor a telephone conversation and take notes. Unless you are unusually speedy you cannot hope to get every word, but you can take down the main points in the way one takes lecture notes. Transcribe such notes at once while they are still fresh in your mind.

Both sides of a telephone call can be recorded on a dictating machine placed near the telephone. Legally, however, the other person must be told that the conversation is being recorded. The recording may be kept for reference, or you may be asked to transcribe the entire conversation or to abstract its important points.

On-the-Spot Dictation

In Illus. 6-3, a secretary has been asked to take notes during an impromptu meeting of advertising executives. At times it is necessary to take dictation within a split second, while standing or working at a desk where there is no cleared space. You may even have to take notes on scratch paper. In order to become accustomed to the awkwardness of rush work, practice taking dictation with a notebook on your knee or while standing using a scratch pad. After transcription, date the notes, fold them to less than page size, and staple them to the first blank page in your regular dictation notebook.

At the Typewriter

Occasionally the executive may ask you to type something as it is being dictated to you. It helps to ask before starting whether the dictation will be long or short so you can determine the placement of the item on the page. Retyping, however, is often required. In the majority of cases where the executive asks you to type something as it is being dictated, the placement is unsatisfactory and insertions or corrections are necessary. Do not stop to erase errors as they are made. It is better

Illus. 6-3
During an
impromptu
conference, the
executive has asked
the secretary to
come in and record
comments on an
advertising layout
under consideration.

to correct errors or retype the page when the executive has finished
dictating and has left your desk.

Printed Forms

The answers to questions on a printed form are frequently dictated. The executive usually works from the form; therefore, the information given will seem sketchy and incomplete. If the dictator does
not identify the numbers or letters of the items being responded to, ask
for them so that you can type the information on the proper lines.

If only one copy of a form is furnished, make a photocopy of the
completed form for the files. If completing printed forms is a new
experience for you, or if you are unsure of the line spacing, you could
make a photocopy of the blank form and practice on it.

LEARNING TO DICTATE

The secretary will find that taking, giving, and transcribing dictation can be done more efficiently if dictation equipment is used. A
deterrent to using dictation equipment is the reluctance of the dictator
to organize thoughts and materials before starting to speak. Although

all equipment provides for playback, correction of dictation, and some type of control with which to alert the transcriber to a transcription problem, a dictator may also fear that the dictation will be imperfect. Some secretaries, accustomed to transcribing and to speaking slowly and distinctly with logical phrasing, have less difficulty in dictating efficiently than do some executives. Refer to Illus. 6-4.

To prepare for giving easily transcribed dictation, first study the instruction book for the equipment until you can operate all of its controls. Dictate a practice item that contains tricky words and figures. After a short interval, play back the dictation and see whether you can distinguish every word and figure.

To produce dictation of which you can be proud it helps to make an outline. The more complex the communication, the more necessary the outline.

Illus. 6-4
When dictating, speak slowly and distinctly and give explicit instructions.

TRANSCRIPTION FUNDAMENTALS

Transcription is a high order skill. It is often performed under rush conditions and involves competency in typewriting, English usage, punctuation, and decision making. The ultimate test of your ability to perform this complicated process is the production of a quality transcript.

Language Skills

The fundamental tool of the secretarial profession is the English language—spelling, punctuation, and word usage. Typewriting style and the ability to use reference books are also important skills of the professional secretary. You must master these fundamentals so that you can flawlessly transmit the dictator's ideas. You—not necessarily the dictator—are the expert in the areas of spelling, punctuation, and word usage. You are responsible for perfection in communication.

If you must work with a specialized or technical vocabulary, read file copies of recent letters and appropriate technical and trade publications. From these sources make a list of words new to you. Learn the meanings of the words, their spelling, and their pronunciations.

To master additional spelling difficulties, compile and maintain your own list of troublesome words. If you persistently write down each misspelling that occurs in your transcription and each word that you have to check in a dictionary, you will have a custom-made list for instant reference.

A secretary must know the rules of punctuation as they apply to formal writing. A paper that is to appear in print or a report to the board of directors must be punctuated with formal correctness. In routine business writing there is a trend to reduce the amount of internal punctuation in a sentence, especially those marks that indicate pauses. Punctuation that indicates pauses, such as commas, semicolons, and colons, is often omitted in a sentence whose meaning is clear without it. But whenever you are in doubt, punctuate fully. Comprehensive punctuation rules are given in the Reference Guide.

Grammar and usage are based on relatively fixed standards used in communicating at a formal or educated level. Since most of the executive's writing is at that level, the secretary must have a mastery of grammar—a knowledge of the system of rules for speaking and writing correctly.

Reference Sources

Dictionaries vary. Compare the very British and formal *Oxford English Dictionary* to *Webster's Third New International Dictionary of the English Language. Webster's* aroused a great furor among scholars when it first appeared because it contained new words that had crept into the language through usage but had never before been listed.

Three recommended desk-size dictionaries that have recently been revised are *Webster's New Collegiate Dictionary* (1981), *The American Heritage Dictionary* (College Edition, 1982), and *Random House College Dictionary* (1975). A desk dictionary should be replaced every five years or so with a current edition. You should turn to the dictionary at transcribing time to learn:

1. The correct spelling of a word, such as *neophyte*
2. The correct spelling of an inflectional form, such as the past tense of *benefit*
3. The preferred form of variant spellings, such as *acknowledgment* or *acknowledgement, judgment* or *judgement*
4. Whether to use one word or two words, such as *highlight* or *high light*
5. Whether to treat a word as a foreign one and underline it, such as *bon voyage* and *carte blanche*
6. How to divide a word at the end of a line, *committal,* for example
7. Whether to use a hyphen to join a suffix or prefix to a word or to form one complete word without a hyphen, such as *pre-Socratic* and *preview; selfsame* and *self-control; businesslike* and *droll-like*

Dictionaries indicate the correct solution to each of these seven situations in different ways. The key to how they are indicated in your dictionary is given in the explanatory notes at the front of the dictionary. (Sometimes this section has an explicit title, such as "Guide to the Use of the Dictionary.") One secretary hyphenated numerous compound words incorrectly because he confused the mark denoting syllabication with the one indicating a hyphen. Careful reference to the explanatory notes will prevent such embarrassing mistakes. When you do locate an important point in the explanatory notes, underline it or enclose it in a frame with pencil for easy reference.

A current and comprehensive secretarial handbook will help you with many transcription problems. At the end of this chapter, several preferred solutions to some common transcription problems are listed. There are also secretarial manuals for special fields like law, medicine, and science, to help you if your work involves specialization. These aids are listed at the end of this chapter. Reference books are discussed more fully in Chapter 16.

TRANSCRIPTION PROCEDURE

To assure efficient transcription, first make certain that the equipment is in good working order; the supply of letterheads, envelopes, and carbon paper is adequate and carefully arranged; reference books are within reach; a pencil is at hand for use in editing notes or jotting down instructions; and correcting supplies are nearby. Familiarize yourself with any procedures that dictate company-wide styles or formats.

Order of Transcription

Transcribe rush and top priority items in the order of their immediacy as indicated by your notes, instructions on the dictating equipment, or your supervisor. Telegrams, Mailgrams, or cablegrams get first attention. Special-delivery letters should be attended to next and, if urgent, they should be presented immediately for signing and mailing. If there is an interoffice memorandum of great importance, it may take precedence over other transcription items. Show your employer that you can make the right decisions as to priorities. Store any transcription items that must be carried over until the next day in one regular place.

Editing and Completing Dictated Items

Before starting to type an item from shorthand notes, read through it intently; edit until it is letter-perfect and ready for smooth, continuous transcription. As you read through each item

Insert punctuation.
Indicate paragraphs.
Correct errors in grammar.
Correct errors in fact.
Eliminate redundancies.
Clarify ambiguities.
Make substitutions for repeated words.

Rewrite poor sentences.
Verify facts (prices, names, etc.).
Write out difficult spellings.
Fill in blanks left by executive.
Find and insert needed information.

If a dictated sentence does not make sense to you, it probably will not be clear to the addressee. When in doubt, ask. If the dictator is close by, interrupt only at an opportune time. Only valid, sensible changes should be made in the dictation, as shown in the following example:

What the Executive Said	**What the Secretary Typed**
Let's meet in Chicago Wednesday morning, January 24. I'll arrive the night before the meeting. Please make a reservation for me at the Drake for the 24th.	Let's meet in Chicago Wednesday morning, January 24. I'll arrive the night before the meeting. Please make a reservation for me at the Drake for the 23rd.

Before you begin to transcribe, double-check any instructions in your notes or at the beginning of a machine dictated item as to format, number of copies, distribution, additions on certain copies, enclosures to be prepared, or whether final copy or rough draft is wanted. In making a rough draft, use wide margins and double or triple spacing to allow for editorial changes.

Number and Kinds of Copies

Some companies require two copies of every letter, one for the individual correspondence file, and another for a chronological file of all letters mailed each day. Materials in this chron file are kept at least a month for quick reference. Whether copies are produced by carbon paper, a copying machine, or word processing equipment will depend on your organization's equipment and methods. Copies can now be obtained from computer input. Most secretaries are delighted that the trend in making copies is away from the use of time-consuming carbon copies.

You will be asked to make and furnish certain individuals and departments with copies of every letter you type relating to subjects of mutual interest. List in your desk manual the persons who should receive copies for each general subject. You can then make the correct number of copies and distribute them properly each time you type a letter. Your notes or dictated instructions which precede items will usually tell you the number of copies needed.

Dating Transcription

Date every transcript. Use the date of transcription if it differs from that of the dictation. It may be necessary to edit the dictation to make it conform to the date of transcription. For example, you might type "your visit *yesterday*" rather than "your visit *this morning*" if you are transcribing dictation that was given the preceding day. On casual typewritten matter use the abbreviated form to date transcripts, 8/28/--, for instance.

Letter and Envelope Styles

Many companies furnish style manuals for use with their correspondence. If you do not receive one, compile your own models from previous correspondence and from style authorities. Study the model letters and envelopes shown in the Reference Guide.

The modified block letter is used most often because of its time-saving features. If you have the choice, you may want to use the simplified letter style. Study the post office recommended format for envelopes (shown in Chapter 8). Use the latest forms of nonsexist salutations—or the omission of the salutation altogether. Note the new ways of indicating reference initials, especially those used for computer entered documents. Using whatever decision-making authority you have, try to modernize the format of your transcription—but never forget that the dictator is in charge.

Proofreading

Although sophisticated word processors can detect a misspelled word or incorrect hyphenation, the machine cannot store all of the words you may use. Besides, many secretaries do not have such sophisticated equipment. You are, therefore, responsible for proofreading. No matter how beautiful a document looks, if there is a proofreading error, the desired reaction is destroyed. A memorandum from the publisher of secretarial materials stated: "The enclosed catalog will *aquaint* you with . . ." Do you think any material was ordered? A ridiculous error, such as reference to a *dump* truck driver as a *dumb* truck driver, lost a valuable customer.

Although speed in producing transcription has increased strikingly, proofreading is not the place to strive for increased output; take your time and proceed painstakingly.

Common Transcription Errors. The top ten transcription errors are letters omitted, substitutions (-ing for -ed, for instance), space omitted, punctuation mark omitted (such as failure to close a quote), transpositions, words omitted, small letter for a capital letter, a full line omitted, a spelling error, or a capital letter for a small letter. Watch for them.

Good Proofreading Techniques. The following techniques are recommended:

1. Use the paperbail method. Roll back to the first line of the copy and use your paperbail to guide your eye as you read line by line.
2. Read the material once for content.
3. Read again for mechanical errors: grammar, spelling, and punctuation.
4. Read from right to left. (Sometimes a copy is easier to proofread because it is inked more heavily than the original.)
5. Wait thirty minutes and reread.
6. Check numbers, especially decimals, and names and addresses with extreme care.

If you are unsure of the accuracy of your proofreading, ask someone else to read aloud from the original as you proofread or ask someone else to proofread your work. (In some word processing centers, proofreading is a particular function assigned to a specialist.)

Keeping It Confidential

There are always several persons in a large office who are inquisitive as to what is currently happening in the executive offices. Transcripts on secretaries' desks (such as finished letters waiting to be signed), letters being typed, and copies in viewing range are often fruitful sources of information. If someone comes to your desk while you are transcribing, roll the letter back into the typewriter, making your action as unobtrusive as possible. Keep transcribed letters covered with a sheet of paper, facedown, or inside a file folder. Copies are just as informative as originals so treat them with the same respect. Many executives now use electric wastebaskets that shred paper that might reveal company secrets.

Reference Notations

Several types of information may be noted below the final signature line. These include reference initials, enclosure notations, copy notations, and filing codes.

Reference Initials. Reference initials are typed a double space below the last typed line in any of several ways.

ty or TY or t (transcriber only)
MP:TY or MP:ty or mp/t (dictator and transcriber)
MP:AG:TY (executive, actual composer of document, and transcriber)

Enclosure Notations. Type enclosure notations a double space below the reference initials at the left margin. Use *Enclosure* or *Enc.* when an item is to be sent in the envelope with the letter.

Copy Notations. Type the names or initials of copy recipients a double space below the enclosure notation. (The sender need not sign copies.) If the sender does not want the recipient of the original correspondence to know that a copy is being sent to someone else, the transcriber should place a slip of paper between the ribbon and the original and type *bc* (blind copy) and the name or initials of the person receiving the copy before removing the pack from the typewriter. The notation *pc* stands for photocopy, and *cc* indicates a carbon copy.

Word Processing Codes. Filing codes are reference notations which identify documents prepared in a word processing center so that they can be located on magnetic media or hard copy. Such codes are not yet standardized. The following example shows one possible handling:

LM/a 2.4

LM is the word originator; *a* is the word processing specialist; *2* identifies Tuesday, the second day of the week; and *4* indicates the fourth document typed by *a* on Tuesday. The *4* also indicates that the document is stored on the fourth magnetic disk or is the fourth hard copy filed behind *Tuesday* in the center's file.

Envelopes

Before removing a letter from the typewriter, drop its envelope between the letter and the platen. When you remove the letter, the envelope will be positioned for addressing. Before removing the envelope from the typewriter, check it against the original source document for accuracy. Slip the addressed envelope, flap side up, over the

top of the letter and its enclosures. The accumulated stack of correspondence is easy to handle, and your employer will find it easy to read
and sign the letters. However, in order to reduce addressing errors,
some employers prefer the addressed side up to match the address on
the envelope with the letter address. On some electronic typewriters
letter addresses once keyboarded can be retained for addressing envelopes automatically.

Enclosures

Whenever an enclosure is mentioned in a letter, there is an
implied instruction to the secretary to obtain the enclosure and attach
it to the letter before submitting it for signature. If possible, collect all
enclosures at the same time. If the enclosure refers to a letter which
passed between the correspondents earlier, do not use the file copy or
the original letter as the enclosure. Instead, prepare a copy on a copying
machine or type a plain copy of the letter and identify it as such.

If an enclosure is small enough not to cover the body of the letter,
attach it to the face. If larger, it is placed behind the letter.

Should it be nececessary to send in a letter for signature without
its enclosures, clip a note to it listing the missing enclosures. Refer to
the example in Illus. 6-5. The note will serve a dual purpose: it will
inform the executive that you have not forgotten the items to be
enclosed, and it will remind you not to mail the letter until the enclosures are at hand.

Submitting the Correspondence for Signature

If rush items are involved, they are submitted as soon as completed. Some executives like to sign the mail at least twice a day. In
other cases, the mail is signed in the afternoon in time to meet mail
schedules (with which the secretary must become familiar). Learn and
follow the executive's preferences in these matters.

The correct arrangement of transcribed material is as follows: the
letter and its envelope are on top, then follow the enclosures, the extra
carbons and the file copy with its notations. If the executive is there,
present the letters faceup. If not, turn the letters facedown to keep
them clean and to prevent their being read.

Most secretaries arrange to be at the executive's desk for the signing session. If questions or concerns arise about the items to be signed,
the secretary can respond immediately.

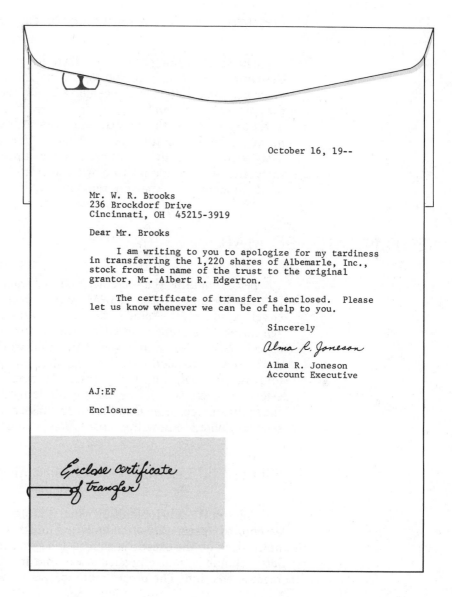

October 16, 19--

Mr. W. R. Brooks
236 Brockdorf Drive
Cincinnati, OH 45215-3919

Dear Mr. Brooks

    I am writing to you to apologize for my tardiness
in transferring the 1,220 shares of Albemarle, Inc.,
stock from the name of the trust to the original
grantor, Mr. Albert R. Edgerton.

    The certificate of transfer is enclosed. Please
let us know whenever we can be of help to you.

    Sincerely

    Alma R. Joneson

    Alma R. Joneson
    Account Executive

AJ:EF

Enclosure

Enclose certificate of transfer

Illus. 6-5
If an enclosure will be bulky or difficult for the signer to handle, the secretary attaches a note to the letter as a signal of awareness of the enclosure and as a self-reminder at mailing time.

    A frequent point of irritation between an executive and a transcriber is the difference between what the executive thinks was dictated and what has been transcribed. There is only one gracious way to handle these differences of opinion . The secretary accepts responsibility for making all corrections and changes. It really does not make any difference who made a mistake. The important thing is to go about correcting it at once, cheerfully and willingly.

Preparing the Correspondence for Filing

The secretary prepares transcribed dictation for filing by stapling the copy of each reply to the top of the incoming letter it answers. Place pertinent letters in the pending file or make tickler entries from the copies. Write each follow-up date on the file copy or on the original letter to show that the date has been set and recorded. Add the filing notation before laying the correspondence aside. The matter of designating *where* to file letters is taken up in Chapter 13. Increasingly, the file notation is made by the dictator or transcriber and typed on the document at transcription time.

SENDING SIGNED MAIL

Before mailing, the secretary makes a final check of all materials. Has the document been signed? Are all enclosures attached? Is the envelope address the same as the letter address? Is the amount of postage correct? If stamps are used, are they securely affixed? In some large offices, secretaries are relieved of the final work of sending out correspondence. Mail clerks collect signed letters and the envelopes and fold, insert, seal, and stamp them. In small offices, the secretary attends to every step of this routine. Modern office equipment, such as the folding machine, makes the routine faster and easier. However, the secretary should know the most efficient manual procedures as well.

Folding and Inserting Letters Manually

A letter is ready for mailing when it is signed and all enclosures are assembled. A secretary often folds and inserts the letters while waiting at the desk for the executive to read and sign the rest of the mail. Every letter should be folded in such a way that it will unfold naturally into reading position. The proper methods are shown in Illus. 6-6.

Sealing and Stamping Envelopes

When all letters are enclosed, joggle the envelopes into a neat stack. All the address sides will be down and the flaps will be opened out. Now pick up the stack, grasp the flaps, and bend them back in order to make them flatter. Holding the short edges of the stack of

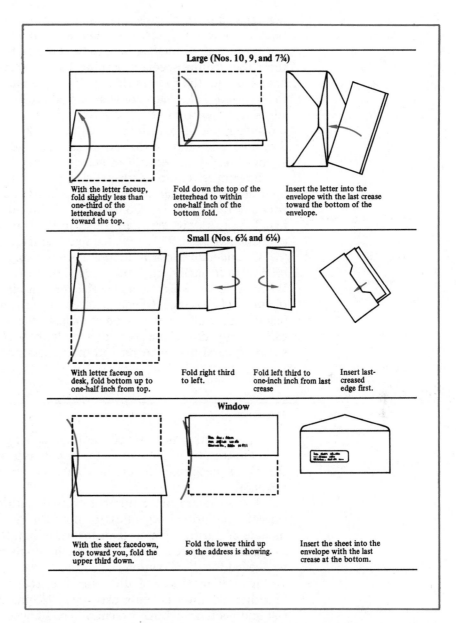

Large (Nos. 10, 9, and 7¾)

With the letter faceup, fold slightly less than one-third of the letterhead up toward the top.

Fold down the top of the letterhead to within one-half inch of the bottom fold.

Insert the letter into the envelope with the last crease toward the bottom of the envelope.

Small (Nos. 6¾ and 6¼)

With letter faceup on desk, fold bottom up to one-half inch from top.

Fold right third to left.

Fold left third to one-inch inch from last crease

Insert last-creased edge first.

Window

With the sheet facedown, top toward you, fold the upper third down.

Fold the lower third up so the address is showing.

Insert the sheet into the envelope with the last crease at the bottom.

Illus. 6-6
Examples of ways to fold letters into envelopes.

envelopes between your hands, drop the envlopes off the bottom of the stack one at a time onto the desk so that only the gummed part of the flap of each envelope is visible. Then take a moistening tube, sponge, or wet paper towel and with one swing of the arm moisten all the flaps at once. Lay the tube aside on a blotter and start sealing the envelope nearest you by folding over the flap. Continue up the column. As you seal each envelope, pick it up and lay it in a stack, flap side up.

If the sealed envelopes are to be stamped by hand, first remove all those that require special stamping. Lay the rest of them out in columnar form with the address side up, leaving enough depth for the stamps to be pasted. Take a strip of stamps that are joined with the horizontal edges together, moisten one stamp at a time on a nearby sponge or moistener, and affix it to an envelope, working from the top envelope down. For strip stamps that are attached at the vertical edges, as rolled stamps are, lay the envelopes across the desk.

Envelopes requiring special stamping should be given individual attention. Those that are to be sent special delivery or to other countries and those that are too heavy for the minimum postage should be handled separately. Write in pencil in the stamp position the amount of postage needed. This penciled figure is later covered by the stamps.

Considerable loss is incurred from using excess postage. Every office should have some kind of postal scale. Weigh every piece of mail. When in doubt, weigh! Small scales for first-class mail are sensitive to fractions of an ounce. Check the accuracy of your scale periodically by placing nine *new* pennies on it; adjust the scale until they weigh exactly one ounce. The post office no longer delivers unstamped mail, so check carefully to be sure all mail is stamped.

SUMMARY

The secretary is involved in the processing of most written documents in the office. Therefore, it is imperative for the secretary to have the skills necessary to produce quality written communications efficiently.

The secretary has a number of predictation responsibilities that must be performed regardless of how the dictation is given. These include preparing a list of items for today's attention, replenishing the executive's supplies, and assembling materials from the files that will be needed for the dictation.

Several methods of dictation are available to the executive. Machine dictation is being used more frequently today because it is fast and economical. An executive can choose from many models of dictation machines and magnetic recording media. Shorthand dictation (dictation by the executive to the secretary in a face-to-face situation) will continue to be used. Many executives prefer to work with a person who can assist them when they are dictating. Electronic shorthand is an adaptation of machine shorthand. The machine records keystrokes on magnetic tape which is read into a computer and translated into words.

The secretary will encounter many types of dictation in the office including routine letters, memos, reports and drafts; instructions for transcribing and composing documents; highly confidential material; telephone communications; on-the-spot dictation; dictation at the typewriter; and dictated answers to questions on printed forms.

Because the secretary may be asked to dictate, he/she must know how to use dictation equipment. The instruction booklet for the equipment should be studied, and dictation should be practiced until efficiency is achieved. Use of an outline when dictating will make the secretary a more effective dictator.

Transcription skills are critical to the written communication process. The secretary must have excellent English language skills. These skills include spelling, punctuation, and word usage. Typewriting style and the ability to use reference books are also secretarial requisites. The secretary is expected to be a communications expert.

To complete the transcription process in the most accurate and efficient manner, the secretary must follow a number of procedures. These include establishing priority items for transcription; editing the dictation before beginning transcription; determining number and kind of copies needed; dating transcription; using appropriate letter and envelope styles; proofreading the transcript; using appropriate reference and enclosure notations; submitting the correspondence for signature; and preparing the correspondence for filing.

After the secretary has made a final check to see that everything is in order, correspondence is folded, inserted in the appropriate envelope, and sealed. Envelopes are then stamped. Large offices may have a mail room that handles these procedures.

SUGGESTED READINGS

Doris, Lillian, and Bessemay Miller. *Complete Secretary's Handbook*, 5th ed. Englewood Cliffs, NJ: Prentice-Hall, Inc., 1983.

Executive Dictation for Word Processing. Rye, NY: Dictaphone Corp., 1985.

Gonzales, Jean. *The Complete Guide to Effective Dictation*. Boston: Kent Publishing Company, 1980.

A Manual of Style, 13th ed. Chicago: University of Chicago Press, 1982.

Matthews, Anne L., and Patricia G. Moody. *The Letter Clinic*, How to Dictate. Cincinnati: South-Western Publishing Co., 1982.

Schrag, Adele F. *How to Dictate*. New York: McGraw-Hill Book Co., 1981.

Soukhanov, Anne (ed.). *The Professional Secretary's Handbook*, A Guide to the Electronic and Conventional Office. Boston: Houghton Mifflin Company, 1984.

Century 21 Shorthand (series). Cincinnati: South-Western Publishing Co., 1975.

Whelan, Doris. *Secretary's Handbook*. New York: Harcourt Brace Jovanovich, Inc., 1978.

LEGAL SECRETARIAL AIDS

Bate, Marjorie D., and Mary C. Casey. *Legal Office Procedures*, 2d ed. New York: McGraw-Hill Book Co., 1980.

DuPree, Garland, and Dorothy S. Namanny. *Legal Office Typing with Practical Applications*, 2d ed. Cincinnati: South-Western Publishing Co., 1984.

Ferrman, Marian. *Legal Secretary's Handbook*. West Nyack, NJ: Parker Publishing Co., 1977.

Gordon, David, and Thomas Hemnes. *Legal Word Book*. Boston: Houghton Mifflin Company, 1978.

Knapp, Mary M. *Legal Terminology*. Skokie, IL: Stenograph Corporation, 1981.

Morton, Joyce. *Legal Secretarial Procedures*. Englewood Cliffs, NJ: Prentice-Hall, Inc., 1979.

Park, William R. (ed.). *Manual for Legal Assistants*. St. Paul: West Publishing Co., 1979.

Roderick, Wanda W. *Legal Studies, To Wit*, Basic Legal Terminology and Transcription, 2d ed. Cincinnati: South-Western Publishing Co., 1985.

MEDICAL SECRETARIAL AIDS

Atkinson, Philip S. and John E. Clement. *Medical Office Practice*, 3d ed. Cincinnati: South-Western Publishing Co., 1984.

Bredow, Miriam, *et al. Medical Office Procedures*, 2d ed. New York: McGraw-Hill Book Co., 1981.

Carlson, Harriette L. *Medi-Speller*, A Transcription Aid. Springfield, IL: Charles C. Thomas, Publisher, 1979.

Ehrlich, Ann. *Medical Office Procedures Manual*. Champaign, IL: Colwell Systems, Inc., 1983.

Saputo, Helen N., and Nancy G. Rutherford. *Medical Secretary's Standard Reference Handbook*. Englewood Cliffs, NJ: Prentice-Hall, Inc., 1980.

Sormunen, Carolee. *Terminology for Allied Health Professionals*. Cincinnati: South-Western Publishing Co., 1985.

SUGGESTED QUICK REFERENCES

House, Clifford R., and Kathie Sigler. *Reference Manual for Office Personnel*, 6th ed. Cincinnati: South-Western Publishing Co., 1981.

Kutie, Rita, and Virginia Huffman. *The WP Book*. New York: John Wiley & Sons, Inc., 1980.

Leslie, Louis. *Twenty Thousand Words*, 7th ed. New York: McGraw-Hill Book Co., 1977.

Sabin, William. *The Gregg Reference Manual*, 6th ed. New York: McGraw-Hill Book Co., 1985.

Perry, Devern J., and J. E. Silverthorn. *Word Division Manual*, 3d ed. Cincinnati: South-Western Publishing Co., 1984.

National Five-Digit ZIP Code and Post Office Directory. Washington, DC: U.S. Postal Service, 1986.

QUESTIONS FOR DISCUSSION

1. As a new secretary to the director of an electronic engineering research laboratory, how would you familiarize yourself with the lab's highly technical vocabulary?
2. How would you handle the situation if the dictator:
   a. Habitually uses out-of-date stereotyped phrases
   b. Makes obvious errors in grammar
   c. Repeats the same conspicuous word several times in one business letter
   d. Refers to secretaries as *she* and executives as *he* in all dictation although your company has a model affirmative action program in operation
   e. Dictates even the most obvious punctuation although much of it is questionable
   f. Mumbles
3. What kinds of changes should the secretary make in dictation? What kinds should not be made?
4. How would you proceed if you dictated a letter to the word processing center that was transcribed in a format that did not conform to your instructions?

5. What directions would you follow in transcribing:
    a. A personal letter to a classmate in charge of a college reunion
    b. A letter about a discount improperly taken. Assume that the invoice in question is handed to you along with the customer's letter.
    c. A reply to a letter of complaint about the service given to a customer by a branch office
    d. A proposed contract for the construction of a new plant
6. Type the preferred plural of each of the following words. Use the Reference Guide to verify and correct your answers.
    a. attorney-at-law
    b. commander in chief
    c. cupful
    d. Fox (proper name)
    e. appendix
    f. judge advocate
    g. notary public
    h. runner-up

PROBLEMS

1. Your executive hands you a letter of invitation to speak at a Rotary Club meeting on December 10. The letter is from David Atchison, Vice-President of the club. His address is 1610 Northway Drive, your city. Your employer asks you to reply stating that the pressure of business makes it impossible to prepare adequately for such a presentation and suggests a substitute, Maria Savitsky, of the Springer Corporation. Prepare an outline for the reply and dictate it to a dictation machine. Ask either a classmate or your instructor to critique your work.
2. Type answers to the following questions. Correct your answers, using the reference books designated at the end of the chapter; cite your authority.
    a. What are synonyms for *agent, integrity, mediocrity*?
    b. What is the correct salutation for a clergyman?
    c. What are the state abbreviations, addresses, and ZIP Codes for the following: Federal Reserve Bank, Kansas City, Missouri; Doctors Hospital, Seattle, Washington; El Paso (Texas) Chamber of Commerce
    d. Should there be a space after the first period in Ph. D.?
    e. How would you punctuate the following sentence: Did he say Are you going
    f. Should *cooperate* and *reread* be hyphenated?

3. One of your greatest assets in producing quality transcripts is your ability to proofread accurately. To test your competency in this area, type the letter which follows, correcting the errors. Retype a mailable copy, if instructed to do so by your instructor. (Refer to the Reference Guide as needed.) Can you locate 18 errors?

Drs. J. M. Miller & H. A. Kahn
Medical Arts Bldg
Omaha, Nebr.

Gentlemen

We have no way of determing from your letter of Feb 10 you needs for additional X-ray equiptment.

We have ask our sales representative Manuel Alvarez to telephone you for an appointment and examine your present machines before he attends next months state physicians convention in Omaha, As you requested I reminded him not tl call on you until after 4 p.m.

In the mean time you may like to examine our latest catlog, so that you can see what is available from our company. It is enclosed

Yours Cordially

Chapter 7

Composing Assignments

Other than face-to-face contact or personal calls, the written word is the most effective way to communicate ideas in business. Often written communications are the only contact others will have with your firm. Your ability to express your ideas clearly, concisely, and correctly will make you an invaluable employee.

It stands to reason, then, that your ability to compose effective messages, either on paper or electronically (using sophisticated technology), will contribute significantly to your employer's success and to your advancement. Whether you are asked to formulate a simple reply to a request for a catalog or to send a message to an applicant who does not qualify for a position with your firm, you will find that these kinds of composing assignments provide opportunities to display your writing ability and your creativity. Each composing assignment tests your educational background and experience.

To help you perfect your composing skills, this chapter presents in capsule form the principles involved in producing communications that express personal concern, build goodwill, and solve business problems. Examples of typical business and personal correspondence that you may be asked to compose are also included.

THE BASICS

When your employer says, "Prepare a reply for my signature," he or she shows confidence in your writing ability. Before you undertake a composing assignment, organize your thoughts in a logical fashion. A simple outline of what you want to say will help you achieve this goal.

The written message often becomes a permanent record and, therefore, has more impact upon the reader than the spoken word has upon the listener. Today, because of the secretary's access to electronic technology, you may be asked to compose electronic messages that go directly to a company president. It is essential, then, that you exercise extreme care in preparing business communications of all types. In certain situations, it may be necessary to revise a document several times until just the right combination of ideas, words, and sentences produces a lasting, favorable impression.

The writing principles presented in this chapter represent a modern approach. A review of basic writing principles will help you recall the do's and don'ts of composing clear, concise, and correct communications. Before you begin any composing assignment, ask yourself, "What does the reader expect?" Isolate the main purpose of your communication and build your message around it. Focus on your reader by writing about his or her interests. Gather and verify facts. Outline major points and place them in an effective order. Finally, draft the letter, making sure that every sentence is clear and that you have supplied complete and correct information.

Set the Proper Tone

Tone makes communication human. It conveys the attitude of the writer and should be used to make a message cordial, tactful, positive, and courteous. By ignoring tone, you may give your reader the feeling that you are blunt, impolite, superior, unfriendly, or given to high-pressure sales tactics. The effective writer controls tone by the careful choice of words. The reader's interpretation of your words will determine the nature of the response to your correspondence.

Personalize Your Message. Even if your letter is written for a mass audience, make each reader feel that it was written to one person—the recipient.

Personal Tone	Impersonal Tone
To help you plan a pleasant vacation, we are enclosing a copy of our new travel brochure.	Our new travel brochure has been published to help clients plan their vacations.

Most business communications suffer from too much attention to the writer's point of view and not enough emphasis on the reader. Such letters lack the *you* attitude. Instead of beginning a paragraph with *I* or *we*, reverse the order and begin with *you*.

Emphasis on the Reader	Emphasis on the Writer
For your convenience, we are enclosing a Banktime Credit Card to help you establish credit in our city.	We are enclosing a Banktime Credit Card to help you establish credit in our city.

Using the reader's name is also a good way to put your reader in the picture. Don't overdo this, however, or you run the risk of sounding too familiar.

Personal	Impersonal
You will be glad to know, Mrs. Lane, that the Bank of Grundy has raised the interest rate on passbook savings to 9 percent.	The Bank of Grundy has raised the interest rate on passbook savings to 9 percent.

Humanize Your Message. Relax and let your letters reflect your personality. Business communications need not be dull and mechanical.

Friendly, Human Tone	Dull, Monotonous Tone
Thanks for your order. We are pleased that you chose us to furnish linens for your new hotel. I have instructed our shipping department to fill your order promptly, and you should receive your first shipment of linens within two weeks.	We are in receipt of your recent order for linens. I have instructed our shipping department to process same immediately. The first shipment should arrive in due course.

Encourage Your Reader. Accent the positive elements in your message. Tell your reader what you *can* do, not what you *can't* do. Bring out points favorable to your reader. If you have good news, tell it in the first sentence. If you have bad news, avoid dwelling on negative terms such as *error, mistake, inconvenience,* and *trouble.* These words merely emphasize the problems you have caused.

Positive Tone	Negative Tone
Because you take pride in owning a Prestige car, we are making a special effort to restore the paint to its original luster. By carefully mixing the proper colors, we can spray	The problem you reported in your complaint of October 6 resulted from an unfortunate error in mixing the paint. It will be necessary to repaint the car, and we regret that we

the car on Friday and let it dry during the weekend. You can drive away on Monday in a car that looks like new.

must keep it over the weekend. We apologize for the inconvenience, but as you know, errors like this are bound to occur.

Be Natural—Write the Way You Talk. A business message should be a substitute for a visit or personal call and should be written in a conversational tone. If your letters or those of your employer contain dull, hackneyed expressions, substitute natural expressions.

Natural Expressions	Hackneyed Expressions
immediately, soon, or <u>supply the specific date</u>	at an early date, in the near future, at your earliest convenience
as you requested, as you stated	as per your letter, in accordance with your request
here is, enclosed is	enclosed herewith please find
this is to let you know	please be advised that
later	at a later date
today or <u>supply the specific date or time</u>	in due course
because or since	in view of the fact, due to the fact that, owing to fact that
Thank you for your letter of (<u>supply the specific date</u>)	I have your recent letter
as you instructed	pursuant to your instructions
this, that, these, those	the above named, the above mentioned
<u>omit (never take your reader for granted)</u>	thanking you in advance

Practice Tact. Tact is knowing what to do or say to maintain good relations with others. It is essential that a letter telling a reader a claim has been denied, a promotion has been disapproved, or employment is being terminated is tactful.

Tactful Tone

Another box of brochures is being mailed to you today. Should the lost brochures show up later, please return them to us. Your first shipment was mailed on October 6 to your Oakland address. We would appreciate your checking with your local post office to see if they are being held there.

Tactless Tone

We cannot understand why you failed to receive the brochures we mailed on October 6. They were sent to you at your Oakland address. Check with your local post office to see if they are being held there. In the meantime, we will mail you another box of brochures. If the lost brochures should turn up, return them to us immediately.

Never Write in Anger. No matter how hard you try to disguise your anger, your words and expressions will give you away. Writing letters that destroy customer relations is something no business can afford to do. The best advice to follow is to cool off and wait a few days before responding. (If your employer violates this principle, you may take it upon yourself to hold the angry letter a few hours or until the next day. Your employer knows this rule of thumb, too, and will appreciate your good judgment.)

Improve Sentence Quality

Today's busy reader has little time for wasted words that do not contribute to the message. Every word should work. Your writing will improve considerably if you let each sentence express one idea.

Keep Your Sentences Short. Short sentences containing fewer than 15 words will give your message impact. They also carry your reader's interest from one set of ideas to another. Caution should be exercised, however, not to put too many short sentences together. Such an arrangement gives your writing a monotonous, unbalanced effect.

A sentence that expresses a thought briefly and clearly is concise. A concise sentence is stripped of superfluous words and, thus, is easy to read and understand. Conciseness is a mark of finesse and skill. It is an important quality for business communications because it saves time—the writer's time, the typist's time, and the reader's time. It can also save paper. To achieve conciseness, state a fact only once. Cut out superfluous words and phrases in each sentence. Beware, however, of the brusque tone that can be created through abrupt conciseness. For instance, "Be here at five," lacks the graciousness of "I'm looking forward to seeing you at five."

Keep Your Paragraphs Short. Your reader will be less likely to ignore your ideas if you present them in short paragraphs. Remember to begin a new paragraph when you change the subject.

Prefer the Short Word. A good vocabulary is essential to precise expression. As a general rule, however, a simple word will have a more powerful effect than a long one that your reader may have to look up. Small words can express big ideas—*God, sun, sea, sky, joy, war.* A waiter is more likely to grasp your meaning if you ask, "Is the *tip* included in the price of the meal?" than if you ask, "Is the *gratuity* included in the price of the meal?"

The trend in business letters is toward short, informal words. They usually create a friendly, personal relationship between the writer and the reader; they also help the writer relax and write naturally.

If a word is long, chances are you should change it to a shorter, more familiar one so that its meaning is clear. Avoid the use of colloquialisms, slang, and coined phrases. There are readers, however, who are scholarly and intellectual. Visualize your reader and use the kind of words suitable to that person.

In the list that follows, look over the words commonly used in business writing and their short, less formal counterparts. Would you say that the short words are always preferable to the long words? that the long words are always preferable to the short words?

A civil tongue means to me a language that is not bogged down in jargon, not puffed up with false dignity, not studded with trick phrases that have lost their meaning. . . . It is direct, specific, concrete, vigorous, colorful, subtle, and imaginative when it should be and as lucid and eloquent as we are able to make it. It is something to revel in and enjoy.

Edwin Newman

approximately	about	inevitable	sure
ascertain	learn	inform	tell
commence	begin	inquire	ask
communication	letter	peruse	read
conflagration	fire	procure	get
demonstrate	show	purchase	buy
encounter	meet	remuneration	pay
endeavor	try	residence	home
gratuitous	free	verification	proof

A handy reference for the secretary's desk, *Roget's International Thesaurus in Dictionary Form*, lists synonyms, antonyms, and related phrases. When a word seems too long, too impressive, or is used too often, check a thesaurus for a substitute.

Avoid Redundant Expressions. Too many words unnecessarily lengthen a communication and sap its vitality. When two or three words are used to express a thought that could be expressed with one word, your writing becomes redundant, causing readers to lose interest.

Here are some examples of redundant expressions that frequently occur in business communications. In each of these examples, only one of the words is needed. To avoid redundancy build a *watch list* of needless words that creep into your correspondence:

mutual cooperation	attach together	free gratis
widow woman	hot water heater	both alike
close proximity	general public	quite unique
future prospect	local resident	is now currently
definite decision	intent and purpose	if and when
continue on	future planning	circle around
refer back	serious danger	settle up
matinee performance	commute to and from	never before in past history
prominent and leading	last remaining	repeat again
penetrate into	seldom ever	total destruction
completely honest	day dawned in the East	vital necessity
most perfect	end result	violent explosion
each and every	regular weekly report	lonely isolation
vital and essential	at the hour of 9	very fatal

Another common error often made by business writers is using comparative forms of words that have no degrees of comparison. If a task is *impossible*, it cannot be *most impossible*. Words such as *honest*, *fatal*, *mortal*, *final*, and *hazardous* are concepts that cannot be compared. Such expressions as a *completely honest*, *very fatal*, and *rather obvious* waste your reader's time.

Strive for Clarity. It would be difficult to estimate how costly unclear statements—statements that leave the reader confused—truly are. A statement like, "All the citizens had a part in appointing the members of the committee, and they think that the project should continue," leaves serious doubt as to whether *they* refers to the citizens or to the members of the committee. Such statements baffle even the brightest readers and could lead to serious misinterpretation. If there is any doubt that what you have written could be misinterpreted, rewrite it.

Use Active Verbs. To make a forceful impression, writers have found that the active rather than the passive voice is helpful. In the active voice, the subject is the doer of the action; whereas in the passive voice, the subject is acted upon. Therefore, the passive voice tends to weaken a sentence. When *forcefulness* is not a factor, however, and the writer wants to concentrate on the *you* attitude, the passive voice may be used to avoid *we* and *I*. The passive voice is also effective in eliminating the generic use of masculine pronouns in describing occupations, life-styles, and so forth. The following sentences illustrate each of these principles:

Forceful	**Weak**
We have approved your loan and have notified your agent.	The loan was approved by us and your agent has been notified.

Nonsexist	**Sexist**
A premium will be given when the customer buys.	When a customer buys, give him the premium.

Use Concrete Expressions. Vague expressions and ambiguous references cloud your meaning and detract from your message. Precise, specific terms will improve the clarity of your writing and make your sentences more forceful. Expressions such as a *good* salary, a *large* crowd, a *few* hours, a *big* sale, and *several* errors are vague. One reader may visualize a good salary as $10,000 while another would consider $25,000 a good salary. After you have written your first draft, check it for fuzzy expressions.

Avoid Negative Expressions. In every kind of communication, words with negative connotations should be avoided. As one business communicator put it, negative words can turn a letter into a brink of war communiqué. Negative words in their kindest usage still have an unpleasant tinge. A list of negative reaction words is given here. You can undoubtedly add others—and you should!

abandoned	claim	failure	misfortune
abuse	collapse	fault	mistake
alibi	collusion	fear	muddled
adverse	complaint	flagrant	regret
apology	criticize	flat	reject
bankrupt	deadlock	hardship	scheme
blame	decline	hazy	so-called
biased	desert	impossible	sorry
beware	disaster	inconvenient	useless
calamity	error	insist	won't
can't	evict	meager	wrong
cheap			

Words of positive connotations improve tone. Use them whenever possible. Compiling your own reference list of positive reaction words will help you become alert to using them. Here are a few:

ability	conscientious	gracious	please
abundant	dependable	gratifying	poised
achieve	desirable	happy	praise
active	determined	kind	progress
admirable	distinctive	lasting	prominent
advantage	diversity	majority	punctual
benefit	effective	merit	steady
beautiful	enjoy	perfect	study
capable	faith	permanent	thorough
cooperate	good	pleasant	thoughtful
cheer	glad		

Use a Forceful Beginning Sentence. Getting started is often the most difficult part of the letter-writing task. Your first sentence should be gracious and establish a point of contact with your reader. *Thank you* is always a good beginning when it is used appropriately and sincerely. When your reader has had previous correspondence with you and is expecting a specific reply, a good way to begin is by assuring your reader in the first sentence that a specific action has been taken. The following examples should be helpful:

Forceful

Thank you for your letter of October 15 requesting a

Weak

Due to excessive demand, we regret we cannot comply

copy of our fall catalog. Because of high demand, we are temporarily out of catalogs, but we will mail yours when our new edition comes off the press next month.

with your request for a copy of our fall catalog. We have had to request an additional printing and will mail you a copy of this edition when it is next available.

Your check for $85 in payment of claim No. 4577 was mailed today.

As you requested, we have instructed our accounting department to mail you a check for $85.

A copy of our brochure, ''Modern Technology,'' is on its way to you with our compliments.

Your request for a copy of our brochure, ''Modern Technology,'' has been received, and we are forwarding a copy to you today.

Although the use of *Dear Mr., Miss, Mrs.,* or *Ms.* combined with a last name is still the most popular form of salutation, many business writers are adopting the *dearless salutation* and the *salute opening* to begin their letters. Because of increased awareness of sexual stereotyping, *Dear Sir, Gentlemen,* and *Dear Madam* are disappearing from salutations. The dearless salutation substitutes some other word for *dear,* and the salute opening incorporates the salutation in the first few words of the opening sentence as illustrated in the following examples:

Dearless Salutation

Salute Opening

Hello, Mrs. Wilkins:

You are right, Mrs. Wilkins, in assuming that the shipment was prepaid.

Good Morning, Dr. Cortez:

Congratulations, Dr. Cortez, on your recent appointment to the Finance Committee.

Use a Gracious Ending. The closing lines are your last chance to make a good impression and achieve a favorable reaction. Here are some important pointers on writing effective closing sentences:

1. *Make the last sentence independent of the complimentary close.* Avoid fragmented endings such as *"Hoping to hear from you soon, I remain."* Fragmented endings are considered outmoded and add nothing to your message.

2. *Omit meaningless phrases.* If you have turned down an application for credit, it is meaningless to say, "Call on me again when I can be helpful."

3. *Make it easy for your reader to reply to a specific request.* Use statements such as "Return the postage-free card" or "Sign the enclosed card, and we'll bill you later."

4. *Look to the future.* Resell your company, its products, and its people. For example a retail clothing store might close its letters by saying, "You are special to all of us at Martin's, and we will work hard to provide you with courteous service and quality merchandise."

5. *Ask for the action you want.* If you want your reader to respond in a certain way, don't imply your expectations. When you can, point out the advantages the reader will gain by reacting favorably to your request. For example, you might say: "Send no money now. Just complete the enclosed order form and you can enjoy the comfort and beauty of your new furniture today. We'll bill you after January 1."

6. *End on a positive note;* but , if you are answering a letter asking for an adjustment, don't apologize. Apologies and negative endings only remind the reader of inconvenience and error. A frank admission of error on your part may win your point, but too many negative words weaken your message. Instead of writing "We regret the inconvenience this error has caused you, but mistakes are bound to occur in an organization as large as ours," use a positive approach: "The situation you described in your letter of October 15 has been corrected, and we look forward to working with you when you again need furniture for your new home."

7. *Don't thank in advance.* This is discourteous: it presumes the reader's willingness to cooperate. It is appropriate to show appreciation in a closing sentence, but never make a statement such as "Thank you in advance."

8. *Stop when you've said enough.* In an attempt to be courteous, many letter writers drag their readers through a maze of words that add nothing to the message. Statements such as "Again, let me thank you for . . . " are redundant and weaken the effect of your letter.

Summary of Letter-Writing Basics

This preceding section covered the basic principles of effective letter writing. Your adherence to the recommended guidelines should help you avoid the most common pitfalls that make letter writing dull and uninteresting. The next time you compose a letter, analyze it against the checklist in Illus. 7-1. If you can answer yes to these questions, your letter conforms to writing techniques that will make a favorable impression on your reader.

CHECKLIST FOR EFFECTIVE WRITING

Can you answer yes to these questions?

_____ Is your message long enough to give complete information but short enough to assure a thorough reading?

_____ Is it clear and easy to read?

_____ Does it present advantages to the reader that encourage the action you desire?

_____ Is it natural, friendly, and conversational?

_____ Is it neat and attractive, indicating that you care about the impression it makes?

_____ Does it indicate a desire to help the reader?

_____ Is it courteous and free of unpleasant, negative, and superior words and phrases that belittle the reader?

_____ Is it forceful and interesting? Is it free from dull, hackneyed expressions? Have you used a variety of words and sentence structures?

_____ Is it personalized? Did you use the reader's name and incorporate the reader's interests?

_____ Does it emphasize the reader through the avoidance of too many sentences that begin with *I, we, our*, and *my*? Does it have the *you* attitude?

_____ Is it free from sexist language and stereotypes?

Illus. 7-1
If you can answer yes to most of these questions, your writing ability is above average.

TYPICAL LETTERS COMPOSED BY THE SECRETARY

The occasions when a secretary is asked to compose material for the employer fall into two categories—assignments of a business nature and those of a personal nature. No matter what the orientation may be, a request to compose a message for the employer's signature is to be regarded as a compliment—a compliment to your ability to do this high-level secretarial task.

Business Correspondence

Generally experienced secretaries are asked to write drafts of reports, speeches, minutes of meetings, difficult letters, and memorandums. This material probably requires the employer's signature. Routine assignments, such as replies to requests for information, transmittal letters, special requests, short messages, reservations, appointment letters, or acknowledgments might appropriately be signed by the secretary or administrative assistant.

If you are just beginning to assume these correspondence duties, you may wish to type a suggested reply to a letter and give it to your employer for editing. This is a good way to familiarize your employer with your ability as a correspondent.

In the course of transcribing your employer's dictation or typing from rough drafts, you may find it necessary to correct grammar, dates, amounts, and sentence structure. Of course, you will do so tactfully and courteously. This is an instance where your knowledge of English fundamentals can be brought to your employer's attention. If you become recognized as an expert in this area, you may find yourself putting the finishing touches on much of your employer's business correspondence.

Acknowledgments. In general, every letter should be answered or acknowledged promptly, preferably the day it is received. In *answering* a letter, discuss the points raised. In *acknowledging* a letter or other materials, merely tell about its receipt and add any other necessary information. Acknowledgment letters may be sent to notify a customer that an order or a request for an appointment has been received. An effective acknowledgment letter will show appreciation; refer to the major points in the letter received; explain the action to be taken in the future; resell the customer on your firm, its products, and its service. Notice how the body of the letter in the sample below incorporates the four important features of an effective acknowledgment:

> Thank you for your letter of October 4 indicating that your order was shipped to Memphis instead of Nashville as you requested. (<u>appreciation</u>)
>
> Your concern about receiving your merchandise in time for pre—Christmas sales is understandable. (<u>major point</u>) Mr. Andrews, our sales manager, is in Atlanta this week; and I will notify him today to authorize a shipment to you from our Atlanta warehouse. (<u>specific action</u>)
>
> We will make every effort to provide you with prompt and courteous service to ensure that you receive your merchandise in time for your pre—Christmas promotions. (<u>resale of company service</u>)

Covering Letters A universal business practice is to inform recipients when money or material is being sent separately. A covering letter tells, with a touch of personal interest, what is being sent, why, when, and how.

A letter of transmittal is also a form of covering letter. It states that the material is enclosed and usually includes pertinent remarks about the enclosure.

When material is to be sent separately, the covering letter should start with the direct approach. Indicate what is being sent and why. Tie in the reader's personal interest if possible.

> Today we mailed you separately a complete set of swatches of our latest collection of decorator fabrics. (<u>what is being sent and why</u>) These should help you select draperies for your new home. (<u>reader's personal interest</u>)

Requests and Inquires. Letters that request personal favors, information, or free materials should be courteous and complete in every detail. Let the reader know exactly what you want; give sound reasons why the reader should comply with your requests. Don't write in a demanding tone; keep in mind that you are the one who wants the favor. Make it easy to reply to your letter and express your gratitude and your willingness to return the favor.

> In the November issue of <u>Office Male</u>, I noticed an article outlining the many opportunities available to male secretaries. The article was both informative and timely, and I would like to have reprints for students who come to me for career counseling.
>
> Enclosed is an addressed envelope. If there is a charge for these reprints, please bill me.
>
> I appreciate your help in providing these informative articles. Your magazine is often helpful in assisting students in planning their careers.

Answers to Inquiries. When you write a letter in reply to an inquiry, try to give a satisfactory answer that will make your reader think you are giving personal attention to the request. If you cannot provide the information requested (for whatever reason), tactfully state your refusal so that your reader will not be offended; don't make excuses.

Express appreciation for the letter and offer additional help when appropriate—this is an excellent public relations tool.

> Thank you for your letter of January 4 asking for a complimentary copy of our booklet on fund raising. The demand for this publication has been so heavy that we ran out of copies before the end of the year. This booklet is being reprinted and will be available by February 1.
>
> In the meantime, if you would like to have our Fund Raiser's Kit, which contains much of the same information plus some of the materials you will need to get started, just write your order on the bottom of this letter. Enclose $3 to cover mailing costs, and we will get a kit in the mail to you.

Reminder Letters. Every secretary keeps a tickler file of items that are pending. Answers awaited, reports due, goods to be received are all recorded in this file. When an item is overdue, the secretary sends a reminder. This is a routine procedure, and the secretary writes the letter without being instructed to do so. Tactful phrasing is imperative, for no one likes to be reminded of negligence or lack of promptness.

To ensure that you are writing tactful reminder letters, never write in an accusing tone. Don't imply forgetfulness on the reader's part. Give complete information and close with a positive look to the future.

> By July 24 we must complete our bids on the new construction on Highway 77 North. We need the quotations that we requested on June 1 to get our bids in on time. Could you possibly have this information sent to our Chicago office by the first of next week? A stamped envelope is enclosed for your convenience.
>
> Your help in securing this contract is greatly appreciated, and we look forward to working with you as the project progresses.

Letters of Recommendation. In writing a letter of recommendation, your employer is putting the stamp of approval on an employee or on a former employee who is seeking another position. Letters of recommendation usually give the reason for writing the letter, outline the duties that were performed by the employee, state the employee's qualifications for the job, and include the recommendation of the writer, as shown in the following example:

> I understand that Mr. J. A. Brandt has applied
> for the position of branch manager in your
> Dayton office. Mr. Brandt worked for us from his
> senior year in college until about a month ago.
> Although his duties were not supervisory in
> nature, he was thorough and accurate in all his
> work. He is very efficient, and his pleasant
> disposition made him very popular among his co-
> workers.
>
> We regret that he has left us, but we are
> delighted that he has found a position that will
> offer him the opportunity he deserves. It is a
> pleasure to recommend him to you. We are
> confident that he will prove himself capable of
> performing any responsibilities you assign him.

Letters of Reference. Unlike the letter of recommendation, the letter of reference reports pertinent information about employees who have left the firm. This type of letter is useful in handling routine inquiries about former employees. An example follows.

> Here is the information you requested about Mrs.
> Janice King who was employed in our mail room as
> a postal clerk from August 1980 until June 1985.
> Mrs. King left us to assist her husband in his
> printing business. While she was with us, she
> performed her duties in a satisfactory manner,
> and we found no reason to question her
> dependability or her skills.

Letters of Introduction. A letter of introduction is usually written to assist a former employee, customer, business associate, or acquaintance. This letter should establish the relationship between your employer and the person being introduced, state the reasons for the introduction, and politely ask the reader for help. Your employer may be called upon to write a letter of introduction to someone that neither the employer nor the employee knows. The letter should be hand-carried and presented to a possible employer who is yet unknown. It is not necessary to begin the letter with the outdated TO WHOM IT

MAY CONCERN. Simply begin the letter with the introduction and omit any form of salutation.

> This letter will introduce Ms. Nancy Adams, who served as my secretary from October 1980 until last May. Ms. Adams is a professional in every sense of the word. She is dependable, loyal, honest, and hardworking. She is leaving us to accompany her husband to Milwaukee. He has accepted a position with the AMB Corporation.
>
> I heartily recommend Ms. Adams to you. Any help you can give her in locating a suitable position will be appreciated.

A sample letter of introduction for a business associate follows:

> Sometime next month a young engineer, Donna Maxey, will call on you in Chicago. Our firm has worked with Donna for the past five years, and we find her to be an outstanding authority on metal design. She is now traveling throughout the Midwest to establish herself in a line of work that she will explain to you.
>
> Please make her feel welcome and extend to her any help you can give.

Negative Letters. Often a letter must be written about unpleasant subjects: *complaints, refusals,* and *mistakes.* These letters require special care.

Complaint Letters. As a company employee, any complaint letter which you receive that is antagonistic to your company must not be taken lightly. A prompt, thorough investigation of the complaint is necessary. Often a company does not even know there is a reason for dissatisfaction, so a genuine complaint letter is usually appreciated.

But what if *you* have a complaint? A good formula to follow in writing your letter is to begin with a positive reference to the trouble, continue with a detailed explanation, and end with a courteous request for an adjustment. See if the following paragraphs meet these criteria:

> On October 16 I ordered a solid cherry nightstand to match the Provantique bedroom grouping I purchased from you on August 29. The

```
nightstand was delivered this morning in the
carton in which it was originally packed. Upon
opening the carton, I discovered that the
nightstand had been packed before the finish had
completely dried. There were impressions of the
cardboard packing on the top of the stand that no
amount of cleaning will remove.

I am expecting guests for the Thanksgiving
holidays and am eager to have the room completed
before their arrival. Will you please have your
truck pick up the nightstand, have it
refinished, and return it to me before
Thanksgiving? If this is not possible, could I
please have another nightstand shipped from the
factory?

I realize that this error was made at the
factory, but I know you will take care of it
before my guests arrive.
```

Refusal Letters. One of the most severe tests of your ability to compose an effective letter will come when your employer asks you to write a letter of refusal. Banks often have to reject loans and employers have to turn down job applicants and refuse requests for favors. Since it is difficult to maintain the reader's goodwill when you must refuse a request, letters of this type require special care.

When it is necessary to refuse a request, use the sandwich technique. Place the refusal between a positive opening statement and a positive closing statement. A positive opening statement softens the impact of bad news. It should contain at least one element upon which both you and your reader agree, but it will not be effective if it sounds artificial or contrived. You should give a detailed explanation leading up to the refusal. Keep it practical and sympathetic. Avoid general statements that substitute for detailed explanations. State the refusal, or imply it strongly. Leave no doubt in your reader's mind. Offer an alternative action if possible and resell your company, its products, and its services. Here is an example of a refusal that uses the sandwich technique:

```
The Provantique bedroom suite that you
purchased from us on August 29 is indeed one of
```

the finest groupings our store has carried. We
are sure it is especially beautiful in your new
home. (positive point of agreement) However,
the Provantique grouping has been discontinued
by the manufacturer, and no matching pieces are
available. Our refinishing specialist tells us
that all attempts to match the finish on the
Provantique grouping have proved unsuccessful.
(explanation leading to the refusal).

May we have John Hendricks, A.S.I.D., our
interior designer, visit you at your
convenience? We have explained your concern to
him, and we are confident his suggestions will
enable you to select a compatible piece of
furniture to complement your Provantique
grouping and enhance your guest bedroom.
(alternative suggestion)

Our adjustment department will call you to make
arrangements to pick up the nightstand. Of
course, the full purchase price will be
refunded, and we will offer you our most
attractive price on any item you select as a
replacement. (resale of merchandise)

We appreciate the opportunity you have given us
to help you furnish your new home. With the
holidays approaching, we look forward to
helping you select any accent pieces you may
wish to acquire to beautify your home at this
festive time of the year. (positive closing)

Mistake Letters. As long as people and computers handle the affairs
of business, mistakes will occur. These errors require letters that are
tactful enough to soothe feelings and maintain harmonious relationships. When you write a letter about a mistake, admit that you are at
fault without the use of pompous phrases and long words. If you forgot
to put an enclosure in a letter, write a brief note of explanation to the
addressee, attach the enclosure, and send a copy of the message in with
the rest of the day's mail to be signed. This procedure lets your
employer know that the enclosure was omitted from the original
correspondence.

It is human nature to want to help a person who admits a mistake, unless that person's mistakes occur too frequently and have severe consequences. Compare your reactions to the mistake letters which follow.

Acceptable	**Unacceptable**
After you called yesterday, I checked our file of advertisements and found that we neglected to include yours in the October issue of <u>Edwardian Times</u>. We are sorry that this happened, and we will give your advertisement preferred placement in our November issue.	Pursuant to your telephone call of October 10, we immediately searched our records to determine what disposition had been made of your ad submitted for publication in the October issue of <u>Edwardian Times</u>. Apparently, through some inadvertent oversight on the part of our editorial department, your ad was omitted from this issue. We hope that delaying the ad for another month will not seriously inconvenience you.

Personal Correspondence

Occasionally your employer will ask you to write personal letters to business acquaintances. Some of these letters may be written without dictation or instruction and submitted to your employer for signature. It is especially important that these letters sound as though your employer had written them. Use the same salutation, complimentary close, and writing style that your employer uses. Personal correspondence should be typed on executive-size stationery or on the executive's personal stationery, if available; otherwise, it should be typed on plain bond paper. Submit your first draft for approval.

The types of personal business letters your employer may write are almost limitless. They may be letters of appreciation, sympathy, recognition, congratulations, introduction or formal acceptances and regrets. Often, because of their personal nature, your employer will dictate these letters; however, should she or he ask you to compose such a letter, consult an etiquette book or an up-to-date handbook on communications.

Letters of Appreciation. A busy executive in the office is usually just as busy on the outside with community activities. For instance, after a year of work on a civic project, your employer may ask you to write a note to committee members acknowledging the contributions they made to the project. For example:

> The work is finally concluded, and it is through your efforts and those of the other members of the committee that we can consider this project complete.
>
> Watching our dream become a reality will be gratifying to each of us. I hope we will have the opportunity to work together on another project for the betterment of our community.

Letters of Recognition. In the course of your employment, you will come to know many of your employer's friends and will recognize their names when you see them in print. If one of them has an article in a current magazine, you may be asked to scan the article and draft a letter complimenting the friend, using the executive's writing style, as in the following example:

> I have just read your interesting, informative article in the current issue of <u>Dynamics</u>. It shows your skill in organizing usually confusing ideas into a clear, pro-and-con presentation that allows valid conclusions to be drawn. Your readers, I know, will commend you for your treatment of this complex subject.

Letters of Sympathy. If death or tragedy occurs in the family of one of the executive's friends, you can draft a sympathy note to be copied in longhand by the executive. A personal note is more thoughtful than a commercial card. It is sincere and usually brief. The words *die* and *death* are seldom used in sympathy notes. Euphemistic phrases, such as *your bereavement, fatal illness, tragic happening,* and *the obituary in the paper* are kinder. Two examples follow.

> We were distressed to read in this morning's <u>Times</u> of the passing of Dr. Cramer. All of us extend to you our sincere sympathy for the loss of a good friend, a respected associate, and a great citizen.

All of us at Benson's extend our sincere
sympathy to you and your family. Mrs. Carter's
loss will be keenly felt here in the office by
those of us who worked with her. Her personal
integrity and good judgment made her invaluable
to us.

We send you our sincere sympathy and affection.

Letters of Congratulations. If there is publicity about the promotion
or professional achievement of one of your employer's friends, you
may draft a letter of congratulations. For example:

Congratulations, Keith, on your appointment as
President of Cober College. Having you as
president will be a great source of satisfaction
to alumni and friends of the college.

Please accept my sincere good wishes for a
productive presidency.

Letters Accepting Invitations. Letters accepting invitations should
convey appreciation and enthusiasm. Details of the invitation might
be repeated to assure the person issuing the invitation that the time,
place, date, and other arrangements are clear. If your employer receives
an invitation to speak (and numerous similar requests), it might be
wise to put together a packet to include with letters of acceptance. The
packet might include a biographical sketch (to be used in introducing
your employer), a list of the special equipment your employer will
need to make the presentation (projectors, recorders, screens, etc.), and
a publicity photograph (to be sent only when requested). If a spouse or
other special guests will accompany the employer, this information
should be included in the letter of acceptance. Give your reader as
much information as possible. This will eliminate the need for additional correspondence that may ask for a biographical sketch, a photograph, and a list of audiovisual equipment needed for the presentation.
Use the following example as a guide to compose acceptances:

Thank you for including me in your plans for the
annual employees' banquet to be held at the
Mario Hotel in New Orleans on Monday, November
14, at 7 p.m.

In keeping with your banquet theme, I have
entitled my remarks, ''The Five A's of Job

Satisfaction." I will do my best to give your employees an interesting twenty minutes.

My wife will accompany me and, as you suggested, we will meet you in the lobby of the hotel at six o'clock.

I look forward to meeting you in New Orleans.

Letters Declining an Invitation. Letters declining an invitation should express appreciation for the invitation but, at the same time, express regret. A specific explanation of the circumstances that prevent acceptance should be given. Specific reasons are more sincere than statements such as "due to circumstances beyond my control," or "because of a previous engagement." These are flimsy excuses and have a ring of insincerity.

Acceptable	Unacceptable
Thank you for inviting me to be your keynote speaker at the artists' forum on August 23 in Portland, Maine.	I regret exceedingly that I must decline your invitation to speak at the artists' forum on August 23.
I regret that a teaching assignment at a print-making workshop during the entire month of August makes it impossible for me to accept.	Circumstances beyond my control make it impossible for me to accept.
It was thoughtful of you to include me in your plans, and I hope you will keep me in mind for next summer's forum; I will not be teaching that semester.	

Letters Canceling Previously Accepted Engagements. Canceling engagements often causes inconvenience, frustration, and ill will and should be done only when a genuine emergency arises. Despite careful planning, there may be occasions when it will be necessary for your employer to cancel a previously accepted enagement. The following model should be helpful in drafting a letter of this type:

```
This is a difficult letter to write because I
know it can only cause you worry and
inconvenience.

On Monday morning I was awakened at home to learn
that our North Brattenborough plant had lost
thousands of gallons of milk because of a leak in
the filtering system. This morning our home
office ordered a massive project to correct this
situation. This unexpected emergency will, of
course, make it impossible for me to speak
before the national symposium in Santa Fe next
Saturday.
```

Guide Letters and Standard Paragraphs. You will soon discover that certain letterwriting situations frequently recur. Many of the letters you compose will cover similar circumstances. When you find an especially effective sentence or term, preserve it for another letter. You can do this by compiling a letter reference manual. The manual should contain samples of letters that reflect your employer's language and typical reactions. Although the preparation of such a reference takes time, it will become one of your greatest time-savers. Here is how to do it:

1. Keep an extra copy of all outgoing letters for a month.
2. Reread them at the end of the month, all in one sitting. As you read them, you will recognize words, phrases, and ideas that frequently recur..
3. Separate the letters into categories; make extra copies of those letters that fit several classifications; underline favorite phrases and other keys to your employer's ways of handling situations; set up a file folder for each classification. Ask yourself the reasons for variations among the letters in the amount of detail used, degree of cordiality, language, tone, and style.
4. Make an outline of the points usually covered by the letters in each category.
5. Pick out the best opening and closing sentences and the best key points tailored to specific situations.
6. Compile a letter guide, using a loose-leaf notebook. Type an outline for model responses to letters in each category on a heavy sheet of paper. Use them as dividers between categories

of letters. Type model opening and closing sentences and
model paragraphs for each category on separate sheets.
7.   When you compose a letter, compare it with the model outline to be sure that you included all necessary parts.
8.   Keep a record of the form used for each letter sent so that you
do not send the same letter to the same person twice.

One of the capabilities of word processing equipment is the storing
of standard paragraphs. It is the secretary's responsibility to store
paragraphs often used by the executive. When you are asked to compose a letter which incorporates standard paragraphs, all you need to do
is play back the stored paragraphs.

OTHER OPPORTUNITIES FOR SECRETARIAL COMPOSITION

Most of your composing assignments will probably consist of letters for your employer's signature; however, you may also be asked to
write interoffice correspondence, prepare press releases, and handle
correspondence to and from foreign offices. Knowing how to handle
these oppportunities for composition will add another dimension to
your effectiveness as a secretary.

Interoffice Correspondence

Written communication among the staff of a company takes the
form of an interoffice memorandum, a style less formal than a traditional letter. (See the illustration of an interoffice memorandum in the
Reference Guide.) The secretary will have many opportunities to compose messages for intracompany distribution. Ordering supplies,
requesting temporary help, and setting the time and place for a meeting are examples of when an interoffice memo might be used. Your
writing approach to this correspondence should be direct and concise.
If your employer requests that you write a memorandum to the staff
scheduling a meeting, your memo might read as follows:

```
The meeting of the sales staff will be held in
Mr. Breese's office at 10 a.m. on May 4. The
items for discussion include the establishment
of sales districts and quotas. Please bring . . .
```

Press Releases

If the publicity for your company is not the responsibility of an advertising department or an outside agency, you may be asked to compose or type brief articles for newspaper or magazine publication. Press releases are unsolicited. They are sent to editors in the hope that they will be published. They must, therefore, be *newsworthy*.

Style. A good press release clearly states all the facts *without* opinion. The italicized words in these expressions are opinions of the writer: *dire* emergency, everyone *should*, *noted* attorney, *signally* honored.

In composing a press release, answer the five W's—*who, what, when , where,* and *why*—plus the *how*. Put the most vital facts in the first sentence, the second most important facts in the second, and so on. This journalistic style is for the convenience of the busy reader and the busy editor. If the release has to be shortened, the editor cuts out sentences beginning at the end of the release and works forward. This leaves the important news intact without rewriting.

Form. A company that submits numerous press releases uses a special letterhead. An example appears in Illus. 7-2. Otherwise, an item is typed on regular letterhead or on an 8 1/2-by-11-inch sheet of bond paper. If a plain sheet is used, the name, address, and telephone number of the company are typed across the top. All press releases should carry the name and telephone number of a person whom the editor can call for additional information. If the news stems from an outside activity of the executive, the secretary uses a plain sheet of paper and gives the executive's name as the contact. Other practices to observe are:

1. Give the date when the news may be published—the release date.
2. Type the release date near the top. Express it in either of these ways: *FOR IMMEDIATE RELEASE* or *FOR RELEASE TUES-DAY, FEBRUARY 2, 19—*.
3. Give the release a title, if possible. This gives the editor an idea of the contents at a quick glance.
4. Double-space the text. Leave generous margins for editorial use. Confine the release to one page, if possible.
5. Center each page number after the first one at the top.
6. Type—*more*—at the bottom of all pages but the last.
7. Type # # # at the end of the release.
8. Send the original and type *Exclusive to* . . . on the release if it really is an exclusive. A carbon copy indicates you are sending the same release to other publishers.
9. Mail the release directly to the editor.

CONTACT: June Huyers
           (812) 555-6408

FOR IMMEDIATE
RELEASE

IBP PLANS EXPANSION

Chicago, November 21, 19--. While addressing a stockholders'
meeting at the Convention Center, President Joseph Miller announced
April 21 as the date scheduled for IBP Corporation's ground-breaking
ceremonies for a five-building headquarters complex estimated to
cost in excess of $75 million. Site of the new development is
company-owned acreage north of the present administration area.
Miller also confirmed IBP's plans to expand its highly sophisticated
computer services operation by building an eight-floor addition to
present facilities. Cost of the new building for computer operations is projected to reach $43 million.

IBP's plans for expansion of plant and operations reflect a
strong corporate optimism based, in part, on a strong commitment
to diversification of products and services. Figures for the last
five years show IBP's sales to have grown 32 percent annually.
This year the corporation anticipates 30 percent growth, and it
hopes to sustain a compound growth rate of 25-30 percent well into
the next decade. Reaction by stockholders to the Miller announcements was very supportive.

Illus. 7-2
A good press
release answers
who, what, when,
where, why, and
how.

International Correspondence

Many corporations do business abroad. Letter style for international correspondence is much more formal and traditional than for
domestic correspondence. Social amenities must be observed meticulously. Although you will probably not compose many letters to for-

eign companies, you may be asked to have messages translated into a foreign language. Then you may have to retype them on your company's letterhead. This can be a real challenge even for the expert typist!

When addressing a letter to a foreign recipient, copy the address *exactly* as it is given. Here, too, style differs. In European and South American countries, the street number *follows* the street name: Nassaustraat 7, not 7 Nassaustraat. In Japanese addresses, many other designations in addition to the street name and number are used to locate the prefecture and the section of the city; all are essential. Here is a list of ten tips for writing international correspondence:

1. Avoid all forms of humor. With the exception of a few countries, American humor is misunderstood overseas.

2. Don't be too familiar. Using first names and inquiring into personal business is sometimes regarded as disrespectful by people in other countries. Proceed slowly in writing to your overseas clients on a first-name basis.

3. Avoid American bias. Using words, phrases, cliches, or slang in a letter to an overseas customer or client may lead to misunderstanding and the loss of business. References to Hollywood, Wall Street, or Watergate may leave your reader at a loss. Using cliches like "You can't teach an old dog new tricks," may be considered offensive to a reader in a country where dogs are considered vile animals.

4. Avoid a condescending tone. Your reader will be quick to detect a superior tone in your letter. Never mention in correspondence that a country is a "developing nation," part of the Third World, or dependent upon the U.S. for aid.

5. Avoid discussing religion or politics unless religion or politics is the business at hand.

6. Expect and give formal courtesy. Although the writer of foreign correspondence may convey "most sincere compliments" or ask "your esteemed favor," it is not necessary for you to respond in kind. It is essential that please, thank you, and other courteous expressions be used generously in international correspondence. Stick to formal styles; use full titles and spell all names correctly.

7. Question tactfully. If you need to know whether the person to whom you are writing has the authority to approve or sign a contract, be very tactful in determining this. Do not in any way question the status of your reader. Position and status are immensely important in many foreign countries.

8. Respect the social customs, religion, and mores of your reader. Be prepared for different standards of conduct. For example, time is essential in most of the correspondence of Americans. However, if you insist upon prompt replies, you

may offend your reader unless the request is phrased tactfully.

9. Don't compete with your reader. Although you may be quite knowledgeable about Belgian lace, Chinese porcelain, Swiss watches, or French wines, don't pit your acquired expertise against that of your reader. It is not wrong to let your reader know that you have knowledge of such things, but don't try to be an expert.

10. Punctuate generously and make only one point in a sentence. Put all figures in writing and confirm oral discussions. Use charts, graphs, and pictures to help clarify your message. Avoid technical business jargon.

SUMMARY

One of the most important contributions you can make to your employer will come from your ability to write effectively. Your willingness to take on the task of composing business and personal correspondence for your employer will make you an invaluable employee.

The letter is the most personal form of written communication. As a secretary, you must know the fundamentals of effective letter writing as well as the proper forms of many kinds of letters—business and personal.

The most important part of any letter is its tone. Tone makes the communication human. It reflects the attitude of the writer, encourages the reader to react favorably, and conveys tact, courtesy, and caring.

Effective letter writers use a natural style that avoids monotonous, hackneyed expressions which sap the vitality of the message. Short words, short sentences, and short paragraphs, the elimination of redundant expressions, and the use of active verbs will improve the clarity of your communications. Concrete words give your writing precision. *Six hours* is far more precise than *a few hours*.

Using a forceful beginning sentence, preparing a gracious ending, and avoiding negative expressions and sexist language will also lead to a more favorable reaction from your reader.

Typical business letters composed by secretaries include acknowledgements, covering letters, requests, inquiries, answers to inquiries, reminders, letters of recommendation, reference letters, letters of introduction, negative letters, complaint letters, refusals, and mistake letters. Letters require special care in composition if they are to make the right impression and evoke favorable responses.

You may also be called upon to compose personal correspondence for your employer: letters of appreciation, recognition, and sympathy;

letters accepting or declining invitations; and letters canceling previously accepted engagements.

To cover situations that frequently recur, you may develop guide letters. These will save you time needed to restructure a separate letter each time the same situation occurs.

There are several other areas where your expertise in composition will be helpful. These areas include interoffice correspondence, press releases, and international correspondence.

Keep in mind that the essentials of effective letters are completeness; clarity; conciseness; courtesy; concreteness; conversational, unbiased tone; and forceful and interesting style.

Effective composition takes work. A well-structured communication of any type omits nothing essential to the message and includes nothing superfluous.

SUGGESTED READINGS

Keithley, Erwin M. and Philip J. Schreiner. *A Manual of Style for the Preparation of Papers & Reports* Cincinnati: South-Western Publishing Co., 1980.

Pearce, C. Glenn, Ross Figgins, and Stephen P. Golen. *Principles of Business Communication*, Theory, Application, and Technology. New York: John Wiley & Sons, Inc., 1984.

Wolf, Morris P. and Shirley Kuiper. *Effective Communication in Business*. Cincinnati: South-Western Publishing Co., 1984.

QUESTIONS FOR DISCUSSION

1. Your employer has been invited to be the keynote speaker for the state convention of Executive Women International. The date of May 5 conflicts with a scheduled presentation of a new line of products to a group of buyers in New York. Your employer asks you to respond. What information should you include in your letter?

2. When you were hired, your employer told you that every letter was an opportunity to build goodwill for the company. What are some of the steps you can take to ensure that the letters you compose build goodwill for the company?

3. If your employer is promoted to a position involving international trade, how can you help write overseas business letters that build goodwill for your company?

4. Your employer says, "Subscribe to *Business Week* for me, please." These are the only details you have. How would you handle this task?

5. Assume that the following are the first sentences of four business letters. What is your reader's response to them?
   a. This is in answer to your letter of July 10.
   b. We cannot send the merchandise you want until we receive payment for the last shipment.
   c. Your ball-point pens are lousy, and we are sending back the whole kit and caboodle of them express collect!
   d. It is with extreme pleasure that we send you the catalog you so graciously requested in your welcome letter of May 7.

6. A former classmate of yours applied for an executive secretarial position in the office of the comptroller of your firm. Your employer has the final word on personnel changes. Because of your friend's lack of accounting experience, another applicant was selected. Your employer is aware of your relationship to your classmate and has asked for your help in drafting the letter turning down the application. Discuss the approach you would take in drafting such a letter.

7. Your employer has asked you to write a letter of introduction for an employee who is leaving the company to go to Phoenix, Arizona. Neither your employer nor the employee has any contacts in Phoenix. How should you begin the letter, and what should be included?

8. Revise the following sentences to make them more euphonious. Use the Reference Guide to check your answers.
   a. The letter was too abrupt and tactless.
   b. The job was just a job to the secretary.
   What euphemisms would you use to replace the italicized words in the following sentences?
   c. We are mailing you a refund since you *claim* there was an error in your bill.
   d. He was *discharged* last August.
   e. He came from a *poor* neighborhood.

PROBLEMS

1. Your employer, Ms. Perry, has just been promoted to the position of personnel manager for your firm. Ms. Perry is a recent college graduate and has a tendency to be verbose. On your return from a workshop in effective letter writing, you are asked to revise the

following letter to conform to good letter-writing practice. Rewrite this letter.

We have your letter of March 16 for which we express our sincere thanks and appreciation. The information your office has kindly supplied us will be most helpful in helping us decide upon the choice of the individual who will make the most substantial contribution to this company.

In the event that any other information should come to your attention regarding the qualifications of this individual, we should appreciate your sending it along to us immediately.

We look forward with sincere pleasure to hearing from you further. In the meantime, if we can return your generous favor, please do not hesitate to call on us.

2. At a recent secretarial workshop, the participants were asked to reduce the text of the following letter to the smallest possible number of words. One secretary got it down to eight words. Can you do as well?

A copy of your pamphlet of "The Human Side" has been handed to the undersigned and in reading the content we have been very much impressed and are wondering if this pamphlet can be secured by subscription and, if so, what are the charges for such subscription. Might we hear from you in this regard at your earliest convenience?

3. Mr. Stanley intercepts the following two letters written by his assistant. He asks you to write acceptable replacements for them. Type each on a half-sheet simulated letterhead.

Dear Mrs. Gau:

Concerning our conversation of last week, we regret the delay of shipment of your order.

We are at a loss to explain why your merchandise has not reached you. The delivery truck picked up the package as requested.

We value your business. Naturally, we will do everything in our power to regain the confidence you have in our company and our products.

Very respectfully yours,

Dear Mr. Franklin:

We are indeed pleased to send you a copy of our recent catalog. In addition, we have alerted our sales representative in your territory, Janet Brinkley, to call for an appointment in your office. You should be hearing from her soon.

In checking our records, we see that we have not yet received your January order. Please let us have the opportunity to continue being of service to you.

Sincerely,

4. One of the important facets of good writing is effective organization. Rearrange the following paragraphs for the most effective message:

    a. The next time you are downtown, drop by our office. A few minutes of careful planning can help you protect your family in case something happens to you.

    b. At Providence Mutual, our counselors can help you set aside a portion of your income for your retirement, the education of your children, a vacation home, or the protection of your family for as little as $35 a month. If you wish, this amount can be deducted from your payroll check.

    c. Have you often stayed awake at night wondering what would happen to your family if something happened to you?

    d. Just call me at 555-1212, and I'll be glad to introduce you to one of our financial planning specialists.

Chapter 8

Handling Outgoing Communications and Shipments

Postal costs are a major expense in every company. Business is making conspicuous efforts to reduce this expense and also to improve postal service. In a large organization, the secretary sends much of the outgoing mail to a mail department for dispatch, but the secretary may also bypass this department by preparing and sending business mail, including packages, directly. In a small office, though, the secretary has complete responsibility for the mail. Transmittal expenses can be greatly reduced by a secretary who is familiar with postal information and services. Rate and procedural changes occur frequently, however, so this information must be constantly updated.

This chapter describes domestic and international mail classifications and explains special mail services. It discusses mail collection, delivery, and the use of money orders. Most important, it makes suggestions for speeding mail delivery and reducing postal expense.

DOMESTIC MAIL CLASSIFICATIONS

Domestic mail includes mail transmitted within, among, and between the United States, its territories and possessions, the Military Postal Service, and the United Nations in New York City.

The U.S. Postal Service divides domestic mail into the following general classes: *first class, priority mail, express mail, second class, third class, fourth class, official and free mail, mail for the blind,* and *mixed classes.* The best source of mailing information is the *Domestic Mail Manual,* which is updated regularly and may be purchased from the Superintendent of Documents, U. S. Government Printing Office, Washington, D.C. 20401. General descriptions of each mail classification, taken from this manual, are given in this chapter. Rates and fees are not provided since they are subject to change. For current information, consult the publications available from your local post office.

First-Class Mail

Airmail, as a domestic category, has been discontinued. All first-class mail has been upgraded to airmail status. If air service is not available, first-class mail is sent by the fastest means available. First-class mail refers to items weighing no more than 12 ounces. Items weighing more than 12 ounces that are to be sent by the fastest available route are called priority mail.

First-class mail includes letters (typewritten, handwritten, carbon copy, or photocopy); post cards; business reply mail; and bills and checks. All first-class envelopes should be sealed.

Because of the need for mail to conform to automated sorting machine measurements, a surcharge (a fee in addition to applicable postage) is assessed on each piece of nonstandard-sized mail. Items subject to this surcharge are first-class letters and postcards that are more than 6 1/8 inches high, 11 1/2 inches long, or 1/4 inch thick. Mail that is less than .007 inches thick, 3 1/2 inches high, or 5 inches long is also surcharged. All envelopes must be rectangular in shape.

Postage for first-class items is charged on the first ounce. If mail weighs more than one ounce, the rate for the second ounce is less than for the first—a fact not realized by a lot of mailers.

Priority Mail

Priority mail, another type of first-class mail, is given a separate classification by the Postal Service. It is relatively new and needs to be popularized. Priority mail refers to first-class mail weighing over 12 ounces. The maximum weight for priority mail is 70 pounds; the maximum size, length and girth combined, is 100 inches. Packages sent by priority mail are given preferential handling and are shipped by air or by selected ground transportation. Packages, either sealed or unsealed, can be mailed at any post office (not in mail collection boxes). Delivery is made within two or three days. Charges are assessed by zones: the longer the travel distance, the higher the rate. Priority mail is often less expensive than overnight express service.

The mailer who wants to send large envelopes by either first-class or priority mail should designate the class on both the front and the back of the envelope to prevent its being handled as third-class mail. Special oversized envelopes with green diamond borders for first-class mail and red diamond borders for priority mail are available to make the mailer's preferences known.

Express Mail

Express Mail is the fastest, most reliable postal service available for sending both letters and packages in most metropolitan areas. There are four service offerings: Express Mail Next Day Service, Express Mail Custom Designed Service, Express Mail Same Day Airport Service, and Express Mail International Service.

> Express Mail Next Day Service is designed for mailers whose needs for reliable overnight delivery do not recur on a regular basis. Mail deposited by a certain time (usually 5 p.m.) at a designated post office or collection box is delivered by 3 p.m. the next day, including weekends and holidays.

> Express Mail Custom Designed Service is offered under an agreement to customers who make regularly scheduled shipments. Each agreement is tailored to meet a customer's individual needs.

> Express Mail Same Day Airport Service provides service between major airports within the United States. The customer takes letters or packages to the airport mail facility (AMF), and they are dispatched on the next available flight to the destination airport. Items are made available for claim by the addressee according to times determined when accepted at the originating airport.

> Express Mail International Service is offered under a service agreement to many countries. On Demand Service, similar to Next Day Service, is available to some countries without a service agreement for the occasional user. International service is constantly expanding with the addition of new countries.

Second-Class Mail

Second-class mail includes newspapers and periodicals. Publishers and news agencies are granted second-class rates if they file the proper forms (obtained from their local post offices), pay the required fees, and comply with the regulations. Such mail must bear notice of second-class entry and be mailed in bulk lots.

You will probably not be responsible for bulk mailings, but you may mail single copies of a second-class publication. To qualify for the second-class rate, the entire publication must be mailed and no first-class material can be included. (To call attention to an article in a publication, the mailer writes *Marked Copy* on the wrapper.) Slit an addressed envelope and roll it around the publication. Use the gummed flap of the envelope to seal the roll, but leave the ends of the publication exposed. Write *Second Class* on the wrapper above the address.

Third-Class Mail

Third-class mail weighs less than 16 ounces. It is used for matter that cannot be classified as first- or second-class mail. The same matter in parcels that weigh 16 ounces or more is considered fourth-class mail. More than half of all mail falls into the third-class category.

Rates charged vary for single piece and bulk third-class mailings. The bulk third-class rate applies to mailings of identical pieces in large quantities to different addressees.

The Postal Service prefers that third-class mail not be sealed so that it can be easily examined. Items mailed at the single piece third-class rate may be sealed, however, if legibly endorsed (marked) *Third Class*. This notation must be printed on the front of the envelope. Third-class mail that is unsealed does not require any endorsement.

Mail that may be sent third class includes merchandise, printed matter, keys, advertising, and so on. Special rates also apply to books, manuscripts, music, sound recordings, films, and the like.

Fourth-Class Mail

The more common term for *fourth-class service* is *parcel post*. It includes all mailable matter not in first, second, or third class which weighs 16 ounces or more.

Parcel post rates are scaled according to the weight of the parcel and the distance it is being transported. Every local post office charts the country into eight zones. Zone charts showing the parcel post zone of any domestic post office in relation to the sender's post office may be obtained free from the sender's post office.

There are both weight and size limits for fourth-class packages according to delivery zones. Size limits are given in total inches, length and girth combined, as shown in Illus. 8-1. There are also special rates according to weight and zone for bound printed matter weighing 16 ounces or more.

Fourth-class packages may be sent unsealed or sealed. Mailing of sealed packages implies that the sender consents to inspection of the contents. A sealed package is treated as parcel post by postal sorters no matter what rate of postage has been paid unless the package is conspicuously marked *First Class*

It is a good idea to include the name and address of both the addressee and the sender inside a parcel post package just in cast the outside address is damaged or becomes unreadable. Also, if the contents of the package are perishable or fragile, put a label on the wrapper that says either *Perishable* or *Fragile.*

Certain kinds of packaged mail are given special low rates. Books without advertising that contain at least 22 printed pages are eligible for a special fourth-class rate; so are manuscripts, if labeled *Special Fourth-Class Mail.* The sender may, however, decide to send manuscripts by first-class mail because the rate difference is inconsequential.

The library rate applies to materials sent to or from libraries, schools, and certain nonprofit organizations. The secretary may use this rate when returning qualifying material to any of the organizations that are permitted to use this rate. The rate is the same to all zones and applies to books, periodicals, theses, microfilms, music, sound recordings, films, and other library materials. The package may

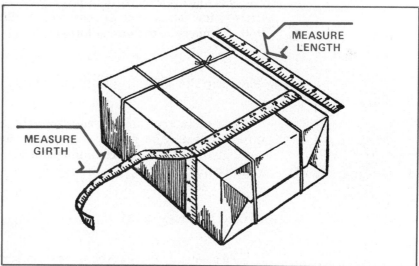

Illus. 8-1   Postal Service Manual

To determine the size of a parcel, measure the longest side to get the legnth; measure the distance around the parcel at its thickest part to get the girth; add the two figures together. For example, a parcel 10 inches long, 8 inches wide, and 4 1/2 inches high measures 35 inches, length and girth combined (10 inches + 4 1/2 inches + 8 inches + 4 1/2 inches + 8 inches). A free pamphlet, "Packaging for Mailing," may be obtained from your post office.

be sealed, but it must be conspicuously marked *Library Rate* on the address side.

It is recommended that the sender consult the local post office before mailing special fourth-class mail or library materials.

Official and Free Mail

Federal government offices and personnel send out official mail without affixing postage. There are two kinds of official mail: franked mail and penalty mail.

A *franked* piece of mail must have a real or facsimile signature of the sender in place of the stamp, and the words *Official Business* must appear on the address side. Only a few persons such as the vice-president of the United States, members and members-elect of Congress, resident commissioners, the Secretary of the Senate, and the Sergeant at Arms of the Senate are authorized to use the frank.

Penalty mail is used for official government correspondence. It travels in penalty envelopes or under penalty labels marked *Official Business—Penalty for Private Use.* Examples of a franked piece of mail and penalty mail appear in Illus. 8-2.

Free mail is sent without postage by the general public. It is limited to a few items, such as census mail and absentee ballot envelopes from members of the armed forces.

Mail for the Visually Handicapped

Some kinds of mail to and from the blind may be mailed free; other kinds may be mailed at nominal rates. If, as a secretary, your work involves sending letters and parcels to or from the blind, consult your local post office.

Mixed Classes of Mail

To ensure delivery at the same time, sometimes it is better to send two pieces of mail of different classes together in a single mailing by labeling the package *First-Class Mail Enclosed* or by attaching the first-class letter to the outside of the package. Delivery time is determined by the mail classification of the package; therefore, a first-class letter attached to a four pound package will go as fourth-class mail.

Previously, if a piece of first-class material was attached to a second-, third-, or fourth-class mailing, the Postal Service required postage

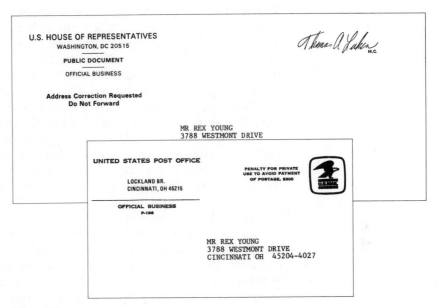

Illus. 8-2
Notice the difference between a franked envelope and a penalty envelope. A
franked envelope must show a real or facsimile signature and carry the
words *OFFICIAL BUSINESS*. A penalty envelope must carry the penalty
warning and the words *OFFICIAL BUSINESS* under a return address.

for both pieces. As the result of a recent ruling, a piece of first-class
mail that is incidental (related) to matter mailed via another class—
except nonmerchandise third-class mail—does not require separate,
additional postage.

SPECIAL MAIL SERVICES

In addition to transmitting mail, the post office provides many
special services. The sender should be aware, however, that fees for
such services may be very expensive.

Registered and Insured Mail

A piece of important or valuable mail can be registered or insured,
depending on its nature.

Registering Mail. First-class or priority mail can be registered. It is the safest way to send valuables through the mail system. The full value of the contents must be declared on a piece of mail being registered because the fee charged is based on an item's worth. There are two sets of fees. Fees depend upon whether or not the sender has commercial insurance covering the matter being mailed. When the value of the shipment is greater than the maximum liability of the post office, special private insurance is usually taken out by the sender.

Each piece of mail to be registered must be tightly sealed along all edges (transparent tape cannot be used) and must bear the complete addresses of both the sender and the addressee. The sender takes it to the registry window where the postal clerk computes the fee.

Insuring Mail. A piece of third- or fourth-class mail, or priority mail containing third- or fourth-class matter, may be insured up to $500. The package is taken to the post office window where the clerk makes out a receipt for it, stamps the package *Insured*, and puts the receipt number, if any , on it. (An unnumbered receipt is given if the package is insured for $15 or less.) After placing the regular and insured postage on the package, the clerk gives the receipt to the sender for filing. If the package is lost or damaged, the post office reimburses the sender according to the amount of its insured value.

If a business frequently sends several insured packages at one time, it may be more convenient to use a mailing book rather than file a separate receipt for each package. Mailing books, which are issued by the post office on request, provide pages for entering the description of insured parcels. The pages of this book are officially endorsed at the time of mailing and become the sender's receipts.

Return Receipts and Restricted Delivery. The sender is always furnished with a receipt showing that the post office accepted a piece of insured or registerd mail for transmittal and delivery. However, the sender often wants legal evidence that the piece of mail was also actually received by the addressee. For an added fee, the sender may obtain a signed receipt, commonly called a *return receipt*, on any piece of certified or registered mail or on any piece of mail insured for more than $15. This service is helpful when there is reason to believe that the addressee may have moved.

A sender who wants a return receipt fills in the receipt number and the addressee's name and address on a postal card form supplied by the post office. Senders also indicate their return address on the reverse of the post card and write *Return Receipt Requested* on the front of the mail. This card is pasted (facedown) along its two gummed edges to the back of the envelope or package. At delivery, the letter carrier removes

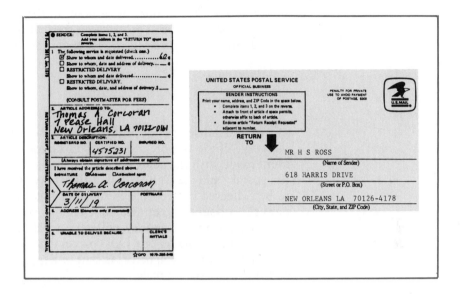

Illus. 8-3
A sender must
complete two sides
of a return receipt.

the card, obtains the addressee's signature on the ungummed side, fills in the information required, and mails the card to the sender. Illus. 8-3 shows both sides of a return receipt.

For an added fee, delivery may be *restricted to the addressee*, only if the piece of mail is registered, certified, or insured for more than $15. The charge for a return receipt is almost doubled if the receipt is requested after mailing.

Business Reply Mail

Business reply mail is used by mailers to encourage responses by paying the postage for those responses. This mail is returned to any valid address in the United States. The mailer guarantees to pay the postage for all replies which are returned. The postage per piece is the regular first-class rate plus a business-reply fee.

Mailgram

An electronic communications service offered by Western Union and the Postal Service is the *Mailgram*. Mailgrams are transmitted over Western Union's communications network to printers in over 141 post offices. Mailgrams are delivered by regular mail carriers the next business day throughout the United States. A *Business Reply Mailgram* is now available. It provides all the features of a regular Mailgram with a built-in response in the form of a business reply envelope.

COD Service

Merchandise may be sent to a purchaser *COD*—that is, *collect on delivery*—if the shipment is based on a bona fide order or on an agreement made with the addressee by the mailer. The sender often prepays the postage and the COD fees, but they may be included in the amount to be collected if agreeable to the addressee. Otherwise the addressee pays the amount due on the merchandise, plus the fee for the money order to return the money collected to the sender. The maximum amount collectible on one COD parcel is $500. If the sender alters the COD charges after the parcel is sent or designates a new addressee, an additional charge is made.

Certificates of Mailing

For a few cents a sender may obtain a very simple proof of having taken a piece of mail to the post office for dispatching. Such proof may be obtained for any kind of mail. The sender fills in the required information on a certificate blank, pastes on the appropriate stamp, and hands this certificate to the postal clerk with the piece of mail. The clerk cancels the stamp and hands the certificate back to the sender as evidence that the piece of mail was received.

This is an economical service for one who is mailing something that is of value to the addressee but who has no obligation or responsibility to pay to have the material insured, registered, or certified. It also furnishes a sender with inexpensive proof of having mailed tax returns.

Certified Mail

Certified mail requires that the addressee's post office maintain a record of delivery for two years. In addition to the regular postage, the sender pays to have the mail carrier obtain a signature from the addressee upon delivery. Certified mail is appropriate for first-class mail that has no monetary value, such as letters, bills, or nonnegotiable bonds. It carries no insurance. If a sender requests a return receipt, an additional fee is charged (see Illus. 8-4).

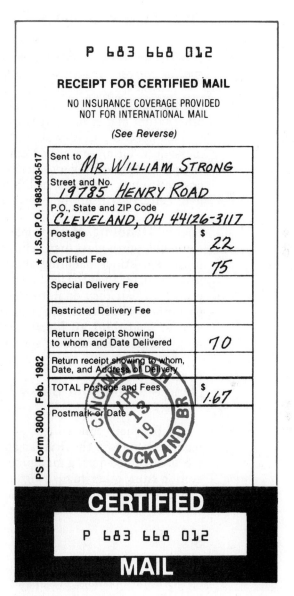

Illus. 8-4
A receipt for
certified mail
shows the itemized
charges for the
service including
the regular postage
fee, the certified
fee, and the return
receipt service fee.

Certified mail has the following advantages: (1) it provides the sender with a means of checking on the delivery of the letter; (2) it provides official evidence of mailing if a postmarked receipt is obtained; and (3) it gives the letter the appearance of importance and urgency. For that reason, it is frequently used by many collection agencies.

Special Delivery and Special Handling

The delivery of a piece of mail may be hurried along by the use of *special delivery* or *special handling services.*

Special Delivery. *Special delivery service* provides the fastest handling—from mailer to addressee—for all classes of mail. Mail must be marked *Special Delivery* above the address. Immediate delivery is by messenger during prescribed hours to points within certain limits of any post office or delivery station. Do not send special delivery mail to post office box addresses, military installations, or other places where mail delivery will not be expedited after arrival.

Special Handling. Most people are not aware of *special handling* for third-and fourth-class mail. The fee for this service, which provides the most expeditious handling and ground transportation practicable, is less expensive than the fee for special delivery. Parcels move with first-class mail, but they do not receive special delivery at the destination post office. The rate for special handling is high. Often it is less expensive to send third- or fourth-class mail first class, unless it is very bulky, rather than request special handling.

Hand Stamping for Bulky Mail

Bulky mail, called *slugs*, should be marked *Hand Stamp* in large red letters on both the front and back of the envelope. Unmarked slugs are often ruined during mail processing. Unless clearly marked for separation from other mail, slugs may be routinely placed in canceling machines which may cause serious damage.

Stamps

Ordinary postage stamps are available in sheet, coil, or booklet form. Postage stamps can be exchanged at full value if stamps of the wrong denomination were purchased or if damaged stamps were received. Envelopes with imprinted stamps are also available.

Precanceled Stamps and Envelopes. *Precanceled stamps* and *precanceled stamped envelopes* may be used only by those persons or companies who have been issued a permit to use them. Also, they may be used only on matter presented at the post office where the precanceled stamps or envelopes were purchased. Their advantage is the saving of canceling time at the post office.

Other Supplies Available from the Post Office. Stamped envelopes in various sizes, kinds, and denominations may be purchased at the post office individually or in quantity lots. For a nominal amount, the post office will have the sender's return request and name and address printed on them when the envelopes are ordered in quantity lots. Two lines of advertising material may also be included.

To facilitate in-company printing of standard messages in batches, postal cards are available from the post office in continuous sheets. First-class postal cards are available in single or double form, the latter kind being used when a reply is desired on the attached card.

Unserviceable or spoiled stamped envelopes and cards (if uncanceled) may be exchanged at postage value. Such exchanges are made in stamps, stamped envelopes, or postal cards.

The post office also sells a *combination mailer*, a large envelope with a No. 10 envelope attached. A combination mailer can be used to mail a third-class enclosure and a first-class letter. Various shipping containers can also be purchased for packing your parcels.

Metered Postage

One of the quickest and most efficient ways of affixing postage to mail of any class is by means of a *postage meter*. The meter prints the postmark and the proper amount of postage on each piece of mail. Metered mail need not be canceled or postmarked when it reaches the post office. As a result , it often catches earlier trains, trucks, or planes than does nonmetered mail.

The postage may be fully automatic, not only printing the postage, postmark, and date of mailing; but also feeding, sealing, and stacking the stamped envelopes. The imprint is usually red and may carry a line or two of advertising. Some models can also print the postage on gummed tape that can be pasted onto packages. The meter registers the amount of postage used on each piece of mail, the amount of postage remaining in the meter, and the number of pieces that have passed through the machine.

The machine itself is purchased outright, but the meter mechanism is leased. In order to use a postage meter, a company must first obtain a meter license by filing an application with the post office where its mail is handled. The application must tell the make and model of the meter. A record of use must be maintained in a *Meter Record Book* supplied by the post office.

The meter locks when the remaining postage supply reaches $10. The user can purchase additional postage before this happens in either of two ways. By the old system, the meter is removed from the machine and taken to the post office for resetting and relocking at the time that new postage is bought. Now a meter can be reset by a telephone-to-computer linkup between the user and the meter manufacturer's computer. The computer supplies coded information to the post office enabling it to collect money for the postage from an approved bank.

Forwarding, Returning, and Remailing

Unfortunately mail does not always reach its final destination on first mailing. Some pieces must be forwarded, returned to the sender, or remailed. Additional postage may or may not be required.

Forwarding Mail. The secretary is often required to forward mail. The following information indicates the extra postage or fee required:

> *First-Class Mail Up to 12 Ounces.* No additional postage is required to forward first-class mail. Change the address and deposit it.

> *Second-Class Publications.* Full postage must be paid at a single piece rate to forward second-class publications. Change the address, affix the postage, endorse it as *Second-Class Mail*, and deposit it.

> *Third-Class and Fourth-Class Mail.* Additional postage at applicable rate must be paid to forward third- and fourth-class mail. Change the address, affix the postage, and deposit it.

> *Registered, Certified, Insured, COD, and Special Handling Mail.* This mail can be forwarded without payment of additional registry, insurance, COD, or special handling fees; however, ordinary forwarding postage charge, if any, must be paid.

> *Special Delivery Service.* This mail will not receive special delivery service at a second address unless a change-of-address card has been filed.

Return of Undeliverable Mail. An undeliverable first-class letter will be returned to the sender free of charge. For undeliverable third- or fourth-class parcels, the sender must pay full postage for the return service. To assure that third- and fourth-class packages are returned, *Return Postage Guaranteed* should be conspicuously placed below the return address.

Undeliverable letters and packages without return addresses are sent to the dead letter office where they are examined. They may be opened to find a return address; so it is wise to enclose completed address labels in all packages . Whenever an address is found, the mail is returned for a fee. Undeliverable dead mail is destroyed or sold.

Remailing Returned Mail. The secretary is always chagrined when mail is returned. Any piece of mail returned rubber stamped "RETURN TO SENDER" and with the reason indicated by a "pointing finger" must be put in a fresh, correctly addressed envelope, and postage must be paid again.

Change of Address

The post office serving you must be officially notified by letter or by one of its forms when you change your address. The old and the new address and the date when the new address is effective must be given. Correspondents should be notified of a new address promptly by special notices or by stickers attached to all outgoing mail. The post office supplies new address cards free for personal and business use.

Recalling Mail

Occasionally it may be necessary to recall a piece of mail that has been posted. This calls for fast action. Type an addressed envelope that duplicates the one mailed. Go to the post office in your mailing zone if the letter is local or to the central post office if the letter is an out-of-town mailing. Fill in a *Sender's Application for Recall of Mail.*

If the mail is an undelivered local letter, on-the-spot return will be made. If the letter has left the post office for an out-of-town address, the post office (at the sender's request and expense) will wire or telephone the addressee's post office and ask that the letter be returned. If the mail has already been delivered, the sender is notified, but the addressee is not informed that a recall was requested.

MAIL COLLECTION AND DELIVERY

A number of plans have been inaugurated by the Postal Service to improve operations and reduce costs. An explanation of some of these plans follows.

Addressing Mail

The ZIP (Zone Improvement Plan) Code was designed to speed mail deliveries and to facilitate the use of automated equipment in the processing of mail. The ZIP Code originally conceived by the United States Postal Service in 1963 was five digits. In 1981 the Postal Service introduced a nine-digit ZIP Code. The ZIP + 4 Code includes the original five digits plus four additional digits preceded by a hyphen. For example, ZIP + 4 Code might be 45227-1035. With four more digits, the Postal Service can pinpoint mail delivery and make ZIP Codes very precise, permitting the fine sorting of mail down to the individual carrier's route. Use of the ZIP + 4 Code is voluntary.

All bulk mailers of second- or third-class mail are required to use ZIP Codes. Failure to do so may subject the mail to a postal rate penalty. When the mail is being sorted, an item with no ZIP Code goes into the reject slot, delaying the sorting operation.

A *National ZIP Code and Post Office Directory* can be purchased from the Postal Service. The directory is updated regularly. Other sources of ZIP Codes are the current edition of the *World Almanac and Book of Facts*[1] and the directory placed in the lobby of most post offices.

To permit the use of scanning machines with limited capabilities for spaces per line, the Postal Service has designed and approved a two-letter abbreviation for each state and abbreviations for cities with long names. The two-letter state abbreviations should be used on all mail if the ZIP Code is included. The list of approved abbreviations is presented on page 854 of this book.

Optical character readers that electronically scan addresses are used in many post offices. They are programmed to scan a specific area on all envelopes, so the address must be completely within this read zone, single-spaced, and blocked in style. The two-letter state abbreviations must be used. Acceptable placement for an address is shown in Illus. 8-5. Optical character readers are discussed in more detail in Chapter 9, "Data and Word Processing."

Bar Codes

The post office uses bar code readers to automate the sorting of mail. A series of bars and half-bars, representing an address, can be

---

[1]Published annually by Newspaper Enterprise Association, Inc., 200 Park Avenue, New York, NY 10166.

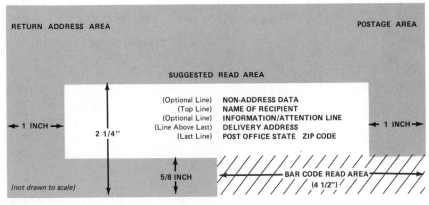

Illus. 8-5
Post office optical character readers are designed to scan a specific area on all envelopes. The illustration shows the read zones within which addresses and bar codes must be placed. The last line of the address must be completely within the white OCR area.

electronically scanned and sorted at amazing speed. The bar code contains the ZIP Code and certain letters and numbers from the address. Bar coding is most often used on business reply envelopes, as in Illus. 8-6, where the code is imprinted along with the address.

Illus. 8-6
Business reply envelope showing bar code.

Presorting Mail

To encourage large mailers to presort mail before depositing it, the Postal Service grants a reduction of a few cents in postage on each presorted piece. To qualify for the reduction, a minimum of 500 first-class pieces must be included in each mailing. For the specifics on presorting, you should contact your local post office.

Postal regulations require five or more pieces of metered mail to be bundled and identified. Presorted bundles of metered mail are indicated by color-coded labels. For example, mail for the same state would be coded with an orange label bearing an *S*, and all mail for the same firm would carry a blue label with an *F* on it.

Mail presorted by ZIP Code moves faster. Large mailers can presort and deposit mail to a specific ZIP Code or to a specific company in one bag. The post office furnishes trays for presorting in preparing mail for deposit at the post office.

The opportunity for postage savings carries the implication that every mailer in an organization must cooperate with the mail room to obtain cost reductions. This means that mail should be sent to the mail room regularly during the day. The practice now prevalent, in which 75 percent of outgoing material reaches the mail room sometime in the late afternoon, prevents many mail room managers from capitalizing on possible reductions.

The secretary who is responsible for mailing should presort mail for speedier handling by the post office. Before depositing mail, separate it into major categories, such as local, out-of-town, precanceled, and metered. It can then bypass one or more preliminary handlings in the post office. Types of presorting vary with the types of individual mailings. For instance, if most of the mail goes to in-state addresses, this mail may be kept separate and identified as "All for (*State*)," thus eliminating one sorting operation.

Post Office Box

It is possible to rent a post office box where mail can be picked up at any time that the post office building is open. Mail can be obtained faster from post office boxes than from carriers.

Vertical Improved Mail (VIM)

Vertical Improved Mail (VIM) is a mail distribution system installed in many new large office buildings. In essence, VIM is the reverse of the familiar mail chute that channels mail dropped from the upper floors into a collection box. Under VIM, all incoming mail is delivered to a central mail room in the building. There postal employees sort it into lockboxes by floors. These boxes are then placed on a conveyor belt and keyed to be ejected automatically to the right floor. There the office personnel pick up and deliver the mail. By this process, the offices on each floor of the building can have continuous delivery of incoming mail. In buildings where lockboxes are not feasible, call windows can be used for frequent pickup of mail.

General Delivery

Mail may be addressed to individuals in care of the *General Delivery* window of main post offices. This service is convenient to transients and to individuals who have no definite address in a city. Such mail is held for a specified number of days and, if uncalled for, is returned to the sender.

Executives on touring vacations or sales representatives who are on the road for several days and do not have specific hotel addresses, frequently ask to have mail addressed in care of *General Delivery* to a city en route. The address can also include the words *Transient* or *To Be Called For*. Such a letter would go to the main post office in a city and be held at the *General Delivery* window for the addressee for 10 days, or up to 30 days if the envelope bears such a request.

Updates of Mailing Lists

The mailer can do a great deal to obtain information about changes of address by using first-class mail marked *Address Correction Requested* and guaranteeing the return postage.

The postmaster will correct any list of local mailing addresses at the expense of the mailer. The list should be typed on cards about the size and quality of postal cards, with one address per card. The name of the owner of the list should be placed in the upper left corner of each card for identification purposes. Cards should be sent only to the post office that serves the address shown on the card. Cards with the addresses of "lost" addressees are distributed to local carriers who fill in the correct addresses or explain other reasons why delivery cannot be made.

Private Mail Delivery

Private carriers also transport mail. Several companies provide overnight letter delivery to most major United States markets. The maximum weight for an overnight letter is two ounces or the equivalent of ten 8 1/2-by-11-inch folded pages. A special pouch is used to deliver an overnight letter.

Some companies use their own employees to deliver unstamped letters between their offices and to companies with whom they conduct a large volume of business. Another time- and money-saving operation is hand delivery of bills.

Automated Mail Room Equipment

For businesses that are interested in improving the capabilities of the mail room, a number of electronic mail handling devices are available to increase the efficiency of mail room operations.

An electronic postage scale can compute domestic and international mailing rates and shipping fees. Any weight restrictions that might prevent mailing are also indicated. The scale interfaces (connects) with a postage meter. An operator can place the scale in letter mode for envelope processing or in parcel mode for dispensing gummed meter tapes for packages. Electronic accounting devices can be attached to mailing equipment to record and print out a daily record of postage totals and piece counts for each department in a company. Accounting devices that interface with mailing equipment enable a company to keep an accurate record of postage expenditures.

Other mail room related equipment, such as folding and inserting machines, address printers, electronic embossers, collators, and copiers, is also being automated. The use of this new equipment enables mail room personnel to keep up with the increasing flow of mail being produced in the office. Illus. 8-7 is an example of an electronic mailing system which weighs letters and packages, computes the most efficient rate, and makes a record of the transaction in one operation.

MONEY ORDERS

Money may be transferred from one person or business to another by use of a *money order*. There are instances in which money orders are the requested form of payment. They are also a convenience to individuals who do not have checking accounts.

Illus. 8-7
Electronic mailing
equipment.

Courtesy of Friden Alcatel

Domestic Money Orders

Postal money orders may be purchased at all post offices, branches, and stations. The maximum amount for a single *domestic money order* is $500. However, there is no limit on the number of money orders that may be purchased at one time. Money orders are also available at a low rate to savings banks depositors and at other businesses, such as drugstores, supermarkets, etc.

International Money Orders

Money may be sent to a foreign country by means of an *international money order* procurable at local post offices. When buying such an order, you are given a receipt for it by the postal clerk, who then arranges for sending the money order abroad. Exact information is required about the payee and the payee's address. If the payee is a woman, you must state whether she is single, married, or widowed. The purpose of the payment should also be stated.

INTERNATIONAL MAIL

The Postal Service participates in an international communications network that provides surface and airmail services for correspondence, printed material, and merchandise to almost any destination in the world. Correspondence and other documents may be transmitted electronically to a few countries through the Postal Service's INTELPOST service.

Classifications of International Mail

International postal service provides *postal union mail* and *parcel post*.

Postal Union Mail. *Postal union mail* is divided into *LC Mail* and *AO Mail*.

LC Mail (letters and cards) consists of letters, letter packages, air letters (aerogrammes), and postal cards.

AO Mail (other articles) consists of printed matter, merchandise samples without salable value, commercial papers, small packets, and matter for the blind.

The postage for letters and postal cards mailed to Canada and Mexico is the same as for the United States. To all other countries, the rates are higher and weights are limited. Letter packages (small, sealed packages sent at a letter rate of postage) are given letter treatment if they are marked *Letter*. A customs label identifying the contents must be attached to each letter package carrying dutiable merchandise.

Parcel Post. Parcels for transmission overseas are mailed by *parcel post* and must be packed even more carefully than those delivered within the continental United States. These packages may be registered or insured. Special handling services are also available. There is no international COD service. A *customs declaration* form must be attached to the parcel with an accurate and complete description of the contents. Since rates, weight limitations, and other regulations are not the same for all countries, the secretary should obtain information from the post office about requirements for a particular shipment.

International Air Postal Services

Rates on letters by air to foreign countries are charged at a fixed rate for a half ounce (except to Canada and Mexico, where rates are the same as in the United States).

Air Letters (Aerogrammes). The post office sells an *air letter* sheet which may be mailed to any country with which we maintain airmail service. It is an airmail, prestamped, lightweight, single sheet that is folded into the form of an envelope and sealed. No enclosures, either paper or other kinds, are permitted. Firms engaged in international trade may print, subject to prior approval of the Postal Service, their own aerogramme letterheads.

AO Mail by Air. Many businesses are not aware of the cheapest and fastest of all international postal services—*AO mail by air*. No export forms are required for most shipments. This service is restricted to samples of such items as merchandise, maps, printed matter, and drawings. It is ideal for shipping small articles and should be investigated by those companies using other air services.

International Air Parcel Post. A minimum of forms is required to ship by *international air parcel post*. This service is available to nearly all countries and is rated on the first four ounces and each additional four ounces according to the country of destination.

Reply Postage

To enclose reply postage with mail going out of the country, use an international reply coupon, called *Coupon Response International*. It is purchased at the post office and is exchanged for stamps by the addressee in the country where it is received. The stamps are then used for postage on the reply mail addressed to this country.

SHIPPING SERVICES

Shipments can be made by air, rail, ship, bus, and truck. The secretary needs to know the advantages of each and the sources to investigate for current information. The following discussion deals with three shipping services: United Parcel Service, courier, and freight.

United Parcel Service

United Parcel Service, Inc. carries packages among all 50 states either by air or truck. Delivery times vary, from overnight to four days, depending on the distance from the place of origin. Parcels are limited to 50 pounds and a combined girth and length of 108 inches. If a UPS driver is unable to make a delivery the first time, the driver will try twice more before a notice is issued to the recipient to pick up the package at the local UPS office. Refused or undeliverable packages are returned to the sender at no extra charge. Rates are based on weights and delivery zones.

UPS also offers 2nd Day Air Service, which is similar to overnight air express offered by many other express shipping companies. UPS makes deliveries and will pick up shipments for a nominal fee.

Courier Services

Courier services are offered by air, van, or bus. Each service offers advantages. Choice of service depends on specific shipping needs.

Air Service. Air Service is the fastest and most expensive means of transporting packages. Many companies provide express air service for letters at a flat rate. The charge for packages varies with the size and weight of the package. Pickup and delivery is included in the fee. Next day delivery is assured to most points in the United States. Some companies guarantee delivery to every address in the 48 contiguous states. Companies such as Emery Air Freight Corp., Federal Express Corp., Purolator Courier Corp., and United Parcel Service, Inc., own their own air fleets and can provide faster service than those using commercial planes. Some airlines also offer express air service for small parcels.

Van Service. Some couriers offer van service within metropolitan areas or to points that are not easily accessible by air. For example, Purolator supplements its air express service by using vans to ship packages up to 70 pounds and 108 inches in length and girth.

Bus Service. If speedy delivery of a package to a small town in another part of the state is necessary, the secretary should consider bus service. This service is particularly useful when destination points are located where there are no airports. Round-the-clock service is offered, including Sundays and holidays. Between many points, same day bus service is available. Pickup and delivery service is available at an extra charge. Most bus lines offer this type of shipping, the most widely known being Greyhound and Trailways. Items are insured free up to $100, and a small charge is added for insurance beyond that value. The size of a package is limited to 100 pounds by Greyhound and 150 pounds by

Trailways. A package must be no larger than 140 inches in combined length, width, and girth with a restriction of five feet in length by Greyhound and six feet by Trailways.

Choosing a Service. With so many choices, the shipper needs to make constant comparisons of costs and services. For current service and rates, call the agencies listed in the Yellow Pages that offer courier service.

Freight Services

Freight is generally thought of as a shipment sent by any method other than mail or courier. It is the most economical service used to transport heavy, bulky goods in large quantities. Because freight shipping is the most complex of all methods, the secretary will probably not be required to select the carrier and to route the shipments. Still, it is good to know a few of the salient facts.

Railroad Freight. Ordinarily when goods are shipped by *railroad freight*, they must be delivered by the shipper (consignor) to the local freight office. When the shipment arrives at its destination, the addressee (consignee) must arrange for delivery or must call for the shipment. Many railroads, however, have instituted door delivery. Trucks operated by the railway company compete with the door delivery service of trucking companies.

More and more, the shipper loads goods into containers at the home location and takes them to the carrier, who transports and delivers the shipment to the consignee with no further handling. Containerized shipping also offers the advantage of better security.

A service called *piggyback* is offered by the railroads to trucking firms for long-distance hauls. Loaded truck trailers are driven to the railway depot in one city, detached from the tractor, placed on railroad flatcars, and moved by rail to another city where they can be unloaded and driven to their destinations. Thus areas not on the regular railroad lines can be reached by this service.

To provide a less-than-carload freight service at a special rate, *freight-forwarding companies* assemble from several consignors shipments that are less than a carload that are going to the same destination. This service allows shippers of small quantities to gain a carload rate from the railroads.

Motor Freight. *Motor freight* is used for both local and long-distance hauls. Truck companies operate coast-to-coast service and have connecting services with local trucking lines. As described above, they often work in conjunction with railroads. Sometimes shipments are held by trucking companies until they have a paying load destined for the same locality. Specialized trucks also carry single commodities such as milk, gasoline, new cars, chemicals, sand, and gravel in truck-load quantities.

Air Freight. Businesses find that the high cost of air freight is partly offset by reduced costs in inventory and in warehouse space. There is also a saving in packing costs, since air shipments do not require the sturdy crating that surface shipments frequently demand. Delivery service is provided without charge; however, there is a small charge for pickup service.

Water Freight. *Water freight* is usually considerably cheaper than any other means of freight transportation. River barges and other vessels on the inland waterways of the United States carry such commodities as lumber, coal, iron ore, and chemicals. Bulky items for overseas shipment are carried in freighters, while passenger lines carry mail and items packaged in crates. Information on services and rates can be obtained from shipping companies.

International Shipments

The market for American products is worldwide. International air cargo service makes it possible to deliver goods to most places in the world within a matter of hours. The bulk of tonnage to foreign markets, however, still moves via *surface* (ships).

International shipments present problems—special packing, complicated shipping procedures, marine insurance, foreign exchange—usually not encountered in domestic trade. The mere handling of communications with a foreign business firm can be a problem in itself.

Shipping Documents. A foreign shipment involves the preparation of a number of documents, such as forms to obtain an *export license* (some commodities), *ocean bill of lading, consular invoice* or *certificate of origin*, and *export customs declaration*. Large manufacturers doing extensive business abroad usually establish export departments (1) to market their products, (2) to execute required export and shipping forms, and (3) to arrange for the actual shipments.

Many small firms use the services of an export broker or Combination Export Management (CEM) firm. This firm performs the same functions as an export department; namely, marketing, processing, and shipping goods.

Some businesses prefer to use the services of a foreign freight forwarder or the services of a cargo agent who specializes in processing foreign shipments. The agent executes required reports and shipping documents and arranges for the actual shipment.

International airlines and steamship companies also maintain departments that assist customers with their overseas shipments.

International Air Cargo. To send a shipment by *international air cargo*, whether you are sending one package or a carload, contact the office of an international airline. The airline will provide instructions for packaging and addressing the shipment and for completing necessary documents, such as *bills of lading* and *customs declarations*. In many cases air freight or air express is less expensive than international parcel post.

SUMMARY

Postal costs continue to be a major expense for businesses. Secretaries who are familiar with postal information and services can contribute to the reduction of these expenses.

Domestic mail includes mail transmitted within, among, and between the United States, its territories and possessions, the Military Postal Service, and the United Nations in New York. Domestic mail is divided into several general classes.

First-class mail includes items weighing no more than 12 ounces. This mail is normally shipped by air service; if air service is not available, it is sent by the fastest means possible. The kinds of mail sent first class are letters in any form, post cards, business reply mail, and such items as bills and checks.

Priority mail is first-class mail weighing over 12 ounces. Packages sent by priority mail are given preferential handling and are shipped by air and selected ground transportation.

Express mail is the fastest, most reliable postal service available for sending both letters and packages. The mailer can choose from four types of service: Express Mail Next Day Service, Express Mail Custom Designed Service, Express Mail Same Day Airport Service, and Express Mail International Service.

Second-class mail includes newspapers and periodicals. Such mail must bear notice of second-class entry and is often mailed in bulk lots.

Third-class mail is used for matter that cannot be classified as first- or second-class mail and that weighs less than 16 ounces. These items include merchandise, printed matter, keys, advertising, etc.

Fourth-class mail is also called parcel post. It includes all mailable matter not in first, second, or third class which weighs 16 ounces or more. There are both weight and size limits for fourth-class packages according to delivery zones.

Official and free mail is used by federal government offices. Franked mail, which requires a real or facsimile signature of the sender, is used by selected government officials. Penalty mail is used for official government correspondence.

Important mail can be registered or insured, depending on the contents. First-class or priority mail can be registered, while third- or fourth-class mail, or priority mail containing third- or fourth-class matter, may be insured. Other special services provided by the Postal Service include business reply mail; Mailgrams; COD (collect on delivery) service; certificates of mailing; certified mail; special delivery and special handling; hand stamping for bulky mail; purchase of stamps and metered postage; forwarding, returning, and remailing of mail when necessary; change of address forms; and recalling mail. These services all require an additional charge.

A number of plans are in use to improve operations and reduce the costs of mail service. The ZIP (Zone Improvement Plan) Code was designed to facilitate the use of automated equipment in processing mail. The ZIP + 4 Code is being used to further pinpoint mail delivery. Bar code readers are also used to automate the sorting of mail. The bar code contains the ZIP Code and certain letters and numbers from the address.

Many companies are automating their mail rooms to cut costs. Automated equipment can provide information that enables the mailer to compare alternative methods of sending mail and choose the most advantageous rate.

Domestic and international money orders, which can be used to transfer money from one person or business to another, may be purchased at all post offices. Domestic money orders can also be purchased at other outlets, such as banks and drugstores.

The Postal Service participates in an international communications network that provides surface and airmail services for correspondence, printed material, and merchandise to almost any destination in the world. Correspondence may also be transmitted electronically to some countries through the INTELPOST service.

In addition to the post office, many other companies provide shipping services. United Parcel Service carries packages among all 50 states either by air or truck. Delivery time varies according to destinations. Courier service is offered by air, van, or bus. The advantages of each service vary. Your choice of service will depend on your specific shipping needs.

Freight services are the most economical way to transport heavy, bulky goods in large quantities. Freight may be shipped by rail, motor, air, or water. Because freight shipping is the most complex of all methods, the secretary will probably not be required to select the carrier.

International shipments present problems, such as special packing, complicated shipping procedures, marine insurance, and foreign exchange. Many organizations have specific departments to handle arrangements for international shipping.

SUGGESTED READINGS

Akers, Herbert A. *Modern Mailroom Management.* New York: McGraw-Hill Book Company, 1979.

BusinessWeek, Administrative Management, The Office, Time, Newsweek, and newspapers carry reports on the postal service as changes are made.

Domestic Mail Manual. Washington: U.S. Government Printing Office. Replaces Chapter 1 of the *Postal Service Manual* describing domestic mail service and gives a detailed description of each class of mail and special services available to the public. Subscription basis only, with changes issued as required.

A Guide to Business Mail Preparation. Washington: U.S. Government Printing Office, Publication No. 25, 1984.

Mailers Guide. Washington: U.S. Government Printing Office, Publication No. 19, 1984.

U.S. Postal Service, Public and Employee Communications Department. *Memo to Mailers.* Published monthly for customers originating significant quantities of mail.

National Directory of Addresses and Telephone Numbers. New York: National Directory of Addresses and Telephone Numbers (updated annually).

National Five-Digit ZIP Code and Post Office Directory is available through local post offices or may be purchased from the Superintendent of Documents, Government Printing Office, Washington D.C. 20401.

QUESTIONS FOR DISCUSSION

1. What alternative methods of sending mail have developed to compete with the U.S. Postal Service? How is the postal service attempting to combat this competition?

2. Discuss precautions that must be taken in the placement of the address on an envelope. Why?

3. Which considerations would influence you to choose certified mail over a certificate of mailing?

4. In what in-company ways can an organization speed the mail without increasing postage costs?

5. Your employer gives you an addressed, sealed envelope containing an income tax return and asks you to mail it. What method will you use to mail this document so that your employer will have legal evidence that the income tax return was mailed? (The federal government will prosecute a taxpayer whose return is not received, even though the taxpayer has a copy of the return and makes a verbal claim that the return was filed by mail.)

6. You are sending a request for a free brochure published in Norway. How can you arrange to enclose adequate postage for mailing the brochure with your request?

7. There are three ways of sending a letter which tells that a parcel post package is being mailed: separately, enclosed with the contents, or in an envelope fastened to the outside of the package. Which do you think is preferable and why?

8. Your employer asked you to mail an important letter to Germany. You are chagrined when it is returned for insufficient postage. The letter weighed one ounce, and you had affixed domestic postage. Why was it returned? How can you prevent the recurrence of such an error?

9. Mail from the home office reaches your city post office around 2 a.m. each morning. However, it is not delivered to your office until the time of the regular mail delivery at 10:30 a.m. Your employer wants to have the home office mail as early as possible so that district sales representatives can be told of price changes. What do you suggest to solve this problem?

10. When would you choose express mail over priority mail?

11. Why is a surcharge justified for mail that does not conform to size standards?

12. The post office recommendations for new address formats have been disregarded by many secretaries. Why? Should you follow them?

13. Why should a business organization assume the responsibility of presorting mail?

14. Fill in the blanks in these sentences, selecting the correct use for the number(s) in parentheses following the sentence. Use the Reference Guide to verify or correct your answers.

    a. Leave _____ blank spaces after all terminal marks of punctuation. (2)

   b. Over _____ employees attended the meeting. (2,000)

   c. The expressway is completed except for a _____ mile exit ramp. (3/4)

   d. Send us your check for _____ to cover the cost of shipping. ($12.00)

   e. The _____ lengths of pipe were shipped on flatcars _____ long. (30', 50')

   f. The company is celebrating the _____ anniversary of its founding. (50)

   g. The course is listed as a _____ semester offering. (1/2)

   h. The interest was calculated for _____ . (1 year, six months, and 9 days)

PROBLEMS

1. Assume that your employer is out of the city on a business trip. How would you go about forwarding each of the following unopened pieces of mail? State whether additional postage is required.
   a. A personal letter
   b. A piece of registered mail requiring a signed return receipt
   c. A letter mailed by your office to the employer but returned because of an insufficient address
   d. A special delivery letter you wish to have forwarded also by special delivery
   e. A parcel post package

2. Set up a three-column table with each column head indicating the information requested in a, b, and c. In the appropriate columns, enter the information required by Items 1-21.
   a. The class of postal service that should be used (if parcel post is chosen, indicate the zone if a chart is available.)
   b. The kinds of fees that must be paid in addition to postage
   c. Special requirements or secretarial procedures
      (1) A photocopy of a letter
      (2) A pen corrected copy of a printed price list
      (3) A library book you are returning by mail
      (4) A letter addressed to a relative of the executive enclosing bonds valued at $500 and registered for full value; return receipt required showing address where delivery was made
      (5) A magazine addressed to a city 30 miles distant and sent at the personal request of the executive
      (6) An 18-ounce sealed package containing a printing plate and addressed to a city 550 miles distant, with special delivery service

(7) A seven-ounce unsealed package of candy to be sent special delivery

(8) A $20 money order addressed to a city 20 miles distant

(9) A box 3' long, 1 1/2' wide, and 1 1/2' high, weighing 40 pounds, addressed to a city 400 miles distant

(10) A sealed parcel weighing five ounces to be sent by priority mail

(11) An eight-pound box of perishable fruit

(12) A monthly statement of a department store to a customer in the same city

(13) A post card to a city 300 miles away

(14) A one-pound parcel containing clothing sent to a city 95 miles distant and insured for $15, return receipt requested at the time the parcel was mailed

(15) A check for $45 to a city 300 miles away

(16) Sixty individually addressed unsealed envelopes containing one-page mimeographed price lists

(17) A five-pound box containing automobile parts addressed to a city 250 miles distant where your employer is stranded in a disabled automobile

(18) A letter sent by certified mail for which a postmarked receipt is requested

(19) A one-pound sealed parcel containing costume jewelry insured for $75 and being transmitted 2,500 miles

(20) A letter containing notice to an heir of an estate for which a return receipt is requested showing where the envelope was delivered

(21) Thirty invitations in unsealed envelopes addressed to out-of-town guests

3. Which service would you recommend to someone living in a metropolitan area in sending the following goods?

a. An engine part for factory equipment that has broken down

b. One thousand copies of a convention program for distribution in two weeks

c. An antique desk inherited by an heir in New Orleans from a relative in St. Louis

d. Ten dozen summer shirts ready for shipment

e. A year's supply of letterheads for a branch office in Osaka

f. Photographs for a resident of a town 30 miles away; the recipient is to take them on a vacation trip the following day

g. Ten dozen summer shirts to replenish stock during a sale

Part Two   CASE PROBLEMS

Case 2-1
ADJUSTING TO NEW EQUIPMENT

When Irene Stamus came to work on Tuesday morning, she was amazed to find that a new electronic typewriter had replaced the familiar electric on her desk. She would have been delighted except for the fact that her employer, Ellen Farrell, had left a 30-page report on her desk with the request that she have it ready for her to present at a 2 p.m. meeting that afternoon when she returned from an out-of-town trip. She found that all the secretaries on the floor had received the same new equipment and that no instruction manuals had been left for the users.

Irene stormed into the office of the manager of administrative services and announced that she was taking the report to an outside agency for typing, would bring it back in time for Ms. Farrell's meeting, and meanwhile would attend a training session given by the typewriter manufacturer on the use of the new machines.

What principle has been violated by the administrative services manager? by Irene? Do you approve of Irene's short-term solution? What long-range action do you recommend?

Case 2-2
CONFIDENTIALITY OF DICTATION

Ida Morgan was in a particularly sensitive position as secretary to Dr. Bryan Barton, director of research and development. She had been warned that the dictation she transcribed often involved confidential information about new processes or products, test results, and analyses of competitors' products.

She was shocked one day when Dr. Barton told her that information about a new product had been leaked to another corporation and would cause the loss of millions of dollars to the company. All employees, even she, were under suspicion. She was so shocked by the implication of her guilt that she could think of no reply.

In trying to assess the blame, she reviewed her relationships with the rest of the staff and remembered that when she returned from lunch one day she surprised Al Johnson, a recently hired junior chemist, as he was rummaging through her desk. His explanation was that he had misplaced the schedule of projects and knew she had another one in her desk.

She also remembered that, although she usually kept the top drawer of her desk locked and the key in her purse, she had neglected to lock the drawer that day. She was so sure that she knew the culprit that she decided to confront Al Johnson and insist that he tell Dr. Barton about his involvement and take full responsibility.

What steps would you take in this situation?

Case 2-3
CARELESSNESS
IN MAILING
CORRESPON-
DENCE

J. J. Payhos, branch sales manager of a large national corporation, was concerned about the disappointing performance of a sales representative under his supervision. He and the corporate sales manager discussed termination of the sales representative's employment.

Mr. Payhos then dictated a stern but courteous memo to the sales representative telling him that he must meet next month's sales quota and increase the number of daily calls if he hoped to stay with the company. At the bottom of the carbon copy which was to be sent to the corporate sales manager, he wrote in longhand, "Hope I wasn't too hard on him, but he has been goofing off long enough. I'll keep you informed of developments."

Two days later Jim Protzman, the secretary who had transcribed the memo, was confronted by an irate Mr. Payhos: "Just look at this. See what you have done! You put the memos in the wrong envelopes." Jim was handed the memo intended for the corporate sales manager. A second notation at the bottom read: "I resign. I never 'goofed off' in my life."

Jim now remembers that when Mr. Payhos sent him on an emergency errand at 4:45, he gave the day's mail to a subordinate and asked him to insert the transcribed materials in the envelopes and see that they were dispatched.

What should Jim say to Mr. Payhos? How should he handle the error with the clerk? What principle is involved?

Case 2-4
NECESSITY FOR
LEARNING
ABOUT MAIL
SERVICES

Louise Weldon had been secretary to an accounting firm for two weeks when she was given these four items to mail on her way home from work: a client's signed income tax return, a package of 200 handouts to be distributed by one of the partners when delivering a speech at a convention on Friday, a letter containing a check, and two magazines that had been borrowed from a colleague by a member accountant.

She sent the tax return and the check by first-class mail and the magazines and handouts by special handling. When she was reprimanded by her employer for her decisions, she said, "You didn't tell me how you wanted the items sent, and besides I was working overtime to get them in the mail anyway."

How should the materials have been sent? Why? What principles did Louise violate by her actions?

PART THREE

INFORMATION PROCESSING: SERVICES/EQUIPMENT/SYSTEMS

The primary purpose of the office is to handle information efficiently and effectively. The office of today exists wherever business information is handled.

Part Three is an overview of the technological advancements that have been made in information handling. Emphasis is given to five components of information handling: input, processing, telecommunications (which makes integration of various technologies possible), replication, and distribution. In addition, approaches to managing information resources (records) are examined.

The secretary must be able to use technologically advanced services, equipment, and systems to perform office functions at faster speeds and lower cost, producing higher quality results. The secretary must also be able to present information to all who need it in an easy-to-use manner. It is important for a secretary employed in an information processing environment to become knowledgeable about office functions that can be handled electronically.

Chapter 9

Data and Word Processing

The explosive growth of data and word processing technology has dramatically benefited the secretary. Increases in secretarial productivity have occurred through the application of data and word processing to office tasks. The time needed to process information has been shortened, freeing some secretaries from day-to-day tasks that often bogged them down.

Today's secretary must be knowledgeable about the impact of data/word processing, what it can do, and how best to make use of its applications. This chapter will give you an opportunity to explore data/word processing. Concepts will be explained, and the equipment used in this rapidly expanding phase of office technology will be described.

DATA PROCESSING DEFINED

The terms *data* and *information* are frequently used interchangeably. However, *data* often refers to unorganized or raw facts, while *information* is the knowledge that results from the manipulation of data.

Data processing involves a series of operations that convert unorganized alphabetical and numerical facts into useful information. For example, with data processing, figures on costs, purchases, sales, inventories, and production can be quickly transformed into useful information for decision making.

COMPUTER SYSTEMS

Data processing today is characterized by computer systems that classify, sort, merge, record, retrieve, transmit, and report large quantities of data. A *computer system*, as shown in Illus. 9-1, consists of

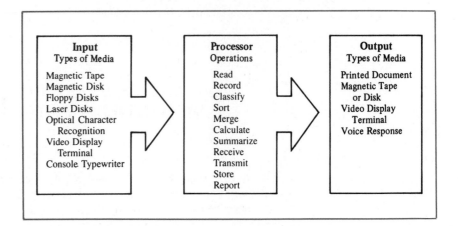

Illus. 9-1
The three
components in a
data processing
system, their
media, and
operations.

input, a central processing unit (the CPU), and output. The manipulation of data within the system is a continuous chain of operations composed of input, processing, and output. Operations are performed by entering instructions into the computer system.

The computer and its peripheral equipment are referred to as the system's *hardware*. *Software* is the term used to indicate programs concerned with the operation of the system.

This section discusses the basic components of computer systems: input media and devices, the central processing unit, output media and equipment, and various computer applications.

Input Media and Input Devices

The term *input* describes the act of introducing data into a computer system. An input medium is the form or the material on which data are recorded for processing. *Input media* range from magnetic tape to voice recognition. An *input device*, considered peripheral equipment to the computer, is used to read the input medium into the system. Input devices vary with the types of input media used.

Magnetic Tape. Magnetic tape is plastic coated with a metallic oxide. It comes in widths of one-half to one inch and lengths of 2,400 to 3,600 feet per reel. Data are recorded on the tape as invisible magnetized spots that, when read into the system, create electrical impulses. A tape drive is used to read the magnetized spots into the computer.

Magnetic tape is considered a *sequential access* medium; that is, what is first on the reel is read first, what is second is read second, and so forth. In other words, in order to locate information halfway through the tape, all the preceding material must be read first. For some business operations, such as the periodic updating of customer accounts, magnetic tape is ideal; but where information is scattered throughout a tape, the computer access time necessary to reach the desired data can delay processing.

Data can be keyed directly to magnetic tape for reading to the computer using a keyboard similar to that of an electronic typewriter. Or, the operator can key data on miniature magnetic tapes in tape cassettes, which the computer can then convert to run size tape for processing.

Magnetic Disks. Magnetic disks are thin, circular, metal plates, coated on both sides with ferrous oxide. In appearance, a file of magnetic disks resembles a stack of phonograph records. Information is recorded and stored as magnetic spots on both sides of a disk, using various key-to-disk devices. Data can be transferred from a disk to a tape for processing by the computer.

Like magnetic tape, disks are durable and erasable. Depending on the nature of the information recorded on a magnetic disk or tape, a second copy may be made to protect recorded information against accidental erasure or destruction. Disks are available in a broad range of speed and storage capacities. Most computer systems today use disks rather than tape.

Whereas magnetic tape is a sequential access medium (the computer must search from the beginning of the tape for desired data), magnetic disks are a *random access* medium (the computer can go directly to any spot on the disk and retrieve desired data). Access time to retrieve information from magnetic disks is shorter than with magnetic tape. Magnetic disks are used in computer installations for large volume storage capacity.

Floppy Disks. The demand for an inexpensive magnetic storage medium was met with the development of a flexible (or floppy) disk. Floppy disks are magnetically coated plastic disks. Their ability to be easily handled makes them popular with users of word/information processing equipment. Many manufacturers now produce diskettes (floppies) that record on front and back surfaces, effectively doubling their storage capacity (see Illus. 9-2).

Laser Disks. A laser disk on which data can be moved, altered, or erased has recently been introduced into the computer market. When a

Illus. 9-2
Word processing
specialists often
record and store
information onto
diskettes.

laser beam strikes a magnetized surface of metallic material, the heat from the beam produces a tiny magnetized spot on the surface of the disk. This is the data-entry process. To read the data, a laser scans the disk and a lens picks up reflections from various spots. To erase, the laser beam heats the magnetized spots, changing them back to their original form. One $5\frac{1}{4}$-inch laser disk will hold up to 250,000 pages of data.

Optical Character Recognition (OCR). Optical scanners read and translate printed or handwritten characters into machine language, transferring the data directly into a computer. Optical character recognition devices are gaining favor as input devices of raw data. There are three basic methods for recording data on a document that can be read by optical scanners: (1) optically readable marks; (2) bar codes; (3) optically readable characters, including handwritten characters.

The optical mark page reader is a device that can sense marks made by a pencil or a pen on specially designed forms. It is used mainly for test scoring, inventory control, and data collection.

Bar codes, a series of vertical lines of varying widths, can be optically read by scanners. The universal product code (UPC), one specialized application of bar codes, is placed on products to expedite checkout at grocery stores.

Some optical scanners can only read data that is recorded in a special typeface. Some scanners can read handwritten data. Machines that read handwriting are extremely versatile in their recognition capability. They can read handwritten numbers, machine printed numbers, imprinted numbers and marks, and some alphanumeric data. Alphanumeric data consist of letters of the alphabet with combinations of spaces, numbers, or special characters.

Video Display Terminals (VDT). A video display terminal has a cathode ray tube (CRT), or a television-like screen, and a keyboard linked to a computer. It is part of an input/output system. The user inputs data through the keyboard of the terminal.

Some terminals do not have the capacity to process data in any way; that is, the terminal only transmits data directly to the central computer for processing. These terminals are sometimes referred to as *dumb terminals.*

Intelligent terminals are normally found at remote sites within various departments of an organization. Preliminary processing, such as verifying data, can take place at these remote sites (see Illus. 9-3). Errors can be corrected before data are transmitted to a central computer. Intelligent terminals increase the processing efficiency of the central computer by reducing the total time for results to reach data users.

Illus. 9-3
The operator
verifies data
visually on a CRT.

Recent innovations have increased the intelligence and versatility of these terminals. One example is the *portable intelligent terminal* that can be interfaced with a telephone line. Such terminals, which may or may not have a television-like screen, use a *bubble memory*. A magnetic bubble stores data on thin film. Bubble memory remains intact even in a power failure. A sales representative calling on customers can enter and store order data (quantities, prices, colors, and sizes) on a portable terminal. Later the data can be printed out as hard copy before being transmitted to a computer in the sales representative's home office. The data can be sent rapidly over telephone lines, permitting the customer's order to be filled almost immediately.

Voice Recognition. A voice recognition unit is capable of converting spoken words into suitable input for a computer. One application of voice recognition units enables an executive to dictate to a computer that is capable of printing out messages.

One type of unit stores a dictionary of several hundred words. Users practice matching the sound of each in the prestored dictionary until the unit accepts their dictation. This system is limited in its application because of its inability to distinguish between words that sound alike: *then* and *than*, *bear* and *bare*, *for* and *far*. The use of incorrect grammar, dialects, and accents also limit the effectiveness of this system.

Another voice recognition system has the capability of asking the dictator to clarify words it does not understand. This unit can take dictation and produce sentences, but it is extremely expensive and will respond only to a limited number of people.

Central Processing Unit

The heart of the electronic data processing system is the CPU. It consists of (1) an internal storage or memory file, (2) an arithmetic/logic component, and (3) a control unit. The central processing unit accepts data from various input devices, processes the data according to the programmer's instructions, and sends results to storage or to an output device. The relationship between the various components of a computer system is shown in Illus. 9-4.

Storage or Memory File. *Storage* (frequently called *memory*, or *memory file*) is the place where computer data and programs are magnetically stored. Storage is organized into thousands of individual locations, each with a unique address. Data can be located in storage in the same manner that a house can be located by a street address. The speed

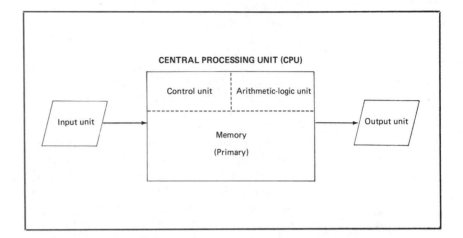

CENTRAL PROCESSING UNIT (CPU)

Control unit | Arithmetic-logic unit

Input unit

Memory

(Primary)

Output unit

Illus. 9-4
The basic computer
system consists of
input and output
devices as well as a
CPU. The CPU
contains memory,
arithmetic/logic,
and control units.

with which the processing unit can locate an "address" and transfer the data to the arithmetic/logic component is referred to as *access time*. Since large processors can perform several hundred operations per second, the access time to stored data is critical. Slow access time uses up valuable computer time.

Most computers have two types of storage: internal (also called primary) and external (or secondary) storage. *Internal storage* is quick access storage. It holds data that are being used at a given time. *External storage* consists of devices, such as magnetic disks, magnetic tape, laser disks, and bubble memory, that hold data until needed. Storing data on external or secondary media is less expensive than storing it internally in the CPU.

Arithmetic/Logic Component. The arithmetic/logic section of the computer is like an electronic calculator that performs addition, subtraction, multiplication, and division. It can also logically compare and select alternate courses of action.

Arithmetic Ability. The arithmetic component consists of adder circuits and accumulator registers. Calculations are performed in the *adder* section at lightning speed measured in *microseconds* (millionths of a second) or in *nanoseconds* (billionths of a second). Naturally this time varies with the size and complexity of the unit. A small computer might require .001 second (a thousand microseconds) to multiply a four-digit number by a five-digit number.

The *accumulator* is that portion of the arithmetic unit where results (answers) of arithmetic operations are temporarily stored until a calculation is complete. A program may direct the computer to do the following:

1. Copy a number from a storage location into the accumulator.
2. Get a second number from a storage location and add it to the number in the accumulator.
3. Multiply the sum of the two numbers (in the accumulator) by 25 and return the answer to storage.

Logic Component. One of the distinctive qualities of the computer is its ability to compare and select alternate courses of action. The computer can be programmed to examine a figure and determine if it is above or below a certain amount. If it is above, the computer will follow one set of instructions. If it is below, the computer will follow another set. After data and a program have been fed into the system, the logic component makes it possible for the computer to complete a sequence of operations automatically. For instance, after data on individual time cards are fed into the computer, it can process a payroll without any further human intervention. It calculates wages; obtains information about withholding allowances; determines withholding tax and social security tax; makes other approved deductions; determines net pay; and prints paychecks. In addition, the computer can store payroll information, produce complete payroll information on each employee, and print W-2 forms (Wage and Tax Statements). A payroll for several thousand employees can be completed within a few hours.

Control Unit. The control unit directs the many functions of the computer system. It seeks instructions from storage files and interprets and executes them. It internally controls operations of input devices, the storage unit, the arithmetic/logic unit, and output devices.

Output Media

Output is defined as information processed by the computer. *Output medium* is the form in which processed information appears. The *output device* is the equipment connected to the system that records or displays processed data. Output can be in the form of magnetic tape or magnetic disks, records, reports, visual displays, or voice responses. By far the most common output medium is the printed document.

Records and Reports. Processed data in the form of records and reports are printed on high-speed printing equipment that usually prints a whole line of characters at one time. Printing technology is discussed later in this chapter.

Magnetic Tape or Disk. Data can be stored on magnetic tape and disks. On magnetic tape, recorded data are stored on one-inch magnetic tapes (similar to audio cassette tapes). With a magnetic disk, data are recorded and stored as a series of electronic spots on an oxide-coated disk.

Video Display Terminals (VDT). The user inputs data and control signals through the VDT keyboard. The computer responds and outputs data on the VDT.

Voice Response. For businesses like airlines, transportation companies, and banks, the most convenient means of data retrieval is a voice response terminal. For example, to check the credit reference of a customer, a bank representative can dial into the computer and a voice will respond with the requested information. The words in a voice response come from a vocabulary stored in the system and are generally restricted to the basic type of information requested.

COMPUTER SERVICES

In response to the growing need for computer access by business organizations that cannot afford their own computers, computer service centers and computer usage arrangements have developed. Examples of these arrangements are leasing, data processing service centers, and information retrieval and exchange centers.

Computer equipment can be leased from the manufacturer and installed on the user's premises. Computer equipment can also be leased through a specialized agency. Under this arrangement, the leasing agency buys the data processing equipment specified by the user and then leases it to the user.

Commercial data processing service centers provide computer service to small businesses without computers. They also handle overflow loads for larger companies that have their own computer installations. Considerable diversity exists among data processing service centers. Well-established centers may provide a range of data processing services, such as analyzing customer requirements, offering consultations, and writing programs and implementing them. Some centers have developed areas of expertise, only processing pension plans, direct mail, or income tax forms, for example. Most service centers offer *batch* processing (the periodic processing of data accumulated over a period of time). Monthly accounts receivable or a weekly payroll are examples of batch processing. This work is done on a fixed schedule.

Information retrieval and exchange centers have evolved to provide subscribers with business, scientific, and technical data by direct connection with computers through telephone lines. For example, a business can subscribe to a local credit rating service that in turn is affiliated with a regional or national credit service. One strategically located center can store the credit ratings of most businesses and millions of individuals in its area.

MAINFRAMES, MINICOMPUTERS, AND MICROCOMPUTERS

A *mainframe computer* is the largest type of computer system in terms of size and is capable of massive data processing operations. Mainframe systems use a variety of input and output devices and several types of internal and external memory devices. The size and capacity of a mainframe and the variety and number of its input/output devices are determined by the data processing requirements of the organization. These computers are usually centralized, process data at high speeds, and have greater storage capacity than mini and microcomputers.

A *minicomputer* is a small, relatively inexpensive computer containing a CPU with one or more input/output devices. It is usually equipped with a CRT and can be used in business to process accounts receivable and accounts payable, enter orders, calculate payrolls, analyze sales, and record inventory. The minicomputer also has some scientific applications.

A minicomputer can serve as a company's complete computer system or as a supplement to a larger installation. In *distributed data processing*, minicomputers, located in areas where processing is required, are linked to a large central computer. Distributed data processing involves the distribution of computing power to locations where that power is needed. Minicomputer systems also give remote sites access to the database of a large central computer.

A major development that has impacted significantly on the office in this decade is the microcomputer. Microcomputers, like the one shown in Illus. 9-5, perform many of the same functions as larger computer systems on a smaller scale. A *microcomputer* consists of a VDT, a keyboard, and a *microprocessor* (a silicon chip smaller than a fingernail). Within a microcomputer, the microprocessor functions as the CPU. This desktop "computer on a chip" has revolutionized the office. Although extremely tiny, the microprocessor has a control unit and an arithmetic/logic unit. The microprocessor chip is used alone in sewing machines, microwave ovens, automobiles, and many other devices to automate one or more functions. Illus. 9-6 is an enlargement of a microprocessor chip.

The microcomputer is generally used in one of two ways. As a stand-alone computer, the microcomputer is capable of performing processing functions without a communication link to any other equipment. Linked to a large computer, the microcomputer eliminates the need for much rekeyboarding and manipulating of data. The microcomputer's intelligence permits processing of information before it is communicated to the larger system's CPU.

Illus. 9-5 Although microcomputers can support printers, they are generally much slower than the printers of larger systems.

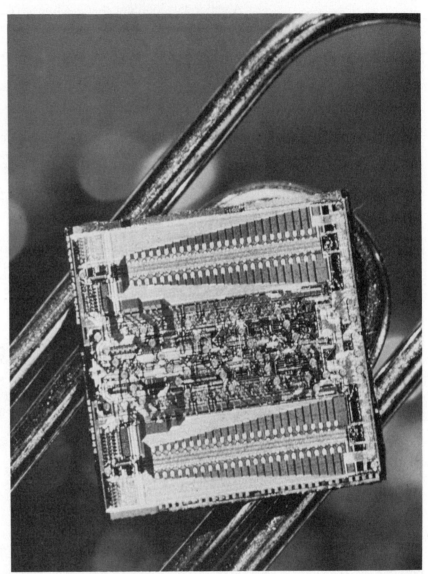

Illus. 9-6
A microprocessor chip is an integrated circuit containing the components of an entire central processing unit.

Courtesy of IBM Corporation

OPERATING SYSTEMS/PROGRAMS

Instructions that tell a computer what to do are called *programs. Operating systems* are internally stored programs that control all computer functions. Operating programs provide step-by-step instructions to the computer to perform such basic functions as how to input information from a terminal, how to print information, how to place information in storage, and how to retrieve data from a disk.

A variety of operating systems is available from equipment manufacturers. Among the better known operating systems are CP/M (for Control Program/Microcomputer), developed by the Digital Research, Inc., and PC-DOS (for Disk Operating System), developed by IBM for use with its microcomputers. These two are probably the most popular operating systems but others do exist: UNIX and Corvus are other available systems.

Software packages that permit users to perform specialized tasks without writing their own programs are available for such functions as word processing, payroll and inventory control, graphics, and file management. In selecting software for a microcomputer, keep in mind that these programs work only with certain operating systems. Before purchasing a software program, be sure that the program is compatible with the operating system your microcomputer uses.

When an organization faces specific problems that cannot be solved by already existing software, programs may be written within the organization. To write programs, special computer languages are used. The ones most commonly used in business are COBOL (Common Business Oriented Language), FORTRAN (FORmula TRANslation), BASIC (Beginner's All Purpose Symbolic Code), Pascal, and RPG (Report Program Generator). To convert these languages into a language that the computer can read, *compilers* or *translator programs* are used to convert them into *machine language*. Compiler programs are available through equipment manufacturers.

THE DEVELOPMENT OF WORD PROCESSING

Word processing, the manipulation of text (words, sentences, and paragraphs), has become a widely accepted tool for increasing office productivity and for improving the quality and speed of written communications. Word processing systems facilitate the handling of written communications through a configuration of specialized personnel, automated equipment, and procedures. Although all three elements are important to the system, word processing equipment is emphasized in this chapter. Much has already been said about the impact of word processing on the secretary.

Early attempts to automate the typing of form letters and other documents were made in the 1930s with the Hoover Automatic Typewriter and the Autotypist. These machines operated on the same principle as the player piano, using punched paper tape to record key-strokes. Some years later, the Robotyper and the Flexowriter appeared on the market. Both of these machines also used punched paper tape to produce large volumes of form letters. These early machines were specifically designed to handle form letters and contracts.

Word processing, as we know it today, emerged in 1964 when IBM introduced the Magnetic Tape Selectric Typewriter (MT/ST). This machine used magnetic tape to record keystrokes. After a document had been keyboarded, the MT/ST would automatically play back the document stored on the tape. It eliminated the need for erasers, correction fluid, and correction tape. Errors could be corrected by backspacing and striking over, enabling the secretary to produce in minutes what had previously taken hours. By saving "useable words," revisions could be made without retyping an entire document. In 1969 IBM replaced the MT/ST with the Magnetic Card Selectric Typewriter (MC/ST), which used a magnetic card, rather than magnetic tape, for storing documents. (Magnetic cards proved to be more accessible than magnetic tape.) By 1973 IBM had introduced an advanced version of the MC/ST, the Mag Card II.

Over the next few years, other manufacturers introduced nondisplay (also called "blind" or "mechanical") word processors, consisting of a high-speed typewriter console equipped with some form of magnetic medium to record and play back text. As the operator typed each character or space on the keyboard, a hard copy was produced by the word processor while a unit recorded the character or space on the mag (magnetic) medium. When a typing mistake was made, the operator simply backspaced and struck over the incorrect letter, word, or phrase. The process of backspacing and retyping erased the error on the mag medium and replaced it with the correct copy. After the text was recorded on the mag medium, additional copy could be inserted or unwanted copy could be deleted.

When the rough draft typing was completed and the copy was edited, the operator inserted a letterhead (or a regular sheet of paper) and any desired carbons into the typewriter console. The machine was placed in playback mode by pressing a button on the console. The machine then retyped the text automatically without error. While retyping, the machine was programmed to respace and reposition words and sentences, control end-of-line hyphens, determine line and page endings, align columns, make high-speed forward and reverse underlinings, and stop for manual keyboarding of variables for form letters. The mag medium used depended on the make and model of the machine. The most commonly used media were mag tape, card, and diskette (floppy disk).

Most offices have replaced nondisplay systems with machines housing television-like screens. Word processors found in offices today are visual display machines that permit an operator to see copy on a screen as it is keyboarded. The combination of a keyboard and screen is often called a terminal or workstation. The terminal provides a partial or full-page display of keyboarded copy that may be viewed before it is committed to magnetic medium. Most word processors use a CRT (cathode ray tube) for visual display. The memory capacity of word processors used to temporarily store words is called the *buffer* or *buffer storage.*

Typing errors are corrected by typing directly over the error. Words, lines, or paragraphs may be added at any point in the copy by moving a cursor, or a movable pointer, to the desired position and striking the appropriate keys. Once copy has been fully edited, it can be scrolled off (transferred) from the word processor's internal memory to magnetic medium for printout, storage, or both.

Display word processors have separate units for keyboarding and printing, each operating independently of the other. This arrangement frees the keyboard console and the display screen to produce new input while copy already stored on the mag medium is played out on the printer. The visual display system incorporates several useful features:

1. *Spelling verification* permits storage of words that are peculiar to a particular business. An engineering firm would find it useful to store engineering terms, for example. This feature detects misspellings and typographical errors by matching the keyboarded word with the stored word. Unmatched words are highlighted on the screen.

2. *Global search and replace* enables an operator to replace designated words in the text in every place where they occur. For example, if you keyboarded *CPA* instead of *CPS*, the global search feature locates every *CPA* in the text and changes it automatically to *CPS* without your assistance.

3. *Wraparound or word wrap* moves a word down to the next line of text when that word is too long to fit within the limits of the right margin.

4. *Word division* hyphenates words according to preprogrammed rules. This feature is only about 85 percent accurate.

5. *Selective search and replace* moves the *cursor* (the movable pointer) to each place in the text where an editing change needs to be made. For example, if you are unsure whether you used accent marks to spell *resume* each time you keyboarded it, this feature would scroll to each place in the text where the word occurs so that you can check for the accent marks.

6. *Justification* automatically adjusts the right margin during playback so that the right margin is even as in typeset copy.

7. *Automatic page, figure, footnote, and paragraph numbering*

places page numbers sequentially on each page. Also, this feature automatically renumbers pages, footnotes, and figure references in the proper sequence should new material be added to the manuscript.

8. *List/merge* combines text from two separate documents during printing. An example would be the combining of names and addresses within the text of a form letter.

9. *Decimal alignment* aligns decimal points when statistical data are typed.

Display systems are often dedicated to performing only word processing functions. However, higher priced systems offer applications in addition to word processing.

TODAY'S WORD/INFORMATION PROCESSORS

Because of the invention of the silicon chip in the mid-70s, the term "word processor" is far too limited to describe the machines used by secretaries today. In many instances, word processing is only one of many functions performed by these machines. Word processors, strictly speaking, are equipped to record, edit, and print text. Recent developments, however, enable the secretary to go beyond the standard word processing tasks of adding or deleting copy, moving paragraphs, and correcting errors automatically. With much of the equipment available today, it is possible for an operator to perform data processing functions as well. Because of the integration of data and word processing functions, the term *word/information processors* is used to describe systems of today.

Newer machines perform sophisticated tasks, such as placing graphics within the body of long reports. By scanning a picture or a graph, a machine, without operator assistance, can insert it where it is needed. The size of the graphic can be reduced or enlarged to fit available space—this is a tremendous time-saver for secretaries who type long, complicated documents. As statistical material is typed, calculations for interest, discounts, and the like are performed simultaneously. Today's word processors process records, edit complex reports, and perform mathematical calculations.

As a result of advances in technology, a wide range of versatile equipment with powerful capabilities is available for word processing. All word/information processing equipment, however, can be classified into two general categories: standalone systems and shared systems.

Standalone Systems

A *standalone system* contains a keyboard, a storage unit, and a printer that operate independently of a central computer system. Most standalones are software-driven. (A special software package is used to instruct the equipment to perform a variety of functions.) Some of these software packages contain data processing instructions. For example, software programs are available that compute invoice extensions and totals. These figures are recorded automatically when the invoice is printed out. Standalone systems include electronic typewriters, microcomputers, and dedicated word processors.

Electronic Typewriters. An electronic typewriter is a low-level word processor with limited memory for storing text to be recalled when needed. Display is usually limited to one or two lines. Only limited revision of text is possible. Automatic features generally include automatic centering, carrier return, underscoring, and decimal alignment. Two of the most popular features on electronic typewriters are phrase storage and format storage. Frequently used words, phrases, datelines, standard complimentary closings, signature lines, line lengths, and tab settings can be stored for later use.

All electronic typewriters have some storage capacity (memory). Those with limited storage capacity must either erase or print out stored copy when the memory becomes full. Newer machines have removable storage which increases a machine's memory.

Office automation experts disagree as to whether the electronic typewriter should be classified as a word/information processor. The machine is slow, has limited storage, and a limited number of automated features. It is, however, less expensive than other forms of word processing equipment and relatively simple to operate.

The electronic typewriter's growth in popularity means that it will soon replace the secretary's standard electric typewriter. Enhanced features, including increased storage capacity, increased visual display, and the ability to communicate with other machines, will continue to make electronic typewriters attractive to office machine users.

Microcomputers (or Personal Computers). The development of word processing software packages, such as WordStar and Scripsit, have given word processing capabilities to microcomputers (the smallest and least expensive of all computers). Since the microcomputer is small enough to fit onto most desktops and inexpensive enough to be affordable by most businesses, it has become increasingly popular as a word/information processor.

Equipment with increased features and speed has fueled the phenomenal growth of the microcomputer industry. Recent microcomputer models are versatile enough to perform these six functions simultaneously: word processing, calculating, graphics, drawing, list creation, and project scheduling. For example, microcomputers can combine sales data with graphics to produce a pie chart. Such versatility has considerably reduced the work involved in producing reports and other complicated documents.

Microcomputers have not only become more versatile, but they are becoming more "friendly" or easier to learn how to use. As the market matures, users of microcomputers will find fewer problems in adapting them to the word processing requirements of their offices. In choosing a microcomputer, the secretary should consider the availability of local service and training, the length of training required to learn how to use the equipment, the quality of the material provided to instruct users in the operation of the equipment (documentation), and the quality of the software available for word processing.

Dedicated Word Processors. Some standalone machines are referred to as *dedicated word processors* because they were designed primarily for word processing. The storage capacity of dedicated word processors has been increased through the use of double density, double-sided diskettes. Twice as many strokes (density) can be stored on a standard diskette and information can be recorded on both of its sides (double-sided). Some standalone word processors use *hard* disks (magnetically coated, rigid disks) for storage to increase storage capacity. The internal memories of standalone systems (buffer memories) are also expanding to permit the storage of more text.

Shared Systems

By linking two or more terminals with other devices (or resources), efficient and cost effective systems can be realized. In a shared system, the central processing unit, terminals, printers, and *disk drives* (the part of the computer system that holds the disk on which word processing programs and documents are stored) are arranged in various ways to enhance productivity. There are three types of shared systems: shared logic, distributed logic, and shared resource systems.

Shared Logic Systems. In a shared logic system, a number of terminals share the logic component and the storage capabilities of a central computer to produce either hard copy (a printed document) or screen-displayed text. A shared logic system greatly increases the capabilities of a single terminal, because the central computer gives each terminal access to processing power and greater storage capacity. However, because the terminals depend on a central computer for logic, they are "dumb" terminals, incapable of operating if the central computer breaks down.

Shared logic systems allow workstations to be placed throughout the company. In some instances, terminals are used for word processing part of the time and for data processing the remainder of the time. A typical example would be a manufacturing firm that uses the same terminal to prepare personalized sales letters and to compute commissions; thus, the terminal is an information processing unit rather than a unit dedicated exclusively to word processing or to data processing.

Distributed Logic Systems. Shared systems that have terminals scattered throughout a building are sometimes referred to as being distributed. A central computer may be used to enhance the capabilities of each terminal, but each operator can access and control jobs independent of the central computer's CPU. In this type of system, the logic (or computing power of the central computer) is distributed to each terminal; hence, the term "distributed logic."

Shared Resource Systems. In a shared resource system, several terminals share the capabilities of one or more resources (or devices), such as printers, but each terminal has its own logic (intelligence) and processing power. A malfunction of one terminal would not affect any other terminal nor would the failure of the main CPU affect any user.

TIME-SHARED SERVICES

Time-shared services link word/information processors with a remote CPU. Such an arrangement represents an expansion of the shared logic concept by permitting several users in a variety of locations to share the costs of a large computer. A time-shared word/information processor is primarily a computer input terminal and a text-altering station. The CPU records the input from the word/information processor, performs text manipulations as directed, and provides the full output through the computer's high-speed printer.

Several terminals may interact simultaneously with one computer through time-sharing. The linkup with a more powerful computer enables the word processing specialist to tap a vast amount of computer-stored information.

The terminal may be connected to the computer by placing the telephone in a *coupler* (a device that connects a keyboard terminal to a telephone line) and dialing the computer's number. The terminal operator must give proper identification before the computer will react. This procedure is followed to ensure confidentiality and security.

Time-shared services are most often used for processing long documents that require extensive text-editing and format change. Users of these systems pay for computer time, telephone use, printouts, storage at the computer center, and the terminal connection.

PRINTER TECHNOLOGY

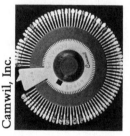

Camwil, Inc.

In order to have a completely satisfactory word/information processing system, the appropriate printer technology is essential; therefore some knowledge of printers is essential for selecting printers that will produce acceptable copy. For many years the Selectric typewriter was used for both input and output in most word/information processing systems. The Selectric (golfball) element was used to keyboard and correct copy before it was stored on a magnetic medium. It was also used to print out the final, edited copy. Newer printers use much faster technology, such as the daisy wheel, a dot matrix device, laser beams, or the ink jet process, to produce documents.

Printer technology can be classified into two categories: *impact printers and nonimpact printers*. Impact printers employ a device (a character bar, a Selectric element, a daisy wheel, etc.) to strike a ribbon against paper to produce a printed character. Nonimpact printers produce images without any physical impact. These printers store the shape of characters in memory and release them onto a page via a special mechanism.

Impact Printers

The two most popular types of impact printers for office work are the *dot matrix printer* and the *daisy wheel printer*. The dot matrix printer stores character shapes in memory. When commanded to print, a series of steel pins strike a ribbon to create a matrix of dots on the paper. As the print head moves across the paper, it prints a portion of each character. As more passes across the paper are made, characters become more complete and legible. The speed of dot matrix printers is usually faster than wheel printers; however, the print wheel produces superior letter quality. Some dot matrix printers, operating at slower speeds, can also produce documents that are of acceptable letter quality.

Daisy wheels print text by rotating characters into position and striking through a ribbon to produce an image. Because of their sharpness and similarity to typewritten copy, daisy wheels are used for letter quality output. Most printers of this type are bidirectional: they print from left to right and right to left alternatively at high speeds. Multiple typefaces are available with daisy wheel printers.

Nonimpact Printers

Nonimpact printers are usually faster and more costly than impact printers. They do not use ribbons or impact to produce images. Among the most commonly used nonimpact printers are *laser and xerographic (electrostatic) printers, ink jet printers,* and *ion deposition printers.*

Laser and xerographic printers (generally classified as electrostatic printers) use a light source, such as a laser beam, to reflect characters and graphic images through a complex of mirrors onto a photo-conductor drum. The drum attracts particles and fuses them with heat and pressure to create an image on paper. This process is similar to copier technology, which is discussed in Chapter 10.

The ink jet printer is capable of extremely high speeds. Its printing mechanism sprays tiny drops of fast-drying electrostatically-charged ink onto a page where characters are desired.

The ion deposition printer is a newcomer to printer technology. It operates in much the same way as electrostatic printers, except no light is required. Electronically-charged particles (ions) are deposited directly onto a drum to form images. The drum transfers the images to paper as print.

EQUIPMENT AND INFORMATION SECURITY

In the open office design where equipment is both highly visible and accessible, security is a major concern. Some computers, for instance, are portable and can easily be taken from an office. Companies can combat theft by affixing serially-numbered tags with the company name on each piece of equipment, using locking devices, or placing the equipment in a locked storage area at the end of each working day.

In addition to possible theft of equipment, information pilferage is also a major concern to computer users. When the confidentiality of information is critical to a firm, the use of computer codes or other access devices should be implemented. Shredders can be used to destroy confidential printouts.

Offices, especially in dry climates, are susceptible to static electricity. Static electricity can cause electronic equipment memory loss, produce inaccurate data, and/or initiate such unwanted action as a printer start-up. Anti-static floor mats, sprays, and dustcovers are used to control this phenomenon.

SUMMARY

The growth of data and word processing technology has expanded many facets of the secretarial profession. Data processing is a series of operations that converts raw alphabetical and numerical data into useful information. Computer systems consist of input equipment, a central processing unit, and output equipment. Floppy disks, laser disks, magnetic tape, magnetic disks, optical character recognition, video display terminals, and voice recognition are examples of input media. The CPU is the heart of an electronic data processing system. It consists of an internal storage or memory file, an arithmetic/logic component, and a control unit. Output media are the forms in which processed information finally appears. Examples include records and reports, magnetic tape or disks, video display, and voice response.

A number of computer services and usage arrangements have been developed for business organizations that cannot afford to buy their own equipment. Leasing, data processing service centers, and information retrieval and exchange are examples of these services.

There are a number of operating systems—internally-stored programs that tell computers what to do—on the market. Caution should be exercised in selecting an operating system to ensure that software packages are compatible with the system. Among the most popular operating systems used in word/information processing today are CP/M and PC-DOS.

The word/information processor evolved from automated typewriters. Word/information processors may be classified in two major categories: standalone systems and shared systems. Standalone systems include electronic typewriters, microcomputers, and dedicated word processors. Microcomputers have in recent years become a very important addition to the standalone group. There are three types of shared systems: shared logic, distributed logic, and shared resources. Time-shared services link word/information processors with a remote CPU.

In order to have a completely effective word/information processing system, appropriate printer technology is essential. Printers can be classified in two categories: impact printers and nonimpact printers. Examples of impact printers are daisy wheel and dot matrix printers. The dot matrix printer does not produce output as high in quality as the daisy wheel printer. Nonimpact printers use a light source or an electrostatic process to produce images. They are high-speed printers.

Equipment and information security is also a major concern in the modern office. Static electricity is another concern of computer users. It must be controlled to prevent equipment memory loss and malfunction.

SUGGESTED READINGS

Adams, David R., Michael J. Powers, and V. Arthur Owles. *Computer Information Systems Development*, Design and Implementation. Cincinnati: South-Western Publishing Co., 1985.

Casady, Mona J. *Word/Information Processing Concepts*, 2d ed. Cincinnati: South-Western Publishing Co., 1984.

Casady, Mona J. and Dorothy C. Sandburg. *Word/Information Processing*, A System Approach. Cincinnati: South-Western Publishing Co., 1985.

Medley, Don B., Allen Smith, and Wilma Jean Alexander. *The Automated Office*. Cincinnati: South-Western Publishing Co., 1985.

Palmer, Janet J. and Charles M. Ray. *Office Automation*, A Systems Approach. Cincinnati: South-Western Publishing Co., 1987.

Shelly, Gary B. and Thomas J. Cashman. *Computer Fundamentals for an Information Age*. Brea, CA: Anaheim Publishing Co., 1984.

Wolff, Terris B. *Microcomputer Applications*, Using Small Systems Software. Boston: Boyd & Fraser Publishing Co., 1985.

QUESTIONS FOR DISCUSSION

1. Since the time spent in keyboarding is greatly reduced with the addition of automated equipment, do you think office automation will improve job satisfaction for the secretary?

2. Secretaries often say rather defensively, "I don't know anything about word processors, since we don't have any in my office." Discuss this attitude.

3. The statement has been made that businesses could not return to manual processing of data even if they wanted to. Why would this be true?

4. Why should a secretary entering the office force today have a background in data processing?

5. How can companies combat the loss of equipment and the pilferage of information in an open office design, where computer data are so accessible?

6. Voice recognition units have been slow in gaining acceptance in the office as input devices to computerized equipment. Why?

7. Select the correct word from the parentheses in each of the following sentences. Refer to the Reference Guide to check your answers.

   a. Every department was (effected, affected) by the budget cuts. The final (effect, affect) of this action will be the elimination of several jobs.

   b. The captain will divide the prize money (among, between) nine players.

   c. All members (accept, except) John were present to (accept, except) the award.

   d. She was (eager, anxious) to change jobs, but the interview left her (anxious, eager) about the added responsibility.

   e. We have (adopted, adapted) the constitution of the national office, and we will (adopt, adapt) it to the objectives of our local chapter.

   f. The shoes and bag (complimented, complemented) her new dress so well that she received many (compliments, complements).

PROBLEMS

1. A number of companies manufacture equipment with word processing capabilities. Each model has certain advantages and limitations. Assume that you have the responsibility of submitting specifications for a word processor to be installed in a newly organized word processing center for your office. Initially the center will be a one-person operation. The correspondence of four executives will be processed by one secretary.

   a. Set up the criteria you will use for selecting the word processor. Gather data on two different models and select one to recommend for purchase. Support your selection with reasons for the decision.

   b. What qualifications would you suggest for the secretary who will staff the newly formed word processing center?

2. Visit a computer installation in your community and prepare a report showing how the use of the equipment has reduced the amount of repetitive labor involved in office work.

3. The following letter is to be mailed to a list of four clients. Using any word processing system available to you, keyboard the letter in block style. Use the addresses below and merge them with the copy. Proofread before printing the copy. Print the four letters on August 16, 19--. Store the copy.

Dear _____:

Thank you for your letter of August 15 requesting our current catalog. Your request has been sent to our printer, who will forward a copy to you as soon as they are ready for distribution.

Our new line of merchandise has been so popular that our supply of catalogs was soon exhausted. You should receive your copy within ten days. Your interest in our products is appreciated.

Sincerely,

John D. Clayborn
President

CLIENTS: Dr. Nancy Nash   Mrs. Blair Cosby
          1101 Kings Mill Drive   270 Palmer Court
          Richmond, VA   Warren, PA
          23225-0012   16367-4592

          Mr. Paul Franklin   Mr. Myron Baxter
          4400 West Avenue   71 Hanna Lane
          Statesboro, GA   Maywood, NJ
          30458-9876   07607-3730

Chapter 10

Reprographics

Reprographics is the multiple reproduction of images. In an office, two kinds of equipment are primarily used for reprographics: copiers and duplicators. *Copiers* (also called copying machines or photocopiers) use an image-forming process to create reproductions of originals. Originals may include typewritten pages, pages from magazines and books, financial reports, photographs, artwork, graphic illustrations, and other legally reproducible materials. *Duplicators*, however, make copies from prepared stencils or masters.

Secretaries need to know how to operate reprographic equipment, how to prepare originals for copying, how to paste up camera-ready copy, and how to make masters for duplication. In many offices, the secretary determines the type of reprographic equipment to be purchased and also assumes responsibility for its control. A thorough knowledge of reprographic equipment and supplies can reduce the expense and the delays often associated with producing multiple copies. It is vital, then, that you understand the reprographic equipment and processes available to you and how to use them effectively.

COPYING MACHINES

During the 70s and early 80s, the copier industry was characterized by a flurry of technological innovations designed to make the task of reproducing images faster, easier, cleaner, and, in some cases, less expensive. For example, the use of microprocessors simplified the design, maintenance, and operation of copiers. The application of microprocessors to this industry also allowed manufacturers to increase the work-saving features of their machines and reduce the number of their operable parts. Major copier manufacturers, such as Xerox, IBM, Canon, and Sharp, continue to focus on the needs of users to simplify the reproduction process; however, the industry is approaching maturity. The once rapid introduction of new technology into the market is slowing down.

Copier Volume Levels/Speeds

Low-volume copiers, often called *convenience copiers*, are simple and easy to operate. Low-volume copiers are placed in readily accessible locations throughout an organization. Time spent traveling to and from the machines is greatly reduced because of their accessibility, and no special skill is required to operate them.

Today's low-volume copiers are small (often tabletop units), relatively inexpensive to purchase, and virtually maintenance-free. Low-volume copiers are capable of producing up to 20,000 copies per month at speeds of up to 20 copies per minute. These machines offer a broad range of features and are used in large as well as in small organizations.

For offices that require 20,000 to 50,000 copies per month, the *mid-volume copier* has become popular in the past few years. It operates at speeds of 21 to 50 copies per minute. The modular design of many mid-volume copiers permits users to customize their machines. When the need arises for a special feature, it can be added easily and inexpensively to an existing machine.

In some organizations *high-volume copiers* are used. These machines are usually operated by trained employees and are equipped with many special features. High-volume copiers operate at speeds of 51 to 90 copies per minute and are recommended for volume levels of 50,000 to 100,000 copies per month.

Copier Image Processing

Copiers seem to be such simple machines. You place the original on a glass surface, select the desired number of copies, and push a button marked "print." Seconds later, copies of the original are released from the machine one after the other. However, from the standpoint of the imaging process used, most commonly used copiers are far from simple.

Electrostatic Process. Most office copiers, like the one shown in Illus. 10-1, use the electrostatic process to produce images and are of two types: *plain paper copiers* (PPCs) or *coated paper copiers* (CPCs). In plain paper copying, a camera throws an image of the original onto a positively charged selenium-coated drum. When a sheet of plain (untreated), negatively charged paper is passed over the drum, the image adheres to the paper and is permanently fixed to it with heat. Coated paper copiers use an electonic process that reproduces images directly onto coated (chemically treated or sensitized) paper. A toner

Illus. 10-1
The electrostatic
copier, like this
plain paper
convenience copier,
is popular in many
offices.

(ink in powdered or liquid form) is used to develop the image on the exposed paper.

Today, most copiers use plain, uncoated paper. If you share the responsibility for selecting copying equipment and supplies, you should be aware that buyers are often confused by manufacturers that claim their machines use plain paper. You should ask, "Will the copier use any kind of paper?" before you buy.

Fiber Optics Process. A recent innovation in the highly competitive office copier market is the use of fiber optics. The fiber optic process uses an array of tiny hairlike strands of glass to replace the lenses and mirrors of electrostatic copiers. These tiny strands of glass transmit images in the form of pulsating light.

The utilization of fiber optics in place of conventional lens and mirror assemblies has occurred mostly in low-volume or convenience copiers. Copiers using fiber optics are slower than conventional copiers because the optics (light source) must remain fixed while paper on a moving platen moves past the light. However, their reliability, energy savings, and low cost have made fiber optics copiers popular in the low-volume copier market.

Intelligent Copiers/Printers

The intelligent copier/printer represents one of the most exciting and most versatile advances in copying technology. An intelligent copier/printer can create images from hard copy (printed documents) or from instructions from computers or word processors. It can also communicate with other intelligent copier/printers. Because the intelligent copier/printer is a hybrid, combining copier and printer capabilities, it is relatively expensive. You will find its major application in large company in-house print shops producing high-volume jobs.

Intelligent copier/printers often use laser technology. A beam of red light (laser) is used to transmit the original onto a sensitized surface; the image is then transferred from that surface to a plain sheet of paper. Because of its speed, laser technology is growing in popularity for producing high-volume jobs like telephone directories.

Intelligent copiers presently on the market can perform the following operations: reproduce hard copy at local or distant locations without operator intervention, communicate with other intelligent copier/printers, print up to 120 pages a minute, merge data from various electronic sources, depict graphic and alphabetic information, print high-quality copy, and operate at a low-noise level. An example of an intelligent copier/printer appears in Illus. 10-2.

Copier Features

Major developments in copier technology during the last decade produced a number of significant new features that have made the copying task easier. Although many of these new features were once only available on expensive high-volume machines, they are now available on a wide range of low- and mid-volume copiers.

If you have a voice in the selection of reprographic equipment for your office, you should consider the desirability of several features as they apply to your job. Some of the broad spectrum of features available on today's copiers are outlined in the paragraphs which follow.

Automatic Document Feed. A device holds a stack of originals and feeds them automatically one at a time over the lighted glass surface

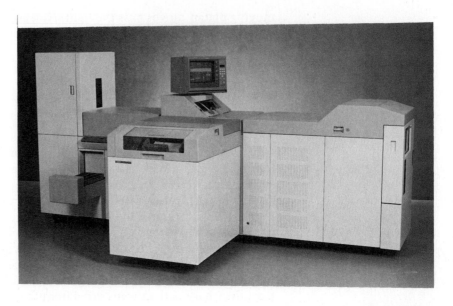

Illus. 10-2
Intelligent copier/
printers are usually
found in an in-
house print shop of
a large company,
producing high-
volume jobs.

for copying. This device eliminates the need to raise the copier cover, to position the original on the glass surface, and to press the button to print each time a copy is made. Most automatic feeders hold up to 50 originals. Other versions of automatic or semiautomatic feeders take originals from the operator's hand and feed them over the glass one at a time. This mechanism is called a *stream feeder*.

Automatic Duplexing. Duplexing is copying on both sides of the page. With automatic duplexing, the operator does not have to reload paper to do each side. On low-volume convenience copiers, however, it is usually necessary to reload paper manually for copying on each side. Copiers that are not designed for duplexing are likely to produce slightly burnt, smudged copies, and excessive duplexing may damage a machine. Although duplexing saves paper and reduces paper handling, it should be done only on machines equipped with this feature.

Exposure Control. This device controls the lightness and darkness of copies. It is especially useful when copying from newspapers or other darker-than-normal originals.

Copy Counter. This device presets the desired number of copies.

Roll Feeding. This feature permits a variety of copies in different sizes to be reproduced. The copier is fitted with a roll of continuous-feed paper that can be cut into various lengths as it is fed through the machine.

Sorter/Collator. This feature allows the copier to produce sets of copies. The copier has a series of bins into which copies are inserted so that a number of sets can be produced at one time. Other types of sorters/collaters produce copies in staggered piles of complete sets inside the machine. A stapler can be added to this feature to finish the collating process by stapling assembled sets.

Color Copying. Color copying is growing in popularity. Several manufacturers produce reliable color copiers; however, because of high per copy cost, their use is usually limited to those situations where color is essential. An attachment to some color copiers makes color "prints" by enlarging color slides on paper. For example, color prints might be made and distributed to an audience after a management presentation from a transparency. (Transparencies are discussed in detail on page 277.)

Job Recovery. It is sometimes necessary to interrupt a "run" to make a few copies of something urgent or to allow someone else to use the machine. When this happens, if your machine is equipped with a job recovery feature, the machine will remember where it was interrupted and afterward return to its place automatically.

Repeat Key or Return to Position. This is a money-saving feature that prevents overcopying. For example, if you are making 20 copies of a document, once you have completed the last copy, the copy counter will automatically return to 1. This prevents the next user from making 20 copies in error.

Reduction and Enlargement. Many copiers are capable of reducing and/or enlarging the size of originals. Varying degrees of reduction and enlargement are available. Usually operators can reduce originals between 64 and 77 percent, but manufacturers are working to provide a greater variety of reduction choices. This feature is useful in reducing computer printouts, drawings, and ledger sheets that are too large to fit into the files. The enlargement feature permits operators to produce copies that are larger than the original. It is useful for sharpening details and making copy more readable. Most manufacturers are offering this feature now and are expanding the variety of ratios available for enlargements.

Instant On. This feature eliminates the need for warm-up time. The copier can be used the minute it is turned on.

Interrupt Key. This is a device that permits the operator to stop the machine at any point.

Automatic Diagnosis. This feature will diagnose copy status and malfunctions. Machines display words or symbols to signal this information. Automatic diagnosis is also available in voice synthesis. "Talking copiers" have the capability of telling an operator what to do or what is wrong. The talking copier gives such commands as "take the original off the platen," "add toner," or "call the service technician."

Help Button. A feature designed to help inexperienced operators, the help button flashes understandable instructions in step-by-step order so that an operator can produce copies correctly. This is probably the most "user friendly" device of all new features.

COPY QUALITY CHECKLIST

If you answer no to any of the following questions, you are not obtaining the highest quality of reproduction from your copying machine.

1. Is the background as white as the original?
2. Is the copy free of specks or spots?
3. Is the copy free of streaks crossing the paper?
4. Is the intensity of the inklike impression similar to the original copy?
5. Does the copier compensate for less-than-perfect originals, such as those with dark backgrounds or light images?
6. Does the copier reproduce a pencil original into readable copy?
7. Does the copier adjust to the reproduction of originals on colored paper?
8. Do both black-and-white and color photographs reproduce clearly?
9. Can the copier produce good copies from such items as labels, card stock, transparencies, vellum, and specialty papers?

COPYING ABUSES

The ease with which copies can be made on reprographic equipment has led to the tendency to make more copies than are needed. This urge seems to be almost irresistible. In addition to overcopying, there is also the cost of unauthorized copying of personal materials: recipes, bowling scores, and personal letters. Although each copy costs only a few pennies, the cumulative total adds many dollars to the monthly copying bill.

To meet the problems of overcopying and unauthorized copying, some companies centralize all copiers in a word processing center or in a reprographic department, assigning full-time operators to the machines. A reprographic requisition form must be submitted with each original. This system has been known to decrease the volume of unnecessary copying by 20 percent. Other companies, however, contend that centralizing copiers increases the time it takes to get copies, takes the secretary away from the workstation, and causes delays. The cost of lost time far exceeds the savings gained by eliminating unauthorized copying and overcopying.

Copiers can be equipped with a device, such as an *autotron*, to ensure that only authorized personnel use machines. Such devices also make it possible to charge copying costs to departments or individuals on a use basis. One such unit employs a counter that cannot be reset by the user. The operator must have a key to activate the machine. When a key is inserted in the lock activating the machine, the counter corresponding to that key records the number of copies made.

Another factor in the mounting cost of copying is the temptation, because of convenience, to use the copier rather than the duplicator to produce multiple copies. Multiple copies of a page or several pages can usually be produced on a duplicator at a third of the cost of reproducing them on a copier or less.

Because of the ease of making photocopies and the availability of copiers in the office, there is a temptation to make copies of valuable personal papers and to use or carry them in place of the originals. There are rules against and penalities for copying certain papers. These papers include driver's licenses, automobile registration, passports, citizenship papers, naturalization papers, immigration papers, postage stamps, copyrighted materials, and securities of the United States government.

DUPLICATING MACHINES

Unlike the copier, which reproduces directly from an original, a duplicating machine produces copies from prepared masters and stencils. The three most commonly used types of duplicating processes are fluid, stencil, and offset. Fluid and stencil duplicators, popular for so many years because of their simple operation and low initial cost, are rapidly being replaced by up-to-date technology.

Fluid (Direct Process) Duplication

The *fluid process*, also known as *liquid, spirit, direct,* and *ditto process,* is used for relatively short runs. Up to 300 copies can be reproduced from one *master set.* A master set has three parts: the master itself, a protective tissue, and a carbon sheet. The master actually produces the copies.

The material to be reproduced is transferred in reverse image to the back of a master by typing, tracing, drawing, or writing. The master is clamped to the cylinder of the duplicator carbon side up. The carbon deposit side of the master comes in contact with chemically moistened sheets of paper as they pass through the machine. A minute portion of dye from the master transfers to the paper, thus producing the copy.

Copies can be produced in purple, black, blue, green, or red. If various colored carbons are used to produce the master, several colors can be reproduced at the same time. Charts, pictures, and ruled forms can be traced onto the master.

Master sets for the fluid duplicator deteriorate when stored too long. You should take this into consideration when you requisition supplies. Stock master sets in small quantities.

Stencil Duplication (Mimeograph Process)

The stencil process involves a different kind of master, a *stencil*, and an inked drum or an inked screen. The stencil is a thin tissue coated with a waxy substance which ink cannot penetrate. Material to be duplicated is transferred to the stencil by one of several methods. Each method results in pushing aside or removing the wax coating, thus exposing porous fibers. The stencil is placed around an inked drum or screen. Ink flows through the exposed fibers to produce the copy as paper passes through the machine.

The quality of reproduction in stencil duplication is superior to that of the fluid process. Several thousand highly readable copies can be reproduced from one stencil, thus making the process practical for both short runs and relatively long runs.

Fast drying emulsion inks make it possible to duplicate on both sides of a sheet of paper without slip-sheeting (inserting a blotting paper between sheets). As many as five colors can be reproduced at the same time by using a special multicolor ink pad.

With the stencil process, near perfect registration (the exact positioning of images and text in correct relationship to each other on a page, in a column, and on a line) can be achieved, making it possible to duplicate fill-ins on printed or duplicated forms. Variable speed controls regulate the lightness or darkness of copies. Up to 200 copies a minute can be reproduced on the single drum machine, and 125 copies a minute can be reproduced on the twin drum machine. These machines may be set to shut off automatically upon completion of a preset number of copies.

Offset Duplication

In *offset duplication* (also known as photo-offset, lithography, photo-offset lithography, and offset lithography), an inked impression is first transferred to a rubber roller and then transferred to paper. Offset duplication is based on the chemical principle that grease and water do not mix. The image area is receptive to a greasy ink; the nonimage area is receptive to water. Thus, the resistance of the ink to water defines the image. Material to be duplicated is typed or drawn onto the front side of an offset master. The master is placed on a cylinder and is inked as it rotates. The ink on the master deposits an image in reverse on a large rubber drum called a *blanket*. The image is transferred from the blanket to paper being fed through the machine by an impression roller pressing the paper against the rubber blanket.

The offset process offers a wide range of possibilities for reproducing printed, handwritten, or typed copy, as well as pictures and drawings. Various colors can be used. Several colors can be reproduced on the same page, but a separate master and a separate run are required for each color. Copies can be run on both sides of a sheet of paper to reduce costs and bulk.

Offset duplicator manufacturers market tabletop machines designed to produce high-quality work at a low per copy cost. (An example appears in Illus. 10-3.) Their objective is to provide a machine

Illus. 10-3
Tabletop offset duplicators are very easy to operate.

Courtesy of A.B. Dick Company

that is competitive for general office copying tasks. The operation of these machines has been so simplified that they may be operated satisfactorily by most members of the office staff.

As many as 10,000 copies can be reproduced from one offset master, and work of the highest quality can be obtained. The wide range of paper and the variety of colors that can be used make the process especially appropriate where visual impact is of major concern.

VOLUME COPIER/DUPLICATORS

One of the most cost-effective developments in office reprographics is the *copier/duplicator*. These machines use the electrostatic imaging process and are designed for high-volume production (100,000 to 200,000 copies per month). An example appears in Illus. 10-4. They are capable of producing 92 or more copies per minute and compete favorably in per copy cost with offset duplicators. They offer the convenience of copiers and the speed and cost advantages of duplicators. They also contain certain desirable automated features not available on duplicating machines (sorters, for example). A sorter assembles duplicated pages in sequence to provide multiple sets of a duplicated document, such as a report. The *on-line* sorter of copier/duplicators allows copies to proceed directly from the copier/duplicator to the sorter without operator intervention. As multiple copies of the first page of the original come off the copier/duplicator, they are automatically separated into a series of bins, one bin for each copy. This process is repeated until all pages of the original have been copied. Each bin will then contain one complete copied set of the original. Similar sorter attachments for duplicators are also available.

In addition to assembling, some copier/duplicators carry the process one step further to include on-line *finishing*. The assembling unit receives the copies, jogs each set, staples it, and deposits it in a removable tray.

Most copier/duplicators produce the number of desired copies of page one before proceeding to page two. Others, however, produce one copy of each page of a report, assemble and finish set one, then proceed to repeat the process and complete set two. The advantage of the latter system is that it is not necessary to wait until all sets have been duplicated before getting the first finished set. The turnaround time—the lapsed time from submission of original to receipt of assembled copies—is reduced.

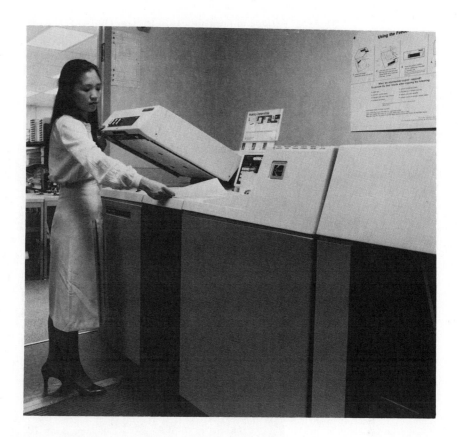

Illus. 10-4
High-volume
copiers are often
located in
centralized
reprographics
departments.

AUTOMATED DUPLICATORS

The copier/duplicator offers the convenience of reproducing copy directly from an original without the intermediate step of preparing a master or a stencil. To compete, manufacturers of stencil and offset duplicators have produced highly automated machines for high-volume users. Basically the automated duplicator combines three machines into an on-line assembly: (1) an automatic master- or stencil-making machine, (2) a high-speed duplicating machine, and (3) a sorter to provide assembled copies. The operator produces the master or stencil on the automatic master or stencil maker and transfers the master or stencil to the duplicator. The duplicated copies feed automatically into a sorter and the operator receives assembled copies. The operation is further automated by some manufacturers. The master or stencil moves via conveyor belt directly from the stencil maker to the duplicator; the operator does not have to intervene to transfer the master to the duplicator. The operator's function is to feed the original into the stencil maker and to set the duplicator for the desired number of copies. These highly automated duplicators are also known as *continuous copy offset systems*. An example appears in Illus. 10-5.

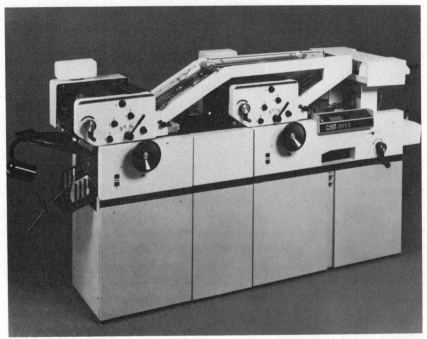

Photo permission of Multigraphics
Div. of AM International, Inc.

Illus. 10-5
In the continuous copy offset system, originals are fed into the duplicator at the right and an offset master is prepared. The master moves on a belt to a machine that processes the master. The master automatically attaches itself to the cylinder of the offset duplicator, where many copies are duplicated very rapidly.

AUXILIARY REPROGRAPHIC EQUIPMENT

Offices use various types of equipment to supplement the work of copiers and duplicators. This equipment is often located in a reprographics department or in a word processing center.

Headliners, Composers, and
Phototypesetters.

Certain kinds of office equipment can produce a variety of type
sizes and styles to improve the visual quality of materials to be duplicated or copied. Such equipment is useful to the secretary in preparing
visually appealing materials, such as important brochures, reports, and
directories. Using this equipment, the secretary can add a creative
touch to what would otherwise be an ordinary looking document.

Headliners. Type composition machines are available for in-office use
to create display type for headlines, subheads, and similar material. By
dialing the letters in a heading one at a time, an operator "typesets"
letters onto sensitized strips of tape. The tape is pasted on the original.
The original is then converted to a master and duplicated. Headliners
are especially useful in preparing originals for transparencies. Because
of the type sizes they can produce, headliners enhance readability.
Illus. 10-6 provides an example of display type produced by a headliner.

The sample was typed on a KROYTYPE lettering machine. Lettering is made on
tape by manually moving a type disk. KROYTYPE machines are small and
inexpensive, offering type disks with 19 commonly used type styles.

This is a sample of headlining

Illus. 10-6
Sample of headliner
lettering.

Composers. Ordinary typewritten documents can be reproduced to
resemble the print found in magazines and advertising brochures. A
VariTyper, an IBM Composer, and word processors can be used to
accomplish this task. These machines have a regular typewriter keyboard and the capability to justify right margins, permit the

interchange of type styles and sizes, and provide proportional letter spacing.

Phototypesetters. The professional quality typesetting that you see in books, brochures, directories, advertisements, and newspapers is achieved through the use of *phototypesetters*. Phototypeset materials exhibit a variety of sizes and styles of type, justified right margins, and proportional spacing between letters and words. A document that is phototypeset can be condensed to use only 50 percent of the space that would be used if it were typewritten. In turn, printing, collating, binding, and mailing costs are reduced. These costs are particularly important when documents must be sent to many people. Also, the amount of filing space is kept to a minimum.

A phototypesetter with its video display and keyboard looks much like a word processor. In addition to the characters on the keyboard, a phototypesetter has composition command keys to code specifications. Examples of composition commands involve type styles, type sizes, line lengths, and space between lines. When information is keyboarded, most phototypesetters record and store it on magnetic disks or diskettes.

For years, initial keyboarding was usually done on word processing equipment. Final copy was processed through an interface unit (black box) that permitted the word processor to communicate with the phototypesetter. The interface translated the copy stored in the word processor into simple commands that the phototypesetter could understand. No rekeyboarding was necessary.

Today some phototypesetters receive input directly from OCR scanners, word processors, or computers. Two different machines that are compatible can interface directly without black boxes. Direct interface greatly reduces keyboarding and proofreading time.

Documents that have been phototypeset are usually duplicated by offset printing. However, many office copiers can also make clean, sharp copies from phototypeset originals. Intelligent copier/printers can reproduce copies by communicating directly with the phototypesetter. The use of intelligent copier/printers bypasses the need to prepare a hard copy of the document before duplicating it.

Finishing Equipment

Collating, stapling, binding, folding, addressing, and signing copies are time-consuming activities. There are machines that perform these paper-pushing jobs quickly and accurately.

Collators. There are collators that operate independently of copiers and duplicators. The operator places piles of papers in the collator's bins, each bin containing copies of the same sheet. When activated, the machine automatically ejects the top sheet from each bin and assembles the sheets in a desired order. Fully automatic collators stack completed sets on a stacking bin. If the collator is semiautomatic, the operator must gather and stack the assembled sets.

Binders. Binding gives a professional appearance to copied or duplicated materials. Equipment consisting of a puncher and a binder is available for both softcover and hardcover binding. There are both manually and electrically operated punching, binding, and stapling machines.

Folding and Inserting Machines. Machines that fold duplicated sheets, such as letters and advertisements, and insert them in envelopes are significant energy-savers and time-savers to businesses that have large mailings. For example, Insertamate Mailing System (distributed by Pitney Bowes) is a fully integrated system that folds, inserts, seals, and meter-stamps mail in one fast, accurate, and simultaneous operation.

Addresser-Printers. The addresser-printer is used to address envelopes to each name and address on a mailing list. The mailing list is recorded on some form of plate or card called the *data carrier*. The data carrier may be a metal or plastic plate or a card with a small stencil or a direct process master insert. A separate data carrier is used for each addressee. As the envelope or addressing tape passes through the addresser-printer, the plate or address card falls in place, one at a time. The address is then duplicated onto the envelope or address tape. The addresser-printer may be manually fed or fully automatic. These machines are called addresser-printers because they may be used for purposes other than addressing, such as preparing inventory cards or monthly bills and routing multiple forms.

Signature Machines. When a large number of original signatures are regularly required, a signature machine can save an employer many tedious hours. Two types of signature machines are available: the *template* and the *ribbon*. As the template machine traces the user's signature from a pattern cut in a template (a thin plate), a mechanical pen writes the signature on the document. The ribbon machine impresses the signature on the document by means of pressure on a ribbon in much the same way a charge card is imprinted. This type of machine is often used for signing checks.

COMMERCIAL AND IN-HOUSE DUPLICATION

According to a national market research organization, the demand for duplicating increases at the rate of 150 billion copies every five years. Many companies are meeting this demand with their own in-house reprographics shops. This growing trend challenges the secretary to provide letter-perfect originals to the reprographics department in an acceptable format.

Some firms will continue to use commercial print shops for handling jobs that cannot be produced on in-house copiers or duplicators and where the volume of work does not justify the purchase of large-scale reprographic equipment. In every city there are commercial shops that specialize in reprographics. These businesses are usually listed in the Yellow Pages under "Letter Shop Service," "Copying and Duplicating," or "Photocopying." Such shops will prepare stencils or masters, run copies, address envelopes, and fold and insert enclosures. They will do the entire job or any phase of it.

If the office does not have adequate reprographic equipment or if time is short, the secretary may need to turn to an outside shop. Factors that must be investigated and compared include (1) rates charged per copy, (2) quality of prepared copy, (3) cost for collating, (4) cost for binding copies, and (5) time needed for completion. The secretary should maintain a file of information about available shops.

SELECTING THE REPROGRAPHIC METHOD

The secretary usually makes the decision as to whether copies are to be produced on the copier, copier/duplicator, duplicator, or by a commercial shop. Several factors enter into this decision: the number of copies required; the urgency; copying and duplicating facilities available in-company and at outside agencies; the quality of reproduction desired; and the cost per copy.

If the number of copies required is ten or less, the copying machine will probably be the least expensive, fastest, and most convenient method. If the number required is 100 or more, the duplicator or copier/duplicator will be the fastest method, will provide the highest quality reproduction, and will result in the lowest per copy cost. However, when the number of copies required falls between ten and 100, the choice comes within the *gray zone*, meaning that your decision is not clearly weighted for copying or for duplicating. The copier/duplicator is economical in this range, but it is a high-volume machine and is usually available only in large companies with a centralized reprographics department. The commercial shop may be the most economical in the 10-to-100-and-above copy range, but inconvenience and the shop's slow turnaround time may preclude its use. The convenience and quality of reproduction by duplicator will depend on whether equipment for stencil and master imaging is available, which duplicator method is used, and which automated features are on the equipment.

PREPARING MASTERS AND STENCILS

Copy to be duplicated may be transferred to an offset or direct process master or to a stencil in a number of ways. The traditional way to image material onto a master or stencil is by typing. Technology, however, has provided new imaging devices that are more convenient, faster, and more versatile than typing. These new devices have been instrumental in keeping the duplicator in a competitive position relative to the copying machine. Imaging equipment is now used extensively in large offices, and the number of small offices purchasing this equipment is growing steadily.

Imaging techniques not only save the time of manually typing and correcting masters and stencils, but offer many other advantages as well. For example, most of the time-consuming process of proofreading the master is eliminated. If the original is correct, the master will be correct. In addition, imaging techniques provide the flexibility of including a printed graph or map, of preparing a four-page folded program, and of including photographs and other materials that would be impractical, if not impossible, to attempt to record manually onto a stencil or master.

Thermal Imaging

Thermographic copiers use the *infrared* or *heat-transfer process* to make images. Material to be copied is placed beneath a heat-sensitive copy sheet. Infrared light is beamed through the sensitized copy sheet onto the original as both are fed through the machine. The heat turns the sensitized paper dark in the same places where the original is dark, thus producing the image.

Although copiers using the thermographic process were the first to be marketed for office use, today the process is used primarily to prepare transparencies for overhead projectors and to laminate documents.

The thermographic copier can also be used to produce stencils and fluid masters. The original is combined with a *thermal stencil* or *master* and passed through the copier. The heat causes an image of the original to transfer to the master which may be immediately run on a fluid or stencil duplicator to reproduce copies.

One limitation of the thermal process is that certain colors will not transfer. However, if a copy of the original is made on a copier utilizing the electrostatic process, this copy can then be used to produce the thermal master.

Photo Imaging

Small desktop offset platemakers can transfer originals to offset masters (plates) within seconds. The original and a chemically sensitized offset master are placed on a flatbed window. When the printing button is pressed, a photographic-type lamp exposes the master. A timer controls the exposure. No film or other intermediate steps are required, and the process is almost error-proof.

Electrostatic Imaging

The process of producing an offset master on a copying machine is almost as simple and convenient as producing a copy of an original. The original is placed in the copier. A sensitized offset master is substituted for the copy paper. The image is transferred from the original to the offset master, which may be immediately used to produce copies on the offset duplicator.

Facsimile Imaging

The *facsimile process*, sometimes referred to as the *electronic scanning method*, is used for preparing stencils and offset masters. The process is an adaptation of the principle of the photoelectric cell. Material to be reproduced is placed on the left drum of a two-drum machine. An electronic (plastic) stencil or offset plate is placed on the right drum. As the drums rotate slowly, a photoelectric eye scans each line. This activates a needle that moves across the second drum. The needle records the image on the stencil or offset master. Drawings, forms, printed and typed copy, diagrams, and artwork (including photographs) can be transferred to a stencil or master with relatively high-quality detail via facsimile imaging. The steps involved in producing a stencil using the facsimile process are illustrated in Illus. 10-7.

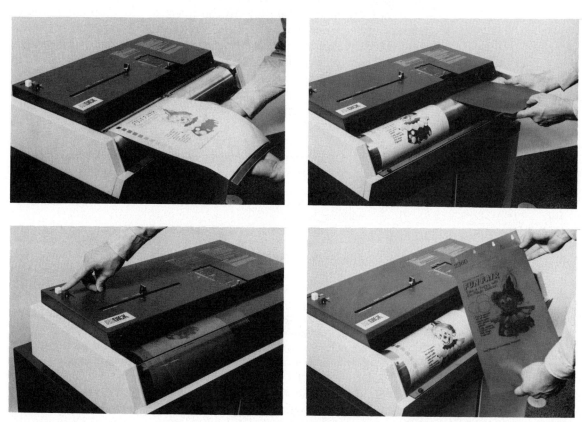

Courtesy of A.B. Dick Company

Illus. 10-7
The four steps in preparing a stencil by the facsimile process are: (1) place the original on one drum; (2) place an electronic stencil or an offset master on the second drum; (3) activate the machine; and (4) remove the completed stencil.

PREPARING TRANSPARENCIES

Making a transparency is a quick process. Before attempting to make a transparency, be sure you have the right film for the machine you are using. You can damage your copier if the film you use was designed for another type of machine. Special film has been produced for plain paper copiers that enables you to make a transparency in much the same way you make a paper copy. Substitute the film for the paper in the copier's paper feed tray, place your original on the platen of the copier, and press the print button.

One type of transparency film is made for desktop convenience copiers and another type is manufactured for the high-volume copier/duplicator systems. There are also many transparency films on the market capable of producing color transparencies on clear film in bright purple, red, blue, or green. Film is also available that produces white-frosted images that project black against clear or colored backgrounds. The following tips should help you get perfect transparencies on your first attempt:

1. If the transparency film becomes separated from its backing sheet, reassemble the sheets by matching the rounded corners.
2. To write or draw on an original, use a No. 2 pencil or a black marking pen.
3. If the transparency is too light or too dark, adjust the exposure dial.
4. If the backing sheet does not peel away easily, the machine is too hot.
5. Some copiers, such as those that use the thermographic process, have a screen carrier to move the original and film through the machine. A screen carrier consists of two sheets of special paper fastened at the top. The original and the film are placed in the carrier before insertion into the copier. The screen carrier transports the packet through the machine.

When your employer is called upon to make an oral presentation, your ability to prepare the proper supporting visuals can not only enhance the presentation, but it can provide you with the opportunity to demonstrate your creative talents. In preparing a transparency or a similar visual to be used before an audience, remember to:

1. Use print that is large enough to be read from any point in the room.
2. Make advance arrangements to have visual equipment, including a screen, in place.
3. Keep the content of the transparency simple; complex visuals tend to confuse rather than clarify.
4. Proofread the copy carefully; a typo can often kill the effectiveness of a presentation and embarrass the presenter.
5. Make full use of color, cartoons, and lettering machines to enhance the content.

6. Mount transparencies in suitable frames and label them for easy handling.

PREPARING CAMERA-READY COPY

Most in-house reprographics departments and commercial printers produce their most professional looking jobs from pasted up, camera-ready copy. Camera-ready copy is ready to be photographed for reproduction. Cutting and pasting copy affords the secretary an excellent opportunity to be creative and to improve the appearance of what would otherwise be an ordinary-looking document. Avoid errors, delays, and frustrations by exercising care in preparing camera-ready copy for reproduction. The printer with whom you work will be able to help you with this task until such time that you become proficient. The following precautions, prescribed by professional printers, will enable you to get good results the first time you prepare camera-ready copy:

1. Use a high-density carbon-based ribbon for best results.
2. Leave at least a three-eighths inch margin. This is the minimum amount of space needed for the machine to grasp an original.
3. Use a razor blade or a utility knife, such as an X-ACTO blade knife, to make smooth cuts.
4. Avoid the use of highly reflective art, slick pictures from magazines, or two or three shades of paper on the same page. They will produce uneven shading in the copy because the camera can detect even the slightest difference.
5. Use rubber cement instead of tape or staples to paste up copy. However, do not let glue ooze from under edges; it will attract dirt and cause shadows around the copy.
6. Avoid overlapping pasted-up portions of copy. Shadows will occur where there are overlaps.
7. Keep the copy clean.
8. Proof the copy carefully (once for content and logic, once for mechanical errors, and again for both). Have someone other than the typist who prepared the copy proofread it.
9. Give complete instructions. If an item is to be duplexed, stapled, collated, folded, or punched, the proper instructions should be given before the job begins.
10. Attach a dummy copy. The dummy should show how the finished product should look. Dummies are of immeasurable assistance to printers and will ensure that you get the finished product you desire.

PAPER FOR DUPLICATORS AND COPIERS

The secretary may be assigned the responsibility for buying paper for the office copier and duplicator. This purchasing problem is complicated because several office copiers use sensitized papers, and each duplicating process requires its own type of paper.

Paper used in duplicating is usually wood sulfite. It comes in a wide variety of colors. The three standard weights for mimeo and duplicating paper are 16, 20, and 24 pounds. Offset paper may carry these same weight identifications or higher weights of 50, 60, or 70 pounds.

Offset paper is either coated or uncoated. Coated paper is designed for high-grade work, offset enamel being the very highest quality. Uncoated paper is used for the majority of in-house work which does not require high-quality results.

Paper for stencil duplicating, unlike that for spirit duplicating, is unglazed and absorbent. Since moisture affects the quality of reproduction and the ease with which paper is handled by machines, duplicating paper should be kept wrapped in the moisture-proof covers in which it is received. It should be stored in a dry place and stacked flat.

Duplicator paper, like other paper, has a top and a bottom side. The best results are obtained by using the paper topside up. The printed label on the package usually indicates the correct printing side.

Avoid overstocking. Most copier papers have a shelf life which should be checked before buying in quantity. Paper for copiers may be purchased in rolls (which use more storage space) and in a variety of precut sizes, such as executive, letter, and legal.

SUMMARY

Reprographics is a relatively new classification of office work that emerged with the advent of copier technology. Reprographics is the multiple reproduction of images. It involves the use of two primary types of equipment: copiers and duplicators.

Copiers use an image-forming process similar to a camera to create copies directly from existing originals. Duplicators, on the other hand, make copies from stencils or masters that must be prepared before copies are reproduced.

The demand for more and better copies has brought about a dramatic change in the field of reprographics. A continuous flow of technological advances has enabled the secretary to produce faster, easier, cleaner, and less expensive copies and has taken much of the drudgery out of the copying routine.

Numerous features are standard equipment on low-volume convenience copiers that were once only available on expensive, high-volume models. These features include copy reduction, enlargement, automatic duplexing, and automatic document feed.

Copiers are commonplace in most offices; but because of easy access, they are often abused by employees who copy personal materials at company expense. Various controls have been developed to prevent this abuse.

As the reprographics market continues to expand, new auxiliary equipment has appeared on the market to simplify and enhance the reprographics task. Collators, sorters, typesetting machines, staplers, signature machines, and the like assist operators in producing professional-looking copies.

In order to produce professional-looking copies, secretaries need to know how to prepare masters, stencils, transparencies, and camera-ready copy. It is also essential to know which reprographics process will produce the highest quality copy at the lowest cost in the shortest time.

SUGGESTED READINGS

Auer, Joseph, and Charles E. Harris. *Major Equipment Procurement.* New York: Van Nostrand Reinhold Co., Inc., 1983.

Manson, Richard E. *The Manager's Guide to Copying and Duplicating.* New York: McGraw-Hill Book Co., 1980.

Pasewark, William R. *Reprographics,* Copier, Offset, Fluid, and Stencil, 3d ed. Cincinnati: South-Western Publishing Co., 1984.

QUESTIONS FOR DISCUSSION

1. Other than producing a copy of an original document, what are some other major functions handled by copiers?
2. The ease of using copiers has led to the copying of all kinds of materials. What are some items that cannot by law be copied?
3. Which reproduction process would you recommend for each of the following projects, assuming that all types were available to you:
   a. 5,000 copies of a form letter to be mailed to sales prospects
   b. Five copies of an order to be distributed to department heads with the least possible delay

c. 300 copies of a notice to be mailed to all sales representatives, announcing a new product

d. 750 copies of a four-page house organ that is issued monthly and contains pictures and illustrations

e. Eight copies of the secretary's minutes of the directors' meeting

f. 150 copies of a price list duplicated each week (The list covers 144 standard items arranged in alphabetical order. Since prices fluctuate, a new price list is prepared, duplicated, and distributed weekly to all sales employees.)

g. 500 preprinted time cards—one time card for each company employee (The title on the card shows the employee's number, name, address, social security number, and number of income tax exemptions.)

h. 1,500 copies of a program cover for a secretarial seminar (you would like to use the CPS key and the Professional Secretaries International emblem on the front and the state seal and motto of your home state on the back.)

4. What kinds of auxiliary finishing equipment may be purchased for copiers and duplicators?

5. Which cost should be itemized to arrive at the cost per copy for copiers and duplicators?

6. What can the secretary do in preparing camera-ready copy to ensure that the print shop will return a professional-looking job?

7. Select the word or phrase which properly completes each sentence. Use the Reference Guide to check your answers.

a. All of us _____ Phillip will attend. (accept, except)

b. I am not _____ to asking questions when I am lost. (averse, adverse)

c. He will _____ to his military experience in his address to the association. (allude, elude)

d. I cannot _____ the course of the committee after they have voted. (altar, alter)

e. Her shoes were the perfect _____ for the new tweed suit. (compliment, complement)

f. The sample is _____ the ones we were shown at the market. (different than, different from)

PROBLEMS

1. There are many makes, models, and types of duplicators and copiers available. Furthermore, each duplicator and copier process offers certain advantages, depending on the specific reproduction

requirements of the office. Careful consideration is required to select the reprographic process and the make and model of machine that will best meet the needs of an insurance office. Prepare a list of the factors you would consider in selecting the process and the make and model of machine to be used in an insurance office.

2. Prepare an instruction sheet clearly explaining procedures for one of the following activities (illustrate your explanation, if possible):
    a. Placing the master on a direct process duplicator and running the copies
    b. Placing the master on the offset duplicator and running the copies
    c. Using a copying machine to make a transparency
    d. Using a heat transfer copier to produce a direct process master, stencil, or transparency
    e. Using a facsimile imaging machine to produce an offset master

3. Your company occupies six floors of an office building. One high-speed copier/duplicator is installed in a central location on each floor, and each staff person uses that machine for copying. You are aware of several problems.
    a. The total cost for copying has been increasing at an alarming rate and you are suspicious that there is much overcopying and copying of personal material.
    b. You have observed that staff members frequently lose considerable time waiting at the copier for the machine to become available.
    c. The copying center has become a quasi-social center for office personnel.
    d. Although the copier/duplicator is centrally located, it is a considerable distance from some of the offices. Secretaries frequently make the round trip to the machine to reproduce only two or three copies.
    e. Senior staff members complain that secretaries are away from their desks too much of the time.
    Prepare a list of recommendations to improve the situation.

4. Because of a recent merger of your company with another firm, copying requirements have increased from 15,000 to approximately 50,000 copies per month. Your employer has been given the task of restructuring reprographic services in your company. You have been asked to provide a list of the major manufacturers of copying equipment suitable for this higher range and to indicate those that maintain local showrooms or sales and service offices. Prepare the list, indicating those that serve your community.

Chapter 11

Basic Telephone and Telegraph Services

The telephone is a vital link between secretaries, their co-workers, and the public. Although you are likely to consider yourself adept in handling this instrument, business phones are quite different and much more complicated than the personal telephone. In this chapter you will learn how to improve your telephone speech and to use appropriate telephone etiquette. You will learn techniques for answering incoming local and long-distance calls and for handling multibutton telephones. You will understand how to take messages and how to record or summarize conversations.

The telegram often accelerates business action. It gets results when other channels of communication prove inadequate. You must know how and when to use telegraphic messages. Chapter 11 concludes with a discussion of the procedures for preparing and filing both domestic and international telegraphic messages.

TELEPHONE EQUIPMENT

Local telephone companies offer single line or multiline service to business customers. Equipment differs with the type of service required. This section describes conventional telephone equipment: the rotary dial, push-button, and key telephones. A discussion of telephone systems is reserved for Chapter 12.

Rotary Dial and Push-Button Telephones

Single line telephones are operated either by a rotary dial or a push-button pad. Because the push-button phone is needed to access certain services (*Touch-Tone* service, for example), it is rapidly replacing rotary dial equipment. Push-button phones are also easier to dial in the dark or in an emergency and by the visually impaired.

Key Telephones

The standard telephone for multiline service is the *key telephone*. In addition to a dialing number pad, key telephones are equipped with a *hold* button and a series of Lucite buttons, each representing a separate telephone line. An example of a multiline key telephone appears in Illus. 11-1. When a particular line is in use, its Lucite button is illuminated. The advantage of the key telephone is that it allows the secretary to make or receive several calls simultaneously from both inside and outside the office. All key telephones operate essentially the same way.

To answer a call:
1. Determine the line to be answered by the flashing signal light.
2. Depress the lighted button, remove the receiver, and speak.

Illus. 11-1
Multiline key
telephones allow
one person to
handle several
lines.

Reproduced with permission of
AT&T Corporate Archive

To place a call:

1.   Choose a line that is not in use (unlighted).
2.   Depress the button for that line, remove the receiver, and make your call.
3.   If you accidentally choose a line that is being held, depress the hold button to reestablish the hold.

To hold a call:

1.   Request permission from the caller to hold the line. (The caller may prefer to call back or have you return the call.)
2.   If the caller is agreeable, depress the hold button. Both the line button and the hold button will return to their normal positions. While on hold, the line button continues to flash.
3.   Place or answer another call on another line. The person on the line being held cannot overhear your conversation.

TELEPHONE TECHNIQUES

Some phase of at least 90 percent of all business transactions is conducted by telephone. This is why many personnel officers check the telephone technique of applicants before hiring them. It is also why companies frequently provide in-service telephone training for all office employees. What a secretary says during a telephone conversation is important. The tactful choice of words in contrast to blunt statements, offers of help in contrast to plain no's, and ease in conducting pleasant, effective conversations come with experience and proper training.

The Voice With a Smile

Your voice over the phone reflects your personality. Make it attractive to callers. If you consider each call an annoying interruption, your voice will reflect a negative attitude. You really cannot afford to answer the telephone indifferently. It is possible that the person calling may be very important—your employer, for instance. Here are eight simple rules to assist you in developing a pleasant telephone voice:

1.   Speak at a normal speed; use rising and falling inflections to avoid monotony.
2.   Use a tone suitable for face-to-face-conversation; keep your voice low-pitched.

3. Speak directly into the transmitter; hold it between half an inch and an inch from your lips.

4. Try to visualize and speak directly *to* the person calling, not *at* the telephone.

5. Try to convey a friendly, intelligent interest.

6. Show that you are wide awake and ready to help the person on the line.

7. Use simple, nontechnical language and avoid slang.

8. End the call by simply saying *goodbye.* Saying *bye-bye* at the end of a conversation leaves a distinctly bad impression.

Telephone Etiquette

Rudeness that would never occur in a face-to-face encounter too often occurs in telephone conversations. Answering the telephone in a courteous manner is essential to good business practice. These guidelines for telephone etiquette are strongly recommended:

1. Answer the telephone immediately, before the third ring, even if you are in the midst of an important job. This practice will not only establish a good relationship with the caller, but will reassure your employer about your competence. In addition, immediately answering a ringing telephone reduces disturbances.

2. *Listen* until you know definitely what the caller wants. If in doubt, ask for a confirmation of your understanding. Nothing is more annoying than telling someone the purpose of a call and then realizing by the response that you were not understood. Listening is one of the most important communication skills. In no place can you demonstrate your mastery of listening skills better than in your telephone conversations.

3. Do not eat, drink, type, or file papers while talking on the telephone. These noises are quickly picked up over telephone lines. These actions can be misinterpreted as a lack of interest on your part.

4. Establish yourself as a helpful person. By being able to speak confidently about your organization and being courteous as well as helpful, you can quickly establish yourself as someone callers can deal with and, most important, as someone that your employer can trust. Here is a chance to widen your sphere of influence.

5. Sprinkle your conversations with *thank you* and *please.* Do not be superficial in your use of these expressions, be genuine: "Thank you *so much*, Mr. Rodrigues, for letting us know that."

6. Never assume the identity of a caller. Only use the caller's name if you recognize the voice. In case of doubt, you should not risk the possibility of making an error in identification.

7. Follow through; don't leave the caller stranded. Go that last mile. Either get the information, transfer the call, or arrange for someone (maybe you) to call back, then *do so*. Promises must be carried out.

8. Keep calls short. Eliminate chitchat; plan conversations before placing calls. Some organizations do not permit employees to make personal calls, but you may occasionally have to make one. In any case, keep personal calls to a minimum and keep them short.

9. Remember that politeness dictates that the person who initiated the call terminate it. If you are to close the conversation, do so courteously and graciously. Suggested wording of your last sentence might be
   a. Thank you for calling, Ms. Levinson.
   b. I'm glad I was able to help you. Goodbye.
   c. You're welcome, Mr. Rogers. Goodbye.

10. If you must terminate a conversation suddenly for any of several reasons, give a plausible, tactfully worded explanation: Examples include: "I'm sorry, Ms. Allen has just buzzed for me to come into her office"; "I'm sorry, someone is waiting for me in the reception room"; or "I'm sorry, I must get out a rush letter for Mr. Barkley."
   Finally, place the receiver in its holder gently. A slammed receiver at the very least is rude and may be interpreted incorrectly.

Enunciation

Secretaries give and take information over the telephone frequently. Enunciation, then, becomes very important. Watch for these frequent causes of inaccuracy: *F* and *S* are often confused, as are *P* and *B*, *T* and *D*, and *M* and *N*. To prevent mistakes, use any simple, easy-to-understand word to identify a letter, such as *D as in David*, *A as in Alice*, *V as in Victor*, and so on. Make it a practice to spell difficult names. It is particularly important that the listener understand any numbers; therefore, the speaker should slightly exaggerate their enunciation. Repeat all numbers. If there is still a question about one digit, give its preceding sequence, as "three, four, *five*," emphasizing the proper number.

The American Telephone & Telegraph Co. recommends the following sentences to improve your diction. *Read them aloud slowly, giving every sound its proper value.* Think about them, too.

1. For distinct enunciation, every word, every syllable, every sound must be given its proper form and values.
2. Think of the mouth chamber as a mold in which the correct form must be given to every sound.
3. Move your lips noticeably.
4. Your teeth should never be kept closed while you are talking.
5. You may know what you are saying, but others won't unless you make it clear to them.
6. Through practice we can learn to speak more rapidly, but still with perfect distinctions.
7. The courtesy of face-to-face conversation, in which the smile is so important, can be conveyed by telephone only through a smiling voice.

INCOMING CALLS

There are specific techniques to follow in handling incoming calls. Every executive has preferences about how calls are to be handled. Although the trend today is for executives to answer their telephones directly, many executives prefer to have their calls screened. If you are working with several executives who are frequently out of the office, it is especially important to learn the preferences of each one. Armed with this information, you can then adopt appropriate procedures. When you must be away from your desk, arrange for a co-worker to answer your phone and explain your telephone procedures to that person.

Identification

How you answer your telephone depends upon whether it is connected directly to an outside line or to the company switchboard. In general, you should answer with a courteous greeting, give the name of the company (department, or individual's office), and follow with your name. You should never answer by simply saying hello or yes. If your telephone is on an outside line, you may answer in the following manner:

> National Supply Company, Sales Department, Miss Hunt speaking.
> *or*
> National Supply Company, Mr. Brandt's office, Miss Hunt speaking.

If the call comes through the company switchboard, the switchboard attendant has already identified the company. Answer as follows:

> Sales Department, Miss Hunt speaking.
> *or*
> Mr. Brandt's office, Miss Hunt speaking.

Most executives and professional people answer their telephones by saying their entire names (first and surname) or surnames only, while secretaries answer by using a courtesy title and their last names. Some offices, however, instruct secretaries to use their first names only in answering calls. In this case, you would answer, "Mr. Brandt's office, this is Susan" or "Mr. Brandt's office, Susan speaking."

Screening Calls

If your employer prefers to have you screen calls or has someone in the office and is obviously too busy to answer the telephone, you should answer all calls. If you answer a call from someone that you recognize as a VIP (Very Important Person), tell the executive who is calling, and put the call through. When the caller provides no identification and you do not recognize the voice, find out who is calling. The abrupt question, "Who is calling?" sounds rude and discriminating. Tactful secretaries phrase their questions like this:

> May I ask who is calling, please?
> *or*
> May I tell Miss Wong who is calling, please?
> *or*
> Miss Wong is in, may I tell her who is calling, please?

After notifying the executive of the caller, put the call through. A buzzer system on the telephone and an interoffice line is used for this purpose. Some executives prefer this kind of screening so that they can immediately address callers by name.

If a caller refuses to provide identification, ask the executive for instructions or ask the caller for a telephone number so that the executive can return the call later in the day.

Executive Unavailable

The secretary has three responsibilities regarding incoming calls when the executive is not available to answer the telephone:

1.   To give helpful but not explicit information to the caller about the executive's schedule and activities.
2.   To get information from hesitant callers.
3.   To take messages and keep a record of incoming calls.

Giving Information. When the executive is not available to answer a phone call, give a plausible explanation, suggest a time when the caller might call back, or possibly suggest that the caller talk to another person. A typical explanation might be:

> Mr. Graham, Mrs. Allen is attending an important conference. May I help you or transfer you to someone who can?
>   *or*
> Mr. Graham, Mrs. Allen is away from her desk at the moment. May I help you?

Avoid dead-end replies such as "Mrs. Allen is not here." Notice in the two preceding examples that the information that was given was not explicit. An executive may not want anything specific communicated to certain callers. *When in doubt, don't be explicit.* Unless you have a certain reason for being so, try to be helpful without being too specific. Note the differences in the following responses:

Specific	*Helpful But Not Explicit*
Miss Ettinger hasn't come in yet.	Miss Ettinger isn't at her desk. I expect her at ten o'clock.
Ms. Smith is in Chicago on business.	Ms. Smith is out of the city today.
Mr. Hubbard left early today to play golf.	Mr. Hubbard won't be in until tomorrow.

Getting Information. Getting information from an unidentified caller is often a problem and a challenge. How can you get both the name of the caller and the purpose of the call before the person says, "I'll call back," and then hangs up? You may have to use an oblique approach. The conversation might develop something like this:

> You answer the call and say, "Ms. Allen is away today. I am her secretary, perhaps I can help you." (Notice that you do not abruptly ask who is calling or what is wanted.) If the caller is hesitant, you might ask, "May I have her call you tomorrow?" If the answer is, "Yes, will you? This is Helen Fox, 555-6412," you might then ask, "Shall I give her any special message, Ms. Fox?" Or you might ask, "Will Ms. Allen know what you are calling about?"

Another approach to take with callers who are hesitant about identifying themselves is to delay stating whether the employer is available to take the call until after the caller has been identified. For example, if the caller asks to speak to your employer, Ms. Smith, you may respond by saying "May I tell Ms. Smith who is calling?" Then follow through by asking the purpose of the call. When you have this information, you can then reveal that your employer is out of the office for the day. Suggest that the caller speak with someone else or indicate that your employer will return the call. Phrase your requests for identification in a courteous and positive way. Examine the following:

Discourteous Requests	Tactful Requests
She wants to know who's calling.	May I say who's calling, please?
If you'll tell me who's calling, I'll see if I can locate her.	She's in a meeting. May I take a message?
Ms. Smith isn't taking any calls this morning.	Will you please wait while I see if she is in?

Taking Messages. As you answer your telephone, pick up a pencil and a telephone message pad. *Keep these supplies handy at all times.* Some firms use small printed slips for this purpose. It is possible to buy books of telephone message forms that are interleaved with carbon sheets. The original message can be put on the executive's desk, and the secretary retains the carbon copy for reference. An example of a telephone message form appears in Illus. 11-2.

Always offer to take a message when your employer is out. Ask the caller to explain any details that you do not understand. Take time to repeat the message; verify numbers and the spelling of all names. If a

TELEPHONE MESSAGE

FOR _Mrs. McDuff._ _____ DATE _8/6/--_

M _r. E. Jones_ OF _Sales_

PHONE NO. _ext. 904_ _____ TIME _9:15_

✓	TELEPHONED		PLEASE PHONE
	RETURNED YOUR CALL		WANTS TO SEE YOU
	CAME TO SEE YOU		WILL CALL AGAIN

MESSAGE _The meeting of the product managers has been postponed until next week._

BY _EJM_

Illus. 11-2
Telephone
messages should
contain all
pertinent data.

call back is indicated, say, "I'll ask Mrs. McDuff to call you when she is free."

After you have recorded the message, add the date, the time, the name and company affiliation of the caller, and your initials. Place telephone messages in order of importance on the executive's desk beside the telephone or in another conspicuous spot. If the executive uses a computer to store messages, enter the telephone message on the computer so that it may be called up by the executive and read from the screen. A secretary to several executives may establish a *message island* which each executive can regularly check.

Always relay messages promptly. If there is no message to report, make a record of the call for the executive's information. When the executive is away, a professional secretary keeps a telephone diary, similar to the one shown in Illus. 11-3, of all calls and messages.

TELEPHONE DIARY OF INCOMING CALLS
August 6, 19- -

Time	Name of Caller	Affiliation	Message or Purpose	Disposition	
				Spoke With	(Call Back) Telephone #
9:15	*Mr. E. Jones*	*sales dept.*	*product man grs meeting postponed*	*E.G.M.*	

Illus. 11-3
This telephone diary can be maintained on a daily basis or prepared when the executive is away.

Transferring Calls

When you receive a call that is not for your extension, or if you believe that someone other than yourself or your employer could better handle the call, transfer it; but avoid giving the caller the run-around. (It is possible that the caller has already been transferred to several extensions.) Your company's image and your own are extremely important. Nothing is more exasperating to a caller than an *I-couldn't-care-less* or *I-have-my-own-work-to-do* attitude. Several techniques can be used to demonstrate to callers that you and your organization want to be helpful.

1. Be sure that the person to whom you transfer the call can actually supply the information the caller seeks. This is your opportunity to demonstrate your understanding of your company's organization and to show that you know who knows what.
2. Look up the extension to which you are transferring the call in the company directory. Tell the caller the number of the extension you are transferring the call to and the name of the person at that extension. Stay on the line until the call is answered.
3. Rather than transferring a call, consider the possibility of getting the information for the caller yourself and returning the call.

Recording Complete or Summarized Telephone Conversations

If your employer wishes to record crucial telephone conversations, the recorder must be equipped with a sound device that emits intermittent beeps to warn the other person that the call is being recorded. You may be asked to type a full transcript or a summary of these telephone conversations. The transcript may be condensed, but it should be typed in dialogue form as indicated on page 786 of the Reference Guide. At other times you may be asked to get on the line and take notes during a conversation. Your employer should introduce you to the caller or mention that you are on the line to record parts of the conversation.

Answering a Second Telephone

You may work with an executive who has a multiline telephone. If two lines ring at the same time, answer one and ask the caller to excuse you for a moment while you answer the other call. Get approval before you put the caller on *hold*. If the second call is local, get the number and offer to call back, placing the call immediately after completing the first call. If the second call is long distance, explain that you are handling another call and excuse yourself long enough to tell the first caller, "I'll be with you in a minute." Complete the long-distance call as quickly as possible. When you get back to the first call, thank the caller for waiting and apologize for the delay.

When a caller is on hold, make an attempt to get back on the line every 30 seconds to report any additional delay. If there will be a long wait, suggest that you return the call as soon as possible so that company lines are not tied up.

In the event you are on the telephone when the second call comes in, follow the same procedure. Your main concern is to dispatch each call efficiently and courteously.

If you are answering calls for another secretary, answer them with the same smile and competency that you display with your own calls. Record all messages and leave them in a readily accessible place. Later double-check with the secretary to make sure the messages were received and understood.

Precautions for Receiving Long-Distance Calls

Long distance will be used more and more often as travel costs rise. You will receive many such calls. To reduce waiting time, a well-trained caller immediately announces that the call is long distance.

Special efforts should be made to get the person for whom a long-distance call is intended on the line without delay. Before you accept a long-distance collect call, be sure that you have your employer's permission.

If the executive is not available to take a long-distance call, listen carefully and record the message completely and accurately. If you receive a person-to-person call for your employer, give the long-distance operator full information as to when the call should be returned. The operator may ask you to have the executive return the call and give you details about completing the return call. If your employer can be reached at another telephone, either locally or in another city, and you believe that your employer will have no objection to receiving a call there, tell the operator where the call can be transferred. If your telephone is equipped with a call-forwarding feature (see Chapter 12, page 323), transfer the call yourself.

Message-Taking Equipment and Services

Equipment and services are available to ensure that telephone calls are always answered, even when no one is around to cover the phones.

Answering, Recording, and Switching Devices. Automatic answering equipment delivers prerecorded messages. The user makes a recording, telling callers the time of return and asking them to leave a message. Upon returning to the office, a secretary copies the machine's messages onto telephone message forms and gives them to the executive.

One electronic innovation to answering machines enables users to call in, revise their recordings, and listen to their messages. Small businesses, such as real estate and insurance offices, find these answering devices especially advantageous. This equipment is attractive to large users as well.

Telephone Answering Services. Unlike automatic answering devices that merely recite impersonal prerecorded messages, the attendant for a telephone answering service is able to exercise judgment and understanding, personally assisting callers. Many businesses invest in answering services as a way of personalizing their offices during hours they are not open. The secretary in an office using such a service should establish friendly relations with answering service personnel, check with the service immediately upon coming into the office, and provide complete information to attendants when the answering service takes over.

Taped Announcements. Almost every telephone user is familiar with taped announcements that report the time of day, the weather, flight information, market information, movie schedules, and the like. It is possible for a business to develop similar announcements, possibly specifying office hours. Some organizations make taped announcements of advertising messages to play to callers waiting for busy lines to clear.

OUTGOING CALLS

In addition to answering the telephone, the secretary places local and long-distance calls. To do this well, a secretary must know how to get maximum service from telephone directories and telephone operators and how to make the appropriate choices regarding service options.

Telephone Directories

Before placing a call, you must locate the telephone number. Sometimes this takes quite a bit of skill. The telephone directory has two parts: the alphabetical directory (the white pages) contains a complete list of subscribers, their addresses, and telephone numbers; the Yellow Pages (the classified directory) contains a list of businesses under headings that are arranged by product or service. Metropolitan areas often publish two types of Yellow Pages, one for businesses and another for consumers.

The telephone directory is a mine of information. Most directories for large metropolitan areas contain in their introductory pages emergency numbers; community service numbers; instructions for telephoning locally, nationally, and overseas; area codes for major cities in the United States; explanations of various types of service; zones for assessing message unit rates (see page 301); a map showing area code distribution; a local postal zone map; long-distance rates to major cities and hours during which rates apply; facts about telephone services and their costs; helpful hints for finding numbers quickly and easily; explanations of billing; and money-saving tips. Part of these explanations may be repeated in a foreign language if there are enough people in a particular geographical area to justify the translation.

A corporation may find it advantageous to keep a collection of telephone directories of cities in which it conducts a large volume of business in a central location. It is also possible to find out-of-town directories of large cities in some hotels, major travel terminals, and public libraries.

The Alphabetical Directory. You can usually locate numbers in the alphabetical directory quickly, but the exceptions make it necessary for the secretary to know the rules for arranging names in alphabetic sequence. For example, there are 21 columns of the surname *Miller* in one metropolitan directory.

Locating various government offices and public services also requires a knowledge of alphabetic lists. They are generally listed under their proper political subdivisions. City offices are found under the name of the municipality; county offices, under the name of the county; state offices, under the name of the state; and federal offices, under *United States Government.* (Government listings are sometimes found in a special blue section at the end of some directories.) Public schools are usually listed under the municipality, then under a *Board of Education* subentry. Parochial schools are listed individually by name.

Identical main entries (*Miller Jeff*, for example) are listed in alphabetic order according to street names. Numbered streets are listed after named streets in numeric order. (*Eighth Street* would follow rather than precede *Second Street.*)

The Yellow Pages Directory. The Yellow Pages directory is a very helpful reference for the secretary. In metropolitan areas, this classified directory of products and services is usually bound separately from the white pages. If an executive wants to talk with "that air conditioning firm on Church Street," an alert secretary would look in the Yellow Pages under *Air Conditioning Equipment & Systems—Supplies & Parts* and find *Tuttle & Bailey, Inc.*, the only air conditioning firm on Church Street.

You should circle every frequently called telephone number in the directory. You should also jot down numbers you look up just in case you get a busy signal when you first dial them. List new or changed numbers on the proper directory page or in a desk directory.

Personal Telephone Directory. Large organizations provide employees with a company telephone directory that lists the telephone numbers of its employees. In addition to this directory, every secretary should keep a personal, up-to-date directory of outside telephone numbers for the executive. (You can look up a number in a personal telephone directory in ten seconds, about a third of the time required to search a larger directory.) In it are listed alphabetically the names of frequently called persons and firms. A thoughtful secretary places a condensed list of these numbers at the back of the executive's daily calendar, beside the telephone, or pasted to a desk extension.

For your personal directory, it is better to use some kind of card or tab insertion scheme rather than a typed list that makes no provision for the addition of names or for name changes. Any list quickly becomes out of date unless a system is devised that provides for additions and deletions. Most secretaries use a small rotary wheel for mounting their personal directories. For making corrections, some secretaries use peel-off labels. A personal telephone booklet may be obtained from the telephone company or blank pages at the back of a directory's white pages can also be used to list the names and numbers of frequently called persons.

Some people prefer not to have their telephone numbers listed in the city directory. Usually Directory Assistance (Information) will not have these unlisted numbers in its records. Only in exceptional circumstances (with the customer's consent) will the telephone company arrange to complete directory-assisted calls to unlisted numbers. Keeping unlisted numbers in a personal directory becomes doubly important since they cannot be found elsewhere.

Business Promotion Listings. A company may list its telephone number in a directory in several ways to promote business. One way to promote business is to list a special reverse-charge toll number, an 800 number. With an 800 number, charges are automatically billed to the called party. A company may also incorporate its toll-free 800 number into its newspaper and television advertising. To determine if a company has an 800 listing, dial 1-800-555-1212. The operator will give this information to you.[1] Hotels and motels often list their 800 numbers nationally with listings that look like this:

> **SHERATON HOTELS & MOTOR**
> **INNS—**
> Reservation Office StLouisMo
> **No Charge To Calling Party 800 325-3535**

Some companies also list their out-of-town numbers in local directories in the hope that they will promote business even if the caller has to pay for the call.

---

[1]A digest of 800 numbers can be ordered from Toll-Free Digest Company, Box 800, Claverack, NY 12513 (telephone: 800-447-4700).

Special Reverse-Charge Toll Service

A business can make its services easily available by telephone in cities where it has no branch office with a special listing in the telephone directory of those cities. These listings permit the caller to make a call as a local one, and the toll charge is billed to the listed number. For instance, a Yonkers, New York company could have a New York City number listed in the New York City directory.

On such incoming calls, the secretary provides complete and cordial help, but is careful not to waste long-distance time (see page 295).

Local Calls

The procedure of placing local calls varies with the kind of telephone equipment in use. If the desk telephone is a direct outside line, simply dial the telephone number. If the line goes through a switchboard, you either dial 9 for an outside line or ask the switchboard attendant for a line by saying, "Outside, please." When you get a dial tone, dial the number.

Secretaries regularly make two kinds of local calls. They will either phone someone with whom the employer will talk, or they place their own calls. Whatever the case, allow ample time for the party to answer the ring.

When placing a call for your employer that goes through a switchboard, ask for the person and/or extension number. When you are connected, indicate the person with whom your employer wishes to speak and immediately identify your employer as the caller. Say something like: "Mr. Norman, please. Ms. Allen of Allen and Lovell calling." If Mr. Norman is unavailable, ask for a convenient time when Mr. Norman can be reached or leave a message for Mr. Norman to call Ms. Allen back, mentioning a time when Ms. Allen will be in her office. Secretaries should make every effort to avoid "telephone tag." Returning calls because executives keep missing each other wastes time.

Always determine if the executive is ready to take a call before placing it. If the switchboard operator or a secretary asks you to put your employer on the line first, be gracious and follow the request. The person who originates the call should wait for the other to respond.

You should jot down what you want to say before you place a phone call. This will help you avoid the embarrassment of having to call back because you forgot something. You will speak with more confidence and effectiveness and make a better impression by knowing in advance what you are going to say.

Introduce yourself properly. Upon being connected, give your own name and, if desirable, your firm's name: "This is Susan Baer of Allen and Lovell." Making a good impression on people over the telephone is just as important as making a good impression in person. When you initiate a call, telephone etiquette requires that you end the call. Do so pleasantly by saying, "Thank you for the information. Goodbye."

Message Units

Within some metropolitan areas, calls between widely separated locations are not considered local calls or long-distance calls but are individually charged as message-unit calls. A *message unit* is a term that describes a standard base rate used to determine the cost of a call. A table of rates in the front of the directory shows the *number* of message units chargeable between telephone exchanges.

Long-Distance Calls

Every time you pick up your phone, you enter a vast 150-billion-dollar system that connects nearly 200 million telephones in the United States. Long-distance calls can be made to all telephones in the U.S.A. and to most other countries and territories throughout the world as well.

Station to Station. Because of the time and money saved through direct distance dialing, businesses tend to use station-to-station long-distance service, except in cases when it is known that the person to be reached may not be readily located. You should dial station to station when you are willing to talk with anyone who answers the telephone or when you are reasonably sure that the specific person you want to talk to is nearby. Charges begin when the telephone or the switchboard is answered. If the person you want is not immediately available to take the call, charges are assessed while you wait for that person to get on the line. For example, if you are trying to reach someone registered at a hotel, the hotel operator may page the lobby and hotel restaurants if that person is not in his or her room. If the operator cannot locate the guest, the call is still fully chargeable to you.

Person-to-Person. A person-to-person call requires operator assistance and is made when you must talk to a particular person or extension. Charges begin when that person or extension answers.

Placing Long-Distance Calls. Long-distance calls may be made by direct distance dialing or through a long-distance operator. In either case, if the call is answered by someone other than the person for whom it is intended, immediately indicate that the call is long distance so that time and money are not wasted.

Direct Distance Dialing (DDD). Most station-to-station long-distance calls are dialed direct. Usually you dial *1* plus the three-digit *area code*, then the telephone number. When you are dialing a long-distance number within your own area code, dial *1* plus the number.

Specific directions for DDD may be found in the front section of your telephone directory. You can obtain the area code from a letterhead (where it is often included with the address), your personal telephone directory, the front of the telephone directory, or the operator. If you have the area code but do not know the telephone number, dial the prefix *1*, the area code, and the number 555-1212. Tell the directory assistance operator the city and the individual or business you wish to call, and you will be given the number. If there is even a remote possibility of future calls, record both the area code and the telephone number in your personal directory.

Dial the number carefully. If you reach the wrong number on any DDD call, promptly report the error to the operator to avoid all charges for the call. If you are cut off before completing a call, inform the operator so that the charges can be adjusted. Sometimes you get a recorded message telling you that your call has not been completed and asking you to initiate it again. If it is evident that for some reason your call is not going through, dial the operator for help.

Operator-Assisted Calls. If you know the area code and telephone number but wish to call person-to-person, collect, on a credit card (also known as calling card), or to have the call charged to another number, you need only routine operator assistance. Dial *0* (zero), the area code, and the telephone number. When the operator answers:

1. Give the name of the person you are calling for a *person-to-person call.*
2. Say "Collect" and give your name for a *collect call.*
3. Say "Credit card call" and give your credit card number for a *credit card call.*
4. Say "Bill to" and give the area code and telephone number to which the call is to be billed *to charge a call to another number.*

For the convenience of credit card customers, special public telephones for credit card users are available at major airports, in some hotels, and in other heavy traffic areas throughout the country. The user simply inserts the card into a slot, enters *0*, then dials the desired number.

If you require special assistance, dial *0*, state your problem, and give the operator whatever information you have. One secretary had to call an official in Washington, D.C., at two o'clock for an employer who expected to be in the local courthouse near another telephone at that time. The secretary explained the situation to the operator, who placed the call at two o'clock to the courthouse telephone but charged the call to the employer's office telephone. Another secretary was asked to get in touch with A. J. Dearing, who was staying at a Pittsburgh hotel. The secretary told the long-distance operator that the only clue to Dearing's whereabouts was that lodging would be at one of Pittsburgh's better hotels. The operator checked the hotels until Dearing was located. The secretary need not hesitate to ask for this kind of service.

Leave-Word Calls. If the party you are calling is not in, you can request a "leave-word call" through the operator. The operator informs the receiving party to call Operator 6, the code for leave-word calls. When the call is returned, it will be paid by your employer.

Time Zones. Time zones are very important to the secretary in placing long-distance calls. A New York office would not call San Francisco before 12 noon because there would be little likelihood of reaching anyone in the San Francisco office before 9 a.m. Conversely, a secretary in Los Angeles would not place a call to Boston after 2 p.m. It is very likely that the office in Boston would close around 5 p.m. Secretaries who place overseas calls should also become familiar with international time zones.

The map in Illus. 11-4 indicates time zones and area codes for the continental United States and adjacent Canadian provinces. A person placing a long-distance call should plan the call to coincide with the business day in the city called. The time where the call originates determines whether day, evening, or night rates apply.

Relative Costs. Calls dialed directly are much cheaper than person-to-person calls. Having a number at hand and dialing the number yourself saves a great deal of money. Calling at night or on weekends is cheaper than calling during the business day. Knowing the relative costs of different services enables customers to use the telephone economically. A table of long-distance rates to many cities is given in the front of every telephone directory. Rates to places not listed are obtainable from the long-distance operator.

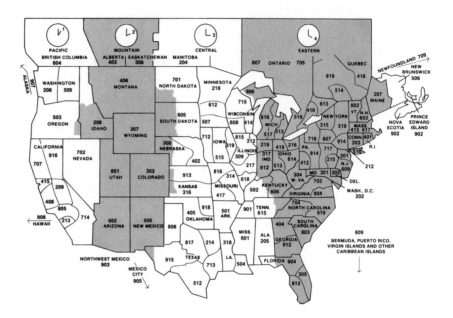

Illus. 11-4
This map shows area codes and standard time zones for the continental United States and Canada.

You must often decide whether to use person-to-person or station-to-station service. You can arrive at the better choice only by considering certain factors, including costs and the whereabouts of the person called. If you were asked to reach a salesperson at the home office, you should probably make a person-to-person call, because the nature of a sales job often requires field work. On the other hand, the manager of a branch office should be in the office most of the time and is usually available to receive a station-to-station call.

Businesses have several options for controlling the costs of long-distance telephoning. Some computer-controlled telephone systems automatically select the least expensive long-distance line for a call. If the least costly outside line is busy, the caller is rung back when the line is available and the number is automatically dialed by the computerized telephone system. Other telephones automatically give priority for long-distance lines to the caller holding the highest rank so that an executive's time spent on long-distance calls is reduced.

Paying for Long Distance. A secretary may be responsible for accepting long-distance charges, accounting for them, reversing them, or obtaining a credit card for an executive on which to charge calls. Many secretaries have found that keeping a record of outgoing long-distance calls (similar to the one shown in Illus. 11-5) helps verify calls and charges.

RECORD OF OUTGOING LONG-DISTANCE CALLS

	Time		Type of Call			Person Called				Caller
Date	Begun	Ended	P/P	S/S	Other	Name	Affiliation	City	Phone #	
8/16	9:45	10:23	✓			Johanna Layman	ARC Corp.	Cleveland	216-321-0995	McDuff

P/P   Person to Person
S/S   Station to Station

Illus. 11-5
In order to verify long-distance calls secretaries often keep a record of pertinent data regarding them.

Obtaining Charges on Toll Calls. Charges for long-distance calls are referred to as *toll charges.* If you need to know the cost of a call, ask the operator *at the time the call is placed* to report the charges. After the call is completed and the cost is calculated, the operator will notify you of the charge. This service is not available on DDD calls.

Cost Records of Toll Calls. For accounting purposes, most companies charge toll calls to specific departments, clients, or jobs. Using records kept at the secretary's desk toll charges can be checked against a bill and charged to the proper departments. Modern equipment performs this accounting function automatically.

The federal government levies an excise tax on long-distance calls. The telephone company collects this tax from subscribers. Tax rates are shown on the customer's bill. A cost record of each long-distance call for accounting purposes requires that this tax be computed and added to each toll charge.

Collect Calls. Long-distance calls (toll calls) can be made *collect;* that is, charges for person-to-person and station-to-station calls can be reversed (or charged) to the number called rather than to the caller. The request to reverse charges, however, must be made at the time the call is placed so that the person called can have an opportunity to accept or refuse the charges. Because collect calls are operator assisted, they are more expensive than DDD calls.

Telephone Credit Cards. Executives who make telephone calls while away from the office may carry telephone credit cards on which to charge calls to their companies. These cards use a code number to initiate calls through the operator or through special credit card telephones. Monthly telephone bills identify credit card calls as such.

LONG-DISTANCE CARRIERS

American Telephone & Telegraph Company had a virtual monopoly over the telephone industry since its inception. Today the industry is deregulated. A number of communication carriers now compete in the direct-dial segment of the long-distance market. In addition to AT&T, the industry leader, MCI Telecommunications Corp., GTE, American Telephone Exchange, and Western Union, to mention a few, provide long-distance service.

Using the new long-distance carriers is relatively simple. By notifying their local telephone company of their preferred long-distance carrier, customers use 1 + the area code + the telephone number to dial long-distance calls with that carrier. This arrangement is known as equal access. Some customers who use more than one carrier must enter a special five-digit company identification code before dialing long distance. The long-distance calls of customers who do not choose a long-distance service are divided up among long-distance carriers according to the proportion of customers who made choices.

DOMESTIC TELEGRAMS

It is frequently necessary in business to send an urgent but brief message. Because they have an attention-getting advantage over letters and telephone calls, telegrams, the oldest form of electronic mail, are often appropriate for these communications. Businesses often use telegrams to confirm bids or approve contracts. Messages might also be sent via a telegram to register a personal opinion with an elected official.

There are two kinds of telegrams: regular and overnight. A *regular telegram* can be sent at any time, day or night, any day of the week. The charge is based on a ten-word minimum, excluding the address and signature. An additional charge is made for each word over ten words. The *overnight telegram* is seldom used because its rate structure is very similar to the regular telegram, and to some extent, it has been replaced by the *Mailgram*. Overnight telegrams are accepted up to 12 midnight for next-day delivery prior to 2 p.m.

Western Union assures delivery of telegrams by telephone usually within two hours. If messenger delivery is required, delivery to most points is assured within five hours; however, a delivery charge is assessed. A report of delivery is available for an additional fee.

Telegram messages may be personally taken or phoned in to a Western Union office. If the message will be taken to a Western Union office, type it on plain paper, company stationery, or a Western Union form. Compose a message that is brief. Avoid ambiguous messages. Saying, for example, "Arrive Monday on the 3:30 flight" does not indicate whether the flight will arrive in the morning or in the afternoon, nor does it indicate the airport or the airline. Use action verbs, avoid unnecessary adjectives, and use numbers instead of words. An example of a clearly worded telegram appears in Illus. 11-6.

If you phone in the message, an operator will type it as it is recorded. Collect complete information before making the call, including the spelling of all names, correct addresses (street, city, state, and ZIP Code) and telephone numbers, and billing information.

If your office does not have a Telex or TWX but the addressee's office does, you can reduce expenses by sending the telegram to the recipient's teletypewriter. (The Western Union operator can obtain the Telex or TWX number.) Mailgrams, Telex, and TWX are discussed in greater detail in Chapter 12.

Follow these guidelines when typing a telegram:

1. Type telegrams in all caps.
2. Prepare a file copy for every telegram. In most cases you will need a copy for your files, one for the accounting department, and (if a confirmation copy is to be mailed) one for the addressee.

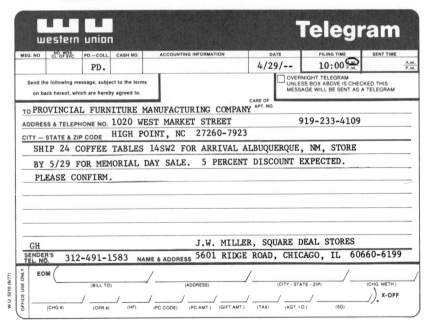

Illus. 11-6
Telegrams may be typed at your desk on plain paper, on a letterhead, or on a form provided by Western Union.

3. Indicate the type of service desired.
4. Include your reference initials in the lower left-hand corner.
5. Include all essential information in the address, including the telephone number.
6. Omit the salutation and complimentary close.
7. To save money, learn and follow Western Union practices for counting letters, words, and symbols:
    a. Dictionary words in any language are counted as one word each, regardless of length.
    b. Figures and nondictionary words, such as *rehab*, *Solarbilt*, *scam*, or *Earthsafe*, are counted at the rate of five characters to the word.
    c. Personal names are counted according to the number of words and initials.
    d. Punctuation marks are neither counted nor charged for regardless of where they appear in the message. Words, such as *Stop*, that are used instead of punctuation marks are charged as words.
    e. Letters, figures, and symbols are counted as fewer characters if written without spaces. For example, NY is one character, but N Y or N. Y. is counted as two characters; 9a.m. is one character, but 9 a. m. is three.
    f. A signature may consist of *any two* of the following items: name of sender, sender's title, name of department, or name of organization. This signature is sent without extra charge.

INTERNATIONAL TELEGRAPH COMMUNICATIONS

Overseas telegrams are sent by underwater cables or by satellite. International messages to land stations are collected and distributed by such companies as Western Union International, Inc., RCA Global Communications, Inc., and ITT Corporation. (Do not confuse the domestic Western Union Telegraph Co. with Western Union International, Inc. These organizations are completely separate and unrelated.) International messages may also be sent by Telex or TWX from your office or by telephone. Communications networks are also available to send messages between ships and shore by radio.

All destinations are not served by all overseas companies. To obtain the fastest service, ask Western Union International for the most direct route before filing an international telegram. However, if you know a preferred route, include the name of the carrier (via ITT, for example) with your message so that it will not be sent to a pool where messages are apportioned equally among carriers, regardless of which carrier provides the most direct route. Designating a carrier is not chargeable.

International time zones should be considered in sending telegrams overseas. Delivery to countries in certain time zones can differ from the country of origin by more than a day. Illus. 11-7 provides a map of the world's standard time zones. You should also be aware that businesses in some countries close at midday and observe shorter office hours, different holidays, and different workdays. You should determine this information prior to filing so that your telegram will reach its destination during working hours.

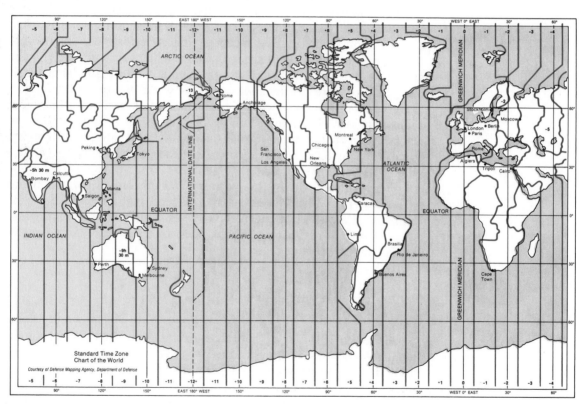

Illus. 11-7
Zones in east longitude are numbered in sequence from 1 to 12 and labeled *minus*; zones in west longitude are numbered 1 to 12 and labeled *plus*. To obtain Greenwich time, the zone number in each zone is either added to or subtracted from the standard time in accordance with its plus or minus sign. For example, Chicago is in the +6 zone. When it is 9:00 a.m. in Chicago, add six hours to determine the Greenwich time of 3:00 p.m. Tokyo is in the −9 zone. When it is 10:00 a.m. in Tokyo, subtract nine hours to determine the Greenwich time of 1:00 a.m.

The Full Rate International Telegram

The full rate telegram is the only class of international telegrams (or cablegrams). Except for the destination country, each word in the name, address, message, and signature is counted as a chargeable word. Codes and ciphers are permissible. One code word may mean several plain language words and, therefore, lowers the cost of the cablegram. Code words are composed entirely of letters. They may be real or artificial words, but they must not contain more than five letters. For example, the code word *KALOP* may be used to cover these statements: *We authorize you to act for us. Will confirm this by mail.* Illus. 11-8 provides some guidelines for producing international telegrams.

Ciphers used for secrecy are usually composed of more than five figures or letters. Cipher words do not fulfill the requirements of either code or plain language. In a message that contains a combination of code, cipher, and plain language, the code and cipher words are charged at the rate of five characters to the word, while plain language is charged at the rate of fifteen letters to the word. Because every word is charged when sending a cable, companies often register a one-word cable address with the telegraph office. Addresses already on file cannot be duplicated. You will notice one-word cable addresses printed on some company letterheads. Record these addresses for future reference when you encounter them.

Frequently a firm in this country and its foreign correspondent will register an identical cable address and restrict its use to the exchange of messages between themselves. This procedure, known as a *reversible address*, eliminates the need for a signature on messages, thus saving the cost of one word.

Other International Services

Although you will probably be concerned mostly with international telegrams, you should know that your organization may use international leased wires to telephone overseas and international Telex for written message transmittal. These services will be performed by special attendants with whom you will work in sending messages overseas.

Improved technology allows equipment used to transmit messages to serve different functions. During business hours, this equipment can be used to transact regular international business communications; during off-hours, it can be used to transmit large volumes of data overseas.

HOW TO PREPARE AN INTERNATIONAL TELEGRAM

Type your city and state.	ATLANTA GA
Type FR (full rate, for immediate delivery).	FR
or LT (lower-rate service, for next day delivery; not available to every country).	LT
Type the registered cable address or the addressee's name and address.	SMITHCO or SMITH COMPANY 14 BAYSWATER ROAD
Type the overseas city and country. Enclose the country name in parentheses.	LONDON (ENGLAND)
Type the text of your message in caps.	TEXT OF YOUR MESSAGE
Type NNNN to indicate the end of your overseas message.	NNNN

Note: In an international telegram, the following symbols must be transmitted in an equivalent form as illustrated.

In Place of:	*Type:*
Dollar Sign ($)	DOLLAR, DLRS, DOLS, or DLS
Cent Sign (¢)	CENTS
Number Sign (#)	NUMBER or POUNDS
Ampersand (&)	AND
Percent Sign (%)	0/0 or PERCENT
Fractions ($\frac{1}{2}$)	Numbers with a slash (1/2)
Quotation Marks (")	Two aprostophe signs (") or UNQUOTE
Semicolon (;)	SEMICOLON
@	AT
Roman Numerals	4, FOUR, or ROMAN 4
Lowercase Letters	UPPERCASE LETTERS

Illus. 11-8
An international telegram must be prepared according to these specifications.

SUMMARY

A very important responsibility of the secretary is handling the business telephone efficiently and courteously. Telephone equipment may be quite basic: a single line with a rotary dial or push-button pad. A key telephone with multiline service may also be used. The advantage of a key telephone is that the secretary can make or receive several calls simultaneously from both inside and outside the office.

The secretary who displays an attractive telephone personality is an asset to any office. Ease in conducting pleasant, effective telephone conversations comes with experience, proper training, and the knowledge of telephone etiquette. Distinct enunciation is a necessity.

In answering incoming calls, the secretary follows the executive's preferences. How you answer your telephone depends upon whether it is connected directly to an outside line or to a company switchboard. Some executives prefer that the secretary screen all calls. In this case, the secretary must learn the identification of the caller before putting the executive on the line. Getting this information is often a task in itself.

When the executive is unavailable to take phone calls, the secretary takes complete messages and records all incoming calls. A telephone message form is used for this purpose. If a call is to be transferred to another office, the secretary should make every effort to be helpful to the caller. If a caller is placed on *hold*, get back to the caller every half minute to report the length of the delay.

Long-distance calls have priority over other calls. The secretary immediately informs the executive of long-distance calls and follows the executive's instructions for handling them.

Secretaries obtain telephone numbers from a telephone directory (white or Yellow Pages), a company directory, or their own records. Long-distance calls are made station-to-station or person-to-person. The secretary is expected to know the relative costs of these options and when to use them. Many offices also require that the secretary maintain a record of all long-distance calls for accounting purposes. With the deregulation of the communications industry, new long-distance carriers are now competing for the direct-dial segment of the long-distance market. Secretaries should be familiar with the carrier their companies prefer to use to make long-distance calls.

When an urgent but brief documented message is required, a telegraphic message is often appropriate. There are two classes of domestic telegrams: regular and overnight. The urgency of the message will determine which type is selected. Techniques for typing a telegraphic message are discussed in this chapter.

International telegrams (or cablegrams) are sent full rate. The secretary must consider time differences when filing a cablegram. If one is on file with the telegraph office, a one-word cable address is often used to reduce the cost of an international telegram.

SUGGESTED READINGS

Branchaw, Bernadine, and Joel Bowman. *Office Procedures for the Professional Secretary*. Chicago: SRA, Inc., 1984. See especially pp. 283-286.

Brochures on specialized topics are available from your local telephone company for distribution to schools and businesses.

From Nine to Five. Chicago: Dartnell Corp. Semimonthly pamphlets on specialized topics. Available from Dartnell Corp., 4660 Ravenswood Ave., Chicago, IL 60640.

McFarland, Emmett. *Secretarial Procedures*, Office Administration and Automated Systems. Reston, VA: Reston Publishing Co., Inc., 1985.

Office Topics. Fairfield, CT: The Economics Press. A biweekly pamphlet sold in quantity to organizations for in-service training.

U.S. Department of Commerce, Office of Consumer Affairs in association with the Bell Atlantic Companies. *A Consumer's Guide to Telephone Service*. Washington: Government Printing Office.

QUESTIONS FOR DISCUSSION

1. Reword the following sentences to reflect better telephone usage.
   a. Sorry, I don't know where Miss Schwartz is. She should be at her desk.
   b. We don't give that information out to the public.
   c. You should have called the purchasing department for that information.
   d. I don't know who handles employee insurance, but Mr. Wallenstein doesn't.
   e. Miss Lombardi is in a conference with the tax consultant.
   f. I haven't got time to look it up, Mr. Kenyon. I have to get this report ready for the committee meeting in 20 minutes.
   g. I haven't the foggiest. I'll ask Marge to fill me in on what happened at that meeting.
   h. Oh, I gave you the wrong information. I thought you were Professor Milligan of New State College. She is writing a book on the same subject.

2. Think of business telephone calls in which you have taken part. Describe techniques used by the other party that pleased you and those that annoyed you.

3. In order to get information from an incoming caller you delay stating whether the executive is available to take the call until you have the identification of the caller. What risk are you taking in using this approach?

4. Examine your local telephone directory. What information is found in its introductory pages? in the Yellow Pages?

5. If your office is located in Philadelphia, between what hours (yours) would you try to reach an office in Salt Lake City by long distance? If your office is in Salt Lake City, between what hours (yours) would you try to reach a Philadelphia office?

6. Which class of long-distance service should you use in trying to reach each of the following persons?
    a. A buyer in a department store
    b. A lawyer who is pleading an important case
    c. A politician who is staying in a hotel at which you made the reservation
    d. Your employer's son who lives in a college dormitory not equipped with Centrex
    e. The city editor of a newspaper

7. Do you think that organizations should adopt a no-personal-telephone-calls policy? Why?

8. Assuming that the following words come at the end of a typewritten page, indicate those words that you can correctly divide by showing where you could make the divisions. Check the Reference Guide to verify and correct your answers.
    a. Among
    b. Edited
    c. Couldn't
    d. Delicate
    e. Filling
    f. September 20
    g. Self-starter

PROBLEMS

1. Locate the numbers for the following in your local telephone directory. Type a list showing the organization or department wanted, the name under which the telephone number is listed, and the telephone number for each item in tabular form.
    a. City hall
    b. Western Union

  c. Fire department
  d. Park or recreation department
  e. Police department
  f. Post office
  g. Public library
  h. Your college or university
  i. The local office of the state employment service
  j. Telephone repair service
  k. Weather information
2. Type a list showing the heading in the Yellow Pages under which you would find the names of subscribers for each of the following:
  a. Office supplies
  b. Windshield repair
  c. Exercise centers
  d. Dry cleaners
3. Type the following excerpts of conversation in acceptable form. Use the Reference Guide to verify and correct your answers.
  a. The opening part of this telephone conversation occurred this Monday, shortly before noon. Mr. Lawrence Bell called Mr. Thomas Green. Bell—Tom, have you come to a decision yet? Green—No, I'd like a day or two more to think it over. Bell—Time is getting short, Tom. I have to know by Wednesday at the latest. Green—I'll sleep on it and let you know the first thing in the morning.
  b. A confidential memorandum to the president of the company reports a conversation that occurred in the executive's office two weeks ago between Steve Douglas and Charlene Duncan: Steve said I talked it over with Nelson, very confidentially, of course, and he thought he could arrange a meeting before the end of this month. Charlene said do you think it was wise to expose our hand. Steve said I don't think talking it over with Nelson can be called exposing our hand. He's trustworthy. Charlene said well it's done now. What about the meeting?
4. Rewrite each of the following messages, using not more than ten words.
  a. THERE WILL BE A SALES MEETING SATURDAY MORNING IN THE OFFICE AT TEN O'CLOCK. PLEASE ARRANGE TO BE THERE. BRING REQUESTED ESTIMATES.
  b. MR. WILCOX WIRED SAYING HE WOULD BE HERE TOMORROW. IS IT POSSIBLE FOR YOU TO COME BACK? MUST KNOW BY THREE O'CLOCK.
  c. IN ANSWER YOUR TELEGRAM SUGGEST YOU OFFER A 40% DISCOUNT TERMS 2% 10 DAYS. DELIVERY TO BE MADE FOB NEW YORK.

5.   Miss Mary Holmes, secretary to Harry Miller, handled the following telephone calls:

a. Mr. Miller was attending a luncheon meeting at the Terrace Hotel and expected back at his desk at 1:30 p.m. At 12:15 his superior phoned long distance from Boston. Miss Holmes said, "Mr. Miller will not be back until 1:30 and cannot be reached until then."

b. At closing time, the long-distance operator had not reached a person with whom Mr. Miller must talk before the next morning. Mr. Miller was going to dinner at his brother's home but would be at his own home until 7 p.m. Miss Holmes said, "Operator, try that number again and keep trying until 7:00 p.m. Mr. Miller will be at 555-8973 in half an hour and will be there until seven."

c. Mr. Miller was playing golf. The long-distance operator informed Miss Holmes that she had a call from Mr. Miller's New York broker, Mr. Adams, who wanted to talk to him as soon as possible. Miss Holmes said, "Mr. Miller is out of the office for the afternoon. If you will tell me where Mr. Adams can be reached, I will try to get in touch with Mr. Miller and ask him to call back immediately. I should be able to reach him within an hour."

d. Mr. Miller was writing copy for an advertising circular and told Miss Holmes that he did not wish to be disturbed under any circumstances before four o'clock. A long-distance call came in from George Herman, his assistant, who was in Baltimore attending a sales conference. Mr. Herman was to leave Baltimore on a three o'clock plane. Miss Holmes told the long-distance operator, "I am sorry, but Mr. Miller can't be reached this afternoon. Ask Mr. Herman if I can help him instead. I am Mr. Miller's secretary."

e. Mr. Miller wanted to make a long-distance call from the office telephone, 555-2219, to Dr. L. K. Holthaus of New Orleans on a personal matter. Miss Holmes did not know Dr. Holthaus's number, but she knew that he was a noted ophthalmologist. She dialed the operator and said, "Operator, this is 555-2219. I want to call Dr. L. K. Holthaus in New Orleans. I do not have the number, but he is a well-known eye specialist. Will you give me the area code and the number, please, so that I can dial him direct."

f. Mr. Miller wanted to call Ms. Houston in the purchasing department of the Acme Company in White Plains, New York, area code 914. Mr. Miller wished to say that on Friday afternoon he would call on either Ms. Houston or her assistant about the new service contract. Could one of them be available for a conference? Miss Holmes made an operator-assisted call.

g. Mr. Miller wanted to call his wife, who was visiting in Akron, Ohio. Her number was 555-0753 and the area code was 216. He said that it need not be a person-to-person call; but he wanted the call charged to his home number, 555-8973. Miss Holmes said, "Operator, this is 555-2219. I want to place a call to 555-0753 in Akron, Ohio. Don't charge the call to this number. It should be charged to 555-8973."

h. Mr. Miller wanted to call Lawrence Taylor of the Lenox Supply Company in Los Angeles about the cancellation of an order. The number was 555-6501; the area code number, 213; the charges were to be reversed. Miss Holmes said, "Operator, this is 555-2219. I want to place a call to Lawrence Taylor of the Lenox Supply Company in Los Angeles. I don't know the number. Tell the switchboard operator there that Mr. Miller won't pay for the call because it is about an order he plans to cancel. Ask Mr. Taylor to pay for it."

i. While Miss Holmes was on the key telephone, a second call came through. She excused herself and answered the second call, which was for Mr. Miller. She depressed the local button to ask Mr. Miller if he would take the call and then transferred it to his line. When she returned to the first call, she found that the caller had been disconnected.

Miss Holmes was surprised when Mr. Miller told her that he had arranged for her to take a five-hour course to improve her telephone technique. She had always thought that she was unusually proficient in this area. Criticize Miss Holmes's handling of the nine calls described above. Indicate what you would have done in the cases that were poorly handled.

Chapter 12

Communication Systems and Services

Chapter 11 discussed the proper techniques for handling the business telephone. You also learned how to prepare and send telegraphic messages. This chapter describes the technological advancements that have been made in the transmission of business communications which every secretary must understand in order to function effectively in the changing office environment.

In the early 1980s, American Telephone & Telegraph Company (AT&T), which had long been the major supplier of telephone transmission services for home and industry, was divided up into a number of smaller organizations. AT&T divested itself of its "Bell System," turning over the day-to-day operation of providing telephone service and equipment to regional telephone companies. Since the AT&T breakup, hundreds of firms have entered the communication industry, producing a bewildering array of equipment and offering a variety of services to individual consumers and to businesses. As a result, office managers and secretaries are challenged to make decisions that will provide the office with the most efficient and the most cost-effective communication system available. Because communication technologies are still developing, these decisions are not easily made.

This chapter begins by defining telecommunications. A discussion of communication networks and information transmission technologies follows. Specific telephone systems, special services, electronic mail, and voice mail are also explained in detail in this chapter.

TELECOMMUNICATIONS DEFINED

The technical meaning of the term *telecommunications* is still evolving. In its broadest sense, telecommunications is the electronic transmission of communication from one location to another. Electronically transmitted communications can take five different forms: data, text, image (maps, graphics, pictures), voice, and video.

Information Technologies and Communication Networks

Developments in the field of electronics have created new and efficient ways of circulating business information. When automation was introduced to the business office, each piece of equipment performed only one function. Each had its own separate technology. The telephone, for instance, only transmitted voices. The computer only processed digital (numeric) data. Secretaries typed dictated material for executives in an immediate area, and the transcripts were sent by conventional means to another location. Reprographic equipment only served to reproduce information at one point.

Today information technologies are integrated. The capabilities of formerly one-function machines have merged. Electronically generated messages can be composed, edited, transmitted, reproduced, distributed, and filed in a fraction of the time that it takes to send a conventional business letter through the mail or to complete a typical telephone conversation. Mail can be electronically "picked up" from the equipment in which it is stored at the convenience of the recipient. It is possible not only to transmit voice, data, image, and text to one or several locations electronically, but to merge all four kinds of information at one receiving point.

Messages may appear on a CRT for reading, be stored in a computer's memory for later recall, or be printed out as hard copy. With the appropriate equipment, all forms of information (handwritten or typed messages, processed/unprocessed data, charts, or voice messages) can be transmitted from point of origin to any distant point or points equipped with the appropriate receiving equipment.

The integration of information technologies, which permits separate technologies to communicate with each other, is often made possible by *networking*. Networking, the linking of computers and peripheral equipment across distances through various communication carriers, occurs on a local and a global scale.

Local Area Networks. Independent of public communication networks, a *local area network* (LAN) provides the means for connecting many types of electronic office equipment into a single system within a one-half-mile radius. Mainframe computers, personal computers, terminals, word processors, and printers, for example, within a building or a complex can be linked by cable to exchange information. In addition, resources, such as the memory of a mainframe computer and the capabilities of a high-speed printer, can be shared. Xerox's Ethernet communication network and Wang's Wang Net are two examples of local area networks.

Wide Area Networks. Besides an internal communication system, many businesses also need access to an external or global communication system. Local area networks (LANs) can tie into a larger network to enable a business to communicate over a greater geographical region. With a *wide area* or *global network*, electronic equipment can communicate within a given city, to another city, or to a foreign country. A business can communicate with its branch offices and with other business firms as well. Satellite and microwave communication systems permit wide area networks.

Transmission Technologies

Methods of electronic transmission include the following technologies: analog and digital transmission, cable and fiber optics, and microwave and satellite communication. While any discussion of these methods could be highly technical, the descriptions which follow will acquaint you with the processes.

Analog and Digital Transmission. Certain communication networks transmit information in either an analog or a digital mode. *Analog signals* transmit data in continuous, smooth sound waves. Voice communication networks, such as telephone lines, are in analog mode. Computer data, on the other hand, is transmitted in the form of *digital signals*; that is, discrete on/off signals. In order for voice and data transmission to be sent over the same network, it must be possible to convert analog signals to digital signals and vice versa. Conversions are made by the use of *modems* (modulator/demodulator) at both sending and receiving locations. A modem converts a digital signal to analog form or an analog signal to a digital form. For instance, an office with only analog transmission (voice) facilities would use a modem to convert digital signals from a computer to analog mode for transmission over its analog line. At the receiving location, a modem would convert the analog signals back to digital form for use by the computer. Illus. 12-1 depicts this exchange of signals.

Digital transmission is regarded as more efficient because it has the capability of sending large quantities of information at very rapid speeds. Most businesses are replacing old analog lines with digital lines. AT&T is also gradually changing over to digital transmission. The development of digital systems for simultaneous voice and data transmission is forecast for the future.

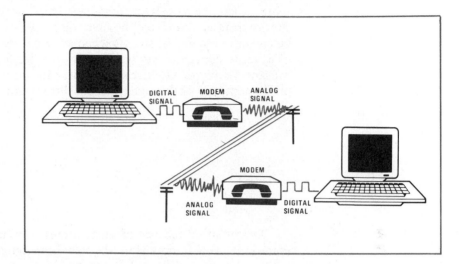

Illus. 12-1
Modems are used to convert digital signals into analog signals for transmission over telephone lines.

Cable and Fiber Optics. The most popular medium through which electrical signals for voice and data communication are transmitted is copper cable. Telephone lines, wire cables twisted into pairs, are an example of cable transmission technology. Computer-generated data are also transmitted to other locations by direct links through cables. A new transmission method, fiber optics, can be used to transmit either analog or digital information. Fiber optics may soon replace the copper cable as a major transmission medium. The fiber optics medium can transmit a greater volume of communication and offers greater security than copper cables. Fiber optics are thin glass-like tubes which transmit light. Electrical signals are first converted to light pulses, then sent over the fiber optics medium. At the receiving station, the light impulses are returned to their electrical signal state.

Microwave and Satellite Communication. The long-distance high-speed transmission of information has been made possible by the development of microwave and satellite technologies. Microwave communications are sent by on-the-ground transmission towers. These towers are strategically located 30 miles apart across the country. Signals are relayed from one tower's antenna to another's until the signals reach their final destination.

Orbiting satellites are a variation of the microwave relay tower system. Generally positioned over 23,000 miles above the earth, they transmit signals in space. Satellite communication is worldwide. In the mid 1980s, approximately 20 satellites were orbiting the earth. Digital signals are sent from earth stations to the satellite which rebroadcasts the signals for transmission to another earth station. Like the other transmission technologies discussed earlier, voice signals can be converted to digital signals when sending and receiving microwave or satellite communication. Many businesses lease or rent the use of microwave and/or satellite communication services through the telephone company or through other satellite communication companies.

TELEPHONE SYSTEMS

Despite the number of alternatives available to businesses for communicating information, the telephone remains the most popular means of communication between two or more persons. The breakup of AT&T has fueled the competition among manufacturers that provide telephone equipment and systems to businesses.

Key Systems

The *key system* links a group of key telephones. Each key telephone permits the user to select an outside or an intercom line. Each individual key telephone also has the same capability of receiving, initiating, and holding calls. Intercom lines are used for conversations and for paging purposes.

AT&T's Com Key 416, shown in Illus. 12-2, is an example of an electronic key system. This system has an ultimate capacity of 16 stations, 4 central office lines, and 2 intercom paths. It has distinctive ringing features so that the secretary is alerted to the type of call being answered. It is possible to set up multiline conferences among the phones in the system by depressing buttons simultaneously. Two people may also converse with each other over the intercom.

A more sophisticated system developed at AT&T is the Merlin. It is equipped with a microprocessor and is software based. Each telephone has buttons for outside lines and buttons for programming Merlin's features. Among its programmable features are automatic dialing, privacy (no one can hear or interrupt a call), and do not disturb (no calls can ring on that phone). The Merlin system can be expanded with additional outside lines, telephones, and custom features.

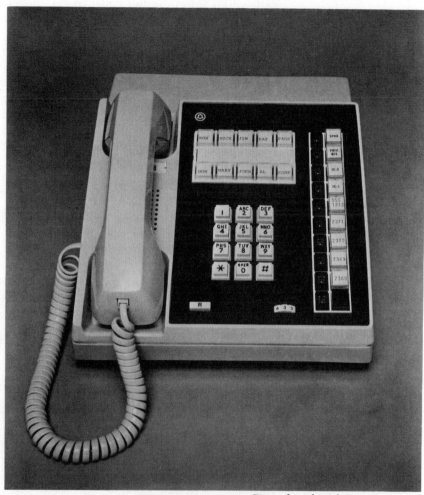

Illus. 12-2
AT&T's Com Key
416 permits users
to select a number
of intercom lines
and a number of
outside lines.

PBX (Private Branch Exchange) Systems

Many businesses have sufficient phone traffic to justify some type of central switchboard. A *PBX system* is found in organizations that have more than 25 telephone extensions. The attendant answers incoming calls and forwards them by touching a button on an electronic console (switchboard). PBX systems offer many features, one of which is *Direct Outward Dialing* (DOD). To place outgoing calls, the caller dials 9 (or another code) to get an outside line, then dials the desired phone number. The assistance of an attendant is not needed in making outgoing or internal calls.

Today's PBX systems, also referred to as *private automatic branch exchanges*, are computer controlled. These systems accept and transmit analog signals. They can be purchased or leased from AT&T or from any number of equipment manufacturers. A computerized telephone system permits a company to acquire new features through periodic enhancements to the computer program. These add-on features (enhancements) can be customized to fit telephone arrangements in each organization.

A more recent development in PBX systems is the *digital PBX*. It has integrated voice and data transmission capabilities. The digital PBX is regarded as a major support component to local area networks (LANs). An example of a digital PBX console appears in Illus. 12-3.

Illus. 12-3
State-of-the-art PBX systems incorporate digital technology to provide secretaries and management a host of information/communication capabilities.

Reproduced with permission of
AT&T Corporate Archive

Centrex (Central Exchange) Systems

One of the frustrations of the modern office is the difficulty of getting through the switchboard. To circumvent this problem, many companies have installed *Direct Inward Dialing (DID)*. Using *Centrex*, or *central exchange*, every telephone in a company has its own seven-digit telephone number. Any caller can direct-dial this seven-digit number from an outside telephone, bypassing the switchboard. Direct calls can be made within a company to any extension in a Centrex system by dialing the last four digits.

Additional features of Centrex include the identification of all outgoing calls. This feature allows the accounting department to apportion long-distance calls and no-charge interoffice calls to the right telephone. It is also possible for one secretary to screen calls to several Centrex numbers.

SPECIAL SERVICES/EQUIPMENT

In addition to basic telephone service, there are many additional telecommunication services available through telephone companies and other equipment manufacturers that directly affect the secretary. Some of these special services and equipment represent significant advances in the communications market, involving savings in time and costs.

Incoming Toll-Free Calling

Through its 800 Service, AT&T offers subscribers volume-discounted long-distance service for *incoming* calls on either an intrastate or interstate basis. For the caller, 800 Service represents toll-free calling by dialing 1 + 800 + the designated phone number. This service is particularly attractive to businesses who want their customers to have easy access to them and their services. Subscribers choose from six levels of coverage based on geographic zones, known as service areas. Service Area 6, which is the broadest service area, includes the continental United States, Alaska, Puerto Rico, and the Virgin Islands. Lower-numbered service areas provide service to narrower geographic zones and lower cost per unit of use. All AT&T 800 Service customers are entitled to a free listing in either the Business or Consumer edition of the *AT&T 800 Service Directory*.

Wide Area Telecommunications Service (WATS)

AT&T also offers volume-discounted long-distance service for *outgoing* calls via its Wide Area Telecommunications Service (WATS). In addition to a tapered discount based on usage, WATS provides time of day and day of week price discounts as well. Like 800 Service, there are six service areas. The broadest coverage, Service Area 6, includes the continental United States, Puerto Rico, the Virgin Islands, Hawaii, and Alaska. Lower-numbered service areas provide WATS service to narrower geographic zones and lower unit prices. In addition to voice, WATS can be used to transmit data and graphics. Similar WATS-like services are also available through other long-distance carriers.

Leased (or Private) Lines

It is possible for a company to lease telegraph and telephone lines for its exclusive use. Special *tie lines* can be used to connect various locations of a business complex in different parts of the same city or in different cities. They provide direct voice contact between separate units of a business and also transmit data. A tie line can connect switchboards, key telephones, and regular telephones. It provides unlimited calling at a fixed monthly charge and is always reserved for the exclusive use of the subscriber.

Many organizations lease private telephone channels for calling their foreign branches or other companies. Volume determines whether leasing lines is cost effective.

Foreign Exchange Service (FX)

A local telephone number can be listed in the directory of a city that is remote from a plant or company headquarters so that calls made to the listed number go through as local calls. For example, the New York City directory might carry the number of a firm located in New Brunswick, New Jersey. The company's New York City clients can, in effect, make local calls to New Brunswick, because the New Brunswick company picks up the long-distance charge. FX does *not* refer to international calls.

Mobile (Cellular) Service

Mobile telephones use radio signals to transmit conversations between individuals in locations remote from the traditional office setting (in trucks and cars, for example). The equipment is made by a number of manufacturers and sold primarily through cellular service carriers. Anyone can make a call to a mobile phone from any telephone, and any telephone can receive a call from a mobile unit. Conversations travel partway by radio and partway by telephone wire through given geographical areas called *cells*. Each cell has a radio transmitter and control equipment that links mobile telephones to computers and the local telephone system.

Pagers

Unlike cellular phones, which permit two-way conversations, *pagers* are signaling devices that alert the holder to contact a predetermined phone number for messages. Pagers are small units that can be attached to a belt or kept in a pocket or in a handbag. A caller activates the pager by dialing a special telephone number. The beeping sound of the pager signals the holder to return the call. Some units have the capability of giving short messages. Others can display the caller's phone number. Pagers are very popular with executives who are often away from the office, yet must keep in contact with office personnel for messages and/or instructions.

Touch-Tone Service

Touch-Tone service utilizes the 12-button push-button telephone. Ten buttons are reserved for dialing numbers zero to nine; two additional buttons allow direct access to a computer center, a dictating center, or other service centers. Touch-Tone phones permit data to be entered into computers via tone transmission.

The Touch-a-matic Telephone

The *Touch-a-matic telephone* has an electronic memory. Frequently called numbers can be stored in the phone's memory and dialed at the touch of a single button. The Touch-a-matic telephone is also equipped with a *last-person-called-button* that enables users to recall the person last talked to before a new number is dialed. An example of a Touch-a-matic phone appears in Illus. 12-4.

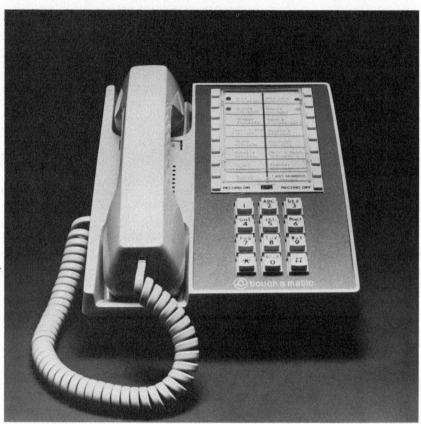

Illus. 12-4
Touch-a-matic
telephone allows
automatic single
button connection
with any of 15
frequently dialed
numbers.

Reproduced with permission of
AT&T Corporate Archive

The Speakerphone

The *speakerphone* has a built-in transmitter and volume control to permit both sides of a telephone conversation to be amplified. The secretary can leave the telephone, walk to the opposite side of the office, look up information in a file, and read it to the caller from this location. Users can hear comments and discussions among several people without being tied to the telephone receiver. The speakerphone expands opportunities for full communication during conference calls. It also makes it possible to deliver lectures over the telephone and have them amplified to classes or conference groups. An example of a speakerphone appears in Illus. 12-5.

Conference Calls

The amount of time that executives spend traveling to and from meetings, combined with the increasing expense of airfare and lodging, make conference calls a particularly cost-effective communication tool. Recent innovations have made it possible to set up conference calls without the assistance of an operator. If your company does not have an electronic switchboard with conference call capability, it is still possible to set up conference calls. For example, if your employer wanted to discuss a marketing strategy with associates in several branch offices across the country, you would call the operator and ask for the conference operator, specifying the locations and names of persons to be included and indicating when the call should be put through. With speakerphones, several persons may listen in on a *two-way conference call* at any one location.

A conference operator may also help you set up a *one-way conference call*. In a one-way conference call, only the voice of the caller is transmitted. Another conference call feature allows you to add a third caller to a conversation that is already in progress.

Illus. 12-5
Speakerphones
have built-in
transmitters and
volume controls
that permit both
sides of a
conversation to be
amplified.

Reproduced with permission of
AT&T Corporate Archive

Overseas Telephone Service

If your company's long-distance carrier provides international service, overseas telephone calls can be dialed direct. If you know the local number of the company being called and have a directory with access codes for the countries being called, you may use *International Direct Distance Dialing* (IDDD) to reach your overseas party in this manner:

1. First, dial the international access code.
2. Next, dial the country code (a two- or three-digit number).
3. Then dial the city routing code (not necessary in small cities with only one code).
4. Finally, dial the local number.

For example, to dial London, dial 011 (the international access code) + 44 (the country code) + 1 (the city routing code) + 123456 (the local number). If you are using a push-button telephone, depress the # button after dialing the number to save connecting time. If you are using a long-distance carrier other than your company's designated long-distance company to make an overseas call, that carrier's five-digit number must be dialed before you dial the international access code. After dialing an international call, allow at least 45 seconds for the call to start. Special pamphlets available from your telephone company can keep you up-to-date on overseas rates and special conditions in various countries.

If your telephone is not capable of handling IDDD calls, dial the operator and give the name of the country to be called, the name of the company wanted, and the name of the person to be reached. Of course, it is essential to consider time zones and to check times during which various overseas rates apply. Consulting a world time zone map (see page 309) will help you decide when to place international calls.

ELECTRONIC MAIL

Communication that is sent to a destination by electronic means is called *electronic mail*. Instead of using the U.S. Postal Service, office support personnel frequently send communications electronically via Telex, TWX, Mailgram, facsimile equipment, and communicating word processors and copiers. An electronic mail system especially designed for managers, a computer-based message system, is also described in this section. Voice mail, another form of electronic mail, is covered separately on page 336.

Telex and TWX

Among the oldest keyboard communication devices, the *teletypewriter* combines the immediacy of the telephone with the documentation and accuracy of letters. Capable of sending and receiving messages, the teletypewriter is a relatively inexpensive means of providing fast communication in writing, 24 hours a day, 7 days a week. An example of a teletypewriter appears in Illus. 12-6.

Illus. 12-6
A teletypewriter's output is in the form of a hard copy.

Western Union

There are two teletypewriter networks, owned by Western Union, to which businesses can subscribe: *Telex* and *TWX* (pronounced *twix*). Both networks can be interconnected. They vary only slightly in how they work and in what they can do.

Type Telex or TWX messages on the stationery your company uses for this purpose. By dialing a special code, you or a message center attendant can send messages on the teletypewriter. An automatic identification assures you that you have reached the person wanted. This automatic identification may be repeated at the end of the transmission, confirming that the message has been received. To send messages, words are punched on a paper tape. It can be corrected before transmission. Paper tapes should be retained for at least one business day in case messages must be retransmitted because lines were unavailable. Newer teletypewriters have screens, disks or diskettes for storage, and limited word processing functions.

Teletypewriters are also used to send Mailgrams, telegrams, and cablegrams. Special applications are possible for organizations that frequently send messages to the same list of people. Western Union's InfoMaster computer system can store addresses on one tape which can be easily merged with a message tape. The InfoMaster can also be programmed for type of delivery—Telex, TWX, Mailgram, or domestic or international telegram—for each message. Other information that will be repeated in future communications may also be stored in Western Union's computer.

Mailgrams

The *Mailgram*, which was introduced in 1970, is a very popular service. It combines Western Union's communication network with the U.S. Postal Service. Customers send messages to Western Union by telephone, Telex/TWX, Mailgram terminals, or communicating word processors. They may also present in person. Mailgram messages are sent over Western Union's computerized communication network directly to the recipient's local post office. Teleprinters type messages on continuous rolls of paper. Later, they are inserted into distinctive blue-and-white envelopes. Delivery is made the next business day by regular postal carriers. Some organizations rent post office boxes into which Mailgrams are deposited as received. In this way, companies can pick up their messages before mail carriers deliver them.

Mailgrams offer several advantages over other forms of communication. They engender a sense of urgency and importance by their special envelopes and telegram format. They receive post office priority.

When received, they are usually opened before the other mail. They are relatively low in cost. An example of a Mailgram appears in Illus. 12-7.

Mailgrams may be sent to several people at different addresses simultaneously. For example, politicians use them widely to influence voters. They can be used to invite people to a function or to cancel one. They are often used in promoting sales. It is possible to detach a reply form from the bottom of a Mailgram, fill it in, and fold it into a business reply envelope to be mailed back to the sender postage-free. Mailgrams can also provide proof of delivery. In filing a Mailgram, follow the instructions for preparing a telegram (see page 307).

Illus. 12-7
Mailgrams unite
Western Union's
communication
network with the
U.S. Postal Service.

Western Union

Facsimile Equipment

Facsimile (FAX) systems are long-distance output copiers. An example appears in Illus. 12-8. These machines read a document at the sending location, transmit the information over telephone lines, and then produce a high-resolution hard copy of the original at the receiving location. No rekeying of text is necessary, making this process virtually error-free. Textual information, graphics, and photographs can be sent across town or across thousands of miles.

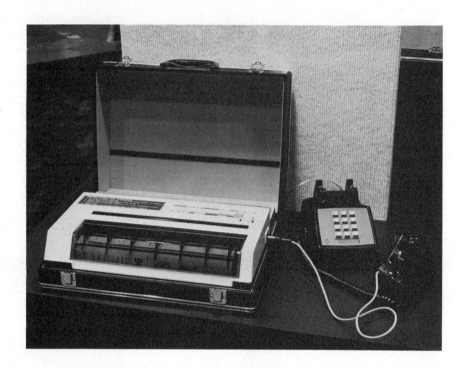

Illus. 12-8
Some facsimile
systems are
portable.

Facsimile equipment is easy to operate and requires only minimal operator training. Variations in manufacturers' equipment do exist, however. A description of how to operate one manufacturer's facsimile system follows:

> To send a facsimile message, place the original in a sender or a transceiver device. The transceiver is identical with the equipment at the receiving location. It is an instrument that can both send and receive messages. To alert the recipient, dial the number to which the message is being sent. Place your telephone receiver in the coupler cradle and press the send button. (The coupler cradle is the resting place for the receiver that connects the two offices.)
>
> To receive a document, place the handset (receiver) in the coupler cradle as soon as you receive the alert. Press the receive button. If you want to discuss the document that you have received, remove the handset from the receiving cradle and begin to talk.

A facsimile is chosen when only one copy of a typewritten page, chart, map, photo, or almost any other type of image is urgently required. Facsimile devices are often used when originals will not reproduce clearly on office copiers. The clarity of an image is an important consideration when handwritten messages or statistical information is being reproduced.

A disadvantage of facsimiles has been the incompatibility of different manufacturers' equipment. Originally facsimiles could be transmitted from one point to another only via identical machines. New switched network services, made possible by powerful computer-based systems, make previously incompatible facsimile machines capable of transmitting messages.

Another disadvantage of facsimiles has been their high cost, since slow transmission time made the necessary telephone use expensive. Advanced technology now makes transmission of a page possible within a matter of minutes. The equipment also includes store-and-forward capability. Messages can be retained, filed, and recalled when wanted. These technological advances have made facsimile transmission a popular medium for utilizing electronic mail.

For best results in sending facsimile messages, clearly legible material is a must. Typewritten material generally transmits well as does handwritten material in black ballpoint pen or heavy pencil. Do not use facsimiles for lengthy documents, unless the cost involved is justified by urgency. Costs can be reduced by taking advantage of reduced night telephone rates. Be sure the office you are sending a facsimile to has compatible equipment. Your company directory, telephone operator, or the person in charge of communications can tell you this, if you are sending an in-company message.

Communicating Word Processors and Copiers

A communicating word processor can exchange information with a compatible word processor via telephone lines. The functions of sending and receiving information are under operator control and supervision. Copy is keyboarded, then stored on a magnetic medium for transmission over telephone lines. At the receiving location, the information can be stored or printed out. Because of storing capability, information can be received after office hours, thus taking advantage of lower night telephone rates. If connected to a Telex or TWX machine, a communicating word processor can input into that electronic mail system. In addition, a communicating word processor can be linked to a computer, becoming a component of a computer-based message system.

Another electronic device which plays a key role in electronic mail is the intelligent copier/printer. This machine can produce hard copies from input received from various devices, including computers and word processors.

Computer-Based Message Systems

Computer-based message systems offer the most promise for increased communication efficiency between and among executives and office support personnel (secretaries and clerical personnel). With this system, on-line computers (computers that are directly connected to each other) exchange information. Messages are keyboarded and transmitted through telephone wires or satellites to receiving terminals. The equipment required to establish a computer-based message system at a typical workstation is a desktop or personal computer with a keyboard and screen. Messages are stored in the computer's files for users to call up on the terminal's screen at their convenience. Producing a hard copy printout is also possible. Changes to messages can be made and return messages sent to the sender.

To send a message, the secretary or executive keyboards the information and the recipient's address. The computer instantly processes the message. To denote priority, the sender labels the message *URGENT* or *PRIVATE*.

VOICE MAIL

Voice mail is a store-and-forward system that combines three elements of communications equipment: the telephone, the computer, and the recording machine. It reduces the necessity of calling several times to reach people by telephone. An executive can record one-way telephone messages when free to record them, and they can be delivered when the recipient is available to hear them. Voice mail is made possible by special equipment attached to both a sending and a receiving telephone. Access into a voice mail system is gained by entering a code on the telephone. A recording then tells the user to dictate the message. At the end of the message, the user dials the voice-mail address of the recipient. (Voice-mail addresses are given to users when equipment is installed.) The message is converted to digital data. The system will attempt to deliver messages immediately. Failing this, the message is filed in the computer's memory. Later, when the recipient dials into the system to obtain messages, the caller's voice is reconstructed.

TELECONFERENCING

Another example of telecommunications technology is *teleconferencing*. Using telecommunications systems, an executive can conduct and/or attend a meeting without traveling to a distant location. Avoidance of travel expenses and time lost in traveling makes teleconferencing attractive to business organizations. Meeting participants communicate electronically using two-way voice, text, or video communication. For a detailed discussion of teleconferencing, refer to Chapter 15, Planning and Facilitating Meetings.

VIDEOTEX/TELETEXT

Videotex and *teletext* are terms used to describe a type of electronic publishing service that makes text and color graphics available through a terminal or personal computer. Videotex service provides two-way interaction between the user and a central computer. Textual information plus graphics in color can be exchanged. Teletext, on the other hand, is a computer-to-user system and communicates textual information only. The user of teletext cannot ask questions or interact with the system.

THE SECRETARY AND COMMUNICATIONS SYSTEMS

The preceding discussion provided a look at the developments in communications systems which affect how business offices exchange information. If you are in or will enter a small professional or traditional office, what does this chapter mean to you in performing your day-to-day duties?

Secretaries have decision-making responsibilities for sending messages that are consistent with office policy and executive preferences. Evaluate each message-sending situation by asking yourself the following questions:

1. How urgent is the message?
2. Is a special impact on the recipient important?
3. Are documentation or reference copies needed?
4. Can another method save costly overtime?
5. What is the least expensive, appropriate way to send the message?

You will compose many types of communications. In addition to originating documents, you will edit them; therefore, sharpen your communication skills. Communications should represent your best efforts at clarity and brevity.

Communication channels bring you in contact with more and more people. Realize that your professional image in representing your organization and your employer will extend beyond the confines of a single office.

You will utilize many of the components of communications systems. Your job will change as new components are added. You will learn to operate new components and understand the functions of others.

The wave of the future is toward executive use of communications systems. More executives will work at home and while traveling, as more sophisticated equipment becomes available. The executive will input material to the secretary's terminal, and the secretary will learn to operate terminals at both the executive and the secretarial desk. If you have your eye on a career in management, your experiences as a professional secretary will put you in a unique position to acquire the background to become an information manager.

SUMMARY

Telecommunication is broadly defined as the electronic transmission of communications from one location to another. These communications can be in the form of data, text, image, voice, and video.

When automation was introduced to the office, each piece of equipment had its own separate technology. Today, such functions as data processing, word processing, and reprographics are now integrated. Integration is made possible by communication networks. A local area network uses cable to connect mainframe computers, personal computers, terminals, word processors, and printers in an office complex. A local area network can also tie into a wide area network, thus expanding the communication to another city or another country. Wide area networks are made possible by satellite communication.

Voice communication networks are in analog mode; computer data, on the other hand, leave the computer as digital signals. In order for digital and analog signals to be sent over the same network, one or the other has to be converted. A modem (modulator/demodulator) is used to perform these conversions. Cable is the main transmission medium of voice and data communication. Fiber optics, thin glass-like tubes which transmit light, may soon replace copper cables as the major transmission medium. Microwave and satellite communication provide high-speed transmission of information over great distances. Satellite communication offers a global network opportunity for business organizations. Microwave and/or satellite services can be leased or rented through the telephone company or from a number of satellite communication companies.

The telephone continues to be the most popular means of communication between two or more persons. With the key telephone system, each individual telephone in the system has the capability of receiving, initiating, and holding calls. Key telephones also make intercom lines possible. A PBX system has a central switchboard and features Direct Outward Dialing. An operator answers incoming calls. A recent development in PBX systems is the digital PBX with integrated voice and data transmission capabilities. The Centrex system features *Direct Inward Dialing* in which every telephone unit in a company has its own seven-digit telephone number.

Special time-saving and cost-saving services and equipment are available for telephone subscribers. They include Wide Area Telecommunications Service (WATS), AT&T's 800 Service, leased lines, foreign exchange service, mobile (cellular) service, pagers, Touch-Tone service, Touch-a-matic telephones, speakerphones, conference calls, and overseas telephone service.

Electronic mail refers to communications that are sent to a destination by electronic means. Electronic mail can be sent by Telex and TWX, via Mailgrams, facsimile equipment, communicating word processors and copiers, and computer-based message systems. All but the last of these services are used primarily by office support personnel. Computer-based message systems are used by management and secretaries. Voice mail, a form of electronic mail, is a store-and-forward system which combines the telephone, the computer, and recording machines.

Teleconferencing allows business people to attend meetings electronically. Meeting participants communicate using two-way voice, text, or video communication. A more detailed discussion of teleconferencing is provided in Chapter 15.

Information can be transmitted electronically by subscribing to videotex or teletext services. Videotex and teletext are terms used to describe types of electronic publishing service. To access these services, a specially equipped terminal or personal computer is needed.

The secretary in a highly technical office environment needs to be extremely knowledgeable about telecommunications. The secretary who works in a smaller, less automated office will have to make decisions regarding efficient methods of sending communications.

SUGGESTED READINGS _____

Blythe, W. John and Mary M. Blyth. *Telecommunications*, Concepts, Development, and Management. Indianapolis: Bobbs-Merrill Co., Inc., 1985.

Casady, Mona J. and Dorothy C. Sandburg. *Word/Information Processing*, A System Approach. Integrating Technology for Information Processing, Chap. 14. Cincinnati: South-Western Publishing Co., 1985.

The Complete Guide to Lower Phone Costs. Washington, DC: Center for the Study of Services, 1984.

Reynolds, George W. *Introduction to Business Telecommunications*. Columbus, OH: Charles E. Merrill Publishing Co., 1984.

QUESTIONS FOR DISCUSSION _____

1. Distinguish between local area networks and wide area networks.
2. What is meant by analog transmission? digital transmission? Give an example of a type of communication in each mode.
3. What function does a modem play in a communication network?
4. A secretary has just learned a Centrex number which the executive may use again. Why should the secretary keep a record of that number?
5. What applications can you think of for cellular service in a business organization?
6. Your office is located in New York City and you are asked to call the accounting division of a company in Paris, France. You are to dial the number directly. During what hours of your business day (9 a.m. to 5 p.m.) would you attempt this call (standard time)?
7. You need to send a one-page document that incorporates text and mathematical calculations. Both your company and the receiving location have a teletypewriter and facsimile capability. Which process would you use? Why?
8. In discussing electronic mail alternatives, this chapter stated that certain forms of electronic mail are used primarily by office support personnel. Computer-based message systems, it was mentioned, were designed with management in mind. Why do you think this distinction has been made?
9. How would a secretary use the voice mail system to increase his/her productivity?

10. Capitalize the appropriate words in the following sentences. Use the Reference Guide to verify and correct your answers.
    a. Our high school provides the senior class with a free booklet on how to find a job.
    b. We will offer a special discount from august 1 through mid-October.
    c. Traffic is always heavy on labor day when students return to the university.
    d. He is known in the music industry as top-ten Martin.
    e. The only bureau in Washington that has current data on the subject is the bureau of labor statistics.
    f. Please include the material on line 6, page 12.

PROBLEMS

1. If you were employed by a well-equipped corporation, which type of communication would you probably choose in the following situations? Give reasons for your choices.
   a. A message to three sales managers in different locations (A reaction is necessary from each.)
   b. A message informing the payroll department in a branch office that data required for issuing paychecks have not been received.
   c. A message containing detailed information about a branch factory's production schedules for the next two months
   d. A message to inquire about prices of a well-known office machine manufactured in a nearby suburb
   e. A message to the production manager in a distant branch factory
   f. A message that must reach 12 sales representatives in different locations by the following morning
   g. A message that will be received after closing hours but must be available when the office opens the following morning
   h. A graph to be used tomorrow in a national sales meeting
2. Visit a technologically up-to-date office and make an oral report to the class on either of the following topics: the company's internal and external telephone system or its electronic mail system. Include reasons why the company selected a particular system. Discuss what kind of equipment is used.

Chapter 13

Information Resource Management

Business records contain information about and evidence of company policies, procedures, operations, functions, and other activities. Any medium—paper, microfilm, computer tape, word processing disk, or the like—can be considered a record or an information resource. In our information society, 45 new pieces of paper are created daily for every worker in the United States; therefore, information resource management is taking on new significance.

As more records are produced, the need for easy access to them for decision making and the need for destroying records when they are no longer useful grows. Consequently, the secretary needs to observe good filing practices and to insist that others with access to records also observe them. This chapter discusses the secretary's filing responsibilities, various methods of manual and electronic filing, equipment and supplies, procedures for filing and retrieving records, the mechanics of good filing, retention and transfer of files, and building company archives (historical records).

THE SECRETARY'S FILING RESPONSIBILITIES

Files are the memory of a business. They may be *centralized* in one location or *decentralized* in various departments or branches. Most secretaries maintain decentralized (in-office) files and also send materials to and secure materials from large central files. In-office files relate not only to the company business for which the executive is responsible; they also contain a number of personal files. The executive's personal files should be kept separate from those that contain company business.

If the company has a records management program, the secretary receives instructions about which materials are to be sent to the central files, which materials may be retained in the executive's files, and how long to keep certain records before destroying them or sending them to a low-cost storage area.

Records managers are primarily concerned with reducing the amount of paper in the files. Their work has been made more demanding by the accessibility of copying machines. The same document may be copied and filed in a half-dozen offices. Since office space is expensive and personnel costs are high, records managers want to avoid filing documents with no reference value, to reduce duplication of copies, and to ensure that superseded material is destroyed when replacements are filed. To save space, they frequently try to reduce executive files. On the other hand, executives fear that they will not be able to refer easily to records that have left their hands; consequently, they have the tendency to build "little empires" that take up space and increase the cost of paperwork. The secretary's task is to reconcile the executive's "empire building" habits with the need to keep in-office files to a minimum; therefore, the secretary needs to understand in-office files and central files thoroughly.

Designing the Files

There is a tendency to restrict one's concept of files to the typical vertical file cabinet so conspicuous in every office. Actually the secretary works with many types of files—card files, project files, files of catalogs, magazine files, blueprint or other outsized material files, tape cassette files, transparency files, files of computer printouts, microform files, open shelf files, and computerized files—in addition to the traditional drawer files with alphabetic, numeric, geographic, and subject captions. Each type of file has a unique function. The secretary's filing responsibilities usually go beyond maintaining existing files to include the designing and installation of various types of files that best serve the executive's need for information. In planning files, three factors must always be considered: findability, confidentiality, and safety.

Findability. Unfortunately files are first thought of as places to *put* materials rather than places to *find* materials; yet the criterion for judging any file system is findability. The efficient secretary makes decisions about where to file an item after considering, How will it be requested? or How can I find it? Materials must be located with dispatch, and only those materials actually wanted should be removed from a complete file. To do this, the secretary must understand what the executive needs. Why provide 250 pages when only 10 are wanted? Safely filing materials is important, but being able to find them promptly is *vital*.

Confidentiality. The secretary is also responsible for the confidentiality of the employer's files. The degree of security required varies. Tight surveillance is required for files and papers marked *confidential, secret, vital, or personal*. Reasonable protection over less sensitive materials should be exercised. If an executive works in a highly sensitive area or industry, there should be a company policy regarding access to confidential and secret materials. In the absence of such a policy, the secretary should work with the executive to establish a policy to safeguard the confidentiality of the executive's files.

Confidential records do not usually leave the executive's office. Before releasing a confidential record (even to your executive's superior), obtain your employer's permission, unless there is a company policy to the contrary. Access to personnel records is regulated by the Privacy Act (see page 653).

Safety. Allied to the need for confidentiality is the secretary's ultimate responsibility for the safety of the records in the executive's office. Many records may be irreplaceable. Secretaries should lock all confidential material in a filing cabinet or vault before leaving the office as a safeguard against prying eyes and fire or water damage. Security systems are built into many new files that automatically lock them when not in use.

Developing an Index

Developing an *index* that indicates how the files are arranged should be a secretarial priority. Chances are, though, none will be available when you begin a new job. Even after a secretary is quite familiar with the files, an index will prove its usefulness: It will help anyone (including an executive or a new assistant) locate material. Do not underestimate its value. A simple index for locating filed material appears in Illus. 13-1.

Communication between secretary and executive seems particularly weak in the filing area. Since the secretary oversees the files, there is the tendency to consider the files the secretary's private domain. Yet the filing system is a joint responsibility. If a secretary and an executive work together in planning the system, the transfer of either of them to another office would not destroy the continuity of the files. A new secretary should not attempt to reorganize the files until considerable insight into the informational needs of the office has been acquired.

Ideas for setting up files may be obtained from professional organizations, publications, and equipment vendors. For instance, sugges-

```
                    FILE INDEX
                      NO. 89
                     CHEMICAL
```

	Location	
	File No.	Drawer No.
Correspondence		
Company	2	1
Government	2	2
Patents	2	3
Personnel Work		
Applications	1	2
Medical	1	3
Security	1	6
Reports		
Company	5	1
Outside	5	3

Illus. 13-1
An index helps
locate filed
material.

tions might be found in an engineering magazine for filing blueprints. Manuals have been published and entire filing systems have been developed to manage the records of insurance, legal, municipal, medical, accounting, and other offices.

It is also possible to buy prefabricated subject file systems for certain types of offices. For example, a prefabricated administration file system is available with subjects and subclassifications preprinted on guides and folder tabs. The manufacturer claims this system provides indexing that is applicable to 90 percent of all basic administrative data.

FILING METHODS

Material should be filed according to how it is identified, how it is called for, and according to rules that are understood by all who use the files. There are four basic filing methods: *alphabetic, subject, numeric,* and *geographic.*

Manufacturers of filing equipment have devised and patented improvements upon these four filing fundamental methods. For example, manufacturers have devised color schemes to expedite sorting, filing, and finding procedures. Techniques for grouping names that are spelled differently but pronounced alike have also been developed. Wheeldex and Datafile are trade names for two such commercial filing systems.

Alphabetic Filing

Most, possibly as high as 80 percent, of all filing done in the office is *alphabetical*; that is, the files are sequenced alphabetically. Furthermore, all filing systems are directly or indirectly based on the alphabetic system. Alphabetic filing is understood by everyone and the filing is *direct*. It is not necessary to consult a subordinate file before filing or finding material in an alphabetic file. The method is based on strict guides for alphabetic indexing as presented in the Reference Guide. An example of an alphabetic file is shown in Illus. 13-2.

Phonetic indexing is a modification of alphabetic indexing. In phonetic indexing, names are arranged by their sound and not by their spelling. Thus, Burke and its variants—Burck, Berk, Berke, Birk, Bourke, Bork, Borck, and others—are filed together. Filing phonetically eliminates problems found in other systems. Errors occurring because of misspellings and poor handwriting are reduced. Phonetic filing is most effectively used with files containing thousands of proper names.

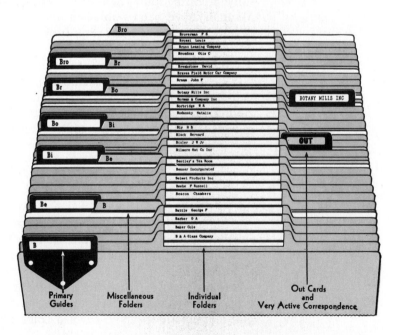

Illus. 13-2
In this illustration of an alphabetic file, four positions are used for captions.

Subject Filing

The nature of some executives' work makes filing some correspondence, reports, and documents under *subject headings* particularly useful. A subject file is actually an alphabetic file. Its captions, though they refer to subjects or topics, are alphabetically arranged.

Clear, concise, and mutually exclusive subject captions are essential to successful subject files. Captions are the key words used in locating filed material. To get an idea of the subjects used in subject filing, examine the Yellow Pages of your local telephone directory. You will see Employment Agencies cross-referenced to Employment Contractors and Temporary Help, and Loans cross-referenced to Banks, Financing, Credit Unions, Mortgages, Savings and Loan Associations, and Pawnbrokers.

Each piece of material is filed under *one subject caption*, but a *relative index* is prepared to support the subject file. This index is basically a cross-reference system. It lists all captions under which an item *may* be filed. To obtain an item from a subject file for which the subject caption is not known, the searcher first consults the relative index to identify all possible headings under which it may be stored.

The time that an executive and the secretary profitably invest in developing a relative index will be saved later when material under a number of captions must be retrieved. If the executive asks for the file on the wage-incentive plans of a rival company, the Green Corporation, it may have been filed under: (1) fringe benefits, (2) incentive plans, (3) personnel, or (4) Green Corporation. The relative index will help locate the appropriate file.

A description of a portion of a subject file is shown in Illus. 13-3. This illustration shows one major subject file heading with its subdivisions.

Notice that the main heading (OFFICE EQUIPMENT) has a number of subheadings. OFFICE EQUIPMENT is subdivided into several categories:

OFFICE EQUIPMENT: Copiers
OFFICE EQUIPMENT: Duplicators
OFFICE EQUIPMENT: Typewriters

Some of these subdivisions may be further subdivided. For example, *OFFICE EQUIPMENT: Typewriters* is subdivided by manufacturer: (IBM, Olivetti, and Silver Reed).

Typewriters is further subdivided by a special classification guide in the fourth position for repairs. Additional classifications depend on the needs of the user.

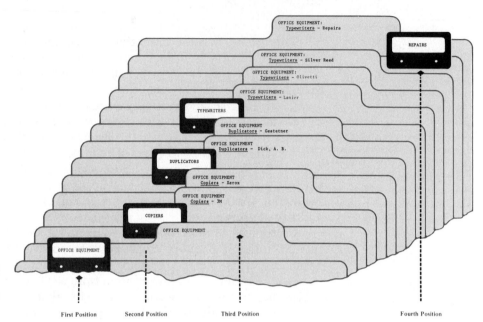

Illus. 13-3
This subject file would be suitable for a purchasing agent or an office manager.

Subject filing presents special retrieval problems because material may be requested under any one of many titles. For this reason one management consultant has said, "To do subject filing well, the secretary must think like the executive." No area of filing requires the exercise of better judgment than does arranging materials by subjects that best indicate their content.

Numeric Filing

Lawyers, architects, engineers, accountants, realtors, insurance brokers, and contractors often assign numbers to their projects and clients. For example, law firms frequently assign case numbers to their work. These numbers become the basis for the *numeric file*. Because anonymity is desired, records of confidential material are commonly filed numerically. A numeric filing plan has four parts:

1. Alphabetic card index
2. Main numeric file
3. Miscellaneous alphabetic file
4. Accession or number book, a record of numbers already assigned

In numeric filing, the alphabetic card index is first consulted to obtain the file number. The item is then located by file number in the main numeric file. If a name or subject is not in the card index, the miscellaneous alphabetic file is searched. It should be obvious from this explanation of numeric filing that it is an *indirect* system. One must search the alphabetic card index before searching the main numeric file for materials.

If the subject file for a small operation (see Illus. 13-3) were converted to a numeric subject file, the main heading for office equipment in the first position might be assigned the number 100. The numeric assignments for each subdivision would then correspond to the numbers shown in Illus. 13-4.

Illus. 13-4
In this numeric subject file, alternate rather than consecutive numbers are assigned. Intervening numbers can be used when a machine from another manufacturer is purchased.

NUMBER	MAIN HEADING First Position	DIVISION Second Position	SUBDIVISION Third Position	SECOND SUBDIVISION Fourth Position
100	Office Equipment			
110		Copiers		
112			3M	
114			Xerox	
116				
118				
120		Duplicators		
122			Dick, A. B.	
124			Gestetner	
126				
128				
130		Typewriters		
132			IBM	
134			Olivetti	
136			Silver Reed	
138				Repairs

Advantages and Disadvantages. Numeric filing has both advantages and disadvantages. It is easy to learn. Misfiling is reduced because numbers are easier to locate and are less confusing than spelled names to file. Furthermore, the alphabetic card index makes extensive cross-referencing possible. A disadvantage of numeric filing is the time-consuming necessity of consulting the alphabetic card index before locating material.

Terminal and Middle Digit Filing. In straight numeric filing, as the files increase, the numbers assigned to them become higher. Because most filing work deals with recent dates, it involves high numbers. In a numeric file of insurance policies, for instance, the most recent policies would have the highest numbers. The higher a number is the more difficult it is to file. *Terminal digit filing* avoids this problem. This filing method divides a number into pairs of digits. For example, insurance policy No. 412010 would be identified as 41 20 10. The last (terminal) digits identify the drawer number; the second pair of digits to the left indicate the guide number in the drawer; and the remaining digits indicate the sequence of the folder behind the guide. Thus, policy No. 41 20 10 would be filed in Drawer 10, behind Guide 20, and in 41st sequence behind the guide (between policy No. 40 20 10 and policy No. 42 20 10). Illus. 13-5 shows a records technician retrieving folders from a terminal digit filing system.

To appreciate the advantage of terminal digit filing, visualize 100 file drawers, each labeled with a two-digit number (00, 01, 02, and so on through 99). Policy No. 2 12 00 would go in Drawer 00, while policy

Illus. 13-5
Research shows the records technicians make fewer filing errors when terminal digit rather than basic numeric filing is used.

No. 2 12 01 would go in Drawer 01, and so on. As consecutive new policy numbers were assigned, the policy materials would be distributed throughout 100 drawers.

Research shows that terminal digit filing saves up to 40 percent of file operation costs by assuring a uniform work load, better employee relations, unlimited expansion facilities, and fewer misfiles. This system has been adapted and modified into triple terminal digit filing (using the last three digits as the drawer number).

In *middle digit filing*, the two middle digits identify the drawer or section; the first two digits, the guide number in the drawer or section; and the final two digits, the sequence behind the guide.

Decimal-Numeric Filing. When used with subject filing, a decimal-numeric classification permits more expansion than does a simple numeric arrangement. The decimal arrangement lends itself to any subject that can be subdivided.

Main headings, major divisions, and first divisions are assigned a number just as they are in the simple numeric arrangement, but a decimal point followed by one or more digits is placed after the number of the first subdivision. The decimal point indicates that there are additional subdivisions. For example, a shoe manufacturer might assign number 444 to women's shoes. A decimal point and a single digit would be added to identify the following:

444	Women's Shoes
444.1	Dress Pumps
444.2	Sandals
444.3	Orthopedic

A second digit after the decimal point indicates an additional subdivision, such as

444.10	Open Toe Dress Pumps
444.11	Open Toe, Open Heel Dress Pumps

Some libraries use a decimal-numeric system, which is used internationally and has been around for almost a century, known as the *Dewey Decimal System*. Engineering firms, governmental agencies, and large pharmaceutical houses also use decimal-numeric filing.

Duplex-Numeric Filing. A duplex number is one of two or more parts separated by a hyphen, space, or comma. It is a useful arrangement for classifying unlimited subject headings with an unlimited number of major divisions and subdivisions. Unlike some other systems, duplex numbers are not assigned to classifications in advance but are assigned to main headings as they are added to the file. Similarly, as major divisions and subdivisions are added to the file, new numbers are assigned in consecutive order to these divisions. For example:

	7		= curriculum
7	-	1	= curriculum design
7	-	2	= curriculum implementation

A subdivision would be indicated by a hyphen and a number:

7-1	-	1	= curriculum design—liberal arts
7-1	-	2	= curriculum design—business

Subsequent subdivisions are indicated by adding a hyphen and a letter or another number. A duplex arrangement is more useful when large numbers (over 100,000) of records are to be filed.

Geographic Filing

Geographic filing arranges records by geographic units or territories. Divisions are made in a logical sequence: nations, states or provinces, cities, and so on. Guides are used for large divisions and subdivisions. Behind each guide, material is filed in miscellaneous folders alphabetically, usually by name of city and then by name of correspondent. Individual folders are filed alphabetically by location, then by name. An example of a geographic file appears in Illus. 13-6.

The geographic file is frequently supported by a card index in which names of companies are filed alphabetically. If the location of a company is forgotten, it may be obtained by referring to the alphabetic card index.

Chronological Filing

When records are filed chronologically, they are arranged in date sequence with the most recent date on top. There are three major types of chronological files: transaction files, suspense (or pending) files, and reading (or chron) files.

Transaction Files. Transaction files store records by the date of transaction. They are useful when records, such as purchase orders or invoices, occur on a daily basis.

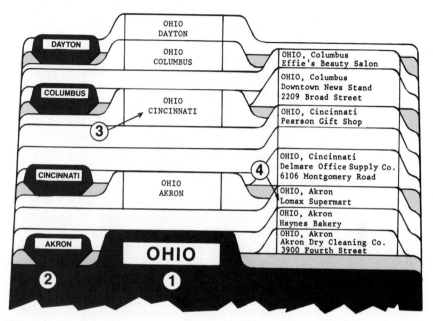

Illus. 13-6
In this geographic file, papers are filed alphabetically by geographic areas as indicated by guides and folders (see No. 1 and No. 2). In the miscellaneous folder for each city (see No. 3), papers are filed alphabetically by the names of correspondents. Individual folders are used for correspondents who have enough communications to warrant a separate folder (see No. 4).

Suspense Files. Suspense (or pending) files serve as reminders of items pending. Items filed in the suspense action file should never become a part of an individual file until the pending action has been completed or a response has been received. Secretaries often maintain a suspense file for busy executives that chronicles the executive's daily activities for a one-month period. The secretary keeps a folder in the desk with 31 separate dividers—one for each day of the month. Behind these is another group of 12 folders—one for each month of the year. Each morning the secretary pulls the chronological suspense file and reviews it to see what the employer must do that day. Wise secretaries check a week or two ahead in order to get signatures, decisions, and so forth before the executive leaves on an extended trip. Things scheduled to occur in future months are filed in the appropriate monthly folder. When a particular month rolls around, the secretary pulls the correspondence from that folder and files it behind the appropriate day guides to ensure that appropriate action is taken on time. Remembering to check the suspense file must become a habit. Failure to do so can result in lost discounts (if bills are not paid on time), missed appointments, and poor relations with customers and clients.

Reading Files. A secretary who must periodically send material to a central file usually keeps a chronological file as a ready in-office reference. This file, sometimes called a *reading* or *chron* (chronological) file, consists of a copy—carbon or photo—of each *outgoing* item, filed in chronological order in a ring binder or in a top bound folder. Such a file can answer many questions—was a letter mailed, to whom was it addressed, when was it mailed, what price was quoted, and was an enclosure mentioned—all without the delay of consulting the central file.

A reading file does not use an index. As a result, if a record is requested without reference to its date, a search of the records is required. This is a time-consuming and frustrating task. To speed the locating of material in the reading file, some secretaries place a sheet with a dated index tab between copies to separate each day's work. It is also recommended that a notation be placed on each copy in the reading file showing where the original correspondence concerning that item is filed. The secretary retains materials in this file for a limited time only, perhaps six months to a year, each month discarding the materials for the earliest month.

Selecting a Method

The basic filing methods used in your office should depend on how materials are identified. If they are identified by name (either personal or company), an alphabetic file system will probably be used. If each client, job, or project is identified by number, a numeric system is appropriate. When the identifying name for the item is a territory or a geographic location, the geographic method will be best. When items are categorized by subject, then a subject file should meet your office needs.

FILING EQUIPMENT

Correspondence is most often filed in drawers or on shelves. It may be placed in folders that rest on the bottom of a drawer or in suspension folders that hang from a metal frame within the drawer or shelf. Two advantages of the suspension folder are that heavy folders do not sag and that folders open wide and slide smoothly on hanger rails. Cards are filed in several ways: in drawers, in boxes, in trays, or in panels, where the captions are immediately visible.

Vertical and Lateral Files

For many years the vertical file was the most popular type of filing equipment. Vertical files remain somewhat popular. They are available in one- to six-drawer units in a wide variety of colors. One important disadvantage of vertical files is that opening drawers requires at least three to four feet of space in front of the cabinet.

The conventional vertical file cabinet, that pulls forward the full depth of the drawer, is rapidly being replaced by lateral files. Lateral files use 50 percent less aisle space and provide up to 100 percent greater accessibility and visibility. The lateral file may be a drawer file that rolls out sideways, or it may be an open shelf file. In executive offices where attractive surroundings are important, the type of lateral file most often chosen has a closed front. Lateral files have drawers that close or cabinets with doors that lift up, slide to one side, or pull down.

Open Shelf Files

In open shelf filing, folders are placed vertically on open shelves. No drawers are involved. Access to folders is from the front. Since open shelves can extend to the ceiling, they can accommodate more material per square foot of floor space than drawer files can. They also require less floor and aisle space, cost less, and require less time to file and find records. In central filing departments like the one shown in Illus. 13-7, open shelf filing is used more often than other kinds of filing equipment.

Tabs identifying the contents of an open shelf file folder project from the side of the folder. Captions are written on both front and back of the tab so that the searcher can locate a folder from either side. Color coding is frequently used with open shelf files for easy visibility. If a whole section is color-coded red, a folder with a green caption is obviously misfiled.

Illus. 13-7
Open shelf files
make it easier for
secretaries and
other office
personnel to file
and find records.
These open shelves
are electrically
powered. They
contract
automatically so
that only one aisle
is open per bay.

Spacesaver Corporation

Mobile Files

Mobile files put records at point of use, permitting what is known as *close support filing*. The concept is to bring a highly active file unit to the operations area rather than forcing the worker to go to the file. Some mobile files are single units that are pushed around like carts. An example of a mobile single unit file, the tub file, is shown in Illus. 13-8. Others are multiple modules that roll on a suspension system from the ceiling. Some are stationary. Trays rotate to give operators access to needed material.

Illus. 13-8
Mobile files bring a
highly active file
unit to the
operations area.

Files for Magnetic Media

The array of equipment for housing magnetic media is almost as varied as it is for housing paper documents. Magnetic media, such as floppy disks, are often filed in plastic library boxes provided by the manufacturer when an order of supplies is delivered. These pop-up boxes hold the media upright on the operator's desk while in use and protect them against environmental contamination when closed.

A variety of desktop modular stands or rotary stands, designed to house flat magnetic media, generally hold large amounts of material. Examples of desktop files for magnetic media appear in Illus. 13-9. One such file holds ten floppy disks in a notebook-like arrangement for easy indexing and accessing by the operator.

Acco International, Inc.

Illus. 13-9
Magnetic media
may be housed in a
variety of desktop
files.

Files for Computer-Generated Material

Provision must be made for filing both computer tapes and computer printouts. Faced with a 15 to 20 percent annual growth rate in the number of computer tapes stored on-site, some companies have replaced fixed-in-place racks with automated mobile shelving. With fingertip pressure on a control button, the operator can move a bay of carriages sideways, right or left, over tracks to open the desired aisle. Tapes have reference numbers and are logged in and out after every access. An example of this type of mobile storage system appears in Illus. 13-10.

Spacesaver Corporation

Illus. 13-10
Shelving units
automatically
shuttle sideways to
eliminate aisles.

Oversize computer printouts are usually filed in special shelves that hold large suspension folders. The need for these special shelves can be minimized by reducing printouts to 8½-by-11 inches for filing in conventional equipment.

Horizontal Files

Horizontal files store materials, such as maps, drawings, and blueprints, that are normally much larger than materials filed in a vertical file drawer in a flat position. They are most commonly found in engineering and architectural offices.

Rotary Wheel Files

Rotary wheel files were designed to make a limited amount of information available within arm's reach. Rotary wheels vary in size from small desktop units, such as the Rolodex, to large motorized floor models. The large desk-size rotary wheel pictured in Illus. 13-11 holds several trays of cards. Each tray rotates independently for easy access.

Illus. 13-11
The rotary file places a large volume of filed materials within arm's reach of the user. In this desk-size file, trays rotate independently.

Delco Associates, Inc.

Visible Card Files

In a visible card file, cards are arranged in shallow metal trays or on upright stands so that one card overlaps another. Only the lower edge of each card shows. Flipping up the preceding card reveals information on the card desired. Cards can be easily inserted and removed from the file and information can be recorded on both the fronts and backs of cards. An example of a visible card file appears in Illus. 13-12.

Visible card files are used extensively for perpetual inventories, accounting records of sales and purchases, and personnel histories. When information must be available quickly, as in answer to a telephone inquiry, visible card files are especially useful. Colored signals provide a visible means of control; for example, a blue signal attached to the visible edge of a customer's credit card may mean *watch credit closely.*

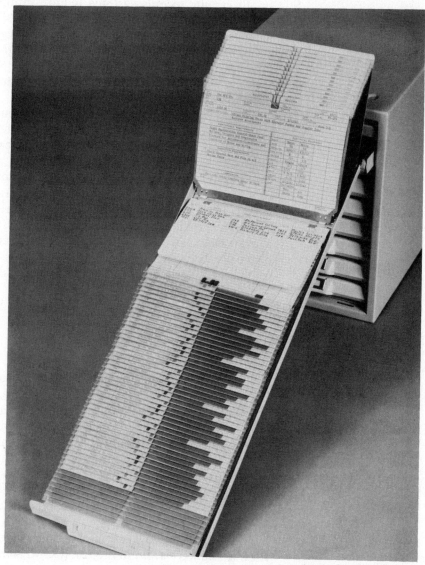

Illus. 13-12
Visible card files are used extensively for situations in which information must be available quickly.

Acme Visible Records

COMPUTERIZED FILING

The processing capabilities and the storage capacity of computers have made electronic storage and retrieval of information a common practice in the modern office. Automated filing equipment, that provides rapid access to large quantities of data, is available from many sources.

Electronic records systems require minimum handling of documents and very little keyboarding. In some systems, incoming correspondence is read by an Optical Character Reader (OCR) and stored in a computer. Outgoing correspondence and other documents produced in-house may also be electronically stored. Some electronic records systems have the capability of storing photographs, signatures, and graphs in addition to text material.

When documents are stored in a computer's memory, they are referred to as *on-line*. In the future, computerized systems will be available in which all related information can be stored in a single database. A *database* is a group of records about a related subject. Conversely, when documents are stored on some medium outside the computer, they are referred to as *off-line*. At present, much off-line storage is on magnetic disks. These disks are relatively inexpensive, and they provide instant retrieval capability. Magnetic disks are comparable to an ordinary file cabinet. As documents are entered electronically, each is assigned a name, number, and entry data. A directory for all stored documents is thus established.

MICROGRAPHICS

Micrographics (the process of creating, using, and storing images and data in *microform*) has merged with computer technology to decrease filing space, reduce misfilings, and increase document retrieval speed. Since the cost of storing documents in a computer is quite high, records managers use microforms extensively, reducing records to a very small size for storage. *Microfilm* is a fine grain, high-resolution film. It is the most common type of microform. An example appears in Illus. 13-13. Images, considerably reduced in size, are stored on reels, in cartridges, on cassettes, on aperture cards, on microfiche, and in jackets.

It is possible to convert information stored in a computer to microfilm. *Computer output microfilm* (COM) is imaged directly from mag-

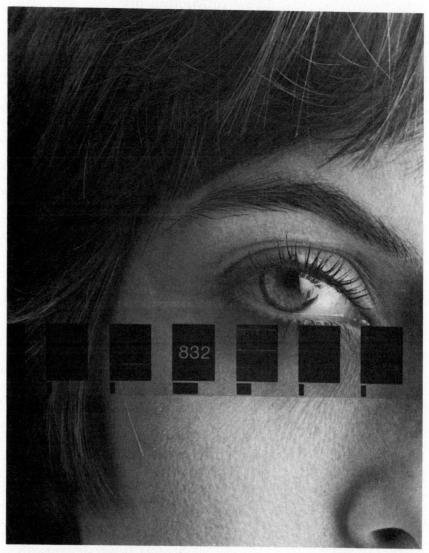

Illus. 13-13
Microfilm
resembles a roll of
16mm or 35mm
film. Images are
produced in
sequence along a
roll.

Eastman Kodak Company

netic tape. The electrical impulses on the tape are converted to visual images and stored on microfilm. Computer input microfilm (CIM) can be converted to electrical impulses, stored on magnetic tape, and used as input. CIM is a relatively low-cost method of rapidly introducing information from a large microfilm file, such as census data, into a computer for processing.

Types of Microforms

A wide variety of user needs and applications has given rise to a number of different forms in which microfilm is made, stored, and used.

Microfilm can be wound onto large *reels* that occupy relatively little space. The disadvantage of storing microfilm on reels is that material cannot be easily located and, therefore, cannot be updated easily.

Cartridges are more convenient than reels for filing microfilm since each roll of film may be wound onto a single cartridge. It is easier to retrieve material from a cartridge than from a reel. Because cartridges can be self-threading, the manual threading necessary with reels is avoided. Microfilm on cartridges is also protected from fingerprints and other damage.

Cassettes are frequently used for filing microfilm. Each cassette contains two spools, the feed and the take-up spool, so that already viewed film can be rewound easily. Microfilm on cassettes can be held in viewing position for reference at a later time.

Microfilm may be more convenient to use if the images are clipped from the film roll and mounted on cards. These are called *aperture cards*. Data may be written on the card or coded by punched holes that permit it to be filed and retrieved manually.

A sheet of film containing multiple images is called *microfiche* (pronounced *microfeesh*). As many as 96 images can be stored on one sheet. Thus, a 96-page report can be recorded on one 6-by-4-inch microfiche. Microfiche can be filed in a card file or in a specially designed book binder.

Strips of film can also be stored in plastic *sleeves* (or *jackets*). Jackets can be updated easily. The images on a single strip of film can be replaced faster and easier than an entire roll of film. Images in a jacket can be copied or read directly from the jacket without removing the film. Jackets are commonly used for personnel applications, medical record files, and credit files.

Microfilm Readers

A variety of readers are available for viewing or reading microforms. There are four basic types of readers. The choice of a reader will depend upon the office environment, the user's needs, the microform used, and cost.

1. *Lap readers* were designed for compactness and personal use. They are available only as microfiche readers.
2. *Portable readers* are lightweight. They may be inserted or folded into a case that is similar to a portable typewriter case.
3. *Desk readers* were designed for use on a table or stand. An example appears in Illus. 13-14.
4. *Reader-printers* allow users to view a microform on a screen and produce a hard copy reproduction of the image as well.

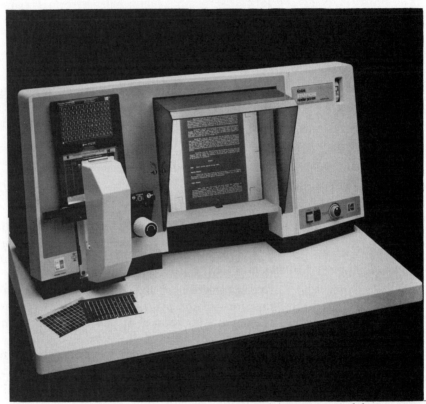

Illus. 13-14
This desktop reader-printer accepts a variety of microforms and produces high-quality prints.

Eastman Kodak Company

Retrieval Systems

A number of retrieval techniques (manual, semiautomated, and automated) that direct the searcher to information on microfilm have evolved over the years. High-speed microform indexing and retrieval systems use computers. *Computer assisted retrieval* (CAR) has the capability to locate or identify microimages (a unit of information, such as a page of text, too small to be read without magnification) by commands initiated through a computer terminal. The computer manipulates an index at very high speeds and provides information for retrieving a desired document. An index serves not only to guide users to the location of the information being sought but also provides a basis for users to screen or select information. The operator of a terminal need only query the computer, and the image is automatically presented to the operator in a matter of seconds. In some systems, information can be displayed at the terminal or printed out as hard copy.

FILING SUPPLIES

Some secretaries purchase their own filing supplies; some requisition them from a stockroom. In either case, a secretary needs to know what filing supplies are available and how to describe each item correctly when ordering.

File Guides

File guides are rigid sheets that divide file drawers into sections. They are frequently attached by a rod to the bottom of the drawer. They come in a variety of tab *widths* or tab *cuts*. A *one-fifth cut* means that the tab occupies one-fifth of the top edge of the guide, permitting five tab positions. Tab positions are identified from left to right as *first position*, *second position*, and so on. An order for guides must specify the cut and position of tabs as one-fifth cut in second position or one-third cut in staggered positions.

Some guide captions come already printed directly on tabs (frequently the case with alphabetic systems), or tabs may be metal or plastic holders into which small typed or printed captions can be easily inserted.

File Folders

File folders come in various styles, weights, cuts, colors, and materials. Tab cuts range from full cut to one-fifth cut with *single* or *double* captions (depth of the cut). Two or more horizontal scores or creases create a flat surface at the bottom of a folder to adjust to the thickness of its contents.

Folders of paper stock come in light, medium, heavy, and extra heavy weights. 11-point paper stock (a point is .001 inch) is medium weight. Some folders are made of thin, durable plastic. For bulky papers, pressboard folders with cloth expansion hinges at the bottom are best.

Folders are also available with built-in fasteners, with metal hooks for suspension from in-drawer frames, and with printed captions. Folders with pockets for holding punched tape, punched cards, or standard size paper can be obtained. It is also possible to color code files by purchasing folders of different colors. Folders that have tab calendars to which plastic markers can be attached to signal dates on which contents should be acted on are also available.

Orders for folders must specify weight, color of stock, size, and position and depth of cut. Orders for folders that will hold any special type of material should contain complete information about the purpose for which the folders will be used.

Folder Labels

Folder labels come in continuous perforated rolls or in self-adhesive strips in a range of colors and in various widths to fit tab cuts. Colored labels and color-striped folders divide a file into color-coded sections. Color coding increases filing accuracy, speeds the filing function, and reduces the time required to find misfiled folders. Colored labels can also aid in transferring materials from active to inactive status. For instance, during a given year, all useful material might be filed in folders with a blue-banded label. When files are reviewed for updating, only blue-banded folders would be considered active.

Cross-Reference Sheets

Cross-reference sheets should be lightweight to conserve space. They should also be in color for easy identification. The secretary can purchase them or have them duplicated in the office.

FILING PROCEDURES

Many papers that should be destroyed are often filed instead. Letters of acknowledgment, letters of transmittal, announcements of meetings (previously noted on the desk calendar), forms and reports already filed in another location, duplicate copies, and routine requests for catalogs and information fall into this category. (In some well-run organizations, routine requests for catalogs and such are returned to the sender with the material.)

Any document that is superseded by another in the file should be removed. When filing a card reporting a change in a telephone number, remove the old one. When a new catalog is filed, destroy the old one.

A temporary file may be kept for materials having no permanent value. Papers in this file are marked with a *T* and destroyed when the action involved is completed.

The government has developed a removal technique to a high level. In many departments of the government, every document receives a date-of-destruction notation before it goes into the file. By continually purging the files of outdated material, a secretary can reduce volume and keep the files up to date.

Preparing Materials for Filing

In addition to files for paper documents, files are maintained in computers and on disks. Filing routines vary with the equipment, but appropriate indexing and coding and adequate cross-referencing are at the heart of any successful system. The term *indexing* means deciding where to file a document; *coding* means labeling a document so that it will always be placed in the same location when refiled.

The increase in the amount of information being filed has led to the development of index entries that include multiple keywords, such as document name, number, author, date, subject, operator, comments, and revision level. Cross-references may be listed either on cross-reference sheets or on the document itself in order to prevent misfiles and retrieval problems. Keywords and other captions should be used freely. A good secretary follows this rule: When in doubt, cross-reference.

In alphabetic filing, material is usually filed according to the most important name appearing on it. A letter to or from a business is usually coded and filed according to the name of that business. If the correspondent is an individual, that person's name is ordinarily used. If, however, an individual is writing as an agent of a business and the name of that business is known, the business name is used instead. Similary, if a business letterhead is used by an individual to write a personal letter, the name of the individual is coded rather than the name of the business. (Complete rules for alphabetic filing sequence are given in the Reference Guide.)

In subject filing, the subject title must be determined from the body of the document. It is then coded according to that subject or according to a number that represents that subject. In numeric filing, the number to be used as a code is determined from the alphabetic card index. In geographic filing, coding is usually done by state and city.

Detailed steps for filing papers are given below:

1. *Conditioning Materials.* To ready papers for filing, remove all pins and paper clips; staple related materials together. Place staples in the upper right corner so that other papers can not be inserted between a pack of stapled sheets in the file. Clippings or other materials smaller than page size should be attached to a regular sheet of paper with rubber cement. Damaged records should be mended or reinforced with tape. If they are not filed in a special place, oversize papers should be folded to the dimensions of the folder and labeled.

2. *Releasing Materials.* When an incoming letter is placed in the filing basket, it should bear a *release mark* indicating that it has been acted on and is ready for filing. This mark may be in the form of the executive's initials, a stamp, the secretary's initials, a code or check mark, a diagonal mark across the sheet, or other agreed upon designation. A check of all attachments will indicate whether they belong to the document. A release mark is not necessary on the file copy of an outgoing letter or on an original letter to which a copy of a reply is attached. A file copy is usually a distinct color.

3. *Indexing and Coding.* Once the secretary has indexed a document (decided where to file it), coding may be done either by underlining or marking on the document the name, word, or number that is to be used as a basis for filing. A colored pencil is commonly used for this purpose. In geographic filing, coding may be done by merely underlining the city and state in the letterhead or in the letter address.

4. *Cross-Referencing.* If there is a possibility that a filed document may be sought under another caption, a cross-reference is made and filed in the second location. Cross-reference forms may be colored or tabbed sheets or cards on which the cross-references are listed. A photocopy or an extra copy of the letter (usually on paper of a different color from the file copy) can also be used as a cross-reference sheet.

    An example of a cross-reference sheet appears in Illus. 13-15. The cross-reference sheet indicates that on May 3 a letter from the Modern Office Equipment Company regarding an exhibit at the Eastern Office Equipment Association convention in Baltimore was received. All correspondence about this convention was filed under Eastern Office Equipment Association. This cross-reference sheet was made and filed under

CROSS-REFERENCE SHEET

Name or Subject _Modern Office Equipment Co._

Date of Item _May 3, 19--_

Regarding _Exhibit, Eastern Office Equipment Assn., Baltimore, MD, June 21-26_

SEE

Name or Subject _Eastern Office Equipment Association_

Authorized by _Joyce Replogle_

Illus. 13-15 Commerically available cross-reference sheets are often colored sheets imprinted with fill-ins. They may also be tabbed, colored cards on which cross-references are listed.

Modern Office Equipment Company. Placing an *X* (for cross-reference) near the name on the original letter indicates that a cross-reference sheet has been filed.

Cross-reference documents that should be filed under more than one name. For instance, a letter from Allen Vincent Company poses a problem. Is Allen a given name or a surname? A regular file should be set up for Vincent, Allen. A cross-reference should be made to Allen, Vincent.

Documents can be cross-referenced by subject. If inquiries have been mailed to several printers asking for quotations on new letterheads, a cross-reference sheet labeled "Letterhead Quotations" may be filed under *Le* listing each of the printer's names. Correspondence with the printers may be filed alphabetically according to their names.

5. *Sorting. Sorting* is arranging papers, including cross-reference sheets, in sequence for filing. When sorting material, the secretary should first make one or two preliminary sortings. For example, in the first sorting, all A to E papers are placed in one group. In the second sorting, papers are put in *A*, *B*, *C*, *D*, and *E* order. It is a simple matter then to put each of these letter groups in correct alphabetic sequence. Sorting for a numeric file should follow a similar procedure.

6.   *Typing Labels.* The one rule that should be observed when typing file labels is the rule of uniformity. The following are useful suggestions (see also Illus. 13-16):

    a.   Type the caption uniformly two or three spaces from the left edge of the label. Position labels uniformly on folders. This practice will prevent captions from being hidden in the file.

    b.   Type the primary reference on the top line in uppercase and lowercase letters. Uppercase and lowercase letters are easier to read than all capitals. If the title is too long for the width of the label, indent the carry-over words on the second line. Omit punctuation marks.

    c.   Type the secondary reference, such as the city and state, on the second line blocked with the first line. If there is a street address, place it on the third line blocked with the preceding lines.

    d.   Spell out an abbreviation if the word is considered in filing. However, if the word is at the end of a name and is not needed for alphabetizing, it may be abbreviated.

Illus. 13-16
The captions at the left are inconsistent in style, punctuation, capitalization, and placement. Captions should be typed in uppercase and lowercase letters as shown at the right.

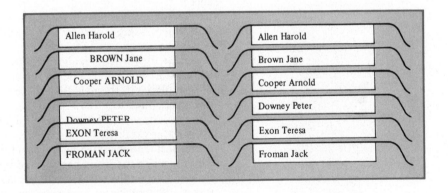

Techniques for Drawer Filing

Use an *individual folder* for letters and other materials to, from, or about one correspondent or subject. For each section use a *Miscellaneous* folder for those individuals and businesses with whom correspondence is infrequent. When five records relating to a person or topic have accumulated in the *Miscellaneous* folder, open an individual folder. File material in the *Miscellaneous* folder in alphabetic order; then, within the alphabetic order, file in chronological order with the most recent date to the front of the folder. Adopt the timesaving guides which follow:

1. Set a definite time for filing every day.
2. File records faceup, top edge to the left, with the most recent date to the front of the folder. When material removed from the file is refiled, it should be placed in correct chronological sequence.
3. Place individual folders immediately *behind* the appropriate guide.
4. Place a Miscellaneous folder at the end of each section of the file, just in front of the next guide. Check Miscellaneous folders frequently to determine if additional individual folders are warranted. Usually an individual folder is made for a person or firm when the accumulated papers amount to five sheets.
5. Use a guide for every 6-8 folders. (Generally, 6-8 folders require about 2.5 centimeters of drawer space.) Keep about 20-25 guides to each drawer.
6. Leave one-fifth of the drawer for expansion and working space.
7. Keep no more than 20-25 sheets in one folder. With bulky files, use scored (creased-at-the-bottom) folders for expansion.
8. Break the files when a folder becomes crowded. Underscore the caption on the old folder in red so that all new material will be placed in the new folder. Date each folder and keep the folders filed together.
9. Use specially scored and reinforced folders for bulky materials, such as catalogs.
10. Avoid accidents by opening only one file drawer at a time. Close it when the filing has been completed.
11. Lift the folder a little way out of the drawer before inserting material so that sheets drop down completely into the folder. When taking a folder out of the files for a short period, pull up the folder directly behind it to mark its place in the file.
12. Do not grasp guides and folders by their index tabs or they will become dog-eared.

Filing Word Processing Materials

When materials are prepared on word processing equipment, documents stored on magnetic media are often indexed and coded for quick filing and retrieval. Floppy disk boxes or standing files (see Illus. 13-9) replace rows of bulky filing cabinets. In some word processing centers, the magnetic medium and the hard copy are filed together.

Handling Confidential Files

Security is always a problem with confidential material—whether in paper or computerized files. Confidential records containing personnel information, new patents, or proposed or in-progress projects, for example, are usually kept under strict security in their respective departments.

If confidential records are in a computerized file, there is always danger that the information will become available to unauthorized personnel. To avoid this possibility, the person requesting a file is assigned a code number that must be entered into the computer before the file is released.

Requesting Material from the Central Files

When the secretary releases material to the central files that will be needed at a definite future date, the item is marked or stamped with the notation *Follow-Up* or *Tickler*. The date on which it will be needed is also noted. Its file folder may also be tabbed with the follow-up date. Frequently, however, the secretary will not know when material will be needed. In these cases, material is requested from the central files when needed by following the usual routine: by telephone, in person, or by a requisition card sent to the filing department. The entire contents of a folder or only specific items in a folder may be requested. An example of a requisition card appears in Illus. 13-17. A telephone request is faster than a written requisition, especially if the information sought can be given orally.

Illus. 13-17
The secretary may request material from the central files on a standardized form such as this.

REQUEST FOR MATERIAL FROM FILES

Name or subject: Mohawk Supply Co.
Address: Boston, Mass.
Date of Material: Latter part of Feb.
Regarding: Adj. on Feb. statement

Date due: 4/6/--
Requested by: Charge date: 4/3/--
Jeannette Morris

The more information the secretary can give to records technicians (names, dates, subjects, addresses, file numbers, etc.), the faster material can be located and delivered. A secretary who is familiar with the central filing system or systems can provide additional leads as to where to locate specific material.

Materials should be returned to the central files promptly. A special problem arises when files checked out to one person are transferred to someone in another department before they are returned to the central files. In some companies, transfers are reported to the filing department on a special form. In any case, records technicians should be informed of the location of all files.

Charge-Out Methods. When an entire folder is taken from the files or when separate items are removed from a folder, a record should be made so that others will be able to locate the materials. Several charge-out methods are in common use. When an individual item is removed from a folder in a paper file, a *substitution card* is usually put in its place. This card indicates the nature of the material, the name of the person who has the material, and the date it was removed. When an entire folder is removed, an *out guide* may be substituted for the folder. An out folder with a substitution card may also be used to take the place of the regular folder. Sometimes the regular folder is retained in the file drawer, and the contents of the folder are transferred to a special *carrier folder*. This practice does not disrupt the filing of new material.

In some companies the original requisitioned material never leaves the central filing area. Instead a photocopy is sent to the person making a requisition. The copy is destroyed when the requesting person is finished with it. Since this practice is expensive and wasteful, it should only be used when it is essential for the original to remain in the central files.

Follow-Up Methods. Secretaries may need to follow up on materials sent to other offices or departments. The daily calendar is frequently used for this purpose. The date for the return is jotted down on the calendar. Another method is to write or type the return date on a card and place it in a tickler file.

Reducing Misfiles

Manufacturers of filing equipment report that the typical office has a 3 percent rate of misfiled records; but, in some cases, the rate is as high as 7 percent. The waste of executive, secretarial, and clerical time because of misfiling is expensive, frustrating, and impacts significantly upon office productivity. In fact, it may cost as much as $80 in executive, secretarial, and clerical time to find one misfiled record. Secretaries should vow to avoid misfiles.

One cause of misfiling is carelessness. Placing a record in a folder without scanning its contents to see if they are related to the document being filed, fastening materials together with paper clips which often also pick up unrelated papers, or putting one folder inside another one are all careless filing mistakes. Another cause of misfiling is not using supplies and equipment as recommended. Secretaries should avoid using too many or too few guides, overcrowding folders so much that their tabs are hidden, overstuffing drawers so that there is inadequate work space, and continuing to file papers in miscellaneous folders when individual folders should have been opened. The final cause of misfiling lies in coding. Using captions that are not mutually exclusive, choosing a wrong title, or using too few cross-references are typical coding errors that lead to misfiles. Illus. 13-18 contains some pointers to help you avoid costly filing mistakes.

If only one paper is lost, it is probably in the wrong folder. Check the folders in front and in back of the correct folder, check between folders, and check the bottom of the drawer. Look in out and in baskets. Don't overlook your employer's desk and your own. Look in the index of files transferred to storage areas. Look under alternate spellings of names and under similar numbers or titles. For instance, if the name you are looking for is Brooks Allen, look under Allen Brooks. If 2309 is lost, look uder 2390. Look in the relative index for other possible captions. If the file is not under CE, look under CA, CO, CU, since the second letter may have been misread.

If an exhaustive search does not locate an item, type all information known about the missing item and date on which the loss was discovered on a sheet of paper. File the sheet where the missing item should be. This practice forestalls a later search for the same item. Also, consider the possibility of obtaining a copy of the lost item from its sender or source.

HOW TO APPRAISE YOUR FILES

Open a file drawer and answer these questions:

How crowded is it?
A tightly packed file drawer slows filing, causes paper cuts, and increases the physical work of filing.

How many file guides have been used?
The purpose of the file guide is to direct the eye to the approximate location of the item sought. Too few guides result in time spent in pushing, pulling, and fingering through the file. If you can place your hand halfway between guides and find the desired folder no more than three or four folders away, you have used an adequate number of guides.

How uniform are the folders?
An efficient file must have uniformly tabbed, logically and consistently arranged folders of uniform size and weight. A conglomerate of folder sizes and tab styles is a sure indication of a sick file.

How have the folders been labeled?
Labels typed in uniform style not only give a neat appearance but save finding time. Time is wasted reading labels that are handwritten, crossed out and retyped, or carelessly positioned on the folder.

How much material is filed in a single folder?
A folder properly scored (creased) and filled will normally hold three-fourths of an inch of material. More material than that will cause papers to "ride up" and become torn or mutilated. Furthermore, the label may be hidden. When labels are hidden, filing speed is greatly reduced.

Illus. 13-18
These five questions will help you appraise your files.

GOOD RECORDS MANAGEMENT PRACTICES

Records management involves the systematic control of records from creation to final disposition. The purpose of records management is to identify, preserve, and protect a company's important documents and to eliminate temporary, useless records with the least possible delay. Experience has shown that as many as 50 percent of some companies' filed records are never retrieved, not even *once*.

The emphasis, however, in records management is not only on the destruction of useless records but also on records preservation and protection. The upsurge in government investigations of corporations, antitrust suits, and price-fixing court cases has made it necessary for companies to be certain they have retained adequate records and that there is no gap in their documentation.

Archives

In addition to the files required for good management, companies also preserve historical records, or *archives*. A secretary to a top executive is frequently responsible for overseeing archives. Usually an organization's archives are kept separate from other records essential for conducting day-to-day business operations.

Material transferred from the central files to the archives should still be indexed in the central files so that they can be located in remote storage. If archives are kept on paper, high-quality rag content paper should be used. A microfilm copy often serves as a backup to paper archives of historical significance.

Retention Schedules

The most efficiently operated companies often have an overall file retention plan for secretaries to follow. Companies use retention schedules to specify how long a document can remain in the office flow; if and when it should be removed to a separate, low-cost records center; and when it should be destroyed. A professionally organized retention plan recommends the following practices:

1. File general correspondence requiring no follow-up for one month.
2. File incoming and outgoing correspondence concerning customers and vendors on routine, promptly settled business; stenographers' notebooks; and expired insurance policies for three months.
3. File bank statements, duplicate deposit slips (except as noted below), work sheets for financial statements, internal reports and summaries (including printouts from data processing equipment and all magnetic tapes and disks), and physical inventories for two years.
4. File canceled payroll checks and summaries, invoices to customers and from vendors, employee data (including accident reports), and completed contracts and leases (as well as similar legal papers) in order to comply with the statute of limitations in affected states.
5. Permanently file books of accounts; minutes of stockholders' meetings; capital stock ledgers and transfer records; corporate election records; certificates on incorporation and corporate charters, constitutions, and bylaws; canceled checks, vouchers, and complete cost data on capital improvements; tax returns and rebated papers; perpetual agreements about pensions, group insurance, and other fringe benefits; deeds; maps, specifications, and plans; patents, trademark registrations, and copyrights; annual reports; organizational charts and procedures manuals; and CPA-certified financial statements.

Because of the enormous volume of output, word processing centers usually have their own retention and disposal schedules. In one typical center these practices prevail:

1. Dictation media are retained one day only.
2. Magnetic media containing original letters that will not be repeated are kept for one week only.
3. Copies of completed material are sent back to the originator without retaining a copy in the center.
4. Each prestructured paragraph that is to be merged with other paragraphs to form a complete letter is reproduced on a separate magnetic medium and is retained until superseded.

Transferring Materials

Plans for storing files are made in relation to the importance of the material and the reduction of costs effected by storing infrequently needed documents in low-priced filing equipment in low-cost rental areas. The possibility of the destruction of vital records by a disaster has caused concern for safe storage—in mountain vaults and caves in some instances and in widely dispersed units in others. Some companies have built their own storage centers, and others have rented file storage space from companies that specialize in providing ready access to stored materials.

Certain types of files can be handled under a *perpetual transfer* plan. When an undertaking is terminated or a project finished the file is closed and transferred. In other cases *periodic transfer* is made. For example, the one-period transfer method takes all material at a designated time from the active files and sends it to the transfer files.

It is all but impossible to avoid consulting some old records. The two-period transfer method tries to avoid this problem. With a two-period transfer, the middle drawers of a file are used for current materials; the upper and lower drawers, for semiactive materials. Semiactive materials are transferred in turn to the inactive files.

A variation of this plan is the *maximum-minimum transfer*. Only inactive material is transferred at regular intervals. For instance, with a transfer date of June 30, 1986, materials filed from January 1, 1986, through June 30, 1986, would not be moved (they would remain in the active files). Materials dated from January 1, 1985, through December 31, 1985, however, would be transferred to storage. New materials would go into the active file until June 30, 1987. Then the files from January 1, 1986, through December 31, 1986, would be transferred, leaving the files for January 1, 1987, through June 30, 1987, in the active files. Each transfer file is labeled with its contents, inclusive dates, and, in some firms, the discard date.

SUMMARY

Every year businesses generate more and more information that must be stored, retrieved, processed, and, in some cases, ultimately destroyed. Consequently, the secretary needs to understand and observe good filing practices.

In order for a filing system to work effectively, the executive and the secretary should plan together. In designing files, attention should be given to findability, confidentiality, and safety of the records. An index should be developed that will indicate where in the files to look for materials.

Materials should be filed according to the designation by which they will be called for and according to the established procedures for the filing method used. There are four basic filing methods: alphabetic, subject, numeric, and geographic. A chronological file is also used as a ready in-office reference. Each filing method has particular advantages depending upon how materials are identified.

Filing equipment is another important facet of records management. The secretary should be familiar with such items as vertical and lateral files, open-shelf files, mobile files, and files for word processing and computer-generated materials. Horizontal files, rotary card files, and visible card files are also available from a number of vendors and have special applications with which the secretary should be familiar.

Microfilm can save space and improve records management efficiency. Computers have made the electronic storage and retrieval of information a common practice in today's offices.

Numerous supplies are available to enhance the efficiency of the records handling task. File folders, guides, labels, and cross-reference sheets should be familiar to the secretary.

In preparing materials for filing, the secretary should condition the materials, see that they have been released for filing, index and code the materials, cross-reference and sort the materials, and type labels. Proven techniques for drawer filing should also be followed. Word processing files and confidential files should be given special attention.

The secretary should also be familiar with procedures for requesting information from central files. Charge-out methods and follow-up methods ensure that files are returned promptly.

Carelessness in placing correspondence in folders, improper equipment, overcrowded folders, and too many or too few guides are some of the reasons for misfiling. Methods for locating misfiled documents should be studied to reduce errors.

Good records management practices include the establishment of complete archives (historical records), the development of sound retention schedules, and the arrangement for transfer of infrequently needed records to permanent storage.

SUGGESTED READINGS

Bassett, Ernest D., David G. Goodman, and Joseph S. Fosegan. *Business Records Control*, 5th ed. Cincinnati: South-Western Publishing Co., 1981.

Johnson, Mina M., and Norman F. Kallaus. *Records Management*, 3d ed. Cincinnati: South-Western Publishing Co., 1982.

Ricks, Betty R., and Kay F. Gow. *Information Resource Management*. Cincinnati: South-Western Publishing Co., 1984.

Thomas, Violet, and Dexter R. Schubert. *Records Management*, Systems and Administration. New York: John Wiley & Sons, Inc., 1983.

QUESTIONS FOR DISCUSSION

1. In what ways has your concept of a secretary's filing work changed since reading this chapter?
2. Filing and records management are commonly used as synonymous terms. What distinction would you make between the two terms?
3. Do you agree with the concept that developing office files is a joint responsibility of the secretary and the executive, or do you think this is the secretary's responsibility alone?
4. How do you think computerized files will alter your secretarial responsibilities?
5. Any communication having reference value should be retained and filed. What are some of the communications that come into or are generated in an office that should be discarded relatively promptly?
6. Companies centralize files for economy and efficiency. Executives, however, tend to resist releasing materials to the central files, preferring to build up their in-office files. What can the secretary do to help resolve this conflict?
7. Your employer asks you to get any correspondence with a Mr. Beal that is available from the central files. Neither you nor your

employer is sure of the spelling of the person's name, nor do you recall the initials. Several years ago, however, there was a person with a similar name involved in an infringement of patent suit against the company. You recall that this person lived in St. Louis. How would you state your request to the central files?

8. If you started to work in a position during a peak period and discovered that many materials were misfiled, that folders and drawers were overcrowded, that materials in folders were not chronologically arranged, and that miscellaneous folders contained materials for which individual folders should have been opened, what would you do?

9. Suggest situations in which each of the following types of files would be advantageous:
   a. Alphabetic
   b. Numeric
   c. Subject
   d. Geographic
   e. Visible card file
   f. Chronological

10. An idiom is an expression or phrase that is somehow peculiar. Although an idiomatic expression is acceptable, it is sometimes illogical in construction or meaning. Retype the following sentences and underscore the idiomatic expressions. Check the Reference Guide to verify your work.
   a. Mr. Grace was tied up in a committee meeting all morning.
   b. We must plow new ground if we are to make our sales quota.
   c. He must live up to the record set by Ms. Evans last year.
   d. We are beating our heads against the wall to solve the problem.
   e. It is impossible to make ends meet on so limited a budget.
   f. Every employee must rise and shine if we are to finish the job today.
   g. She puts up with Mr. King's poor dictation habits, and he puts up with her poor telephone techniques.

PROBLEMS

1. You are administrative assistant and secretary to the sales manager in an organization that has no automated filing equipment. The following items have been seen by the manager and are ready for action. Indicate what disposition you would make of each one. For instance, a notice of an interoffice meeting would be entered on the desk calendar and then destroyed. If an item is retained,

indicate under what name or subject it would be filed. (A separate file is kept for the manager's personal items.)

a. A reminder notice for the next weekly meeting of the Sales Executives' Club

b. A new catalog from Brown and Brown, a firm that provides sales incentive plans (The old catalog is in the files.)

c. An application for a sales position from Wanda Higel

d. Copy for the *Weekly Sales Newsletter*, which is sent to the sales manager by Lloyd Giroux, editor, for final approval before it goes to the reprographics department

e. A letter from an applicant for a sales position thanking the manager for the initial interview

f. An announcement of fall courses at a local college (Employees who take job-related courses are reimbursed by the company for their tuition costs.)

g. A notice that the sales manager's office subscription to *Sales Management* has expired

h. A letter from Rosa Di Lorenzo asking to change her appointment from Wednesday to Friday at the same hour

i. A completed chapter of a book titled *Prognosis of Sales Ability* (The name of the chapter is "Psychological Testing.")

j. A copy of the manager's expense account for the preceding week

k. A requisition for a new dictating unit for the manager's use

l. A car rental contract covering automobiles for sales representatives in the Chicago area

m. A quarterly report of XY Corporation in which the manager holds stock

n. An interoffice memo from the president of the company approving the manager's request to hold a sales training conference at Lake Crystal on September 18-20

o. A letter from an irate customer complaining about the treatment received from the Little Rock area sales representative, Herman Beckwith

p. A catalog from Hertz Company about its blanket quarterly service contract for company rentals

q. Safety regulations applying to all departments in the home office

2. On July 18 your employer, Evelyn Forbes (credit manager), dictated the following letter to be sent to Mr. Frank W. Russo, 421 East Oak Street, Columbus, Ohio, 43210-3223.

Dear Mr. Russo: On June 4 you wrote us that you had purchased the Oak Street Market in Columbus and that you would assume all the market's obligations. At that time the market owed us $86.15 on Invoice No. 3310. On June 13 you ordered more goods for $52.60 at 2/10, n/30. The old bill incurred by the Oak Street Market is now sixty days overdue and your own order of $52.60 remains unpaid. We wonder if something is wrong, Mr. Russo. Won't you write us at once, either enclosing your check for the two invoices or letting us know when we may expect payment. Yours very truly.

You are then told by the credit manager to follow up in ten days with Form Letter 5, if the account is still unpaid. If no action has been secured in 20 days, you are to send Form Letter 8.

a. Type the letter and one carbon copy in good form so you can prepare the carbon copy for filing.
b. Prepare a cross-reference sheet (see page 370) and cross-reference the letter.
c. Release the letter for filing.
d. Prepare a follow-up card for the tickler file.

Case Problems _____

Clint Hobson is office manager for a large transportation company. His secretary, Rhonda Manning, often sends revenue forecasts to the executive vice-president in New York. These forecasts are sent over a microcomputer network. In the interest of time, Mr. Hobson suggested that Rhonda keyboard the reports, proof them on the screen, and then transmit them. On two recent occasions, the reports contained serious errors: $10,000 was transmitted as $100,000 and $5,000 was transmitted as $50,000. Although these errors were caught "at the top," numerous telephone calls ensued, resulting in embarrassment for the local vice-president. Rhonda was blamed for the errors; however, after checking the originals, she discovered that the first error was made by Mr. Hobson, and the second was her typographical error.

How should Rhonda handle this situation? Should she confront Mr. Hobson about his error? Or, should she assume the blame for both errors, apologize to Mr. Hobson, and develop safeguards so that similar errors won't happen again?

Case 3-2
CAUGHT IN THE
MIDDLE—
EMPLOYER'S
REQUEST FOR
PREFERENTIAL
TREATMENT

Jean Smith, copywriter for an advertising agency, handed a 24-page market analysis to her secretary, Judy Dale, saying, "Take this down to reprographics and tell them that this is a rush job. We have to have ten copies, collated and bound, by four o'clock tomorrow, even if they have to let some of their other work go until later."

Aware that her employer had a reputation for making everything a rush job, Judy approached Joe Santini, supervisor of duplicating, with the written job order in hand and said cautiously, "Listen, Joe, Ms. Smith is really in a bind. She has to have ten copies of this market analysis by four o'clock tomorrow, and she knows that she can depend on you to get her out of this crisis."

Joe was unimpressed. "You tell that boss of yours that she has to learn that there are other people in this company who need duplicating. She just has to wait her turn. Look at that pile of work orders. Do you think she has any right to ask to be put ahead of those requisitions? I've done my last rush job for Madam Smith."

Judy considered her alternatives. Should she try again by revealing confidential information that a million dollar contract was riding on that report? Should she accept Joe's refusal and, if so, what should she say to Ms. Smith? What else might she suggest to get the report finished by the deadline?

**Case 3-3
BEING A ROLE
MODEL**

Jane Edwards has developed a company-wide reputation for handling nuisance calls and for appeasing angry customers. Recognizing this ability, the receptionist, who has been in her position for only two months, has begun to transfer all such calls to Jane's desk. Jane realizes that this is a compliment to her tact and diplomacy, but she knows that it keeps her from her assigned responsibilities. Her employer is unaware of the amount of time consumed in this activity.

Should Jane continue to take the calls, should she discuss the situation with her employer, or should she take other action?

**Case 3-4
TELEPHONE
ABUSE**

Jonathan Kaye is secretary to William Vandiver, president of Vanguard Industries, located in San Francisco. As part of his duties, Jonathan supervises three employees located in a room adjoining his office. He reviews communications and copying expenses and often makes recommendations concerning office procedures. For some time he has been concerned about the rising costs of WATS calls. This month his telephone line (one of two company lines) was charged with over 40 hours of use, an increase of 20 hours. Since the company is charged for all calls over ten hours/month, the bill was substantial. To Jonathan's dismay ten of the hours were reported after 5 p.m. when the office was closed. Considering that Vanguard Industries is in the Pacific Time Zone, it is unlikely that use of the WATS line after 5 p.m. could be for business purposes. Jonathan suspects that one or all of his supervisees is making long distance calls on the WATS line after business hours.

What should be Jonathan's plan to control the use of the WATS line? Should he confront the employees in his section?

Case 3-5 BUILDING A GOOD RELATIONSHIP WITH RECORDS MANAGEMENT PERSONNEL

Marty Byrnes is secretary to Mark Janowitz, an attorney in charge of shareholders' relations. Marty was usually annoyed by the type of service she received from the records management administrator, Phyllis Downe. She thought that the department was inefficient and frequently slow and often said so.

One day a crisis developed because of the possibility of a lawsuit instigated by a shareholder. Marty telephoned Ms. Downe to request records that had not been referred to in ten years. Ms. Downe told her that the files were, of course, on microfilm. It would be impossible to get them in fewer than four days. Prior requests had to be taken care of first, and the department was shorthanded. Nobody was immediately available to locate the records by reading the microfilm.

Marty said, "But this is an emergency. Mr. Janowitz wants those records by four o'clock today." Ms. Downe replied, "Sorry, but that will be impossible unless Mr. Janowitz or you want to go 50 miles to the microfilm records center and get them yourselves."

What short-term action can be taken? what long-term action? What principles are involved?

ADMINISTRATIVE SUPPORT SERVICES: TRAVEL AND CONFERENCES

Today's business executive seems to be constantly attending meetings either on company premises, at a location in the community, or at a distant branch office. Consequently, secretaries spend an increasing amount of time planning and following through on travel arrangements. Assisting in the organization of business meetings and reporting their outcomes are two additional secretarial responsibilities directly associated with business travel. These two responsibilities, two tasks which secretaries particularly enjoy, require a great deal of ingenuity and resourcefulness. The college-trained secretary should have little or no difficulty meeting these challenges.

Chapter 14

Expediting Travel Arrangements

Although the technology exists for executives in different geographic locations to hold conferences electronically, many business matters are best addressed in face-to-face discussion. A secretary, therefore, can expect that an executive might have meetings in Los Angeles at 10 a.m. one day, in Atlanta the next, and at home the day after. Out-of-town meetings necessitate arrangements for airline flights, hotels, and ground transportation. Working with either the company's transportation department, with a travel agent, or doing research independently, a secretary secures travel information, obtains the executive's approval, then makes reservations that suit the executive's needs. These arrangements, of course, must conform to the company's established travel policies.

This chapter begins by discussing who is responsible for making business travel arrangements. Types of domestic travel—air, train, and automobile—are also discussed. Facets of international travel are covered in detail. The remainder of the chapter is devoted to the secretary's specific responsibilities when planning a trip, when the employer is away, and when the employer returns to the office.

COMPANY POLICIES REGARDING TRAVEL ARRANGEMENTS

Travel arrangements may be handled by a transportation department within the company, by an outside travel agency, or by the secretary. The secretary's first concern in handling travel arrangements is to learn the company's policies. Who handles travel arrangements? What airline, hotel, and other credit cards are issued and what procedures are authorized for their use? How are employees reimbursed for travel expenses? What restrictions does the company have as to per diem (per day) travel expenses? How are travel funds obtained? Which hotels offer business discounts?

Transportation Department

In large organizations, actual reservations for travel are expedited by a transportation department or by a central travel service that maintains close contact with all carriers. A transportation department has complete official guides for airlines and railroads and deals with special reservation agents who serve only large-volume buyers. In a large organization, a secretary would inform the transportation department of a proposed trip and of the time preferences of the executive. The transportation department would then suggest possible schedules to be approved by the executive. When a decision is made, the secretary would complete a transportation voucher. This form would be sent to the transportation department for its records. The department would then either issue or obtain tickets and distribute credit cards to authorized personnel.

Travel Agencies

In recent years the business world has turned increasingly to travel agencies to make their travel arrangements. By the very nature of its specialization, a reputable agency can cut through the maze of constantly changing fares, flight schedules, and classes of service that has emerged since the deregulation of the airline industry. Even some companies with transportation departments use travel agencies to save time and costs. In fact, it is estimated that 90 percent of all major corporations now use travel agencies.

Travel agencies are paid commissions by airlines, railroads, hotels, and other services booked for a client. Although travel agencies have a policy of not charging clients for their services, some agencies are beginning to do so, particularly for trips involving extensive planning.

Travel agencies offer their clients help in planning an itinerary, obtaining tickets, selecting and making hotel reservations, and arranging for rental cars. Their service also includes free delivery of tickets to the traveler. Because of their contacts in the travel industry, agents may be successful in obtaining reservations when none are available to the public. Some agencies extend credit. Most will accept major credit cards.

If you are asked to choose a travel agency for your employer, determine which agencies specialize in business travel and seek a recommendation from a satisfied business traveler. Look for membership in the American Society of Travel Agents (ASTA) or the Association of Retail Travel Agents (ARTA).

The Secretary

If a business organization has neither the services of an intracompany transportation department nor the regular services of a travel agency, the secretary works directly with airlines, hotels, car rental agencies, etc., to make all travel arrangements. The alert secretary will soon discover the employer's preference for hotel chain, airline, and seat location. Consulting the executive about these preferences and remembering them from trip to trip alleviates some of the mental and physical stress of planning a trip and thus contributes to its overall effectiveness.

AIR TRAVEL

Most people traveling on business prefer to fly, especially on long trips, because they save time. Today a traveler can breakfast in New York, lunch in Chicago, and dine in San Francisco. Supersonic transport planes cross the Atlantic from Washington to Paris in a little over three hours.

Not only speed but comfort prompts many business travelers to fly. Wide-bodied jet aircraft that connect the large cities of the United States with each other and with foreign cities are equipped with large away-from-seat lounges. They also have in-flight movies and recorded entertainment. Some travelers prefer smaller jets, which provide similar comforts.

The electronic age gives executives traveling by air the advantage of keeping in close contact with operations at home. On some flights, air-to-ground telephone service is available. Payment for these calls is by an approved credit card.

The deregulation of the airline industry has produced a number of new airlines; thus, more flight alternatives are available and competition in fares is growing. For example, most major airlines are supported by regional lines that fly to cities where passenger traffic does not support jet service. A passenger traveling from a metropolitan area to a small city may fly to that destination on a small jet or on a propeller aircraft.

Classes of Flights

Most airlines have two kinds of flight classifications: first-class and coach. An additional section, business class, is also available on some flights.

First class serves complimentary meals during conventional meal-times and generous refreshments. Several attendants are available to take care of passenger needs. Seats are wider, farther apart, and provide more legroom than those in the coach section. First-class fares are considerably higher (50 percent or more) than coach or economy fares.

Coach (or economy) serves a complimentary meal or snack when the plane is aloft at mealtime (on most airlines). Coffee, tea, or soft drinks are available at no charge. Coach passengers often sit three abreast, have less legroom, and occupy narrower seats than first-class passengers.

Business class is available on some wide-bodied aircraft. Business-class seating is directly behind first class; legroom and complimentary meals are similar to first class. Business-class fares are only slightly more than coach fares.

Many organizations have a policy that only high-ranking executives travel first class. The secretary should learn this rule before making travel arrangements. Even though an executive may be entitled to first-class accommodations, coach reservations will probably be adequate for short trips. On a long trip, the added comfort makes a first-class reservation desirable.

Services Offered

Meal service differs among competing airlines. On certain domestic flights, a choice of entrée is offered and meals to accommodate special diets can be ordered. Some no-frills airlines have instituted a new practice—they charge for meal service.

Shuttle service is available between certain cities, such as New York/Boston, New York/Washington, and San Francisco/Los Angeles. Passengers board the plane without reservations, and the flights leave at frequent intervals as soon as the plane is filled. Passengers can purchase tickets at shuttle locations at self-ticketing machines or pay their fares aloft with cash, credit card, or personal check. Only carry-on luggage is accepted on some shuttle flights.

On most domestic flights, each passenger is allowed to check three pieces of luggage: one measuring not more than 62 inches in girth; another, not more than 55 inches; and the third, not more than 45 inches. Some luggage may be carried aboard without charge if it fits under a seat in front of the passenger or in an enclosed compartment overhead. Passengers who have luggage in excess of the allowed amount are charged excess baggage rates in addition to the regular fare.

Air Fares

Air fares are constantly changing. In addition to first-class, business, and coach fares, domestic airlines offer special discount rates for night flights, for excursions that comprise a definite number of days, for certain weekend trips, and for tickets purchased in advance. Reduced rate night flights are not appropriate for most business travel.

In addition to the discounts cited above, major airlines also offer frequent flyer incentive programs. A variety of rewards to passengers who accumulate travel mileage with an airline are available. Examples of such rewards include upgrading in class of service (purchase a coach ticket for first-class seating), fare discounts, and free round-trip airline tickets.

Flight Schedules

Airlines publish flight schedules and make them available in airports, major hotels, and travel agencies. Although schedules are not uniform in structure among airlines, Illus. 14-1 (a sample schedule not intended to be valid), shows the ease with which flight schedules can be read. The example is a schedule of all Trans World Airlines, Inc. (TWA) flights between Albuquerque, New Mexico, and New York/Newark airports.

Notice that there are four flights daily from Albuquerque to the New York City area (Flights 402, 94, 454, and 240); however, Flight 454 does not operate on Saturdays. None of these flights are nonstop. Three of these daily flights (402, 94, and 454) show scheduled stops that do not require a change of airplane. These are called *direct flights*. Two of the direct flights land in Newark, just across the Hudson River from New York. The other direct flight lands at Kennedy in New York. In order to land at La Guardia Airport, which is nearer to Manhattan than Kennedy, a change of airplane is necessary.

An executive from Albuquerque planning a business trip to New York would most likely prefer Flight 94. It has only one stop and no change of planes. The 4:55 p.m. arrival time (local time) gives the executive time to check into a hotel and rest before an evening engagement and prepare for an appointment the next morning. The schedule indicates that this particular flight is a wide-body aircraft and, therefore, may offer business class. Note also that a meal is served on this flight. This schedule does not show that Albuquerque is on mountain standard time. A passenger loses two hours flying east from that time zone and gains two hours flying west from New York City.

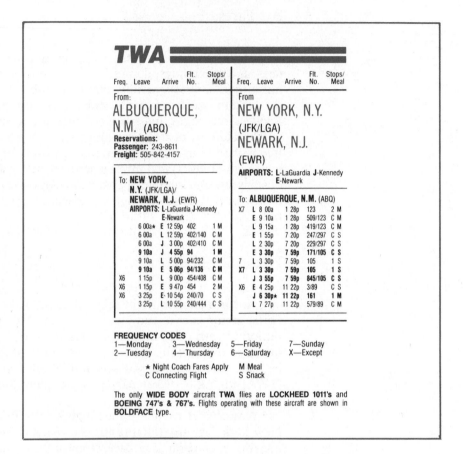

Illus. 14-1
This schedule of
TWA flights
between
Albuquerque and
New York can be
interpreted easily.

In returning to Albuquerque the executive has a choice of three direct flights (123, 105 and 161) departing either La Guardia or Kennedy airports. Flight 123, although not available on Sundays, is a likely choice because it arrives in Albuquerque in the afternoon giving the executive time to check in with the office. The other direct flights do not arrive until early or late evening. If the executive would be traveling on a Sunday and wanted to arrive in Albuquerque in the early afternoon, either flight 509/123 or 419/123, departing from Newark and La Guardia respectively, would be selected.

In researching information on flights, the secretary should be aware that travelers normally have flight preferences in the following order:

1. Nonstop flights to the destination
2. Direct flights to the destination
3. Connecting flights to the destination using the same airline

4.   Connecting flights to the destination using another airline (Airplane gates may be a considerable distance from each other; in some airports, gates may be in different terminals.)

You should present possible flight schedules to the executive according to these preferences. You should also be aware that, like New York City, many cities have more than one airport. In making connecting flight reservations, be especially careful to book the connecting flight from the same airport.

Official Airline Guides

The transportation department of a corporation may subscribe to the *Official Airline Guide, North American Edition* and its optional supplement on fares. Published by Official Airline Guides, Inc., 2000 Clearwater Drive, Oak Brook, IL 60521, this guide provides complete information on direct and connecting flights, departure and arrival times, stops en route, and ground transportation availability. Other informative publications for the traveling executive are the monthly *OAG North American Pocket Flight Guide* and the quarterly *OAG Travel Planner and Hotel/Motel Guide.* Subscribers receive updated materials automatically. Telecommunications technology permits subscribers to access the *OAG North American and Worldwide Electronic Edition* via computer terminals. This electronic edition updates airline schedules for the world weekly and for North American flights daily.

Using the *Official Airline Guide*, the secretary can research the most convenient available flights and present alternative plans for the employer's approval before initiating the actual reservation. This publication (according to the edition used) also gives information about airport facilities, distances from airports to city centers, limousine service (time, fares, and pickup points), hotels, car rentals, and airport taxi service. The *Official Airline Guide* is simple to use once you understand the general method of presentation. Keys to the abbreviations and symbols used are listed on its preliminary pages. Flight information is listed alphabetically by the destination city, then alphabetically by cities from which flights to the destination city are available. For example, suppose your employer is to fly from Atlanta, Georgia to Tulsa, Oklahoma. You would turn to the "TO TULSA" section in the guide. Under "TO TULSA," you would locate the "FROM ATLANTA" listings. You would find a flight schedule similar to that shown in Illus. 14-2. Reading the boldface print at the top of the schedule, you learn the following:

1. Tulsa is on central daylight time (CDT).
2. TUL is the city/airport code for Tulsa.
3. Atlanta is on eastern daylight time (EDT).
4. ATL is the city/airport code for Atlanta, Georgia.

To TULSA, OKLAHOMA **CDT TUL**

From **ATLANTA, GEORGIA-CONT.**

M-ATL D-PDK B-JAO G-JGL P-JAJ F-FTY T-JAE

	7:46a	M	10:31a	T	AA	552	FYBQM	M80	B	1
					AA 552 DISCONTINUED AFTER 1JUL					
	8:42a	M	9:35a	T	DL	677	FYBQM	73S	S	0
X6	9:10a	M	12:06P	T	AA	165	FYBQM	72S	B	1
					AA 165 DISCONTINUED AFTER 1JUL					
X6	9:10a	M	12:08P	T	AA	165	FYBQM	72S	B	1
					AA 165 EFFECTIVE 2JUL-18JUL					
	3:37P	M	4:30P	T	DL	1053	FYBQM	73S		0
	6:50P	M	7:40P	T	DL	1159	FYBQM	D9S	D	0
							EX 4JUL			
			CONNECTIONS							
	7:46a	M	8:41a	DFW	AA	461	FYBQM	M80	B	0
E- 2JUL	9:40a	DFW	**10:34a**	T	AA	552	FYBQM	M80		0
X7	**7:50a**	M	7:58a	MEM	RC	863	FYBQM	DC9	S	0
	9:05a	MEM	**10:12a**	T	RC	801	FYBQM	DC9		0
6	**8:00a**	M	8:10a	MEM	CC	940	FYBMV	727	B	0
	9:05a	MEM	**10:12a**	T	RC	801	FYBQM	DC9		0
X7	**8:20a**	M	8:50a	STL	OZ	686	YBQMV	D9S	B	0
	10:10a	STL	**11:18a**	T	OZ	763	YBQMV	D9S		0
	8:31a	M	9:16a	ORD	UA	591	FYBQM	72S	B	0
D-15JUL	9:44a	ORD	**11:27a**	T	UA	375	FYBQM	73S		0
	8:31a	M	9:16a	ORD	UA	591	FYBQM	72S	B	0
E-16JUL	9:54a	ORD	**11:37a**	T	UA	375	FYBQM	73S		0
X6	**9:10a**	M	10:05a	DFW	AA	893	FYBQM	M80	B	0
E-20JUL	11:15a	DFW	**12:08P**	T	AA	165	FYBQM	72S		0
6	**9:10a**	M	10:05a	DFW	AA	837	FYBQM	72S	B	0
E- 5JUL	11:15a	DFW	**12:09P**	T	AA	165	FYBQM	M80		0
D-12JUL										
6	**9:10a**	M	10:05a	DFW	AA	893	FYBQM	M80	B	0
E-19JUL	11:15a	DFW	**12:09P**	T	AA	165	FYBQM	M80		0
	9:30a	M	9:59a	STL	TW	399	FYBMK	727		0
	10:55a	STL	**12:06P**	T	TW	27	FYBMK	M80		0
	9:35a	M	10:15a	ORD	AA	281	FYBQM	M80	S	0
	11:20a	ORD	**12:58P**	T	AA	529	FYBQM	72S	S	0
X7	**9:38a**	M	10:05a	STL	EA	252	FYHQK	D9S		0
	10:55a	STL	**12:06P**	T	TW	27	FYBMK	M80		0
X67	**9:45a**	M	9:55a	MEM	CC	240	FYBMV	727	B	0
	12:15P	MEM	**1:19P**	T	RC	809	FYBQM	DC9		0
	9:46a	M	10:50a	DFW	EA	615	FYHQK	D9S	S	0
	12:01P	DFW	**12:55P**	T	DL	904	FYBQM	D9S		0
	10:15a	M	11:10a	DFW	DL	167	FYBQM	767	S	0
	12:01P	DFW	**12:55P**	T	DL	904	FYBQM	D9S		0
	11:20a	M	12:03P	ORD	UA	993	FYBQM	727	L	0
	1:09P	ORD	**2:52P**	T	UA	361	FYBQM	73S	L	0
X6	**11:27a**	M	11:35a	MEM	RC	823	FYBQM	DC9		0
	12:15P	MEM	**1:19P**	T	RC	809	FYBQM	DC9		0
	12:34P	M	1:01P	STL	EA	274	FYHQK	D9S	L/S	0
	2:15P	STL	**3:29P**	T	TW	87	FYBMK	727		0
	1:30P	M	2:25P	DFW	DL	887	FYBQM	L10	L	0
	3:05P	DFW	**3:59P**	T	DL	802	FYBQM	D9S		0
							EX 4JUL			
	2:01P	M	2:56P	DFW	AA	401	FYBQM	M80	S/	0
E- 2JUL	4:02P	DFW	**4:56P**	T	AA	342	FYBQM	M80		0
	2:15P	M	2:45P	STL	OZ	684	YBQMV	D9S		0
	3:25P	STL	**4:33P**	T	OZ	581	YBQMV	D9S		0
	2:55P	M	3:05P	MEM	RC	803	FYBQM	DC9		0
	4:05P	MEM	**5:17P**	T	RC	641	FYBQM	DC9		0
	3:15P	M	4:10P	DFW	DL	715	FYBQM	757	S	0
	4:46P	DFW	**5:40P**	T	DL	1078	FYBQM	73S		0
	4:49P	M	5:44P	DFW	AA	263	FYBQM	M80	S	0
E- 2JUL	6:35P	DFW	**7:29P**	T	AA	223	FYBQM	72S		0
	5:10P	M	5:39P	STL	TW	67	FYBMK	727	D/S	0
	6:50P	STL	**8:08P**	T	TW	487	FYBMK	727		0
	5:29P	M	6:14P	ORD	UA	529	FYBQM	727	D	0
E-16JUL	6:59P	ORD	**8:46P**	T	UA	745	FYBQM	73S	D	0
	5:30P	M	6:15P	ORD	UA	529	FYBQM	727	D	0
D-15JUL	6:59P	ORD	**8:46P**	T	UA	745	FYBQM	73S	D	0
X6	**5:40P**	M	6:10P	STL	OZ	688	YBQMV	D9S	D	0
	6:55P	STL	**8:40P**	T	OZ	521	YBQMV	D9S		1
	5:55P	M	6:46P	MCI	EA	385	FYHQK	72S	D	0
	7:30P	MCI	**8:20P**	T	EA	216	FYHQK	D9S		0
	6:35P	M	6:39P	MEM	RC	853	FYBQM	DC9	S	0
	7:55P	MEM	**9:02P**	T	RC	717	FYBQM	DC9		0
	6:45P	M	6:49P	MEM	DL	427	FYBQM	72S	S	0
	7:55P	MEM	**9:02P**	T	RC	717	FYBQM	DC9		0
	7:40P	M	8:35P	DFW	AA	479	FnYnBQM	M80	D	0
E- 2JUL	9:52P	DFW	**10:46P**	T	AA	271	FnYnBQM	M80		0
	8:25P	M	9:20P	DFW	DL	199	FnYnQMBn	L10		0
	9:59P	DFW	**10:53P**	T	DL	241	FnYnQMBn	D9S		0
							EX 4JUL			

Illus. 14-2
This schedule, taken from the *Official Airline Guide*, should help plan a business trip from Atlanta, Georgia to Tulsa, Oklahoma. (Not intended to be valid.)

Notice that most of the flights are nonstop, as indicated by the *O* at the far right. Select a flight based on your employer's time preference and the availability of the flight. Consider the following:

1. The first flight of the day is at 7:46 a.m. This flight operates daily.
2. It arrives in Tulsa at 10:31 a.m.
3. It is an American Airlines flight, Flight 552.
4. A number of fares including first class (F), coach/economy (Y), and coach/economy discounted (B, Q, and M) are available.
5. The aircraft is a McDonnell Douglas DC9 Super 80 (M80).

Under "CONNECTIONS," you find a listing of connecting flights. If an executive wanted to go to Dalla/Fort Worth for a brief conference at the airport and then to Tulsa, it could be arranged via a connecting flight. Notice that

1. American Airlines Flight 893 leaves Atlanta at 9:10 a.m. and arrives in Dallas/Fort Worth at 10:05 a.m.
2. The connecting flight, American Airlines Flight 165, leaves Dallas/Fort Worth at 11:15 a.m. and arrives in Tulsa at 12:08 p.m.
3. A number of fare options are available.
4. The aircraft on the connecting flight is a Boeing 727-200 (72S).
5. Both flights are nonstop.
6. Breakfast is served aboard Flight 893.

Flight Reservations and Ticketing

Flight reservations may be made by telephone, in person at the airport terminal, in an airline ticket office, or at a travel agency. After choosing a flight, the traveler asks the airline reservations agent to check for the availability of space at the desired fare structure. Space is confirmed by means of computer equipment that records and stores flight reservations from all ticketing stations. If your employer prefers to travel coach/economy, and that particular section of the plane is booked, first class or business class may be available. If so, check with the executive to see which class should be booked.

A ticket for an in-person reservation is issued at once; otherwise, it is mailed to a specified address or held for pickup at the ticket office or at the airport. Payment can be made by cash, by check, or by credit card. An organization with a transportation department usually has the authority and the supplies for issuing tickets in-house. Most travel agencies have this capability as well.

Even when a trip involves several destinations and several airlines, only one ticket is issued (by the airline on which the flight originates). Passengers who do not know their continuing flights can purchase an open ticket and make reservations later. Data for any changes in ticketed flights are merely attached to the original ticket.

When checking in for a flight, a passenger receives a boarding pass and, on most flights, is assigned a specific seat in either the smoking or nonsmoking section of the plane. On some airlines seat assignments are made when a ticket is purchased.

Airlines allow customers to make telephone reservations with credit cards. If payment is by credit card, the secretary must know the credit card number and its expiration date. Many organizations issue air travel credit cards to key personnel. Other companies maintain charge accounts with various airlines and are billed regularly for authorized travel.

Redemption of Unused Plane Tickets

Unused tickets or unused portions of plane tickets can be redeemed by submitting them to the issuing airline or travel agency. If payment was with a credit card, the refund is processed through the card account. If the ticket purchase was through a travel agency, the agent processes the refund. In the case of lost tickets, a waiting period of 120 days is imposed before a refund is made because there is the possibility that a lost ticket could be used by someone else.

Airport Services

Airport limousines shuttle travelers between downtown locations and airports, usually at lower rates than taxis. In some cities, limousines call for passengers at key hotels; in others, they depart from downtown ticket offices or downtown airline terminals. If the limousine leaves from a downtown airport terminal, a passenger may check in for a flight at that terminal. If the limousine leaves from a point other than a terminal, passengers check in at the airport.

Limousines may also shuttle passengers between two or more airports serving one city. A handy reference for frequent flyers which outlines transit options, rates, and schedules between airports and city centers is *Crampton's International Airport Transit Guide.*[1]

Helicopters may also be available at some airports to transport passengers to a nearby airport or to a downtown location. Check airline timetables for this information.

Major airlines also operate flight clubs. Travelers may join a flight club for a moderate annual fee. Many executives find it less tedious to wait for planes in flight club lounges than at busy airline gates.

Company Owned Planes

Many corporations own one or more planes. They do so to reduce travel time for executives more than is possible by commercial aviation. Companies who have branch offices or plants in inaccessible outlying areas also find it necessary to maintain aircraft transportation for their personnel. Coordination of company planes is made by an in-house transportation department. Many companies observe the precaution of limiting the number of top officials who can fly in the same plane (private or commercial) to protect continuity of management in case of an accident. Chartering planes is another option businesses have to transport personnel to areas not served by regional airlines.

TRAIN TRAVEL

Traveling long distances by train is a luxury busy executives cannot afford. Using commuter trains within metropolitan areas, however, is another matter. Amtrak, the nations's coast-to-coast railroad, offers Metroliner service between Boston, Washington, DC, and points in-between. Improved service has enabled Amtrak to compete with airlines in this commuter market. On these special trains, a seat is reserved when a ticket is purchased. Because of heavy demand, tickets should be bought well in advance.

The secretary can become familiar with rail services by consulting the *Official Guide of the Railways.* This guide is issued monthly and contains schedules of all railway and steamship lines in the United States, Canada, Mexico, and Puerto Rico.

---

[1]This guide is available from Crampton Associates, P.O. Box 1214, Homewood, IL 60430 for $2.45 plus postage.

RENT-A-CAR TRAVEL

Business executives often rent cars during out-of-town trips. Both airline and railroad timetables indicate cities with rent-a-car service. Automobile rental companies publish directories of their rental agency locations both here and abroad, listing daily rates and mileage charges at each station. You can arrange for a rental car by calling the local office of a car rental agency or by using its toll-free number. It is also possible to arrange for a car rental through an airline. Since rates differ depending on car makes, the number of days leased, weekday or weekend travel, and anticipated mileage, check several agencies for the best price.

When ordering a rental car, indicate the make and model of car wanted, where it will be picked up, the number of days the car is needed, and the method of payment. Most car rental agencies accept major credit cards. They also provide maps, dining guides, entertainment guides, etc., to clients who may be unfamiliar with the area.

The American Automobile Assocation provides its members with travel guides for any contemplated trip. Several oil companies and insurance companies also map routes on request. In addition to these sources, bookstores and travel agencies also stock many handy dining and lodging guides.

HOTEL/MOTEL RESERVATIONS

There are several ways to make a hotel/motel reservation. If there is sufficient time, you may write for a reservation. You may also make reservations by telephone. Chains, such as Hilton and Sheraton, have communication systems that reserve rooms in any of their hotels worldwide through local offices. Other major hotels maintain local offices in major cities. Toll-free 800 numbers for these hotels can also be found in the telephone book. Most airlines make hotel and motel reservations for their passengers. Some have a business tie to a particular chain: for example, United Airlines and the Westin Hotel Co. Reservations for lodging should include the following kinds of information:

1. *Indicate the kind of room you desire.* Note whether you need one room, several rooms, or a suite of rooms. If you prefer a certain room location (close to an elevator, for example), a certain floor, a room with a view, etc., say so.
2. *Indicate your choice of accommodations.* Do you prefer a double bed? a tub or shower bath?

3. *Indicate the approximate or relative rate.* Do you want a medium-priced or a luxury-priced room?
4. *Give the names of the persons in your party.*
5. *Give the name of your company.* Commercial or convention rates may apply to business guests.
6. *Indicate the date of arrival and the approximate time of registration, if known.* Request a *guaranteed arrival* if you know that arrival will be after check-in-time. The room will be held, but the guest will be billed even if the room is unoccupied. Generally, reservations must be cancelled 24 hours ahead of time.
7. *Inquire about transportation services.* Ask if the hotel has a courtesy car that provides transportation between the airport and the hotel. If so, indicate flight number and arrival time.
8. *Indicate the number of days lodging is needed.*
9. *Indicate the method of payment.*

After a reservation is made, request a confirmation record or a confirmation number that the executive can use when registering. Rooms are at a premium in many cities, and a confirmed reservation is a good precaution.

To simplify their accounting, some hotels and motels ask that a deposit *not* be sent. Small operations may require a deposit.

In canceling hotel reservations, obtain a cancellation number for your records, particularly if the reservation was guaranteed. It is also recommended to get the name of the hotel clerk, in case the cancellation request is not recorded.

INTERNATIONAL TRAVEL

During the past three decades, American business firms of almost every size have expanded their operations or their interests internationally. These multinational companies generally have an international division within their organization and branch offices in foreign cities. A secretary to a top executive in a multinational firm will probably plan international as well as domestic travel.

General Considerations

Planning for foreign travel differs in several ways from planning for short, domestic trips. For instance, an executive traveling from New York to London crosses five time zones. Travel experts estimate that it takes the human body *one* day to adapt fully for each time zone crossed. Body rhythms and cycles are disrupted, and changes in body temperature and heart rate occur. These changes are the effect of *jet lag*. If possible, a secretary making international travel arrangements should schedule a flight that will allow an executive one day of rest before a scheduled meeting in London. For the return trip, two days are recommended for the traveler to adjust physically and psychologically to the time difference. If it is not possible to schedule a full day of rest before a London meeting, schedule a flight that arrives the night before. On the return, schedule a flight that arrives either on a Friday or Saturday, giving the executive the weekend to rest.

Another difference between domestic and foreign travel is in arranging appointments. Both because of possible difficulties in getting around in a foreign city and because of the slower pace at which foreign business is conducted, the American visitor will want to keep appointments to two or three a day.

Holidays are different in each country. In planning a trip, check to see if a holiday occurs during the period. For instance, in Italy many business firms close down for vacation the entire month of August.

Learning the customs of the countries to be visited is important to the success of a business visit. An excellent reference is the *Countries of the World and Their Leaders Yearbook* published by Gale Research Company. This yearbook gives background information about each country, health recommendations, methods of travel, and so forth. Most of the international airlines now publish guides for conducting business in Europe and the Far East. In addition, the U.S. Department of State publishes a series of pamphlets entitled *Background Notes on the Countries of the World,*[2] which should be very useful to the secretary of a traveling executive. Another reference is *The Multinational Executive Travel Companion*, published annually.[3] Both publications contain information about important trade fairs, holidays, time differences, climate, hotels and restaurants, office hours, important business contacts, currency exchange, business etiquette and customs, and invaluable hints for improving business contacts.

The business card is an important adjunct to the business call. A card with English on one side and the appropriate foreign language on the reverse side would be an asset to a traveling executive. A card is always presented by a caller; therefore, a business visitor can easily use up a supply of 200 cards while attending a business fair. The European

---

[2]Available from the Superintendent of Documents, Government Printing Office, Washington, DC 20402

[3]A pocket-sized guide published by World-Wide Business Centres, Inc., 575 Madison Avenue, New York, NY 10022.

business fair has no counterpart in this country. An entire year's output of a product may be sold during such a fair.

Abroad it pays to bring gifts—judiciously. There are many subtleties to the art of international gift-giving. Where possible, offer a gift which is company associated, such as a pen with a company logo. What pleases a customer in London may be offensive to a Tokyo counterpart. A present to the wife of a business contact in Europe will be accepted graciously, but a present to the wife of a Near Eastern businessman is offensive. As with gifts, the practice of tipping may not be appropriate. Asking advice of a resident of the country being visited may be beneficial.

Services of a Travel Agency

In lieu of a well-established company transportation department, a travel agency can be of great help in planning a foreign trip. The secretary to an executive who travels abroad frequently will find the following services of a travel agent almost indispensable:

> Making hotel and rent-a-car reservations
> Listing available transportation
> Suggesting itineraries and procuring tickets
> Notifying you of the required travel documents and how to obtain
> > them
> Supplying currency conversion rules and obtaining foreign
> > currency
> Explaining baggage restrictions
> Obtaining insurance for traveler and baggage
> Listing port taxes (Most international airports levy a port tax from
> > $1 to $3. An international transportation tax is also imposed
> > on each international passenger departing from the continen-
> > tal United States.)
> Providing information about visas
> Arranging for the traveler to be met by a representative or a
> > limousine
> Supplying information about vaccinations and inoculations
> Explaining customs regulations
> Giving average temperatures

Passports

The first requisite for foreign travel is a *passport*. A passport is an official document, issued by the Department of State, granting permission to travel. It authenticates a person's right to protection in the host country. For travel in most countries outside the United States, a passport is necessary. U.S. citizens are not required to carry passports in Canada, Mexico, Bermuda, the West Indies, or Central America, although proof of citizenship may be requested. For example, a visitor to Mexico must have a tourist card and carry proof of citizenship.

Passport application forms can be obtained from a travel agent; from passport offices in Boston, Chicago, Los Angeles, Miami, New Orleans, New York, Philadelphia, San Francisco, Seattle, Honolulu, and Washington; from the passport office in local federal buildings; or from designated post offices. For your nearest passport office, look in the White pages. Most telephone directories list a number for passport information under "United States Government, Postal Service."

In order to obtain a passport for the first time, an applicant is required to appear in person before an agent of the passport office or before a clerk of a federal or state court authorized by law to naturalize aliens. The applicant must present the following papers:

> The completed passport application
> Proof of United States citizenship (birth certificate, baptismal certificate, or certificate of naturalization)
> Proof of identification bearing signature and description, such as a driver's license
> Two signed duplicate photographs *taken by a photographer* within the past six months
> The passport fee

If the applicant is going abroad on a government contract, a letter from the employing company is required showing the applicant's position, destination, purpose of travel, and proposed length of stay.

As soon as a passport is received, it should be signed and the information requested on the inside cover should be filled in. During overseas travel, a passport should always be carried and *never* left in a hotel room. Loss of a passport should be reported immediately to the nearest passport office or, if abroad, to the nearest consulate. Business travelers should also carry a letter from the business they represent that describes the nature and the duration of their visit.

A person holding an expired passport must reapply for a current passport. A renewal application may be obtained from the nearest passport office or designated post office. The applicant completes the form, signs and dates the application, attaches two signed duplicate photographs taken within six months of the date of the application, and encloses the expired passport and the passport fee. These materials are mailed to the nearest passport office.

A passport is valid for ten years from date of issue. Since processing a passport application may take up to six weeks, persons contemplating foreign travel should keep their passports in order. Secretaries to traveling executives should note passport expiration dates in the tickler file. An example of a passport appears in Illus. 14-3.

Many Americans who travel abroad in the future will use electronic passports that can be read by a machine. When inserted in a special machine, the passport will display a coded symbol invisible to the unaided eye. Electronic passports should speed the passage of travelers through borders and reduce the fraudulent use of United States passports. A long-term goal of the system is the linking of passport reading machines to a central computer that will keep track of international travelers.

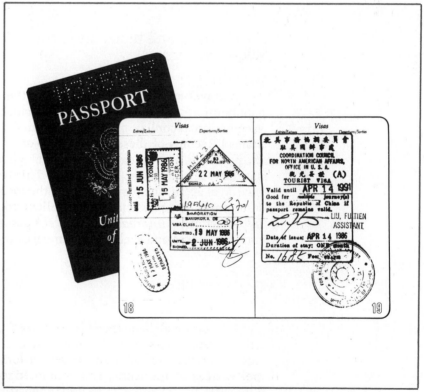

Illus. 14-3
This is a page from a valid passport. When a traveler enters a foreign country, an immigration officer may stamp the passport with a visa stamp (date of entry and allowable length of visit). When the visitor leaves the country, the passport is stamped with an embarkation stamp.

Visas

A *visa* is a permit granted by a foreign government for a person to enter its territory. It usually appears as a stamped notation in a passport indicating that the bearer may enter the country for a certain purpose and for a specified period of time. Take special note of the effective dates of a visa. Anyone in doubt as to the necessity of obtaining a travel visa should contact the consulate of the particular country or a travel agent before leaving the United States. Consular representatives of most foreign countries are located in principal cities. Their addresses can be found in the *Congressional Directory*, available in many public libraries, or in the Yellow Pages of major cities under "Consulates." A traveler who intends to work in a foreign country should check to see whether a work permit is required.

Vaccination and Inoculation Requirements

A travel agent or the consulate of the country to be visited can supply information about required *vaccinations* and *inoculations*. (A vaccination record is no longer required for reentry to the United States.) Records of these vaccinations and inoculations are signed by the physician and validated by the local or state health officer on International Certificates of Vaccination. This form may be obtained from the travel agent, the passport office, the local health department, or in some cases, the physician. An excellent government booklet, *Health Information for International Travel*,[4] describes a number of possible travel ailments and includes seven pages of health hints.

Overseas Flights

International plane travel is basically the same as it is for domestic flights. Jumbo jets that seat more than 200 passengers are usually flown. Services include large passenger lounges, a choice among several entrées at mealtime, and containerized baggage compartments. Baggage is always stored in an upright position and unloaded swiftly by bringing the containers to the customs area.

---

[4]Available from the Superintendent of Documents, Government Printing Office, Washington, DC 20402. Request Stock Number 017-023-00147-7.

On international flights there are two classes of flights: first class and economy or tourist. Business class, similar to first class, is offered on some flights. Gourmet meals and beverages are served in first class. Beautiful china, crystal, and silver are used; and the service of flight attendants is outstanding. In tourist class, meals meet a lesser quality standard.

Baggage limitations vary, so the secretary must check this information when making reservations. Passengers must reconfirm international flights within 72 hours.

Fares vary with the season of the year and according to the length of stay. The only way to keep abreast of air fares is to consult the airline reservation agent or your travel agent for special excursion rates. An international flight schedule of a foreign airline is more complicated than a domestic schedule, because timetables for foreign airlines are usually based on the 24-hour clock. Illus. 14-4 explains the 24-hour clock.

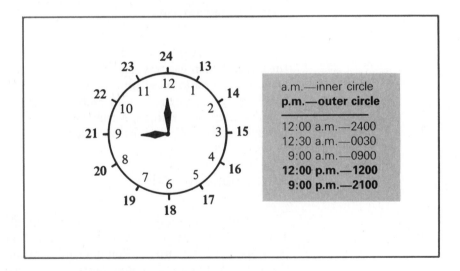

Illus. 14-4
The 24-hour clock assigns a number from 1 to 24 to each hour of the day.

Train Transportation

Most foreign railroads provide three classes of service: (1) *first-class* accommodations seat four to six persons in a compartment, (2) *second-class* accommodations seat six to eight persons, and (3) *third-class* accommodations seat passengers on wooden, unupholstered seats. Reservations are necessary for first-class travel. Passengers carry on their luggage; therefore, it is recommended that passengers carry two small pieces of luggage rather than one large bag.

Sleeping accommodations on trains require first-class tickets. Reservations well in advance of the trip are recommended, for it is often difficult to obtain sleeping car accommodations. Extra-fare trains, carrying first- and second-class sleepers, are only available on the most important international routes.

Restaurant cars are attached to most express trains. Before a meal, the dining car conductor comes through the train and takes reservations. The meal is served in most countries at an announced time at one seating only.

A Eurailpass entitles the holder to unlimited train travel in 16 Western European countries during the length of time specified on the ticket. All travel on a Eurailpass is in first class. Several foreign railway systems maintain ticket and information offices in major cities in America. The Eurailpass must be purchased before a traveler leaves the United States.

Hotel Reservations

Hotel reservations can be made through a travel agent or through the airline. Business travel guides indicate which hotels provide secretarial services and meeting rooms. Breakfast is often included in the hotel charge in Great Britian and frequently in the Netherlands. In other countries in Europe, a continental breakfast, consisting of a hot beverage and a roll, may be included.

Automobile Rentals

Rented automobiles are as readily available in large foreign cities as in the United States. Flight schedules indicate whether this service is available at the airport. Rentals can be arranged by travel agents in this country. In most foreign countries, a United States driver's license is sufficient to operate an automobile; but to be on the safe side, travelers may obtain an International Driving License from the American Automobile Association, either here or in Europe, for a small fee.

TRAVEL DETAILS HANDLED BY THE SECRETARY

The groundwork for a trip will probably be laid during a conference between the executive and the secretary. For example, if your employer in Omaha were to visit a factory in Philadelphia on Monday, March 2, keep appointments in Brussels on March 4, meet with an executive in Paris on March 5, return to Omaha by way of New York, have a one-hour conference at the New York airport, and be back in Omaha on the evening of March 9, you would arrange all the details of the trip.

Planning the Trip

Planning a trip requires checking transportation schedules, researching hotel information, and making reservations. In the case just cited, you would route the executive by air to Philadelphia, from Philadelphia to Brussels, from Brussels to Paris, from Paris to New York, and from New York back to Omaha. If your company has a transportation department, you should consult with someone in that department first. The transportation department, in all likelihood, would handle all reservations and make suggestions concerning hotels as well. If your company does not have a transportation department, you should contact a reputable travel agency, obtain and study current airline timetables, and discuss possible flight plans with airline reservation agents and with the travel agency. You should also obtain pertinent information about hotels and motels. Travel agencies are especially knowledgeable about hotels. *The Hotel and Motel Red Book*,[5] the *Hotel and Travel Index*,[6] and directories published by the American Automobile Association are also good sources of hotel information. These sources list the number of rooms in a hotel, discuss rates, and indicate whether lodging is on the European or the American plan. Under the European plan, the rate represents the cost of the room only. Under the American plan, the rate includes the cost of meals as well. Most commercial hotels are operated under the European plan.

Room rates are quoted for one night's lodging, but many hotels offer reduced rates for daytime-only occupancy. If an executive will be in a city for a few hours for a short meeting, a hotel room makes a good headquarters. In order to be assured of accommodation before the afternoon check-in hour, it may be wise to reserve a room for the previous night and to pay in advance.

---

[5]Published annually by Pactel Publishing, 1600 S. Main Street, Suite 280, Walnut Creek, CA 94596

[6]Published quarterly by Ziff-Davis Publishing Co., One Park Avenue, New York, NY 10016.

Always check the distance from the airport to the hotel and from the hotel to the meeting place. Nothing is more disconcerting than to find oneself across town from an appointment location.

A travel worksheet, such as the one shown in Illus. 14-5 can be useful in accumulating information and finalizing trip plans. An executive's itinerary can be prepared from the information provided on this form.

TRAVEL WORKSHEET

Employee _____   Date _____

Dates of Trip _____

Mode of Travel: Commercial Air _____   Company Plane _____   Train _____   Automobile _____

Date	Destination	Time (Local)		Flight/Train No.	Class of Service	Meals	Date Confirmed
		Departure	Arrival				

Ground Transportation Requirements (limousine, rental car, courtesy car):

Date	Time	Place	Type	Date Confirmed

Hotel Reservations :

Date	Destination	Estimated Arrival Time	Date of Departure	Name of Hotel/Motel	Date Confirmed

Travel Funds:

Cash Advance $ _____   Company Credit Cards Required?: Yes ___ No ___

Company Check $ _____   Specify: _____

Traveler's Checks $ _____   _____

Illus. 14-5
Travel worksheets are used to finalize trip plans.

Preparing an Itinerary

Preparing a comprehensive *itinerary*, a detailed outline of a trip, is an important secretarial function. Foresight and analysis are required to prepare it. (The usual itinerary, which is prepared by a travel agency if you use its services, covers only flight information for arrivals and departures.) A comprehensive itinerary serves as a daily appointment calendar and includes helpful reminders. An executive may request a number of copies of an itinerary for associates and family so that mail and messages can be forwarded and emergencies reported.

You should set up a file on a trip as soon as it enters the planning stage. In the file, place the travel worksheet, purchased tickets, reservations, confirmations, an appointment schedule, and any factual information that may be needed for scheduled meetings. Everything that pertains to the trip should be in this file. When it is time to prepare the itinerary, the file can be sorted into chronological sequence. Illus. 14-6 shows the detail and thoroughness with which an itinerary should be prepared.

Illus. 14-6
This itinerary is a combination of travel and appointment records and reminders.

```
                    ITINERARY FOR K. B. CUNNINGHAM

                           March 1-6, 19--

SUNDAY, MARCH 1  (Omaha to Philadelphia)  No direct flights available.

    4:15 p.m.    Leave Omaha on American Flight 23.  Change in Chicago to United Flight
                 302 leaving at 6:15 p.m.  Dinner served.
    10:21 p.m.   Arrive in Philadelphia.  Guaranteed arrival reservation at Warwick Hotel
                 (confirmation attached).

MONDAY, MARCH 2  (West Chester Plant)

    Take Southeastern Pennsylvania Transportation Authority Conrail commuter train from Penn
    Center Station.  Frequent service.  (Papers in briefcase.)

TUESDAY, MARCH 3  (En Route to Brussels)

    9:00 a.m.    Leave Philadelphia on American Flight 2 to La Guardia Airport (New York)
                 to connect with Sabena Flight 34 to Brussels.
    11:00 a.m.   Leave for Brussels.
    5:00 p.m.    Arrive in Brussels.  Reservation at Intercontinental Hotel (reservation
                 attached).

WEDNESDAY, MARCH 4  (Brussels)

    9:00 a.m.    Interview at La Societe Generale, Room 913, with Johann Schmidt about
                 development of European office in Brussels (prospectus in briefcase).
    1:00 p.m.    Lunch at La Maison du Cygne with Madame Helene Moal and three colleagues
                 for same purpose (prospectus in briefcase).  (Confirm by telephone after
                 11:00 a.m.)
    5:00 p.m.    Leave for Paris on Sabena Flight 711 to Le Bourget Airport.  Dinner
                 served.
    6:21 p.m.    Arrive in Paris.  Reservation at the George V Hotel (reservation
                 attached).

THURSDAY, MARCH 5  (Paris)

    10:00 a.m.   Appointment with Martha Dillon at Citibank, 43 Rue de la Paix (financial
                 statements in briefcase).
    8:30 p.m.    Dinner at Maxim's with Roger Symonds (telephone 45-334).

FRIDAY, MARCH 6  (En Route to Omaha via New York)

    12:00 Noon   Leave from Charles de Gaulle Airport on TWA Flight 803.
    2:55 p.m.    Arrive at Kennedy Airport where Tom McQuiddy will meet your flight with a
                 car.  Conference at International Hotel at airport (daytime reservation
                 enclosed).  (Papers in McQuiddy folder.)
    4:45 p.m.    Leave Kennedy Airport for Chicago on TWA Flight 347.
    6:07 p.m.    Arrive at O'Hare Airport in Chicago.
    6:45 p.m.    Leave Chicago on United Flight 779 for Omaha.
    7:51 p.m.    Arrive at Omaha airport.
```

Some executives prefer to carry an itinerary prepared by a travel agency and a separate appointment schedule, similar to the one shown in Illus. 14-7, on their business trips. An appointment schedule isolates appointments on one easy-to-read form. It should include the times, names of persons having appointments, how to get in touch with them, appointment locations, and other remarks.

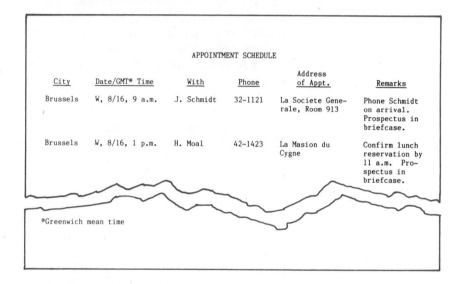

APPOINTMENT SCHEDULE

City	Date/GMT* Time	With	Phone	Address of Appt.	Remarks
Brussels	W, 8/16, 9 a.m.	J. Schmidt	32–1121	La Societe Gene-rale, Room 913	Phone Schmidt on arrival. Prospectus in briefcase.
Brussels	W, 8/16, 1 p.m.	H. Moal	42–1423	La Masion du Cygne	Confirm lunch reservation by 11 a.m. Pro-spectus in briefcase.

*Greenwich mean time

Illus. 14-7
An appointment schedule isolates appointments on one easy-to-read form.

Carrying Travel Funds

Ask the executive whether you are to get money for the trip from the company's cashier or from the bank. If it is an overseas trip, determine whether there are any restrictions in the amount of currency that may be taken into countries to be visited. You can order packets of foreign currencies through the bank or a travel agent. Foreign currency can also be purchased from automatic vending machines in most international airports.

Traveler's Checks. *Traveler's checks* must be purchased by the person who will use them and by nobody else. Traveler's checks are sold in denominations of $10, $20, $50, and $100, for a small fee, depending on the amount purchased. Some banks issue them without charge, especially during certain times of the year. Illus. 14-8 is a photograph of a traveler's check.

Each traveler's check is numbered and printed on a special kind of paper. The purchaser signs each check before an agent of the issuing company. To cash one of the checks, the purchaser countersigns the check in the presence of the person cashing it.

MasterCard International Inc.

Illus. 14-8
The purchaser
signs this traveler's
check in the
bottom left-hand
corner. On cashing
this check, the
purchaser
countersigns the
check at the top.

Traveler's checks are like cash. They almost constitute personalized money, because anyone other than the purchaser must forge the purchaser's name on each check in the presence of another person in order to cash it. The secretary should prepare a record in duplicate of the numbers and the amounts of the checks issued, one for the files and one of the executive to carry so that reimbursement can be immediate in case the checks are lost or stolen.

It is now possible for an American Express card holder to obtain a special personal identification number to buy traveler's checks. This number and an American Express card are used to obtain up to $500 in American Express traveler's checks from automatic tellers located in large airports.

Money Orders. Secretaries may obtain travel funds for executives through money orders. A money order is a form sold by banks, post offices, express companies, and telegraph offices stating that money is to be paid to the person named on the form. An example of a money order appears in Illus. 14-9.

Letters of Credit. A letter of credit is used when extensive travel is involved or when the amount of funds required for a trip is relatively large. The cost of large amounts of money through a letter of credit is considerably less than the cost of traveler's checks. A letter of credit is obtained from a local bank. It indicates the amount the holder is entitled to draw on the issuing bank. To obtain funds, the holder presents the letter of credit to a designated bank in the foreign city. The amounts drawn are recorded on the letter so that the balance is always

Illus. 14-9
Money orders are
convenient forms
of payment because
they can be
purchased in so
many places.

known. The disadvantage of carrying a letter of credit is that it can only be used during banking hours.

Credit Cards. Multipurpose credit cards, such as American Express, VISA, MasterCard and Diner's Club, permit holders to charge practically any service or goods to a personal or company charge account. Secretarial responsibility for credit cards is in requesting renewals on those that expire and in keeping serial numbers on file. Itemized bills for credit card purchases help secretaries prepare expense reports and enable executives to verify expenses.

Obtaining Insurance

Companies sometimes buy blanket insurance policies to cover executives while they are traveling on company business. In addition, companies usually have rules governing the purchase of travel insurance at airports. The secretary is expected to investigate company policy about travel insurance and follow through to see that the executive is appropriately covered.

Assisting in Departure

The secretary is frequently charged with packing the executive's briefcase. This is an important responsibility, for the effectiveness of any business trip is determined by the accessibility of relevant material.

As soon as you learn of an impending trip, start assembling materials and other necessary papers that must be taken along in order to avoid any last minute crisis. Start immediately to procure tickets and other required documents for the trip. Check the appointment book and ask how your employer wants to handle any scheduled appointments or meetings. Go through the tickler and the pending file. Discuss matters to be handled in your employer's absence and determine who is responsible for making decisions. Check whether rent, insurance, or income tax payments will be due before the trip is over and get instructions for handling them. Write any letters that will increase the effectiveness of the trip. Decide how expected mail is to be handled. Find out *who* is responsible for *what* during the trip. Just before departure, hand the executive the following:

Travel tickets (also a schedule of alternate flights)
Itinerary (a detailed one and a thumbnail copy on a card)
Hotel and motel confirmations
Car rental arrangements
Travel funds
Address book (including addresses of any people to be visited in the area)
A personal checkbook and expense account forms
A company telephone directory
A supply of business cards
A supply of stamps (for domestic use only)
Typed address labels for letters to known correspondents, such as the executive's family, secretary, or the president of the company
Notebook, pen, pencil
Dictation recorder and recording media
Appointment papers (A separate envelope for each appointment is recommended. Include copies of relevant correspondence, lists of people to be seen and their positions in their companies, and memorandums about matters to be discussed.)
Personal items, such as medication or extra eyeglasses
Favorite reading materials, crossword puzzles
Copies of company brochures, if requested
Extra camera film, chewing gum, mints
Luggage identification tags
Any maps and instructions that may be useful

In addition to the items above, the following should be included for foreign travel:

Money packets of foreign currency and traveler's checks

An International Driving License (unless it has been determined that a United States driver's license is sufficient)

Notes about reconfirming reservations for foreign flights at least 72 hours before departure

Passport, International Certificates of Vaccination, and baggage identification labels for foreign travel

AN OFFICE AWAY FROM HOME

Many hotels today in such cities as Boston, Houston, Chicago and New York offer complete business centers, providing secretarial services for traveling executives. Where a business center is not available, a hotel concierge can most likely find professional secretarial help. The National Association of Secretarial Services (NASS), representing nearly 1000 service bureaus, publishes a directory of member bureaus by city and by specialized service. This directory can be ordered from NASS, 240 Driftwood Road SE, St. Petersburg, FL 33705. Another organization, known as Omnioffices, advertises that it can provide an office for out-of-town business executives in 14 locations in 9 different United States cities. These offices offer telecommunications capability, mail and telephone service, secretarial support, and conference space. Close to O'Hare airport in Chicago, a company called EasyKeys rents private work rooms equipped with microcomputers. Software is available at a nominal charge. EasyKeys employees can also be hired on a short term basis to perform some tasks.

In a joint venture with Diner's Club, Headquarters Companies rents offices or conference rooms to any Diner's Club cardholder in its offices in 47 cities for as little as two hours duration. Full secretarial support can be arranged. Finally, Mutual of Omaha is making its airport offices in Pittsburgh, Detroit, Richmond, and Los Angeles available to travelers for a fee. It is estimated that as these conveniences become more popular with the traveling public, more offices away from home will be established.

WHILE THE EXECUTIVE IS TRAVELING

While the executive is on a trip, the secretary assumes increased responsibility for smooth operation of the office. Members of the management team share the decision-making role involving problems usually handled by the employer. It is better for secretaries to discuss a perplexing situation with an executive who has been designated to handle crises than to assume too much authority. Routine matters, of course, should be promptly taken care of by the secretary.

The executive who wants to keep in touch with the home office usually telephones the office daily, especially if the company has 800 Service. If you expect your employer to call you, you should keep notes about situations you want to discuss. Many secretaries keep a daily log of incoming calls, letters, and visitors so that when the employer calls they can be discussed.

Your performance while the executive is away is just as important as it is when the executive is present. Other employees may be quick to notice whether you are busy or frittering away time. A competent secretary organizes work so that there is little idle time. During an employer's absence, complete tasks that you have not had time to do, such as reorganizing the files.

Upon return the executive will be grateful and pleased if you have taken care of routine matters, kept records of office activities for review, and arranged matters that require attention in terms of their importance. Materials that have accumulated for the executive's return should be separated into two groups: (1) matters already taken care of by you or by others and (2) matters to be handled by the executive personally.

You should place the first group in a folder marked "Information Only." The second group goes into a folder marked "Important." Just before presenting the folders, you should arrange materials in logical order, with the most important on top. A list of future appointments and engagements should be included in the "Important" folder.

If the trip is long, the executive may ask you to forward copies of documents that require personal attention (refer to pages 127-129 for instructions). Two copies of mail may be sent to the traveler—one to the destination on the itinerary and one to the next point to be visited, in case mail service is slower than expected.

FOLLOW-UP ACTIVITIES

After the executive returns to the office, a flurry of activity is required to wind up a trip. Follow-up activities include filing the expense report, composing thank-you letters, and updating the files.

Expense Report

Some firms advance funds for travel. Periodically, or when a trip is over, the executive submits a complete report on expenses incurred. In other companies, executives advance their own funds and are reimbursed later. In either case, the executive must keep an accurate record of the dates and times of travel, the conveyances used, and the costs. Most organizations require receipts for hotel and other accommodations and for any expenses above an established minimum. The traveler's word is usually taken for the costs of taxis, meals, and tips; but usually these costs must be itemized. Receipts are required, however, for entertainment expenses. The date, cost, place, nature of the entertainment, the business purpose, and the names of the persons included must be specified. For further information on allowable business expenses, consult a current copy of the Internal Revenue Service's Bulletin 463, *Travel, Entertainment, and Gift Expenses.*

Expense report forms are usually provided by the company. Follow the company procedures manual in preparing expense reports, obtaining the necessary signatures, and submitting them to the financial division. The secretary should check the executive's expenses against previous reports to make sure that the amounts for such items as taxis and meals are reasonable and that flight and rail fares are correct. Reimbursement is frequently held up until all expenses are approved by the auditor's office.

Letters

Thank-you letters must be sent to show appreciation for favors during the trip. The need for other letters will be generated by the nature of the trip.

Files

After materials are unpacked and returned to the files, duplicate files can be destroyed. The secretary updates the files to reflect any changes originated by the trip.

SUMMARY _____

For most executives business travel is considered a necessary part of their responsibilities. Unless a trip is under 300 miles, executives generally travel by air. The secretary is responsible for setting travel arrangements in motion by either contacting an in-house transportation department, a travel agency, or airline reservation agents. Specific company policies regarding travel must be followed in making reservations.

Airline fares, flight schedules, and classes of service are constantly changing. Airlines publish flight schedules on a regular basis. For up-to-date information, however, consult the *Official Airline Guide, North American Edition* or the *OAG North American and Worldwide Electronic Edition.*

Hotel/motel reservations are made by telephone or, if time permits, by letter. Several hotel/motel directories are available which provide information on rates and services.

Planning for a trip abroad requires more time and preparation than for short, domestic trips. The service of an intracompany transportation department or a travel agency is almost a necessity. The executive and the secretary will have a number of questions concerning foreign travel that are best answered by a reputable travel agency. For travel in most countries outside the United States, a passport is necessary, and it takes time to acquire one.

When the secretary becomes aware of an impending trip, a travel file is opened and a travel worksheet is prepared. Appointments are made and an itinerary is compiled. Travel funds are arranged and all necessary documents and files set aside.

While the executive is away, the secretary is responsible for the smooth operation of the office. After the trip an expense report with the required receipts is prepared, follow-up letters are composed, and the files are updated.

SUGGESTED READINGS

Barish, Frances (ed.). *Frommer's Guide for the Disabled Traveler,* United States, Canada, and Europe. New York: Simon & Schuster Inc., 1984.

Braganti, Nancy L., and Elizabeth Devine. *The Traveler's Guide to European Customs and Manners.* Deephaven, MN: Meadowbrook Books, 1984.

Lehmann, Armin D. *Travel and Tourism.* Indianapolis: Bobbs-Merrill Educational Publishing Co., 1978.

North, Susanna. *Traveling Alone,* A Practical Guide for Business Women. New York: Sovereign Books, 1980.

Soukhanov, Anne (ed.). *The Professional Secretary's Handbook,* A Guide to the Electronic and Conventional Office. Boston: Houghton Mifflin Company, 1984.

The Travel Agent. Published twice weekly by American Traveler, Inc., 2 West 46th Street, New York, NY 10036.

TWA Ambassador. Published monthly for Trans World Airlines, Inc. by Paulsen Publishing, Inc., 420 Lexington Avenue, New York, NY 10170. Other airlines also provide special periodicals free to business customers. Examples include Pan American's *Getting Around Overseas*, and Air Canada's *Business Traveler's Guide to Canada.*

QUESTIONS FOR DISCUSSION

1. What are the secretary's responsibilities for travel arrangements if there is an in-company transportation department?
2. In what ways can you inform yourself about changes in air and rail travel? Just to show that you are alert to such changes, report any recent travel plan not described in this chapter.
3. What are some of the services travel agencies provide to the business traveler?
4. Why do you suppose that many companies will not permit several of their executives to fly on the same plane?
5. If your employer travels on an airline that has a frequent flyer program, what type of record would you suggest to your employer to keep track of this mileage?
6. What procedures should the secretary follow to renew a passport and obtain the necessary visas and traveler's checks for an employer?
7. If your employer were planning to visit five countries overseas on a business trip, what type of information about the countries would you provide?
8. Just after your employer has left on a somewhat lengthy business trip by plane, you discover the itinerary, reservation letters, and appointment schedule on your desk. What should you do?
9. While your employer is away from the office on an extended trip, how would you use your office time?
10. Correct the capitalization of the following sentences. Refer to the Reference Guide to verify and correct your answers.
    a. The space age will provide modern man with a new frontier.
    b. Reserve room 12 of the student center for our meeting.
    c. U.S. route 64 runs east and west; U.S. route 77 runs north and south.
    d. He is well known as a professor of asian culture and polynesian music.

   e. Our Professor Griggs has taught history at the university of
      Texas for many years.
   f. The students will hear president Mason speak at the first ses-
      sion on Monday.
   g. We are unusually busy during the spring and summer months;
      most of the tourists are gone by early fall.

PROBLEMS

1. Working individually, or as a member of a team as your instructor
   directs, recommend the best services available for a trip to Miami,
   Florida, for a two-day student convention, using travel schedules
   provided in your classroom.

2. You are secretary to Jonathan Ames, Ames Industries, located in
   St. Louis, Missouri. You have made the following travel arrangements for Mr. Ames beginning Monday, November 2. Type an
   itinerary in proper format.

   TWA Flight 140 leaves St. Louis at 9:49 a.m., arrives La
   Guardia airport at 12:50 p.m. Meal served on this flight.
   Reservation at Whitson Hotel; confirmation in brief-
   case. Appointment at 3:00 with Steven B. Hoover,
   Smith Oil Corporation, Rockefeller Plaza. Dinner and
   show with Aunt Rose at 7 p.m. She will meet Mr. Ames
   in his hotel lobby. Tuesday meeting at 10 a.m. with
   Mary Parker, Sales Manager, Larga Products, 243 Park
   Avenue. Lunch at the New York Club, 61 Central Park
   South at 1:00 with Arthur Lemont and Beth Arlington
   of J. Thomas Advertising Agency. All materials in briefcase. Dinner at 7 with the Hargroves in their apartment
   at 42 East 62nd Street. Wednesday Mr. Ames has a 9:30
   interview with Ralph W. Carlson for production manager position. Application is in briefcase. Mr. Carlson is
   to call Mr. Ames to discuss a meeting place. At noon
   Mr. Ames is to give a speech at the Wire Products Manufacturers' Conference in the Whitson's Dining Room
   C. Speech in briefcase. At 3:30 take hotel limousine to
   La Guardia Airport for TWA Flight 495 leaving at 5:55
   p.m., arriving St. Louis at 7:50 p.m. Meal served.

Chapter 15

Planning and Facilitating Meetings

Ask executives how they spend most of their workday, and invariably their responses will be "in meetings." In today's business world, more and more decisions involve group decision making; therefore, today's executives spend more time in meetings than at any time in the past. A recent survey has found that meetings take up to 35-40 percent of an executive's time.[1] Meetings may be informal, involving two or more employees, or they may be more structured and formal, involving many participants and a prepared agenda. A meeting can be face-to-face or take place over the telephone, via computer, or through a closed circuit television hookup.

Executives often assume leadership roles in the community. They also attend annual conventions, conferences, and numerous workshops and symposia where they exchange ideas with people with similar interests and learn of new developments that will improve their job performance. Participation in these community and professional functions may require an executive to assume part or all of the responsibilities for planning a function.

This chapter discusses informal business meetings, multinational meetings, formal meetings, and conferences and conventions. Technological alternatives to face-to-face meetings are also discussed. The secretary plays a significant role in making meetings effective. The secretary is involved in planning and facilitating meetings, from the initial planning stage through the follow-up. All of these responsibilities are explained in detail in this chapter.

---

[1]"Holding Fewer, More Structured Meetings Saves a Manager's Time," *Office Administration and Automation* (January, 1985), p. 7.

INFORMAL OFFICE OR COMMITTEE MEETINGS

Informal office meetings are held on company premises with company personnel and/or visitors. Informal meetings do not involve complicated arrangements and may be scheduled or unscheduled.

If an informal meeting has been scheduled, participants have been previously notified and should have a calendar notation to remind them of the time and place. Some secretaries send participants written reminders or telephone them the day before a meeting. If a participant is late, the secretary should call that person to determine if he or she plans to attend. For unscheduled meetings, the secretary uses electronic calendaring, if available, or the telephone to arrange a convenient meeting time. Once the time is agreed upon, a note confirming the time and place should be sent to all participants.

If a meeting takes place in the executive's office, the secretary makes sure that the room is in good order, that enough chairs are available, and that all the needed materials are assembled. One way to create an atmosphere of relaxation is to provide refreshments—even if Styrofoam cups, plastic spoons, instant coffee or tea, and powdered cream are used.

During the meeting, the secretary may be asked to take notes. Recommended conference procedure suggests that the chairperson summarize actions and reiterate conclusions as they are reached. The secretary taking notes of a meeting for such a chairperson is lucky. Many office conferences, however, are informal discussions where opinions are exchanged, conclusions are reached, and recommendations are made with no observance of protocol. In these cases the secretary, working alone, is expected to summarize the meeting and to distribute copies of the report to all participants. If, during the meeting, it is agreed that certain conferees should take a specific action, the secretary should send each a copy of the report *with the agreed upon action underlined.* For short, informal meetings, a summary may be made in memo form. An example appears in Illus. 15-1.

Many departments have a weekly "stand up briefing" on Monday mornings. Because these meetings are intended to be short, the secretary need not make special provisions in the executive's office, unless told otherwise. Generally no report of this briefing is required.

MULTINATIONAL MEETINGS

A new experience for American businesses involves attending and conducting meetings where some of the participants do not speak English. Multinational meetings involving non-English-speaking manage-

```
                    M E M O R A N D U M


                                              October 21, 19--


        TO: √R. Edison
            F. Marco
            J. Monroe
            S. Renberg


        The Budget Committee met in Mr. Monroe's office on Mon-
        day, October 20, 19--, to discuss the group health plan
        and the parking lot resurfacing.  All members were
        present.

        Mr. Marco stated that the dental health plan is now in
        operation, and the anticipated premium for the year is
        $6,000.

        Mr. Renberg reviewed bids for resurfacing the company
        parking lot.  The lowest bidder was Root Construction
        Company at $8,025.  The work will begin Saturday,
        October 25.

        Mr. Edison agreed to develop guidelines for budget fore-
        casts and to present them at the next meeting of the
        Committee.


                                        Joyce Anderson
                                        Joyce Anderson
                                        Secretary to Mr. Monroe
```

Illus. 15-1
A summary of an
informal meeting
in memorandum
form is prepared
and signed by the
secretary.

ment officials are likely to be formal in nature, requiring extensive planning and the preparation of a business agenda. Rank (or protocol) may be an important concern with international visitors and should be carefully observed by meeting hosts and administrative staff.

Secretaries assisting with a multinational meeting may be asked to arrange for an interpreter to attend the meeting or to have the interpreter prepare audio tapes in the language of the non-English-speaking members. The secretary might also help the interpreter prepare special overhead visuals and handouts in the foreign language or languages. Ensuring effective communication during multinational meetings takes a great deal of time and preparation on the part of the executive/ secretary team. If minutes of such a meeting are to be produced, the secretary should use a tape recorder for a verbatim record. Afterward the interpreter and the executive should be consulted before typing the report.

Not all multinational meetings require this type of preparation. Many foreign nationals speak English; however, in any multinational meeting, it is wise to use standard speech, omitting slang and regional expressions.

Secretaries may also facilitate a multinational meeting by developing packets of information for foreign visitors. Packets may include a list of ethnic restaurants, points of interest, important telephone numbers, a city map, and general information about the community.

FORMAL OFFICE MEETINGS

As soon as you know that a formal meeting is to be called, your responsibilities as a meeting facilitator begin. You must schedule a meeting room, send out meeting notices, prepare the agenda, and perform a host of other duties. To keep meeting materials organized, you should set up a file folder. Use the name of the meeting and the date as the tab caption. Place every bit of relevant information that crosses your desk during the planning stages into this folder.

Reserving the Meeting Room

When the executive says, "Call a meeting on budget requests for next Wednesday afternoon at two o'clock," the first detail to take care of is reserving the meeting room. Since meetings of three or more people are customarily held in a conference room, the secretary immediately checks to see if a company conference room is available. The room should be signed out with the person in charge. The number of people attending the meeting and the time required should be noted.

If the meeting is to be held in a hotel, the secretary reserves an adequately sized room with seating facilities. The location and hour of the meeting should then be posted on the announcement board in the lobby and in the elevators. If a meal is included, the menu, the serving time, the method of payment, and the number of guests are discussed with the hotel's banquet manager. You will find that hotels do not normally charge for meeting rooms if the meeting includes meal service. In making these arrangements, keep a record of the names of hotel personnel you contact. If something must be done at the last minute, such as requesting additional chairs for the conference room or an additional place setting at the dining table, this list will be helpful.

Notices of Meetings

The secretary's responsibility for notifying participants of a meeting frequently involves five steps:

1. Making calendar notations
2. Preparing the mailing list
3. Composing the notice
4. Typing and sending notices
5. Handling the follow-up work

Making Calendar Notations. You should make notations on a calendar as a reminder to prepare and send notices. Make the notations on dates far enough ahead to allow time for the notices to be composed, reproduced, and delivered several days before the meeting. Notices that arrive too early may be forgotten. A notice for an office conference of staff personnel could be delivered the day before a meeting, but an office conference of traveling salespeople might require two weeks' notice. You should also make a calendar notation to confirm your conference room reservation a few days before the meeting.

Preparing the Mailing List. Mailing lists of persons to receive meeting notices are kept in several ways. If your organization has word processing equipment, a mailing list can be put on one input medium and merged with another input source containing the actual notice. A word processing center could easily handle this type of routine work. The secretary would be responsible for submitting an alphabetized list of persons to receive the meeting notice and for informing the center of any changes as they occur. The word processing center would be responsible for producing the properly addressed notices.

The secretary should keep a record of the names, addresses, and telephone numbers of persons who are to receive specific notices. This information can be stored electronically in an address label format for printouts or kept in card files. If you use cards, type the addresses in either of two ways: either invert the name for easy filing (and follow with the address that will appear on the notice) or type the name and address exactly as it will appear on the notice, perhaps underlining the last name as a filing aid. Type an identifier beside each address. For example, type *AMS* to indicate that the addressee belongs on the mailing list for Administrative Management Society meetings (see Illus. 15-2). File cards alphabetically according to last names. Cards may also be filed under the name of the committee, group, or team.

```
  JONES, Maxwell                        (AMS)

    1501 Mirimar Street
    Dayton, OH  45409-3528

    513-429-3372
```

Illus. 15-2
Inverting names on mailing list cards makes them easier to file.

How you prepare address labels depends on the type of equipment available. You can make labels on a copier using a master mailing list typed in address label format by placing $8\frac{1}{2}$-by-11-inch sheets of blank labels in the paper tray. If your mailing list is stored electronically, continuous sheets of blank labels can be inserted into a printer.

A mailing list must be kept up to date. In addition to making reported changes as they occur, the secretary should verify the current addresses of members at least once a year.

Composing the Notice. Simple meeting notices can be composed by the secretary for the executive's approval. The notice of the previous meeting is a good model to follow if it specifies the day, the date, the time, the place, and either the purpose of a special meeting or the fact that it is a regularly scheduled one. If required to prepare an agenda, the secretary should send a request for agenda items along with the notice of the meeting.

Before a notice of an official meeting, such as a stockholders' meeting, is sent out, the legal department should check the organization's bylaws. For instance, the bylaws may state that no dividends can be voted on unless the question of dividends is discussed at the meeting; therefore, the notice of the meeting should include this information. In preparing a notice for such a meeting, the secretary is guided by the official secretary of the company, generally a lawyer.

A notice of an upcoming stockholders' meeting should also include a form on which the shareholder may sign a *proxy*. Signing a proxy authorizes someone else to vote the stock if the shareholder is absent from the meeting. Because the notice of a stockholders' meeting must include a detailed agenda of the business to be transacted, the reasons for soliciting the proxy, and other information specifically required by law, it is usually prepared by the corporate legal department.

Typing and Sending Notices. For small meetings, participants are notified either with a typewritten memo or by telephone. For large meetings, a notice is reproduced and distributed. Illus. 15-3 shows a notice sent to members of a finance committee, announcing the day, date, time, place, and purpose of a meeting.

Postcard notices should be attractively typed. The message should be neatly displayed. A simple, double-spaced form is acceptable for short notices. Some secretaries underline important words.

Illus. 15-3
This notice of a finance committee meeting identifies members of the committee. The name of the recipient is checked off.

November 19, 19--

To the Finance Committee

   Donald Wang
   C. B. Newman
√ Marian Sternberg

The Finance Committee will meet in the second floor conference room at 10 a.m. on Tuesday, November 24.

Please bring comparisons of last year's budget with actual results in your division as of October 31 so that we can make preliminary estimates of changes that will be necessary next year.

J. J. Young

Fill-in notices of meetings that recur on a regular basis may be duplicated at the beginning of the year so that only the date, program topic, and other pertinent information is necessary to complete the notice. Some meetings or conferences are of such importance that the announcement is typed or duplicated on letterhead. If only a few participants are involved, a tabular listing of the names of those to receive the announcement may be typed in place of the usual single name, address, and salutation. With the tabular listing, the salutation is a general one, such as *Dear Member* or *Dear Committee Member*. Modern usage permits the omission of the salutation entirely. An individual letter to each person is sometimes used, but it is a time-consuming procedure, unless word processing equipment is available. Keeping a copy of meeting notices which contain the date of mailing is a precautionary measure that all secretaries should adopt.

Handling the Follow-up Work. Follow-up duties consist chiefly of recording who and how many will or will not attend the meeting. If return postcards were furnished, follow-up is merely a matter of sorting the cards into the *will's* and *will not's*. But usually telephoning several persons for a definite yes or no is required.

One executive, who is secretary of a civic luncheon club in a large city, sends out duplicated notices one week before monthly meetings. Two days before the meeting, the executive's secretary telephones anyone who has not responded to ask whether they plan to attend. An easy way to note attendance plans is to keep a record on which names, acceptances, and refusals are listed (see Illus. 15-4). When this record is complete, the secretary informs the hotel or restaurant of the number of reservations.

RECORD OF TELEPHONE VERIFICATION

Meeting *Production Management*   Date *Tuesday, October 15, 19—*
Time   *10:00 a.m.*   Place *Home Office, Conference Room 2*

Date Called	Name	Will Attend	Unable to Attend	Remarks
9/29	Angela Larsen	✓		
9/29	Sam Highland		Conflicts with plant opening in Denver	

Illus. 15-4
This record is useful to determine the number of reservations to be made for a meeting and if a quorum will be present.

With a fairly small group, the secretary may call all persons expected, or their secretaries, to inquire if they plan to attend, adding in explanation that a final check on probable attendance is being made. Some members may be unable to attend for last-minute reasons; others may explain that they will be late. Fortified with such knowledge, the chairperson is assured of a *quorum* and can call the meeting to order promptly. A quorum is the number of voting members that when present is sufficient to transact business.

Preparing the Order of Business (Agenda)

Every formal meeting should follow a systematic program that has been planned and outlined in advance. This program is usually called the *order of business*. It is called the *agenda* in academic and business meetings. The term *calendar* is used at meetings of some legislative bodies, such as a city council. A review of the bylaws and the minutes of previous meetings (properly indexed for easy cross-reference) is an invaluable aid in preparing an order of business and in helping the presiding officer to carry out the agenda in an effective manner.

Sometime before the meeting you should remind the executive who is to preside over the meeting to prepare the order of business. If you know the purpose of the meeting, you can type the agenda in rough-draft form following the order of business in general use by the organization. Be sure to review the minutes of the last meeting to determine if any unfinished business should be included on the agenda. Then submit this rough draft and a copy of the previous meeting's minutes to the executive for revision or approval.

In some organizations a *tentative* agenda is distributed to the membership for their information and additions. If no additional items are submitted, the tentative agenda becomes the final order of business and is redistributed to all members. If additional items are submitted for consideration, a *final* agenda is prepared and sent to the membership. If the agenda includes a discussion of a proposed plan, a copy of the proposal should accompany it. An example of an agenda is shown in Illus. 15-5.

The order of business may be set forth in an organization's bylaws. If not, the usual order is as follows:

1. Call to order by the presiding officer
2. Roll call (either oral or taken by the secretary)
3. Announcement of quorum (not always done)
4. Reading of the minutes of the previous meeting (Sometimes the minutes are circulated before the meeting and this step is omitted.)

```
                    AGENDA FOR THE REGULAR MEETING

                               of the

                    COMMITTEE FOR A DOWNTOWN MALL
                         May 15, 19--

        I.   Call to Order          Randy Anderson, Chairperson

       II.   Reading of the Minutes  Alan Updike, Secretary

      III.   Treasurer's Report      Susan Novak, Treasurer

       IV.   Old Business

                   Government Regulations, Walter Franks
                   Special Funding Measures, Letitia Alberiche

        V.   New Business

                   Architect's Concepts, William Chaney
                   Rerouting Traffic, Officer Nelson
                   The Tulsa Experience, Mayor LaFortune

       VI.   Adjournment
```

Illus. 15-5
A typical agenda is
typewritten and
double-spaced.

5.   Approval of the minutes
6.   Reports of officers
7.   Reports of standing committees   } *Copies of these reports are*
8.   Reports of special committees   *usually given to the*
secretary.
9.   Unfinished business (taken from the previous minutes)
10. New business
11. Appointment of committees
12. Nominations and elections
13. Date of next meeting
14. Adjournment

A group that is meeting for the first time appoints a temporary chairperson and a temporary secretary. Later in the initial meeting, the group elects permanent officers or appoints a committee to nominate officers and to draw up a constitution and bylaws.

Last Minute Duties

The secretary's first duty on the day of the meeting is to check the meeting room to see that the air in the room is fresh; that there are enough chairs, ashtrays, matches, paper, pencils, clips, and pins; and that any requested equipment, such as a portable chalkboard, an overhead projector, or a VDT, is in place. Your employer may ask you to place a "Thank You for Not Smoking" sign in the meeting room.

Many small business meetings are recorded on tape. The secretary makes arrangements for setting up the recording machine, often operating the tape recorder and taking notes as well. In order to identify voices on a tape, during the meeting, use a form, similar to the one shown in Illus. 15-6, to record each speaker's initial comments.

Illus. 15-6
To identify the speakers at a taped meeting, this form allows the secretary to record the speaker's name and first phrase.

Speaker's name_____
Identifying phrase_____

Speaker's name_____
Identifying phrase_____

Speaker's name_____
Identifying phrase_____

Assemble materials in a file folder for the executive, arranging them in the order in which they will be needed as indicated by the agenda. In addition, give a copy of *Robert's Rules of Order Newly Revised*, the organization's bylaws, a list of those who should attend the meeting, and a list of standing and special committees to the executive to take to the meeting.

If you are to take the minutes, take a copy of the agenda, the attendance list, the minutes book, a seating chart (if necessary), ballots, and any other material that may be required during the meeting.

Use the attendance list to mark off member's names as they enter the room and to record early departures. The attendance list can also be useful if you need to make introductions. You may wish to prepare a *minutes skeleton* from copies of the minutes of previous meetings (see Illus. 15-7) to use as a guide in taking notes. Study the agenda and become familiar with the names of those who are to present topics so that you can easily record these names during the meeting. If you miss

FUTURE SECRETARIES ASSOCIATION

Clem Community College Chapter

February Meeting
Symthe Hall, February 22, 4:00 p.m.

Call to Order -- *Jan Rodgers, President*

Roll Call -- *53 members present*

Reading of the Minutes *dated January 24.*
  Approval of the Minutes   *The minutes were approved as read.*

Officer's Reports
  Vice-President -- *Nothing to report.*

  Treasurer -- *Monthly finance report read. Current balance of $432.50 accepted.*

  Social Chairperson -- *Induction of new members scheduled for April 5. Food & entertainment committees under the direction of Roberta Stevens.*
  Publicity Chairperson   *Results of membership drive—16 new members.*

  Chapter Advisor -- *Nothing to report.*

Old Business
  1. *Margaret Sandy reported last week's bake sale profit: $31.90.*
  2.
  3.

New Business
  1. *Trip to Medical Transcription Services Inc. scheduled for March 14. Those interested should see Jan Rodgers.*
  2.
  3.

Date and Time of Next Meeting -- *March 30*

Adjournment -- *5:15 p.m.*

Illus. 15-7
Secretaries use minutes skeletons as guides to record all pertinent matters presented in a meeting.

a name, jot down some distinguishing characteristic of that person and ask the presiding officer for help after the meeting.

Unless you have previously done so, make arrangements so that there will be no telephone interruptions during the meeting. Before leaving your desk to take the minutes, double-check to see that you have all necessary recording supplies and other materials with you. It is most embarrassing to leave a meeting for things that should already be there. It advertises that a secretary is not very thorough. On the other hand, offering to get records on subjects that arise unexpectedly shows a secretary's willingness to be of help. Before leaving a meeting room, however, get permission from the presiding officer.

Parliamentary Procedure

If you understand parliamentary procedure, you can report meetings more accurately. You can also unobtrusively call the attention of the chairman[2] to any violations of parliamentary rules. Therefore, you should review important points of parliamentary procedure before going to a meeting. You should also review the rules for handling motions that are outlined in Illus. 15-8.

Parliamentary law has been defined as "common sense used in a gracious manner." Its purpose is to arrive at a group decision in an efficient and orderly manner. Parliamentary procedure is based on four principles:

1. Courtesy and justice must be accorded to all.
2. Only one topic is considered at one time.
3. The minority must be heard.
4. The majority must prevail.

Most business is transacted through main motions, which require a majority vote for adoption. A member addresses the chairman (by saying "Mr. Chairman" or "Madam Chairman" as the case may be), is recognized, and makes a motion. Another member seconds the motion. After the motion has been made and seconded, the chairman states the motion, names both the one who made it and the one who seconded it, and calls for discussion. When the discussion ends, a vote is taken, usually by voice. The chairman announces the result: "The

---

[2]During the 20th Convention of the National Association of Parliamentarians, members passed a resolution to use the term *chairman* instead of *chairperson* to address the presiding officer.

RULES FOR HANDLING MOTIONS

Types of Motions	Order of Handling	Must Be Seconded	Can Be Discussed	Can Be Amended	Vote Required[1]	Vote Can Be Reconsidered
MAIN MOTION						
To present a proposal to assembly	Cannot be made if any other motion is pending	Yes	Yes	Yes	Majority	Yes
SUBSIDIARY MOTIONS[2]						
To postpone indefinitely action on a motion	Has precedence over above motion	Yes	Yes	No	Majority	Affirmative vote only
To amend [improve] a main motion	Has precedence over above motions	Yes	Yes, when motion is debatable	Yes, but only once	Majority	Yes
To refer motion to committee [for special consideration]	Has precedence over above motions	Yes	Yes	Yes	Majority	Yes
To postpone definitely [to certain time] action on a motion	Has precedence over above motions	Yes	Yes	Yes	Majority	Yes
To limit discussion to a certain time	Has precedence over above motions	Yes	No	Yes	⅔	Yes
To call for vote [to end discussion at once and vote]	Has precedence over above motions	Yes	No	No	⅔	No
To table motion [to lay it aside until later]	Has precedence over above motions	Yes	No	No	Majority	No
INCIDENTAL MOTIONS[3]						
To suspend a rule temporarily [e.g., to change order of business]	No definite precedence rule	Yes	No	No	⅔	No
To close nominations[4]		Yes	No	Yes	⅔	No
To reopen nominations	These motions have precedence over motion to which they pertain	Yes	No	Yes	Majority	Negative vote only
To withdraw or modify a motion [to prevent vote or inclusion in minutes][5]		No	No	No	Majority	Negative vote only
To rise to a point of order [to enforce rules or program][6]		No	No	No	No vote, chairman rules	No
To appeal from decision of the chair [must be made immediately][6]		Yes	Yes, when motion is debatable	No	Majority	Yes
PRIVILEGED MOTIONS						
To call for orders of the day [to keep meeting to program or order of business][6]	Has precedence over above motions	No	No	No	No vote required[7]	No
Questions of privilege [to bring up an urgent matter—concerning noise, discomfort, etc.]	Has precedence over above motions	No	No	No	Majority	No
To take a recess	Has precedence over above motions	Yes	Yes, if no motion is pending	Yes	Majority	No
To adjourn	Has precedence over above motions	Yes	No	No	Majority	No
To set next meeting time	Has precedence over above motions	Yes	Yes, if no motion is pending	As to time and place	Majority	Yes
UNCLASSIFIED MOTIONS						
To take motion from table [to bring up tabled motion for consideration][8]	Cannot be made if any other motion is pending	Yes	No	No	Majority	No
To reconsider [to bring up discussion and obtain vote on previously decided motion][9]		Yes	Yes, when motion is debatable	No	Majority	No
To rescind [repeal] decision on a motion[10]		Yes	Yes, when motion is debatable	No	Majority or ⅔	Yes

1. A tied vote is always lost except on a motion to appeal from the decision of the chair [see "Incidental Motions"] when a tied vote sustains the decision of the chair.
2. Subsidiary motions are motions that pertain to a main motion while it is pending.
3. Most incidental motions arise out of another question that is pending and must be decided before the question out of which they arise is decided.
4. The chair opens nominations with "Nominations are now in order." Nominations may be made by a nominating committee, by a nominating ballot, or from the floor. A member may make a motion to close nominations, or the chair may declare nominations closed after assembly has been given a chance to make nominations. The voting is not limited to the nominees, as every member is at liberty to vote for any member who is not declared ineligible by the bylaws.
5. The mover may request to withdraw or modify his motion without consent of anyone before the motion has been put to assembly for consideration. When motion is before the assembly and if there is no objection from anyone in the assembly, the chairman announces that the motion is withdrawn or modified. If anyone objects, the request is put to a vote.
6. A member may interrupt the speaker who has the floor to rise to a point of order or appeal, call for orders of the day, or raise a question of privilege.
7. Orders of the day can be changed by a motion to suspend the rules. [See "Incidental Motions."]
8. Motion can be taken from the table during the meeting when it was tabled or at the next meeting.
9. Motion to reconsider may be made only by one who voted on the prevailing side. A motion to reconsider must be made during the meeting when it was decided or on the next succeeding day of the same session.
10. It is impossible to rescind any action that has been taken as a result of a motion, but the unexecuted part may be rescinded. Notice must be given one meeting before the vote is taken, or if voted on immediately, a two-thirds vote to rescind is necessary.

Illus. 15-8
Parliamentary procedure governs the proceedings of many kinds of meetings.

motion is carried (or defeated)." If anyone calls "Division," the chairman asks for a show of hands or a standing vote. If a majority demands it, the vote must be taken by ballot. Illus. 15-9 discusses several basic methods of voting.

BASIC METHODS OF VOTING

1. *Voice vote* is the most common voting method since it is the easiest and fastest way of determining a vote outcome. If the vote is in doubt, another voice vote or a show of hands may be taken. Responses in favor are either *yeas* or *ayes*; against, *nays* or *noes*.

2. *Show of hands or rising* vote is used when a motion requires a definite number of affirmative votes, such as two-thirds. The secretary and possibly others appointed by the presiding officer are responsible for counting the votes.

3. *Roll call* vote may be required by the bylaws of an organization for particular motions or may be decided upon by a motion from a member. The presiding officer states the responses to be used in voting for or against the motion. Members not voting may be asked to respond by saying, "Present" or "Abstain." Names are called in alphabetical order and the vote is given. The presiding officer is named last and votes only if it would affect the result. The roll call record is made a part of the minutes of the meeting.

4. *Ballot vote* allows for a secret vote and is commonly used for elections or important matters brought before the organization. Printed ballots, as in the case of elections, generally are prepared before the meeting. For matters arising at the meeting requiring a ballot vote, slips of paper are distributed to the membership for voting use.

Illus. 15-9
There are four
basic methods of
voting.

> *Announcement of Results: The affirmative vote is given first, followed by a statement to the effect that the motion passed or the motion was defeated.*

After a main motion has been made, a member of the body can propose an amendment to the motion. If the proposal is seconded, it is discussed. The proposed amendment must be voted upon before the main motion can again be considered. After announcing the action on a proposed amendment, the chairman states that the original motion plus the amendment is now before the house if the amendment carried. If the amendment was defeated, the original motion is acted upon.

If a motion involves two actions rather than one, a member can move that the question be divided for voting; then each part becomes a separate motion. If a motion is so bogged down that further discussion would seem a waste of time, and if two-thirds of the voting members agree, a member can "move the question," forcing an immediate vote.

If the motion to move the question loses, discussion continues. When it becomes obvious that further information is needed, a motion can be made to refer the matter to a committee, which is then named by the chairman.

A motion can also be made to *table* a motion (to delay further discussion or action). A seconded motion to table must be voted upon at once. A successful motion to table permits the group to consider more important business and sometimes allows a motion to die, although a tabled motion may be taken from the table by a majority vote. (A surer way to kill a motion is to move that the motion be postponed indefinitely.)

Members may question the chairman about the way business is being conducted at any time. If a member says, "I rise to a point of order," the chairman must decide, without debate, if a rule has been broken or rely on a parliamentarian for advice. By unobtrusively calling the attention of the chairman to any violations in parliamentary procedure, the secretary can prevent embarrassment. Slipping a brief, tactfully phrased note to the chairman is sufficient to alert her (or him) to an error or an omission in procedure.

Privileged motions have precedence over others. One privileged motion is "to call for orders of the day." This motion, without debate, forces the chairman to follow the agenda.

The Secretary at the Meeting

If you are asked to take notes at a meeting, familiarize yourself ahead of time with matters that may be discussed by reading the minutes of previous meetings, the agenda, proposals, and other information that might be brought before the membership. This background information will help you set up the order of your note taking or supplement a recorder if the meeting is being taped. Select a chair next to the presiding officer and concentrate on taking notes as unobtrusively as possible.

Your first duty may be to report whether a quorum is present. A rapid check can be made by using a membership list. While taking notes, you may have to ask to have something repeated. You may say, "I did not get that," or you may give a prearranged signal to the presiding officer, such as raising your left hand slightly. The presiding officer will ask that the point be repeated. The bylaws of some organizations require that the person making a motion submit the motion to the secretary in writing so that it will be exactly phrased in the minutes. Some secretaries prepare blank motion forms and distribute them to members before the meeting begins (see Illus. 15-10). Even with written motions, you should take the oral motion down verbatim to be sure that the written motion conforms to the oral one. Copies of complicated reports or presentations should be given to you to attach to the minutes.

You are not expected to take down the meeting word for word. Too many notes, however, are better than too few. You are responsible for getting everything important in your notes, especially motions, amendments, pertinent discussions, and decisions. If you cannot decide whether a statement is important, you should record it. It can be dropped from the final draft if it later seems inconsequential.

```
Motion _____

_____

_____

Made by _____

Seconded by _____

Vote for _____    Vote against _____

Abstentions _____

Absent during voting _____

Summary of discussion _____

_____

_____
```

Illus. 15-10
Because an organization's bylaws may require members to submit motions in written form, blank motion forms may be distributed before a meeting begins. Persons making motions would record them on blank forms and hand them to the secretary. When a motion reached the floor, the secretary would use the form to record all pertinent data regarding it; i.e., who made the motion, who seconded it, votes for and against, abstentions, and a summary of the discussion.

Some essential parts of the minutes may not be specifically announced at the time of the meeting. For example, the date, time, and place of the meeting and the name of the presiding officer may not be stated. The roll may be called; but if it is not called *the secretary is expected to observe and to record* all details of attendance including who attended, who did not attend, who arrived late, and who left early. The last two items of information are important in recording action on measures voted upon. (Those not wishing to go on record with their votes may absent themselves from a part of the session for just that reason.) To report as present a person who left the meeting during an important transaction could have serious consequences.

If you are depending on a taped report of the meeting as the source for the minutes, you should have two recorders set up in the room. Activate the second recorder immediately after the first tape is used. In addition, you will need to make notes of *items that are not likely to appear in the recording:* the names of those attending, the official title of the speaker, who said what, the time of the meeting and adjournment, the names of those voting yes and no to motions, the names of those coming in late and leaving early, and possibly any difficult names and words that may cause confusion in transcription. If you outline the proceedings during the meeting, you can more easily make necessary insertions when you work with the taped report. Keep the tapes until the minutes have been signed and formally approved by the membership.

If it is the secretary's duty to read the minutes of the last meeting, they should be read in an intelligible manner and in a voice loud enough that everyone in attendance can hear what matters were considered and what decisions were made. After the minutes are read, the presiding officer asks for corrections and additions. Usually this is a mere formality, and a voice vote approves the minutes as read. In some cases, however, corrections or additions are made. When this happens, the minutes should not be retyped. The changes should be made in red ink on the original copy of the minutes. Corrections and additions become a part of the minutes of the meeting at which they are made. Some organizations appoint a minutes committee to examine the minutes before the next meeting and report to the membership whether the minutes are in order or what changes should be made.

The order of business follows the agenda. The story of every motion, passed or defeated, must be recorded in the minutes. The name of the person making the motion, the complete motion exactly as stated, the name of the person seconding it, a summary of the pros and cons given, including the names of those speaking to the issue, and the decision by vote all must go into the secretary's notes. Motions written out by their originators and committee reports are important source documents.

After the business of the meeting is completed, the date of the next meeting is announced, usually just before adjournment. After the meeting has been adjourned, the secretary collects copies of all papers read and all committee reports so that they can be made a part of the minutes. (Committee reports are attached to the minutes.) If in doubt, the secretary should verify the correct spelling of names and the correct phrasing of motions before leaving the meeting room.

Follow-up Work after the Meeting

A great deal of work always follows a meeting. Aside from putting the meeting room back in order and preparing the minutes, the secretary should note items that require future attention on office calendars. Individual letters to those newly elected to membership, to those appointed to serve on committees, and to those requested to perform certain tasks should be written. A check should also be made to see that appropriate thank-you letters are written. The secretary should be especially diligent in processing all forms necessary for prompt payment of honoraria, fees, and expense accounts that the meeting's sponsors are obligated to pay.

Resolutions. Often an organization wishes to formally express its opinion or will in the form of a resolution. A resolution may be presented at the meeting in writing, or afterward the secretary may be instructed to prepare one. After a resolution is composed and typewritten, the secretary is responsible for having it signed, distributing it, and incorporating it into the minutes. A resolution may express sympathy, voice approval of stated objectives, or recognize achievements. An example appears in Illus. 15-11.

Preparing the Minutes. Accurately reporting actions taken during a meeting is the most important part of preparing minutes; yet, sometimes it is difficult to report what is *done* at a meeting when the record reports only what is said. It is a challenge for even an experienced secretary to winnow the pertinent facts from a written or a taped record of a meeting.

The minutes of a meeting vary with the degree of formality required. The minutes of an office conference are often very compact and simple. If the secretary finds that grouping the minutes around a central theme is clearer than preparing them in chronological order, the minutes of an informal meeting may be prepared in this fashion. The minutes of a meeting of a large organization are often complex. The efforts of individual members are often recognized and letters from former members may be read. Official minutes of a formal nature

Illus. 15-11
A resolution is
usually a formal
statement. Each
paragraph begins
with *WHEREAS* or
RESOLVED typed
in capital letters or
underlined.

```
                            RESOLUTION
                       Adopted October 11, 19--

        WHEREAS, Judith Monique has been a member of the legal
            firm of Killian, Longhill, Paganne, and Monique for the
            past twelve years and during this time has contributed
            significantly to the professional prestige of our com-
            pany as well as to its monetary success; and

        WHEREAS, Ms. Monique is leaving the organization to accept
            an appointment as judge of the district court of New
            Jersey; therefore, be it

        RESOLVED, that the members of this firm go on record as
            expressing their sincere appreciation of Ms. Monique's
            services at the same time that they wish her well in
            the judgeship for which she is eminently qualified;
            and be it

        RESOLVED FURTHER, that our Secretary send a copy of this
            resolution to the governor of the state of New Jersey.



        Lucian Paganne                      K. L. Killian
        Lucian Paganne, Secretary           K. L. Killian, Senior Member
```

(corporate minutes, for example) must be prepared in the order of occurrence, contain complete details, and include the exact wording of all motions and resolutions.

Sometimes the original copy of the minutes is placed in the minutes book only. In other cases, copies of the minutes are made and distributed to members after they have been officially approved.

If it is known that the minutes will be referred to at another meeting, copies are often prepared with line numbers typed in the left margin. It is easy for speakers to refer to *page 3, line 17*, and have the membership follow the discussion.

Sample formats for the preparation of minutes are presented in Illus. 15-12 and in Illus. 15-13. Notice that the minutes answer what, where, when, who, and why. Minutes should be written in complete sentences in past tense. When preparing minutes, follow these suggestions:

1. Use plain white paper.
2. Capitalize and center the group's official title or the nature of its work.
3. Single- or double-space the minutes and allow generous margins. Double-spaced minutes are preferred. Indent paragraphs five to ten spaces.

```
MEETING OF THE COMMITTEE TO STANDARDIZE OFFICE FORMS

February 17, 19--

The Committee held its organization meeting in the private
dining room in the company cafeteria at 12 noon.

Those present were Thomas Healey, L. D. Livovich, Margo
Margolis, and Merville Perry.  Madeleine Marshall was absent.

By unanimous vote Miss Margolis was elected chairperson,
and Mr. Livovich was elected secretary.

The following actions were taken.

Collection of Forms Currently in Use.  Using the corpora-
tion organization chart, Mr. Healey will assign each member of
the Committee a definite number of departments from which to
collect all forms presently being used.  These forms are to be
collected by March 1.

Research on Forms Control.  Mr. Livovich will obtain from
the company librarian a list of books already available in our
library on forms control.  He will bring these books to the next
meeting of the Committee so that members can volunteer to study
those of greatest interest to them.  He will also research Books
in Print and request that the librarian purchase new books that
would be useful.  Mr. Perry suggested that the number of new
books requested be kept to five, and the group concurred.
```

```
The meeting was adjourned at 1:15 p.m.

February 17, 19--                        L. D. Livovich
       Date                             L. D. Livovich
```

Illus. 15-12
In this sample,
paragraph point
headings are used
to indicate subject
captions and
separate motions.

4. Prepare the minutes with the agenda's subject captions. Record each different action in a separate paragraph.

5. Establish that the meeting was properly called and that members were properly notified. Indicate whether it was a regular or a special meeting.

6. Give the names of the presiding officer and the committee's official secretary.

7. Indicate whether a quorum was present; provide a roll of those present. At official meetings, list those absent.

8. Prepare a rough draft of the minutes for approval by your employer before preparing them in final form.

9. Transcribe the minutes while they are still fresh in your memory. If that is impossible, take the notes home and read through them, securing them in mind for accurate transcription the next day. If the minutes for a meeting that you did not attend are dictated to you, be sure that you get all the pertinent data from your employer at the time of dictation.

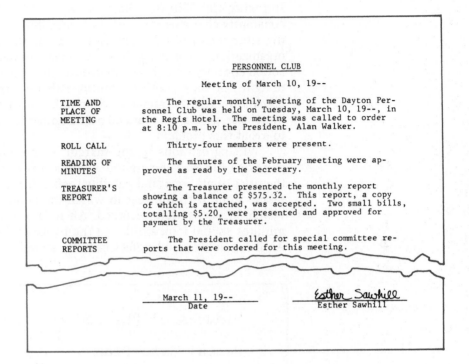

PERSONNEL CLUB

Meeting of March 10, 19--

TIME AND
PLACE OF
MEETING
> The regular monthly meeting of the Dayton Personnel Club was held on Tuesday, March 10, 19--, in the Regis Hotel. The meeting was called to order at 8:10 p.m. by the President, Alan Walker.

ROLL CALL
> Thirty-four members were present.

READING OF
MINUTES
> The minutes of the February meeting were approved as read by the Secretary.

TREASURER'S
REPORT
> The Treasurer presented the monthly report showing a balance of $575.32. This report, a copy of which is attached, was accepted. Two small bills, totalling $5.20, were presented and approved for payment by the Treasurer.

COMMITTEE
REPORTS
> The President called for special committee reports that were ordered for this meeting.

March 11, 19--
Date

Esther Sawhill
Esther Sawhill

Illus. 15-13
In this sample, subject captions are typed in the margins.

10. Capitalize such words as *Board of Directors, Company, Corporation,* and *Committee* in the minutes when they refer to the group in session.

11. Use objective and businesslike language. Do not include personal opinions, interpretations, or comments. Record only business actions, not sentiments or feelings. Such phrases as *outstanding speech, brilliant report,* or *provocative argument* are out of place in the minutes. Where gratitude or appreciation is to be expressed, it should take the form of a resolution.

12. Give the name of each speaker. Try to summarize the gist of each person's discussion about a motion, including reasons presented for and against its adoption. (A recently formed organization interested in improving business records for historical purposes decries the lack of information in the minutes of company meetings at all levels. This organization stresses the value of summaries.)

13. Number pages at the bottom.

14. Send official minutes to the secretary of the organization or to the presiding officer or both, for signatures. At the end of the minutes, type a line for recording the date of their approval.

Indexing the Minutes. Because the membership of organizations is constantly changing, sometimes groups find themselves in embarrassing situations because they do not know the regulations which the organization, as a body, has previously passed. They may take an action contrary to required procedure; they may violate their own regulations; or they may pass motions that contradict each other. The preparation and maintenance of an index of an organization's minutes by subject, giving the year and page number of each action taken, helps to avoid this problem.

Writing captions in the margin of the minutes book facilitates preparing file cards for its index. File cards should be captioned with the titles of motions (and possibly their subtitles) on which action was taken, along with the year in which the group acted and the page on which decisions were recorded. An index card for an organization's minutes should look similar to the index card shown in Illus. 15-14. An index could also be electronically stored in a computer.

Illus. 15-14
An index card concerning an organization's dental care plan might look like this.

```
Minutes of the Budget Committee

Dental Care Plan


          January 13, 1982,   p. 1
          February 16, 1982,  p. 1
          March 16, 1982,     p. 1
```

Other Duties. Some organizations require members to attend all meetings or a specified number of meetings per year. If attendance is required, the secretary's records are extremely important and will be periodically reviewed to determine which members should be replaced for violating the attendance requirement. If you are responsible for keeping a detailed record of attendance patterns, a form similar to the one shown in Illus. 15-15 might be used if an organization met monthly. This form could easily be adapted for other time periods.

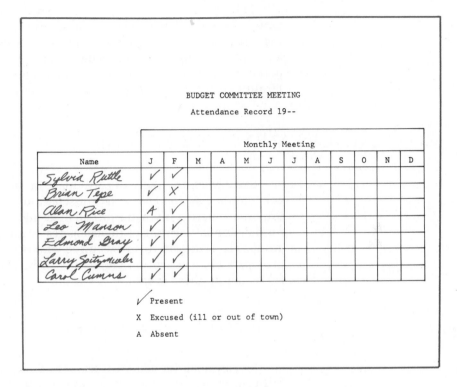

BUDGET COMMITTEE MEETING

Attendance Record 19--

Name						Monthly Meeting							
	J	F	M	A	M	J	J	A	S	O	N	D
Sylvia Ruttle	✓	✓										
Brian Tepe	✓	X										
Alan Rice	A	✓										
Leo Manson	✓	✓										
Edmond Gray	✓	✓										
Larry Spitzmuler	✓	✓										
Carol Cumms	✓	✓										

✓ Present

X Excused (ill or out of town)

A Absent

Illus. 15-15 Secretaries are often responsible for keeping an accurate record of attendance patterns.

Corporate Minutes

Corporations are required by law to keep minutes of stockholders' and directors' meetings. Stockholders usually meet once a year, but directors' meetings are held more frequently. These minutes are extremely important legal records.

The minutes of a corporation are kept by a corporation secretary, a full-time executive. Stockholders' and directors' minutes are usually kept in separate books. These minutes books must be carefully guarded against the substitution or removal of pages. Prenumbered pages signed and dated by the corporation secretary, watermarked pages, and keylock binders that can only be opened with carefully guarded keys are ways to protect corporate minutes from tampering.

Corrections resulting from the reading of the minutes at a subsequent meeting are written in and the incorrect portions are ruled out in ink. These changes are initialed in the margin.

The minutes of a corporation identify the membership of the group, show the date and place of the meeting, tell whether the meeting is regular or special, give the names of those attending, and contain a complete record of the proceedings. The official secretary of the corporation has full responsibility for their completeness, accuracy, and legality even though a regular secretary may type them.

CONFERENCES AND CONVENTIONS

Executives are likely to participate in numerous conferences and conventions. A *conference* is a discussion or consultation on some important matter, often in a formal meeting. A *convention* is usually a formal, annual meeting of the delegates or members, of a professional group. The secretary to an executive who is in charge of a convention or is part of a convention program, will be involved in planning and following-up these events.

Secretarial Planning Responsibilities

Preparations for some conferences and conventions requires the full-time efforts of a secretary for an entire year. Months of painstaking work are necessary to handle such details as selecting the meeting location, contacting speakers, preparing publicity and registration materials, and planning meals and social functions.

The Meeting Location. An annual convention of a professional association or similar group requires special facilities. For this reason, conventions are often held in hotels or in civic centers. At least one room large enough to accommodate all registered participants is required. In addition, a number of small conference rooms for group discussions and adequate facilities for dining and social functions are needed. A block of rooms for out-of-town participants must also be reserved, usually at a special rate. In selecting a meeting location, the secretary seeks the assistance of hotel or convention bureau staffs. Estimates of attendance should be available from either the executive or from the previous year's attendance figures.

Session Speakers. You may be asked to make the initial contact with prospective speakers. If you have plenty of time before the convention program is printed, you may communicate with them by letter: otherwise, phone calls are necessary. The date and the location of the convention, the name of the convention, the expected attendance at the speaker's session, the preferred topic, and presentation length should be discussed in the initial contact with a prospective speaker. Finally, the matter of fees and expenses must be addressed. If the speaker agrees to make a presentation, ask about the type of audiovisual equipment and room arrangement desired. The form shown in Illus. 15-16 would be useful for gathering this information. Also, ask the speaker to send a biographical sketch and, if required, a recent photograph. Confirm final arrangements by letter. (The secretary to an executive who makes several conference presentations a year should have a packet of materials including a biographical sketch, photograph, requests for certain types of equipment, and a floorplan of a preferred room arrangement prepared in advance for conference coordinators.)

Illus. 15-16
This form helps gather information on what type of equipment and room arrangement speakers prefer.

```
                    EQUIPMENT REQUISITION

Session _____        Date _____  Time _____

Room _____        Room Capacity _____

Seating Accommodations:

    Speaker's Table _____     Chairs _____

    Chairs for Participants _____
                                    Date        Operator
Equipment Required                  Ordered     Required

Tape/Cassette Recorder              _____    _____

Chalkboard                          _____    _____

Easel for Chart                     _____    _____

Overhead Projector                  _____    _____

35 mm Projector                     _____    _____

Screen                              _____    _____

Videotape Recorder                  _____    _____

Slide Projector                     _____    _____

8 mm Projector                      _____    _____

Microphone                          _____    _____

Lectern                             _____    _____

Television Monitor                  _____    _____


Room Arrangement Preference (Indicate Preference):

Round Table _____    Horseshoe _____    Classroom _____
                                        Tables ___  Chairs ___
```

Publicity and Registration. Publicity material, including the convention program and instructions for advance registration, must be prepared and mailed to prospective participants. You may be responsible for selecting the printer as well as proofreading and distributing publicity materials. You may also be involved in preparing news releases. In addition, you may be asked to collect and deposit registration fees.

When participants check-in for a convention, they receive give-away items, a roster of participants, a name tag, meal tickets, and miscellaneous literature. You may be asked to obtain and assemble these materials into an attractive packet for distribution at convention time.

Other Preconvention Duties. Some speakers may ask you to make hotel reservations for them. If so, ask the hotel to send the speaker a written confirmation. As a special courtesy, you may also arrange for each speaker to be met and escorted to the hotel.

The hotel staff assists the secretary in deciding the menu for meals and other social functions. Generally, a budget has been determined for these functions and menus are selected with the budget in mind. If there is to be a speaker's table, determine the proper seating order and prepare the necessary place cards.

Many conventions involve displays and exhibits of the latest equipment and/or techniques of a particular profession. Floor space for each exhibit is assigned by contract; therefore, the secretary may be responsible for typing and mailing contracts. A floor plan of the exhibit area is helpful in keeping track of assignments.

Duties at the Conference

The secretary is challenged at every turn to perform efficiently during the conference. Even with the best of planning, problems are bound to occur. Most last-minute problems can be avoided by alert, well-organized secretaries. Although you may not be involved in the registration process, you should check to see that registration tables are set up and that all the registration packets are conveniently arranged. A typewriter and stationery supplies should be available at the registration table. It is up to you to see that microphones work and that service people are on hand during presentations. This may involve checking union regulations. You must remember to send complimentary tickets to the spouse of the luncheon speaker, to position session signs, to direct traffic, to have ice water at the lectern, to check the number of chairs on the platform, to check that the table is draped, and to provide place cards for the speakers' table and arrange them with a sense of protocol. As a general rule, arrange for the chairman or host of the meeting to sit at the center of the table. The most distinguished guest or speaker sits to the right of the chairman, and the next most distinguished person sits to the chairman's left. If there is a lectern at the table, seat the host and the most distinguished guest to one side of the podium. The remaining places at the table are filled according to rank.

For each speaker's session, you should verify that the equipment in the room is in good working condition. You must see that the projectionist is available when the speaker wants to show films or slides. You make sure that the room is darkened during these presentations. If printed material accompanies a presentation, arrange to have it distributed. If there are not enough copies, make arrangements for additional copies to be made.

Conference Follow-Up

Secretaries are often responsible for conference groundwork and follow-up work. They should not, however, be concerned with the writing of the conference report, only with the processing of it.

Conference participants often want a copy of the proceedings. This service might be covered by the registration fee, or an additional charge might be made. In any case, the secretary may be responsible for securing mailing addresses of those entitled to a copy of the proceedings.

If papers are read at a conference, each speaker is usually asked to submit the paper prior to (or at) the meeting so that it can be printed in its entirety or abstracted. Permission from the speaker must be obtained prior to publication. One of the secretary's follow-up responsibilities is to obtain a copy of all papers for publication.

The conference reporter needs only to report the discussion following the presentation of a paper. Conference reports may be made from a tape recording or from summary notes. Sometimes the speaker is asked to prepare the summary. The conference reporter then becomes responsible for organizing the speaker's summary, editing it for uniformity of style, and writing introductions, conclusions, or recommendations.

Other follow-up duties include arranging for the return of any equipment on loan to the convention and picking up papers, supplies, and other things belonging to the convention that are left behind. Speakers and distinguished guests should be assisted in checking out of the hotel and in reaching transportation. Thank-you letters must be sent and expense reports must be compiled and processed. A final task for the secretary might be to compose recommendations for subsequent meetings, based on experience gained from this one.

TELECONFERENCING

Using today's technology, meeting participants do not have to be in the same room to communicate effectively. In fact, they do not have to be in the same city. *Teleconferencing* enables two or more persons in different geographic locations to communicate electronically. Teleconferencing is effective for informal meetings, sales meetings, training sessions, and as an adjunct to formal, structured meetings, annual conventions, and other conferences. It is estimated that teleconferencing could substitute for 35 percent of all business meetings involving travel.[3] Audio (voice) transmission, video (pictorial) transmission with audio, and computer messages are forms of teleconferencing. Illus. 15-17 shows several executives participating in a video conference.

Illus. 15-17
Specially equipped meeting rooms in hotels are ideal environments for teleconferences.

Hilton Hotels Corporation

---

[3]Nancy B. Finn, *The Electronic Office* (Englewood Cliffs, NJ: Prentice-Hall, Inc., 1983).

Audio Conferencing

Audio teleconferences involve only the transmission of sound. Audio conferencing is also called *audio teleconferencing, voice teleconferencing, telephone conferencing,* and *conference calling.* Audio conferencing capabilities have been available since the 1950s. Connections are made by using a conference operator or by using a circuit where each participant dials a special access code. Audio conferencing works well in sharing information, making announcements, giving status reports, and making future plans.

The secretary's responsibilities in planning and executing a successful audio conference can be extensive. The secretary may prepare and send an agenda and other handouts prior to the conference, give instructions to the conference operator, introduce and establish the order of speakers, transmit graphics over facsimile equipment (see page 333), standby until the conference is concluded, and take minutes of the meeting.

Video Conferencing

Video conferencing, in addition to having audio capabilities, provides televised pictures of participants at conference locations. When a still photograph of each participant is sufficient, *freeze frame* is used. *Slow scan* video, in which the image on the screen changes approximately every 60 seconds, is another possibility. The method which most closely resembles a face-to-face conference, however, is *full motion (live)* video.

During the pictorial and verbal interchange, text, graphics, and data can be sent back and forth via intelligent copiers (see page 261) and facsimile equipment. Another device which can enhance a video conference is the *electronic blackboard.* An electronic blackboard is used like an ordinary blackboard. Chalk strokes are transmitted over telephone lines and received on television monitors. As with an ordinary blackboard, part or all of the information can be erased. The electronic blackboard is particularly effective in creating and displaying graphics.

In a video conference the presenter is the person shown on the screen at the time and attendees are those participating at different locations. There are definite advantages in using video conferencing as a means of reducing travel costs; however, the elimination of socialization, the inability of observing firsthand the reaction of attendees, and the high cost of the video conferencing itself ensure that video conferencing will not entirely replace face-to-face meetings. Major hotel chains have installed equipment and communication lines necessary for video conferencing to attract companies to hold conferences on their premises. The secretary in charge of a video conference must contact participants to schedule a time for the conference, arrange for the equipment and an operator, and schedule a conference room. Handouts or conference materials must be mailed and distributed prior to the conference. For reporting or summary purposes, the secretary may be in attendance or replay a tape recording at a later time.

Computer Conferencing

Using computer terminals, meetings can be held (either simultaneously or on a delayed basis) with groups of people in various geographic locations. Participants input messages to other members of the group on computer terminals that are linked by telephone on a national or international computer network. All records of discussions and document transmission are stored. Computer conferencing is like a business meeting except that everyone is not necessarily present at the same time. There may be discussion between two participants or a group discussion among several members, but all participants do not have to be in a group at the same time. One could arrive at 9 a.m. and see what another member did at 11 p.m. the previous evening. Computer conferencing may include a range of graphic capabilities, such as slides, transparencies, sketches, and handwritten notes. Computer conferencing appears to work best when tasks are clearly identified and users are comfortable using keyboards.

A secretary's responsibilities concerning computer conferencing may be to notify the executive when messages are received, to input messages, to obtain additional information, and to call other executives to ask for their input. Prior to the conference, the secretary may be responsible for preparing graphics and other documentation.

SUMMARY

Within a business organization, the majority of decisions are made during or as a result of business meetings; therefore, it is no surprise that executives spend up to 40 percent of their time in meetings. Meetings may be informal, involving two or more company employees, or they may be structured, involving many participants and a prepared agenda. Executives also attend community-related meetings and professional conferences and conventions. The secretary to such an executive may be involved in conference preparation and follow-up. In addition, the secretary may be responsible for recording the minutes of many different kinds of meetings which require different levels of secretarial skill.

For informal scheduled meetings, the secretary's responsibilities include reminding members of the meeting, preparing the meeting room, and preparing a summary of the meeting for distribution to members. If an executive calls an unscheduled meeting, the secretary must quickly determine a mutually agreeable time for the meeting.

A special meeting situation arises if one of the members does not speak English. The secretary may be asked to contact an interpreter.

Formal meetings require scheduling a meeting room, sending out meeting notices, preparing an agenda, and a number of last-minute duties. The secretary who is to record the minutes of a formal meeting comes to the meeting prepared with an attendance list, the agenda, the minutes book, ballots, and any other material. For example, a copy of *Robert's Rules of Order Newly Revised* should be available for the executive's reference. If the secretary is to read the minutes of the previous meeting, they should be read in an intelligible manner and in a voice loud enough to be heard. Any corrections to the minutes are made in red ink on the original copy. After the meeting, the secretary is responsible for such follow-up activities as preparing resolutions, typing and indexing the minutes, and distributing the minutes for signatures. A company officer, generally the corporation secretary, prepares the minutes of the corporation. The secretary to a corporation secretary performs the planning and follow-up duties required for formal meetings.

Annual conferences or conventions can require the full-time services of a secretary for an entire year. Many hours of work are involved in selecting the convention site, contacting speakers, preparing publicity and registration materials, and performing other preconvention duties. During the conference, the secretary makes sure that the equipment in the room is in good working order. The secretary often assumes the role of a troubleshooter and attempts to solve problems before they occur. Responsibility for recording a convention's minutes is delegated to professional recorders. The secretary may be in charge of the distribution of the minutes, however. Finally, a significant secretarial contribution to conference planning is making recommendations for next year's conference.

The time and expense involved in travel to and from meetings is making teleconferencing technology attractive to many business organizations. Teleconferencing (audio, video, computer) enables two or more persons in different geographic locations to communicate electronically without leaving their offices. Secretarial responsibilities differ with each teleconferencing method. Although an alternative to face-to-face meetings, the technological advancement which teleconferencing represents is not perceived as a substitute to the traditional meeting environment.

SUGGESTED READINGS

Baber, Lina G. *Office Practices and Procedures*. Columbus, OH: Charles E. Merrill Publishing Company, 1982.

Becker, Esther, and Evelyn Anders. *The Successful Secretary's Handbook*. New York: Barnes & Noble Books, 1984.

Newman, Pamela J., and Alfred F. Lynch. *Behind Closed Doors*, A Guide to Successful Meetings. Englewood Cliffs, NJ: Prentice-Hall, Inc., 1983.

Palmer, Barbara C., and Kenneth R. Palmer. *Successful Meeting Master Guide for Business and Professional People*. Englewood Cliffs, NJ: Prentice-Hall, Inc., 1983.

QUESTIONS FOR DISCUSSION

1. How could an efficient secretary have improved the last organized meeting you attended:
   a. Before the meeting?
   b. During the meeting?
   c. After the session?
2. An unscheduled meeting of the Personnel Committee has just been called and must be held within the next two days. Can you foresee any difficulty if the secretary uses electronic calendaring to set the date and time for this meeting?
3. Discuss methods of keeping a mailing list current.
4. Your employer has planned a meeting with ten people in the company conference room. You have arranged for a recorder to tape the conference.
   a. Why is it a good practice to have two recorders in the room?
   b. If you are to type the minutes, what type of information will the recorder not provide?
5. Give examples of the types of information a secretary responsible for taking minutes would take to the meeting.

6. While taking notes during a meeting what should the secretary do in the following situations:
    a. An unidentified person makes a motion
    b. A person makes a motion that lacks clarity and rephrases it several times before it is voted on
    c. The presiding officer entertains a new motion before the motion on the floor has been disposed of
7. What are some of the preliminary responsibilities of a secretary to an executive in charge of an annual convention?
8. How do the secretary's responsibilities differ in arranging a meeting for an executive and two company employees in the following situations:
    a. Over the telephone
    b. In the executive's office
    c. When one of the employees does not speak English
    d. Via a computer network
9. Retype the following sentences. Show the correct possessive form of the word in parentheses. Refer to the Reference Guide to correct and verify your answers.
    a. Do you want copies of the (teacher) or the (student) handbook?
    b. We bought ($8) worth of stamps.
    c. I have not heard of anyone (else) dismissal.
    d. My (brother-in-law) business is for sale.
    e. Eleanor (Jones) reelection will ensure progress for the state.
    f. Have you read the (Morgan Company) report?
    g. There were several (women) groups in the parade.

PROBLEMS

1. Attend a local public meeting. Record the minutes and type them in an acceptable format.
2. You have been asked to prepare a resolution of appreciation for the services of Miss Janet Godfrey, who has just completed two terms as the first president of the Secretarial Department Club. She was instrumental in getting the College of Business to award a Secretary-of-the-Year plaque at the annual awards banquet. She also represented the organization on the Council of Student Groups on campus.
3. After a recent conference for which you made most of the arrangements and wrote the minutes, the following complaints were made:
    a. A participant could not locate the meeting room, which had been changed the morning of the meeting.

b. Two participants were incorrectly identified in the minutes.

c. One participant complained that the motion she made was incorrectly recorded in the minutes.

d. Two participants who were given specific post-conference responsibilities did not perform them and gave the excuse that they had forgotten what had transpired.

What should you do next time to prevent recurrence of these problems?

4. Your employer, Henry C. Campbell, is secretary of the Denver Credit Managers Association. The regular monthly meeting of that organization was held on Thursday, June 22, at 6:30 p.m., at the Palace Hotel. Mr. Campbell gives you the following notes for the minutes of that meeting. You are to type the minutes in good form, using headings in the margins for each paragraph.

Called to order—8 p.m. by Ralph Riopelle, President.

Number of members present: 16. Charles Bavin, Vice-President, absent.

Minutes of May meeting read by the secretary and approved.

Treas. report—present bal. $572.68. Accepted (copy of report given to you by Mr. Campbell). No bills presented for payment.

Budget Committee—Rene Betz, Chairperson. Motion to accept moved and seconded. No discussion. Motion carried.

Membership Com.—Herbert Smith, Chairperson, introduced two new members, J. E. Gary and R. C. Baldwin.

James Steer introduced Donald Durst of Atlanta as speaker. Subject: "Trends in Installment Credit." Question and answer period followed.

Mr. Riopelle announced July 27 date of next regular meeting.

Motion for adjournment carried—9:37 p.m.

Case Problems

Tony Alvarez, secretary to the sales manager of ASD Company, went to lunch with Mary Turner and Jack Lewis, sales representatives, who had just submitted their travel expense forms for a sales conference at Mount White Inn. The conference was held some distance from the home office, and each one had driven a car to get to the hotel. Jack said, "I hope that our mileage figures are somewhat alike, Mary. I added 75 miles and included a visit to a customer in Brookfield, though I must admit that I didn't make that call. I did get a telephone order from there that day, however. You know, with today's inflation, we can't possibly live on the expense allowance that the company gives us."

Mary answered, "Yes, I know, Jack. We haven't had an adjustment in a year. I don't intend to lose money on my expenses either, so sometimes I have to juggle my figures a bit. I don't overestimate my actual travel expenses, but my expense accounts aren't exactly accurate either. Besides, everybody does it."

Then Jack said, "I know we just had that memo from our sales manager asking us to cut down on travel expenses because the company had such low third quarter earnings. I don't see much chance for a change in our travel allowance this year." He turned to Tony and said, "Tony, I have an idea. Why don't you suggest to Ms. Wolf that we be given a more reasonable figure?"

What should Tony say? What action, if any, should Tony take?

Ms. Elverson came back from a trip and complained to her secretary, Lilli LiQuan, about the airline she had traveled on. Lilli had made the arrangements through Marie Koch, an employee in the company's transportation department. She knew that Marie chose the airline over other airlines with parallel schedules.

Lilli had a friend who was an airline reservation clerk, handling corporate travel accounts only. She decided that she would discuss the best schedules and accommodations with him for a trip to Chicago that three company executives were to make the following week. She decided on the round-trip flights, telephoned Marie to give her specific requests, and asked her to make the actual reservations.

Marie said indignantly, "Don't tell me which flights to choose. What are you trying to do—take my job away from me?"

Lilli tried to appease her by saying, "But Ms. Elverson doesn't like to travel on the airline on which you always put our executives. I was just trying to be helpful."

What is the proper line of authority in this situation? What principle should Lilli follow in trying to handle the situation without troubling Ms. Elverson?

**Case 4-3
EXPANDING
DUTIES**

Frank Larson was secretary to Robert Holmes, manager of telecommunications for CXD. This multinational corporation had just purchased equipment for teleconferencing. Frank attended briefings on the use of the equipment and was given all the instructional manuals connected with its use. He did not, however, study the manuals because of the pressure of his other duties.

The first tryout was to be a conference between the president of the company and its five regional vice-presidents. Mr. Holmes wanted this to be a stellar performance. Unfortunately the full motion video that was planned was unsatisfactory. Mr. Holmes asked Frank to supply freeze frames. Because he had not studied the material that had been given him, Frank did not know what a freeze frame was and had made no provision for obtaining the photographs.

After the pictureless conference, Mr. Holmes blamed Frank for not having had the backup pictures available. He pointed out that the instructions warn that they are necessary in case anything goes wrong with a conference as planned.

Frank replied, "I'm sorry, Mr. Holmes. However, I don't really think that I should be blamed. I'm a secretary, not an engineer. I don't believe that I should have to know how to cope with that complicated equipment."

What principles are involved in Frank's reaction?

ADMINISTRATIVE SUPPORT SERVICES: RESEARCH AND ORGANIZATION OF BUSINESS DATA

An area of secretarial responsibility which requires intellectual curiosity and creativity is the research and organization of information for business reports. Organizing data into understandable and readable form is a high-order skill. The secretary who types a final report must have the capability of preparing a visually attractive document that often incorporates tables, charts, and other graphics.

To accomplish these duties, the secretary may work with special tools, such as VDTs and plotter/printers. The professional secretary, therefore, must keep informed of the technological advancements that provide new ways in which data and text are processed in the office.

Chapter 16

Collecting Business Information

Oftentimes before business decisions can be made, detailed reports, involving time-consuming research, must be prepared and thoroughly examined. Depending on the nature of the report, the information in it may be used by the executive or by the secretary. Researching and organizing business data gives the secretary an opportunity to show initiative and to work without supervision—two qualities which often lead to recognition and promotion. College-trained secretaries should be particularly adept at finding information, and for this reason, should welcome research assignments which ask them to do the following:

Verify the accuracy of data submitted in support of a proposal.

Gather data an executive needs to prepare a proposal.

Examine possible solutions to a problem, the advantages and disadvantages of certain solutions, and the opinions of authorities.

Gather and organize information the executive will need in preparing a speech, in writing an article for a professional magazine, or in contributing to a project.

Review personnel needs due to increased work load.

Research the financial condition of certain companies.

Compare product sales in a given category or territory.

Update information for a report or proposal.

Review information sources on a continuing basis.

To accomplish these activities, the secretary locates information and presents it in a proper format. This chapter will assist you in becoming a knowledgeable researcher of business information. Chapters 17 and 18 discuss ways of organizing data for effective presentation.

WHERE TO LOOK FOR INFORMATION

Information may be found in the executive's office, in the office files, in a company library, in an outside library, or in a computer database. An executive undoubtedly subscribes to technical publications, belongs to trade or professional organizations, and acquires specialized reference books for a personal office library. These are also good sources of business information. If the company you work for provides secretaries with desk reference materials, you have additional sources for checking facts.

Libraries

Many large corporations maintain a company library and have a technically trained librarian on staff. In addition to a librarian, many companies have a research staff that locates information by request. In this case, the function of the secretary is to provide accurate and exact requests for information. In other situations, the secretary must locate information in the company library without assistance.

It may be necessary to go outside the organization for information. The first logical outside source is the public library. A number of cities have public libraries with specialized business departments that provide invaluable assistance to business patrons.

The *specialized library* is another source of information. *The Directory of Special Libraries and Information Centers*, published by Gale Research Company of Detroit, lists the location, size, and specialty of these libraries. For example, local chambers of commerce frequently maintain libraries on commercial and industrial subjects. Many business, technical, and professional societies also maintain excellent libraries, although access is generally limited to members. County and federal court buildings and university law schools often house extensive law libraries. Many cities provide municipal reference libraries for the public as well as for city employees. Hospitals and colleges of medicine maintain medical and surgical libraries. Art, history, and natural history museums have specialized libraries, as do colleges and universities. Some newspapers have large library collections that are open to the public. The U.S. Department of Commerce maintains regional offices in principal cities, making its publications available for public use through these offices.

Computer Databases

Computer databases are like electronic libraries. They are important information sources for the researcher. Collections of data (databases) on many different subjects are stored in large, central computers. A company with adequate computer facilities can subscribe to an information service that maintains many databases. By keying in a special code, subscribers can access different databases. Information may appear on a CRT or it may be printed out. This is known as an on-line database search. If the computer searches its database after a researcher has signed off the computer, or if the desired citations or abstracts are sent to the researcher through the mail, the search is off-line. Generally off-line searches are less expensive than on-line searches. There are three general categories of database services: financial, general business/research, and special purpose.[1]

1. *Financial.* Perhaps the best known financial database service is the *Dow Jones News/Retrieval* which compiles stock quotations from the New York Stock Exchange, the American Stock Exchange, and the over-the-counter market. It also stores the full text of news stories from *The Wall Street Journal* and other Dow Jones sources.

2. *General Business/Research.* This category of database services is divided into on-line research services and on-line library services. The largest on-line research service is Lockheed Information System's *Dialog* which covers over 200 general news, science, and business databases. Other services in this group are *Bibliographic Retrieval Services* (BRS) and Mead Data Central's *Lexis* (legal references). On-line library services include *The Source* and *Compuserve.*

3. *Special Purpose.* Examples of special purpose database services include *NewsNet,* a collection of business newsletters and press releases, and the *OAG North American and Worldwide Electronic Edition.*

Directories of on-line databases can be found in most libraries. Examples of these references include Cuadra Associates, Inc.'s *Directory of Online Databases* and *DataPro Directory of Online Services.*

Research libraries, university libraries, and most public libraries subscribe to one or more database services. For some searches, the researcher may be able to use the service at no charge or for a minimal charge. For more complicated searches, however, a library staff member performs the search and an hourly fee is charged.

---

[1]Seymour, Jim, "Data Bases: Managers Go On-Line," *Today's Office* (September, 1984), pp. 36-40.

USING THE LIBRARY

When a subject requires extensive research, the secretary usually goes to the library to do the work. For purposes of review, a library has the following sections:

A circulation desk, where books are checked in and out
A reference area, where noncirculating reference materials are shelved
Card, microform, or computer Catalogs
Book Collections
Reserve Collections
Periodical Collections
Vertical Files
A media/audiovisual center
A sound recordings collection
A microform reading center

If you are unfamiliar with the library, a brief stop at the information reference desk to outline the purpose of your visit can save considerable time. The reference librarian at the information desk is usually very willing to assist researchers in locating the information sources they need. Some libraries offer tours to acquaint users with their facilities. A library tour would undoubtedly prove helpful to a new user.

Telephone Reference

Reference librarians provide a very valuable service to the business community. A phone call to the specialists can give you the answer to most questions, trivial or practical. The telephone numbers for the reference desks of most libraries are listed in the telephone directory.

In order to save time, callers should get straight to the point. Ask for the source of information, if the librarian does not supply it. If your question is too specialized or too technical, ask to be referred to another library division or to an outside source for assistance.

Finding Information

The experienced researcher consults library indexes, guides, and catalogs as the first step in the process of finding information. These sources are generally located near the reference desk.

Books. The library's *card catalog* indexes books by subject, title, and author. The card catalog may be in card form, in microform, or stored in a computer. The card catalog indexes the contents of the library just as a book's index lists its topics. Many cards contain cross-references that tell researchers where similar or related information may be found. Catalog cards are usually uniformly printed and available to libraries from the Library of Congress. An example of a card from a card catalog appears in Illus. 16-1.

Dewey Decimal System. The Dewey decimal system classifies library collections by subject. Most public libraries use this system. Subjects are divided into ten general classifications, numbered from 000 to 900. Each major class can be subdivided indefinitely by using the decimal point: 126.1, 126.2, 126.21, 126.211 are subdivisions of one class. Under this system, business information is found in the 650s.

Library of Congress System. Some research libraries use the Library of Congress system to classify their collections. This system uses a combination of letters and numbers. With this system, business information is found under the social sciences category, *H*.

Published Indexes. An annual publication in several volumes, *Books in Print*, lists all books included in publishers' catalogs, by author, title, and subject. The listings by subject are particularly helpful in developing a bibliography of current books on a given topic. These books are normally shelved in the reference section of the library.

Illus. 16-1
The author card in
a library catalog
contains many
kinds of
information.

```
330.219 ◄─ CLASSIFICATION (OR CALL) NUMBER

                  Amacher, Ryan C. ◄─ AUTHOR'S NAME
TITLE OF ──────►Principles of economics/ Ryan C. Amacher,
BOOK,      Holley H. Ulbrich. --3rd ed.-- Cincinnati:
AUTHOR(S) South-Western Publishing Co., 1986.
FACTS OF       x, 914 p. : ill. ; 24 cm. ◄── TEXT PAGES AND
PUBLICATION                                    SIZE OF BOOK

                  Includes bibliographies
                ISBN 0-538-08671-8 ◄─INTERNATIONAL STANDARD
         JOINT AUTHOR ENTRY                    BOOK NUMBER
SUBJECT ──────►1. ECONOMICS.  I. Ulbrich, Holley H., joint
ENTRY      author.  II. Title.


           ╱HB171.5.A397 1986  ╱330.219        85-50939 ╲
         LIBRARY OF CONGRESS   DEWEY DECIMAL   SERIAL NUMBER
         CLASSIFICATION NUMBER CLASSIFICATION  OF CARD
                               NUMBER
```

The *Cumulative Book Index* (or the *CBI* as it is familiarly identified) is an index of books printed in English from all over the world that are still available from publishers. The CBI lists books by author, title, and subject. These extra-large volumes are normally shelved in the catalog department of the library or at a reference desk. Other indexes that list sources of current information in special fields are the *Biological and Agricultural Index, Applied Science and Technology Index, Business Periodicals Index, Education Index, Social Sciences Index,* and *Engineering Index Annual.*

Pamphlets and Booklets. Valuable information is often published in pamphlet, booklet, or leaflet form. Such material is cataloged by subject and title in the *Vertical File Index of Pamphlets* (a subject and title index to selected pamphlets), published monthly. A typical entry from this index appears in Illus. 16-2.

Illus. 16-2
Much valuable information is published in pamphlet, booklet, or leaflet form.

> **JOB hunting**
> How to get your first job. 24p nd Inst of food technologists 221 N La Salle st Chicago Il 60601 $5 send payment with order
> Booklet offers pointers for job-hunters. Sections include: writing resumes, networking, typical questions asked by employers during interviews (such as "Why should I hire you?" and "What do you know about our company?"), "negative factors evaluated during an employment interview frequently leading to rejection of the applicant", and a list of further readings.

News. Summaries of newspaper and magazine reports from over 50 domestic and foreign sources is published in a one-volume, loose-leaf booklet known as *Facts on File Weekly World News Digest.*

The New York Times Index is another valuable reference for locating sources of information in newsprint. Supplements to this index are published monthly; cumulative editions, annually. Entries are arranged alphabetically under subjects. *The Wall Street Journal* publishes a similar index.

Magazines. The best index on general magazines is the *Readers' Guide to Periodical Literature.* This guide is a cumulative author and subject index to articles appearing in popular periodicals.

Preparing Bibliography Cards

The first consideration in selecting material for examination is the *date of publication*. If current information is desired, an article on laser beams published ten years ago would be of little value. The second consideration is *content*. Some indexes describe the types of information found in publications. Such descriptions help researchers to focus their search.

You should prepare a bibliography card for each reference you choose to examine. On a 5-by-3-inch card, record the library call number, the author's name, the title of the publication (and the article's title, if it is in a periodical), the publisher, date of publication, and page references.

Number the cards in the upper right corner in sequence, as shown in Illus. 16-3. The number that is thus assigned to a source is used to identify all notes that are taken from it. This method saves a great deal of time in identifying sources. Bibliography cards serve as a permanent and detailed record of a researcher's sources.

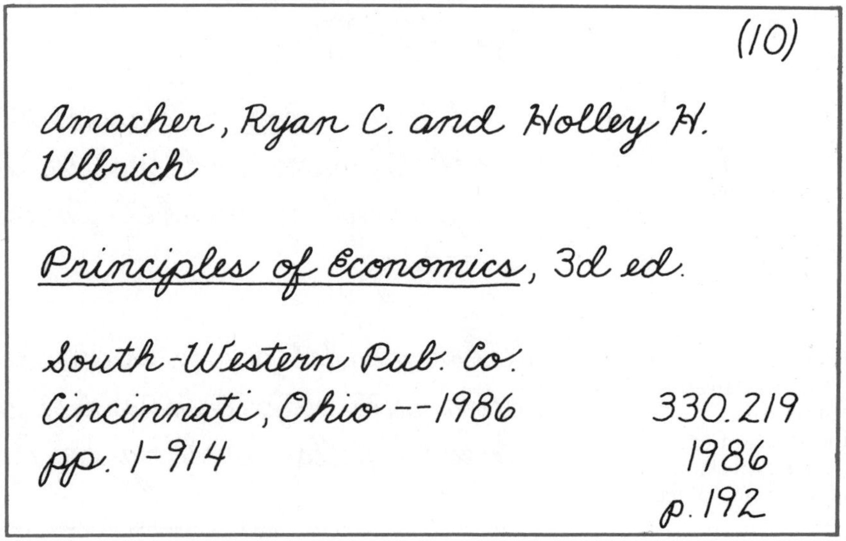
(10)

Amacher, Ryan C. and Holley H. Ulbrich

Principles of Economics, 3d ed.

South-Western Pub. Co.
Cincinnati, Ohio --1986 330.219
pp. 1-914 1986
p. 192

Illus. 16-3
Bibliography cards provide researchers with a permanent record of their sources.

Taking Notes

The secretary is now ready to study, evaluate, accept or reject material, and record references on individual sheets or cards, 6-by-4 inches or larger. By using cards or sheets of uniform size instead of a shorthand notebook, a complete set of references can be sorted for use in drafting the outline and writing the report.

Compiling Reference Cards. Each reference card should list the following information in a standard form (see Illus. 16-4):

1. Page numbers should be written in the upper left corner. (Do this first to avoid omitting them.)
2. Sources should be cited according to the number on its bibliography card.
3. Topics should be noted in a conspicuous position.
4. Information should be exactly quoted or summarized. It is important that you make a distinction for your employer between what is a summary statement and what is a direct quotation. A direct quotation is written word for word and enclosed in quotation marks, and any omissions from the original are indicated by ellipses. (Reproducing an author's work without express permission is in violation of the copyright laws.)

Illus. 16-4
This reference card summarizes information on Post-Keynesianism taken from source #10.

> *pp.* 372-375   (10)
>
> <u>Post Keynesianism</u> stresses the role of market power and institutional rigidities in preventing market forces from working.
>
> When market power is concentrated, business often cuts output instead of prices when demand falls, resulting in unemployment.

Abstracting. It may be more convenient to provide notes in abstract form rather than on reference cards. Abstracting is the process of taking the important ideas in a document and recording them in your own words. To prepare good abstracts, you must develop the ability to pick out important points and express them in summary form. Abstracts may be prepared in single-spaced or double-spaced form. An example appears in Illus. 16-5. Skillfully prepared abstracts can save the employer a great deal of reading time. A reference in abstract form should be identified as such. The source and page numbers should also be identified. Before preparing an abstract, check with the library to see if its computer database service provides abstracts of your reference sources.

Illus. 16-5
To prepare good abstracts, you must be able to pick out important points and express them in summary form.

```
                            ABSTRACT


        Murphy, Alma A.  "Information Processing in the Modern Office."
        The Mechanized Office (October 10, 1986), p. 43.†

            Office work involves inputting, processing, and outputting
        information.  Information is frequently inputted at the keyboard
        of a word processor or computer-linked terminal.  Information
        is processed through the use of hardware (computers and word
        processors) and software.  Printed material, also called hard
        copy, is by far the most common form of output.  Information
        can also be displayed on a VDT.  Other forms of output include
        microfilm, magnetic tape, and magnetic disks.  This article
        gives further evidence of the merger of data and word processing.
        More and more manufacturers are introducing equipment that
        performs both data and word processing functions.



        †CITATION GIVEN IS FICTITIOUS
```

Copying Material. Most libraries provide typewriters and copiers at a nominal cost. Because of the likelihood of errors in recording numerical data, statistical tables should be copied by machine. When library publications can be borrowed, take material to the office to reproduce numerical data. Librarians will sometimes lend a noncirculating reference book for a limited time. Libraries are eager to cooperate with business people and want them to make full use of their collections.

SOURCES OF GENERAL INFORMATION

Information sources are updated and revised constantly, and new materials are published regularly. It is necessary, therefore, to update references (including this chapter) with current sources.

Atlases

An atlas is a collection of maps and statistical information regarding populations and geographic areas. *Rand McNally Commercial Atlas and Marketing Guide*, available in most libraries, contains not only geographic maps but also many economic maps. Its primary emphasis is on the United States. Other atlases include sections on the solar system, world climate, and world energy resources.

Dictionaries

One would naturally expect that secretaries frequently use reference sources. Even though the office may have a large unabridged dictionary, secretaries often keep an up-to-date desk-size dictionary within arm's reach. *Webster's Ninth New Collegiate Dictionary*, for example, is a valuable addition to the secretary's reference shelf.

There are also innumerable specialized dictionaries: bilingual ones for use in writing and translating foreign correspondence and technical ones that focus on specialized business subjects, such as accounting, economics, data processing, telecommunications, and insurance.

New developments outdate technical dictionaries rapidly. Only the most recent editions can be considered dependably up to date.

Directories

Hundreds of directories are shelved in the reference section of the library. Some directories are available through computer database services. One type of directory, the city directory, is especially useful to local business firms. Most directories, however, are national in scope and serve special industrial and professional fields. For a listing of more than 5,000 American and foreign directories, consult *The Directory of Directories*. (For subscription information contact the Gale Research Company, Book Tower, Detroit, Michigan 48226.)

City Directories. A city directory provides a listing of residents of a city by name, by address, and by telephone number. These directories are not published by the municipality they serve but by private concerns for a profit. Not all large cities have a city directory. Unlike the telephone directory, city directories list telephone numbers in numerical order with addresses and occupants' names indicated. Current and back issues of city directories are kept at libraries for the convenience of business users. The local library's collection of directories may contain that city's city directory and also the directories of other cities in the state and of major cities throughout the country.

Special Directories. Special directories include the following:

1. *American Medical Directory* lists the names of physicians in the United States, Canada, Puerto Rico, and the Virgin Islands. It provides information on the year licensed, medical school attended, board certifications, etc.
2. *Who's Who in America* is a biographical directory of notable living Americans from the fields of science, politics, sports, education, etc. There are also selective *Who's Who* references, such as *Who's Who of American Women* and *Who's Who in American Law.*
3. The *National Directory of Addresses and Telephone Numbers* lists alphabetically and by categories 75,000 U.S. corporations, giving full names, street addresses, ZIP Codes, area codes, and telephone numbers. The multivolume *Thomas Register of American Manufacturers* and *The Million Dollar Directory* (three volumes) index names of businesses involved in similar enterprises.
4. The *Directory of American Firms Operating in Foreign Countries* and *Major Companies of Europe* (two volumes) list businesses and office addresses of companies doing business overseas.
5. The *Encyclopedia of Associations* lists the names, addresses, and officers of trade, business, labor, legal, educational, religious, and cultural organizations.

Encyclopedias

An encyclopedia is an excellent reference source. Only two are mentioned here. In addition to general information, the *Encyclopedia Americana* provides information on American cities, manufacturing, and commerce. The *Encyclopaedia Britannica* contains useful information on European countries and cities.

Government Publications

The United States government is a prolific publisher and a major source of information for the business executive. Some government publications may be subscribed to and purchased. Others are found on file in the reference department or business section of the public library or in a municipal reference library. Large cities usually have a depository library. Depository libraries are designated by law to receive all or part of the material published by the government. The reference librarian at your local library can tell you the location of the nearest depository.

For a comprehensive list of all publications issued by the various departments and agencies of the United States Government, consult the *Monthly Catalog of U. S. Government Publications*. Included in this comprehensive list of government publications are those for sale by the Superintendent of Documents, (Government Printing Office, Washington, DC 20402) and those for official use only.

Proceedings and debates of Congress are given in *The Congressional Record*. The official directory of the United States Congress, *The Congressional Directory*, provides information on the legislative, judicial, and executive branches of the federal government. The *Congressional Staff Directory* publishes the names of the Washington staff personnel of members of Congress and those serving committees and subcommittees. The *United States Government Manual*, the official handbook of the federal government, provides information on the purposes and programs of most government agencies and lists the top personnel of those agencies.

Publications of the Bureau of the Census are based on data from censuses taken in various years. They include information on population, housing, business, manufacturing, and agriculture. Full census reports provide complete information. The *Statistical Abstract of the United States* (annual), however, summarizes statistics about area and population, vital statistics, education, climate, employment, military affairs, social security, income, prices, banking, transportation, agriculture, forests, fisheries, mining, manufacturing, and related fields.

The U.S. Department of Commerce publishes the *Survey of Current Business* (issued monthly), which reports on the industrial and business activities of the United States. Publications of the Department of Agriculture provide agricultural and marketing statistics and information for increasing production and agricultural efficiency. Department of Labor publications deal mostly with labor statistics, standards, and employment trends. The Department's official publication is the *Monthly Labor Review*.

Economic and agricultural data on many subjects may be acquired from various state governments. The secretary should address inquiries to the departments of health, geology or conservation, and highways; to the divisions of banks, insurance, and statistics; to industrial and public utilities commissions; or to the research bureaus of state universities. Pertinent information about executive, legislative, and judicial branches of state governments is given in the *Book of the States*, which is published every two years by the Council of State Governments.

Yearbooks

Yearbooks are annual summaries of statistics and facts. *The World Almanac and Book of Facts*, which is the most popular book of this type, contains many pages of statistics and facts preceded by an excellent index. One reference librarian has said, "Give me a good dictionary and *The World Almanac*, and I can answer 80 percent of all questions asked me." It covers such items as stock and bond markets; notable events; political and financial statistics on states and cities; statistics on population, farm crops, prices, trade and commerce; educational data; and information on postal services. Because of its wide coverage and low price, the secretary might request the executive to purchase a copy of *The World Almanac* each year for office use. Another yearbook of this type is the *Information Please Almanac*.

The *Statesman's Yearbook* provides factual and statistical information on countries of the world. Data are provided under the following headings: type of government, area and population, religion, education, justice, defense, commerce and industry, and finance. The *International Yearbook and Statesmen's Who's Who* includes biographical sketches of over 10,000 political leaders and general information on international affairs and foreign relations.

SOURCES OF BUSINESS INFORMATION

Sources of business information are constantly revised, and new materials are published regularly. The list of specific business sources that appears in this chapter, therefore, should be supplemented with new sources as they appear.

General Subscription Information Services

Management often subscribes to information services relating to general business conditions. These services present information from sources that are more direct and specialized than those found in popular publications. A service may publish information in loose-leaf form so that superseded pages can be destroyed and new and additional ones easily inserted. It may be the secretary's duty to see that the new pages are filed in their proper place. Information services also provide data through computer database systems. Examples of these information services include the following:

> Babsons Reports, Inc. (370 Washington Street, Wellesley Hills, MA 02181) publishes a weekly bulletin, *Investment & Barometer Letter*.

> The Bureau of National Affairs, Inc. (1231 25th Street NW, Washington, DC 20037) in its *Daily Report for Executives* reports government actions that affect management, labor, law, taxes, finance, federal contracts, antitrust and trade regulations, international trade, and patent law.

> The Kiplinger Washington Editors (1729 H Street NW, Washington, DC 20006) publishes a weekly newsletter, *The Kiplinger Washington Letter*, that analyzes and condenses economic and political news.

> Predicasts, Inc. (1101 Cedar Avenue, Cleveland, OH 44106) publishes three indexes of literature appearing in hundreds of worldwide trade and financial journals, newspapers, and government reports. These indexes are published monthly; cumulative indexes are compiled quarterly and annually.

Specialized Subscription Information Services

The secretary should also be acquainted with some of the specialized subscription services for business fields.

Credit. Dun & Bradstreet Credit Rating Service (One World Trade Center, New York, NY 10048) collects, analyzes, and distributes credit information on retail, wholesale, and manufacturing companies.

Financial. Most brokerage houses provide investment information to prospective and present customers. Moody's Investors Service, Inc. (99 Church Street, New York, NY 10007) produces a number of financial publications, such as *Moody's Bond Survey* and *Moody's Handbook of Widely Held Stocks*. Standard & Poor's Corp. (25 Broadway, New York, NY 10004) publishes a number of handbooks and guides, such as *Standard & Poor's Register of Corporations, Directors and Executives;*

Stock Guide; and *Stock Summary*. Information is also available from Standard & Poor's through computer database services.

Labor. The Bureau of National Affairs, Inc. (1231 25th Street NW, Washington, DC 20037) publishes a number of labor statistics in its *Labor Relations Reporter*.

Law/Tax. Commerce Clearing House, Inc. (4025 W. Peterson Avenue, Chicago, IL 60646) publishes *Topical Law Reports* in loose-leaf format. A few of the topics covered are federal tax, labor, state tax, social security, trusts, and aviation.

Prentice-Hall, Inc. (Englewood Cliffs, NJ 07632) publishes information in loose-leaf format on laws, rules, and regulations with interpretations and comments. Examples are *Executives Tax Report* (weekly), *Lawyer's Weekly Report*, and *Accountant's Weekly Report*.

Management. *Management Contents*, published biweekly by Ziff-Davis Publishing Co., (2265 Carson Drive, Northbrook, IL 60662), provides tables of contents of 350 business and management journals and other information services.

Real Estate. The *Real Estate Guide*, published by Prentice-Hall, Inc., (Englewood Cliffs, NJ 07632), covers all practical aspects of real estate operation.

Trade. The Bureau of National Affairs, Inc., in addition to providing general business services, also publishes *Antitrust and Trade Regulation Report*, the *United States Patents Quarterly*, and other trade information sources.

Newspapers and Periodicals for Executives

Two newspapers are of particular interest to the business community. *The New York Times*, a daily newspaper covering world, domestic, and financial news, contains a special section on business in daily editions. *The Wall Street Journal*, primarily an investor's newspaper, covers current business news and lists daily stock reports.

Countless periodicals of interest to business executives exist. For this discussion, periodicals are divided into two categories: general and specialized.

General Periodicals. The alert secretary scans general business magazines received at the office for material that may be of immediate or possible interest to the executive. Examples of general business magazines that your office may subscribe to include the following:

> *Barron's* is a national business and financial weekly published by Dow Jones & Company, Inc.
>
> *BusinessWeek* is published weekly by McGraw-Hill, Inc. It covers factors of national and international interest to business executives. Statistics reflect current trends.
>
> *Dun's Business Month* is published by Dun & Bradstreet Publications Corporation. It covers finance, credit, production, labor, sales, and distribution.
>
> *Forbes*, a magazine of corporate management for top executives, is published by Forbes Inc.
>
> *Fortune* is published biweekly by Time Inc. It features articles on specific industries and business leaders. It also analyzes current business problems.
>
> *Nation's Business* is published monthly by the U.S. Chamber of Commerce. This business magazine focuses on political and general topics.

Specialized Periodicals. It is common for a company to belong to several trade associations. In addition, the executive may belong to several professional associations. These associations issue regular magazines to their members, publishing articles and statistics of current interest. *The Standard Periodical Directory* lists nearly 67,000 American and Canadian periodicals. The *Business Periodicals Index* is the primary source of information on a wide range of articles appearing in business periodicals.

When seeking data on a specific magazine or newspaper, the secretary might consult *Ayer's Directory of Publications* (newspapers and periodicals) or *Ulrich's International Periodicals Directory*. They provide information on the names of publications, editors, publishers, dates established, and technical data, and geographic areas served. Another source of specialized magazines is the *Readers' Guide to Periodical Literature*. More than 100 well-known magazines, such as *Architectural Record, Changing Times, Consumer Reports, Foreign Affairs, Monthly Labor Review*, and *Time* are indexed in each issue. Articles are cataloged under appropriate subject headings.

Handbooks

Handbooks are published in many areas of business. They are highly factual surveys about particular fields. A few of the many handbooks that are published in the business field are *Personnel Administration Handbook*, *Office Administration Handbook*, and *Sales Manager's Handbook*.

A number of handbooks have been written for the legal secretary, the medical secretary, the real estate secretary, and secretaries in other specialized fields. A partial list of these handbooks can be found on pages 159-161.

Secretary's Reference Shelf

The secretary may collect many worthwhile reference books, or the executive may purchase them for office use. A useful, inexpensive reference, *How to Use the Business Library*, is a valuable adjunct to any business library. Other sources of information that the secretary should have easy access to include the following:

An abridged encyclopedia. *The Columbia Encyclopedia* in one volume is particularly strong on biography and geography.

An annual book of statistics. The *Statistical Abstract of the United States*, *The World Almanac & Book of Facts*, and the *Guinness Book of World Records* are good sources of statistical information.

An atlas or gazetteer. The *Rand McNally Illustrated World Atlas* or *Webster's New Geographical Dictionary* are good choices.

A thesaurus. *Webster's Collegiate Thesaurus* is quite thorough.

A book of quotations. Bartlett's *Familiar Quotations* or *The Home Book of Quotations: Classical and Modern* are good sources for memorable quotations.

A book of etiquette. *The New Emily Post's Etiquette* or *Amy Vanderbilt's Complete Book of Etiquette Revised* are two excellent references.

A ZIP Code directory. The *National Five-Digit ZIP Code and Post Office Directory* is the standard reference for this information.

A handbook of parliamentary procedures. *Robert's Rules of Order* is a comprehensive guide for parliamentarians.

A manual of style. *The Elements of Style with Index* by Strunk and White is a favorite among all types of writers.

A communications manual. The *Executive's Desk Manual of Modern Model Business Letters* by Lloyd H. Geil is popular with many secretaries.

A technical handbook that relates to the executive's work. The *Handbook of Modern Accounting* by Davidson and Weil would be a good choice for an accountant's office.

SUMMARY

When researching business information, the secretary may use the company library, the local public library, a specialized library, and/or a computer database service. Libraries generally subscribe to at least one database service; companies which need current sources of information are likely to subscribe to a database service as well.

The secretary should be familiar with the various sections of the library. A stop at the information desk or at the reference desk is enough to direct a researcher to needed information. The index of books in a library is the card catalog. The card catalog can be in microform or on computer. Library collections are classified under the Dewey decimal system or under the Library of Congress system. Business information is found in the *650s* under the Dewey decimal system and in the major category of *H* under the Library of Congress system. The annual publication, *Books in Print*, lists all books included in publishers' catalogs by author, title, and subject. Pamphlets and booklets are catalogued in the *Vertical File Index of Pamphlets*. Magazines are listed in the *Readers' Guide to Periodical Literature*.

When taking notes, a bibliography card for each reference source should be prepared. Separate reference cards are then written for each topic. A distinction should be made on reference cards between direct quotes and summary statements.

Atlases, dictionaries, directories, encyclopedias, government publications, and yearbooks are sources of general information. Business information can also be found through specialized subscription information services, such as *The Kiplinger Washington Letter* and the *Investment & Barometer Letter*. Specialized subscription information services are also available in the areas of credit, finance, law, tax, management, real estate, and trade.

Two newspapers are of particular interest to the business community: *The New York Times*, with its special daily section on business, and *The Wall Street Journal*. Numerous general periodicals appeal to business executives. These include *BusinessWeek, Fortune,* and *Nation's Business.* The *Business Periodicals Index* indexes a wide range of articles appearing in business periodicals.

A number of business handbooks can be found in the reference section of most libraries. A popular handbook among office managers is the *Office Administration Handbook.*

In addition to secretarial handbooks and a dictionary, the secretary's reference shelf might include a copy of the *Statistical Abstract of the United States,* a book of etiquette, and a Zip Code directory.

SUGGESTED READINGS

Baker, Robert K. *Doing Library Research,* An Introduction for Community College Students. Boulder, CO: Westview Press, 1981.

Brownstone, David M., and Gorton Carruth. *Where to Find Business Information,* A Worldwide Guide for Everyone Who Needs the Answers to Business Questions, 2d ed. New York: John Wiley & Sons, Inc., 1982.

Chandler, G. *How to Find Out,* 5th ed. Elmsford, NY: Pergamon Press, Inc., 1982.

Gates, Jean K. *Guide to the Use of Libraries and Information Sources,* 5th ed. New York: McGraw-Hill Book Company, 1983.

Johnson, H. Webster, Ernest L. Maier, and A.J. Faría *How to Use the Business Library,* 5th ed. Cincinnati: South-Western Publishing Co., 1984.

QUESTIONS FOR DISCUSSION

1. How would your approach differ in taking notes on a magazine article available on a library shelf and one available only in a computer database to which you have access?

2. What are the advantages of using a computer database service in researching information over traditional sources, such as periodicals, books, and standard reference works?

3. In your new position as secretary to the administrative manager of a business consulting firm, you have been given permission to purchase three desk reference books. Which books would you choose? By what criteria would you make these choices?

4. If your employer asked you to go to the public library to obtain a copy of an article appearing in *Forbes,* how would you locate the article?

5. In choosing a reference book, how can you be sure that you have the latest edition of the book?

6. Where is the nearest depository of government publications to your school?

7. If your employer is involved in scientific research and gives highly technical dictation, where would you turn for help in learning the vocabulary?

8. Determine how long the following materials should be retained in an office. In each case, which factors would determine your decision?
   a. Catalogs from suppliers
   b. Back issues of professional and technical magazines
   c. Advertisements of competitive firms
   d. House organs
   e. Copies of *Who's Who in America*

9. Decide whether you would use the italicized words in the following sentences dictated by your employer. Check the Reference Guide to verify and correct your answers.
   a. *Fewer* errors were made in the letter typed on the word processor.
   b. New technology makes it possible to spend *less* hours on routine work.
   c. *Less* work is required to operate the new copier.
   d. There are *less* dollars in the budget this year.
   e. A few *are* going to the conference.
   f. Only a few *plans* to vote.

PROBLEMS

1. Problem 4 in Chapter 18 will ask you to prepare a business report. In preparation, you are now to do the necessary reading, prepare bibliography cards, and take notes. Choose one of the following topics as the subject of your report:
   a. Data Processing Versus Word Processing: Who Should Be in Charge of Information Processing?
   b. Business Ethics: A Revived Interest in the Business Community
   c. Improving Personal Security in the Office
   d. The Paperless Office and How It Works
   e. Orientation Training for Office Workers
   f. The Use of Job-Related Tests in the Selection of Office Employees

     g. Privacy Laws and Office Records
     h. How the Supervisor Supervises Workers Effectively
     i. The Secretary's Role in the 1990s
     j. New Office Positions in the 1990s

2. You are employed as a secretary to an executive of a major food processing firm. Your employer has asked you to compare computer database services in terms of subject matter and price for on-line availability in your office. Limit your comparison to two services and type your recommendation in memorandum format.

3. Assume that you are secretary to Randolph Parker, general counsel for a subsidiary of a major manufacturing firm. Your employer has just been transferred to the home office. He tells you that he has at least ten crates of books to be unpacked and arranged on his bookshelves. You are to supervise the arrangement of the books on the shelves and to devise a system of control, since Mr. Parker expects that many of the staff will want to use his materials. What is your plan of action for arranging the books on the shelves? Explain your system of control.

4. Prepare a list of your sources of information to determine the following:

     a. Who is the chairperson of the board of American Telephone & Telegraph Company? Where will you find biographical data about this person?

     b. What is the address of the national headquarters of the Administrative Management Society? What is the total membership?

     c. What was the population of Seattle, Washington, at the last official census?

     d. Who are the members of the Washington office staff of a senator from your state?

     e. What is the total circulation and the advertising rate of *BusinessWeek*?

     f. What is the annual crude petroleum production of Saudi Arabia?

     g. What products are manufactured by Harold L. Palmer Company, Inc., Livonia, Michigan?

     h. What are the five principal business centers located in the state of Illinois?

     i. What is the London address of NCR Corporation?

     j. What is a quotation on the use of time?

Chapter 17

Presenting Statistical Information

Business and government organizations compile statistical information for internal consumption, for customers, and for the public at large. Annual reports, technical reports, proposals, bids, advertising brochures, and oral presentations all make generous use of numerical data. To make statistical data more readily understood, business communicators use tables, charts, and graphs. A well-constructed table or chart can often communicate a statistical concept more quickly and more clearly than numbers alone.

Computer technology has made a significant contribution to management decision making. Through computers, executives have quantitative (numerical) information—information that is pertinent to every facet of business operations—at their fingertips. Secretaries, too, are working with numerical data more than ever before. Tables and graphs, compiled from computer printouts, are essential to business reports and make excellent visual aids at conferences. Often it is the secretary who keys in the commands on a computer that processes numerical data into pie charts, tables, graphs, and other visual forms.

Giving life to figures, which well-planned tables and graphs really do, calls for a thorough knowledge of the techniques of table and graph construction, good planning, and imagination. Several steps are involved in this type of work. The secretary's responsibility in regard to each one is discussed in this chapter.

THE SECRETARY'S RESPONSIBILITY

Chapter 16 discussed the secretary's responsibilities for gathering and organizing data for effective communication. When a complicated graph for a report or conference is needed, the secretary must know what type of graph will best display the designated data. The secretary has several options for producing graphs and tables: A computer may be commanded to print out an appropriate graph or table; the secretary may arrange for an in-house artist to produce the graph or table or hire a free-lancer; or the secretary may prepare the graph or table freehand or with mechanical aids. However, before attempting to present data in graphic form, the secretary must become familiar with the principles of compiling, organizing, and classifying data.

COMPILING AND ORGANIZING DATA

The data with which secretaries work come from many sources. Some data compiled within a company are provided in the form of computer printouts. Other information, however, is obtained from such secondary sources as magazines, yearbooks, and reports of outside agencies. In order to organize data from several sources into an easy-to-read format so that totals can be obtained, averages and percentages calculated, and information summarized, secretaries use working forms. The process of transferring facts from source documents to working forms is called *compiling* data. The simplest compilation of data is a tabulation. An example of a tabulation appears in Illus. 17-1.

The Leisure and Recreation Corp.
Summary of Operations
For the Year Ended December 31, 19--

Sales and Revenues
(In Thousands)

Divisions	First Quarter	Second Quarter	Third Quarter	Fourth Quarter	Total for Year
Recreation					
Lawn and Garden	$25.6	$30.2	$39.4	$42.7	$137.9
Bicycles/Motorcycles	20.5	29.4	36.4	46.2	132.5
Sporting Goods	19.5	23.6	33.0	45.0	121.1
Marine Products	29.6	32.7	33.2	33.0	128.5
Total	$95.2	$115.9	$142.0	$166.9	$520.0
Recreational Vehicles					
Campers	$42.9	$45.2	$70.5	$90.2	$248.8

From Annual Report of the L&R Corp.
Compiled by R.C. 1/31/-- Checked by DN.

Illus. 17-1
A working form should indicate the source of the data, the compiler, and the checker.

METHODS OF CLASSIFYING DATA

The objective of compiling data is to organize information into meaningful classifications. Data can be classified in any of five ways: (1) alphabetic sequence, (2) kind, (3) size, (4) location, or (5) time.

1. An *alphabetic sequence* of data is often used when the data are compiled in alphabetic order to make comparisons between distinct units. For instance, total sales by individual sales representatives are often provided in alphabetic sequence with the names of the sales reps in alphabetic order.
2. A grouping of data by *kind* is used when the data are kinds of objects, characteristics, products, and so on. An example of a grouping by kind would be a table that classified retail trade into several main groups, such as food stores and apparel stores. Under each of these kinds of stores, data would be listed for each store in that group.
3. *Size variations* may be shown in two ways. In an *array*, data are listed in ascending or descending order. A table of the 50 largest ports in the world arranged in descending order of net tonnage would be an array. In a *frequency distribution*, data is arranged according to each size class. A frequency distribution is used instead of an array when data can be grouped advantageously in classes. For example, tables of age distribution may be grouped according to the number of persons between the ages of 10 to 14 and 15 to 19 instead of listing data for each age (10, 11, 12, etc.) individually.
4. A *location listing* is used to show data by geographic units, such as cities, states, and countries. Real estate data are often listed this way, as are commodity sales on a national scale.
5. *Time-of-occurrence* or *time series listings* are very common. A listing may be made by days, weeks, months, years, decades, and so on. Illus. 17-2 combines an alphabetic sequence of data in a time series listing by years.

After data have been collected, they may be translated into averages or percentages so that comparisons can be made. To say that sales in Dallas were 35 percent greater this month than last month is easier to interpret than to say that sales last month were $50,000 and this month, $67,500. Or it may be more helpful to know the average salary of employees in the purchasing office than to know the highest and the lowest salary paid. The use to be made of the data determines whether an average or a percentage will be of most value.

Illus. 17-2
Machine tabulation
has supplanted
manual
compilation of
data. From input
media, the
computer
calculates and
prints data on
perforated,
accordion-folded
sheets.

```
                        ELECTRONICS, INC.

                SALES & NET EARNINGS (IN MILLIONS)
                   FOR THE 5 COMPANY DIVISIONS

                           1984-1987



    DIVISION          YEAR          SALES      NET EARNINGS

    AEROSPACE         1984          1,611          44
                      1985          1,916          75
                      1986          1,972          76
                      1987          2,099          95

    CONSUMER          1984          3,097         148
                      1985          3,214          86
                      1986          3,288         108
                      1987          3,307         198
```

Averages

One way to help the reader understand a set of figures is to compute an average. (An *average* is a single value used to represent a group.) But which of the three averages in common use should you choose? The one used most often is the *arithmetic average* or, more technically, *arithmetic mean*. It is the sum of two or more quantities divided by the number of quantities. If the weekly payroll for 120 employees is $33,000, for example, the average pay is $275.

The *mode* is a second kind of average. It is the value that recurs the greatest number of times in a given series. The data are arranged in a frequency distribution to determine the mode. For example, the mode in the following distribution is the class interval $260.01 to $270.00, because the greatest number of salaries falls in that range.

Weekly Earnings	No. of Employees
$250.01—$260.00	2
260.01— 270.00	26 ← *MODE*
270.01— 280.00	19
280.01— 290.00	9
290.01— 300.00	5

The *median* is an average of position; it is the midpoint in an array. In order to determine the median, data must be arranged in an array; that is, in either ascending or descending order. To find the median it is necessary only to count the number of items in an array and locate the midpoint. For example, assume that five students have the following amounts in their checking accounts:

Student A	$1,500
Student B	750
Student C	500 ←—*MEDIAN*
Student D	100
Student E	20

The median is $500, but the mean is $575. Obviously the mean is affected by extremes (The student with an abnormally large checking account and the one with almost nothing have a significant impact on the mean.) This is why the median is usually selected as the average that comes nearest to indicating the true state of affairs when there are extreme cases in the data.

Percentages

Percentages make it easy to grasp the relationship of various quantities to one another. For example, to say that 900 consumers were satisfied with their new color televisions has less significance than saying "900 consumers, or 30 percent of 3,000 consumers, were satisfied with their color TV purchases."

Percentage relatives or *index numbers* are used to compare the extent or the degree of change. They are relative because they are based on a clearly defined value at a specific time. An example of a percentage relative is the consumer price index (CPI). It measures the average change in price over time for a fixed basket of goods and services. For example, since 1967 (the *base year*, which is expressed as *100*) prices have increased 150 percent for those specific goods and services. The CPI is then expressed as 250.

PRESENTING DATA EFFECTIVELY

It is the secretary's responsibility to determine the most effective presentation for numerical data. Tables are preferred over graphs when exact figures are used. When well constructed, they are easy to read for reaching conclusions. Charts and graphs are better for highlighting comparisons and trends, when quick identification of relationships is important.

Tables

Three types of tables are used in business reports: *general purpose* tables, *special purpose* tables, and *spot* (or informal) tables. General purpose tables are usually placed in an appendix and numbered consecutively. Most tables of statistical data in business reports are special purpose tables. The table on page 486 is a spot table. Spot tables are unnumbered and appear within paragraphs of a report.

A table should be self-explanatory. It should be simple and designed for rapid reading. The incorporation of too many elements in one table detracts from its readability and effectiveness. When planning a table, keep one question in mind: Precisely what is this table to show? All data that do not apply should be excluded.

After a table has been developed, a chart or graph may be used to dramatize the material presented in it. In other words, the chart does not replace the table; it supplements it. *Tables provide details; charts present relationships.* Charts alone will not satisfy readers who seek exact data.

Planning the Table Layout

A well-balanced table can be typed perfectly the first time, if the work is carefully planned. Facts and the figures to be tabulated must be analyzed carefully before headings and column arrangements are determined. The best method of planning a table is to make a rough draft.

If you are using an electronic typewriter or a word processor, the automatic features of the equipment will make producing a perfect table on the first try much easier.

Suggestions for Typing Tables

Before typing a table, you should review the rules governing table construction. Only by considering a number of details can you hope to produce a satisfactory tabulation.

Table Captions. Most tables include a table number, a main title, a secondary heading, column or boxed headings, and stub (left column) headings. Only the main title is typed in all capital letters. The other headings are typed with initial capital letters only. Illus. 17-3 shows the important parts of a table.

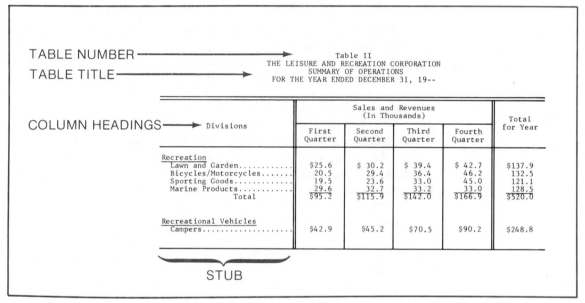

Illus. 17-3
This table was typed from the working form shown in Illus. 17-1. Leaders and skipped lines have been used to improve readability. Note that figures are shown in thousands; thus, $95,200 is shown as $95.2.

Table Numbers. Tables should be numbered consecutively throughout a report. Arabic or Roman numerals can be used. Numerals follow the word *table* typed in all capital letters or with an initial cap only (Table 1, Table I, TABLE 1, TABLE I). The table number is the first caption line; the main table title is the second. Both precede the body of the table.

Main Title. The title should be complete and clearly worded. The main title of a table and its other headings should make the table self-contained. If the data represent a period of time, the title or secondary headings should indicate the period covered. Include internal punctuation in the title, but no terminal period.

If a title requires more than one line, break at a division of thought using single spacing. Avoid ending a line with a preposition. The title should be divided so that second or third lines are shorter than the preceding line(s). The table title should not extend beyond the margins of the table.

Poor Title Construction

THE PROFESSIONAL SECRETARIES INTERNATIONAL
ANNUAL CONVENTION, HYATT REGENCY HOTEL, HOUSTON, TEXAS
MAY 19-23, 19--

Good Title Construction

THE PROFESSIONAL SECRETARIES INTERNATIONAL
ANNUAL CONVENTION, HYATT REGENCY HOTEL
HOUSTON, TEXAS, MAY 19-23, 19--

Abbreviations. In order to save space, abbreviations may be used in column headings; but they should never be used in titles or secondary headings.

Columns. Each vertical column must have a heading. Column headings must clearly identify items in the column and be centered over the column.

Column headings may be numbered consecutively from left to right with the numbers enclosed in parentheses. Columns of related data should be placed closer together than other columns. Major groups of columns can be indicated by wider spaces or by double vertical rules between columns.

Alignment. The left margins of tabulated words and phrases, such as line headings in a table, should be kept even. With figures, usually the right margin must be kept straight. When decimal fractions with different numbers of places to the right of the decimal point are listed, the decimal point must be kept in vertical alignment. Type $+$, $-$, and $\pm$ signs close to figures at the left. Use dashes, leader points, or a blank space to indicate omissions in a column.

Correct Alignment

MULTIPLY	BY	TO OBTAIN METRIC
Miles per hour	1.6	Kilometers per hour
Pounds	0.45	Kilograms
Square feet	0.09	Square Meters
Ounces	28.35	Grams

Incorrect Alignment

Miles per hour	1.6	Kilometers per hour
Pounds	0.45	Kilograms
Square Feet	0.09	Square Meters
Ounces	28.35	Grams

Amounts. A comma should be used to separate every three digits in amounts, but it should not be used with the digits after a decimal point. For example, 1,125.50161 is correct; 1125.501,61 is not.

Dollar signs should be used with the first amount in a column and with each total. This also is true of columns of percentages or like symbols (pounds, kilograms, etc.)

Correct	*Incorrect*
$1,456.26	$1,456.26
362.35	$ 362.35
18.46	$ 18.46
$1,837.07	$1,837.07

Leaders. Lines of periods, or *leaders*, aid the reader by guiding the eyes across a wide expanse of space from one column to another. Leaders are usually typed with a single space between periods. Periods on successive lines should be in vertical alignment.

To vertically align leaders, notice whether you type the periods in the first line on an odd or even number on the typing scale. If you type the first period on an odd number, all subsequent lines of leaders should begin on odd numbers. It is sometimes necessary to leave an extra space at the beginning of a leader in order to align periods. Your finished copy should look like this:

Night school classes 45
Art classes 47
Fashion design and clothing 52

Spacing. Tables can be entirely single-spaced, double-spaced, or a combination of single and double spacing. When long columns are single-spaced, skipping a line every three, four, or five rows improves readability.

Rulings. Rulings improve the appearance of a table. They may be typed with the underline key or made with pencil, ball-point pen, or India ink. A double ruling the entire width of the table is made two lines below the title. Single rulings the width of the table should divide column headings from the rest of the table. A single ruling of the same width should also end the table. If used, vertical rulings separate columns and should extend from the double ruling at the top to the bottom single ruling as shown in Illus. 17-4.

Illus. 17-4
Vertical lines may be used to separate columns; however the ends of the table may be left open. Footnotes are placed directly below the table and are identified with lowercase letters.

Table V
AVERAGE BUSINESS LETTER COSTS FOR THE YEAR 1986[a]

Cost Factor	Average Cost per Letter	Percentage of Total Cost
Secretarial Time	$2.48	27.80[b]
Fixed Charges[c]	2.57	28.81
Dictator's Time	2.46	27.58
Nonproductive Labor[d]	.74	8.30
Mailing Cost	.41	4.60
Materials	.26	2.92
Totals	$8.92	100.01

[a] Based on data supplied by the Dartnell Corporation, Chicago.
[b] Expressed to the nearest 1/100 of 1%.
[c] Depreciation, overhead, rent, light, and similar items.
[d] Time lost due to waiting, illness, vacation, and other causes.

Units. The unit designation of data (inches, pounds, and so forth) must be given. Generally this information is provided in the main heading or a subheading.

Footnotes. If the meaning of any item in a table is not clear or must be qualified, an explanation should be given in a footnote. Footnotes are sometimes used to indicate the source of the data. Footnotes are single-spaced. The source footnote is typed first followed by any footnotes referring to specific items in the table. To identify footnote references in numerical data, use symbols (*, #, †) or lowercase letters. A number used to reference a footnote could be confused as being part of the numerical data. Illus. 17-4 shows proper footnoting.

Reference. The name of the person responsible for the preparation of the table should be indicated on a file copy. When the data come from a secondary source, such as a publication, the source should be footnoted.

Variety and Emphasis. Italics, boldface, type of different sizes and styles, varying the placement of the column totals, and using different colored ribbons can add variety to tables and emphasize the relationships in them. There are other ways to add variety and emphasis to tables. Footnotes and column headings can be typed in elite type, and the body of the table typed in pica type. Changing the type font provides even wider variations. Also, a wide carriage typewriter and oversize paper can be used for a table that cannot be accommodated on standard equipment and paper.

Checking the Typed Table

Every typewritten table must be checked for accuracy. Proofreading requires the help of another person. One person should read from the source document while the secretary checks the typed copy. Reading figures is an oral technique that has a fairly definite prescribed routine. The words in the following examples that are connected by a hyphen should be read as a group; the commas indicate pauses:

718	seven-one-eight
98,302	nine-eight, comma, three-oh-two
24.76	two-four, point, seven-six
$313.00	three-one-three even (or no cents) dollars
77,000	seventy-seven thousand even

For copy in columnar form, read down a column rather than across the page. If the table includes totals, the amounts in each column should be added and checked.

After the accuracy of the typed table has been verified and errors corrected, the original draft of the table and its source should be filed in a personal folder kept by the secretary or attached to and filed with the file copy of the final draft. If anyone who reads the table discovers an error, the filed copy of the original data will enable the secretary to determine whether the error occurred in the source or whether the error was made in the process of typing the table.

Graphic Presentation

A graph is a statistical picture. It presents numerical data in a visual form that is easy to analyze and remember. Taking hard facts and organizing them in visual form to make comparisons, to emphasize contrasts, and to bring out the full force of a message is a challenging opportunity.

You can construct graphs on your typewriter, on your word processor, or with the help of commerically available kits, such as Chartpak and Zipatone. These kits contain self-adhering bar and line tapes in various designs and colors. With these materials, an amateur can make charts that are very effective—even dramatic. Commercial artists can help you with more complicated presentations.

Alphabet lettering packs, such as those offered by 3M, can also help the secretary produce effective graphics. Lettering machines, which produce large, bold typefaces, are ideal for overhead transparencies, conference presentations, and slides (see the discussion on headliners, composers, and phototypesetters in Chapter 10). The secretary should have a basic knowledge of the various types of graphs. Set up a folder of typewritten and commercially prepared graphs and insert notes concerning their suitability for certain data.

Preparing Charts and Graphs

If you are to prepare a chart or graph, it is best to rough out a working copy first. The materials you need include graph paper, correcting fluid, templates of plotting symbols (circles, squares, computer symbols), a protractor and compass, a ruler, a lettering guide or rub-down letters, and a black felt-tip pen. When the final copy is prepared, the graph should be framed on the paper. The bottom margin should be slightly larger than the top margin. The margins on the sides should be equal, unless the pages are to be bound at the left. If guidelines are marked lightly in pencil, they can be erased after the inking is completed.

In a report having several charts or graphs, it is common practice to number them consecutively. A chart or graph is labeled *"figure"* to distinguish it from a table. The word figure is typed with an initial capital letter followed by an Arabic numeral. The title of the chart or graph follows the figure number. The caption is generally typed below the chart or graph but can appear above the illustration. Also, numbering may not be necessary for an isolated chart or one used as a transparency during a presentation.

The source of the data and the date of compilation are placed below the chart. When this information is omitted from the presentation copy, it must be recorded on the working copy.

Line Graphs. A commonly used type of graph is the *line graph. It is most effective in showing fluctuations in a value or a quantity over a period of time.* Variations in production, sales, costs, or profits over a period of months or years can be effectively illustrated with line graphs. Thus, the line graph is a good choice for depicting a comparison of trends over a period of time. The line graph shown in Illus. 17-5 emphasizes the relationship between the total sales of foreign and domestic branches of a company over a five-year period. Refer to Illus. 17-5 and follow these suggestions for preparing line graphs:

1. Prepare a working copy on printed graph paper and the final copy on 8½-by-11-inch plain paper.
2. Place periods of time on the horizontal scale at the bottom of the graph (on the x-axis) and record variations in quantities on the vertical scale (on the y-axis).
3. Always show the *zero* point. To prevent the curve from occurring too high on the chart, show a "break" in the chart with two wavy horizontal lines to indicate the part that you have omitted.
4. To avoid distortions, plan the size of your graph. It is good practice to make the width at least *1½ but not more than 1¾ times the height.* Curves can appear very steep or quite gradual, depending on the relation of height to width.
5. If possible, position all lettering horizontally on the chart.
6. *Work with no more than four or five curves on a graph.* Use a legend or a key to identify each curve. Make each curve distinctive in character by using different colors or by using heavy solid lines, light solid lines, broken lines, dots, or dots and dashes.

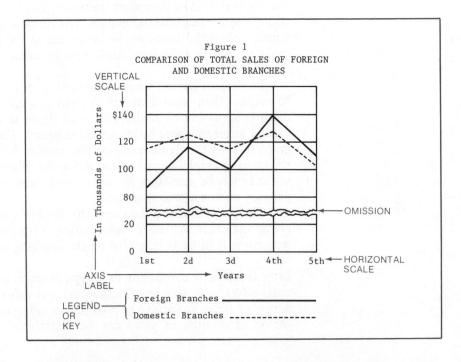

Illus. 17-5
Although this line graph only shows two curves, as many as four or five can be plotted.

Bar Graphs. The bar graph presents quantities by means of horizontal or vertical bars. Variations in quantity are indicated by the lengths of the bars. The width of the bars is constant.

A bar can represent a single value or be stacked; that is, segments of the bar represent different components of the whole bar. The bar graph is most effectively used to compare a limited number of values, generally not more than four or five. *They are often used in time series and frequency distributions.* Refer to Illus. 17-6 and follow these suggestions for preparing bar graphs:

1. Leave one-half to a whole bar width between single bars. Bars can be contiguous, having no spaces between them. This type of bar graph is called a *histogram*.
2. Except for time series, the quantities indicated on bar graphs should begin with *zero*. If a graph starting at zero makes the graph too tall or too wide, show a "break" in the graph. Omit that portion after zero which all bars incorporate.
3. When possible, arrange bars in ascending or descending order according to lengths. If they are arranged according to time, chart the earliest period first.
4. Bars may be in outline form, solid, or cross-hatched. If the bars represent different things, shade or color them for contrast. When bars are shaded or crosshatched, provide a legend or a key for identification.
5. To type a bar, use uppercase letters (X, W, N, or $); strike X over 0); or use a combination of letters and characters.

Illus. 17-6
This bar graph was prepared for a transparency. Note that the chart is unnumbered and that the caption is at the top.

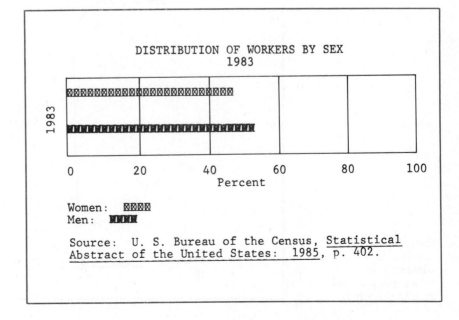

Circle Charts. The circle chart, sometimes called a *pie chart*, is an effective way to show the manner in which a given quantity is divided into parts. In this type of illustration, the complete area of the circle represents the whole quantity, while the divisions within the circle represent the parts. Thus, the chart shows not only the relationship of each part to the whole but also of each part to every other part.

The circle chart may be used to present such data as how the sales dollar is spent; how taxes paid by a firm are divided among local, state, and federal governments; or the percentage of store purchases made by men compared with those made by women. Refer to Illus. 17-7 and follow these suggestions for preparing circle charts:

1. Convert data into percentage form. Let the area of the circle equal 100 percent.
2. Arrange the elements to be plotted according to size, largest first.
3. Draw a circle that is from two to five inches in diameter by using a template or a compass.
4. Determine the size of each segment. If a protractor is used, the circumference of the circle equals 360 degrees; thus a segment representing 10 percent would be 36 degrees. If a protractor is

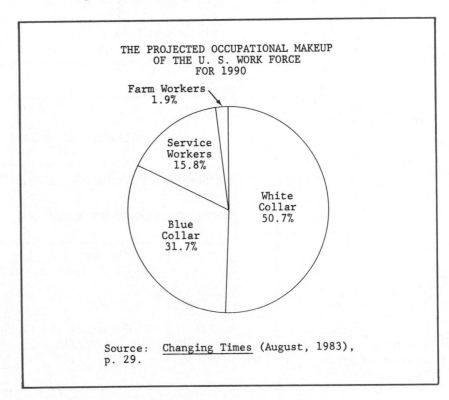

THE PROJECTED OCCUPATIONAL MAKEUP
OF THE U. S. WORK FORCE
FOR 1990

Farm Workers
1.9%

Service
Workers
15.8%

White
Collar
50.7%

Blue
Collar
31.7%

Source: *Changing Times* (August, 1983), p. 29.

Illus. 17-7
Circle charts illustrate the relationship of each part to the whole.

not available, divide the circumference of the circle into four equal parts (each part representing 25 percent). Each fourth part may in turn be divided into halves (representing 12½ percent segments). Follow this plan until the size of desired segment is obtained.

5.   Starting at the top of the circle (at 12 o'clock) and moving in a clockwise direction, mark off each segment, beginning with the largest segment. The sequence of segments may be changed, however, to permit emphasis on a specific element.

6.   If space permits, identify each segment by a caption inside the segment. Type the titles of the sections horizontally.

7.   Shade segments to provide contrast and to dramatize proportions.

Pictorial Charts. One of the more interesting developments in graphic representation is the use of pictorial charts, or *pictographs*. They are generally an adaptation of one of the other types of graphs in which drawn symbols are used to represent the types of data being charted. For example, a bar chart showing fire losses may be illustrated with a streaming fire hose, the length of the stream varying with the amount of the loss. The growth of telephone service may be shown by drawings of telephones arranged in a line, each telephone representing so many thousand telephones.

A secretary may not be expected to do the actual artwork for a pictorial chart but can be expected to devise a suitable chart by cutting and pasting appropriate symbols and making a copy on a copier. When a chart is produced by a commercial artist, the secretary is responsible for planning the graph and overseeing the work of the arist.

Illus. 17-8
This pictorial chart uses money to illustrate the rise in WR Corp.'s sales from March to December.

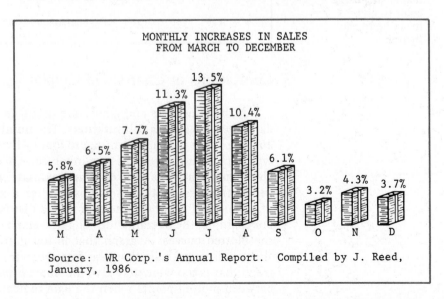

MONTHLY INCREASES IN SALES
FROM MARCH TO DECEMBER

13.5%
11.3%
10.4%
7.7%
6.5%
6.1%
5.8%
4.3%
3.7%
3.2%

M   A   M   J   J   A   S   O   N   D

Source: WR Corp.'s Annual Report. Compiled by J. Reed, January, 1986.

Map Charts. Maps are often used to depict quantitative information, particularly when comparisons are made between geographic areas. After the selection of the proper map, refer to Illus. 17-9 and follow these suggestions in preparing a map chart:

1. Outline geographic areas, using color, shading, or cross-hatching.
2. Provide a legend to explain the meanings given to the colors, shadings, or cross-hatchings.
3. If quantities are involved, figures can be placed inside geographic areas. Other symbols representing quantities, such as dots, may also be used.

Illus. 17-9
To illustrate a report on recreational facilities, the secretary constructed this map chart, using color to give meaning to the figures.

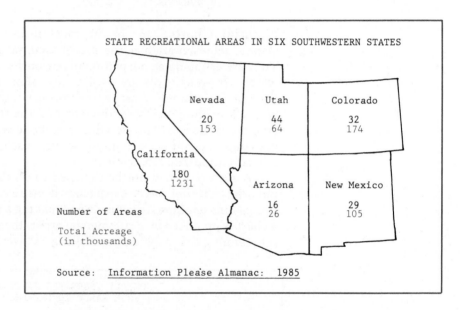

Limitations of Charts and Graphs

Although charts and graphs are useful in presenting comparative data, they have certain limitations. The number of facts presented on any one graph is usually limited to four or five. It is best to use a table when six or more elements are involved. A second limitation of most charts and graphs is that only approximate values can be shown. A third limitation is that is is possible for a graph to be drawn with mathematical accuracy and still give a distorted picture of the facts. For example, the overall width of a line graph determines the angles of the plotted curves. A graph that is too narrow may indicate much sharper rises and falls than the data indicate. In the same way, a line graph that is too wide may give the impression of gradual fluctuations between plotted points when the data indicate sharp increases.

Flowcharts

One of the most widely used tools in office management is the flowchart. It traces a unit of work as it flows through the office. Symbols with connecting lines are used to trace a step-by-step sequence of the work from point of origin to point of completion. Basic flowchart symbols are shown in Illus. 17-10. A template can be purchased for drawing these symbols. While the meaning of each flowchart symbol has become fairly standardized, a key can be provided to prevent any misunderstanding.

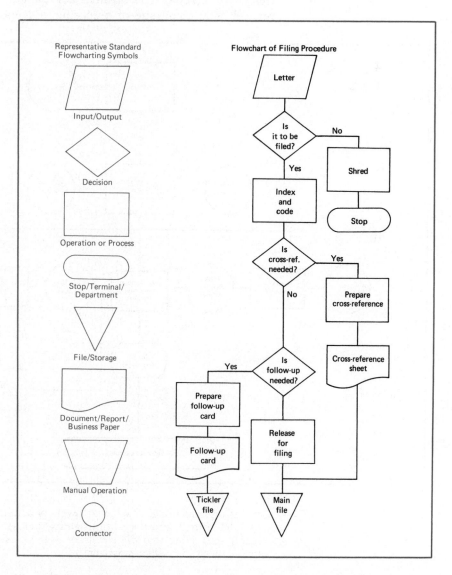

Illus. 17-10
A flowchart traces
a unit of work as it
flows through the
office.

Organizational Charts

An organizational chart is a graphic presentation of the structure of a business. It points out responsibility relationships and answers two basic questions: (1) What are the lines of authority (who reports to whom)? and (2) What are the functions of each unit (who is responsible for what)? Illus. 17-11 answers these questions.

A business organization is seldom static. New personnel, new divisions, new responsibilities, and the realignment of old responsibilities create change. The organizational chart, therefore, is frequently revised. The technique of preparing and updating an organizational

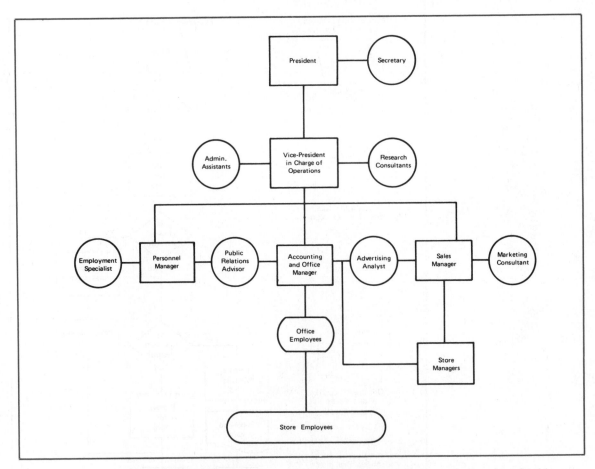

Illus. 17-11
On this organizational chart, four levels of administrative authority are clearly identified, and the administrative staff is differentiated from the support staff. Note that the secretary to the president is not under the supervision of the office manager.

chart is part of the know-how that every secretary needs. Suggestions for preparing an organizational chart include the following:

1. Keep the chart simple. A complex chart can confuse more than it can help.
2. Responsibility should flow downward with each level clearly defined. Lines of authority should be easily identified.
3. When intersecting a line is unavoidable, the *pass symbol* (a half-circle "detour" in an otherwise straight line) is used.
4. Different symbols differentiate policy-making positions (line) from support positions (staff).

The organizational chart in Illus. 17-11 shows line-and-staff relationships. Such a chart is supplemented with a functions chart on which the responsibilities of each position are identified. To show both authority relationships and functional responsibilities on one organizational chart detracts from its visual simplicity.

Wall Charts

Magnetic wall charts, like the one shown in Illus 17-12, display numerical and factual information, such as schedules, production gains, and equipment utilization. Wall charts can also be used to plot the progress of important projects.

Illus. 17-12
This wall chart is used for keeping track of jobs in process.

COMPUTER GRAPHICS

Computer graphics equipment permits people and machines to exchange graphic information at electronic speeds. Some employees work directly with charts, curves, sketches, and drawings on VDTs (see Illus. 17-13). An image can be reviewed, moved, redrawn, altered, erased, recorded in memory, or printed out via a plotter/printer or a film recorder. (A plotter/printer is an output device that uses pens to "draw" on paper.) Depending on the equipment and software package in use, bar, pie, line charts, and organizational charts can be produced in a myriad of colors, patterns, and type styles. Transparencies and color slides of professional quality can be made in color from computer-generated graphics as well. Secretaries with access to computer graphics systems must know how to operate the system to select, display, and produce the most appropriate graphic for the data at hand.

Illus. 17-13
Some software packages convert large amounts of numerical data into colorful graphs.

Courtesy of IBM

SUMMARY

Data, whether in reports, advertising borchures, annual reports or speeches, must be presented so that figures are easily understood by the reader or the listener. Graphics in the form of tables and charts enhance comprehension. Businesses with computer graphics capability have an important source for improving communication at all levels.

The secretary in today's office environment works with numerical information on a daily basis. In order to present data in an appropriate format, the secretary must know which graphics will display the data most effectively. If the secretary is asked to compile data from source documents, it must be organized so that totals, averages, and percentages can be obtained. Data can be classified in any of five ways: alphabetic sequence, kind, size, location, or time.

When exact figures are required for a study, tables are preferable to charts or graphs. Charts and graphs are better to show comparisons and trends, when quick identification of relationships is important.

Producing a well-balanced table requires careful planning. Following the rules of table construction is imperative. Most tables include a table number, a main title, a secondary heading, column or boxed headings, and a stub. The main title of a table should be in all capital letters. Each column must have a heading; abbreviations can be used. Figures must be aligned properly. To enhance the readability of the table, leaders and rulings can be used. Footnotes should be given to clarify any of the data and to provide the data's source.

A graph presents numerical information in picture form. By using the proper materials, a secretary can prepare a graph that is suitable for a report or an oral presentation. A commonly used graph is the *line graph*. It is most effective in showing fluctuations in a value or a quantity over a period of time. The *bar graph* illustrates quantities by means of horizontal or vertical bars. It is used in time series and frequency distributions. When a given quantity is divided into parts, the *circle or pie chart* is an effective graphic. The circle represents the whole quantity while the divisions within the circle represent the parts. When preparing a chart or graph, the secretary should keep in mind that these visuals have limitations: The number of elements that can be shown is limited to four or five and their values can only be approximations. Further, although mathematically accurate, a chart can give a distorted picture of the data. Other kinds of charts include pictorial charts, map charts, flowcharts, organizational charts, and wall charts.

Many businesses now have computer graphics capability. Charts and graphs can be produced in color on paper, on film, or on transparencies. In addition to knowing how to operate the equipment, the secretary working with computer graphics must know what graphic will best display the designated data.

SUGGESTED READINGS

Cardamone, Tom. *Chart and Graph Preparation Skills*. New York: Van Nostrand Reinhold Co., Inc., 1981.

Himstreet, William C., and Wayne M. Baty. *Business Communications*, 7th ed. Boston: Kent Publishing Company, 1983.

Keithley, Erwin M., and Philip J. Schreiner. *A Manual of Style for the Preparation of Papers and Reports*, 3rd ed. Cincinnati: South-Western Publishing Co., 1980.

Lefferts, Robert. *Elements of Graphics*. New York: Harper & Row Publishers, Inc., 1981.

Pearce, C. Glenn, Ross Figgins and Steven P. Golen. *Principles of Business Communication*, Theory, Applications and Technology. New York: John Wiley & Sons, Inc., 1984.

QUESTIONS FOR DISCUSSION

1. How do the secretary's responsibilities differ in chart preparation if computer graphic capabilities are
   a. Available
   b. Unavailable
2. Give two examples based on college enrollment figures to illustrate the necessity for extracting information from raw data so that appropriate decisions can be made.
3. What kind of graph should be prepared to present data in each of the following situations:
   a. Proof that a company has initiated affirmative action programs within the past three years
   b. The total yearly cost of going to college during the past five years
   c. Tuition rates at state supported and private colleges over the past ten years
   d. Amounts spent on research in six divisions of a large corporation over the past three years
   e. The division of energy costs among five departments of a firm
   f. The number of male employees compared with the number of

female employees of a company for each year of a five-year period

g. The locations of ten manufacturing plants in the United States

h. The monthly schedule of assignments for 20 employees.

4. Corporations usually use graphs extensively in their annual reports to stockholders. Financial tables and statements, however, are generally used in presenting data to boards of directors and to banks. Why are graphs used in the one case and tables in the other?

5. A consultant firm with a total of 50 employees reported in a community wage study that its average wage (arithmetic mean) was $20,000. An examination of the records revealed that the firm had ten executives, each receiving $70,000 a year. What would be your criticism of the reported average wage figure?

6. In the following sentences, insert synonyms for those enclosed in parentheses or revise the sentence so that there is no doubt as to its meaning. Check the Reference Guide to verify and correct your answers.

   a. The state legislature meets _____ (every two years).

   b. The vacancies were posted _____ (twice a year).

   c. The board will meet _____ (every two months).

   d. We report to the home office _____ (twice a month).

PROBLEMS

1. The total sales of a women's wear company are $828,000. Sales were distributed among four product lines as follows:

Purses	$250,000
Millinery	125,000
Cosmetics	275,000
Hosiery	178,000

   Convert the amount of sales of each line to a percentage of total sales. (Refer to the Reference Guide, page 860.) Prepare a circle chart showing these percentages.

2. Prepare an organizational chart depicting the structure of the company where you now work or have worked.

3. The following figures represent the sales volume for Innovative Products for two years. Prepare a line graph of the data. What does the graph imply about seasonal fluctuations and general performance for the two years?

	First Year	Second Year
January	$86,857	$114,273
February	69,623	92,526

March	38,972	64,159
April	34,284	60,844
May	40,485	69,273
June	37,737	76,294
July	40,852	74,858
August	46,085	82,437
September	49,592	80,158
October	55,846	83,628
November	54,249	87,849
December	61,292	94,958

4. Before establishing a policy on sick leave, your employer asks you to make a study of the number of days 70 employees in the Des Moines office were absent from work because of illness and other causes (excluding vacations). You obtain the total number of days each employee was absent. They are as follows:

26	8	17	15	17	14	13
16	7	5	47	20	25	19
12	20	11	15	9	4	41
18	27	19	11	19	12	13
8	3	44	18	24	17	15
18	14	13	10	2	37	20
28	16	15	15	14	11	9
1	32	19	30	18	11	12
10	6	13	15	33	17	21
16	11	13	8	7	14	12

a. Prepare a frequency distribution of the days absent. Use a classification interval of five days (one work week), such as 1 to 5, 6 to 10, and so forth. Determine the percentage of employees who were absent in each frequency interval.

b. Type a table with an appropriate title and column headings.

5. The following amounts are sales per day of a product for 25 days in April:

$118.23	$ 9.61	$107.16	$ 10.66
41.32	18.23	26.31	94.33
91.73	27.11	83.17	101.09
63.24	16.94	67.92	89.31
36.74	78.26	74.26	
18.92	124.36	68.31	
87.65	97.08	17.08	

a. Prepare a tabulation in pencil of the sales so that you can determine the median. What is the median sale for April?

b. Calculate the arithmetic average or mean of the April sales.

Chapter 18

Assistance with Writing Reports, Procedures, Speeches, and Publications

In this electronic age, large and small businesses alike depend heavily on information generated by computers. Through the use of computers, management has access to more numerical information than ever before. This increase in the volume of available data has led to the creation of more and different types of reports. Many businesses feel that the more current information is, the better management can function, making sound decisions.

As business becomes more complex, so do management problems. Every year millions of business reports are written which propose solutions to the complexities of business problems. Generally it is management personnel who must digest and react to the information presented in these reports.

This chapter discusses the preparation and presentation of business reports, company procedures, and other manuscripts. It gives specific instructions for the organization of reports and illustrates techniques for making material visually attractive and interesting. A section on speech typing is also included.

REPORT WRITING

A business report transmits objective information to one or more persons and is written for a specific business purpose. A report is used to plan, organize, and implement business operations; it contains factual information presented in clear, concise language. It can be written by an employee of a firm for internal use, or for a business client; it can also be prepared for a company by an independent authority.

Written reports for internal use may be circulated either *vertically* (up and down the company ranks) or *horizontally* (across management lines). Reports may be either *formal* (written) or *informal* (both written and oral). Written reports may take the form of an interoffice memorandum, a letter, or a bound manuscript.

Report-Writing Routine

There is considerable difference in the routine for writing a report and the routine for writing a letter. The originator or an assistant follows these steps in preparing a business report:

1. Collects information
2. Formulates an outline of the contents
3. Checks logic of content organization
4. Drafts the report for first typing
5. Rechecks the organization of material and edits sentence by sentence for clarity and correctness before the second typing
6. Checks the organization and editing again before final typing

In gathering information for a report, the writer reviews both primary and secondary information sources. Primary sources include personal observations, questionnaires, surveys, interviews, and experiments. Secondary sources refer to published documents.

The language of reports is objective, emphasizes factual information, and is free of any personal bias or opinion. Reports are generally written in the third person without *I's*, *we's*, and *you's*. Substitutions for these first person and second person pronouns, such as the *writer* or *researcher*, are also frowned upon. Illustrations of objective and personal writing styles follow:

Objective	*Personal*
A *study* of office correspondence at Henderson Associates *supports* the need for a word processing center.	After making a study of office correspondence at Henderson Associates, we recommend establishing a word processing center.

The present verb tense or a combination of present and past tense is used for report writing. For example, a discussion of how a study was conducted or when investigations were made is written in the past tense, because these actions are no longer in process. Some reports discuss all actions as having taken place in the past, in which case the past tense would be used throughout the report.

Originators vary in their skill in writing reports. Every originator, however, edits and polishes successive drafts until the final report is as clear, concise, and logical as possible.

The Secretary's Responsibility

The secretary plays an important part in the preparation of business reports. The secretary closely follows the report-writing routine discussed previously. It is not unusual for a secretary to be involved in each step of the report-writing routine, from collecting information to the final typing of the report. The important secretarial responsibility of producing attractive reports is made easier by the use of the many automatic features of word processing equipment and/or electronic typewriters. (For a discussion of these features, see pages 87-88.)

In addition, the secretary is responsible for editing reports for clear language, redundancy, spelling, punctuation, and figures and computations. It should be apparent that the secretary's contributions to the report-writing process are significant.

The Form of the Report

Depending on the nature and circulation of a report, its form may be a letter, an interoffice memorandum, or a formal bound manuscript. Some companies have style sheets for all or for special reports. Style sheets standardize report formats. If a style sheet is not available, the writer follows a consistent pattern.

Letter Reports. Letter reports are external reports prepared for clients outside the firm. These reports follow a letter format and include all letter parts. They are prepared on letterhead stationery, single-spaced, with one-inch side margins. Special headings, such as an introduction, a summary and/or conclusions and recommendations, are common in letter reports. These headings are centered or typed at the left margin and should be underscored. Tables are used to display numerical data and are referenced in the text. Tables should begin and end on the same page. As with most reports, the language is objective, written in the third person, and free of statements that show personal bias.

Interoffice Memorandum Reports. Memorandum reports are internal communications formatted in memo style. An example of a memorandum report appears in Illus. 18-1. These reports are single-spaced and may include side headings for introductions, discussion, summary, conclusions, and recommendations. Tables and supporting data are attached to the memorandum. Memorandum reports may be written in a combination of first, second, and third person. The circulation of the report determines the writing style. For instance, a report for upward distribution would probably be written in objective, third person style; one being distributed horizontally would be more informal.

DI Drayer Industries   Interoffice   Memorandum

        TO: Edward F. Bullard, President   DATE: October 10, 19--
      FROM: Lucille Stanford
   SUBJECT: Status Report--Employee Volunteer Program

To accomplish our goal for more community involvement by our company and personnel, a study has been made of our community needs. In addition, a survey of our staff has been made to determine the members' interest in participating in volunteer community projects. A skeleton plan of such a program follows:

Identification of Community Projects

Utilizing the interview technique, members of the Public Relations Department visited with local Chamber of Commerce officials, social welfare agencies, independent agencies, and personnel in the mayor's office to identify projects suitable for our proposed volunteer program. As of today, a list of 150 projects, with their descriptions, has been identified. Some projects require group efforts, while others can be accomplished by one individual. One of the most pressing needs found in our survey was the lack of fire protection services in Burday Township. Attachment A provides a listing of projects and their descriptions.

Matching Employee Interests to Projects

When the program is finalized, information about the community projects will be publicized in the company magazine and posted on all available bulletin boards. Employees will be asked to apply for projects of interest to them. A volunteer coordinator will interview applicants and make the assignment to specific projects.

Implementation of the Program

A volunteer coordinator will be selected to head the program. This individual will devote full time to this project. Employees will be given at least five hours of released time to fulfill their project duties. The coordinator will be responsible for the appointment of the employee to the selected project and evaluate the employee's contribution. The coordinator in collaboration with employee volunteers will be responsible for preparing a report at the conclusion of each project.

Policy Statements

The next step in our plan for a volunteer program for Drayer Industries is to develop policy statements. These documents will be available for your study by the first of next month.

LS:RT
Attachment A

Illus. 18-1 Interoffice memorandum reports are single-spaced documents. They may be written in first, second, or third person, depending upon their circulation.

Formal Reports. A short formal report may consist of only the body or informative text. A long, formal report may have, in addition to the body, various introductory parts and supplements including:

Introductory Parts	Sturdy cover or title page (or both)
	Preface or letter of transmittal, including acknowledgments
	Table of contents
	List of tables, charts, and illustrations
	Summary
Body of the Report	Introduction, including purpose of the report
	Main body of the report
	Conclusions and recommendations
Supplementary Parts	Appendix or reference section
	Bibliography
	Index

Notice that the summary *precedes* the main body of the report. This arrangement benefits the busy executive who may be interested in or have time to read only a synopsis of a report. Those who need or want complete information will read the entire report.

Of the three main parts of a report (introductory, body, and supplementary), the body is usually developed first and typed in all but final form before the other parts are prepared. For this reason, this chapter discusses the development of the body of a report first.

DEVELOPING THE BODY OF THE FORMAL REPORT

The originator of a report is responsible for what the report says and what it implies. The writer who has access to a secretary will sensibly and logically work with that individual as a team in the preparation of a report.

The Outline

A methodical writer first makes a topic outline or framework containing all the important points that will be covered in the report. The outline is usually submitted to a superior for approval. This outline may later serve as the table of contents. Headings for a report may also be taken from the outline.

No main heading or subheading in an outline ever stands alone. For every *I* there is at least a *II*, for every *A* a *B*. (If an outline contains a single heading, it is probably part of another point, or misplaced, or irrelevant.) Headings should be phrased accurately and concisely *in parallel style*, as shown in Illus. 18-2. Main headings, *I* and *II*, should be parallel. Subheadings under the same main heading should be parallel. For example, under one main heading, the subheadings may be noun phrases, while the subheadings under another major heading may be verb phrases. Headings can be short constructions beginning with nouns, verbal nouns, or verbs; long constructions that tell the story; or complete sentences. Once a style for headings is established, it must be consistent and parallel throughout.

```
                  DESIGNING A BUSINESS FORM

        I   PURPOSE OF THE FORM

            A.  Systems Analysis

                1.  Definition of the Problem
                2.  Discussion of the Facts
                3.  Analysis of the Results of the Study
                4.  Recommendation

            B.  Preparation of the Proposal

                1.  Rationale for the Study
                2.  Discussion of the Systems Analysis

        II  FORM DESIGN

            A.  Type of Information
            B.  Space Requirements
            C.  Sequence of Information
```

Illus. 18-2
Notice that each heading in this outline is introduced by a noun.

The Rough Draft

A carefully written formal report is typed one or more times in rough-draft form. A rough draft is generously spaced. Although accurately transcribed, rough drafts give little thought to final form or appearance. The purpose of a rough draft is to get the writer's thoughts on paper; to provide something tangible to edit and improve. Preparing a rough draft is not a waste of time; rather, it is a vital step. In typing rough drafts, the secretary follows these practices:

1. Use paper that is less than letterhead quality but sufficiently strong to withstand erasing during the editing process. Many offices use colored paper for rough drafts.
2. Do not make carbon copies unless they are expressly requested. If an extra copy is needed, a copy can be made on a copier.
3. Provide plenty of room for edits. Use triple spacing and wide margins on all four sides. Indent paragraphs five spaces.
4. Type X's or draw a line through errors, unless the machine is self-correcting.
5. If a quotation is several lines in length, single-space and indent it in the same form as it will appear in the final copy, because changes in quoted matter are unlikely to be made.
6. Type footnotes at the bottom of the page, on a separate sheet, or as shown in Illus. 18-3.
7. Material for an appendix should be typed in final form and labeled Appendix (or Exhibit) A, B, and so forth. Keep this material in a file folder for safekeeping until the report is completed.
8. Type insertions made after the rough draft is typed on separate pages. Number each insertion according to the page where the insert is to be made followed by a capital letter to indicate the position of the insert on the page. For instance, insert 3B would be the second insert to be made on the third page.
9. Number each successive rough draft and date it. Each page is numbered in sequence and sometimes carries the draft number and the date.
10. Carefully check and proofread each successive draft so that subsequent drafts contain valid material.
11. Save all rough drafts until the report is completed and presented. Even though it has been superseded, a writer may decide to use material from an earlier draft.

Illus. 18-3
Footnotes typed in this style are retained in correct position if copy is rearranged during editing.

A simple method of incorporating a footnote into a rough draft

is to type the footnote immediately below the line in which

the reference number appears.[1]   Separate the footnote from the

---

[1]Rita Sloan Tilton, J. Howard Jackson, and Estelle L. Popham, Secretarial Procedures and Administration (9th ed.; Cincinnati: South-Western Publishing Co. 1987), p. 513.

---

text by typing lines across the page above and below it.

TYPING THE BODY OF THE FORMAL REPORT

The final version of a report measures the originator's skill in concise, logical writing and the secretary's skill in sustained, attractive, meticulous typing and in proofreading. To be sure that each page is uniformly typed, the secretary carefully studies the report format, then designs a page layout and prepares a job instruction sheet. Margin and line spacing are planned to enhance readability. If the secretary has a word processor or an electronic typewriter, these instructions can be programmed into the machine. A dictionary and a punctuation guide should be nearby.

Most reports require multiple copies. Most office managers prefer that report originals are typed on good quality paper and photocopied for distribution or that the original is typed on a master for reproduction.

If carbon paper is used to make copies, keep the original and the carbon copy of each page together in the order in which they were typed until they are ready to be proofread and corrected. Never leave carbon paper in a set of typed pages because pressure on the pack will transfer carbon onto the typed pages. Do not paper clip pages together because the clip leaves crimp marks.

Place the carbon copy on top of each set of pages to protect the choice ribbon copy. Since the bottom carbon copy is used for proofreading and marking corrections, any illegibility will be revealed. In this way, an illegible copy will not be passed on inadvertently and be proved useless. If any figures on a set of pages are especially unclear, consider the set unusable.

Page Layouts

There are two kinds of typed page layouts. The *traditional* layout looks much like a printed page from a standard textbook; the *nontraditional* layout creatively arranges and displays units of typing. The successful secretary is alert to ways of presenting facts in nontraditional and in traditional ways. By varying margins, line spacing, indentations, capitals and lowercase letters, spacing between letters and words, and underlining; using white space generously; and devising charts, drawings, and graphs, the secretary can achieve results that will greatly enhance the effectiveness of a report.

Job Instructions. Typing a report of many pages must be organized in advance and controlled while in process so that it can be carried through to a successful completion. To accomplish this task, prepare a job instruction sheet. Cover every point about type style, form, placement, and format. Try to answer in advance every question that will be raised. Be sure to specify the following:

1. Kind and size of paper to be used
2. Weight and finish of carbon paper (if used)
3. Number of carbon copies (if required)
4. Kind and type style of typewriter or word processor to be used
5. Page format, including
     Paper guide scale number
     Left margin (specify number on machine scale)
     Right margin (specify number on machine scale)
     Top margin (specify for first page and following pages)
     Bottom margin (specify number on line guide [see page 516])
     Vertical spacing (single, double, or other)
     Paragraph indentation (specify number of spaces)
     Tabulation indentation (specify number of spaces)
     Tabulation indentation (specify for outline level I, A, 1, a, etc.)
     Tabulation spacing (single or double)
     Headings (provide examples and placement [see page 519])
     Subheadings (provide examples and placement [see page 519])
6. Placement of computer printouts, tables, and graphs (see page 521)
7. Quotations (see page 519)
8. Enumerations (see page 521)
9. Footnotes (see page 520)
10. Instructions for numbering pages (see page 522)
11. Handling of typed pages awaiting assembly (see page 514)
12. Instructions for proofreading (see page 531)
13. Number of copies required
14. Instructions for collating (see page 531)
15. Instructions for binding (see page 532)
16. Distribution of copies
17. Disposal of original draft or electronic media

Indentations. Paragraphs may be typed flush with the left margin or indented 5, 10, 15, or even 20 spaces. Formal reports are usually double-spaced and have paragraph indentations. For single-spaced reports, double-space between paragraphs. In blocked double-spaced work, triple- or quadruple-space between paragraphs. Indentations make for easy reading, regardless of the line length of the body.

Margins. There are several techniques you can use to maintain even top and bottom margins in reports. For instance, if you are typing the entire report yourself, a *top and bottom line guide* should be sufficient. Make your own guide by typing line numbers down the extreme right edge of a second sheet. Position this guide at the back of the carbon pack or behind the top sheet with the line numbers showing along the right edge, as shown in Illus. 18-4.

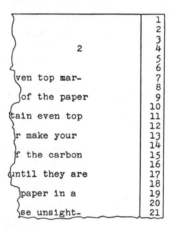

Illus. 18-4
To make a line guide, number lines in ascending order, 1-33, starting at the top to mid-page. Starting at mid-page, number lines in descending order, 33-1, to the bottom of the page.

Another device used to maintain even side, top, and bottom margins is a *special guide sheet*.[1] This guide is particularly useful when several typists are working on one report. A special guide sheet is typed on ordinary bond (or onionskin, if carbon copies are required) and is placed directly behind the page being typed. If a report is being typed in a word processing center and the originator prefers a certain format, the secretary prepares a guide sheet and sends it to the center with the manuscript.

The guide sheet shown in Illus. 18-5 for a leftbound manuscript would be ruled with a dark ink or a colored pencil so that it would be visible through the top sheet. Observe the following:

1. In the *upper right corner* and *centered at the bottom,* short lines for page numbers leave a $\frac{1}{2}$-inch top and a 1-inch side margin or a $\frac{1}{2}$-inch bottom margin, as desired. Usually only if the manuscript is bound at the top are pages numbered at the

---

[1]Adapted from Erwin M. Keithley and Philip J. Schreiner, *A Manual of Style for the Preparation of Papers and Reports* (3rd ed; Cincinnati: South-Western Publishing Co., 1980)

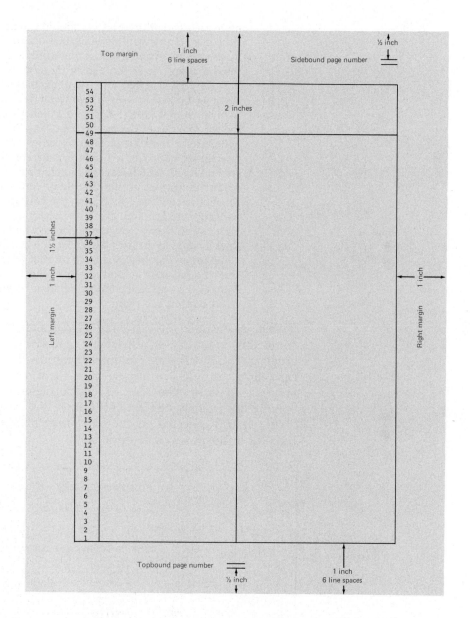

Illus. 18-5
A special guide
sheet is ruled in
dark ink so that it
will be visible
through the page
being typed.

    foot. However, if a first page of an unbound or leftbound man-
uscript is to be numbered, the number is centered at the foot
of the page, as for a topbound manuscript.

2.   The vertical rule $1\frac{1}{2}$ inches from the left indicates the left
margin setting. The extra $\frac{1}{2}$ inch is for binding.

3.   The vertical rule 1 inch from the right indicates the right
margin setting. Keep the right margin as even as possible. No

more than two or three letters should extend beyond this vertical line. Use a word division manual to check end-of-line hyphenations. Avoid hyphenating words at the end of the first line on a page or at the end of more than two consecutive lines; never end a page with a hyphenated word. Do not end or begin a line with a one- or two-letter syllable.

4. Two horizontal lines (1 inch and 2 inches from the top) mark the top margins of the manuscript. The first page of a report part (letter of transmittal, table of contents, chapter) begins on line 13, which leaves a 2-inch top margin. Subsequent pages start on line 7, which leaves a 1-inch top margin. (Position the typewriter to type on the first line *below* guide sheet rules.

5. The horizontal line 1 inch from the bottom edge of the paper indicates the last line available for typing. Plan to leave at least two lines of a paragraph on a page and carry at least two lines forward to the next page. Plan the last line of the body to allow for any footnotes that go on that page.

6. The vertical rule at center shows the horizontal centering point of the page, the point equidistant between the marginal rulings at left and right.

Titles. An attractively arranged traditional or nontraditional title commands attention—a respectable objective of a title page. Several arrangements of titles are possible. Traditionally, titles are typed in all caps, in upper and lowercase letters, in a spread, with extra space between words, or in boldface. Underscoring is optional. Titles of three or more lines may be distinctively framed. An unconventional arrangement, though centered on the page, may in itself be asymmetrical. Illus. 18-6 illustrates these options.

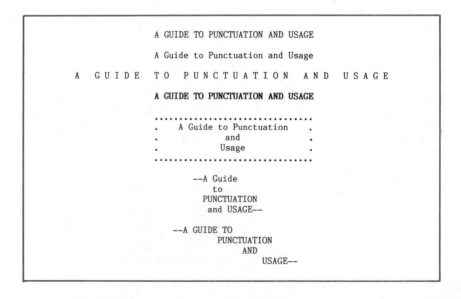

Illus. 18-6
The title of a report may be arranged in a traditional or nontraditional way.

Every typewritten title is a part of a picture. Therefore, select a style that is attractive in width and weight and that is in satisfying proportion to the dimensions of the typed page. It is hard to *visualize* which form of title is best, so experiment with sizes, weights, and arrangements.

Headings and Subheadings. Headings and subheadings are used to guide a reader through a report. (Headings and subheadings are often referred to as *degree headings* [first, second, third degree headings, for example].) They should answer two questions: Do they clarify content and increase readability? Is their construction parallel to other headings?

In general, headings and subheadings parallel the outline. (Note the arrangement of headings in this book. They cue the reader to the relative importance of subject matter.) Centered and capitalized headings are superior to centered headings with capitals and lowercase letters. Also, centered headings are superior to side headings.

Before typing a report, the secretary prepares a job instruction sheet, indicating the form and position of each heading and subheading, of each margin and indentation, and of all line spacing. Illus. 18-7 shows a portion of a job instruction sheet that deals with headings.

Illus. 18-7
A job instruction sheet specifies the type style and placement of headings.

```
                   PLACEMENT OF HEADINGS AND SUBHEADINGS

   Title of Report,        All capitals, underscoring optional
   Chapter Number, and     Use 10-pitch type and begin two inches from
   Chapter Title              the top
                           Center each line horizontally
                           Triple-space to first line of main heading

   No. 1 Heading (Main)    Initial capitals, underscoring optional
                           Center each line horizontally
                           Triple-space to first line of typing

   No. 2 Heading (Sub)     Initial capitals, underscored, flush with
                             left margin
                           Double-space to first line of typing

   No. 3 Heading (Sub)     Initial capitals, underscored, typed at
                             paragraph indentation point
```

Quoted Matter

Reports often quote material from other sources, either directly or indirectly, and must give credit to these sources. For indirect quotations or references, a footnote providing the source suffices. Direct quotations are handled in the following ways:

1. Quotations of *fewer than four lines* are typed in the body of the paragraph and enclosed in quotation marks.
2. Quotations of *four or more lines* are usually typed without quotation marks, single-spaced, and indented from the left margin or from both margins.
3. When a quotation of *several paragraphs* is not indented, quotation marks precede each paragraph and follow the final word in the last paragraph only.
4. A *quotation within a quotation* is enclosed in single quotation marks.
5. *Italicized words* in a quotation are underscored.
6. *Omissions* are shown by ellipses—three periods with a space before, after, and between each period (. . .) within a sentence. Use four periods if the omission comes at the end of a sentence.
7. *Inserted words (interpolations)* are enclosed in typewritten *brackets*. Parentheses cannot be used. Since they often occur naturally in the text, the reader will be unable to identify interpolations if parentheses are used.
8. A source for a quotation should be footnoted, unless the source is identified adequately in the text.

Permission to quote copyrighted material must be obtained from the copyright holder when reports are to be printed or duplicated for public circulation. (Material published by a governmental agency is not copyrighted.) Full information should be sent to the copyright holder with the request to reprint including the following:

1. The text leading up to the quotation or a copy of the page that includes the quotation
2. The lines to be quoted (Underscore the lines on the page)
3. The source line or the complete footnote
4. The title, publisher, and date of publication in which the quoted matter will appear

Footnotes

Three methods of footnoting are used in business reports. They are the traditional method, the textual citation/reference method, and the scientific/technical method.

Traditional footnotes are typed at the bottom of the page on which the citation appears or at the end of the article or chapter. Footnotes are numbered in sequence throughout each section or throughout the entire report. Footnote numbers, called superscript numbers, are raised slightly above the line of print at the citation point and at the footnote location.

Secretaries using electronic equipment which does not have a superscript feature can use the textual citation/reference method. At the citation point in the body of the report, give the name(s) of author(s), publication date, and page number enclosed in parentheses. The bibliography follows the same format as the traditional bibliography, but is entitled "References."

Another method follows the procedure used in scientific and technical publications. Footnotes are numbered consecutively followed by a colon and the page number of the reference in the bibliography. For example, *15:30* indicates the fifteenth reference in the bibliography and page 30. The bibliography is arranged in numerical sequence according to the order in which footnotes appear in the body of the report. A variation of this format is to type the references in the bibliography in alphabetical order and number them. Footnotes are then numbered according to the numbers assigned to them in the bibliography.

Styles of typing traditional footnotes may be reviewed in the Reference Guide on page 855. A guide for typing bibliographies can also be found in the Reference Guide.

Enumerations

When typing enumerations, align the first word of the second line with the first word in the previous line (called a *hanging indent*). Do not return to the left margin or begin under the number. For example:

1. Our recruiting program will begin in September, and our objective will be to hire as many qualified young women as we can find for the vacancies.
2. Our training program will run for one full year. The first three months will be devoted to the orientation of new employees.

Computer Printouts, Tables, and Graphs

Computer printouts, tables, and graphs can be incorporated into the body of a report. Explanations of these illustrations precede their placement in the text. They can also be labeled as exhibits and placed in the appendix. Tables and graphs can be reduced on some copiers. If this is the plan, make the reductions before typing the manuscript, so that proper space allowance can be made. Too many computer tables or graphs detract from the readability of the discussion. Unless absolutely necessary to the discussion, lengthy tables should be placed in the appendix.

Numbering Pages

Unless you are using equipment with an automatic pagination feature, wait until the manuscript is typed in final form before typing page numbers. If making carbon copies, number the top sheet of each carbon assembly in pencil as it is completed to keep unnumbered copies in order. If only an original is being made, number pages in the top right-hand corner in pencil. Only after supplements and preliminary pages have been typed, should page numbers for the body be added.

The title page of a report is considered the first page and is not numbered. Subsequent preliminary pages are numbered in small Roman numerals (*ii, iii*) at the bottom center. For leftbound manuscripts, Arabic numerals without periods are used to number the body of the report and supplementary parts (appendix, bibliography, index). Numbers are typed $\frac{1}{2}$ inch from the top in the upper right corner. Numbering the first page of a report is optional. If it is numbered, the number is centered $\frac{1}{2}$ inch from the bottom of the page. After page 1, pages are numbered consecutively throughout the report.

PREPARING AND TYPING OTHER PARTS

The order in which the other parts of a report are prepared varies, but inserting page numbers on the table of contents must be one of the last steps. This section provides guidelines for preparing supplements and preliminary pages.

Appendix or Reference Section

In a formal report, an *appendix* or *reference section* contains supporting tables, statistics, and similar reference material. Items in an appendix are numbered Appendix A, B, and so forth and are listed in the table of contents. Some reports call the appendix "exhibits" and number items Exhibit A, B, and so forth.

Bibliography/Reference List

All references mentioned in a report should be included in a traditional bibliography. References used in the study, but not specifically cited, should be in the bibliography also. A report that is based on a study of published materials frequently includes a bibliography of source material. Such a bibliography is called a *selected bibliography*. Many business reports are based on factual information compiled within the company, and there is no need to refer to outside source material.

Sometimes the secretary is asked to prepare a *comprehensive bibliography* of all material published on a subject during a designated period of time. An *annotated bibliography* contains an evaluation or a brief explanation of the content of each reference. An example of a reference in an annotated bibliography follows:

> Tilton, Rita Sloan, J. Howard Jackson, and Estelle L. Popham, *Secretarial Procedures and Administration*, 9th ed. Cincinnati: South-Western Publishing Co., 1987.
>
> *This text is designed to prepare secretaries for job entry and advancement. It provides a comprehensive picture of present-day office technology. The Reference Guide at the back of the book is invaluable to the secretarial trainee and to the secretary on the job.*

A bibliography reference is very similar in form to a footnote in that it cites the author's name, the title of the publication, the publisher, and the date. The name of an editor, a translator, or an illustrator may also be included. The price and complete details on the number of illustrations, plates, diagrams, etc., can be included, if this information will be of value to those who will use the bibliography. Specific chapters or sections and their inclusive page numbers may be stated, if the entry refers only to a certain part of the book or periodical; otherwise, page numbers are omitted.

Type the word "bibliography" approximately two inches ($1\frac{1}{2}$ inches, if 10 pitch is used) from the top of the page in capital letters. References are given in alphabetic order, or references may be listed alphabetically within designated sections, such as chapters. The first line is typed flush with the left margin; succeeding lines are indented. Each reference is single-spaced with a double space between references. Refer to the Reference Guide for the proper presentation of a bibliography.

Index

An *index* is included only when it is felt that there will be occasion to use it. A detailed table of contents usually suffices. When an index is necessary, the secretary underlines each item on each page that should be included in the index in colored pencil. Each underlined item and its page number are written on a separate slip, as shown in Illus. 18-8. Completed slips are then sorted into alphabetic order, and an index is prepared from them.

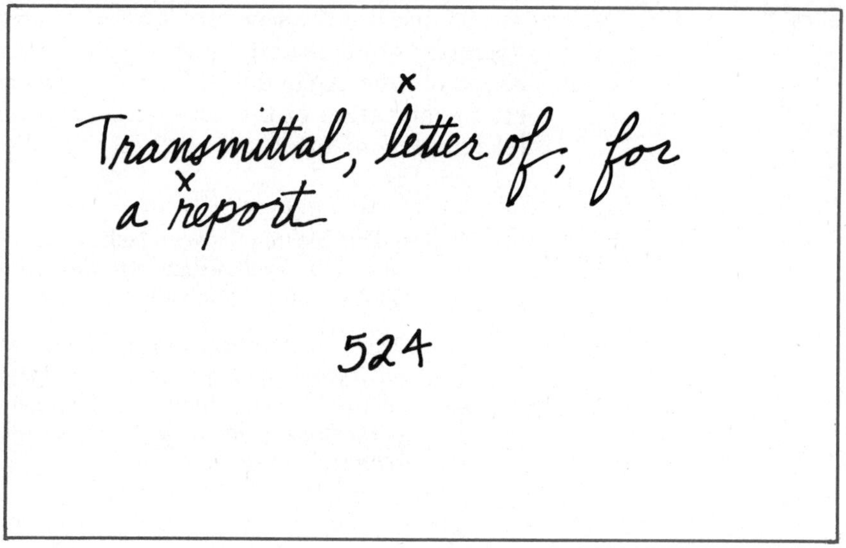

Illus. 18-8
This is an index slip for an item from this book. The X's indicate that cross-reference slips for *Letter of transmittal for a report* and for *Report, letter of transmittal for* were made.

Letter of Transmittal

A *letter of transmittal* is often bound into a report and performs a function similar to a preface. It gives authorization for the report, its purpose, details of its preparation, the period covered, acknowledgments and other similar information. A letter of transmittal helps the reader understand the depth and breadth of a report and arouses interest in studying it (see Illus. 18-10).

The language of a letter of transmittal is more personal than the objective style of a report. It is typed on regular business letterhead and is signed in ink.

Summary

The *summary* is a concise review of the entire report and its find-ings. It includes a statement of the problem, its scope, the method of investigation, conclusions, and recommendations. It is objective in nature and is written to give the reader a clear understanding of the facts in the report. The length of the report determines the length of the summary; however, recommended style is to limit the summary to one page. The word "summary" is typed 2 inches or $1\frac{1}{2}$ inches (if 10 pitch is used) from the top of the page. Double-space the summary; use the same side margins as used for the report. An example of a summary appears in Illus. 18-12. The first page of the report for which this sum-mary was typed appears in Illus. 18-13.

Title Page

Even a report of five or ten pages is enhanced with a *title page*. The title page should be simple if the report is typed in traditional form. If the report is typed in nontraditional form, a distinctive, nontraditional title page should be designed. Attractive borders can be made using the *m, x,), (, *, ',* or " keys.

The title page contains essential facts for identifying a report. Usu-ally a title page contains the title, for whom it was prepared, by whom it was submitted, the date, and the place of preparation. An interoffice report may require only the title and the date. The writer should approve the content and the arrangement of the title page. Illus. 18-9 shows a well-balanced title page.

Table of Contents

After paging a report, the secretary prepares the table of contents. The contents usually include preliminary parts, the main division, (if applicable), main topics or chapter titles, subheadings, and page num-bers (Roman and Arabic). The word used for a report's major divisions, such as "section," "chapter," "part," is typed in all capital letters at the left margin after the preliminary parts. Main headings begin at the left margin and subheadings are indented two or three spaces. Leaders are commonly used. Rough out the table of contents to get an idea of its vertical and horizontal length before deciding on the final style. Illus. 18-11 is an example of a typical table of contents.

```
*****************************************************************************

                          A FEASIBILITY STUDY

                               OF THE

                    WORD PROCESSING CENTER CONCEPT


                    *****************************



                            Prepared for

                         Electro-Mag Company
                       1606 North McVickers Street
                          Chicago, Illinois



                    *****************************



                            Submitted by

                      Management Research, Inc.
                      2500 Diversey Parkway, West
                          Chicago, Illinois


                            June 30, 19--


*****************************************************************************
```

Illus. 18-9
A title page
identifies essential
facts concerning a
report.

June 30, 19--

Mrs. Agnes B. Harper
Electro-Mag Company
1606 North McVickers Street
Chicago, IL 60639-5124

Dear Mrs. Harper:

The feasibility study, authorized by you on January 1
of this year, concerning the establishment of the word processing
center concept in your organization is now complete.

The study included a thorough investigation of your company's
written communications requirements and a series of conferences
at random with management personnel and employees in the office.
An attitude survey of the clerical staff was also made.

It is recommended that the Electro-Mag Company establish
an experimental satellite word processing center in the Sales
Department and that a work measurement procedure be adopted for
this center. After a period of six months, it is suggested that
an evaluation be made of the center's productivity. This evaluation
will determine whether the concept should be implemented in the
Accounting and Manufacturing Departments.

Working with you and your staff has been a pleasure. Our
gratitude is expressed to the many employees of the Electro-Mag
Company who cooperated with us in making this study.

Yours very truly,

Jean J. Torres

Jean J. Torres
Director of Research

ii

Illus. 18-10
A letter of
transmittal may be
less formal in style
and tone than the
body of the report.

TABLE OF CONTENTS

iii

Illus. 18-11
A table of contents uses leaders to enhance readability.

SUMMARY

The feasibility study of the word processing center concept for the Electro-Mag Company indicates the desirability of implementation for the company. Immediate advantages will be realized in the rapid delivery of error-free sales proposals, in the capability of sending original copies of sales letters to prospective customers, and in the ability to meet the deadlines faced by the company in many of its written reports. The change to the system concept of producing written transcripts will result in long-term reduction of clerical costs in terms of personnel needs and supervisory time.

Therefore, the following recommendations are submitted:

1. The Electro-Mag Company establish an experimental satellite center in the Sales Department.

2. A work measurement study be made during the trial period of six months.

3. Six word processing stations be established in the center under the direction of two supervisory personnel.

4. An evaluation of the productivity of the center be made at the end of the trial period.

The results of the evaluation will determine whether additional centers should be established in the Accounting and Manufacturing Departments.

iv

Illus. 18-12
The length of a summary varies with the length of the report, though one-page summaries are preferred.

A FEASIBILITY STUDY

OF THE

WORD PROCESSING CENTER CONCEPT

Introduction

This section discusses in detail the problem of the study, the purpose of the investigation, and the definitions of concepts used throughout the report.

The Problem

The establishment of word processing centers in the Electro-Mag Company is explored to determine whether the concept can meet the ever growing communication needs of the company without an increase in per page costs. Random conferences with management personnel and surveys of the clerical staff are evaluated.

Purpose of the Report

Because of the increase in the written communication requirements of the Electro-Mag Company and the need for a reduction of clerical costs in this area, this feasibility study has been undertaken to determine whether the word processing center concept can accomplish these objectives. All factors involved in the output of written communications are considered. These factors are then studied in a cost analysis within each department of the company.

Illus. 18-13
The first page of a leftbound report usually contains the title of the report and a short introduction.

PROOFREADING, FINAL CHECKING, COLLATING, AND BINDING

After all the typing is finished, four important steps remain: proofreading, final checking of mechanics, collating, and binding. If the report is typed in the word processing center, these activities are performed in the center. The originator's secretary also proofreads the report.

Proofreading

Each typed page of the final copy of the report is proofread word for word and figure for figure. A practical plan is to use a copy for proofreading, boldly marking all corrections on it and filing it permanently. The careful proofreader goes through the material at least twice. The first time, the copy is checked against the final draft for accuracy of typing and for omissions; the second time, for consistency of style and form. If possible, proofread the copy with the help of another person.

Final Checking

After corrections have been made, make a final check. Many embarrassing errors have been caught during this final proof. Check the following items *on each set* of a report unless a copier was used:

1. Final corrections
2. References to page numbers, tables, or figures
3. Sequence of pages (It is necessary to check page sequence for each set even when a copier has been used.)

Collating

The final report is submitted in complete sets, with the original on top. Assemble copied sets in reverse order; that is, the bottom page is laid out first, faceup. In this way, you can see any blank or mutilated pages during assembly. When you have collated a complete set, joggle the pages until they are exactly aligned.

Binding

Binding is the last step in preparing a report. The most popular form of binding is the staple. When only one staple is required, position it diagonally in the upper left corner. When a wider margin has been left for binding at the top or at the left, use two or three staples along the wide margin, parallel with the edge of the paper. If a report that is to be stapled is too thick, use double stapling. Insert staples in proper position from the front and a second set in the same spots from the back.

Some offices prefer sturdier and more permanent types of binding. Some of these bindings require special supplies and equipment, such as metal eyelets, punches, wire spiral devices, or plastic combs. Convenient and attractive report covers in transparent plastic with a snap-on spine are available from most office supply stores.

PREPARING COPY FOR PUBLICATION

Most of the duties associated with preparing a manuscript for publication are assigned to the secretary. (If a word processing center is available, the actual typing of the manuscript would be done in the center.) Since a typesetter will set text in type exactly as it appears in manuscript, it is imperative that punctuation and spelling be correct. The secretary always keeps a file copy for ready reference of all manuscripts sent to the typesetter.

If possible, the secretary should discuss format with the person who is typing or word processing the manuscript. Together they should develop a style sheet specifying the type to be used for main headings and subheadings, for footnotes, for the bibliography, and for captions.

Manuscript

Publishers usually specify manuscript format. It then becomes the secretary's responsibility to see that the manuscript meets the publisher's standards. In general, a manuscript to be typeset should meet the following specifications:

1. Type all copy double-spaced on one side of $8\frac{1}{2}$-by-11-inch sheets. Leave generous margins. Quoted material or other

text to be set apart should be single-spaced and indented on both sides.

2. Key all typewritten copy to its exact position on a page layout.

3. Number all sheets in the upper right corner. Two or more compositors may work on the same assignment; so correct numbering is imperative.

4. Type incidental changes, or write them clearly in ink, between the lines or in the margins.

5. Typewrite a long addition on a separate full-size sheet; give it an insert page number and indicate the point at which the insertion is to be made.

6. Draw a heavy line through words to be omitted.

7. Give explicit directions. With the help of a compositor, specify size and style of typefaces and the amount of leading (space between lines) desired.

8. Use a single underline to indicate *italics*, a double underline for SMALL CAPS, and a triple underline for REGULAR CAPS. To indicate boldface, use a wavy underline.

9. Number footnotes consecutively. They may be typed on the page to which they pertain between full width rules directly under the line in which the reference occurs or at the bottom of the page but separated from the text by short lines. Footnotes may also be typed in sequence on a separate sheet.

10. If a photograph is to be included, type the caption on a separate piece of paper and paste it on the bottom edge of the picture.

11. Provide titles. Number tables and illustrations consecutively with Arabic numerals. Send a full list of all tables and illustrations with the manuscript.

12. Include a title page showing the title, the author's name and address, and perhaps the date.

13. Include the author's vita sheet, if requested.

14. Send the original copy to the printer. Do not fasten the sheets together. Keep them flat by placing them between cardboard or in a strong box.

15. Send the manuscript by first-class mail.

Magazine Articles and Press Releases

An executive may occasionally be asked to submit an article for magazine publication. The secretary simplifies the editor's job of judging the space needed for the article by typing a sample paragraph from a recent issue of the magazine line for line. In this way, the average line length and the number of lines to an inch of printed material is determined. Headings for the copy should be consistent with those used in the magazine. This information becomes the style sheet for the article. A covering letter giving the approximate number of words in the article also aids the editor.

If the approximate length requirements of the article are provided by the publisher, the secretary types a rough draft version with double spacing in the average line length of the magazine copy. This copy is given to the executive with a close estimation of the amount of space presently accounted for. As revisions are made, the executive can lengthen or shorten the article. Copies of published material should be kept in a file so labeled.

Press releases should be addressed to the city editor unless another person, such as the financial editor, is specified. Publicity and news releases are discussed in Chapter 7.

Reading Proof

It is customary for typesetters to submit proofs. The secretary usually checks the proof for errors, but the executive should be given an opportunity to approve revisions.

The first proof is usually in galley form. Galleys are long sheets containing columns of typeset copy. Each kind of error or change to be made to the galley is indicated by a proofreaders' mark (illustrated in the Reference Guide on page 858). The place of the correction is indicated in the text, and the kind of correction to be made is written in the margin on the same line. If there is more than one correction in a line, proofreaders' marks in the margin are separated by conspicuous diagonal lines.

The typesetter submits a second proof in page form. This new proof must be meticulously read and corrected. Page numbers and page headings are shown in this proof and are usually checked in separate individual operations. Page proof is often the final opportunity for the author to catch errors and to make changes.

PROCEDURES WRITING

Procedures writing has been called "verbal flowcharting." It lists the logical sequence of activities involved in a given task step by step. Procedures writing serves to control as well as to communicate. It controls how things are done as it instructs employees in the steps to follow in recurring operations.

Writing good procedures seems deceptively simple, but eliminating extraneous material is extremely difficult. Effective procedures writing is one of the most valuable forms of writing because it enhances productivity and saves business time and money.

Writing procedures is a sophisticated process. Successful procedures writers do a great deal of research and involve management and support personnel in the process (see Illus. 18-14). In fact, some companies assign one person to write procedures, thus maintaining uniformity. It is important that procedures be written in a simple, direct style, using terms that will be easily understood by all who will be expected to interpret and follow them.

Procedures for a department or for an operation are usually collected in a loose-leaf notebook that can be updated by adding and deleting pages as new procedures are issued. This notebook is commonly called a *procedures manual*. It is helpful to include an index in the manual for easy reference.

Illus. 18-14
In all manner of writing, careful research is the foundation for accurate information.

A Sample Procedure

The establishment of word processing centers in most large companies necessitated the development of procedures for submitting work to the centers. You might be asked to write some of the procedures that affect your office. Assume that your input is requested for developing a procedure to submit work to the center. There are at least four formats that you can use in writing procedures: traditional, improved traditional, job breakdown, and playscript.

Traditional. Traditional format features a prose writing style in paragraph form.

> A word originator who has a hard copy document to be typed by the Word Processing Center prepares the document in readable form with complete instructions and attaches it to Form 101 WP, the Word Processing Center Job Ticket, and sends to the Word Processing Center.

> The Word Processing Manager enters the document on Form 102 WP, the Work Log, and notes the date and time on the Job Ticket. The manager then assigns the work to one of the Word Processing Specialists.

> The Word Processing Specialist types the final document in appropriate form, makes the required number of copies, then submits the document and any copies to the Word Processing Coordinator for proofreading and distribution. A messenger delivers the completed work to the originator for signature and mailing.

Improved Traditional. The improved traditional format uses enumerations, tabulations, spacing changes, and underlinings to emphasize the importance of certain actions.

> A word originator who has a hard copy document to be typed by the Word Processing Center
> 1. Completes Form 101 WP, giving detailed instructions
> 2. Attaches Form 101 WP to the document
> 3. Sends to the word processing center

> The Word Processing Manager enters the document on the Work Log (Form 102WP), noting the date and time, and gives to a Word Processing Specialist for typing.

> After typing the document, the WP Specialist submits the work to the Word Processing Coordinator for proofreading and distribution. A messenger delivers the work to the originator for signature and mailing.

Job Breakdown. With the job breakdown format, the logical sequence of action is related in a series of steps. Key points caution employees where mistakes are likely to be made. The *steps* tell the employee what to do; the *key points* tell how to do it. Every *step* may not have a *key point*, but there may be more than one *key point* for each step in an operation.

Steps	*Key Points*
1. Prepare hard copy document.	1. Be sure that the document is in readable form.
2. Attach to Form 101 WP, Word Processing Center Job Ticket.	2. Include complete instructions and all necessary information.
3. Send to Word Processing Center by messenger.	3. Note the time the work was picked up.
4. Receive completed work from the Word Processing Center.	4a. Check to see that directions were followed and all information is included.
	4b. Verify number of copies.
	4c. Check to see if envelope is included and is the right size.
5. Sign and mail.	5. Any changes require the return of the document to the center.

Playscript. The playscript format answers the question, "Who does what?" It utilizes the team approach in completing office tasks. The actor is easily identified, and what the actor does starts with an action verb in the present tense. According to the developer of this technique, playscript is really a type of flowchart. Any step that flows backward rather than proceeds by forward action can immediately be spotted. Gaps in the logical sequence of steps can also be quickly detected.

Responsibility	*Action*
Word Originator	1. Prepares document in readable form including complete instructions.
	2. Attaches Form 101 WP, Word Processing Center Job Ticket, and sends to the center.
Word Processing Manager	3. Enters the document on Form 102 WP, Work Log, noting the date and time on the job ticket.
	4. Assigns the work to a WP Specialist.

Word Processing Specialist	5. Prepares final document in appropriate form and number of copies.
	6. Submits to Word Processing Coordinator.
Word Processing Coordinator	7. Proofs work and prepares for distribution.
Messenger	8. Delivers to originator for signature and mailing.

Selecting the Format

A traditional person or a traditional company will probably adopt the improved traditional format. A more venturesome author in search of an eye-catching arrangement will probably choose the job breakdown or the playscript. In a procedure involving one operator, the job breakdown might be chosen, for it has the advantage of cautioning against wrong moves. It looks more complicated than the playscript, however. The playscript probably will be selected for writing procedures involving more than one worker.

SPEECH TYPING

Busy executives involved in professional and civic organizations will have many opportunities to make oral presentations. Some executives prefer to use only an outline of their ideas to assist them during their speeches. Others prefer to have their speeches typed word for word, particularly if the topic is technical in nature. If only an outline is required, the secretary follows the outline format on page 511. Several copies of an outline or a typewritten speech should be made. One copy of a speech is retained in a topic file; another is for the executive to use to make additions or deletions. In typing an entire speech, the secretary should follow these suggestions:

1. Set the machine for triple or quadruple spacing.
2. Use a 10-pitch type font.
3. Set the machine for a five-inch writing line (some executives prefer a four-inch writing line).
4. Affix an adhesive-type note at the bottom margin before inserting the paper in machine. This note is useful in maintaining an even bottom margin.
5. Number the pages.
6. Place the final draft of a speech in a loose-leaf binder so that pages will be kept in order during the presentation.

Speakers often provide handouts to the audience to supplement a presentation or provide copies of the speech itself. Color-code handouts, so the speaker can refer to them by color and avoid confusion. Most speakers recommend that handouts be distributed after the presentation or when the audience is to use them. If it is necessary to hand out material before a presentation, place them in envelopes with instructions not to open until a specified time.

To clarify or explain key points, speakers use visual aids (see Chapter 10). The preparation of transparancies, flip charts, or slides is a secretarial contribution. If transparencies are used, tape each transparency to a frame and number them according to the order of presentation. Notes also can be conveniently taped to these frames to cue the speaker. Highlight an outline or the text of a speech with a yellow felt-tip pen to call attention to when a transparency is to be presented. Place transparencies and a copy of the speech in order in a box or a briefcase large enough to accommodate them. Bulky handouts should be wrapped or put in a box and delivered to the meeting location in advance of the presentation.

An additional secretarial contribution to an executive's speech-giving duties is to keep a file of poems, jokes, quotations, and cartoons that the employer may use in preparing a speech. Included in this file should be a list of speech topics for future presentations.

SUMMARY

The vast amount of information generated by computers has led to more and different types of reports. Reports are either formal (written) or informal (both written and oral). Written reports take the form of interoffice memorandums, letters, or bound manuscripts.

The report originator follows a set routine in gathering information and formulating the report. The secretary's role follows closely the report-writing routine of the writer. In addition, the secretary is responsible for producing an attractive manuscript, free from grammatical, spelling, and proofreading errors.

The preparation of a formal report begins with a topic outline. The second step is the rough draft, which may be edited and retyped many times. When final draft manuscript is ready to be typed, the secretary designs a page layout and prepares a job instruction sheet. A top and bottom margin guide helps maintain these margins. A special guide sheet assists the typist in keeping side, top, and bottom margins even. The secretary also discusses several arrangements of the title on the title page and the format of headings and subheadings with the typist. Instructions for typing quotations and footnotes are given. When computer printouts, tables, and graphs appear in a report, explanations of these illustrations must precede their placement in the text. Lengthy tables and graphs, unless they are absolutely necessary to understand the discussion, should be placed in an appendix. Numbering the pages of the body of a report is delayed until the report is in final form. Preliminary pages are numbered in small Roman numerals; the body of the text, in Arabic numerals.

Parts of a formal report include the appendix, bibliography, index, letter of transmittal, summary, title page, table of contents, and the body. The appendix is for supplementary documents. The bibliography should include all references used in the study. A selected bibliography or a comprehensive bibliography may occasionally be compiled by the secretary. If a report is very long, an index may be needed. The letter of transmittal is more personal in style than the body of the report. It gives authorization for the report, its purpose, and other details of the report-writing process. A summary provides a concise review of the entire report and its findings. The title page must contain essential facts for identifying the report including the title, for whom it was prepared, by whom it was submitted, the date, and the place of preparation. After paging the report, the secretary prepares a table of contents.

After all the typing is completed, the manuscript must be proofread carefully, possibly with the help of another person. All figures appearing in the manuscript should be checked. Finally, the manuscript is collated and bound.

When preparing copy for publication, a number of steps should be followed. For magazine articles, the secretary types material according to guidelines of the particular magazine. Press releases are addressed to the city editor or another appropriate editor.

Office procedures change with technological advancements. The secretary may be required to list the logical sequence of activities involved in new procedures. The secretary can choose from the traditional format, the improved traditional format, the job breakdown style, or the playscript arrangement to write procedures.

When asked to type a speech, the secretary should follow suggestions given in this chapter. If the executive requests transparencies, flip charts, or slides, the secretary arranges for this work to be done. The same is true with any handouts to be distributed to an audience.

SUGGESTED READINGS

Carr-Ruffino, Norma. *Writing Short Business Reports*. New York: McGraw-Hill Book Company, 1980.

Duncan, Charles H., *et al. College Keyboarding/Typewriting*, 11th ed. Cincinnati: South-Western Publishing Co., 1985.

Keithley, Erwin M., and Philip J. Schreiner. *A Manual of Style for the Preparation of Papers and Reports*, 3d ed. Cincinnati: South-Western Publishing Co., 1980.

Matthies, Leslie H. *Documents to Manage By*. Stamford, CT: Office Publications, Inc., 1982.

Matthies, Leslie H. *The New Playscript Procedure*. Stamford, CT: Office Publications, Inc., 1979.

QUESTIONS FOR DISCUSSION

1. Why is it important that reports follow a definite order of arrangement and that mechanical rules are followed to prepare them?

2. If you were assigned the responsibility for typing a long report, which questions would you ask and what items would you decide for yourself before you started typing?

3. Assume that you and two other secretaries will type the final copy of a formal report for your immediate supervisor. How will you make sure that all pages are properly formatted? How will you proofread the work?

4. Reports written in the third person can be dull reading. How can a secretary assist the report writer in making the report interesting reading?

5. Who and what determine the format of a company's procedures manual?

6. If you had obtained all the data available on a certain subject and an executive had drafted a report based on this information, what would you do if in the morning's mail you received a business magazine containing an article that covered a new angle of the subject? Would you call the executive's attention to the new material, knowing that it would mean a rewrite job?

7. In what ways is the secretary's role that of a facilitator when assisting the executive in preparing an oral presentation?

8. Retype the following sentences by expressing the numbers in parentheses correctly. Check the Reference Guide to verify and correct your answers.
   a. He held the check for _____ days. (7)
   b. The check for _____ pays for a copier that is _____ years old. ($40, 12)
   c. The typewriter was purchased approximately _____ years ago along with _____ _____ drawer file cabinets. (12, 5, 3)

PROBLEMS

1. Type each of the following titles twice (eight different arrangements). Divide the titles into two or more lines if necessary, and center each line horizontally on the page. Allow six line spaces between titles. Indicate which of the arrangements you prefer.
   a. Career Paths in Word Processing Centers
   b. How Information Processing Creates Total Business Systems
   c. The Mature Woman Returns to Work in the Business Office
   d. The Increasing Ranks of the Male Secretary

2. Using 8½-by-11-inch paper, set up three columns and title them as follows:
   a. Change Desired in the Text
   b. Proofreaders' Mark in the Text
   c. Proofreaders' Mark in the Margin

   Practice using proofreaders' marks by showing how you would make the changes indicated below:
   (1) Insert the word *more*.
   (2) Change the word *readnig* to *reading*.
   (3) Delete the word *usually*.
   (4) Show a space in *ofthis*.
   (5) Even up the left margin where letters have been set too far to the right.
   (6) Write the word *think* in all caps.
   (7) Show an apostrophe in the word *womens*.
   (8) Capitalize the word *congressional*.
   (9) Insert a hyphen in *selfemployed*.
   (10) Indicate a new paragraph.
   (11) Italicize the word *usually*.
   (12) Correct the capitalization of these words: History, Algebra, Social Studies, and English.
   (13) Show that you want the capitalization of the word *Washington* to stand.
   (14) Transpose *two only* to *only two*.
   (15) Use less space between words.
   (16) Use small caps for this heading: Characteristics of New Process.
   (17) Use quotation marks around *shot in the arm*.
   (18) Indicate no paragraph.
   (19) Indicate that type does not match.
   (20) Delete the hyphen in *readily-available service*.
   (21) Insert a comma between *pens* and *and*.
   (22) Center and type in solid caps the heading: *Introduction*.

(23) Change *thimk* to *think*.

(24) Indicate leaving more space after a colon.

(25) Increase the amount of space between lines.

(26) Move copy to the left to align.

(27) Indicate correct spelling of *state room*.

(28) Delete the apostrophe in *it's*.

(29) In the title, *A Manual of Style for the Preparation of Papers and Reports*, the words *and Reports* have been crossed out. Indicate that these two words should be retained.

(30) Delete the comma: *He finished the report, and got it on his superior's desk before leaving the office that afternoon.*

3. Type an outline of an article on the topic of ergonomics appearing in any recent issue of a magazine.

4. From the bibliographical notes that you prepared for Problem 1 in Chapter 16, develop a business report on one of the ten topics given (or a topic of your own choice which your instructor has approved). Use graphs or tables if you think they will improve your presentation.

5. Assume that you are sharing the responsibility for typing the report in Problem 4 with two other secretaries. Type a set of job instructions and a special guide sheet for you and your team to follow in typing the report.

6. Using information in the Reference Guide, type a footnote and a bibliography entry for the following:

    a. An unsigned article, "Helping the Disabled Join the Business World" published in May, 1986, on page 52 of *The Office*

    b. A book by Letitia Baldridge, *Complete Guide to Executive Manners*, published by Rawson Associates, a New York City publisher, in 1985 (The footnote refers to page 65.)

    c. A chapter written by Dennis L. Mott entitled "Time Management" in the National Business Education Yearbook, No. 18, *The Changing Office Environment*, edited by Margaret H. Johnson, and published by the National Business Education Association, Reston, Virginia in 1980 (The chapter appears on pages 142-150.)

    d. An article by Marshall B. Bass entitled "The Changing Secretary" in the May, 1986 issue of *The Secretary* (The article is on page 3.)

7. As administrative assistant in a government procurement office, you are assigned the supervision of two young assistants. You have given them the responsibility of opening and sorting the office mail. You decide to prepare a procedural statement in playscript style covering this activity. Before you begin writing, analyze the

cycle of the operation, determine the actors involved (the two assistants, mail messenger, and yourself), analyze each action in the operation, and identify any office forms used in the process. Write the statement of procedures. (You may wish to refer to Chapter 8).

Case Problems _____

**Case 5-1
PLAGIARISM**

Marie Gaines is secretary to William Duvall, marketing director for Freeman Company, an air filter manufacturer located in Seattle, Washington. Mr. Duvall is to give a presentation before the National Association of Air Filter Manufacturers. Marie assisted him in researching information for his talk. Yesterday Marie finished the first draft of the handout material that will supplement Mr. Duvall's speech and placed it on his desk. Today, Mr. Duvall brings the handouts to Marie and says "This is ready to go to press. I'll need at least 100 copies for my session. You will note that I deleted three footnote citations. I really see no reason to clutter the copy with them. Let's take a chance that no one will miss them." After Mr. Duvall leaves Marie's workstation, she studies the handout and is surprised to see which footnotes Mr. Duvall deleted. One indicated where a number of questionable conclusions were taken, another referred to statistical results of a marketing survey, and the other cited recommendations for changes in a filter product made by a manufacturer in the field. Marie believes that deleting these footnotes amounts to plagiarism and could be a source of professional embarrassment for Mr. Duvall. She certainly doesn't want this to happen.

What should Marie do?

**Case 5-2
SECRETARIAL
DECISIONS**

Jim Harper has been secretary to Ms. Juanita Sanchez, branch manager, for five years. He has typed many reports for publication, sometimes adopting nontraditional formats to highlight important points and make the reports more attractive. Ms. Sanchez has accepted these changes, sometimes complimenting him on the innovative arrangements.

Jim is surprised, therefore, when he receives a memo from Ms. Sanchez stating that henceforth all reports for publication are to be typed in traditional styles. Jim is annoyed that the reasons behind this new directive were not discussed with him before the decision was made.

Should he accept the instructions without question, or should he ask to discuss it with Ms. Sanchez?

**Case 5-3
DELEGATING
WORK**

Carmen Reynolds was put in charge of producing a 78-page medical report. She met with each of the three typists assigned to the job, gave instructions as to style, handed them a prepared guide sheet, and requested each typist to read Chapter 18 of this book. The work had to be completed within two days so that Dr. Johanna Spector, her employer, could take it to a meeting at which she was to be the featured speaker. Carmen received the completed work for assembling for presentation to Dr. Spector just two hours before the deadline.

She was horrified to discover that one typist had used a typewriter with 10-pitch type, although the other two had used 12-pitch type; one had typed footnotes in textual citation/reference method; and one had typed headings in solid caps while the other two had used initial caps only and had underscored them.

She showed the variations to Dr. Spector and said, "I am just sick about the way this report looks. You would think that these typists could follow instructions. What can be done now?"

Dr. Spector replied icily, "Nothing, absolutely nothing. I will have to tell the people at the symposium that I will mail them a copy of the report next week. Heaven knows how I can get all their addresses. But, Carmen, I am very unhappy with the way you handled this. After all, you were the one in charge. I had thought that you could handle a simple assignment like this one."

Was Carmen at fault? What did she do wrong? If she talked with you about the problem, what advice would you give her for handling such a situation?

**Case 5-4
UNETHICAL
BEHAVIOR OF
THE EXECUTIVE**

Sally Fong is secretary to Harold Rose, vice-president, Research and Development, for Haskins Leather Processing Company. Mr. Rose has asked Sally to type a proposal to research the feasibility of producing a new type of automatic lock for suitcases.

The preceding week Sally had had dinner with her friend, Tom Lamston, who is also employed in the Research and Development unit. Tom had enthusiastically discussed a new automatic lock that he had invented and intended to patent.

At the office Sally looked carefully through Mr. Rose's proposal for mention of Tom as the inventor of the lock, but it was not there. Mr. Rose had taken full credit for the invention himself.

Where do Sally's loyalties lie?

ADMINISTRATIVE SUPPORT SERVICES: FINANCIAL AND LEGAL PROCEDURES

Keeping financial records, doing personal banking for the employer, handling investments and insurance matters, and preparing payroll present the secretary with an opportunity to learn and grow professionally. The extent to which the secretary becomes involved in these tasks depends upon a number of variables: the size of the business or office, the function of the division in which the secretary is employed, and the secretary's specific tasks or assignments. The financial interests of the executive for whom the secretary works also influence the scope of the secretary's financial responsibilities.

The topics in Part Six will contribute to the secretary's professional and personal growth. As a wage earner and a financially responsible individual, the secretary needs to understand banking services, ways to record and analyze investments and insurance policies, how to organize financial data for the preparation of income tax returns, and the significance of certain legal terms and forms.

Chapter 19

Financial Responsibilities

Complete and accurate financial records are essential to the survival of any business. Your understanding of basic financial services and procedures can help you become a valuable employee. Not only will you be able to aid your employer, but as you learn more about the financial operation of your firm you will learn how to handle your own finances more effectively.

The amount of financial responsibility assigned to you depends upon the nature of the executive's work. Many executive secretaries handle company funds *and* the personal financial records of the employer. Some executives turn all personal financial records including checkbooks, paychecks, dividend checks, credit card records, and personal bills over to their secretaries. Other executives prefer to keep their financial records confidential and delegate only those financial matters that relate to the company to the secretary.

The type and size of the firm that employs you in addition to your employer's preferences define the extent of your financial responsibilities. For example, if you work for a large corporation, your responsibilities may be limited to approving bills for payment, handling your employer's personal records, handling petty cash, or arranging for foreign remittances. On the other hand, if you work for a small company or for a doctor or lawyer, handling all of the financial matters of the business may be one of your primary duties.

Although the total time spent each day performing financial duties may be comparatively small, their importance must not be underestimated. Financial responsibilities are exacting and confidential. They are exacting because they involve handling other people's money. They are confidential because financial data are always highly restricted pieces of information.

STANDARD FINANCIAL PRACTICES

Because of business' increasing need for financial services, banks and other financial institutions are constantly upgrading procedures to simplify banking tasks. The goal of most bankers is to achieve the transfer of funds from one account to another electronically. This goal, however, is not being realized as rapidly as bankers had hoped; therefore, traditional practices and methods are still an important part of the secretary's responsibilities.

Handling Checks

Accepting a check in person or through the mail requires precautions to assure that the check is valid. Examine the date to see that the check is not post-dated (dated later than the current date). Check the amount to determine that the amount of payment is correct. The amount written in figures must agree with the amount written in words. Finally, make sure that an endorsement, if required, has been properly made. To have a deposited check returned by the bank because it was improperly written is time consuming and inconvenient. Before depositing a check, while details are still available, be sure to record information needed for accounting purposes on a receipt form or in a record book.

A secretary with financial responsibilities must be identified at the bank as representing the employer. If the secretary is to sign checks for the withdrawal or payment of personal or company funds or to endorse and cash checks, the bank must be authorized to honor the secretary's signature. The employer may be required to sign a special authorization form or to arrange for the secretary's signature to be added to the signature card on file at the bank. Some banks require that the secretary be issued a power of attorney to perform these functions.

Proving Cash

You might have the responsibility for receiving cash payments and making change and payments from a cash drawer. This responsibility will necessitate proving cash at the beginning or end of each business day. Since you will be held personally responsible for this money, it is essential that you establish a system for protecting these funds. Should you relinquish custody of the cash drawer to another employee, prove the cash before doing so and ask for a receipt to protect yourself. To prove cash efficiently, use a form similar to the one shown in Illus. 19-1.

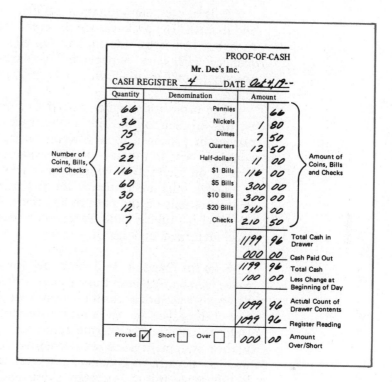

PROOF-OF-CASH		
Mr. Dee's Inc.		
CASH REGISTER 4 DATE Oct 4, 19--		
Quantity	Denomination	Amount
66	Pennies	66
36	Nickels	1 80
75	Dimes	7 50
50	Quarters	12 50
22	Half-dollars	11 00
116	$1 Bills	116 00
60	$5 Bills	300 00
30	$10 Bills	300 00
12	$20 Bills	240 00
7	Checks	210 50
		1199 96 Total Cash in Drawer
		000 00 Cash Paid Out
		1199 96 Total Cash
		100 00 Less Change at Beginning of Day
		1099 96 Actual Count of Drawer Contents
		1099 96 Register Reading
Proved ☑ Short ☐ Over ☐		000 00 Amount Over/Short

Number of Coins, Bills, and Checks

Amount of Coins, Bills and Checks

Illus. 19-1
A form for proving
cash provides an
accurate receipt of
a cash drawer's
contents.

Depositing Funds

To make a deposit, the secretary presents a deposit ticket in duplicate (or a passbook) to the bank teller listing the amounts being deposited. The deposit itself—currency, coin, endorsed checks, and money
orders—should accompany the deposit ticket.

Coins and Bills for Deposit. If coins and bills are in sufficient quantity, banks prefer that you put them in money wrappers. Money wrappers can be obtained from any bank. Coins are packed in paper rolls as
follows:

Denomination	Number of Coins to a Roll	Total Value of Coins in Roll
Pennies	50	$ .50
Nickels	40	2.00
Dimes	50	5.00
Quarters	40	10.00
Halves	20	10.00

Bills of each denomination are made into packages of $50, $100, and so forth. The packages are separated into all-of-a-kind groups with each bill laid right side up and top edge at the top. Torn bills are mended with tape. A paper bill wrapper—a narrow strip with the amount printed on it—is wrapped tightly around the bills and securely glued.

The depositor's name or account number should be stamped or written on each roll of coins and package of bills. Receiving tellers do not count packaged money when taking deposits; rather, someone counts it later in the day. If the depositor's name or account number appears on each roll or wrapper, mistakes can be easily traced.

Loose bills are counted, stacked right side up with the largest denominations on the bottom and the smallest ones on top, and fastened with a rubber band. Extra coins are counted, placed in an envelope, identified, and sealed.

Checks for Deposit. In order to deposit a check or money order, the payee (person to whom the check is written) endorses it on the back. Banks also accept checks for deposit that are endorsed by a representative of the payee. In fact, a bank may accept an occasional check that lacks an endorsement. Some banks stamp the back of such a check with a statement such as, "Credited to account of payee named within—absence of endorsement guaranteed." Notwithstanding the last sentence, it is the secretary's responsibility to endorse every check for deposit. If the name of the payee is written differently from the account name, endorse the check twice: first, as the name appears on the face of the check and, second, the exact way the account is carried. A rubber stamp endorsement (showing the name of the bank, the name of the account, and the account number), may be obtained from the bank where the employer banks or from an office supplies store. Using a rubber stamp to endorse checks saves time. Companies that receive large numbers of checks can use a machine that endorses checks at a high rate of speed. A handwritten signature need not be added to a rubber stamp or machine endorsement. There are several standard endorsements:

1. *A restrictive endorsement* is one in which some condition restrains the negotiability of the check or renders the endorser liable only upon a specified condition or conditions. "For deposit only" or "Upon delivery of contract" are two examples of restrictive endorsements. A restrictive endorsement is commonly used when checks are being deposited. Checks endorsed "For deposit only" need not be signed personally by the depositor but can be endorsed or stamped by the secretary.

The "For deposit only" qualification automatically keeps the check from being used for any purpose other than for deposit to the account of the payee.

2.   An *endorsement in full* or a *special endorsement* (see Illus. 19-2A) gives the name of a specified payee, written before the endorser's signature. This endorsement identifies the person or firm to which the instrument is transferred. A check endorsed in this way cannot be cashed by anyone without the specified payee's signature. The words "Pay to the order of Marilyn Royer" in the illustration identify the name of the person to whom the check is being transferred. For further transfer, Marilyn Royer must endorse the check again.

3.   A *blank endorsement* (see Illus. 19-2B) consists simply of the signature of the payee, making the check payable to any holder. This endorsement, therefore, should never be used except at the bank immediately before the check is being deposited or cashed. A check should never be endorsed at the office or sent through the mail with a blank endorsement. If it is lost, the finder can turn it into cash.

Illus. 19-2A   Illus. 19-2B

An endorsement in full allows the endorser (Noel Carson) to transfer a check to a designated payee (Marilyn Royer). A check with a blank endorsement may be cashed by any holder.

The person or business that accepts an endorsed check (unless stated otherwise in the endorsement) assumes (1) that the check is genuine and valid, (2) that the endorser has received value for it, and (3) that, if necessary, the endorser will reimburse the holder of the check if the bank refuses to process it.

Magnetic Ink Numbers. The American Bankers Association has adopted a uniform system of MICR (magnetic ink character recognition). This system allows a bank to preprint its bank number and the depositor's account number in magnetic ink characters in a uniform position at the bottom of checks and deposit tickets. When a bank receives a check, the date, amount of the check, and other coded information also are recorded in magnetic ink characters at the bottom of the check. Optical character recognition (OCR) equipment sorts the checks according to bank and account numbers, computes totals, and posts to depositors' accounts electronically.

Illus. 19-3 shows a preprinted deposit ticket for an MICR system; Illus. 19-4 shows a check identified by magnetic ink characters.

Deposit Tickets. Many types of deposit tickets are used. Most banks have deposit tickets designed especially for use with automated equipment. The deposit ticket shown is designed for automated processing.

If you wish to receive a portion of the total amount listed on the deposit slip as cash, you may "split" the deposit. This can be done, for example, when your employer asks you to deposit a salary check and to bring back a specific amount of cash. Your employer should not restrict the endorsement in this case, since you are not depositing all the money.

Illus. 19-3
A deposit ticket designed for automatic processing uses magnetic ink numbers to identify the depositor's account.

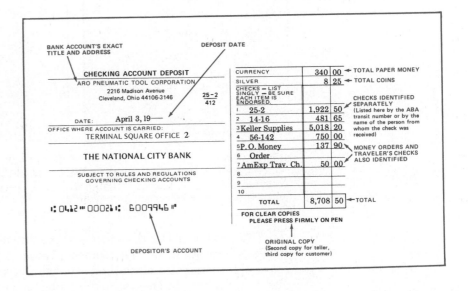

Each depositor has an account number with which the bank's automated equipment identifies the depositor's account; therefore, the account number must appear on the deposit ticket. The bank provides the depositor with a supply of deposit tickets either preprinted with the account number in magnetic ink characters or with space provided for the depositor to record the account number.

Illus. 19-4
Note that the
series of magnetic
ink identification
numbers at the
bottom of this
check are the same
as those on the
preprinted deposit
ticket in Illus. 19-3.

ABA Transit Numbers. Each bank in the United States has an ABA (American Bankers Association) transit number. This number is usually printed on checks in their upper right-hand corners. It identifies the bank for clearinghouse functions in the following manner:

$\dfrac{25\text{-}2}{412}$

25	identifies the city or state
2	identifies the specific bank in that city or state
4	identifies the Federal Reserve District
1	identifies the Federal Reserve Branch in that district
2	identifies the number of days required for the bank to clear the check

Some banks require each check listed on a deposit ticket to be identified by using the two top ABA transit numbers, in this case 25-2, unless the check is drawn on the bank in which the deposit is made. In this case, the check is identified by the name of the maker of the check.

Listing Checks. When a large number of checks are regularly deposited, common practice is to list the checks on an adding machine and to attach the tape to the deposit ticket. Only the total is recorded on the deposit ticket. Some banks prefer that all checks be shown on the deposit ticket and provide large deposit tickets for such use.

Using the Night Depository

Some businesses use the *night* or *after-hours depository* to deposit funds collected after banking hours. The bank provides the depositor with a bag in which to lock the deposit. The depositor then can drop the bag through a slot when the bank is closed. On the next banking day, a bank teller unlocks the bag and makes the deposit. The depositor later stops at the bank to pick up the empty bag and the deposit receipt.

If the depositor prefers, however, the bank will leave the deposit bag locked until the depositor arrives to make the deposit personally.

Banking by Mail

Depositing by mail has become very popular because it saves time. The secretary in a small office may make all or most deposits by mail. All checks must be endorsed "Pay to the order of (name of bank)" or "For Deposit Only," signed, and listed on a deposit slip. The deposit ticket and endorsed checks are placed in an envelope and mailed to the bank or are dropped in the night depository. Currency should never be deposited in this manner unless sent by registered mail. By return mail the bank sends the depositor a receipt, along with a new mail deposit ticket and envelope.

Using a Checking Account

Banks provide checks in a variety of forms. Checks with attached stubs, pads of checks with interleaved copy sheets, and checks with attached *vouchers* (a form used to record the purpose and other details of the payment) are a few of the available forms. In companies where all disbursements must be made by check, voucher checks, like the one shown in Illus. 19-5, and a check register are used. A *check register* is a special journal containing a chronological and serial record of all voucher checks issued. Such a system ensures close control over cash disbursements. Many businesses use prenumbered checks imprinted with the name of the business. The secretary is responsible for ordering a new checkbook before the old one is completely used. Banks usually enclose an order sheet in the back of these checkbooks to make reordering easy.

Completing Check Stubs. Complete the stub *before* you write the check. Failure to do so frequently results in the details of a check being forgotten. In addition to showing the number of the check, the date, the name of the payee, and the amount, the stub should provide other data for classifying or breaking down the disbursement for accounting or tax records. For example, if the check is a part payment, an installment payment, or a final payment, that fact should be noted. If the amount covers several items (such as payment for two or more invoices), each should be listed. If the check is in payment of an insurance premium, the name of the insured and the policy number should be listed.

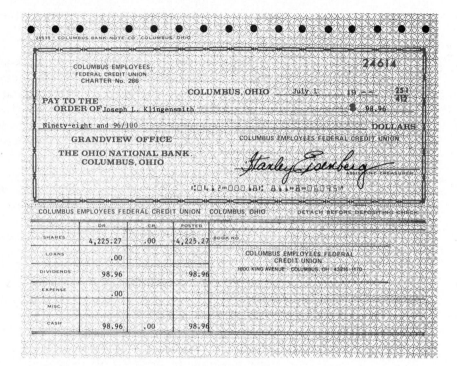

Illus. 19-5
A voucher check
consists of the
check and a
detachable stub
that shows the
purpose of the
check and various
data necessary for
record keeping.

Writing Checks. A check is a negotiable instrument (can be substituted for cash) and imposes certain legal responsibilities on the maker. It must be written with care to ensure that no unintended liability is created. For example, an altered check is not cashable. If a bank honors such a check, it must assume any resulting loss. However, if it can be shown that the maker failed to use reasonable precautions in writing the check, thus making an alteration difficult to detect, the maker must assume any loss. Consequently, always type checks or write them in ink. Never use pencil.

Never cross out, erase, or change any part of a check. If you make an error, write "VOID" conspicuously across the face of both the check and the stub. Save a voided check and file it in numerical order with canceled checks. Since it is easy to alter the impressions made by a worn ribbon, type checks with a fresh ribbon. Keep the checkbook in a safe place, and guard its confidentiality.

Writing Checks for Cash. A check for funds for the personal use of the account holder can be written to "Cash" (as the payee) and signed by the account holder. A check so written is highly negotiable. Anyone in possession of it can turn it into money. The cautious person, therefore, only writes checks for cash on bank premises. (The bank asks the person receiving the money to endorse the check, even though the payee is "Cash.")

The secretary is often responsible for keeping the executive supplied with cash. On banking days, the secretary simply asks, "Do you need money?" If so, the secretary writes the check for cash and either presents it for the executive's signature or, if authorized, signs it. To cash a check made out to "Cash" and signed by the employer, the secretary endorses the check when it is presented at the bank. Checks made out for cash are risky. If lost, they can be cashed by anyone. Unless the secretary is well known at the bank, positive identification will be required. After cashing the check, the secretary should keep the currency separate from personal funds. Place the money in an envelope, seal it, and protect it until delivery.

As a special service some banks provide depositors with a check-cashing or bank check guarantee card. This card, which is a form of identification, guarantees that the bank will honor the card holder's check up to a specified amount. Check-cashing cards facilitate the cashing of personal checks at stores and at other banks.

Checking Accounts That Pay Interest. Funds deposited in checking accounts may draw interest. Banks and savings and loan associations nationwide offer NOW (Negotiable Order of Withdrawal) accounts. Some credit unions pay interest on share-draft accounts, which are like NOW accounts. Most financial institutions offering this service require a minimum balance. A service charge is imposed on accounts that fall below the minimum balance. For example, one financial institution may require you to keep a minimum balance of $500 in your checking account to earn interest. If your balance falls below $500, there is a flat $2 monthly maintenance fee plus 15 cents for each check paid on the account.

Before depositing money in an interest-earning checking account, you should investigate the offerings of several financial institutions. Some of the questions to ask include the following: How much interest is earned? Is a minimum balance required? What if I go under the minimum? Will a traditional noninterest-bearing checking account serve my purposes just as well?

Stopping Payment on Checks

Unless a check has been cleared by the bank upon which it was drawn, payment can be stopped. It may be necessary to stop payment on a check that has been lost, stolen, or incorrectly written. Most banks charge for this service. Before placing a stop-payment order, ask about the fee. If the fee is more than the check, then stop-payment procedures would not be worthwhile.

To stop payment go to the bank or telephone the bank's stop-payment desk. Give the name of the maker, the date, the number and amount of the check, the account number, the name of the payee, and the reason that payment is to be stopped. The bank teller will search the checks on hand or call up the account on a VDT to see if it has cleared the bank. If it has not, the teller will process the stop-payment request. You must then dispatch either a letter of confirmation or a stop-payment form supplied by the bank. When you are sure that the stop-payment request is in effect, write a replacement check, if necessary. Most banks will honor a request to stop payment for a limited time only. If additional time is needed, a new request must be filed with the bank.

Reconciling the Bank Balance

Each month the bank returns *canceled checks* (checks that have cleared the bank during the month) to account holders with a statement that lists each deposit, each withdrawal, interest earned, and service charges. Account holders then check the accuracy of their checkbooks against the bank statement and file canceled checks as proof of payment.

When you receive a statement, compare the final balance on the statement against the checkbook balance. Any difference between these two balances must be accounted for. This process is called *reconciling the bank balance*.

Many banks print instructions and a form for reconciling the bank balance on the back of the bank statement. This printed form may be used, or the reconciliation may be typed on a separate sheet and attached to the bank statement.

In order to reconcile a bank statement, you need the records of checks now outstanding. Keep canceled checks inside folded bank statements and file statements chronologically. You may file checks numerically in a separate place. Save canceled checks. They are evidences of payment and constitute legal receipts. The retention period for canceled checks should be established by company policy.

Some banks offer a *check truncation*, *check retention*, or *check safekeeping* service whereby the bank keeps your canceled checks instead of returning them to you. You receive a monthly statement listing the number and the amount of each check that cleared the bank. You have a right to a copy of any canceled check you may need; however, the bank usually assesses a fee to provide such a copy.

Following Up on Outstanding Checks

Investigate any check that has not cleared the bank within a few weeks of its date of issue. The payee may not have received the check or may have misplaced or lost it. A letter or telephone call to the payee will clarify the matter. If the check is lost, cancel the old check in the checkbook, forward a stop-payment order to the bank, and issue a new check.

Using a Safe-Deposit Box

A *safe-deposit box* may be rented from the bank. A safe-deposit box is a metal box that is locked by two keys into a small compartment in the bank's safe-deposit vault. The bank has very strict rules about access to safe-deposit boxes. The customer must register each time entry to the box is requested. A bank employee accompanies the customer to the box, opens one of the locks with the bank's key, and opens the other lock with the customer's key. The box itself is then removed from the vault and taken by the customer to a private room. Safe-deposit boxes may be used to store securities, wills, insurance policies, notes, gems, and other small valuable articles. Rent is usually billed annually and deducted from the customer's checking account balance.

The executive must sign a special banking form if the secretary is to have access to the safe-deposit box. The secretary may have two responsibilities relative to safe-deposit boxes: (1) to maintain a perpetual inventory of its contents in duplicate (one copy is kept in the box; the other, in the office) and (2) to guard the key carefully.

ELECTRONIC BANKING

Because millions of checks are processed by banks in the United States each year, a number of new procedures have been developed by the banking industry to reduce dependence on checks. Most of these new procedures employ electronic fund transfers (EFTs), which permit the transfer of funds from one depositor's account to another and cash withdrawals without the use of checks.

Computer and electronic technology has made EFT an acceptable substitute for checks and cash in many places. Each EFT service is designed to hold down the rising costs of handling checks and to provide a variety of banking conveniences. EFT services are available in many forms.

Automatic Teller Machines

At shopping centers and other convenient locations, automatic teller machines, like the one shown in Illus. 19-6, provide 24-hour banking. Automatic tellers are used for cash withdrawals, to transfer funds, to make deposits, to make payments on certain loans and bank credit card accounts, to borrow funds in limited amounts, or to obtain the current balance of an account. To use an automatic teller, the depositor inserts a plastic card and punches in a personal identification number (PIN). This number or code is known only to the depositor and the computer, unless the depositor reveals it to others. Federal law requires all automatic tellers to issue receipts.

Illus. 19-6
Automatic tellers dispense cash to users electronically.

Direct Deposits or Withdrawals

You may authorize specific deposits, such as a paycheck or a social security check, to be credited to your account automatically on a regular basis. You can also arrange to have recurring bills, such as insurance premiums and utility bills, paid automatically. Employers may use

EFT to deposit payroll checks directly to banks designated by employees thus eliminating the need to write large numbers of payroll checks each pay period. This service also saves the employee a trip to the bank to make a deposit.

Pay-by-Phone Systems

After preauthorizing your bank to do so, you can call your bank and instruct it to pay certain bills or to transfer funds between accounts. To pay by phone, a Touch-Tone telephone is necessary. You must also provide the bank with your personal identification number (PIN) and an access code. Each pay-by-phone transaction appears on a monthly statement from your bank.

Point-of-Sale Transfers

Point-of-sale transfers let you pay for retail purchases with a debit card. This card is similar to a credit card with one important exception: the money for the purchase is immediately deducted from your bank account and transferred to the store's account. In other words, the amount of the purchase is deducted from the customer's checking account as soon as the customer's identity and the availability of funds is confirmed.

Point-of-sale (POS) terminals permit transfer of amounts from a purchaser's bank account to the store's bank account without the use of a check. The terminal is connected by telephone circuits to the bank's computerized accounting data center. When a customer makes a purchase, the cash register operator inserts the customer's bank-issued debit card into the store terminal. Using a telephone, the clerk dials the bank's computer storage facilities to connect the store terminal to the bank's data center. The clerk then enters the amount of the purchase on the store's terminal keyboard. The customer keys in an individualized code number. The computer responds by authorizing the purchase, deducting the amount from the customer's checking account, and adding it to the merchant's account. Not a single piece of paper changes hands. The customer receives a monthly bank statement that describes checkless transactions in a form similar to a credit card statement.

Rights/Responsibilities

You will encounter EFT in one form or other as you transact routine banking for yourself or your employer. It behooves you to know your rights and responsibilities when handling EFTs. Each time you initiate an EFT at a terminal (automated teller machines or point-of-sale transfers), you get a receipt. Periodic statements must also be issued for all EFTs. Many banks use a single statement system that reports all transactions—deposits, withdrawals, savings, and EFTs—on one form. You have 60 days from the date a problem or error appears on your statement or terminal receipt to notify your bank. If you fail to notify the bank within 60 days, you may find yourself without recourse. Under federal law the bank has no obligation to conduct an investigation if the 60-day deadline is missed.

If you report an error within 60 days, the bank must investigate the problem within 10 business days after notification to tell you the results of the investigation. If the bank needs more time, it may take up to 45 days to complete an investigation. In the meantime, the bank must replace the amount in dispute. The money is then available for the customer's use. It must be paid back to the bank if the investigation reveals that no error was made.

If an EFT card is lost or stolen, notify the issuing bank within two business days. You will then lose no more than $50 if someone else uses your card. If you do not notify the bank within two business days, you may lose as much as $500, if your card is used without your permission. The best way to protect yourself in case your card is lost or stolen is to notify your bank by telephone and to follow up the call with a letter.

When you use EFT, the federal law gives you no right to stop payment. There is one case, however, when you can stop payment. If notice is given to the bank at least three days before a payment is scheduled, preauthorized payments, such as a regularly paid utility bill, can be stopped. This right does not apply to any bills such as loan payments, that you owe your bank.

Smart Cards

Some banks are replacing traditional debit and credit cards with a new kind of computerized card with memory, *a smart card*. A smart card contains a tiny computer chip and is almost fraud proof. Eventually, smart cards will be used to store patients' medical histories, to withdraw money from a bank account, to make retail purchases, and to record insurance information.

Retailers foresee that the smart card will enable a buyer to present a card, containing a preset amount of money, to a cashier. The amount of a purchase is deducted from the card. When the total preset amount in the card's memory is used, the customer takes the card to the bank to have another amount deposited into the card's memory. This system eliminates considerable paperwork, risk, and the time it takes to verify customers' credit cards at checkout counters.

PAYING BILLS

An executive seldom turns over the task of paying personal bills to a new secretary. It is one of the responsibilities that a secretary acquires or assumes over a period of time. First, the secretary may be asked to address envelopes. Then, when rushed, the executive may say, "Will you please write these checks for me." When asked, a secretary should be ready to demonstrate the capability of handling this responsibility. *Bill paying* consists of the following:

1.   Be sure that the bill has been approved for payment. Sometimes charges are made for purchases that have not been received. DO NOT pay a bill until such matters have been cleared with your employer.
2.   Verify each charge and check the computations on each bill.
3.   Fill in the check stub. (Be sure to itemize and identify the payment. Stubs are important for accounting purposes and in preparing income tax returns.)
4.   Make out the check.
5.   Write on the face of the invoice or the statement the date, the number, and the amount of the check.
6.   Address the envelope.
7.   Tear off the invoice or statement stub to be mailed with the check.
8.   Attach the stub from the bill to the check and insert both under the flap of an addressed envelope to present to the executive for signature.

Verifying Bills

The secretary should verify the price, the terms, the extensions, and the additions on all bills. *Invoices* (an itemized list of purchased goods) must be checked against quoted prices and terms or against records of previous prices paid. Monthly *statements* (details of an account showing the amount due at the beginning of the month, purchases and payments made during the month, and the unpaid balance) can be verified by comparison with invoices and sales slips, check stubs, and other records of payments made on the account.

Bills for services, such as utilities, are usually accepted as they are, although the toll statement with a telephone bill is checked very carefully. Explore preauthorized bill payment service, if provided by your bank, to save time in writing checks for utility bills. Before paying bills for professional services, the secretary should obtain the personal approval of the executive.

Credit Card Statements

Rub the identification numbers on all credit cards with a heavy pencil. Lay all cards face down on the glass of a copier with space between them to make a one-page record of all credit cards. On the copy, write the name of the contact you must notify if the card is lost or stolen. File for ready reference.

To avoid carrying large amounts of cash or traveler's checks, many business and professional people use credit cards (such as American Express, Diner's Club, VISA, MasterCard, CHOICE, and Carte Blanche). Credit card statements also are helpful in preparing expense reports and in verifying travel and entertainment expenses for income tax reporting.

When making a purchase with a credit card, the purchaser signs a bill or receipt and receives a copy. A monthly statement for charges made to that card during the month is issued. The executive may delegate the responsibility for checking the monthly credit card statement to the secretary. This requires careful inspection of the signature on each receipt and a comparison of the amount on the enclosed receipt with that on the receipt given at the time of purchase.

Filing Paid Bills

A logical system should be set up for filing paid bills, for they provide the key to canceled checks. If there are only 10 to 20 bills each month, the secretary can place all of them in one file folder. If there are many, an alphabetic file may be set up; or a subject file may be used to keep all utility bills, insurance bills, bills for supplies, and so on together. Whenever a question arises concerning the payment of a bill, the secretary should be able to locate the annotated bill on which the date, the check number, and the amount paid were written. Retrieving the canceled check from the files for evidence should not present a problem.

Making Payments by Other Forms

Although most payments handled by the secretary will probably be made by ordinary check or by electronic fund transfer, one of several special checks or money orders that can be obtained at the bank (usually at a nominal charge) may be used on occasion.

Certified Check. A regular depositor's check that is guaranteed by the bank on which it is drawn is called a *certified check*. To obtain such a check, the secretary takes the employer's personal check to the bank and asks that it be certified. After seeing that sufficient funds are in the account to cover the check, a bank official stamps the check "CERTIFIED," adds an official signature, and immediately charges the account with the amount of the check. An example of a certified check appears in Illus. 19-7.

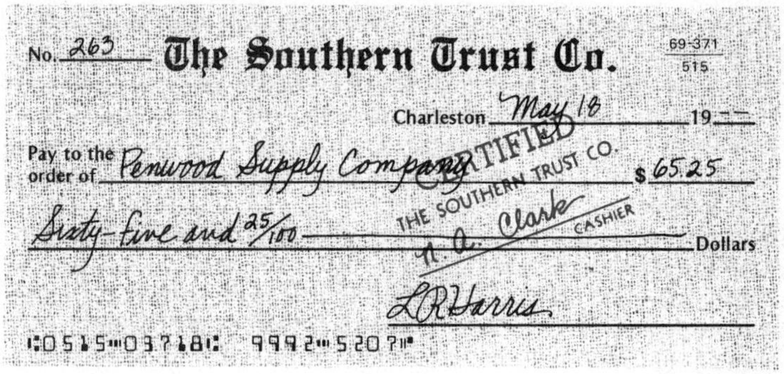

Illus. 19-7
A certified check is guaranteed by the bank on which it is drawn.

Official Check. A check written by the bank on its own funds is known as an *official check*. (It is sometimes known as a *cashier's* or a *treasurer's check*.) Official checks may be used by depositors and by persons who do not have checking accounts. The amount of the check plus a service fee is paid to the bank teller who then writes the check to the specified payee. Recommended practice is to have the official check made payable to the purchaser who must then endorse it in full to the ultimate payee. The canceled check is proof of payment. An example of an official check appears in Illus. 19-8.

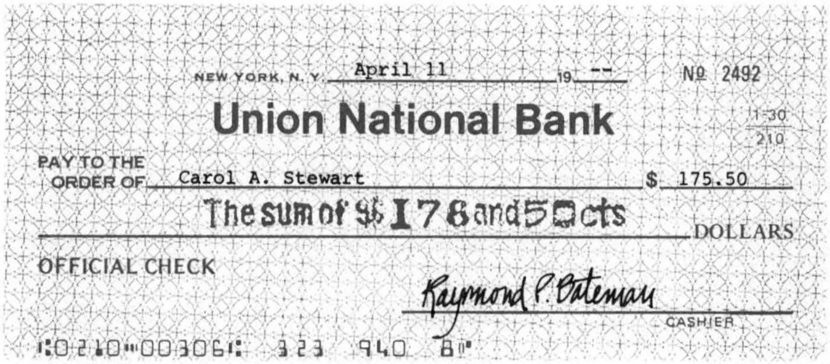

Illus. 19-8
An official check is also known as a cashier's check or a treasurer's check.

Bank Draft. A *bank draft*, as shown in Illus. 19-9, is a check written by the bank on its account in another bank located in the same or in another city. A purchaser pays the bank the exact amount of the draft plus a small fee for issuing the draft. Properly endorsed, the bank draft can then be cashed at the bank on which it is drawn. It differs from an official check only in that the bank draft is drawn by the bank on funds it has on deposit in another bank; an official check is drawn by the cashier on funds in the cashier's own bank.

The bank draft is used primarily for the transfer of large sums from one city to another specific city. The recipient of the draft can then be sure that adequate funds are in hand before taking certain action, such as releasing a shipment of merchandise, signing a deed, or starting work on a contract.

When there is need to transfer funds quickly, the bank communicates with its corresponding bank and directs it to transfer funds to a designated person or company. This process provides a quick, convenient, and safe method of transferring large amounts of money.

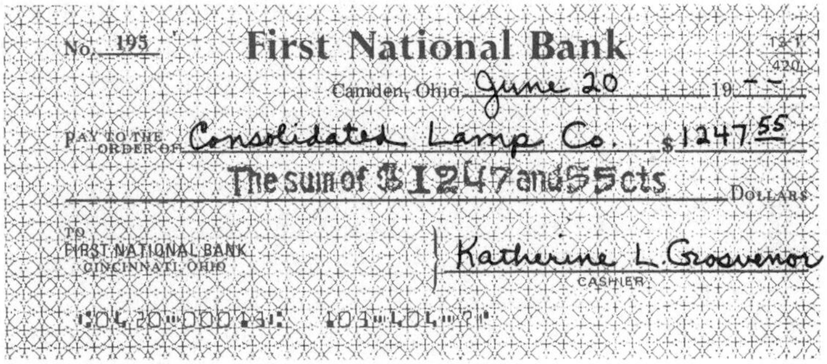

Illus. 19-9
A bank draft is used primarily to transfer large sums of money from one city to another.

Bank Money Order. A *bank money order* (also known as a *personal money order* or a *registered check*) is similar to that issued by the post office. It is sold primarily to persons without checking accounts who wish to send money through the mail. It can normally be cashed at any bank at home or abroad; it is negotiable and transferable by endorsement. The amount of a single bank money order generally cannot exceed $500, but there is no restriction on the number of bank money orders that may be issued to the same person to be sent to the same payee. The purchaser of a bank money order is given a receipt.

The bank money order is more frequently used than an official check or a bank draft when the amount of money transferred is relatively small. It differs from an official check in that the names of both the purchaser and the payee appear on the money order. An example of a bank money order appears in Illus. 19-10.

THE FIRST NATIONAL BANK

50-31
213

SYRACUSE, N. Y. ___May 9___ 19__ ___ NO. 299033

PAY TO THE ORDER OF The Collier Corporation

NOT VALID FOR AMOUNT OVER TWO HUNDRED DOLLARS

The sum of $22 and 50 cts

Paula Dean
SIGNATURE

621 Cary, Syracuse NY
ADDRESS

⑈0213⑈0031⑈0⑈ 136 18904⑈

Illus. 19-10
A bank money order is usually sold to persons without checking accounts.

THE PETTY CASH FUND

Payments of small amounts for postage, bus and taxi fares, collect telegrams, donations, delivery charges, and incidental office supplies are frequently made from a *petty cash fund*. In many instances the fund is entrusted to the secretary.

The size of the fund varies according to the demands made on it. If the fund is large, it should be kept in a locked cash box and stored in the office safe at night. If it is small, it can be kept in a small box or an envelope. In any event, the fund should be locked at night in a desk drawer, a file drawer, or the safe.

The petty cash fund is usually set up with a stipulated amount: $40, for example. Each replenishment of the depleted fund brings it up to $40 again. For example, after disbursements of $38.50 have been made from the fund, there should be $1.50 on hand. A reimbursement check to the petty cash fund would be for $38.50. The employer may prefer to write a check for a full $40 each time or only for the amount of the cash disbursements. A purely personal fund can be any size desired.

In replenishing the petty cash fund, the secretary should prepare a summary report of all disbursements. Each disbursement should have a voucher for accounting purposes. If vouchers are consistently used, the total money in the cash box plus the total of the vouchers should equal the amount of the fund.

Keep a record of vouchers and disbursements. Balance the record whenever the funds get low—or periodically, if the employer prefers. Some of the expenses itemized in a petty cash record may be tax deductible; therefore, file these records and examine them at tax return time. Make petty cash entries at once, for they are difficult to recall later. A practical petty cash voucher is shown in Illus. 19-11.

```
┌─────────────────────────────────────────────────────────────┐
│                                                             │
│   PETTY CASH VOUCHER                            No. 56       │
│                                                             │
│   $ ____10.00____              Date __January 4, 19--__      │
│                                                             │
│   PAID TO ____post office_____   │
│                                                             │
│   FOR _____stamps_____   │
│                                                             │
│                    Received Payment ___RLReed_____    │
│                                                             │
└─────────────────────────────────────────────────────────────┘
```

Illus. 19-11
Stationery stores
sell pads of petty
cash vouchers (or
receipt forms).

THE TREASURER'S REPORT

Although the responsibilities of a treasurer vary in different organizations, the primary responsibility of this officer is to act as banker. This officer's duties, whether as treasurer of a corporation or of a professional organization, are to receive and disburse funds and to report the financial condition of the organization.

Prior to preparation of the treasurer's report, you should file receipts for every payment in chronological order. Pay particular attention in accounting for money received. The treasurer's report consists of a statement of the amount of money on hand at the beginning of a designated period, the amount received during that period, the amount paid out, and the balance at the end of the period. The treasurer's report is prepared for general information. A detailed listing of separate payments is not necessary. Too much detail is useless and makes the report difficult to understand.

Examples of a treasurer's report are shown in Illus. 19-12 and 19-13. These reports can be varied to fit the needs of most organizations. If the list of receipts and expenditures is extremely long, a separate schedule of these can be attached to the report.

The treasurer's report may or may not be signed, but the treasurer's name should appear somewhere on the report. When the treasurer's report is submitted, it is referred to an auditing committee for examination and verification.

TREASURER'S REPORT

As Treasurer of the Oakland Chapter of AMS, I submit the following annual report:

The balance on hand at the beginning of the year was $1,150.76. Money received from all sources totalled $2,450.24. During the year expenses amounted to $1,250.00. The balance at the end of the year was $2,351.00.

An itemized statement of receipts and expenditures is attached.

Respectfully submitted,

Franklin P. Willis
Franklin P. Willis
Treasurer, AMS

Illus. 19-12
A treasurer's report in narrative form outlines an organization's expenses and income in short paragraphs.

CREDIT AND COLLECTION INSTRUMENTS

The secretary's financial responsibilities may extend to such credit and collection instruments as notes and drafts. Because these papers can be transferred or negotiated by the holder to someone else, they (together with checks and other substitutes for cash, such as money orders) are known as *negotiable instruments*. For instruments to be classified as negotiable, the following elements must be present:

1. It must be in writing and signed by the maker or drawer.
2. It must contain an unconditional promise or order to pay a definite sum.
3. It must be payable on demand or at a fixed or determinable future time.
4. It must be payable to the order of the payee or to the bearer.
5. It must identify the maker (person who signed the instrument) with reasonable certainty.

```
                    FINANCIAL REPORT FOR FISCAL YEAR 19--
                        Kelly P. Barnes, Treasurer




RECEIPTS AND DISBURSEMENTS

Beginning Cash Balance . . . . . . . . . . .                     $119,700

Receipts
      Cash Sales . . . . . . . . . . . . . . .   $ 19,200
      Collection on Accounts Receivable  . . .    134,908
      Interest Earned on Investments . . . . .      1,300
            Total Receipts . . . . . . . . . .                    155,408

Total Cash Available . . . . . . . . . . .                      $275,108




Disbursements
      Payments on Purchases of Merchandise . .   $125,740
      Selling Expenses . . . . . . . . . . . .     17,500
      Administrative Expenses . . . . . . . .      17,000
      Taxes . . . . . . . . . . . . . . . . .       1,425
      Miscellaneous Expenses . . . . . . . . .     11,300
            Total Disbursements . . . . . . . .                  $172,965

Ending Cash Balance . . . . . . . . . . . .                     $102,143
```

Illus. 19-13
A treasurer's report
(statement form)
itemizes receipts
and disbursements
in balance sheet
form.

Notes

A *promissory note*, more commonly referred to as a *note*, is a promise by one person (known as the *maker*) to pay a certain sum of money on demand or at a fixed or determinable future date to another person or party (known as the *payee*). A promissory note is shown in Illus. 19-14.

Illus. 19-14
With this
promissory note,
Monica Shaw (the
maker) promises to
pay James Bailey
(the payee) $660 at
the end of four
months.

$660.00 ___ Phoenix, Ariz. August 7 19==
Four months ___ AFTER DATE ___ PROMISE TO PAY TO
THE ORDER OF James Bailey
Six hundred sixty 00/100 ___ DOLLARS
PAYABLE AT Second National Bank
VALUE RECEIVED WITH INTEREST AT 16 %
No. 13 ___ DUE Dec. 7, 19== ___ Monica Shaw

Frequently collateral is requested to pledge the payment of a note. In this case, the instrument is called a *collateral note*. Collateral can be salable securities (stocks, bonds), a real estate mortgage, or anything that represents ownership and is exchangeable. When an obligation is fully paid, the collateral is returned to the borrower. If the note is not paid, the creditor can convert the collateral into cash.

Some notes bear interest paid at maturity when the *face* of the note is due. On a discounted note, the loan-making agency deducts the *interest* in advance (known as the *discount*) from the face of the note. The remainder is called the *proceeds*. For instance, a borrower who receives a three-month discounted note for $2,000 at 12 percent will receive $1,940 (2,000 × .12 ÷ 4 = 60). The full $2,000 must be paid when the note is due.

The amount and the date of a partial payment are written on the back of the note. When a partial payment is made, the secretary should make certain that the payment is recorded on the back of the note, for the note is held by the lender until it is paid in full. If payment is made in full, the endorsed note should be turned over to the secretary. It then becomes a legal record that the obligation has been discharged.

Commercial Drafts

A *commercial draft* is a written order by one person to another to pay a sum of money to a third person. It is generally used as a collection device. In the commercial draft shown in Illus. 19-15, Ankromm and Son owe $539.62 to King and Wilson. King and Wilson give this draft to their bank in Topeka for collection. The bank forwards the draft to its bank in St. Louis, which presents it for payment to Ankromm and Son. When the draft is paid, the proceeds are sent to the Topeka bank and then to King and Wilson.

Illus. 19-15 is a *sight draft*, because it stipulates payment "at sight." A *time draft* is payable at a future time and reads "thirty days after date" or some other stipulated period of time.

Drafts are frequently used as a means of collecting for goods shipped by freight before delivery. The merchandise is shipped on a *bill of lading* (a written account of goods shipped) prepared in triplicate and signed by a freight agent. A draft is attached to the original bill of lading and sent by the seller to the bank in the town of the buyer. When the merchandise arrives, the purchaser pays the draft at the bank, obtains the bill of lading, and then presents the bill of lading to the freight carrier to obtain possession of the goods held at the local freight office.

Illus. 19-15
A sight draft is sometimes used by creditors to collect overdue accounts.

$539.62   Topeka, Kansas,   January 3 19 - -
At sight   PAY TO THE
ORDER OF Ourselves
Five hundred thirty-nine 62/100   DOLLARS
VALUE RECEIVED AND CHARGE TO ACCOUNT OF
TO C.R. Ankromm & Son | King and Wilson
No. 20   St. Louis, Missouri | L.B. King, Secretary

Foreign Remittances

In the past decade, financial transactions on a global basis have increased considerably. The responsibilities for handling such transactions make it essential for the secretary to understand legal restrictions and the available methods for making remittances to foreign countries. When a payment or a remittance is to be made to a person or business firm in a foreign country, currency, money orders, or a foreign bank draft may be used.

Currency. United States currency or foreign currency purchased through your local bank may be sent abroad. Most foreign countries regulate the amount of currency that may be so transferred. Your bank will advise you as to these legal restrictions. Currency payments, of course, should be sent by registered mail. The financial section of major newspapers carries foreign exchange tables that show the value of foreign currency in U.S. dollars and vice versa on a specific day. A telephone call to major banks and travel agencies will provide an answer to most currency conversion questions. You should keep a recent currency conversion table if your job requires receiving or disbursing international currencies.

Money Orders. Either your bank, local post office, Western Union, or an express company can arrange for money to be sent abroad. A money order is generally payable in the currency of the country to which it is sent. These money orders are speedy, but can be expensive.

Foreign Bank Draft. A bank draft payable in a foreign currency can be purchased at your local bank. As with currency, most foreign countries limit the amount of money that may be transferred. The bank arranges for the transfer of the draft, or the purchaser may transfer it by mail or other means. This method of payment or transfer of funds should be used when large amounts are involved.

SUMMARY

The degree of financial responsibility assigned to the secretary depends upon the size of the firm and the personal preferences of the employer. In large companies, special departments are responsible for extending credit, collecting accounts, keeping financial records, and making decisions relating to services offered by financial institutions. On the other hand, a secretary in a small firm, such as a doctor's or a lawyer's office, may be responsible for all functions that relate to that organization's bank accounts. Some top executives expect their secretaries to assist them with personal financial records and banking in addition to company accounts.

Whether the secretary's financial duties are extensive or limited, a basic knowledge of banking practices helps the secretary understand the firm's financial operation. In almost every job, the secretary may be expected to perform some, if not all, of these functions: make bank deposits, write checks, cash checks, pay bills, reconcile bank statements, handle petty cash, record incoming funds, and arrange for foreign remittances. Preparation of a treasurer's report, banking by mail, stopping payment on a check, using proper endorsements, filing canceled checks, using a safe deposit box, handling credit card records, and selecting the proper credit and collection instrument may also be a part of the secretary's duties. An awareness of transactions made possible by new technology and the ability to use efficiently such services as direct deposits and withdrawals, automatic teller machines, point-of-sale transfers, pay-by-phone systems, and other electronic banking services are often required.

A knowledge of financial practices and procedures offers the secretary an opportunity to assume increased responsibilities and to improve career opportunities. Financial records are vital to the survival of every organization. To be entrusted with them is an indication of the employer's confidence in the secretary's ability.

SUGGESTED READINGS

Bowden, Elbert V., and Judith Holbert. *Revolution in Banking*, 2d ed. Englewood Cliffs, NJ: Reston Publishing Co., Inc., 1984.

Jessup, Paul F. *Modern Bank Management*. St. Paul, MN: West Publishing Co., 1980.

Kamerschen, David R. *Money and Banking*, 8th ed. Cincinnati: South-Western Publishing Co., 1984.

QUESTIONS FOR DISCUSSION

1. As Judith Hill was leaving for lunch, her supervisor, Edith Romero, asked her to deposit a customer's check in the bank. Mrs. Romero endorsed the check by writing the company name and her initials on the back of the check. Judith placed the check in her purse. During lunch and before the deposit was made, Judith lost her purse.
   a. What poor business practices were evident in this situation?
   b. Upon discovery of the loss, what should Judith do?
2. Many top level executives expect their secretaries to assist them with their personal financial records and banking. This may include writing checks to pay personal bills, keeping the executive's checking account, keeping records of the executive's investments, and so forth. Is this use of company paid secretarial time on the part of the corporate executive ethical? Is it the secretary's responsibility to conform or to refuse?

3. Your job requires that you accept cash payments and make change for customers. If a customer who made a payment earlier in the day returns to your office telling you that her change was $10 short, what action would you take before returning the money?

4. What is meant by electronic fund transfers? Why has EFT been introduced by banks? What is the bank's responsibility to depositors who use EFT?

5. Your employer asks you to submit a plan for establishing and maintaining a petty cash fund in the office. What major elements would you include in your plan?

6. When a bank draft is purchased, it may be drawn in favor of the person or business to whom payment is being made. It may also be drawn in favor of the person purchasing the draft and endorsed by the purchaser to the creditor. Which do you think is the better method? Why?

7. Explain what shipping and payment procedure would be used to permit a fruit grower in California to receive payment for a rail shipment of fruit at the time of delivery to an Atlanta dealer. The fruit grower wants the Atlanta dealer to know before making payment that the fruit arrives in accordance with the conditions of the order.

8. If necessary, correct the following sentences. Use your Reference Guide to check your answers.
   1. All the documents bear his daughter's-in-law signature.
   2. Its almost too late to issue the notice for a meeting in June.
   3. The singer signed her autograph in both Ruth and Mandy's book.
   4. The project will require three years' work.
   5. All the childrens' accounts were closed before Christmas.

PROBLEMS

1. Your office has a $50 petty cash fund that is stored in a small metal box and locked in a file cabinet at the end of the day. Entries are made in a petty cash book that contains the following columns: Cash Received, Cash Paid, Postage, Office Supplies, Donations, and Miscellaneous. The largest single expenditure permitted from the fund is $5. Prenumbered petty cash vouchers are used. Since you are turning the responsibility for the fund over to an assistant, prepare written directions, specifying details for the following:
   a. Safekeeping the fund
   b. Making payments from the fund
   c. Replenishing the fund

2. Assume that you are completing the year as treasurer of your chapter of Professional Secretaries International. You must submit your annual report to the board of directors at the next meeting. Prepare the report from the following data in statement form:

> You began the year with $522.42 in the bank. Receipts during the year consisted of $860 in dues; dinners, $232; seminar ticket sales, $208.40. Disbursements consisted of: national dues, $516; printing, $46; postage, $7.50; paper and supplies, $25; jewelry, $41.81; dinners, $232; convention expenses, $400.40.

3. The following checks, bills, and coins are to be deposited:

Checks

ABA 43-45	$ 225.80
ABA 18-24	18.50
ABA 63-785	1,346.00
ABA 2-77	7.50

Bills

Five $20 bills
Twelve $10 bills
Thirty-five $5 bills
Sixteen $2 bills
One hundred ten $1 bills

Coins

21 halves
42 quarters
52 dimes
36 nickels
76 pennies

a. Determine the total amount of the deposit.
b. Indicate specifically how the checks, bills, and coins should be prepared for deposit.

4. Today is August 10. Your employer has approved the following bills and has asked you to write checks today:
a. Manhattan Rental Agency for rent on his condo in New York City due August 15. Amount: $1,100.
b. Newtown Life Insurance Agency for premium on his automobile insurance due August 12. Amount: $348.75.
c. Atlas Office Interiors for credenza for his office at home. This bill allows a 5 percent discount if paid by August 10. Amount: $865.00.
d. EXXON for gasoline and automotive service due August 12. Amount: $117.50.

e. Marty's Flower Shoppe for flowers for his daughter's wedding due August 15. Amount: $351.

Your employer's check register shows a balance in his personal account of $2,750. Payday is August 15. Total the bills to see if there is enough money in the checking account to cover them. What recommendations would you make to your employer to prevent an overdraft, if there is not enough money to cover the checks, or to prevent the balance from falling below the $200 minimum.

Chapter 20

Investments and Insurance

As an experienced secretary or administrative assistant, you may be required to maintain and supervise records pertaining to securities, real estate, and insurance. These records are vital to the financial health of your company and are needed to determine property values, income and loss for tax purposes, and for settling insurance claims. Unless your employer's holdings are vast enough to justify the employment of a professional investment counselor, you will need to understand the language of investments and the workings of financial markets.

SECURITIES

A corporation can obtain capital by issuing stock or by borrowing money through bonds. *Stocks* are evidence of ownership in the corporation; *bonds* are evidence of creditorship; that is, of a loan to the corporation.

Stocks

Ownership in a corporation is divided into units known as *shares of stock*. A stockholder is an owner of one or more shares of stock. This ownership is shown by a paper known as a *stock certificate*. The stockholder receives *dividends* in return for an investment in the corporation. Dividends are paid from the earnings of the company either in cash or in additional stock known as a *stock dividend*.

A corporation can issue a designated number of stock shares. The term *authorized shares* refers to the maximum number of shares a corporation can issue. A corporation generally seeks authorization for more shares than it expects to issue. *Issued stock* represents the portion of authorized shares that has been issued and sold to investors.

The remainder, consisting of the difference between authorized and issued stock, is called *unissued stock*.

From time to time a corporation may reacquire its shares from investors. If a corporation acquires stock either by gift, by purchase, or as compensation for certain actions, it is called *treasury stock*. Corporations can eventually either resell treasury shares or retire them.

The number of a corporation's *outstanding shares* equals shares issued less treasury shares. Outstanding shares indicate the available supply of shares in the hands of investors.

Kinds of Stock. Stocks fall into two general classes: *common* and *preferred*. Holders of common stock are usually the only ones who have the right to vote at stockholders' meetings. The rate of dividends paid on common stock is not fixed.

Preferred stock usually has a fixed dividend rate and is senior to common stock in the first payment of dividends and in the first distribution of assets if the company is liquidated. Preferred stock may be *cumulative* or *noncumulative*. With cumulative preferred stock, any unpaid preferred stock dividends accumulate and must be paid before any distribution can be made to holders of common stock. Noncumulative preferred stock does not contain a provision to pay dividends in arrears.

Preferred stock also may be *participating* or *nonparticipating*. It is participating only if the stockholder is entitled to share with the holders of common stock in any additional dividend disbursement after an agreed rate is paid on the common stock.

Some preferred stock is *convertible*; that is, the owner has the privilege of converting it into a specified number of shares of common stock at any time. Most preferred stocks are *callable*; that is, they are redeemable at the option of the issuing corporation at the redemption price specified in the stock certificate.

Stock may be *par value* or *no par value*. *Par value* refers to the value ($1, $5, $10, $100) printed on the stock certificate. This printed value has no significance in determining the market price of the stock, which is measured by the stock's earning power—past, present, and future. Many companies today, therefore, do not print any value on their common stock. It is then known as *no par value* stock.

Stockholders' Meetings. Stockholders' meetings are held annually. Members of the board of directors are elected at this meeting by stockholders present or by proxy. The board, in turn, elects the officers of the company at one of its regular meetings.

A notice of a stockholders' meeting, accompanied by a proxy form and a proxy statement, is sent to each stockholder entitled to vote. The notice gives a description of the business that is to be transacted. A *proxy* is a legal instrument assigning one's voting privilege to a specified person or persons. If directors of the corporation are to be elected, the proxy statement indicates the names of the persons nominated for whom the stockholder's proxy will be voted. The stockholder may vote in person by attending the meeting or vote by mail by signing the proxy.

If the executive usually attends stockholders' meetings, the dates of these meetings should be recorded on the secretary's and the executive's calendars. If the meeting is held out of town, the secretary may also be expected to make travel arrangements. It may also be necessary to request a ticket to the meeting from a broker.

Annual Reports. Most companies send annual and, usually, quarterly, reports to stockholders. Such reports usually include a review of the company's activities and its financial statements. Some executives study these reports carefully and then keep them. If this is your employer's habit, file them with other such reports or in a separate folder for that stock.

Bonds

A *bond* is a certificate containing a written interest-bearing promise to pay a definite sum of money at a specified time and place. Interest due on bonds must be paid to bondholders before stockholders can share in the profits of the company. For this reason, bonds are considered safer investments than stocks. The ownership of bonds does not give the investor voting rights in the company.

There are two general classes of bonds: *coupon bonds* and *registered bonds*. Coupon bonds are payable to the person holding them. If the bond or the interest coupons are lost or stolen, they can be converted into cash by the holder. Coupon bonds, therefore, present a security responsibility to the secretary who is entrusted to care for them. Bonds should be kept in a safe-deposit box.

Coupons representing interest earned are cut from the bonds on or after their due date and presented at a local bank for collection. Some banks make a small charge for this collection service. Bond coupons can be listed on a bank deposit ticket.

Registered bonds are less responsibility for the secretary. Such bonds are registered by the issuing organization which mails the interest and principal payments to registered holders. If the bond is lost, the owner still receives the payments, and the bond certificate can be replaced.

Corporate bonds are usually issued in $5,000 units. The selling price, however, is quoted as a percentage of the par value. Thus, if a $5,000 bond is said to sell at 97⅝, it actually sells at $4881.25; that is, at a discount of 2⅜ ($118.75) from its maturity value.

Interest on bonds issued by a municipality, a state, or certain other political subdivisions is exempt from federal income tax. These bonds are known as *tax-exempt bonds*.

Other types of bonds available to investors include *mortgage bonds*. Mortgage bonds are backed by mortgages on specific properties. A *general mortgage bond* is usually backed by a blanket mortgage on all the fixed capital assets of a corporation. *Convertible bonds* can usually be converted into common stock at a specific price or ratio. They are sometimes convertible to preferred stock or other types of bonds. *Guaranteed bonds* are guaranteed by firms other than the corporation that issues them. Principal (the original amount of money invested), or interest, or both may be included in the guarantee. A *debenture bond* is a promissory note backed solely by the general credit of the issuing company; it is not secured by any specific property. Sometimes debenture bonds are issued with the provision that payment of interest will depend upon earnings. Such bonds are called *income bonds*.

> The best kept secret in the American economy is how it works.
>
> Robert L. Hielbroner

Securities Trading

Most stocks and bonds are purchased and sold through a stock exchange, such as the New York Stock Exchange, the American Stock Exchange (Amex), the Midwest (Chicago) Stock Exchange, the Pacific Coast Stock Exchange, or the Toronto Stock Exchange. A number of small organized exchanges are found in different parts of the country in large cities. On the New York Stock Exchange, only securities listed on the exchange are traded; the American Stock Exchange and other exchanges permit trading in unlisted securities.

Some stocks and bonds are purchased in the *over-the-counter market*. The over-the-counter market is not a place but a method of doing business; that is, transactions are handled privately through a bank, a broker, or a securities dealer and do not go through any of the stock exchanges. A buyer or seller of the security is located, and the sale price is arrived at by negotiation. Most over-the-counter transactions are limited to unlisted securities (stocks and bonds of relatively small local companies that are not listed on an exchange).

Buying and selling stocks and bonds on the stock exchange is handled through a *broker*. Stock certificates sold through brokers are not passed from owner to owner; rather, the seller turns in the certificates to the broker who sends them to a transfer agent for cancellation. The transfer agent employed by the corporation is usually a bank. The transfer agent keeps a record of the specific owners of stock certificates by name and number. The agent fills in a new certificate with the name of the new owner, writes in the number of shares the certificate represents, has it signed and countersigned, and forwards it to the broker for delivery to the new owner or for deposit to the credit of the owner's account at the brokerage firm. Some brokerage firms hold all stocks and bonds owned by an investor and send a statement or inventory of holdings, listing the amounts received as dividends or interest, to clients each month.

A *mutual fund* represents a pool of money contributed by investors and managed by professional money managers. Funds sell shares to investors and use the money raised to purchase securities. Stocks and bonds make up the portfolio of most funds. An individual investor in a mutual fund is offered a chance to own (indirectly) an interest in many companies and many types of securities. Mutual funds are also available to investors who want to purchase specialized securities, such as government bonds, health stocks, or gold stocks.

Shares in most mutual funds may be bought or sold at any time. The price of each share fluctuates daily. The investment is not insured; therefore, it is possible that one could lose money because of fraud, economic upheaval, or mismanagement. However, because mutual fund portfolios are diversified, the risk of a loss is reduced.

Stock Market Information. The financial pages of leading newspapers report daily stock transactions at major exchanges. The number of shares sold and the selling price for all stocks listed and traded that day on each exchange are reported. An example of a stock table appears in Illus. 20-1. Sales and prices of bonds and the share price (or net asset value) of mutual funds are also reported in separate tables.

In addition to the daily stock market report and other financial news that appear in newspapers, information on security prices, trends, and business conditions may be obtained from such sources as *The Wall Street Journal, BusinessWeek, Barron's, Financial World, Forbes, The New York Stock Exchange Monthly Review, American Investor, Moody's Handbooks,* and *The Commercial and Financial Chronicle.* Several large brokerage firms and some banks also publish special reports on securities.

There are a number of investment advisory services. The most widely used services are those offered by Moody's Investors Service and Standard & Poor's Corp. Most of these services analyze the stock market and provide investors with detailed information on companies, stocks to watch, stocks that represent good buys, and stocks to sell.

They also analyze an individual's stock holdings and provide other data that an investor may need. These services are also available from the broker with whom an investor has an account (see also Chapter 16).

19-- High	1 Low	2 Stock	3 P-E Ratio	4 Sales 100s	High	5 Low	6 Close	7 Net Chg.
55 1/2	37 1/4	AbbtLab 1	15	1357	46 1/4	45 1/2	46	- 3/4
53 1/4	36 1/4	AetnaLf pf 2	..	9	48 1/2	48 3/4	48 1/4	- 1/2
46 3/4	26 3/8	Boeing la	10	645	42	40 1/2	41 3/4	+1 3/8
7	5 1/2	CaroPw 1.72b	8	529	22 1/4	22 3/8	22 1/2	- 5/8
14 1/2	10 1/2	CloroxCo .52i	10	352	12 1/2	12 1/8	13 3/8	+ 1/8

NEW YORK STOCK EXCHANGE COMPOSITE TRANSACTION*

Illus. 20-1

1. To date this year, Abbott Laboratories common stock has sold at a high of $55.50 (55½), and at a low of $37.25 (37¼).
2. The rate of annual dividend paid per share based on the last quarterly or semiannual declaration was $1.00. Special and extra dividends are noted by a legend letter. In this illustration, the legend letters should be interpreted in the following manner:

   a—also extra or extras
   b—annual rate plus stock dividend
   i—declared or paid after stock split
   pf—preferred stock

3. The price-earnings ratio of 15 means that the current selling price for Abbott Laboratories stock is 15 times the annual earnings per share.
4. During the day, 135,700 shares of Abbott Laboratories stock were sold.
5. The highest price the stock reached during the day was $46.25; the lowest price was $45.50. (Stock quotations are in eighths of a point [dollar]. Thus, 76⅛ means a price of $76.125 per share.)
6. The last (closing) price for Abbott Laboratories was $46.00.
7. The difference between today's closing price and yesterday's closing price for Abbott Laboratories stock was down ¾ (or down 75 cents). (A plus sign indicates an increase, and a minus sign indicates a decrease.)

Market Averages. A number of stock averages are designed to serve as barometers of the stock market; that is, they indicate whether the market is rising or falling. Probably the best known are the Standard & Poor's Index and the Dow-Jones Averages. The Standard and Poor's Index is based on the price of 500 stocks and is computed hourly each trading day. The Dow-Jones Averages include four separate averages: one for industrial stocks (stocks of industrial corporations), one for rails, one for utilities, and a composite average of 65 stocks intended to measure trends in all divisions of the market. Market averages are published in leading newspapers and are reported on television and radio.

Market Terminology. Learning the language of the investment world requires a special effort. If you are new to the task of handling investments, you may find some terms and phrases puzzling. The following list of standard stock market terminology will assist you in your efforts to handle this aspect of your job efficiently:

A *bear market* is a declining market. A *bear* is someone who believes that the market will decline.

Bid and offer is the price at which a prospective buyer will purchase and the price at which a prospective seller will sell. This quotation involves over-the-counter sales.

Blue-chip stock is the common stock of a company nationally known for high quality, the wide acceptance of its products, service, and its ability to consistently show a profit and to pay dividends in good times and bad. These stocks are relatively high priced and offer low yields (the measure of return in an investment) as compared to other stocks. Bonds issued by blue-chip companies are called *gilt-edged bonds*.

A *bull market* is a rising market. A *bull* is someone who believes that the market will rise.

A *day order* is good only for the day on which it is given. A *GTW Order* is good for this week. A *GTM Order* is good this month. A *GTC Order* (or open order) is good till canceled.

A *discretionary order* is an order that gives the broker the privilege of determining when to execute it.

An *ex-dividend* is the term used when a company declares a dividend to be paid to all stockholders as of a given future date. Stock sold during the intervening period may be sold *ex-dividend*; that is, the *seller*, not the *purchaser*, receives the unpaid declared dividend.

A *limited order* instructs the broker to buy or sell a security at a certain price only. If the transaction cannot be consummated at the designated price, the order is not executed.

A *market order* instructs the broker to buy or sell a security at once. No price is designated and the order is executed "at the market"; that is, at the best price obtainable.

Stocks that are listed on the stock exchanges and traded in 100-share units are called *round lots*. An order for anything less than 100 shares is known as an *odd lot*. A small additional commission is charged for handling *odd lot* transactions.

A *short sale* occurs when an investor sells short; that is, the investor sells securities that she or he does not own in anticipation of buying them later at a lower price. To negotiate the sale, the broker borrows the stocks temporarily.

Stock rights represent a corporation's plans to sell additional stock. Each existing stockholder may be given a stock warrant indicating the number of shares that he or she is entitled to purchase at a designated price, usually slightly below the market price. A stockholder who chooses not to exercise stock purchase rights has the option of selling the rights to another party.

A *stock split* occurs when a company issues to each stockholder a specified number of additional shares for each share the stockholder now owns. For example, in a three-to-two split, the stockholder receives three shares in exchange for each two shares owned. A company may split its stock to lower its market value.

A *stop order* instructs the broker to buy or sell "at the market" whenever a security moves to a specified quotation (price).

The *yield* is the percentage of return for one year on one share of stock computed at the current market price or at the price paid by an owner.

A Brokerage Transaction. To understand the procedure of a brokerage transaction, follow this hypothetical case:

1. The purchaser (or the purchaser's secretary) places an order with a broker to buy 25 shares of U.S. Steel common *at the market* (generally by a telephone call). (The secretary makes a full memorandum of the order. The date, the time, and the order placed are noted. The broker *executes* the order on that date—the trade date.)

2. When the broker makes the purchase through the stock exchange, an invoice (called a *confirmation*) for the purchase of the stock is sent to the buyer. (The invoice for the purchase or sale of securities is called a *confirmation* because the broker is acting as an agent and is confirming by means of the invoice the instructions received. The confirmation lists the name of the stock and description, the number of shares purchased or sold, the price per share, extension, commission charge, tax, postage, and total. The secretary compares the confirmation with the memorandum to make sure the order has been carried out correctly.)

3.   The purchaser or the secretary sends a check to the broker by the settlement date (which is five business days after the trade date).

4.   The broker arranges for the transfer of the stock to the purchaser. (If the executive has the brokerage company retain the stock, the executive's account is credited and the stock is reported on the next monthly inventory statement. The broker may also collect dividends and interest, which are also shown on a detailed monthly report. This simplifies income tax preparation. If the executive retains his or own stock certificates, the certificate is forwarded by registered mail. If delivery is made to the executive, the secretary, upon receipt of the stock, records the stock certificate number on the confirmation and transfers all information from the confirmation to the executive's permanent record. The secretary may attach the confirmation to the stock certificate or file the confirmation chronologically under the broker's name so that it will be available when the stock is sold. The sales confirmation may be filed with the copy of the executive's income tax return.)

Delivery of Securities. When securities held personally by the executive are sold, ordinarily the secretary or a messenger delivers them to the broker's office. Or they are insured and sent with a covering letter describing the securities in full by registered mail. Include the owner's name, the company name, amount, and certificate number for each stock certificate or bond enclosed. Request a return receipt. Keep in mind that stock certificates are valuable and should be treated as such.

Records of Securities. One good rule for the secretary to follow in keeping financial records for securities is to use a separate page or card for each lot. Illus. 20-2 is a card record of Detroit Edison common stock. If your employer's stock holdings are extensive and you have access to a computer, consider storing this data on a computer. It will enable you to update information quickly and to retrieve vital investment data instantly. Otherwise, a separate record card or sheet for stock transactions should be kept for each lot of securities. Purchases and sales are recorded on the front of the card as illustrated. Dividends are recorded on a ruled form on the back of the card. A metal tab can be used to indicate the dates on which to expect dividends. The card should show where the securities are kept. The "where kept" notation is important information that should be recorded for any valuable paper. Papers tucked away in unusual safekeeping spots known only to the owner are often difficult to find in the owner's absence.

JAN	FEB	MAR	APR	MAY	JUN	JUL	AUG	SEPT	OCT	NOV	DEC

(Dividend Date)

STOCK: Detroit Edison, common   DIVIDENDS: Mar., June,
BROKER: Merrill Lynch   Sept., Dec.
FILED: Safe deposit box, City National

Date	Certificate Number	How Acquired	No. of Shares	Cost per Share	Total Cost*
1/18/--	H21601	Purchased	100	14 1/2	1,486.00
5/20/--	H29861	New cert. for H21601 after sale 40 shares	60		
12/4/--	H32504	5% stock dividend	3		

*Includes postage, insurance, and commission.

RECORD OF SALES						
Trading Date	Shares Sold	Selling Price	Gross Amount	Int. or State Tax	Commission Paid	Net Amt. Received
5/20/--	40	16 3/4	670.00	2.43	11.25	656.32

Illus. 20-2
A card record of the purchase and sale of stock must be meticulously maintained.

Stock Certificate Numbers. When all the stock covered by one certificate is sold, the certificate is surrendered to the broker as part of the sale. When only a portion of a block of stock covered by one certificate is sold, the certificate is also turned over to the broker; but the investor receives a new certificate for the unsold shares. This sale requires a change in the certificate number on the stock records. For example, in Illus. 20-2, 40 shares that were sold were from the block of 100 shares covered by Certificate H21601. The new certificate number for the 60 unsold shares is also recorded.

The executive should have at hand a typed alphabetic list of securities (see Illus. 20-3). Usually this list is typed in triplicate: one copy is for the executive's desk, one is for the files, and one is for the secretary's records. Each purchase of stock for a given company made on different days or at different prices should be listed separately. If the employer's securities are stored in a computer and the list is kept current, an up-to-date computer printout can be obtained on request.

Illus. 20-3
Three copies of an
alphabetic list of
securities are
usually kept. In
addition to the
executive's copy
and the secretary's
copy, a file copy is
maintained.

LIST OF SECURITIES (CURRENT AS OF 5/17/--)

Date Purchased	Security	No. of Shares	Price per Share	Total Cost
1/18/82	Johns-Manville	240	13 3/4	$ 3,420.00
8/13/82	Mead Corp. Prf. 2.80	200	20	4,000.00
4/14/82	Pfizer	200	50 3/4	10,150.00

United States Treasury Securities

The United States Treasury raises funds to finance the debt of the federal government by selling securities to the public through twelve Federal Reserve Banks and any of their branches. Treasury securities consist of bills, notes, and bonds. Treasury securities may be purchased at a Federal Reserve Bank without charge. An application to purchase government securities must be accompanied by full payment. For a fee, Treasury securities may also be purchased from commercial banks or other financial institutions or a broker.

Treasury securities are backed by the full taxing power of the federal government; therefore, interest and return of the principal (face value of the security) are guaranteed. Interest earned on Treasury securities is exempt from state and local income taxes but subject to federal income tax.

United States Treasury Bills. A Treasury bill is a short-term security sold at auction on a regular basis by the United States Treasury. Treasury bills mature in 13, 26, or 52 weeks. Bills are sold in minimum amounts of $10,000 and in multiples of $5,000 above the minimum. Purchases are limited to $500,000 for each new offering. Purchasers receive a nonnegotiable receipt instead of an engraved certificate at the time the security is issued. This receipt is evidence of a book entry at the Treasury that establishes an account for the purchaser.

Interest is earned by purchasing Treasury bills at a discount and redeeming them at face value. For example, if your employer purchased a 26-week, $10,000 (face value) bill on June 1 for $9,556.36, the discount would be $443.64. A check for the amount of the discount would be mailed by the Federal Reserve Bank on the date the bills were issued.

Every week on Monday, 13- and 26-week bills are auctioned. The bills are issued on the following Thursday. Fifty-two week bills are offered and issued only once a month. At maturity, the Treasury mails a check for the face value of the bills, unless an automatic reinvestment of the face value at maturity has been requested.

Treasury bills are among the best known and most popular short-term investments for corporate and individual investors. Because of their safety, liquidity, and exemption from state and local income taxes, Treasury bills are frequently included in a company's portfolio of investments.

Treasury Notes and Bonds. Treasury notes and bonds have a longer maturity than Treasury bills. Notes have a fixed maturity of not less than one year and not more than ten years from date of issue. Bonds usually have a fixed maturity of more than ten years. Bonds are available in multiples of $1,000. Previously issued notes must be purchased in the securities market through a broker or a commercial bank. Treasury notes and bonds are issued in registered form. The owner's name appears on the face of the security, and interest is paid only to the registered owner by a United States Treasury check. Treasury notes and bonds pay owners a fixed rate of interest twice a year.

Investment Certificates

Investment certificates provide attractive alternatives for both individual and corporate investors. This form of investment is popular because these certificates are virtually risk free. Investment certificates provide a relatively high rate of return and can be purchased without the payment of fees, commissions, or administrative costs.

Institutions issuing investment certificates usually require that funds remain on deposit for a designated period of time. A substantial penalty is imposed for early withdrawal of the deposit. Interest is usually paid to the investor quarterly, semiannually, or annually. With some certificates, the interest is paid monthly. Once the certificate has been purchased, the rate of interest is fixed until the certificate matures.

A minimum investment ranging from $100 to $10,000 is required by most financial institutions. The minimum required depends upon the type of certificate and the issuing institution.

A negotiable *certificate of deposit* (CD) is a marketable receipt (can be sold to others) for funds that have been deposited in a bank for a specified time. Negotiable CD's are offered by banks in major money centers in denominations ranging from $25,000 to $10,000,000. The original maturity period can range from one to eighteen months, but most have a maturity date of four months or less. Income from negotiable CD's is taxable at all levels of government; the rate of return is similar to that of Treasury bills. When the certificate matures, the owner receives the full amount deposited plus earned interest. Negotiable CD's may be obtained from financial institutions without the cost of a commission. These certificates are low risk, short term, and readily convertible to cash.

REAL ESTATE

A secretary may be assigned tasks related to real estate holdings. These tasks include caring for valuable papers necessary to real estate transactions, doing the banking work, and keeping simple, complete records of income and expenses. Accurate records and a systematic method of following through all real estate transactions prevent costly errors and delays. Should you be responsible for following through on a real estate closing, you should check carefully to see that you have correctly calculated city and county taxes, sales tax, insurance premiums, and commissions. To protect your employer, you should also check carefully all deeds, leases, checks, mortgages, and the like. Keep in mind that every record involving the transfer of real estate is vital to the completion of the transaction.

Buying Property

When real property is purchased, the title of ownership is transferred by means of a properly executed written instrument known as a *deed*. There are two types of deeds: *warranty deeds* and *quitclaim deeds*. In a *warranty deed* the grantor or seller warrants that he or she is the true and lawful owner with full power to convey the property and that the title is free, clear, and unencumbered. In a *quitclaim deed*, the grantor quits claim to the property; that is, the grantor relinquishes claim but does not warrant or guarantee the title.

When a deed is transferred, it must be signed, witnessed, and acknowledged before a notary public. It should be *recorded* on public record at the courthouse in the county where the property is located. Deeds, mortgages, and leases are valuable legal documents and should be kept in a bank safe-deposit box or in a fireproof vault or safe. Other terms frequently used when the title to real estate is transferred include the following:

1.   The *abstract of title* is a history of the transfers of title to a given property briefly stating the parties to and the effect of all deeds, wills, and legal proceedings relating to the land.

2. *Amortization* is a mortgage or loan repayment plan that permits the borrower to retire the principal of the loan through regular payments at stated intervals.

3. *Appurtenances* are rights of way or other types of easements that are properly used with the land, the title to which passes with the land.

4. *Easements* are privileges regarding a special use of another person's property, such as right of way to pass over the land, to use a driveway, or to fish in a stream.

5. *Escrow* is the delivery of a deed or other property to a custodian who in turn makes final delivery to the transferee when specified conditions have been satisfied.

6. *Fixtures* are those articles that are permanently attached to real estate, such as buildings, fences, and the electrical wiring in a building.

7. *Foreclosure proceedings* are legal processes used to satisfy the claim of the lender in case of default in payment of interest or principal on a mortgage.

8. A *junior (second) mortgage* is a mortgage that is subordinate to a prior mortgage.

9. A *land contract* is a method of payment whereby the buyer makes a small down payment and agrees to pay additional amounts for the property at intervals. (The buyer does not get a deed to the property until a substantial amount of the price of the property is paid.)

10. A *mortgage* is a formal written contract that transfers interest in a property as security for the payment of the debt. (Mortgages must be signed, witnessed, and recorded in the public record the same as a deed. The law considers the mortgagor [the borrower] the owner of the property during the period of the loan.)

11. An *option* is an agreement under which an owner of property gives another person the right to buy the property at a fixed price within a specified time.

If your employer invests heavily in real estate, you should be familiar not only with the terminology of real estate transactions, but you should know how to protect your employer's investment as well. Federal law requires the preparation of a *Federal Truth in Lending Statement* to be presented to loan applicants for the purchase of real property. This statement contains considerable detail including the amount of the loan, the amount of the down payment, the amount to be financed, escrow fee, finance charges, annual rate of interest, method of payment, due date of each installment, and security for the loan among other things. This statement, when presented to the loan applicant for signature, indicates that the disclosure statement has been received.

Property Records

Permanent records of property are kept for several reasons: to determine the value of the property, to show outstanding debt, to use in tax reporting, and to use as a basis for setting a satisfactory selling price. A separate record should be kept for each piece of property and should include information similar to that shown in Illus. 20-4.

Illus. 20-4
Keep a property record for each piece of property. At the end of each year, all income and expenses related to each piece of property can be conveniently organized for the preparation of the income tax report.

Type and Location of Property	Commercial Property 127 North Webster Avenue Tucson, AZ 85715-8635
Title in name of Robert C. and Mary K. Folley	
Date Acquired	2/21/--
Purchase Price	$97,500
Mortgage(s)	Main Savings and Loan $40,000 First Federal Bank 5,000
Assessed Evaluation for Taxes	$59,000
Remarks	Deed is filed in home safe

Income from Rentals			Mortgage Payments Interest & Principal			Expenses		
Date	Item	Amount	Date	Item	Amount	Date	Item	Amount
2/10	Rent	510.00	2/28	I+P	310.00	3/10	Taxes	500.00
3/10	Rent	510.00	3/31	I+P	310.00	3/10	Water	48.20
4/10	Rent	510.00	4/30	I+P	310.00	4/16	Plumb.	46.85

Investment Property. Property held for rental income or to be sold at a hoped-for profit is *investment property*. The secretary's employer may own several pieces of investment property, or the business may be employed to manage it for other owners for a fee. Managing property means negotiating with tenants, keeping the building in repair, collecting rents, paying expenses, and so on.

A secretary may prepare *leases* for tenants to sign. Printed lease forms are also available in stationery or legal supply stores. Pertinent facts must be filled in on these leases and signatures affixed. These lease forms should be checked with an attorney to be certain they set forth the exact conditions desired. Illus. 20-5 provides an example of a lease form.

APARTMENT LEASE

Date _February 10, 19—_

PARTIES   _Julia Diaz_   (hereinafter referred to as Lessor) hereby leases to _Henry Nichols_ (hereinafter referred to as Lessee) the following described property:

PREMISES   Apartment No. _3_ at _301 Park Place_ in _Sussex, WI_ for use by resident as a private residence only.

TERM   This lease is for a term commencing on the _1st_ day of _March_ 19—, and ending on the last calendar day of _February_, 19—.

AUTOMATIC RENEWAL   If Lessee or Lessor desires that this lease terminate at the expiration of its term, he or she must give to the other party written notice at least 30 days prior to that date. Failure of either party to give this required notice will automatically renew this lease and all the terms thereof except that the term of the lease will be for one month. This provision is a continuing one and will apply at the expiration of the original term and at the expiration of each subsequent term.

RENT   This lease is made for and in consideration of a monthly rental of _Four Hundred Fifty (450)_ Dollars per month payable in advance on or before the 1st day of each month at _504 Town Line Road_. If the rent is paid by the 5th of the month, Lessee shall be entitled to a deduction of _Ten (10)_ Dollars per month; provided however that any monthly rental payment not received by the 5th of the month shall be considered delinquent. If Lessee pays by check and said check is not honored on presentation for any reason whatsoever, Lessee agrees to pay an additional sum of $10.00 as a penalty.

In the event that the rent is not paid by the 10th of the month, Lessee shall be deemed to be in default; and Lessor shall have the option to cancel this lease effective on midnight of the 14th day of the month. On or before the termination date, Lessor shall deliver written notice of Lessor's election to cancel this lease to Lessee's premises.

Lessor acknowledges receipt from Lessee of the sum of _Four Hundred Forty (450)_ Dollars which is prorated rental for _30_ days from the date of commencement of this lease to the 1st day of the following month.

SECURITY DEPOSIT   Upon execution of this lease contract, Lessee agrees to deposit with Lessor, the receipt of which is hereby acknowledged, the sum of _Two Hundred (200)_ Dollars. This deposit, which is noninterest bearing, is to be held by Lessor as security for the full and faithful performance of all the terms and conditions of this lease. This security deposit is not an advance rental and Lessee may not deduct any portion of the deposit from rent due to Lessor. This security deposit is not to be considered liquidated damages. In the event of forfeiture of the security deposit due to Lessee's failure to fully and faithfully perform all the terms and conditions of the lease, Lessor retains all of his or her other rights and remedies. Lessee does not have the right to cancel this lease and avoid his or her obligations thereunder by forfeiting the said security deposit. Deposit refund will be mailed.

Illus. 20-5
This form could be stored on a disk. The variables, which are handwritten here, could then be keyed in as the lease is played out on the word processor or microcomputer.

Lessee shall be entitled to return of said security deposit within 30 days after the premises have been vacated and inspected by Lessor provided (1) said lease premises are returned to Lessor in as good condition as they were at the time Lessee first occupied premises, subject only to normal wear and tear and (2) after all keys are surrendered to Lessor. Lessor agrees to deliver the premises broom clean and free of trash at the beginning of this lease and Lessee agrees to return same in like condition at the termination of the lease.

Notwithstanding any other provisions expressed or implied herein, it is specifically understood and agreed that the entire security deposit aforesaid shall be automatically forfeited as liquidated damages should Lessee vacate or abandon the premises before the expiration of this lease, except where such abandonment occurs during the last month of the term of the lease, Lessee has paid all rent covering the entire term, and either party has given the other timely written notice that this lease will not be renewed under its renewal provisions.

OCCUPANTS   The leased premises shall be occupied by the following persons only: _Henry Nichols_

PETS   No pets are allowed to live on the premises at any time. However, this provision shall not preclude Lessor from modifying any lease to allow pets by mutual written agreement between Lessor and Lessee.

SUBLEASE   Lessee is not permitted to post any "For Rent" signs or to rent, sublet, or grant use or possession of the leased premises without the written consent of Lessor and then only in accordance with this lease.

DEFAULT OR ABANDONMENT   Should the Lessee fail to pay the rent or any other charges arising under this lease promptly as stipulated, should the premises be abandoned by Lessee, should Lessee begin to remove furniture or any substantial portion of Lessee's personal property to the detriment of Lessor's lien, or should voluntary or involuntary bankruptcy proceedings be commenced by or against Lessee, then in any of said events Lessee shall be ipso facto in default and the rent for the whole of the expired term of the lease together with the attorney's fees shall immediately become due. In the event of such cancellation and eviction, Lessee is obligated to pay any and all rent due and owing through the last day said premises are occupied.

In the event that during the term of this lease, or any renewal hereof, either the real estate taxes or the utility costs, or both, should increase above the amount being paid on the leased premises at the inception of this lease, the Lessee agrees to pay his or her proportionate share of such increase and any successive increases. Such payment or payments by Lessee shall be due monthly as increased rent throughout the remainder of Lessee's occupancy; and all such sums may be withheld from Lessee's security deposit if not fully paid at the time Lessee vacates the premises. A 30 day notice will be given to Lessee before any increase is made.

OTHER CONDITIONS   A temporary visitor is one who inhabits the property for no more than ten (10) days.

_____

Executed in duplicate at _301_ _Park Place_ this _10th_ day of _February_, 19 _--_.

Julia Diaz
Lessor

Henry Nichols
Lessee

The secretary keeps detailed records of income and expenses on each piece of investment property because all income and those deductible expenses must be reported on tax returns. To keep accurate data on each unit, the secretary should follow the plan suggested here:

1. Set up an individual file folder for each rental unit; that is, each suite of offices, each apartment in a building, or each house. Identify each unit on the file folder by number or address. (An alphabetic index of tenants' names and their rental locations makes a helpful cross-reference.) File in this folder everything pertaining to the rental unit, including correspondence, the lease, bills for repairs and improvements, lists of any special fixtures or furniture, and rental amount.
2. Use a miscellaneous folder (or folders) for the building in general to take care of items that cannot be charged to a specific rental unit, such as janitorial service, repairs to the exterior of the building or corridors, taxes, and such.

A record of all receipts and expenses paid can be written directly on each folder, or on a card or sheet filed inside each folder. Preferably such records should be kept on separate sheets in a loose-leaf book where the chance of their being lost is considerably reduced.

Although you might feel that a file folder gives you ready access to information concerning your employer's real estate holdings, storing the information in a word processor or a microcomputer greatly enhances the efficiency of handling such records. By storing the data on a diskette, you eliminate the tedium of updating records manually. All information relating to property can be recorded, stored, updated, retrieved, and printed or displayed on the screen at your workstation. Most large firms with extensive real estate holdings use computers to store property data of all types. Computers allow large quantities of data to be stored in a small space and vital data are instantly available upon request.

Banking money collected from investment property and the payment of bills for such property should be handled carefully. It is extremely important that deposit slips be completed so that every deposit can be identified. Every check stub should be labeled so that charges corresponding to a specific rental unit or building are accurately noted.

Personal Property Records. To provide necessary information in event of death or other contingency, the secretary is often asked to keep a file of the executive's personal property, an inventory of household goods, a description and the location of family jewels and heirlooms, insurance policies, and the names and addresses of certain key people involved in the executive's personal affairs. This information should be placed in sealed envelopes, labeled, and kept in a safe-deposit box or in a fireproof office safe.

Tickler Card File

There are many recurring expenses concerning property. Mortgage payments (usually due monthly), tax payments (due annually or semi-annually), and insurance premiums (due annually) are a few of these recurring expenses. Income property rents are usually due on a certain day each month. To make sure that income is received when due and that recurring expenses are paid on time, tickler cards should be prepared and continually refiled under the next pertinent date. An example of a tickler card for a mortgage payment appears in Illus. 20-6. In addition to interest and mortgage payments, use tickler cards to keep track of the following:

1. *Taxes.* Indicate for each kind of tax payment the kind of tax, the payment date, the amount, to whom to make the check payable, where to send the check, and whether or not a return must accompany the payment.
2. *Insurance premiums.* Indicate the renewal and due dates and the amount of the premium.
3. *Rent receipts.* For each rental unit show the location, the amount of rent, the name and mailing address of the tenant, and any special information regarding collection or interpretation of rent payments.

Illus. 20-6
The tickler card for a monthly mortgage payment identifies the property, the file date, the due date, the amount of the payment, to whom payment is to be made, and where the check is to be sent.

```
File date:  12th of each month

Mortgage payment due:  15th of each month
(Mail check no later than the 12th)

Duplex, 906 Seneca Street

Amount of check:  $225.00

Make check to:  Estate of Frank Foster
Send check to:  Willis and Thompson
                148 Baker Bldg.
                110 W. 7th Street
                Fort Worth, TX  76102-6537

Final payment date:  April 15, 1988
```

In companies where computers are used to store property records, automatic reminders of due dates for mortgages, rents, and taxes are built into the system. In some computerized tickler systems, when rents are due, the computer automatically prints out statements. Such systems also issue checks in payment of taxes and mortgages. All the secretary has to do is mail the forms. Such a system relieves the secretary of dependence upon manual devices for remembering dates. Whatever system is used, the secretary should bear in mind that missing a due date can lead to financial loss, serious inconvenience, or both.

Source Materials

An employer who has extensive real estate holdings or is engaged in the real estate business may subscribe to an information service, such as the Mortgage and Real Estate Executive's Report. There are also a number of periodicals that specialize in providing current information on real estate. *Real Estate Weekly*, *The Real Estate Review and Mortgage Banking Monthly*, *National Real Estate Investor*, *Appraisal Journal*, *Journal of Property Management*, and *Construction Labor Report* are titles of periodicals of particular interest to real estate executives.

INSURANCE

Insurance guarantees the protection and safety of persons and property. There are many different kinds of insurance, as Illus. 20-7 shows. A secretary may have definite responsibilities for handling an employer's insurance. These responsibilities go beyond those assumed by the employer's insurance agent or broker and include the following:

1. Checking policies when received to determine if coverage is as agreed upon and conforms to the law (in some instances)
2. Maintaining adequate records of
   a. Payments of premiums
   b. Follow-up of expirations
   c. A summary record of insurance coverage program
3. Canceling policies when necessary
4. Reporting claims
5. Storing policies and related documents in a safe place

Premium Payments and Renewals

Insurance premiums are payable in advance. Those on property insurance are usually paid annually or for a term of three to five years.

TYPES OF INSURANCE

Personal insurance protects against the results of illness, accident, and loss of income because of illness, accident, or death.

Life:	Universal life	Health:	Hospital care
	Limited payment life		Medical fees
	Ordinary life		Surgical fees
	Term		Loss of income

Property insurance protects the insured from financial loss resulting from damage to property.

Automobile collision
Burglary and employee
  theft
Fire
Fire—extended
  coverage—windstorm,
  lightning, riot, strike
  violence, smoke
  damage, falling aircraft
  and vehicle damage,
  most explosions
Plate glass
Standard boiler
Valuable papers
Vandalism

Marine: Barratry
Burning
Collision
Mutiny
Piracy
Sinking
Standing

Liability insurance (casualty) protects the insured against claim of other people if injury or property damage is done to others.

Automobile liability
Bailee insurance
Elevator insurance
Libel and slander

Premise and operations liability
Public liability
Product insurance
Workers' compensation

Credit, fidelity, and surety insurance protects against losses from bad accounts (credit), employee embezzlement (fidelity), and title (surety).

Illus. 20-7
Types of insurance
are varied and
numerous.

Premiums on life insurance may be paid annually or in monthly, quarterly, or semiannual installments.

Many life insurance policies allow a grace period of 28 to 31 days in making premium payments. If the premium is due and payable on August 16, payment of the premium may be made any time before September 16. If the premium notice does not specify a grace period, the secretary should ask the insurance company if a grace period is allowed.

All insurance-related correspondence should include the *policy number*. If the correspondence relates to a claim, include the *claim number*.

Checks in payment of premiums must be drawn in sufficient time to have them signed and sent to the insurance company or agent before the expiration date. It is the secretary's responsibility to avoid any insurance policy lapse caused by failure to make a premium payment.

In addition to seeing that premiums are paid, the secretary should also arrange for the cancellation of policies when protection is no longer needed. A policy can be canceled by telling the insurance company or agent of the cancellation and returning the policy. The premium for the unexpired period of the policy is refundable. The secretary should place a follow-up in the tickler file to check on the receipt of a premium refund.

Insurance Records

A beginning secretary may be fortunate enough to inherit a summary of the employer's personal insurance commitments. More likely, however, no records will be available. If necessary, compile a summary from insurance policies on file in the office and from notices of premiums due as they are received in the mail.

Methods of keeping insurance records vary, but in general these records consist of an insurance register and a premium payment reminder, usually a tickler card. The register should contain information similar to that shown in Illus. 20-8. Some secretaries record insurance policies on separate sheets in a small loose-leaf notebook; thus,

Illus. 20-8
Columns to provide appropriate information can be added to the insurance register as needed. When a policy expires, draw a line through the description to indicate that the policy is no longer in force.

INSURANCE REGISTER

Company and Name of Agent	Policy No.	Type and Amount	Date Issued	Amt. of Premium	Date Due	Grace Period
N.Y. Life V. Getty	29 22 84	Ord. Life on Mr. B. $50,000	3/2/55	$563.00 Semian	2/2 8/2	30-day
N.Y. Life V. Getty	37 86 21	Term $25,000 on Mrs. B.	1/9/68	$107.25 Annual	5/6	30-day
Conn. Gen. T. Ramsey	H261 162	Fire on household goods $25,000	1/12/72	$249.00 Annual	12/12	

when a policy is no longer in force, the sheet can be removed. Others prefer to use a separate register for each type of insurance (life, property, and liability) or to store them in a computer database or on a diskette. The executive's personal insurance and that of the business should be kept in separate registers.

Use a separate tickler card or set up a computer file for each policy according to premium payment date. This helps avoid the lapse of a policy or a penalty for late payment. Illus. 20-9 shows an example of the type of information that should be included on a tickler card for insurance premiums.

Illus. 20-9
File a card for each insurance policy in a tickler file. It provides a convenient record and serves as a reminder for renewals and premium payments.

```
File Date:  December 26, 19 —

Expiration Date:  January 4 each year

Type:  Fire insurance on office furniture

Amount:  $15,000

With:  Mutual Insurance Co.
       5352 First St., City

Policy No.:  X438832
Date of Issue:  January 5 each year
Premium:  $117.20
Policy Filed:  First National Bank
```

Property Inventory

The importance of keeping an up-to-date property inventory can be fully appreciated only by someone who has experienced a fire or burglary loss. To present a claim for a loss, the insured must furnish a complete inventory of the destroyed, lost, damaged, and undamaged property with cost and actual cash value. This is difficult to do after the loss has taken place. A property inventory also serves a second important purpose. It shows how much insurance should be carried. Property values change; and unless the inventory is updated periodically, property may be overinsured or underinsured.

The secretary in a small office should assume the responsibility for compiling an inventory of the furniture and equipment in the office. In addition, the executive should be encouraged to provide details for an inventory of furniture and valuables at home. All inventories should be periodically updated. A computerized inventory is easy to update. Photographs should be stored with an inventory to assist in the claims settlement in case of loss.

Storage of Policies and Inventory Records

Since insurance policies must be examined occasionally for data on coverage, beneficiaries, rates, cash value, endorsements, and the like, the policies should be readily available in a safe place. If the policies are kept in a file, you may find it convenient to remove them from their protective envelopes and place each policy in a separate folder. Label the front of the folder with the name, address, and telephone number of the agent and the policy number. This system makes it possible to file with each policy any important correspondence, itemized lists of property covered, endorsements, and other pertinent data that affect the conditions of the insurance contract. When insurance policies are stored in the office, there is always the possibility of their loss by fire. As a precaution, type a list of the policy numbers, insuring company, coverage, and amount. Your employer should store this list in a safe at home. Thus, if office records are destroyed, they can be reconstructed from this list.

Since an insurance policy *is* a contract, discard it when it has expired to keep your files cleared. First, however, call or write the agent to make certain that no claim on the policy is pending and that it has no continuing value.

Fidelity Bonds

A *fidelity bond* is insurance on an employee's honesty. Most employers carry this insurance on employees who handle large sums of money. The bonding company investigates the employee's character and the supervisory and control methods in force in the employer's business. No bond is sold if the applicant's character is questionable or if office conditions make it easy to embezzle company funds.

Blanket fidelity bonds covering all employees are bought by banks and other financial institutions. They protect against losses by embezzlement, robbery, forgery, and so on.

To be asked to take out a fidelity bond is not a bad reflection on your character. Actually it indicates that you are considered competent to be entrusted with company funds.

Action in Emergency

When disaster strikes, you have an opportunity to prove that you are a coolheaded, responsible person who can think and act quickly. Others may be so excited and involved in the emergency that they fail to think of procedures. Insurance companies make these suggestions:

> After a fire, as soon as the situation is under control, notify the insurance company immediately by phone and confirm the call by letter. The insurance company may be able to have an inspector on the scene to witness the damage and save a lot of paperwork later on.

> Immediately report to the police any losses by theft.

> Keep accurate and separate records for cleanup, repairs, and charges made by outside contractors. These charges become part of the insurance claim.

> When an accident occurs, interview witnesses on the spot. Signed statements carry much weight and refresh memories in settling claims. If possible, take pictures.

WHERE-KEPT FILE

In the event of the sudden death of an executive, the family will need certain financial information immediately. The secretary can be of great assistance in such an emergency, if a folder containing up-to-date information has been maintained. The following information might be included in such a folder:

> *Bank Accounts*—the name and address of each bank in which an account is kept, the type of account, the exact name of account, and the name of bank contact (if the executive has one)
>
> *Birth Certificate*—where it can be found
>
> *Business Interests*—list of the executive's business interests
>
> *Combination to company safe or vault*
>
> *Credit Cards*—record of names and account numbers
>
> *Income Tax Record*—where past returns are filed; the name and address of the tax consultant
>
> *Insurance Policies*—location of insurance records (If these records do not contain detailed information on life, health and accident, hospitalization, and medical insurance policies, the information should be placed in the folder. The name and address of the insurance adviser should be filed also.)

Real Estate Investments—location of detailed property records

Passport—where it can be found

Safe-Deposit Box—the name of the bank, the box number, and location of key

Social Security—the social security number

Stocks and Bonds—location of detailed investment records

Tax Accountant—name

Will—location of the original and copies of the will; date of the latest will; name of attorney who prepared the will; executor's name and address

ADMINISTRATIVE FUNCTIONS

The secretary may be expected to perform a number of administrative functions related to the company's and the executive's property, investments, and insurance coverage. The college-trained secretary has a background of courses in economics, accounting, business law, and, in some cases, real estate and insurance. All these courses contribute to a secretary's competency. You may be asked to do the following:

1. Prepare a prospectus on stocks that are under consideration for investment. This activity involves checking investment service reports to gather data on products, past performance, background of company officials, forecasts for the area and for the company, comparison with competitors, and so forth. Such data are also available in the business section of a public library and in special libraries.

2. Update the investment portfolio of the company or of the executive. The updating process involves analyzing the rate of yield on each investment, profit trends, and the outlook for the company. For some classes of stock, it may be necessary to prepare charts showing fluctuations in the market and to update them at regular intervals.

3. Supervise and follow through on repairs and improvements made to investment property. Frequent visits to the location of the property and careful study of repair and construction contracts are necessary.

4. Handle the details related to the sale or purchase of real estate. This activity involves such details as having the title searched, obtaining title insurance, and processing and recording the deed.

5. Review at regular intervals the insurance policies in force and arrange for revision in insurance coverage in keeping with changing values of property. The responsibility includes canceling unneeded policies and being alert to new insurance needs.

6. Process an insurance claim. This responsibility involves compiling the records necessary to support a claim including cost records, appraisal of loss, and proof of loss.

SUMMARY

Accurate records of all securities, real estate, and insurance transactions are extremely important. Although the services of a realtor, an insurance agent, and a stockbroker may be used, the secretary may also keep records on property income, insurance coverage, and stock dividends.

In order for the secretary to perform financial functions effectively an understanding of the different kinds of stocks, bonds, and other securities held by the employer is necessary. Knowing how to prepare for stockholders' meetings and understanding the operations of securities markets is also essential. The ability to read and understand financial periodicals and stock quotations, trends, and business conditions depends upon the secretary's awareness of market terminology and the procedures of brokerage transactions. Keeping records either manually or on a computer are necessary to determine which investments— stocks, bonds, mutual funds, Treasury notes, bonds and bills, or savings certificates—represent the most profitable investment.

A secretary may also be commissioned to perform tasks related to the executive's real estate holdings. Caring for valuable papers necessary to real estate transactions, doing banking work, and keeping accurate, complete records of income and expenses are a few of the tasks the secretary may regularly execute. A knowledge of legal terms, forms, and procedures frequently used in real estate transactions helps the secretary handle these duties.

The insurance portfolio of an executive usually includes several types of insurance and may involve a number of policies. Accurate records are required to ensure that premiums are paid on time to avoid lapsing policies. The executive may delegate to the secretary the responsibility for canceling policies and reporting claims.

The secretary may be asked to take out a fidelity bond, if large amounts of money are handled on the job. Fidelity insurance is not a negative reflection on the character of the secretary. Rather, it indicates the secretary's competence to handle financial matters.

Should an emergency occur, the secretary should know what action to take and where financial documents are kept. To provide quick access to the executive's financial records, the secretary should keep an up-to-date folder of essential information concerning the employer's bank accounts, birth certificate, credit cards, safe combination, insurance policies, and the like.

The secretary may also be expected to perform a number of administrative functions related to the property, investments, and the insurance coverage of the company and the executive. Examples of these administrative duties include updating investment portfolios, preparing an investment prospectus, following through on a real estate closing, and processing insurance claims.

SUGGESTED READINGS

Greene, Mark R., and James S. Trieschmann. *Risk and Insurance*, 6th ed. Cincinnati: South-Western Publishing Company, 1984.

Insurance Information Institute, 110 William Street, New York, NY 10038, makes various publications available to educators. (Write for information.)

Unger, M. A., and George R. Karvel. *Real Estate*, Principles and Practices, 7th ed. Cincinnati: South-Western Publishing Company, 1983.

The Wall Street Journal, The National Observer, Barron's, and *Changing Times* all contain articles of significance to investors.

QUESTIONS FOR DISCUSSION

1. A secretary whose employer invests in securities must know a number of stock market terms. What does each of the following terms mean? (Refer to outside sources for the meanings of terms with which you are not familiar.)

bear market	market value
blue-chip stocks	mutual fund
book value	option
bull market	over-the-counter
ex-dividend	rails
growth stocks	sleeper
industrials	stock dividend
investment companies	stock split
margin	utilities

2. If a stockholder is dissatisfied with the way a corporation is being managed, what can be done?

3. Assume that you are treasurer of a professional organization that has accumulated $18,000 in a checking account. This amount represents a ten-year surplus of funds. Keep in mind that approximately $5,300 is required for annual operation, that your chapter will host a national convention in 18 months, and that funds must be withdrawn in advance to meet convention expenses.

What would you suggest to the board of directors as a good investment?

4. Cite three major reasons for investing in Treasury bills rather than in common stocks.

5. Your employer is considering an investment in Xerox Corp. You are asked to compile a report on the stock. What type of information would you include in the report? Indicate your information sources.

6. In addition to stock prices, what information does the financial section of the newspaper contain? Would you recommend that a secretary read this section regularly?

7. In the event of fire or theft, all financial records (including stock certificates, bonds, and insurance policies) may be lost. What precautions should a secretary take or suggest to the employer that will minimize such losses?

8. An owner of a small grocery store with six employees wishes to be protected against all possible insurable losses. Which types of insurance should be obtained? Include the building in which the store is located.

9. When the employer's automobile was involved in an accident, it was discovered that the insurance policy had lapsed because of nonpayment of premiums. The employer was extremely critical of the secretary. The secretary's defense was that the premium notices and follow-ups had been placed on the employer's desk. Furthermore, this was personal business and the employer's failure to act was not the secretary's responsibility. Do you agree with the secretary's position?

10. Your employer invests heavily in real estate and has given you complete charge of the collection of rent and the disbursement of funds for expenses related to the operation of various properties. You have been asked to complete the necessary forms for an application for a fidelity bond. What would be your reaction to such a request?

11. Convert these Roman numerals to Arabic ones. Consult the Reference Guide to verify your answers to the following:
    a. On a church corner stone: "Erected A.D. MCCMLXXVIII."
    b. The new shuttle will be named "Spartacus MM."
    c. The old certificate was dated "MCXIII."
    d. The bonds were issued in lots of "X."
    e. Write the following years in Roman numerals: 1930, 1978, current year.
    f. Show an easier-to-read way to write the following amounts: $5,800,000; 7,600,000,000.

PROBLEMS

1. Your employer owns all the following securities:
   200 shares of American Natural Resources, common (ANatR)
   100 shares of Coca Cola, common (CocaCol)
   75 shares of Consolidated Edison, 5% preferred, (ConE pf 5)
   5 bonds of New York Telephone (NY Tel 4½s 91)
   200 shares of Standard Oil of Indiana (StOInd)
   500 shares of Union Oil of Canada (Union Oil)
   a. Prepare a report showing the current market value of your employer's security holdings. (Use the closing price of the security on the date of the report.)
   b. Your employer purchased the shares of American Natural Resources stock at $25. A quarterly dividend of 66 cents per share is declared. Determine the rate of yield on the investment and the rate of yield at the current market price.

2. Your employer owns stock and carries several insurance policies. The insurance policies are on the employer's spouse, son, home, and automobile. You decide to set up a tickler file to keep track of the employer's stocks and insurance policies. Make a list of the type of information you would include on the card about each.
   a. Security
   b. Insurance policy

3. Your employer owns a professional building valued at $220,000. The building houses 18 offices. Six offices rent for $600 a month, ten for $500, and two for $350. All of the offices were rented throughout the year except four of the $600 offices, which were vacant three months while being redecorated. The management fee is 6 percent of the rental income. The following additional expenses were incurred during the year to operate the building:

repairs	$13,835
janitorial and maintenance service	980 per month
supplies	2,400
utilities	4,400
taxes	9,860
redecoration	11,250
miscellaneous expenses	975

   Prepare a report showing the income, expenses, and net income for the year and the annual percentage of return on the investment for this building.

4. On a sheet of paper construct a form on which you can conveniently record income (as it is received) and expenses (as they are paid out) during the year for the operation of the building in Problem 3.

Chapter 21

Payroll and Tax Records

Payroll work in many firms has been computerized. In large companies, a special payroll department handles much of this work; nevertheless, the secretary is often responsible for input to the payroll system. The extent of your payroll responsibilities, therefore, depends on the size and function of the office in which you work.

If your responsibilities include payroll work, you should be familiar with the laws governing payroll records, deductions from gross pay, and minimum wage regulations. Payroll functions must comply with federal and state legislation; therefore, extreme accuracy is required.

Whether or not your work includes payroll responsibilities, your employer may depend on you to assist in preparing annual income tax returns. This does not mean that you must be a tax expert. It does mean, however, that throughout the year you should collect pertinent income tax data so that they are available at tax time.

PAYROLL PROCEDURES

One of the most demanding responsibilities of a secretary in charge of payroll is the maintenance of essential pay records. These records are necessary to determine pensions, vacations, seniority, eligibility for company benefits, wage and salary increases, promotions, and employment references. They also enable the executive to determine when to hold performance reviews and which employees to transfer or dismiss. In addition to maintaining these vital records, you should understand the forms and reports required by the Federal Insurance Contributions Act (Social Security) and the Fair Labor Standards Act as well as pertinent local legislation.

It is the secretary's responsibility to keep all payroll information confidential. From the calculation of the first time card to the writing of the payroll check, payroll facts must be protected. Computation sheets, carbon paper, and one-use ribbons must be destroyed to keep inquisitive persons from gaining payroll information and damaging morale. No matter how tempting, the professional secretary never discusses payroll information and is adept at dealing with co-workers who persist in inquiring about the income of others. If interrupted while working on the payroll, never leave your workstation until you have placed all confidential information in a locked drawer.

Fair Labor Standards Act

There are primarily two classes of remuneration: *wages* at a rate per hour and *salaries* at a rate per week or month. Persons receiving wages are usually paid only for the hours they work; salaried personnel are usually paid for the full pay period even though they may be absent from work for brief periods. To differentiate, employees are called *hourly or salaried*. Office employees are frequently paid salaries, although paying office employees on an hourly basis is also common.

Most hourly employees come under the provisions of the *Fair Labor Standards Act*. This act sets a minimum hourly wage and requires each employer to keep a record of the hours worked by each hourly employee. Also, each hourly employee must be paid at least $1\frac{1}{2}$ times the regular hourly rate for all hours worked in excess of 40. (For example, an employee who makes $10 an hour must be paid $15 an hour for overtime.) Salaried employees are excluded from the provisions of the Fair Labor Standards Act. Some companies pay overtime for all work in excess of a specific number of hours worked per day. In other companies, no overtime is paid salaried workers, but compensatory time off is given instead.

The Fair Labor Standards Act does not require the filing of overtime reports to any government office, but records must be kept on file for three years on hourly (or nonexempt) employees for perusal any time a government examiner chooses to look them over. Detailed information about this legislation may be obtained from the nearest office of the Wage and Hour Division, Department of Labor.

Social Security

In 1935, Congress passed the Social Security Act to provide income when earnings are reduced because of retirement, disability, or death. Social security is a tax based on earnings and, as such, represents a payroll deduction. Since 1935, the Social Security Act has been amended several times.

Under the social security system most business, farm, and household employees and self-employed persons receive an income in old age and survivor benefits in event of death. Social security also provides a nationwide system of unemployment insurance and hospital and medical insurance benefits (Medicare) for persons of age 65 or over.

To cover social security benefits, both employees and employers are taxed in equal amounts. Medical insurance (for persons of age 65 or over) is optional and is financed jointly by contributions from the retired insured person and from the federal government.

Social Security Numbers. Each employer and employee must obtain a social security number for government and accounting purposes. The number on your card is used to keep a record of your earnings. An employer's social security number is called an *identification number.*

To obtain a social security number, file an application with the nearest social security office or with the post office. You will receive a card stamped with your number. If the card is lost, a duplicate can be obtained. If you change your name or need to make other changes, contact the Social Security Administration. The secretary may find it convenient to have the following social security forms on hand:

> Application for a Social Security Number (or Replacement of Lost Card)
> Request for Change in Social Security Records
> Request for Statement of Earnings

The Social Security Administration recommends that each employee request a statement of earnings every three years to make sure that individual earnings have been reported properly. This information can be obtained by sending a signed letter with your date of birth and social security number to or by filing Form SSA-7004-PC with the Social Security Administration, P.O. Box 57, Baltimore, MD 21203. A post card on which the postage is prepaid is also available for this purpose at any social security office.

FICA (Federal Insurance Contributions Act) Tax Deductions. Amounts withheld from employees' earnings (for social security) under this act are based on a percentage of earned wages. For the past few years, this percentage and the maximum wage base against which the FICA tax is applied have increased. Under the Social Security Act both the employer and the employee pay *FICA taxes* at the same rate. The present tax rates and those scheduled for the future (subject to change by Congress) are shown below:

PRESENT AND FUTURE FICA TAX RATES (PERCENTAGES)

Year	Employee	Employer	Self-Employed	Wage Base+
1985	7.05	7.05	14.10	39,600
1986	7.15	7.15	14.30	42,000
1987	7.15	7.15	14.30*	45,000*

*Estimated
+ Maximum earnings subject to FICA tax.

If you earned $45,000 in 1985, your deductions for social security ended when your salary reached $39,600, the wage base for that year. In other words, you earned $5,400 on which no social security tax was levied.

FICA tax is deducted from an employee's wage each payday; these amounts are accumulated and forwarded together with the employer's FICA tax payments to the Internal Revenue Service Center for the region. To illustrate, assume that an employee earns $200 a week and is paid at the end of each week. At the rate of 7.15 percent, $14.30 would be deducted from the employee's pay and the employer would contribute an equal amount. At the end of the quarter (13 weeks), the employer would remit $371.80 to the government.

Self-employed persons (farmers, architects, and contractors, for example) contribute to social security at a higher rate than other wage earners because they are, in effect, employers and employees. Self-employed persons pay their FICA tax simultaneously with their income tax.

Unemployment Compensation Tax

Employers are subject to an unemployment tax. This tax provides funds from which unemployment compensation can be paid to unemployed workers. In most states, unemployment taxes are only paid by the employer. The employer must pay both a federal tax and a state tax to provide funds for unemployment compensation. The state tax rate varies from state to state, but the federal portion of the tax is calculated at 0.80 percent on a wage base ($7,000 in 1984) paid to each employee per calendar year.

In states where an unemployment tax is levied on employees as well as employers, it is deducted by the employer from the employee's wages. The amounts deducted from employees' pay and the employer's contribution are submitted to the state on a quarterly basis. Special forms are used to report these contributions.

Income Tax Deductions

The federal government requires employers to withhold an advance payment on income tax from an employee's wages. Amounts withheld are remitted to the regional Internal Revenue Service Center at the same time FICA taxes are paid. The term "wages" incorporates wages, salaries, commissions, bonuses, and vacation allowances. The following forms are needed for income tax deduction purposes:

Form W-2	Wage and Tax Statement
Form W-3	Transmittal of Income and Tax Statements
Form W-4	Employee's Withholding Allowance Certificate
Form 501	Federal Tax Deposit
Form 940	Employer's Annual Federal Unemployment Tax Return
Form 941	Employer's Quarterly Federal Tax Return
Form 8027	Employer's Information Return on Tip Income and Tip Allocation
Form 1099 MISC	Miscellaneous Income (This form is used to report payments of $600 or more per calendar year to people not treated as employees—consultants, subcontractors, and the like—for services performed.)

The amount of income tax withheld depends on earnings and the number of personal exemptions the taxpayer claims. Each employee must file an Employee's Withholding Allowance Certificate (Form W-4) with the employer immediately upon reporting for work to claim exemptions. In addition to one personal allowance, the following exemptions, subject to revision, may be claimed:

1. An allowance for a spouse (unless the spouse claims his or her own exemption)
2. An allowance for each dependent (unless the employee's spouse claims them)
3. An allowance if the taxpayer or spouse is 65 or older or blind

The amount of tax withheld is then computed from a table provided by the Internal Revenue Service.

A number of cities and states tax personal income. The percentage of deduction and the form of payment vary. One city may have the employer deduct 1 percent from every payroll check issued and remit these deductions at the end of each quarter. Some states and cities require individuals to file annual income tax returns.

Other Payroll Deductions

In addition to the deductions required by federal and state legislation, other payroll deductions for hospital care insurance (hospitalization), group insurance premiums, stock and bond purchases, and such may be made. In most firms, these deductions are voluntary, and usually the authorization for these deductions may be canceled by the employee at any time.

Most paychecks include an itemized listing of all deductions made from the employee's wage. This information is usually provided on a stub attached to the check which may be removed and retained by the employee when the check is cashed. At the end of each year, the employer is required to furnish each employee with a Wage and Tax Statement (Form W-2) that shows an employee's total earnings and tax deductions. One copy of Form W-2 must be attached to the individual's income tax return form.

Time Records

Some hourly workers and some salaried workers use a time clock to punch in and out each time they enter and leave their places of employment. At the end of the payroll period, cards are collected and wages are computed from the time clock stampings. Illus. 21-1 is an example of a time card.

Instead of using a time clock, salaried employees may sign in and out, or the secretary may be responsible for checking each person in and out daily on a time sheet. Time records are not always necessary for computing salaries, but such records may be the basis of paying overtime earnings or balancing compensatory time off with overtime worked. There are various reports, however, that require records of the overtime and the compensatory time off of salaried employees.

SOC. SEC. NO.	696-44-2878			
			PAY PERIOD ENDING	4/30/--
CLOCK NO.	12			
NAME	Nancy Daniels		WITHHOLDING TAX EXEMPTIONS	1

REG. HOURS	RATE	AMOUNT	F.I.C.A. TAX	TOTAL EARNINGS
35½	4.10	145.55	9.95	170.15
O.T. HOURS	RATE	AMOUNT	INC. TAX WITH.	TOTAL DEDUCTIONS
4	6.15	24.60	26.80	40.60
TOTAL HRS.		AMOUNT	GROUP INS.	NET PAY
39½			.50	129.55
			HOSP. 3.35	
			OTHER	

Day							TOTAL Hours
1	8⁰⁴	12⁰¹	12⁴⁸	4³²			7¼
2	7⁵⁴	12⁰²	12⁵²	3⁵⁸			6¾
3	7⁵⁸	11³⁰	12⁵⁴	4³⁶			7
4	7⁵⁹	12⁰³	1²⁸	4³¹			7
5	7⁴⁶	12⁰²	12⁴⁹	4³⁰	5⁰⁰	9⁰⁵	11½
6							
7							
	IN	OUT	IN	OUT	IN	OUT	39½
	MORNING		AFTERNOON		OVERTIME		

Illus. 21-1
A time clock was used to stamp this card each time the employee arrived for and left work.

Payroll Records

Federal legislation requires employers to keep payroll records. These records usually include a payroll register, similar to that shown in Illus. 21-2. In addition, an employee's earning record (Illus. 21-3) is usually kept for *each* employee for at least four years. (Pension records

	EMPLOYEE	S M	EXEMP.	EARNINGS			DEDUCTIONS				NET PAY	CHECK NO.
				REG.	OVER-TIME	TOTAL	F.I.C.A. TAX	WITH-TAX	HEALTH INS.	TOTAL	AMOUNT	
1	Allen, Joanne	S	1	620.00	31.00	651.00	43.62	172.90	18.00	234.52	416.48	123
2	Bauer, Thomas	M	2	560.00		560.00	37.52	103.80	28.00	169.32	390.68	124
3	Cowan, Rhonda	S	1	480.00		480.00	32.16	110.00	18.00	160.16	319.84	125
19	Scott, Martha	M	2	520.00		520.00	34.84	91.40	28.00	154.24	365.76	141
20	Weyer, Louis	S	1	480.00	48.00	528.00	35.38	97.40	18.00	150.78	377.22	142
	TOTALS			10,340.00	1,059.00	11,399.00	763.73	2,246.80	424.00	3,434.17	7,964.47	

PAYROLL REGISTER — FOR PERIOD ENDING March 31, 19--

Illus. 21-2
Standard forms for payroll registers may be purchased at a stationery store, or they may be custom-designed and duplicated.

Illus. 21-3
Individual earnings records for each employee must be kept. Specific requirements determine the number of columns and the data recorded.

EMPLOYEE'S EARNINGS RECORD

	19-- PERIOD ENDING	EARNINGS			DEDUCTIONS				NET PAY
		REG.	OVER-TIME	TOTAL	F.I.C.A. TAX	WITH-TAX	HEALTH INS.	TOTAL	AMOUNT
1	1/15	520.00		520.00	34.84	91.40	28.00	154.24	365.76
2	1/31	520.00		520.00	34.84	91.40	28.00	154.24	365.76
3	2/15	520.00	26.00	546.00	36.58	94.50	28.00	159.08	386.92
4	2/28	520.00		520.00	34.84	91.40	28.00	154.24	365.76
5	3/15	520.00		520.00	34.84	91.40	28.00	154.24	365.76
6	3/31	520.00		520.00	34.84	91.40	28.00	154.24	365.76
QUARTER TOTALS		3,120.00		3,146.00	210.78	551.50	168.00	930.28	2,215.72
YEARLY TOTALS									

NAME	ADDRESS	SOC. SEC. NO.	KIND OF WORK	DEPT.
Scott, Martha	261 Rose Avenue	561-245-4800	Secretary	Sales
NO. DED. 2	Atlanta, Georgia	MARITAL STATUS M		

are usually retained permanently.) Data from the payroll register are transferred periodically to the employee's earning record, preferably each pay period. The employee's earning record provides quarterly totals for the required quarterly tax reports and for annual totals. Even though the laws affecting payroll taxes change from time to time, comprehensive records, similar to those illustrated, provide the basic data from which to compile almost any type of payroll tax report. A calendar of payroll procedures, suggested records retention schedules, and explanations of government requirements concerning payroll procedures are summarized in Illus. 21-4.

CALENDAR OF PAYROLL PROCEDURES

On Hiring a New Employee

Have the employee complete *Form W-4*. Record employee's social security number and the number of his or her exemptions. File Form W-4 in a safe place.

On Each Payment of Wages to an Employee

Withhold the proper amount of income tax and FICA tax by referring to instructions and tables supplied by the Internal Revenue Service and by the city and state (if necessary). Make all other authorized deductions. On a payroll check stub or on a separate statement, record total wages, amount and kind of each deduction, and net amount for each employee.

Within 15 Days after the Close of Each of the First Two Months of Any Calendar Quarter

If withheld income tax and FICA tax total $200 or more, but is less than $2,000, by the last day of the first and/or second month in a calendar quarter, the full amount must be deposited in a Federal Reserve Bank or other authorized bank by the 15th of the following month. (Use *Form 501*.) If the total amount of undeposited tax is less than $200 by the last day of the second month of a calendar quarter, the full amount may be paid with *Form 941*.

On or before Each April 30, July 31, October 31, and January 31

File *Form 941* with the regional Internal Revenue Service Center. Remit with it the full amount due; that is, the total amount of income tax and FICA tax withheld during the quarter less the total deposited with *Form 501*. State unemployment returns are usually filed at this time.

On or before January 31 and at the End of an Employee's Employment

Prepare *Form W-2* showing the total wages, total wages subject to withholding for income tax, the amount of income tax withheld, the total wage subject to FICA tax, and the amount of FICA withheld. The government prepared Form W-2 consists of four copies. Two copies are given to the employee, one copy to the Internal Revenue Service Center, and one copy to the employer. Some large firms print their own W-2 forms with five or six copies. These additional copies are given to the city and state (for records of income tax withheld) if they require them.

On or before January 31 of Each Year

File *Form 940* to report payment of federal unemployment taxes. In general, employers are required to file state unemployment tax returns quarterly.

By February 28 of Each Year

File *Form W-3*. It is a summary of total income tax withheld and is used as a point of comparison between taxes withheld as reported on all W-2's and on all quarterly 941's

Retain payroll records for a period of four years.

Illus. 21-4 Employers must file a number of forms throughout the year for income and FICA tax purposes.

FILING WITH MAGNETIC MEDIA

The Internal Revenue Service, the Social Security Administration, and state tax departments encourage employers to use magnetic media to file reports. Details on how to provide tax data on magnetic media are available at most IRS and Social Security Administration offices. You may also write to the Magnetic Media Coordinator at the nearest IRS Service Center or to the attention of the Magnetic Media Coordinator at the Social Security Administration, P.O. Box 2317, Baltimore MD 21203.

THE EXECUTIVE'S INCOME TAX

The secretary can assist the executive in the preparation of his or her annual income tax return by:

Being alert to items that the executive must report as income and to items that may be taken as deductions, credits, and adjustments

Accumulating such items throughout the year with supporting papers and records for use at income tax time

Keeping a supply of appropriate current tax forms and schedules
Seeing that returns are filed and payments made

The performance of these duties demands a basic understanding of what constitutes taxable income, which deductions are allowable, and how to organize tax-related material.

Income Tax Files

Income tax files generally consist of income and deduction records, supporting computations and memorandums, previous years' tax returns, and a current income tax file folder or portfolio. To avoid the possiblity of filing current tax materials with those of previous years, use large expansion portfolios and file all income tax material related to a given year in that portfolio. Label the folder "Federal Income Tax, 19--." All supporting records of income tax returns should be retained for several years.

At the beginning of each year, a portfolio should be set up for tax data (bills, canceled checks, reports, itemized listings, receipts). Thus, when it is time to prepare the executive's tax return, all the essential records and reference materials have been accumulated.

Records of Taxable Income

A record of the executive's personal income may be maintained in a special record book in which each item is individually recorded. In most instances, however, no separate record book is kept. Instead, records of taxable income consist mainly of deposit slips to which identifying notations have been attached, receipts, statements of earnings and deductions, dividend distribution statements, statements of interest income on savings accounts, etc. Since personal income derives from many sources and accumulates at irregular intervals, the secretary must be able to identify taxable income and must see that a notation on each income item gets into the tax portfolio.

Wages, Salaries, and Other Compensation. Gross earnings (earnings before deductions for income tax, retirement contributions, employee pensions, hospitalization, insurance, etc.) from wages, salaries, commissions, fees, tips, and similar sources of income are taxable. Awards and prizes of money or merchandise, amounts received in reimbursement for expenses in excess of actual business expenses incurred, and bonuses are also taxable income.

Dividends. Cash dividends are generally taxable. Stock dividends, however, may or may not be taxable. Since some dividends may be wholly or partially exempt from taxation, a complete record of all dividends should be maintained. Dividends which are not taxable can be eliminated when the tax return is prepared.

At the beginning of the year, corporations usually send stockholders a form (Form 1099) to report the total amount of dividends paid to the addressed stockholder the previous year. Watch for and file this information in the income tax portfolio. If your employer uses a broker to manage investments, the broker provides a detailed statement of reportable dividends and interest. These statements are helpful in keeping track of income from investments and determining what is reportable at tax time.

Interest. With the exception of interest on tax-exempt securities, all interest is taxable. Thus, interest received from corporate bonds, mortgage bonds, notes, bank deposits, personal loans, accounts in savings and loan associations, and most United States government bonds should be itemized and recorded.

Gains on Sale or Exchange of Property. Profit from the sale of property (including real estate, stocks, and other securities) is fully taxable. Capital gains are taxed at the same rate as other income. In 1987, the top capital gains rate is set at 28 percent.

Proceeds from Annuities and Endowment Life Insurance. A portion of income from annuities and endowment life insurance is taxable.

Rents. Income received from rents is taxable. The owner of property from which rents are received is entitled to deductions for depreciation, mortgage interest, taxes, repairs, insurance, agent's commissions, and other ordinary and necessary operating expenses. Property records should be kept on each rental unit owned.

Royalties. Royalties include income received from writings, works of art, musical compositions, inventions, and patents. All expenses incurred in producing a property that provides a royalty income are deductible.

Income from a Profession or a Personally Owned Business. All income from a profession or a personally owned business is taxable after deductions for all ordinary, necessary operating expenses have been made.

Nontaxable Income. The secretary should strive to keep as complete a record of all income as the working situation permits. Incomes that are not taxable or incomes from which deductions can be made should be examined and properly excluded or recorded by the tax consultant at the time the tax return is prepared. The secretary should *not* assume the responsibility of judging whether or not income is taxable.

Records of Tax Credits and Deductions

A detailed record of allowable tax credits and deductions should be kept in the tax portfolio. Allowable tax credits and deductions lower a taxpayer's taxable income and include such things as charitable contributions and child care expenses. Because tax laws change frequently, some existing authorized deductions may be eliminated, reduced, or modified.

Alimony. Alimony or other payments in lieu of alimony under a decree of divorce or of separate maintenance are allowable as a personal deduction. Such deductions are taken in the year of payment by the spouse making the payment but are taxable income to the spouse receiving the payment. Child support payments, however, are neither deductible nor taxable.

Bad Debts. Nonbusiness bad debt losses are deductible as short-term capital losses, if they are supported by documentation and are non-family loans.

Casualty or Theft Losses. Losses resulting from fire, storm, flood, or theft are deductible, if not reimbursed by insurance. Damage to the taxpayer's automobile resulting from an accident or theft would be deductible to the extent not covered by insurance. The taxpayer must absorb the first $100 of each casualty and theft loss.

Child and Dependent Care Credit. A tax credit for expenditures for child care (when parents are working) and for disabled dependents is allowed up to a designated amount under certain conditions.

Contributions. Contributions to organizations or institutions devoted primarily to charitable, religious, educational, scientific, or literary purposes are deductible. Examples are contributions to schools and colleges, churches, hospitals, American Cancer Foundation, Girl Scouts, Salvation Army, and United Appeal. Charitable gifts to individuals, political organizations, social clubs, or labor unions are not deductible. Limited contributions to political parties are deductible.

Nonreimbursed expenses for the use of an automobile, postage, out-of-town telephone calls, etc., that are incurred while serving in a campaign to collect funds for a charitable, religious, or educational organization are considered a contribution to the organization and are deductible as such.

IRAs. The deduction for individual retirement accounts for workers is $2,000. The deduction for a nonworking spouse is $250. IRA deductions are not allowed for taxpayers whose adjusted gross income before the IRA deduction exceeds $50,000 ($35,000 for singles) and who are covered by employers' pension plans.

Interest. Not all interest paid on personal debts is deductible. Interest paid on bank loans, installment loans on automobiles, and credit card purchases is not deductible. Mortgage interest is deductible as long as it's on a person's main residence or a second home.

Medical and Dental Expenses. Medical and dental expenses are not restricted to those of the taxpayer but may also include the taxpayer's family and dependents. Medical insurance premiums and medical expenses in excess of 7.5 percent of adjusted gross income are deductible. If premiums are paid by an employer, they cannot be deducted by the taxpayer. To claim these deductions the taxpayer is required to furnish the name and address of each person or agency to whom medical and dental expenses were paid, the amount, and the approximate date of payment.

Taxes. Personal taxes (state or local income taxes, personal property taxes, and real estate taxes are deductible.

Business Expenses. Traveling expenses incurred in connection with one's business or profession for which reimbursement is not received are deductible. These expenses include airline tickets, excess baggage charges, airport transportation services, car rentals, automobile expenses, bus and subway fares, taxi fares, meals (only if away overnight), hotel/motel expenses, tips, telephone/telegraph expenses, laundry, and stenographic services. These expenses are deductible only to the extent that they exceed 2 percent of a taxpayer's adjusted gross income.

Travel expense reports, like the one shown in Illus. 21-5, are important tax-reporting documents. Expenses may be forgotten if they are not recorded promptly. At the completion of each business trip, the secretary should obtain data needed to complete a report of travel expenses from the executive. Unless the expenses are reimbursed by the corporation, the report should be filed with receipts in an income tax portfolio.

```
                      TRAVEL EXPENSE REPORT

  From/to   Houston to Chicago              Date(s)  Feb. 5-7, 19--

  Purpose   To attend convention of National Dental Trade Association

                                                        Cost

  Transportation   Air/coach                          $292.00

  Hotel            Conrad Hilton - 2 nights            128.00

  Meals            2/5      $19.00
                   2/6       22.00
                   2/7       19.50                      60.50

  Other            Tips             $ 9.00
                   Taxi             12.50
                   Convention reg.  12.00
                   Airport parking   8.00               41.50

                                          Total        $522.00

  Receipts attached

     Hotel
     American Airlines
     Convention registration
```

Illus. 21-5
Preparing a travel expense report is an important tax-reporting procedure.

Only 80 percent of entertainment expenses for business purposes (customers, clients, etc.) are deductible. The spouse of an out-of-town guest may also be included. Meals, tips, and theatre and other tickets are recognized entertainment costs. Even club dues are deductible, provided the club is used primarily for entertaining business guests. Deductions for entertainment, however, are subject to detailed examination by the Internal Revenue Service. Many companies place limits on travel expenses based upon management level. These limits include a daily amount for meals, lodging, and entertainment. Any verified amount that is spent by your employer for business purposes that is not reimbursed by the company is deductible. A detailed record, similar to the one shown in Illus. 21-6, should be prepared and supported by receipts, if the total cost is $25 or more. Guests and business connections should be identified. At the end of each day, the secretary should check the appointment book and flag any appointment that involved deductible expenses. The next day the needed information can be obtained from the executive, the report can be prepared and filed with attached receipts in the income tax portfolio.

X GRILL		36234
SERVER	PERSONS	TABLE NO.	NUMBER

McKenna's Restaurant

2	Onion soup	3.20
3	Shrimp cocktail	9.00
2	Special salad bowl	8.00
2	Filet sole	8.00
1	Small steak	6.00
5	Coffee	5.75
3	Pecan pie	4.50
	SUBTOTAL	44.45
	SALES TAX	2.22
	TIP + 15%	7.00
	TOTAL	53.67
SIGNATURE	Betty Randall	

GUEST LIST

(Business Entertainment)

Date   April 10, 19--

Guest(s)   George Snyder
              Frank Fletcher
              Mary Lossi
              John Malinowski
              (All of V. M. Massey Co.)

Explanation   Lunch at McKenna's to discuss
              contract renewal

Total cost $46.67 plus 15% tip, $53.67
              Receipt attached.

Illus. 21-6 Entertainment expenses that exceed $25 must be supported with a receipt.

Business gifts up to $25 in value per recipient per year are also deductible. Each gift deduction, however, must be supported by a record showing the date, the cost, the reason for giving, and the name and business connection of the recipient.

Many executives use credit cards to pay for travel and entertainment expenses. The secretary should identify each travel and entertainment expenditure on the monthly credit card statement and file it, or a copy, in the income tax portfolio.

Other Deductions. Other allowable deductions that apply in specific cases are safe-deposit box rentals (if income-producing items are stored in the box), subscriptions to investment publications, cost of uniforms and their upkeep, union dues, moving expenses (within certain limitations), and the cost of job-related educational expenses. These miscellaneous deductions are allowable only to the extent that they exceed 2 percent of adjusted gross income. The secretary should add to the master list of deductible items those items that are pertinent to the executive's situation.

Tax Guides and Forms

Studying an income tax guide will help the secretary be of more assistance to the executive in handling income tax materials. The secretary should also become familiar with various tax forms, know how to choose the proper ones, and know where to find them. Illus. 21-7 provides a summary of several important forms for individual income tax purposes.

Tax Guides. The following publications can be obtained from the Internal Revenue Service free or for a nominal charge: *Your Federal Income Tax, Tax Guide for U.S. Citizens Abroad and Alien Residents, Tax Information for Home Owners, Energy Credits for Individuals, Tax Guide for Small Business,* and *Child and Disabled Dependent Care.* Also available are *Travel, Entertainment, and Gift Expenses; Tax Exempt Status for Your Organization; Credit for the Elderly and Permanently and Totally Disabled; Tax Information for Divorced or Separated Individuals; Tax Guide for Selling Your Home.* Inexpensive tax guides can also be obtained at bookstores.

Tax Forms. One set of blank tax forms in duplicate is mailed to each taxpayer; additional copies for drafting the return may be obtained from a local office of the Internal Revenue Service or from banks and post offices. They may also be reproduced on a copier. (The Internal Revenue Service has ruled that reproduction of tax forms, schedules, and supporting data on office copiers is acceptable.) Forms may be prepared in pencil and reproduced on a copier to avoid the necessity of recopying or typing the form. Copies of all supplementary information and supporting data, such as receipts, statements, expense reports, and other items that may be attached and mailed with the tax return, should be made on a copier and filed before a return is mailed.

Typing and Mailing Tax Returns

The tax return contains confidential information. It should be typed by the secretary, not by an assistant. Before typing, each figure must be checked for accuracy; then the return must be typed and proofread carefully. Before mailing the form, the secretary should check to see that it has been properly signed and that materials to accompany the return have been securely attached to the finished form as directed.

Space is provided on federal tax forms for the signature of the preparer, if other than the taxpayer. This does not mean the signature of the secretary who has merely collected tax data or typed the form. The space is for the signature of a tax consultant or attorney who prepared the return and who assumes responsibility for its validity.

Since mailing tax returns is a very important responsibility, the secretary should mail them personally. Do not put them in the regular office mail, send them through the mail department, or trust them to a clerk or anyone else to post. The secretary should note on the file copy the exact time and place where each return was mailed. A certificate of mailing may be obtained from the post office as legal proof that the return was mailed. If such a certificate is obtained, attach it to the file copy of the return.

If a declaration of estimated tax was made, the secretary must remind the employer when quarterly tax payments are due (April 15, June 15, September 15, and January 15). A good idea is to place cards in the tickler file at appropriate points.

FORMS FOR FILING INDIVIDUAL INCOME TAX RETURNS

File on or before April 15 following the close of the calendar year.

Form 1040 (U.S. Individual Income Tax Return)

This two-page return, also known as the *long form*, is used for any amount of income. All deductions are listed in full, and all computations are made by the taxpayer. The appropriate schedules must also be filed with Form 1040. There are many different kinds of schedules. The IRS provides copies upon request. They include:

Schedule A for reporting itemized deductions
Schedule B for reporting interest and dividend income
Schedule C for reporting business and professional profits and losses
Schedule D for reporting capital gains and losses

Other special forms are available to report moving expenses, casualties and thefts, the sale and exchange of a principal residence, and employee business expenses.

Form 1040-ES (Estimated Tax for Individuals)

This form is filed by every citizen who can reasonably expect to receive more than $500 in taxable income other than wages. If tax withheld does not cover 80 percent of the tax shown on last year's income tax return, estimated tax payments must be made quarterly. If all income is subject to withholding, no estimated tax payments are required. Estimated unpaid tax may be paid in full when the declaration (Form 1040-ES) is filed, or it may be paid in four equal installments (payable on April 15, June 15, September 15, and January 15). The first installment payment must accompany the declaration.

Illus. 21-7
You should be familiar with Form 1040 and Form 1040-ES.

A packet of 1040-ES forms is mailed to taxpayers along with preprinted vouchers and a worksheet to help compute estimated tax. Keep the worksheet in the tax portfolio. Use the preprinted vouchers to speed the processing of estimated tax payments and reduce errors. File the vouchers in the tickler file.

Late Filing

The taxpayer who files a late tax return is assessed a penalty. An individual, however, may obtain an automatic two-month extension beyond the April 15 deadline by submitting Form 2688, Application for Extension of Time. Additional extensions are granted only under certain circumstances.

Tax Assistance

Should questions occur regarding the preparation of tax returns or while computing payroll deductions, the IRS has a problem resolution program for taxpayers who are unable to solve problems through normal channels. By calling a toll-free number in your area and asking for the Problem Resolution Office, misunderstandings and misinterpretations can be cleared up.

SUMMARY

Federal and state laws require all employers to keep detailed payroll records. Time records must be maintained, employee earnings and deductions must be recorded, payroll checks must be prepared, and tax reports must be submitted. In large firms, much of this work is done in a special payroll division. Unless employed in that division, a secretary would have few, if any, of these duties to perform. In a small office, however, the secretary may handle all payroll work. Obviously, then, the extent of a secretary's payroll duties is determined by the size and function of the office or company in which the secretary works.

Payroll work is exacting and demands mathematical accuracy. In addition to the responsibility of safeguarding all payroll information, the secretary must understand the forms and reports required by the Federal Insurance Contributions Act, the Fair Labor Standards Acts, income tax laws, federal and state unemployment compensation acts, and pertinent local legislation.

Regardless of the secretary's payroll responsibilities, every secretary can assist the employer in the preparation of annual income tax returns. Throughout the year, the secretary can systematically collect income tax data so that facts and figures are readily available when income tax time comes. No employer expects the secretary to be a tax expert, but the secretary's willingness to assume a helpful role in the tax preparation process is one that almost every employer appreciates.

To assist in the tax preparation process, the secretary should keep a supply of current tax forms and schedules on hand, maintain accurate records, file supporting documents, notice items that are deductible and items that must be declared as income, and see that returns are filed and payments are made on time. Knowing where to go for assistance with tax problems and knowing the procedures for late filing are also helpful.

SUGGESTED READINGS

Bower, James B., and Harold Q. Langenderfer, *Income Tax Procedure.* Cincinnati: South-Western Publishing Co., 1986. *Issued annually.*

Keeling, B. Lewis, and Bernard J. Beig. *Payroll Records and Accounting.* Cincinnati: South-Western Publishing Co., 1986. *Issued annually.*

Circular E: Employer's Tax Guide, Cincinnati: Internal Revenue Service, undated.

QUESTIONS FOR DISCUSSION

1. Does it build employee morale to make available to all employees salaries paid to co-workers? Support your answer.
2. Why should a secretary not employed in a payroll department be familiar with payroll procedures and payroll taxes?
3. Why is the self-employed person taxed at a higher FICA tax rate than other workers?
4. One of your assistants, who is your senior in age and tenure has the habit of arriving a few minutes late each morning. As a corrective measure you ask each member of your staff to sign in and out each day. There is opposition to your regulation from other members of your staff on the grounds that they are salaried, not hourly, employees. What is the difference between a salaried and an hourly employee, and how would you respond to this objection?
5. Assume you are employed in a small office (four employees) and your employer asks you to take complete charge of payroll records, including preparing and submitting all payroll tax reports. Where could you obtain assistance to help you prepare for and carry out this assignment?
6. It is said that the secretary's role in the preparation of the employer's income tax return is an assistant's role. What does this mean to you?

7. The Internal Revenue Service requires a taxpayer to document all traveling and entertainment expenses for which a tax deduction is claimed. What is the secretary's role in compiling this important information?

8. What precautions should the secretary observe in typing and mailing the employer's income tax return?

9. As an employee, you will be required to pay social security tax (FICA tax), which will be deducted from your paycheck. This tax can be a large amount of money. Assuming that your career will extend over 40 years, what is your reaction to this law?

10. If necessary, correct the following sentences. Use the Reference Guide to check your answers.
    a. The principle on the loan must be paid before June 1.
    b. We must raise additional capitol for expansion of our new plant.
    c. There is considerable disagreement between our many stockholders.
    d. The contract's terms are precise.
    e. Send us 35 8-column worksheets.

PROBLEMS

1. Obtain one of the following payroll forms, study the instructions for completing it, and be prepared to present a description of the form and the method of completing it to the class.

    SS-4   Application for Employer Identification Number
    SS-5   Application for a Social Security Number
    941   Employer's Quarterly Federal Tax Return
    W-2   Wage and Tax Statement
    W-4   Employee's Withholding Allowance Certificate

2. To accumulate information for a tax file, a secretary must have some understanding of taxable income and allowable deductions. From the following list, select those income items that are taxable and those expenses that are deductible. Arrange the items alphabetically and type them in a convenient form for reference. You may need to check reference sources to identify the tax status of certain items.

    Income Items

    Payment for writing magazine article
    Interest from municipal bonds
    Bonus from employer

Prize (paid vacation to a resort for the "Best Idea" contest)
Rent received on property inherited from a relative
Dividends on corporation stock
Interest on U.S. government bonds
Merchandise received from employer
Interest on deposits in savings and loan association
Payments from accident insurance
Property inherited from a relative
Payment for a speech to a service club (not related to business)
Royalties received from a patent
Profit from sale of building lot originally planned for home

Expense Items

Contribution to an old friend
Tips paid for service while on business trip
Federal income tax paid during year
Interest on loan on family automobile
Contributions to the Girl Scouts
Contribution of $25 to a political party
Interest on loan on home
Driver's license fee
State income tax
Property loss resulting from theft (not covered by insurance)
FICA
Retail sales tax (state)
Employment fees paid to agency
Life insurance premiums
Traveling expenses to and from the place of employment
Union dues
Repairs on home
Gift costing $25 given to a customer
Expenses incurred in acting as chairman of United Appeal fund drive

3. John O'Brian is paid $6.20 an hour and an overtime wage of $1\frac{1}{2}$ times his hourly rate. All hours over 40 are considered overtime. He worked 48 hours during the last week in March.
   a. What are his gross earnings for the week?
   b. If the FICA tax rate is 7.15 percent and an $18.30 federal income tax deduction and a 2 percent state income tax deduction are made, what are his net earnings?

4. Assume that you are secretary to three executives in the same firm. All three have asked for your assistance in preparing their individual income tax returns. In order to submit the proper information to the CPA who will prepare their returns, design a questionnaire you could give to these executives to obtain vital information concerning their tax status.

Chapter 22

Producing and Processing Legal Papers

Increased numbers of government regulations during the past two decades have made compliance with local, state, and federal legislation a matter of prime importance in most businesses. Laws pertaining to employee privacy, civil rights, malpractice, consumer protection, taxes, and environmental protection have influenced significantly the secretary's need for a knowledge of the law and legal procedures.

Obviously the scope and the amount of legal work that a secretary performs varies from office to office. A secretary in a corporate office that deals with the nonlegal aspects of a business may perform only an occasional law-related function. On the other hand, the secretary in a legal office works full time in an environment where legal terminology, documents, and procedures are the core of all activity. The work is so specialized that legal secretaries have their own association that administers a training and certification program. In large law offices, word processing technology is having a dramatic impact on the functions of the legal secretary. Much of the repetitive typing, copying, and proofreading that formerly constituted a significant part of a legal secretary's work is now being done by word processors, computers, and copiers. This technology makes legal secretarial work less clerical and more professional. It has enabled some legal secretaries to become legal assistants or researchers.

This chapter introduces the secretary to the processing of legal papers. It describes some of the more commonly used legal documents, discusses secretarial procedures related to preparing them, outlines some legislation with which secretaries should be familiar, and suggests reference sources to which the secretary may turn for assistance.

Eventually, you may find legal work attractive and decide to become a trainee in a law firm, in the legal department of a large corporation, or in the government. You can build upon the content of this chapter with specialized training to become a professional legal secretary (PLS), a paralegal, or a legal assistant. You may even decide to study law and prepare for the bar. Regardless of the type of firm that

631

employs you, your work as a legal office worker will involve some contact with documents, correspondence, vocabulary, and procedures related to the law.

FREQUENTLY USED LEGAL DOCUMENTS

Business transactions frequently involve parties from different states. Complexities and problems arise in preparing legal documents which cover conflicting laws of the federal government and the fifty states. To expedite legal procedures, a number of uniform *statutes* (laws) have been enacted, the most recent and most important one from a business standpoint being the Uniform Commercial Code. The legal documents described here conform to this code.

Contracts

Many people are concerned with the legalities of buying and selling goods, property, and services. Every buying and selling activity constitutes a contract between or among buyers and sellers. A *contract* is an enforceable agreement, either oral or written, which involves legal rights and responsibilities. A contract may be in the form of an oral agreement, a sales slip, a memorandum, a promissory note, or a letter. Some contracts, such as those for the purchase of real estate, must be in writing. All important contracts should be written, although it is not a legal requirement.

Content. In typing a contract, the secretary should see if the following essential information is included:

> Date and place of agreement
> Names of parties entering into the agreement
> Purpose of the contract
> Duties of each party
> A statement of the money, the goods, or the services given in consideration (as payment for) of the agreement
> Time element or duration involved
> Signatures of the parties

Prepare enough copies of a contract so that each party will have a file copy. (If a contract is prepared in a law office, an additional copy is made for the law office files.) When an executive sells services by contract (as engineers, architects, builders, and real estate representatives do), the secretary may use a standard form; but, usually there are items peculiar to each contract that make it necessary to vary a standard contract's fill-ins each time. Printed forms are available for most common legal documents. Since some contracts must follow a statutory model or must contain specified provisions, it is recommended that the secretary use a printed form or follow legal advice when preparing specific provisions of a legal document.

Care Before Signing. All contracts should be carefully read by all parties before they are signed. Not only will mistakes, misunderstandings, and fraud be avoided but content will be clarified with regard to (1) what responsibilities are assumed by each party, (2) exactly what is offered at what price, (3) how payment is to be made, (4) whether or not material can be returned, and (5) when and how the contract can be terminated.

Contracts Made by the Secretary. The secretary often acts (in a legal sense) as an executive's deputy; that is, the secretary knowingly—and sometimes unknowingly—executes contracts. The secretary, therefore, should exercise caution in making commitments; in requesting work to be done by outside agencies; in quoting prices or making offers to purchase; and in signing purchase orders, repair orders, sales orders, or other agreements. Such commitments may be contractual.

When signing an agreement (contract) generated by the secretary, the executive usually relies on the secretary's recommendation. The mere fact that the secretary presents a contract to an executive for signature implies the secretary's endorsement of its content. For example, the secretary may make all the arrangements for the purchase of a new machine. The executive signs the contract on the presumption that the secretary has checked all details and has verified that the contract is correct, understood, and proper. By attaching an annotation of a contract's important points, the secretary can save the employer the time of reading "the fine print."

A contract copy should be carefully filed. It is a legal instrument, necessary for prosecuting any deviation from the contract. It is a good idea to place a contract in a No. 10 envelope and mark plainly on the outside, "Signed contract between. . . . " The contract can be filed permanently under the appropriate name, in a separate file for signed contracts, or in a safe-deposit box. In some companies, legal papers are kept in asbestos envelopes as a protection against fire.

Legal firms with access to word processing equipment store standard forms in memory. When a contract, deed, will, lease, or other standard document is needed, the stored document is played out and the secretary keys in the variables. This capability has made word processing very popular in law offices.

Proof of Claim in Bankruptcy

Our legal system provides a process by which honest but over-extended debtors can be relieved of their financial obligations and start over economically. The process, called *bankruptcy*, was originally intended to benefit creditors (those to whom money is owed). Bankruptcy forces debtors (those who owe money) to pay creditors from property turned over to the court. This action prevents debtors from concealing their assets and paying only selected creditors. The Bankruptcy Reform Act of 1978 modernized bankruptcy laws. Today a bankruptcy petition can be initiated by the debtor or by creditors. Only federal courts may rule in bankruptcy matters.

Should your employer be involved in collecting money from a bankrupt debtor, you may be required to prepare a *proof of claim*, which is a written statement signed by the creditor, or an authorized representative, stating the claim against the bankrupt and the basis for the claim. An example of a proof of claim appears in Illus. 22-1. The proof of claim must be filed within six months after the first meeting of the bankrupt's creditors. Creditors may lose their claims if they fail to file on time.

Within a reasonable time after a debtor has filed for bankruptcy, the bankruptcy court must call a meeting of unsecured creditors (those who do not have access to property or other assets that can be used to satisfy a debt). (The debtor supplies the court with a list of creditors so that the court may notify them of the meeting.) For example, a vendor can repossess office furniture to satisfy a debt, thereby securing the vendor's claim to the debtor's assets. On the other hand, a vendor supplying fuel oil to the bankrupt cannot repossess fuel oil that has been consumed; therefore, the oil vendor is an unsecured creditor.

The secretary should also have some knowledge of the priority of claims. For example, creditors who hold a mortgage as security for payment are not affected by a debtor's bankruptcy. With the mortgage they hold, they may exercise their rights of foreclosure or repossession to obtain payment of their claims. Unsecured creditors share in the remaining assets of the bankrupt in priority order established by the court. The secretary's ability to provide a proof of claim and to assist the employer in the timely presentation of evidence will result in considerable savings and reduce the stress associated with such litigation.

Wills and Codicils

Requirements regarding the drawing of wills and codicils are rather technical and vary among states. Hence, they should not be drawn without proper legal supervision or direction.

United States Bankruptcy Court

In re _____

Case No. _____

Debtor(s)   Claim No. [*For office use only*] _____

PROOF OF CLAIM

1. This proof of claim is made for the claimant named below by the undersigned individual who states that he is duly authorized to make this proof of claim on behalf of the claimant, which is: *(Check the appropriate line)*
    _____ An Individual   _____ A Partnership   _____ A Corporation   _____ Other

2. The correct name and address of the claimant, and the account number, if any, to which all notices and distribution checks should be mailed is stated below:
    _____ Account No. _____

    _____

    _____

3. This claim is based upon: *(Check the appropriate line)*
    _____ A note, contract, or other writing. The original or duplicate copies are attached, or, if not, an explanation is attached.
    _____ An open account. An itemized statement showing the date due is attached.
    _____ Other consideration (or ground of liabiity). Explain and attach documentation.

4. No judgment has been rendered upon the claim, except _____

5. The debtor was at the time of the filing of the petition, and still is, indebted (or liable) to the claimant as follows:

    [A detailed explanation of additional charges, including an itemization, basis for inclusion and computation, should be attached.]

    | PRINCIPAL | $ _____ |
    | PLUS ADDITIONAL CHARGES | $ _____ |
    | TOTAL | $ _____ |
    | LESS PAYMENTS/CREDITS | $ _____ |
    | BALANCE DUE | $ _____ |

6. This claim is free from any charge forbidden by applicable law and excludes any interest accrued after the date the case was commenced.

7. This claim is an unsecured claim, except to the extent that the security interest, if any, described in paragraph 8 hereof is sufficient to satisfy the claim. (If priority is claimed, give amount and written explanation.)

8. NO SECURITY INTEREST IS HELD FOR THIS CLAIM EXCEPT: _____

    _____
    (If security interest in property of the debtor is claimed, it is claimed under the writing referred to in paragraph 3 or under a separate writing, the original or duplicate of which is attached hereto. If not attached, give written explanation. Evidence of perfection is also attached.)

9. The *FAIR MARKET VALUE* of the property on which the claimant has a lien is $ _____ .
    (Do NOT use balance due unless it is fair market value.)

File this form, *IN DUPLICATE*, with:

CLERK'S OFFICE, U.S. BANKRUPTCY COURT   Signed: _____
Post Office Box 676
Richmond, VA 23206

_____
(Type or print name & title, if any)

DATE: _____

Penalty for presenting fraudulent claim: Fine of not more than $5,000.00 or imprisonment for not more than five years, or both — Title 18, U.S.C. 152.

COPY 1 — COURT COPY

Illus. 22-1
A proof of claim in bankruptcy must be presented to the court within six months after the first meeting of creditors.

Wills. A will is a legal instrument whereby a person provides for the disposition of property after death. A *testator* (man) or *testatrix* (woman) is one who makes a will. One who dies without having made a valid will is said to die *intestate*. A *nuncupative* will is an oral will. It is valid only as to personal property; land may not be devised by a nuncupative will. A will in the handwriting of the testator is called a *holographic* will. A *joint* will is one executed by two or more persons. A will that sets forth provisions conditional upon the occurrence of a specified event is called a *conditional* will. Such a will might be written before a person undergoes a serious operation.

A will may be *revoked* by mutilation, alteration, cancellation, destruction, or the execution of a new will. Every will should contain a provision stating that any and all previous wills are revoked even though the testator does not remember ever having made another will.

To *probate* a will is to prove its validity to the court for the purpose of carrying out its provisions. An *executor* (man) or *executrix* (woman) is named by the testator to carry out the provisions of a will. If a person dies intestate, the courts will appoint an *administrator* (man) or *administratrix* (woman) to settle the estate of the deceased.

Codicils. A *codicil* is a supplement that makes a change in a will, deletes or adds something to it, or explains it. It must be signed and witnessed with all the formalities of the original will.

A person asked to *attest* (witness) a will or codicil need not read the provisions and, of course, does not try. The attestant merely witnesses the signature of the testator and assures the beneficiaries that the testator was in sound mind when the will was signed. A will presented for witnessing should have only the signature area visible, to prevent a chance reading of its contents.

Copyrights

Creative work reproduced for sale or public distribution may be *copyrighted*. Copyrighting applies not only to printed matter, such as books and periodicals, but also to photographs, pictorial illustrations, musical compositions, maps, paintings, and movies.

To copyright is to register a claim with the federal government to a piece of original literary or artistic work. A copyright grants an exclusive right to reproduce a creative work or to perform it publicly. Registering is done either by the originator of the work or by the one reproducing and marketing copies. Copyrighting prevents a dishonest or careless person from stealing another's creative work and marketing it. A copyright endures for the life of the author plus fifty years after the author's death. It ensures that public broadcasters and others cannot use a copyrighted work without the originator's consent and provides guidelines under which classroom and library copying of material is permitted. A copyright can be obtained by filing an application for copyright with the Copyright Office, Library of Congress, Washington, DC 20559.

Petitions

Secretaries are often called upon to prepare petitions for employers or for organizations to which they belong. A *petition* is a document containing a formal written request. An example appears in Illus. 22-2. Writing a petition requires an orderly expression of ideas in clear, concise language. It should be forcefully presented in a respectful tone. Petitions are usually presented in one of the following styles:

1. The reasons for the petition are stated in the order of their importance and are followed by the request. Each reason is usually preceded by the words "inasmuch as" or "in view of the fact that."

2. An explanation of who is making the request is stated first. For example, "We, the undersigned residents of Colby Circle Apartments" would open the petition and be followed by the request and the reasons for it.

PETITION TO THE CITY COUNCIL

We, the undersigned residents of the city of Norwood, respectfully call your attention to the fact that automobile accidents are frequently occurring in areas where large recreational vehicles and business vans are parked on street corners, obstructing the view of drivers entering intersections.

Inasmuch as it has been the concern of city council for many years to reduce the number of accidents occurring on our city streets, we urgently request that a local ordinance be passed to prohibit the parking of large recreational vehicles and business vans of any type on street corners where the view could be obstructed.

NAMES	ADDRESSES
Mr. & Mrs. Greg C. Clements	902 Clarion Avenue
Anne Williams	3730 Smith Rd.

Illus. 22-2
This petition begins with an explanation of who is making the petition.

Affidavits

An *affidavit* is a written declaration made under oath that the facts set forth are sworn to be true and correct. The word itself means "he has made oath." An affidavit, made by an *affiant*, must be sworn to before a public officer (such as a notary, a judge, or a justice of the peace). For example, evidence of citizenship is required before an applicant can obtain a United States passport. If the person seeking a passport has no birth certificate, an affidavit from a relative declaring that the passport applicant was born in the United States may be used. An example of an affidavit appears in Illus. 22-3.

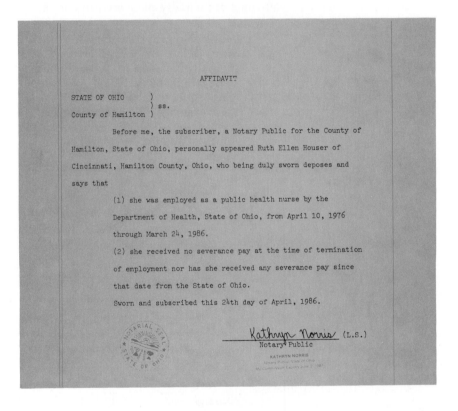

Illus. 22-3
An affidavit may be typed on ruled legal paper, as illustrated here, or it may be typed on unruled paper. It must be signed by a notary public, judge, or justice of the peace.

Power of Attorney

A legal instrument authorizing one to act as an agent for another is known as *power of attorney*. An example appears in Illus. 22-4. Often an employer gives a secretary power of attorney to perform certain specified functions. For example, the secretary may be authorized to sign checks and other legal documents for the executive. A power of attorney may be made for an indefinite period, for a specific period, or for a specific purpose only. Only a secretary with unquestionable professional integrity earns this decidedly weighty responsibility.

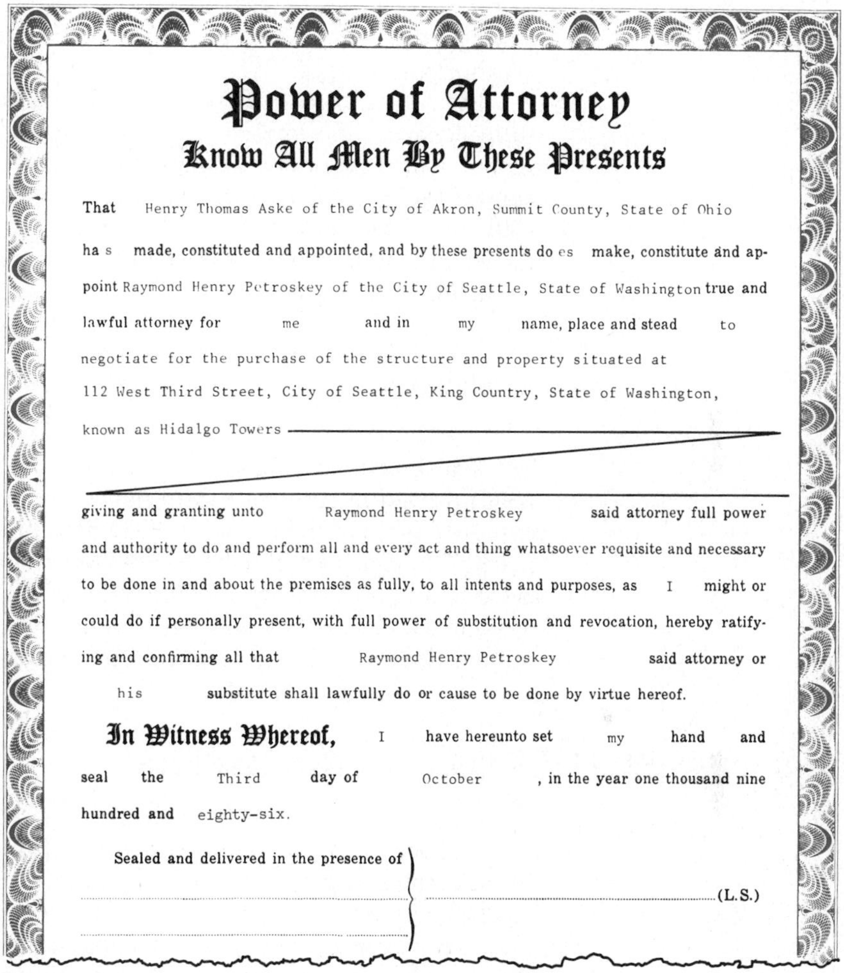

Power of Attorney

Know All Men By These Presents

That Henry Thomas Aske of the City of Akron, Summit County, State of Ohio

ha s made, constituted and appointed, and by these presents do es make, constitute and appoint Raymond Henry Petroskey of the City of Seattle, State of Washington true and lawful attorney for me and in my name, place and stead to negotiate for the purchase of the structure and property situated at 112 West Third Street, City of Seattle, King Country, State of Washington, known as Hidalgo Towers

giving and granting unto Raymond Henry Petroskey said attorney full power and authority to do and perform all and every act and thing whatsoever requisite and necessary to be done in and about the premises as fully, to all intents and purposes, as I might or could do if personally present, with full power of substitution and revocation, hereby ratifying and confirming all that Raymond Henry Petroskey said attorney or his substitute shall lawfully do or cause to be done by virtue hereof.

In Witness Whereof, I have hereunto set my hand and seal the Third day of October , in the year one thousand nine hundred and eighty-six.

Sealed and delivered in the presence of

....(L. S.)

....

Illus. 22-4
A power of attorney is notarized in a form similar to that shown in Illus. 22-3.

Should the executive have power of attorney for someone else, the secretary sets up a special file and records all executions. These records will not only protect the employer, but they will serve as a vital source of information to the person who granted the power of attorney.

Patents

A *patent* grants an inventor the exclusive right to make and sell a new and useful art, machine, manufacture, or composition of matter.

Literature on the procedure for securing a patent can be obtained through the Office of Public Affairs, Patent and Trademark Office, Washington, DC, 20231.

Legal specialists are usually employed to prepare a patent application. A patent application is the first step in negotiations between the Patent and Trademark Office and the inventor. A patent must be applied for by the inventor. After the patent has been granted, it can be sold outright or leased, in which case the inventor is paid a royalty for its use. A patent expires at the end of 17 years and can be renewed only by an Act of Congress.

Trademarks

The Patent and Trademark Office also registers trademarks for goods moved in interstate commerce, giving evidence of the validity and ownership of the mark by the registrant and of the right to use the mark. The registration term covers twenty years. However, during the sixth year of registration, an affidavit must be filed with the Patent and Trademark Office showing that the trademark is being used or that its nonuse does not signify intention to abandon the mark.

RESPONSIBILITIES FOR LEGAL PAPERS

The secretary may type legal papers, fill in printed legal forms, and witness the signing of completed papers. It may be necessary to have legal papers notarized; that is, acknowledged by a notary public. A notary public acknowledges that a document was actually executed by the person or persons who sign it. For convenience, it may be practical for the secretary to become a notary public, thus avoiding the inconvenience of having to go outside the office for this service. Finally, the secretary may be responsible for recording of the legal paper.

Notary Public

Notarial commissions are issued by the secretary of state, the governor, or other designated state official. Application blanks are furnished upon request by the appropriate official in the state in which the commission is sought, or they may be bought at a stationery store. Usually a fee and an examination are required. Certain citizenship qualifications must also be met. Most states also require bond, which may be applied for with the application. A notary public can purchase *error and omission* insurance to protect against financial liability.

The notary's appointment states the county or counties in which authority to notarize has been granted. The commission's expiration date is also stated. It is necessary to buy a notary public seal and a rubber stamp. The former is used to emboss the document with a seal that shows the name of the county in which the notary is commissioned to act and the seal of the state. The rubber stamp shows the date when the commission expires. Each notary receives local rules and instructions that must be observed.

A notary does not scrutinize the document being certified. The notary gives the oath and verifies that the signature or signatures are genuine. If you should become a notary, remember not to be curious about what is in the paper you are certifying.

If the secretary is not a notary public, arranging to have papers notarized becomes a secretarial responsibility. The names of two or three notaries public convenient to the office should be obtained. Sometimes it may be necessary to arrange a meeting time with the notary public and to notify all parties involved.

The notary public witnesses affidavits and signs *acknowledgments* and *verifications* that are executed under oath. In an acknowledgment, like the one shown in Illus. 22-5, the person swears that the signature appearing on a document is genuine and was made of free will. A verification is a sworn and signed statement of the truth and correctness of the content of a document. All necessary signatures must be completed before the notary public signs the document.

Illus. 22-5
An acknowledgment of a notary public attests that the signature on a document is genuine.

```
STATE OF OHIO   )
                ) ss.
County of Summit)

        On October 3, 1986, before me, a Notary Public, in and for

said County and State, personally appeared Henry Thomas Aske, known to

me to be the person whose name is subscribed to the within instrument,

and acknowledged that he exectued the same.

        IN TESTIMONY THEREFOR I have hereunto subscribed my name and

affixed my seal of office the day and year last above written.


                Lawrence E. Philpot      (L.S.)

        My commission expires June 10, 1987.
```

Preparation of Legal Papers

Legal papers can be divided into two classes:

1. *Court Documents.* These vary considerably and must follow the specifications of the particular city, county, state, or federal court in which they are filed. They include such documents as *complaints, answers, demurrers, notices, motions, affidavits, summonses,* and *subpoenas.*
2. *Noncourt Legal Documents.* These include such legal papers as contracts, wills, leases, powers of attorney, agreements, and many others. They give formal expression to legal acts and are legal evidence if court action or litigation becomes necessary.

The form of legal papers is standardized in some respects; in others, it varies with the wishes of the court and with the personal preference of the employer.

Paper Size. Traditionally all legal documents are typed on $8\frac{1}{2}$-by-13- or 14-inch hard-to-tear white paper called *legal cap.* Legal cap is printed with a red or blue vertical double rule $1\frac{3}{8}$ inches from the left edge and a single rule $\frac{3}{8}$ inch from the right edge. *Brief* paper, $8\frac{1}{2}$-by-$10\frac{1}{2}$ inches, also with ruled margins, is used for legal briefs and memorandums; for some documents, each line on a sheet is numbered. Although some courts still require legal cap for court documents, there is a trend toward using standard $8\frac{1}{2}$-by-11-inch sheets because this size can be microfilmed easily for storage in court files.

All federal courts now require $8\frac{1}{2}$-by-11-inch paper. In an effort to standardize, many city, county, and state courts are also adopting shorter papers for legal documents. Before typing a court document, the secretary should learn the requirements of the particular court.

Copies. Multiple copies of legal documents are usually required. For example, all parties to a contract receive a copy, file copies are necessary, and the attorney retains one or more copies for the office. Copies can be made on a copier; the secretary types only one original and makes copies from the original. In some offices, the secretary types an original and a file copy on color-coded tissue paper. All other copies are made from the original on the copier. *Copies* can be used and referred to as *duplicate originals.* They must, however, be signed and made to *conform* in all respects to the original (to contain all the copy shown on the original).

After a paper has been *executed* (the original and duplicate originals have been made valid by necessary procedures, such as signing, witnessing, notarizing, and recording), all distribution copies and the office file copy must be *conformed* by typing in the signatures, dates, and all other data that were added in executing the paper.

Type. For legal papers, pica type is preferred and may be required for court documents. In any case, do not use script, italic, or gothic typefaces.

Margins, Spacing, and Centered Titles. On paper with printed marginal rules, type within the rules by one or two spaces. On ruled paper, use 1½-inch left and at least ½-inch right margins. Top margins are 2 inches on the first page and 1½ inches on subsequent pages. Bottom margins are 1 inch.

For most legal papers, use double spacing and triple-space above side headings. Some legal secretaries recommend that a triple space be made between paragraphs to provide flexibility for limited changes on any page without making it necessary to retype the entire instrument. Very long documents are sometimes single-spaced to avoid exceptional bulkiness.

Two inches from the top of the first page, type the title of the paper in all capitals, and center it between the rules. Divide at a logical point and double-space a heading that is too long for one line. Leave two blank line spaces below the title.

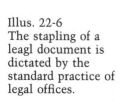

To ensure that no line of an original legal document has been omitted in retyping, hold line-for-line typed copy beside the original or align the copy over the original and hold them up to a bright light.

Stapling and Punching. Legal documents protected by legal backs should be stapled on each side at the lower edge on the top fold of the legal back about one inch from the side of the backing sheet. Staple legal documents prepared without legal backs, regardless of whether the document is an original or a copy, one inch from the top of the page on both corners (see Illus. 22-6). Try to avoid removing staples from documents fastened to a legal back. Once a will has been stapled, it becomes invalid if taken apart unless each page is initialed in the handwriting of the one who made the will.

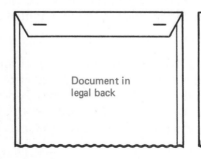

Document in
legal back

Multipage unbound
legal document

Illus. 22-6
The stapling of a leagl document is dictated by the standard practice of legal offices.

A two-hole punch with punches set 2¾ inches apart is used in legal offices to prepare documents for filing. All pages to be filed should be punched at the top center.

Hyphenation. Learn the preference of the office that employs you. Sometimes the last word on a page must not be hyphenated; sometimes a divided last word is recommended to make the unwarranted insertion of pages more difficult. Avoid dividing words at the end of other lines.

Paragraphs. Indent ten spaces for paragraphs. To make difficult any unwarranted insertion of pages, do not end a page with the last line of a paragraph. Carry over two or more lines to the next page. The one-page contract in Illus. 22-7 was typed on legal cap. Notice the paragraph format.

Quoted Matter and Land Descriptions. For quoted matter and land descriptions, indent five to ten spaces from the left margin; retain the right margin if desired, or indent five spaces. Indent another five spaces for a new paragraph in the quoted material. Indented quotations may be single spaced.

Page Numbers. Legal documents frequently go through a series of drafts. Number and date each draft. Label the first typing, "first draft" and date it; the second, "second draft" and date it, etc. Keep all drafts and media until the final document has been typed and processed.

Center page numbers one-half inch from the bottom edge. Always number the first and last page of every document.

Dates. Spell out single-digit *ordinal* dates and type the year to conform. (An ordinal number is one that signifies rank or place in a sequence: first, second, tenth, etc. A *cardinal* number is used in simple counting to indicate how many: one, two, ten, thirty, etc.) For example, you would type *the first day of June, nineteen hundred and eighty-seven,* but for a double-digit date, you would type, *the 15th day of June, 1987.* Date every legal paper. If the last paragraph does not include the date, type the date on the last line immediately preceding the signature lines.

Numbers. Numbers with legal significance (amounts of money, periods of time) have traditionally been written in both words and figures. Figures follow words in parentheses. For example, *Five Thousand Dollars ($5,000),* or *Ten (10) barrels of oil,* or *Sixty (60) days* (but *six-month period*) would be typed as shown here.

CONTRACT

THIS CONTRACT made and entered into this fourth day of January, nineteen hundred and eighty-six, by and between ROBERT LEYLAND ROBINS of the City of Tampa, County of Hillsborough, State of Florida, doing business under the name of ADORN MANUFACTURING COMPANY, and referred to as the firm in this contract, and JANICE WEBBER LOGAL of Bradenton, Manatee County, State of Florida, WITNESSETH:

1. JANICE WEBBER LOGAL shall enter the services of the said firm as a products representative for them in their business of manufacturing cosmetics for the period of one year from the 12th day of October, 1983, subject to the general control of said firm.

2. The said products representative shall devote the whole of her time, attention, and energies to the performance of her duties as such representative, and shall not either directly or indirectly, alone or in partnership, be connected with or concerned in any other business or pursuit whatsoever during the said term of one year.

3. The said products representative shall, subject to the control of the said firm, keep proper books of account and make due and correct entries of the price of all goods sold and of all transactions and dealings of and in relation to the said business, and shall serve the firm diligently and according to the best abilities of all respects.

4. The fixed salary of the said products representative shall be Ten Thousand Dollars ($10,000) per annum, payable in equal semimonthly installments.

Date: January 4, 1986   /s/ _____
                                  Adorn Manufacturing Company

                              /s/ _____
                                  Janice Webber Logal

Illus. 22-7 Observe that the copy is double spaced, that paragraphs have been indented ten spaces, that names of the parties to the contract are in all caps, and that dates conform to suggested patterns for legal papers.

Use the dollar sign with a number in conformity with the spelled-out version: *Sixty Dollars ($60)* or *Sixty (60) Dollars.* Capitalize all words of an amount: *Three Hundred Seventy-Five and 45/100 Dollars ($375.45).* Some offices type dollar amounts in all capitals.

Reference Notations. On the first page of a file copy in the upper left corner, type the full names of the recipients of all copies of the document.

After preparing multiple copies of a legal paper that requires many signatures, flag the appropriate points for each signer, using a different color flag for each one.

Names and Signature Lines. If you know the exact signature that is to be used, type it in the body of the document in exactly that way. If you do not know the form of the signature, use the legal name. The full two or three names of the person without abbreviations or initials is the legal name. The legal signature of a married woman combines her maiden name with her married name, such as Dorothy Keller Brown, not Dorothy Ann Brown. Personal titles (Mr., Mrs., Ms., Miss) are not used; ordinarily neither are professional titles. To permit easy reference and identification, it is common practice to type the names of individuals, businesses, agencies, and institutions named in a legal document in all capitals.

At the end of a legal paper, type the lines for required signatures. These signature lines cannot stand alone on a page; arrange the body so that at least two lines of text appear on the page with the signatures. The lines extend from the center to the right margin, with two or three blank line spaces between them. Signature lines for witnesses begin at the left margin and extend to the center.

Some secretaries lightly pencil in the respective initials on the lines on which each is to sign. Other secretaries use a small "x" to mark the spot. In some jurisdictions, names must be typed under signature lines. Names are typed on signature lines after the word "signed" or the abbreviation "Sgd." on file copies.

Seals. The abbreviation "L.S." (*locus sigilli*, meaning "place of the seal") frequently appears at the end of lines on which parties to a paper sign their names (see Illus. 22-5). This abbreviation has the legal significance of a wax seal. State laws determine whether or not a legal paper requires a seal.

Insertions. At the time of signing a legal paper, an insertion may be requested. An insertion is valid if the signers endorse it by writing their initials in ink near it.

Erasures and Corrections. Each page should be typed accurately, for an erased and corrected error can cast doubt on the validity of a document if it occurs in a vital phrase. (Neither may an omission be inserted between lines to avoid retyping a page.) For example *"four* thousand acres" erased and changed to *"forty* thousand acres" or *"June 6"* changed to *"June 5"* may raise a question of validity. An error in a single word in the straight text can usually be erased and corrected without question, but avoid erasing figures, dates, names, and places. If they must be erased, have the correction initialed. Word processing has made erasing almost obsolete in those offices where word processors are used.

Proofreading. The secretary who is unfamiliar with legal work should be particularly careful in proofreading and in questioning terms that are not understood. Novices have typed "the plaintiff praise" for "the plaintiff prays" or the "Court of Common Please" or the "Court of Common Police" rather than the "Court of Common Pleas." Referring to a notary public as a "notary republic" is embarrassing. If you are not sure about a term, ask for assistance or consult an authoritative text.

Property descriptions, quoted material, and all figures and dates that appear in legal documents should be proofread twice, because a minor discrepancy can be the basis of litigation. Read a second time aloud to another person. Identify all capital letters, punctuation marks, and abbreviations.

Standard Legal Forms

Undoubtedly your employer will engage legal counsel when preparing important legal papers. If, however, certain types of papers are often used, such as leases or deeds, forms given in legal reference books can be used as guides. Avoid indiscriminate copying of such forms, because laws vary from state to state, and laws also change.

Legal Forms. Stationery stores that supply legal offices carry preprinted forms for such common documents as affidavits, agreements, deeds, leases, powers of attorney, and wills that concur with local laws. These are called *legal forms* or *law blanks*. Look in the Yellow Pages under "Legal Forms" for sources of supply. Some legal forms are purchased in pads. Insert a reorder reminder approximately three-fourths of the way through each new pad.

Many legal forms consist of four pages, printed on both sides of one sheet of 8½-by-28-inch paper folded once to make four pages of 8½-by-14 inches. The form for the endorsement is printed on the fourth page. With this arrangement, binding of pages at the top is unnecessary, and a cover is not used. When the front page (page 1) is turned, pages 2 and 3 read as one continuous page down the full inside length of the document. Legal forms may be bound in a number of ways as Illus. 22-8 and Illus. 22-9 show.

Fill-Ins on Legal Blanks. Fill-ins may range from a single letter or figure to words, phrases, or long lines of text. Printed lines are usually not provided in the blank spaces; therefore, the typist must align the typing line with the printed line. Use the printed margins for typing full lines. As a precaution, rule a "Z" in ink to fill deep unused space (see Illus. 22-4).

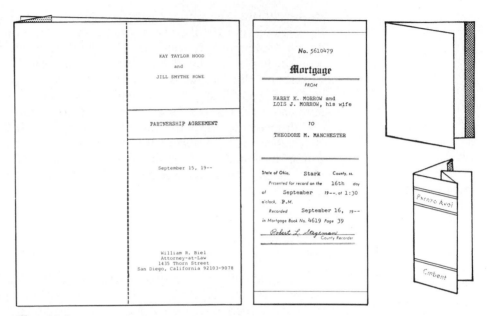

Illus. 22-8
A description of the legal paper within may be typed on the outside of a cover or on a printed legal back. The correct folding of a legal back is shown at the right. Some offices file folded documents in tall, narrow files with the descriptions in view.

Carbon Copies of Legal Blanks. To ensure the best possible alignment on carbon copies of printed forms, check the forms to be sure that all copies were printed at the same time. Most forms carry a legend which indicates when they were printed. For example, *60M 7/6/--* indicates that 60,000 copies were printed on July 6, 19--. Roll the matched set carefully into the typewriter, then insert the carbons. Because aligning is difficult, you may prefer to type each blank individually, checking each one against the source document. If you do this, type *COPY* on all but the original.

Riders. When the space allotted for filling in conditional clauses or other provisions in a legal blank is not large enough for the typewritten insert, leave sufficient space after the last line to permit a slip of paper containing the rest of the typewritten material (called a *rider*) to be pasted to the document. Use legal cap for the rider, and cut off any unused part of the sheet. Fasten the rider securely to the document and fold the rider to fit neatly within the backing sheet.

Forms File. Many legal documents that the secretary types are adaptations of previous ones. A forms file of commonly typed legal docu-

Illus. 22-9
To protect a legal document, a single backing sheet (legal back or cover) with dimensions that are about 1 inch wider and 1½ inches longer than the instrument may be used. This sheet is a high-grade, heavy paper and is usually blue. Pages are inserted under the one-inch fold at the top of the backing sheet. An eyelet or staple is placed at each side. Backing sheets may be color-coded to differentiate types of documents.

```
                      PARTNERSHIP AGREEMENT
            THIS AGREEMENT, made in the City of San Diego,
    State of California, on the 15th day of September, 19--,
    between KAY TAYLOR HOOD and JILL SMYTHE ROWE, both of San
    Diego, California,
            WHEREIN IT IS MUTUALLY AGREED, AS FOLLOWS:
            1.  That the parties hereto shall, as partners,
    engage in and conduct the business of a worldwide travel
    agency.
            2.  That the name of the partnership shall be THE
    WORLDWIDE TRAVEL-EASE AGENCY.
            3.  That the capital of the partnership shall be
    the sum of Twenty Thousand Dollars ($20,000); and each party
    shall contribute thereto, contemporaneously with the execution
    of this agreement, the sum of Ten Thousand Dollars ($10,000)
    in cash.
            4.  That at the end of each calendar year the net
    profit or net loss shall be divided equally between the parties
    hereto, and the account of each shall be credited or debited
    as the case may be, with her proportionate share thereof.

                                    Kay Taylor Hood
                                    Kay Taylor Hood

                                    Jill Smythe Rowe
                                    Jill Smythe Rowe

    Signed and delivered
    in the presence of
```

ments, therefore, can be an important time saver. Accumulate this file by making an extra carbon or photocopy of representative legal documents when they are first typed. In the margin, add helpful notes regarding the number of copies to be prepared, the distribution of the copies, and other pertinent data. In time, the file will contain most, if not all, of the legal documents produced in the office. You can then consult the file to determine the exact procedure for any document contained therein. Legal secretaries consider their forms file to be their most valuable reference source.

WORD PROCESSING AND THE LEGAL OFFICE

Most large and many small legal offices are equipped with automated word processing equipment. Standard paragraphs that have been court-tested make up a significant portion of many legal documents. By storing these paragraphs, they can be retrieved automatically, quickly, and error-free. This leaves the operator only the task of filling in the variable materials. Typographical errors and erasures in certain critical places in a legal document can disqualify the document for court purposes. Word processors produce error-free typing and save many hours of proofreading time.

Computer networks have been established to serve legal offices. These networks carefully store and index legal material—cases, decisions, opinions, and reviews—in large computer banks. For a fee a legal office can access a vast amount of stored information and save hours of research. For example, the computer network can be instructed to print out all the court decisions dealing with a specific point of law. This information usually comes into the legal office of subscribers via some form of computer terminal. In many cases this terminal is a word processor that reproduces materials stored on magnetic media within the legal office and receives output from the legal computer network in response to a request.

THE PARALEGAL/LEGAL ASSISTANT

In the early 1970s when the American Bar Association recognized the need for administrative support personnel to free attorneys from many of the details associated with the practice of law, the position of *paralegal* or *legal assistant* was created. There is no difference in the meaning of these titles; the paralegal and the legal assistant perform the same duties.

A paralegal/legal assistant is an individual who works under the supervision of a licensed member of the legal profession. An attorney utilizes the services of a paralegal in much the same way as a physician would use those of a nurse. Some of the duties performed by a paralegal include the following:

1. To conduct the initial client interview
2. To follow up on an investigation of factual information
3. To research the law pertaining to litigation
4. To draft legal documents
5. To prepare various legal motions

6. To handle exhibits used in court
7. To prepare documents for the dissolution of a marriage, to collect accounts, handle claims, and probate wills

Duties actually performed depend on the nature of the law practice and the needs of attorneys. To be a paralegal, you must be willing to accept professional responsibility, have an interest in and an aptitude for the law, and be completely oriented toward serving the attorney who employs you. Your work must be of unquestioned accuracy.

The educational background required to become a paralegal varies widely. Since the program is relatively new, there are various programs designed to train paralegals. Some of these are degree programs offered by colleges and universities. Others are six-month courses offered by special schools throughout the country. There are over 200 schools offering paralegal programs today. Some states offer a certification program leading to the professional designation of certified attorney's assistant. To obtain this certification, a paralegal must pass a qualifying examination. Local state bar associations have details on paralegal programs offered in various states. The paralegal field is growing in demand and prestige. It offers an excellent career opportunity for the secretary with a special interest in the law and could serve as excellent preparation for law school.

In 1981 the National Association of Legal Assistants (NALA) established a certified legal assistant (CLA) program to promote high standards and professionalism among legal assistants. The CLA program involves the successful completion of a two-day examination; evidence of continuing education must be submitted to NALA periodically in order to maintain certified status. Information on the CLA examination may be obtained from NALA Headquarters, 1420 S. Utica Street, Tulsa, OK 74104.

THE SECRETARY'S KNOWLEDGE OF THE LAW

Some elements of business law affect the day-to-day operation of every office. Because of the importance of your role as a guardian of information, a working knowledge of the laws that directly pertain to your company will add to your efficiency and prevent costly litigation. Business law is extensive and complex, and the secretary is not expected to be an authority on legal matters. However, most companies have established policies that govern the handling of information pertaining to the company, its clients, and its employees.

It is not uncommon for executives and secretaries to unknowingly violate legislation safeguarding equal employment opportunities and the privacy of personnel information. It is essential that every secretary be familiar with the company's policies and federal legislation regarding these areas.

Equal Employment Regulations

A secretary who works closely with the personnel department of a company should be especially familiar with regulations concerning recruiting, screening, hiring, and terminating employees, since these regulations are frequently violated. If you share the responsibilities for interviewing and selecting employees, you should know about the discriminatory nature of certain questions. Before asking any preemployment question, consider these two points: Is the question job related? Does the question eliminate a disproportionate number of minorities? If the answer to this last question is yes or maybe, omit it.

Because regulations change rapidly, it is necessary that you keep up-to-date. The Equal Employment Opportunity Commission issues periodic guidelines for employers about employment regulations. (For further information contact the Director, Equal Employment Opportunity Commission, Room 412, 2401 E Street NW, Washington, DC 20507.) Three significant regulations governing equal employment are:

1. Every employer who is engaged in interstate commerce and employs at least 15 people is required to make employment decisions without consideration of race, creed, color, sex, religion, or national origin. Additionally, an employer may not segregate or classify employees or applicants in any discriminatory way. This includes advertising jobs as male jobs or female jobs.
2. All employers of 20 or more persons are prevented from making employment decisions based on age for persons between 40 and 70.
3. Employers must provide equal pay for men and women working in the same business at jobs requiring equal skill, effort, and responsibility under similar conditions.

Employee Information and Privacy Legislation

With the increasing sophistication of computerized record keeping systems, the public has become concerned about the kinds of information being collected, how the information is used, and who has access to it. The federal government responded to these concerns by passing the Freedom of Information Act in 1966 (FOIA) and amending it in 1974 with the Privacy Act. Both of these acts apply only to records kept by federal agencies, but it is possible that national legislation will be passed to ensure the privacy of employee records in private industry as well. Some states have already passed legislation to permit employees access to their own personal records.

The collection, dispersal, and access to personnel information is usually covered by company policy. The secretary should have a copy of these policies and be alert to requests for information from outsiders. Some companies give only directory information to outsiders. Directory information consists of the employee's job title and dates of employment.

Knowing what you are permitted to tell a caller about company employees can save your employer the cost and inconvenience of a lawsuit if the wrong information should be given. Personnel and payroll records should be made available only to authorized users. If in doubt about what information can or cannot be given, always refer to a higher authority.

SUMMARY

Secretarial work inevitably involves contact with legal vocabulary, legal documents, legal correspondence, and legal procedures. The extent of this involvement depends upon several factors. The secretary in a legal office spends a majority of the workday handling legal documents and procedures. However, an executive secretary in a corporate office may deal with legal documents only occasionally. Regardless of the extent of a secretary's legal work, it demands accuracy and requires some basic understanding of the essential elements of a contract; how to file a proof of claim in bankruptcy proceedings; and the requirements for drawing wills, codicils, affidavits, a power of attorney, and other legal documents.

Regardless of the legal responsibilities assigned to the secretary, familiarity with commonly used legal documents—contracts, proofs of claim, wills and codicils, copyrights, petitions, affidavits, powers of attorney, and patents—is basic to the efficient performance of legal tasks. Responsibilities for the preparation of legal papers may include typing legal documents, filling in legal forms, and witnessing the signing of completed papers. The secretary might find it convenient to become a notary public in order to witness affidavits, wills, acknowledgements, or verifications.

Preparation of legal papers involves work on two classes of documents: *court documents* (affidavits, demurrers, motions, and the like) and *noncourt* documents (leases, wills, contracts, powers of attorney, etc.).

Court requirements vary from state to state regarding the preparation of legal documents. The secretary should learn the court's and the employer's standards for paper size, copies required, type styles, stapling and punching, hyphenation, paragraph indention, page numbers, and how to handle quoted matter and land descriptions. Understanding how to type dates, numbers, reference notations, signature lines and understanding how to handle insertions, erasures, and corrections is also necessary.

Proofreading is an essential skill. Secretaries unfamiliar with legal work should question terms that are not understood. A knowledge of legal forms and how to appropriately fill in legal blanks, to make carbon copies of printed legal forms, to attach riders, and to establish a forms file add to the legal secretary's effectiveness.

In many law offices, word processing technology is having a dramatic effect upon the functions of the legal secretary. Much of the repetitive typing, copying, and proofreading that formerly comprised a significant part of the work of a legal secretary has been automated with word processors, computers, and copiers.

Some secretaries become legal assistants/paralegals. Certification programs to become a professional legal secretary (PLS) or a certified legal assistant (CLA) have been established to professionalize legal secretarial work.

The daily operation of every business is in some way affected by the law. It is not uncommon for secretaries and executives to unknowingly violate legislation regulating equal employment opportunities and the privacy of personnel information. Most companies have policies to meet this legislation. It is essential that every secretary be familiar with these policies.

SUGGESTED READINGS

Anderson, Ronald A., Ivan Fox, and David Twomey. *Business Law*, 12th ed. Cincinnati: South-Western Publishing Co., 1984.

Black's Law Dictionary, 5th ed. St. Paul, MN: West Publishing Co., 1979.

Docket. A bimonthly magazine published for members of the National Association of Legal Secretaries, 3005 East Skelly Drive, Suite 120, Tulsa, OK 74105.

Martindale-Hubbell Law Directory. Summit, NJ: Martindale-Hubbell, Inc. *A four volume reference published annually listing lawyers and their addresses, a digest of the laws of the 50 states, and patent, trademark, and copyright law.*

Namanny, Dorothy S., and Garland C. Dupree. *Legal Office Procedures,* 2d ed. Cincinnati: South-Western Publishing Co., 1984.

National Association of Legal Secretaries. *Manual for the Legal Secretarial Profession,* 2d ed. St. Paul, MN: West Publishing Co., 1974.

Oran, Daniel. *Law Dictionary for Non-Lawyers.* St. Paul, MN: West Publishing Co., 1985.

Reilly, Theresa M. *Legal Secretary's Word Finder and Desk Book.* Englewood Cliffs, NJ: Prentice-Hall, Inc., 1974.

QUESTIONS FOR DISCUSSION

1. Should an employer be involved in collecting money owed by a bankrupt, what are some of the duties that might be assigned to the secretary? What knowledge of bankruptcy proceedings should the secretary have?

2. Answer the following questions relating to the preparation of a power of attorney:
   a. What variables are usually typed on a power of attorney form?
   b. What may be done to prevent the fraudulent insertion of additions after the power of attorney form has been signed?
   c. If the power of attorney is to authorize the bank to accept checks drawn on the company bank account when signed by the secretary, how many copies should be made of the document itself?
   d. How can you be sure that all copies of a printed legal form are identical?

3. How does legal typing differ from manuscript typing in the following areas:
   a. The use of hyphens to divide words
   b. Numbering pages
   c. Ending a page with the last line of a paragraph
   d. The acceptability of erasures and corrections

4. Assume that you are a notary public. In what way do your responsibilities differ when you sign an agreement for monthly machine repair service and when you notarize an affidavit?

5. The secretary in an adjacent office asks you to witness the signatures on a contract. When you reach the office, you find that the signatures have already been affixed. What would you do?

6. Your employer asks you to rush out a legal paper that must be signed by persons waiting in the office. You type it quickly, check it even more quickly, and hand it in. After the signers leave, you notice you made a serious error in a date. What would you do?

7. What precautions are required regarding signatures on legal documents?

8. One reference source states: "When making photocopies of the Will or Codicil, IT IS NEVER TO BE UNSTAPLED OR TAKEN APART." What is a codicil? Why should the will or codicil not be unstapled when preparing copies?

9. Many Latin words and phrases are used in legal documents. What is the English translation of each of the following Latin terms?
   a. *corpus juris*   f. *pro tempore* (or *pro tem*)
   b. *de jure*   g. *quasi*
   c. *et al.*   h. *quod erat demonstrandum* (Q.E.D.)
   d. *loco citato*   i. *scilicet (ss)*
   e. *prima facie*   j. *sic*

10. Why would an employee want access to information kept in a personnel file?

11. A *conversion* is the unconventional use of a word, such as using a noun as an adjective or a verb as a noun. Select the words in the following sentences that have been converted to unconventional parts of speech. Consult the Reference Guide to check your answers.
    a. The Board railroaded the appointment of the chairman.
    b. Many performers skyrocket to fame after their first appearance in Las Vegas.
    c. We bicycled all over Europe.
    d. Her peaches-and-cream complexion is envied by all her friends.
    e. He glassed in the porch to enjoy the winter sun.
    f. We catnapped on the plane.
    g. They can jet to Asia in a few hours.

PROBLEMS

1. It has been recommended that a secretary accumulate a file of legal forms for reference purposes. Prepare a typing instruction

sheet that could be inserted in the front of such a file. Include typing instructions for:

a. Margins
b. Spacing
c. Paragraph indentation
d. Writing dates
e. Paging
f. Writing figures
g. Typing names
h. Typing quoted matter
i. Preparing forms for signatures
j. Fill-ins in legal blanks
k. Correction of errors

2. Assume that you wish to become a notary public in your state.

   a. From your library, from a notary public, or from some other source, obtain the name and address of the designated official in your state who issues notary public commissions.

   b. Obtain from the designated official the specific requirements for the commission in your state. Type a summary of the various requirements.

3. You are a notary public commissioned in Storey County, Nevada. Mr. Toni Nuvamsa asks you to prepare an affidavit for his signature stating that he, Toni Nuvamsa, is a member of the Apache Indian tribe and has resided for the past 18 years at 2323 North Canyon Drive, Reno, Nevada. Prepare the affidavit using the one shown in Illus. 22-3 as a guide. Use the current date. Sign the form as the notary public.

4. Mr. Edward Thomas Stanek, who lives at 134 North 10th Street, Cleveland, Ohio, owns a building located at 3150 North Platt Street, Orlando, Florida. Mr. Stanek wishes to give Rebecca Mary Ploeger of 86 Professional Drive, Orlando, authority to sell the building and the land for him and to execute in his behalf all papers necessary for the transfer of the property. Prepare the power of attorney. Use the form in Illus. 22-4 as a guide. Your form, however, will be typewritten in place of using a printed form illustrated. Use the current date. Complete the notary public statement that constitutes part of the power of attorney.

5. Using the partnership agreement shown in Illus. 22-9 type an original and two carbons of the partnership agreement for Helen Bates Royzet and Martin Charles Cassi, both residents of Columbia, South Carolina. They are forming a partnership to operate a tax accounting service to be known as the Star Tax Service. Each agrees to invest $25,000 in the business. Profits and losses are to be distributed annually and divided equally between the partners. Use the current date.

6. Use a diskette to prepare a bill of sale to be stored on a word processor or a microcomputer. Use the following form as a guide. The variables are indicated by letters.

BILL OF SALE

THIS INDENTURE made the ___a___ day of
_____b_____, 19__c__, BETWEEN
_____d_____

_____,
party of the first part, and _____e_____

_____,
party of the second part;

WITNESSETH: That the said party of the first part in consideration of the sum of $_____f_____ paid by the party of the second part, the receipt of which is hereby acknowledged, shall sell, convey, and confer unto the party of the second part, the following personal property:

_____
_____g_____
_____

_____
_____h_____
_____

Part Six   Case Problems _____

Case 6-1
WHOM DO YOU TRUST?

Norma Surry is secretary to Al Menton, a senior vice-president. As part of her responsibilities, Norma organizes Mr. Menton's tax records to be turned over to his certified public accountant. She also pays his personal bills. Mr. Menton is divorced, lives alone, and travels a good part of the year.

Recently, while Mr. Menton was on an extended business trip, a Mr. Edmunds, who introduced himself as Mr. Menton's investment counselor, came by the office. After introducing himself, he produced a questionnaire and asked Norma questions regarding Mr. Menton's income, investments, indebtedness, and bank balances. Mr. Menton had no appointment scheduled for Mr. Edmunds, and a quick check of her Rolodex revealed that Mr. Edmunds was not listed in any of Norma's records.

How should Norma handle this situation?

Case 6-2
CONFIDENTIALITY OF INFORMATION

Joyce Newman is secretary to the company comptroller. Her job involves handling confidential payroll information. She often has lunch with Connie Vernon, who is secretary to Marvin Keller, an inquisitive junior executive in the sales department. Mr. Keller sometimes joins the secretaries for lunch in the company cafeteria. Each time he has indirectly asked Joyce to divulge salaries of certain employees.

If you were in Joyce's position, how would you handle this situation?

Case 6-3
CENTRALIZED FINANCIAL CONTROL REFLECTS ON SECRETARY'S HONESTY AND EFFICIENCY

Sharon Strong is secretary and office manager for a large medical practice owned and operated by Dr. David I. Hohenshill, Dr. Herman A. West, and Dr. Anthony Petrelano. Dr. Hohenshill is the senior partner; Drs. West and Petrelano have been practicing for only a few years.

Sharon has complete charge of the firm's checking account, petty cash, office payroll, and accounts receivable. She signs all checks and is responsible for paying bills and collecting delinquent accounts. The office staff consists of Ellen Broyles, who works only 20 hours per week. Ellen is responsible for billing, correspondence, and the inventory of prescription drugs. The only other employee is a maid, Anne

Carpenter, who works five days a week. Anne sometimes helps with errands.

Sharon has been with the firm for ten years and has seen it grow from a few patients seen daily to as many as 110 patients a day. In the past ten years, the office has moved twice to accommodate larger numbers of patients. In that time, however, no new equipment has been purchased except an IBM Selectric typewriter on which Ellen types bills and correspondence. The telephone system has been updated once in the past ten years.

Because of the larger number of patients in and out of the office daily, most of Sharon's time is spent making appointments and updating patient records. Consequently, all billing, ordering of supplies, and collection of accounts has been left to Ellen who is woefully behind. Patients sometimes receive their bills as long as 45 days after their visits. Several patients have complained of errors.

Because of some questionable charges to an insurance company for the treatment of a patient, Dr. Hohenshill hired an outside auditing firm to conduct an audit of the firm's records. The audit was completed last October. It is now February and the auditor's report arrived this morning containing the following notations:

1. Written procedures for handling petty cash are not being followed as outlined in the office manual. The account is seldom used, and Sharon often forgets to make a note of cash advances to Anne and Ellen.
2. Some patients received bills for treatment 45 days after an office visit.
3. There is no evidence of executive approval of checks. Dr. Hohenshill countersigned all checks several years ago, but turned the entire responsibility over to Sharon last year.
4. Some accounts receivable are 60 days past due.
5. Several documents in the files bear no evidence of executive approval. Sharon has processed all insurance claims in the past without approval from the doctors.

These notations caused Sharon a great deal of concern inasmuch as she felt that they cast a negative reflection on her integrity and her efficiency. She feels that she is overworked and understaffed.

What corrective action should Sharon recommend to the doctors?

YOUR PROFESSION: PLACEMENT AND ADVANCEMENT

You are now ready to determine your future in the secretarial profession. First, you must make some basic decisions regarding your preferences for field of secretarial specialization, location, and size of the office. A self-evaluation of your interests and abilities will assist you in making these decisions. Once you have accepted a position, work diligently in accomplishing your duties. By making significant contributions to the job and to the employer, you can advance to a position of increased responsibility. With continued education, you can aspire to a management position.

As you enter the field, set your career goals and work toward them steadfastly. In this way, you can reap the dividends of added prestige, greater responsibility, and financial remuneration.

Chapter 23

Selecting the Right Position

Earlier in this book, you learned that qualified secretaries are very much in demand today. In the foreseeable future, the demand for competent, professional secretaries will increase. You also read that salaries are on the rise. Now, as you are about to complete your final term of formal secretarial instruction, you should begin to make some fundamental decisions about your career. As you prepare for employment, you will find many career options available to you; therefore, many decisions must be made in selecting the right position. For example, you must decide if you would prefer to specialize in a medical, legal, government, education, or technical field. You have the choice of working in small or large companies and of working for one person or several. The location of the office may also affect your career decision. You may prefer to work in the heart of town or in the expanse of suburbia. You may want to be a secretary in your own hometown, in a distant city, or even in a distant land. It's really up to you. All these decisions are yours. Well-qualified applicants have no difficulty getting the secretarial position they want in the office, location, and specialization of their choice.

This chapter will prepare you to make some decisions about your career choices. The important steps in the employment process—preparation of a personal data sheet, application forms, and interview techniques—are discussed. The chapter concludes with a discussion of special interest to the part-time job seeker and to the experienced job applicant. Useful suggestions for job hunting and preparing a personal data sheet are provided.

TYPES OF OFFICES

The size of an office and its location determine the type and extent of benefits afforded employees. Although many secretaries work in the downtown areas of cities, where salaries are usually higher than those in outlying districts, attractive positions are open in the suburbs and in smaller towns. From a secretary's viewpoint each type of office and location offers certain advantages.

Small Offices

Many secretaries prefer to work in small offices because small offices enable them to perform a wide variety of duties. The small office is an excellent training ground for all facets of secretarial work. There is usually no one but the secretary to answer the telephone, greet callers, do the filing, handle the petty cash, duplicate materials, sort and send out the mail, and purchase supplies. Examples of one-secretary offices are those maintained by attorneys, architects, engineers, accountants, doctors, dentists, insurance agents, schools, and branch offices.

Personnel Policies. One of the advantages of working in a small office is freedom. Working hours are usually established, but the secretary in a small office knows the volume of work so thoroughly that when time permits, or personal circumstances require, a lunch hour may be extended or an early leave may be taken.

Small offices usually have general personnel policies rather than clearly defined ones. This may or may not be to the advantage of the secretary. There may be no limit to sick leaves and emergency absences, or there may be no provision for them at all. There also may be no insurance or retirement benefits.

There are, however, a few definite disadvantages to working in a small office. Generally salaries have limits. The ceiling for salaries may be set by circumstances of the business and not by the competence of the secretary. Instead of giving specified salary increases at definite intervals, the employer is likely to consider each salary increase individually. Another disadvantage is the absence of social opportunities in the work environment.

Administrative Opportunities. In some small offices, the secretary assumes a great deal of administrative responsibility, but is rarely given an administrative title. Advancement is in terms of salary, not title. Small offices necessitate close working relationships; therefore, an employer soon learns the capabilities of the secretary and will increasingly expand that position to include more and more responsibility. Depending upon the nature of the work, the employer may be out of the office much of the time, and the secretary virtually runs the office.

An office with three and four secretaries frequently provides excellent opportunities to gain supervisory experience. In such situations, the senior secretary may supervise the work of the office staff in addition to the other duties of the job.

Large Offices

The work of the secretary in a large office tends to differ in many respects from that of the secretary in the small office. In the large office, many business routines are performed by special departments. Telephone duties are handled by switchboard operators; postal and shipping chores, by mailing and shipping departments; ordering supplies, by the purchasing department. On the other hand, the secretary in the large office may handle travel details, research business information for the executive, draft reports, sit in on conferences, and perform other important services.

In some large offices, typing and nontyping duties of the secretarial position may be separated, with the word processing center assuming most of the typing responsibilities. The secretary may choose whether to follow the career paths available in a word processing center or those in administrative support areas. Both of these options let the secretary enjoy the benefits of membership in a large organization.

The opportunity for advancement in a large organization to supervisory and administrative positions is good. Secretaries to top management in large firms are frequently administrative assistants in both duties and title.

Personnel Policies. Personnel policies are clearly defined and must be followed in large offices. Singling out an individual employee for special privileges can be damaging to office morale. The personnel policies of a large company are usually very explicit about such matters as the following:

> Hours of work, lunch hour, and rest periods
> Overtime pay or compensatory time off
> Eligibility for vacation, length of vacation
> Number of days allowed annually for sick leave
> Paid holidays
> Salary range for each job, frequency and extent of salary increases
> Fringe benefits
> Job descriptions
> Job classifications

Fringe Benefits. Many businesses and government agencies offer fringe benefits to their employees. They are called *fringe* because they are outside the realm of salary, and sometimes outside the realm of taxable income. In some instances, these benefits cost an organization an additional 30 to 50 percent of wages paid. Common benefits include the following:

Group life insurance
Medical examinations
Medical and hospitalization insurance
Long-term disability benefits
Company stock purchase plan
Profit-sharing plans
Pension fund
Bonuses
Employee credit union
Company educational seminars and conferences
Tuition refunds for job-related course work
Membership expenses in professional organizations
Company subsidized cafeteria
Recreational facilities
Dental insurance
Child care services

A company may pay for all or part of an employee's insurance premiums, make substantial contributions to the pension fund, and provide office space for an employee-operated credit union. Some companies allow employees to choose their own package of benefits. Generous vacations, holidays, and sick leaves are becoming more and more common. Liberal maternity benefits have been written into many company policy manuals. Finally, some firms such as retailers and commercial airlines, offer attractive purchase or travel discounts to their employees.

OPPORTUNITIES FOR SPECIALIZATION

There are unlimited opportunities for the qualified secretary to specialize in a particular field. For most secretaries, a decision to specialize usually comes after having had some experience in general office work. Some office experience, training in business fundamentals and secretarial skills, and an interest in the area of specialization are prerequisite to making this decision. Although there are many areas of specialization, this book can discuss only a few of them.

The Medical Secretary

A long-established and rapidly growing area of secretarial specialization is that of the medical secretary. You may work in a doctor's or dentist's office, a clinic, a hospital, a pharmaceutical company, a public health facility, or even in an insurance company.

Although desirable, special training is not essential; learning on the job is always possible. A knowledge of Latin, however, is helpful in understanding the terminology. Courses in German also will prove helpful. Independent business schools, community colleges, technical colleges and institutes, and some four-year colleges and universities offer programs for training medical secretaries. Besides training in office skills and medical dictation, curriculums include a number of science courses, the study of medical terminology, records management, and accounting procedures. Specialized handbooks are available for the medical secretary. The secretary who is contemplating this field would be wise to examine such a handbook.

In the one-doctor office, the secretary may serve as receptionist, bookkeeper, transcriber of case histories, secretary, and office manager. Sterilizing instruments and taking temperatures may be required. Medical secretaries must also observe the principles of medical ethics by keeping patients' records confidential.

In large medical offices and in hospitals, the secretary's work consists of transcribing patients' records from machine dictation and of smoothly, pleasantly, and comfortingly handling patients. Regardless of the size of the office or organization, the secretary must be familiar with the meaning and the spelling of medical terms, with professional office procedures, and with medical and hospital insurance forms. Illus. 23-1 should give you an idea of the work environment of a medical secretary employed by a large hospital.

To keep current in the field, the medical secretary should join the American Association of Medical Assistants, a professional organization for office staff, nurses, technicians, and assistants employed by physicians or accredited hospitals. This organization sponsors a certification program, publishes a bimonthly magazine (*The Professional Medical Assistant*), and holds an annual convention.

To be eligible to take the certification examination, candidates must meet certain requirements. Training acquired in a medical assisting program and experience in the field are necessary. The examination has three categories. The *general* category tests knowledge of medical terminology, anatomy, physiology, behavioral science, medical law, and medical ethics. The *basic administrative procedures* category covers oral and written communication, bookkeeping, insurance, and

Illus. 23-1
The work of a medical secretary is demanding. Keeping patients' records safe and confidential is an important aspect of this work.

office administration. The *basic clinical procedures* category tests examination room techniques, sterilization procedures, medications, and other clinical procedures.

The Legal Secretary

The legal secretary must have a command of the English language and excellent typewriting and transcription skills. The work of a law office is exacting; an inaccurate record can be extremely expensive to the firm. Working long hours—most of them under pressure—a legal secretary must have a thorough knowledge of legal procedures and a real interest in the law. Most law offices are equipped with word processors or with computers with word processing capabilities; therefore, knowledge of these technologies is imperative.

The National Association of Legal Secretaries holds an annual convention and publishes the NALS *Docket* bimonthly. This organization sponsors through its chapters free training programs, an employment service, and a Professional Legal Secretary examination and certification program. To be eligible for the PLS examination, an applicant must have had at least five years' experience as a legal secretary and must provide the names of two attorneys as references. An applicant with a bachelor's or an associate's degree may file for a partial waiver of the experience requirement. The two-day examination consists of seven parts: written communication skills and knowledge; human relations and ethics; legal secretarial procedures; legal secretarial accounting; legal terminology, techniques, and procedures; exercise of judgment; and legal secretarial skills.

The legal secretary's work is highly varied and involves extensive contact with clients. Occasionally secretaries become so fascinated with the profession that they prepare to be a legal assistant (see Chapter 22) or go to law school.

The Educational Secretary

Every community offers employment opportunities for educational secretaries. The secretary to top school officials in a large city system has duties similar to those of the secretary in business and industry. On the other hand, the secretary in the office of a small school performs vastly different duties including taking dictation, keeping records, ordering materials and supplies, supervising student aides, scheduling facilities, working on master schedules, and planning group meetings. This secretary also meets school visitors and has close contact with students, teachers, and parents.

The National Association of Educational Office Personnel is the professional organization for secretaries in this field. The organization seeks to upgrade the profession by sponsoring a continuing academic program, conducting conferences, and distributing three publications (*The National Educational Secretary, Beam,* and *Crossroads*). The NAEOP also sponsors a Professional Standards Program that issues seven kinds of certificates (basic, associate professional, advanced I, II, III, bachelor, and master) based on education, experience, and professional activity. A college degree is required for the bachelor's certificate and a master's degree for the master's certificate. To be eligible for the examination, an applicant must be a member of the association.

The Technical Secretary

The technical secretary serves engineers and scientists who are at home in the laboratory but not in the office. To conserve the time of highly paid scientific and engineering personnel, many companies provide each top-level scientist and engineer with assistants to perform routine functions, freeing the scientist for creative work. The secretary is the member of this support team, assuming the burden of office administration and minimizing distractions and interruptions.

The technical secretary is probably as much an administrative assistant as a secretary. The work includes not only the usual secretarial duties but such additional responsibilities as handling all or most of the correspondence (from composition to mailing); maintaining the office technical library; gathering materials from libraries or computer databases; and proofreading, editing, and handling all details incident to the publication of scientific papers. The secretary prepares engineering reports, checks materials against specifications and standards, and orders materials in compliance with specifications. The work is demanding and exacting, but the pay is exceedingly rewarding. A strong background in mathematics, science, and technical terminology is a definite asset; advancement requires continued study. Illus. 23-2 should give you an idea of the qualifications employers look for in a technical secretary.

When you work as a technical secretary, you can expect to undergo security clearance if you are employed in a company having contracts with the United States Department of Defense. The maintenance of strict security control is becoming important to other companies as well, because of the possibility of pirating formulas, research findings, advanced designs, and so forth. The technical secretary must know how security is maintained for each classification from restricted data to top secret.

The Public Secretary

As the title implies, the public secretary is in business to serve the public. People (usually traveling executives) often need someone for dictation and transcription or similar short-term jobs. For this reason, the office of a public secretary is equipped with word processing and communication equipment and is usually located in a hotel, off the main foyer of a large office building, or at an airport facility. The public secretary charges by the hour or by the job and may work for as many as a dozen persons each day. The work ranges from taking highly technical dictation to recording speeches and testimony of witnesses, to typing legal documents, to running errands for a busy executive. A public secretary is usually a notary public as well.

Highly qualified secretaries usually find this field gratifying and exciting. Only someone with a broad education, sufficient financial resources, a wealth of office experience, the temperament to cope with the pressure of deadlines, and the highest level of skills should attempt

TECHNICAL SECRETARY

Dynamic young medical research institute needs qualified technical secretary to support quality control division. Highly proficient in all phases of office procedures with top skills. Must be able to work without supervision. Background in mathematics and sciences helpful. Salary commensurate with ability. Excellent benefits. Call Ms. Alvarez at 555-6782 for appointment.

TRIANGLE RESEARCH INSTITUTE
5770 Waycross Drive
Bala Cynwyd, PA 19004-2139

Illus. 23-2
An advertisement for a technical secretary stresses that a background in science or mathematics is desirable.

to enter the field. In the right location, the income is high; but much of the work is performed under pressure.

The Temporary Service Secretary

One of the fastest growing service industries today provides part-time office help. Kelly Services, Inc., Olsten Corp., and Manpower, Inc., are a few of the organizations specializing in temporary service. Others are listed in the Yellow Pages and are widely advertised in general publications. These organizations offer a corps of temporary workers to be deployed wherever required. It is estimated that over two million people work as temporaries each year. They help the office that experiences intermittent periods of heavy work load, they fill in for employees who are on vacation or ill, and they provide the one-half secretary for the $1\frac{1}{2}$-secretary office.

Many firms are entirely staffed with permanent temporary employees. In addition to rendering a service to business, some temporary service agencies provide their temporaries with training on word processors, computers, and related office equipment. These organizations also provide a means of organized part-time employment to a large number of persons who are unable, because of family obligations or other duties, to devote themselves to year-round, full-time jobs. A temporary position permits a flexible schedule and a choice of job locations close to home. It also enables a person to acquire experience before applying for a full-time job or reentering the job market after a long absence. To be happy in temporary work, the secretary must be flexible, confident, and adaptable to change.

The work of a temporary secretary is varied. Calls for assistance come from all types of offices. The agency attempts to match the requirements of the job with the competencies of the temporary worker. Temporaries can be selective in the jobs they accept, as well. Many a secretarial trainee in college has found that being an office temporary for the summer is one way to gain a wide variety of experience in a short time. At the same time, being a temporary helps a secretary determine what type of company would be the most appealing to work for full time.

The Government Secretary

More secretaries work for the government than for any other type of business or organization. Government positions offer certain advantages, such as assured annual salary increments, job security, a sound retirement system, and the opportunity for advancement based on merit. A secretary trained in office administration, who has initiative and ambition, can advance to a position of great responsibility in government service. Being a government employee does not necessarily mean working in Washington, DC (where 12 percent of all U.S. government civilian positions are located) or for the federal government. Wherever there is a military installation, veterans' hospital, weather station, or federal bureau office, there are federal employees. State and local governments (combined) employ far more office workers than does the federal government. Government jobs are found in towns and cities in America and in foreign countries.

The federal government, all states, and many municipal governments have a civil service merit system in which jobs are classified and appointments are made on the basis of examination results. As a student, you can obtain a certificate of proficiency in typing and shorthand from your college, but you must take the written civil service examination of verbal and clerical abilities to qualify for these jobs. The federal government is now following the practice of *self-certification* in typewriting and shorthand. An applicant who certifies a typewriting skill of 40 or more words a minute and shorthand at 80 need not take the tests. The applicant is also graded on education, training, and experience.

Stenographic posts are classified in the federal government as GS3 (General Schedule 3) through GS6, and it is possible for a secretary to advance to GS7 and 8. There is a standard base salary, with annual increments, for each GS rating. For high-cost areas, such as Alaska and Hawaii, cost-of-living increases are given.

For the first years of government service, an employee is considered *career conditional*; after three years, the status changes to *career permanent*. This classification means that you can apply to any federal agency without further testing. Also, if you leave government service and return within three years from the date of your termination, you do not lose accumulated sick leave. In addition, unused sick leave hours count toward an early retirement date.

The United States is divided into ten regions with an Office of Personnel Management in each. Also, there are over 100 Federal Job Information Centers. These centers are listed in telephone directories under "United States Government." If a center is not listed in your directory, the toll-free number for the center in your state can be obtained by dialing 800-555-1212. To obtain information about a position, write to the Office of Personnel Management in the region in which you wish to obtain employment or telephone your local Federal Job Information Center. If you are interested in working in Washington, DC, write to the Office of Personnel Management, 1900 E Street, NW, Washington, DC 20415.[1]

The Foreign Service Secretary

Does the prospect of serving as a secretary in the Americal Legation in Berlin, Tokyo, Paris, London, or Copenhagen interest you? If so, you should examine the employment opportunities in the Foreign Service, the United States Information Agency (USIA), the Agency for International Development (AID), and the Departments of Army, Navy, and Air Force.[2] The Department of State has Foreign Service offices in over 300 cities worldwide.

Work in a foreign country can be thrilling, but also exacting. It calls for a special kind of person. U.S. Foreign Service personnel are on display 24 hours a day. Each staff member represents the United States and contributes to the success of our mission overseas. The Department of State, USIA, and AID, therefore, carefully screen all foreign

---

[1]To learn more about federal employment, order *Federal Personnel Guide* from Federal Personnel Publications, P.O. Box 274, Washington, DC 20044. Published annually in January, this guide explains hiring processes, pay schedules, retirement programs, insurance, and so forth.

[2]Information about foreign employment through the United States Information Agency and the Agency for International Development can be obtained by writing to these agencies in Washington, DC.

service personnel; and requirements are high. The basic requirements for a secretarial position in the Foreign Service are as follows:

21 years of age
United States citizen
High school graduate or equivalent
Passing grade from a qualifying examination covering clerical ability, spelling, typing, shorthand
Good health
Minimum of three to five years of progressively responsible experience in clerical, secretarial, or administrative employment. (Education beyond high school may be substituted for part of the experience requirement.)

Competency in a foreign language is not required. If, however, you should have ambitions to advance to the position of a staff officer in the Department of State, the ability to speak and write a foreign language is required. Extensive study of a foreign language in college will be a strong plus factor when your application is evaluated.

The pay for Foreign Service secretaries is comparatively good, with additional allowances for housing, cost of living, and special compensation for hardship posts. For information, write to the U.S. Department of State, Foreign Service Personnel Office, *Foreign Service Secretaries Brochure*, Washington, DC 20520. The booklet, *Federal Jobs Overseas* (BRE-18), can be obtained at any area office of the Office of Personnel Management.

SURVEY OF EMPLOYMENT OPPORTUNITIES

A review of the help wanted advertisements in most newspapers will show that the highly qualified, college-trained secretary is in a position to pick and choose. The problem, then, is one of job selection. There are many dimensions to the selection process, as these questions reveal:

1. Do you want to work in your local community, or do you hope to find employment in a new location? in a large city? in a different part of the country? abroad?

2. Which organizations relate to your special interests in art, music, sports, medicine, accounting, social work, research, writing, politics?

3. How do your education and skills match the job requirements of your career goal?

4. Would you prefer to work in a one-secretary office or in a large organization?
5. What are you looking for in a job? Do you want a job that offers security? no pressure? competition? responsibility? advancement? prestige?
6. What is the average salary for the position you are seeking?

Psychologists say that the key elements of job satisfaction are a sense of responsibility, satisfaction of achievement, opportunity for growth, recognition from employer, and a feeling of being needed. The right choice is not the result of luck but of careful analysis and action.

Before you begin your job search, take a few minutes to prepare a job prospect list. Decide how you will evaluate a company. Set goals and objectives for yourself. Then begin to execute your plan.

Developing a Job Prospect List

No good sales campaign is ready for action without a *prospect list*. Your job prospect list should include potential employers who can offer the kind of employment opportunity you are seeking in terms of location, size, interest appeal, permanence, and job satisfaction.

College Placement Office. The placement office of your college can give you expert help in developing your prospect list and can assist you in making job contacts. Complete all forms necessary for registration promptly. Get acquainted with the placement office personnel. Discuss your employment needs with them freely and often. If they arrange a job interview for you, always report to them after the interview. Solicit their advice and let them know you appreciate their assistance.

Free Employment Agencies. Employment agencies are a good source of prospective positions. Any person seeking employment may register without charge with a state employment office. Registration includes a comprehensive interview and a skills test so that you can be properly classified according to your abilities, personality traits, training, and experience. In order to keep on its active list, you must communicate with that office regularly.

Other free employment services are available in some metropolitan areas. For instance, JobNet, located in Bedford, Massachusetts, offers a free computerized job finding service to job seekers. Consult the classified section of your newspaper for employment agency listings.

Private Employment Agencies. A private employment agency performs for a fee three functions: It acts as an agent for the job seeker, as a recruiter for the employer, and as a job market information center. Many agencies have a computerized database of job candidates which they make available to employers and to job applicants. In about two thirds of the jobs listed, employers pay the fee. In some states, regulatory bodies set limits on fees charged by agencies. An applicant registering with an agency signs a contract in which the fee terms are stated. (As with every written contract, read carefully before you sign. Be sure that you understand the conditions of the contract.) After a contract is signed, the applicant is assigned a counselor. Inform the counselor of all employers you have contacted before coming to the agency so that you will not be obligated for the fee if a job arises from your previous contacts. A major advantage of a good agency is that it carries out a complete job hunt for the applicant, thus relieving the job seeker of much of the repetitive detail work involved in job hunting. Another advantage is that the agency serves as a third party representative for the applicant with prospective employers.

Private employment agencies perform a valuable service for the employer as well. The staff of the agency can expertly screen, test, and interview each applicant. The company then interviews only those who meet the company's specified qualifications. Because many businesses use private agencies exclusively, keep in mind that many desirable positions are available only through such agencies.

A private employment agency should be selected carefully. Don't hesitate to interview the agency to determine its professionalism. For a directory of reputable agencies, write to the National Association of Personnel Consultants, 1432 Duke Street, Alexandria, VA 22314. This directory will be especially helpful in locating an agency in a distant city where you would like to obtain employment. Agencies listed in this directory subscribe to a code of ethical practices. Some agencies are a part of a recruiting network which can put you in touch with member agencies in other cities. You might also contact the Better Business Bureau to determine if any agency has been reported for unethical practices.

Newspaper Advertisements. The classified section of the newspaper is an excellent source of information for the job seeker. Besides providing an employment picture of the community, skill requirements and current pay rates for secretarial positions are often stated. You do not need to meet every specification of an advertisement, only most of them. If a particular advertisement appeals to you, carefully follow the directions given for making an application.

In reviewing the help wanted section, notice that these advertisements do not specify male or female or in any way indicate a preferred age of an applicant. Federal law prohibits employers and employment agencies from classifying jobs by sex (unless it is a realistic occupational qualification) or by preferred ethnic group or age level. In fact, some advertisements will state that the company is *an equal opportunity employer*.

Firms that advertise for help in the classified columns sometimes use a blind advertisement (see Illus. 23-3). A *blind advertisement* is one in which a key or box number is used for your reply and the firm name is not mentioned. A legitimate blind advertisement is used because the firm does not want to be bothered with interviewing large numbers of applicants. Most employers notify present employees before running a blind advertisement. This prevents the possibility of an employee answering a blind ad and being embarrassed for doing so. Blind advertisements are sometimes used just to get names of sales prospects by someone who has something to sell.

Illus. 23-3
Blind
advertisements ask
applicants to reply
to a newspaper box
number.

TOP DRAWER

Interested in art, music, theater, sports? A new magazine that will cover all aspects of life in the exciting city of Chicago is looking for an exceptional secretary. You must have excellent skills, good judgment, be able to supervise the support staff, work effectively under pressure, and be eager to accept challenges and responsibility. Opportunities for creativity in the areas of writing, photography, graphics, and design abound. Strong background in English a must. This position offers you a ground floor opportunity to go as far as your abilities will take you.
Send resume to Box 119, Sun Times, Chicago, IL 60601-5047

Friends, Relatives, and Associates. Include friends, friends of your family, business people with whom you have had some kind of contact, student alumni groups, and former instructors to gather names for your job prospect list. Inform them that you are seeking a position and that you would appreciate their help.

Another source for job leads is a professional organization, such as the National Federation of Business and Professional Women's Clubs. This organization maintains a talent bank of members for referral to employers seeking women to fill middle- to top-level management jobs. Special interest groups, such as Forty Plus, also provide employment information to members. If someone refers you to an opening, it is a matter of courtesy to let that person know the outcome.

Other Sources. The Yellow Pages of your telephone book provide a classified list of the local businesses to which you might apply. Make a list of those companies where you would like to work. Take the initiative to visit their personnel offices. This is a most effective way of securing employment. For instance, if you are interested in a position in an insurance company, the Yellow Pages will list all local companies. Make an appointment for an interview or send your personal data sheet and a letter of application to the personnel department.

Do not forget that the government is a major employer. You will find federal and state employment offices listed in the telephone directory.

Become an avid reader of the daily newspaper and watch all news items that give clues to possible job contacts. New businesses are constantly opening, and articles relating to jobs, changes, or expansions often appear in the newspaper.

Job Prospects in Other Locations. A number of information sources may be used to obtain job prospects in a distant city or area. In addition to the directory of the National Association of Personnel Consultants (see page 676), copies of the leading newspapers from cities across the nation can be examined at your local library. Telephone directories for major cities are also kept in many public libraries. Trade association directories are helpful in providing addresses of companies and chambers of commerce maintain directories of local employers.

Learning about a Company

After you have compiled a job prospect list, you should exhaust all means of getting information on each of the firms on your list. Telephone to find out the employment manager's name. Inquire of your friends, acquaintances, and instructors about the firm. Check library reference materials and computer databases to learn of the company's financial condition. Examine the company's advertisements in papers and magazines. Study the annual report of the firm. A copy of an annual report can usually be obtained by sending a request to the company.

Many large companies publish brochures describing their job opportunities and employment policies. Your college placement office may have these brochures on file. If not, send a request to the company. If it is a small firm, consult the chamber of commerce and the Better Business Bureau. Use separate file folders to accumulate pertinent material on each company.

Many firms will be eliminated from your list as you proceed in this information-gathering campaign. When your information is complete, group your prospects according to jobs you are best fitted to fill. Select prospects that offer the best chance for employment and which will provide an interesting future.

Evaluating a Company

How do you judge a company as a potential employer? There is no sure test, but answers to the following questions may help:

1. *What is the reputation of the company in the community?* The community image of a company is the sum of many things including employee relationships, reputation for progressive management, sponsorship of community projects, fair employment practices, and general leadership in civic and business activities.

2. *Is the company an equal opportunity employer?* Is it known to discriminate in employment in the areas of race, creed, color, national origin, age, or sex?

3. *How satisfactory are employer-employee relationships?* Do employees seem to have a common bond of enthusiasm, or are there undercurrents of distrust and backbiting?

4. *Is the business financially stable?* A business that is not economically sound cannot give its employees a sense of financial security. Its wage policies and employee benefits will always depend on the profit picture.

5. *Is the company expanding?* A growing organization usually offers opportunities for advancement.

6. *What opportunities for training and advancement are provided?* Companies that provide special training programs or pay college tuition merit special consideration.

Don't overlook opportunities in small offices—you may be happier there—or in a new company that is just getting under way. Being on the beginning team can be exciting and rewarding.

PREPARATION OF AN APPLICATION

A fundamental step in preparing to make an application for employment is to take an inventory of your knowledge, skills, strengths, and weaknesses in terms of the requirements of each particular position. What skills, understandings, and special qualities will the employer be seeking? What type of experience will be expected? Do you have unique qualities that would be an asset in the position? What weaknesses in your preparation or background might the employer note? What plan do you have to correct these weaknesses? The preparation of a personal data sheet will assist you in making this analysis.

Your Personal Data Sheet

Sometimes called a *résumé* or *personal history*, a personal data sheet is a concise, positive presentation of your background and abilities. Because your purpose is to gain a personal interview, your data sheet must arouse interest in your unique qualifications. It must be short, preferably one page; if too long, it dulls the interest. It must be a reflection of you. Do not use a copy from a textbook or one written by a friend.

Some large employment agencies and corporations code and enter information furnished on an applicant's data sheet in their computer system. When an opening occurs, the computer is searched for the names of applicants meeting the specific requirements of the job.

There are two types of personal data sheets: a *chronological data sheet* is a record of your work history; a *functional data sheet* emphasizes job titles and job descriptions. In the latter, a summary statement of experience is given, followed by a list of job functions and their descriptions. The names of employers and dates of employment follow this section or can be omitted. An example of a chronological data sheet appears in Illus. 23-4.

Authorities do not agree on the merit of attaching a photograph to a data sheet. Some believe that a photograph places the personnel officer in a position of possible discrimination, since the photograph illustrates age, sex, and race. Yet other authorities think that a photograph can be of assistance in getting an interview. If you decide that a photograph will be helpful, be sure that it is a businesslike pose of approximately billfold size.

You will use your data sheet in a number of ways. Send it with letters of application. Give copies to friends, relatives, and business acquaintances to pass on to prospective employers. Your college placement office will need one or more copies. Always take a copy to an interview. Use it to supplement an application form.

Make sure that your data sheet is expertly typed on good quality white paper. Try to use an electronic typewriter or a word processor to give your résumé a professional look. Use wide margins and leave

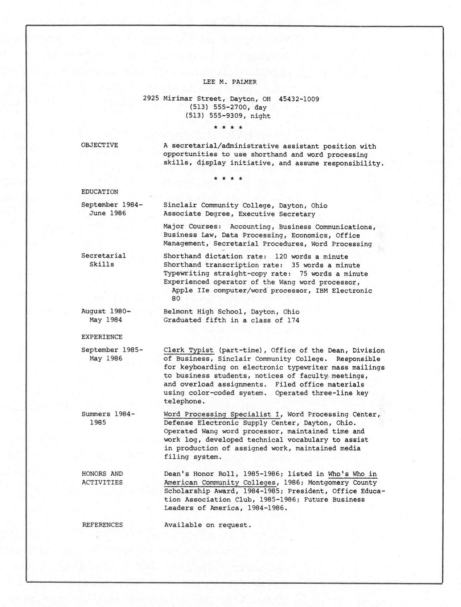

LEE M. PALMER

2925 Mirimar Street, Dayton, OH 45432-1009
(513) 555-2700, day
(513) 555-9309, night

* * * *

OBJECTIVE   A secretarial/administrative assistant position with
                     opportunities to use shorthand and word processing
                     skills, display initiative, and assume responsibility.

* * * *

EDUCATION

September 1984–   Sinclair Community College, Dayton, Ohio
June 1986   Associate Degree, Executive Secretary

                     Major Courses: Accounting, Business Communications,
                     Business Law, Data Processing, Economics, Office
                     Management, Secretarial Procedures, Word Processing

Secretarial   Shorthand dictation rate: 120 words a minute
Skills   Shorthand transcription rate: 35 words a minute
                     Typewriting straight-copy rate: 75 words a minute
                     Experienced operator of the Wang word processor,
                       Apple IIe computer/word processor, IBM Electronic
                       80

August 1980–   Belmont High School, Dayton, Ohio
May 1984   Graduated fifth in a class of 174

EXPERIENCE

September 1985–   Clerk Typist (part-time), Office of the Dean, Division
May 1986   of Business, Sinclair Community College. Responsible
                     for keyboarding on electronic typewriter mass mailings
                     to business students, notices of faculty meetings,
                     and overload assignments. Filed office materials
                     using color-coded system. Operated three-line key
                     telephone.

Summers 1984–   Word Processing Specialist I, Word Processing Center,
1985   Defense Electronic Supply Center, Dayton, Ohio.
                     Operated Wang word processor, maintained time and
                     work log, developed technical vocabulary to assist
                     in production of assigned work, maintained media
                     filing system.

HONORS AND   Dean's Honor Roll, 1985-1986; listed in Who's Who in
ACTIVITIES   American Community Colleges, 1986; Montgomery County
                     Scholarship Award, 1984-1985; President, Office Educa-
                     tion Association Club, 1985-1986; Future Business
                     Leaders of America, 1984-1986.

REFERENCES   Available on request.

Illus. 23-4
A chronological
data sheet provides
a record of an
applicant's
education and work
history.

plenty of blank spaces between sections. Your data sheet's appearance
says as much about you as does its content. Many an applicant has lost
the opportunity for an interview because of messy corrections, poor
format, misspelled words, or grammatical errors on a data sheet or on
an accompanying application letter. Although interviewers prefer an
original copy of a data sheet, a copy made on a good quality copier is
acceptable. Carbon copies are frowned upon by interviewers.

Personal Data. Every data sheet must include the job seeker's name, address, and telephone number. This identification should appear as a heading for the information that follows. It is no longer necessary to provide such personal information as age, height, weight, sex, marital status, or social security number. If, however, you consider it to your advantage to include this information, then do so.

Objective. This section gives you the opportunity to identify the specific position you seek, your long-range career goals, or both. Some authorities believe, however, that this information belongs in a cover letter, thus leaving space in the résumé for mentioning your accomplishments. If you have varied experience and can qualify for a number of office jobs, you should not include a detailed objective that may disqualify you for positions for which you would like to be considered. From the reader's standpoint, an objective provides instant knowledge of the sort of job you are seeking.

Education. Include complete, pertinent information about your educational background. Begin with facts about your most recent educational experience.

Schools Attended. List all colleges and universities that you have attended and the high school from which you were graduated. List the most recent schools first and give dates of graduation, diplomas received, degrees conferred, awards, and scholarships.

Major Subjects. Business courses that you completed should be listed. Include also courses specifically related to the position for which you are applying. For example, in applying for a secretarial position in an advertising office, you might list English, art, and psychology courses taken.

Secretarial Skills and Abilities. Give your speed in shorthand dictation and transcription. Indicate by manufacturer's name the electronic equipment you have used in your work experience. List separately the business machines that you can operate and indicate your operating ability. Overrating your abilities, however, may give your application a tone of superiority that may unfavorably impress your potential employer.

Work Experience. List your work experience in reverse order (on a chronological data sheet) or in the order of its importance to the position in question (on a functional data sheet). For example, in applying for a secretarial position, list office experience (full and part-time) first, giving inclusive dates of employment, the name and address (city and state only) of the employer, telephone number, the title of the position held, and a brief description of your job duties. Use action verbs to describe your duties. If your work involved the supervision of others, be sure to include that fact. And don't forget to mention promotions. Omit any reference to salary earned.

If you are like most college students whose experience is limited to part-time and summer employment, you should include the dates and descriptions of your employment history on your data sheet. Even if your part-time and summer jobs did not involve office work, they should be listed. They are often indicative of your willingness to work and your ability to get along with other people.

Special Interests, Abilities, and Accomplishments. Your extracurricular activities, special interests, and achievements give the prospective employer an indication of what kind of person you are and how you would fit into the office; therefore, you should list:

1. *The extracurricular activities in which you have participated and the offices you have held.* Holding a responsible office in one group may be more impressive than listing membership in virtually every organization on campus.
2. *Special honors received.* Awards and scholarships are evidence of your ability and perseverance.
3. *Special achievements (if they have implications for the position you are seeking).* Your ability to read or speak a foreign language, awards for English composition or original writing, or special training in some field of science may be the specific point that influences an employer to grant you an interview.

References. You will need to have at least three references in mind when you begin your job search. The longer and better they have known you, the more valid will be their evaluation of your abilities.

If you have had no experience, consider using instructors of business subjects or administrators who have firsthand knowledge of your training and can evaluate your work potential. Avoid using the names of close relatives or your minister (unless the job is church related) for a work reference. You must secure permission to use anyone's name as a reference before submitting it to a prospective employer.

Upon leaving a job, request a letter of reference from your employer. This letter may be especially helpful to you if you are moving to another city or state.

Authorities do not agree on including references on the data sheet. The majority suggest that references be furnished upon request. An employer usually asks for the names and addresses of references during the interview or when you are completing an application blank. If you include your references on your data sheet, make clear your relationship (i.e., former employer or teacher).

Other Information. You may include the date that you are available for employment and information about your willingness to relocate on your data sheet. *Save matters concerning salary and your reasons for leaving previous employment for the interview.*

Your Application Letter

An application letter is another document used by the job seeker to obtain a personal interview. It may be the only document to describe your qualifications, or a data sheet may be attached to it. Like the data sheet, the application letter should be individually and faultlessly typed and limited to one page. It should highlight experience that is related to the job in question. Bear in mind, too, that your letter is one of many that the employer receives. Thus, it should be unique in order to set it apart from all the rest.

Solicited and Unsolicited Application Letters. An application letter is *solicited* if you are responding to a help wanted advertisement or if you are writing at the request of an employer (frequently a part of the screening process). A personal data sheet should accompany a solicited letter. The letter will expand on your special qualifications for the position and will indicate why you are interested in the company.

Unsolicited application letters can be written to discover an opening or to follow up a reported opportunity. An unsolicited letter format can be used repeatedly with carefully made adaptations to meet the special requirements of different types of jobs. An unsolicited application letter need not include a data sheet. The letter should include a summary of your previous experience and a discussion of your capabilities and how they relate to the position you are seeking. If you are granted an interview, then you can present your data sheet tailored specifically to the available position.

Basic Parts of an Application Letter. Whether solicited or unsolicited, your letter should include the following parts:

1. An interesting first paragraph that tells why you are writing commands attention. Three examples of interesting first paragraphs follow:

    Mr. Grant Lehman suggested that I write to inquire whether you have an opening for a technical secretary in your Research and Development Division.

The position of secretary described in your advertisement in today's issue of the *Sentinel* is a challenging opportunity. May I be considered for the position?

Mr. Ron Radtke, head of the Administrative Services Department at Eastern Community College, tells me that you have a secretarial position open for a graduate with stenographic and word processing training. Will you please consider me an applicant?

2.   A statement indicating why you are interested in joining the company (if the name of the company is known), or in lieu of that, an expansion on what you know about the requirements of the position you are seeking. The use of quotation marks in the examples which follow indicate that the words appearing in the advertisement have been incorporated into the letter of application.

Your company is well known in our community for its superior products, recent plant expansion, and benefits to employees. From what I have learned about LKM Company, I would be proud to be part of your "future growth."

Words, such as "responsible" and "administrative ability," in your advertisement's description of the available position immediately appealed to me. These words mean that you are looking for an individual who can show initiative, work without supervision, and assume some of the administrative tasks of the employer. I believe that my training at Madison Technical College has qualified me to say "I am up to the task."

3.   A closing paragraph should ask for an appointment for an interview or other definite action.

Because I cannot be reached by telephone during business hours, I shall telephone your office on Friday morning to ask for an appointment for an interview.

I should like very much to come to your office to talk with you about the position. When I telephone you on Wednesday morning, will you please let me know a time that would be convenient for you to see me?

Guides for Writing Application Letters. There is no one formula for writing an effective application letter, but studying the sample letter of application in Illus. 23-5 and observing the following guidelines, should make the task less formidable:

1.   *Address the letter to an individual.* A letter directed "To Whom It May Concern" may never concern anyone. Find out

2925 Mirimar Street
Dayton, OH 45432-1009
April 10, 1986

Mr. Howard Edmonds, Personnel Director
Harmon Manufacturing Company
1604 Stanley Avenue
Dayton, OH 45432-2342

Dear Mr. Edmonds:

TELLS WHY YOU ARE WRITING
The Placement Office at Sinclair Community College has told me of the opening in your office for a graduate with a background in shorthand and word processing. I understand that the position requires a large volume of dictation in addition to routine office duties and provides an opportunity to assume administrative responsibilities. I believe I meet your requirements and would like to be considered for this position.

TELLS WHY YOU ARE INTERESTED IN THIS COMPANY
While enrolled in the Executive Secretary Program at Sinclair, I had the opportunity to tour a number of industrial firms in our city. Of those I visited, your company offices, your operations, and the friendliness of your staff impressed me the most. I hope to become a part of your dynamic organization.

REFERS TO YOUR DATA SHEET
You will see from the enclosed data sheet that I have acquired a high level of secretarial and word processing skill. You will also note that I have supplemented my course work at Sinclair with on-the-job experience during the summers and during my last year at Sinclair.

REQUESTS ACTION
Since it may be difficult to reach me by telephone during working hours, I shall call your office next Tuesday to schedule an appointment at your convenience. I am looking forward to discussing this position with you.

Yours very truly,

Lee M. Palmer

Lee M. Palmer

Enclosure

Illus. 23-5
A letter of application must arouse a reader's interest in your suitability for a particular job.

the name and title of the person in charge of employment and use them. This information may be obtained from the switchboard operator of the company. The use of the name (correctly spelled) and title personalizes the letter and makes a favorable first impression. Obviously you cannot address your letter to an individual when you are replying to a blind advertisement.

The correct address form and salutation for such a letter is shown here:

Box H-816
Charlotte Observer
Charlotte, NC 28202-2555

Ladies and Gentlemen:

Good Morning!

2.   *Use the you approach.* Your application letter is a sales letter, and the product is you. You must convince the prospective employer how you can serve that company. Tell about yourself from the perspective of the employer. Avoid using these expressions: *I want, I did this,* and *I did that.* Show that you understand the requirements of the position and demonstrate how your qualifications meet the employer's needs.

3.   *Be honest, confident, and enthusiastic.* Your application letter should show a proper, not exaggerated, appreciation of your ability. Above all, be *honest.* Your letter should be neither boastful nor deprecating. Employers are experts in detecting insincerity. Be specific about the position you want and the things you can do: You may be called upon to prove your claims. Do not be apologetic. If your experience is limited, you need not call attention to the fact. Concentrate on your positive qualities.

4.   *Be concise.* If you enclose a personal data sheet, omit a detailed treatment of your education and experience in your letter. Your letter should be an invitation to read the data sheet. The statement, "I am enclosing information about my training and experience," does little to persuade the reader to continue to your data sheet. Stimulate interest. "An examination of my personal data sheet will show that I am well prepared by training and experience for secretarial work," or "My extracurricular activities, described in the enclosed personal data sheet, have prepared me to work with other people" are examples of sentences that arouse a reader's interest.

5.   *Make action easy.* You are more likely to win an interview by saying, "I shall call you on Friday morning to see if you wish to arrange a personal interview," instead of saying "May I hear from you?" The purpose of the application letter is to get an interview. If you obtain one, your letter has done as much as you can expect it to do.

6.   *Give the letter eye appeal.* Make your letter attractive and absolutely faultless in conformity with the best rules of business letter writing. Anything you say will be worthless if your message contains a typographical error. There must be no flaws in spelling, grammar, punctuation, typing, arrangement, spacing, placement, or wording. You should use a good quality

bond paper of standard letter size. Your envelope should match the paper in quality. Letterhead paper should not be used. Your complete address (but no name) should be typed as the heading.

7. *File a copy of each application letter that you write.* It is a good idea also to keep records of your interviews. A form, similar to the one shown in Illus. 23-6, is useful for keeping track of this information.

Illus. 23-6
Use this form to record your mailings and interview follow-up dates.

APPLICATION LETTER AND DATA SHEET
MAILINGS

Date	Individual/Firm Name	Follow-up Date	Receipt Ack.	Interview Date	Follow-up Date	Action Plan
4/10	Howard Edmonds Harmon Manuf. Co.	4/16		4/23		

THE INTERVIEW

The hiring process usually involves two interviews. The first takes place in the personnel department; the second, within the department where the position is available. An invitation for an initial interview gives you an opportunity to learn more about the company and the position and it also provides an opportunity to discuss your career aspirations, training, and specific skills. Go to the interview armed with information about the company, its products, and its reputation in the community.

The *first interview* typically lasts half an hour, which is ample time to exchange information and questions. During this interview, you must make a good impression. The interviewer will form opinions based on your general appearance, your voice, diction, posture, attitude, and personality. Enthisiasm for your career will be noted. The interviewer will evaluate how you answer questions and how your abilities match the company's requirements. In short, your performance during this first interview, plus your data sheet and application form, provide a volume of information about you. If you are interested in the position, aim for a second interview at the departmental level. A successful interview doesn't just happen. The job seeker must prepare to make a good first impression.

Guides to a Successful Interview

Tend toward the conservative side in dress and appearance (see Illus. 23-7). Men should wear business suits; women, a suit or tailored dress. Nails should be clean and well manicured. Hair should be clean, trimmed, and simply styled. Make sure that you are satisfied with your appearance before you leave for the interview. It is a good idea to get a good night's rest and to hold a dress rehearsal prior to the interview.

A card, a letter, or a note of introduction to someone in the organization can be helpful. It may be a referral card from your placement or employment agency office or a note on the back of a business card from a reference. This communication should put you in contact with the one you want to see.

Anticipate questions the interviewer will ask. If you have thought through the possible questions, you will be less likely to be caught off guard during the interview. Plan your answers. Do not talk too much nor too little; strive for the happy medium. Have a positive attitude. Remember, first impressions are extremely important. Before an interview, use the pre-interview checklist shown in Illus. 23-8 to be sure you are well prepared. Guidelines for conducting yourself during an interview are also provided.

The Application Blank. You may be asked to complete an application blank before you are interviewed. The application blank is a vital part of the hiring process. Many applicants are eliminated entirely on the basis of the way they fill out the application. Therefore, never treat it casually. Read it through carefully before you begin to fill it out.

Application forms are usually planned with care. Every question serves a purpose for the interviewer. By law, you need not reveal your age, marital status, or the number of your dependents.

In completing an application, be careful that you follow instructions. For instance, print your name when the instructions tell you to print; put your last name first, if you are so requested. The way you fill out the form reveals far more about you than you realize.

The general neatness of the form is important. Good handwriting is desirable. No one in any office wants to decipher a scrawly, illegible hand. An application form to be typed may be a disguised part of a typing test, so it should represent your best work.

Illus. 23-7
A well-prepared
interviewee
conveys confidence
and competence.

The Interviewer's Method. The employment director or a member of the personnel department usually conducts the preliminary interview. If a favorable impression is made, the interviewer sends the applicant to the supervisor who will oversee the job applicant's work (if hired) for a second interview.

An interview may be informal or structured. During a structured interview, the interviewer asks a series of questions in the same order to all applicants. This technique is often reserved for the second or third interview and for administrative positions. The initial interviewer generally uses an informal method which follows this pattern:

1. Establishes rapport with the applicant.
2. Indicates who will make the final selection.
3. Reviews the applicant's work experience record.
4. Asks questions related to the available job.
5. Leads into the closing of the interview.

The interviewer will question you to encourage you to talk. Many of the questions will be routine and, although answered on your personal data sheet, may be asked again merely to put you at ease and to give you an opportunity to express yourself. Be sure to listen to questions. Ask for clarification if you do not understand the question. Some typical questions include:

Where did you attend college?
What is your special training for this work?
What business experience have you had? By what firms have you been employed? Why did you leave your last job?
Why do you want to work for this company? (What an opportunity to show that you know something about it!)

Two laws (Title VII of the Civil Rights Act and the Age Discrimination in Employment Act) prohibit the interviewer from asking questions of a personal nature concerning race, ethnic origin, religion, age, and marital status. You may, however, volunteer this information. A good rule to follow is to provide facts about your personality, education, and work history that are to your advantage.

The interviewer may ask a few questions to catch applicants off guard. Some of these questions may seem unusual and perhaps presumptuous, but they are all part of the interview technique and have a purpose. Some questions of this nature and examples of possible answers are given here.

Questions	*Possible Answers*
If you were starting college over again, what courses would you take?	I would major in the same field.
How much money do you hope to make by the age of 30?	At least 50 percent more than my entry level salary today.
What do you plan to be doing in your career five to ten years from now?	I plan to hold a CPS and be an administrative assistant to an executive.

Do you prefer to accomplish work with others or by yourself?	This depends on the nature of the work (then provide an example).
Do you think you have done the best scholastic work of which you are capable?	(This answer will vary. Be honest.)
What special interests do you have?	Sports, reading, cooking.
What have you learned from some of the positions you have held?	To work under pressure and to work with many types of individuals.
What are your future educational plans?	To prepare for the CPS examination.
What personal characteristics do you believe are important in your field?	Pleasant personality, cooperation, willingness to accept responsibility.
What do you think determines a person's progress within a company?	Performance on the job.
Why did you choose the secretarial field?	I like the office environment; I enjoy the skills required in the secretarial field.

If you have had business experience, it is quite logical that your previous employment will be a point of discussion in the interview. You will probably be asked why you left your last position. Be prepared to answer this question and be sure to emphasize positive—not negative factors. Be truthful but brief. It is tactless and unethical for you to say anything detrimental about any former employer or firm for which you have worked, regardless of any personal feelings you may have. Always speak well of former employers. Nothing is gained by doing otherwise. Other questions that an interviewer might ask include the following:

What do you expect your references to say about you when I call them?
How well do you work under pressure? Give an example.
What goals would you hope to achieve with our company?
How would you describe yourself?
What people have influenced your life? How?
Why should we hire you?
What two or three accomplishments have given you the greatest satisfaction?

Describe a typical day on your last job.

What do you consider your strengths? your weaknesses? (Give positive weaknesses, such as being too exacting, which are used by employers to describe good workers.)

A PRE-INTERVIEW CHECKLIST

1. Are you properly dressed and groomed?
2. Have you gathered all the information you need about the company concerning its products, its policies, its status in the community?
3. Do you know the interviewer's name? If not, obtain it from the receptionist before the interview.
4. Have you mentally formulated answers to the interviewer's routine questions? Are you prepared for any unusual questions that the interviewer may ask?
5. Have you a list of questions to ask the interviewer?
6. Have you practiced the interview with a friend?
7. Be sure to take the following items:
   a. Your personal data sheet
   b. Your social security card
   c. A complete school transcript showing dates of attendance
   d. A tabulated summary of your college courses
   e. A record of your business skills and personal accomplishments (unless included on your personal data sheet)
   f. Letters of reference (Some personnel experts question the value of open letters of recommendation. You may decide to omit them.)
   g. List of personal references
   h. Your employment record, including dates, names, addresses of employers, duties performed, names of immediate supervisors, and salaries
   i. List of questions you wish to ask the interviewer
   j. A pen and well-sharpened pencils
   k. A small notebook for dictation (you may be asked to take an employment test)
   l. A good pocket-size dictionary
   m. Correction materials
   n. A personal appointment calendar

DURING THE INTERVIEW

1. Leave your coat in the reception area.
2. Wait to sit down until invited to do so.
3. Refrain from smoking or chewing gum.
4. Keep your voice well modulated.
5. Look directly at the interviewer when speaking or listening.
6. Control your nervous habits and maintain good posture.
7. Refrain from overtalking or undertalking.
8. Avoid interrupting the interviewer.
9. Be pleasant to everyone you meet in the office.
10. At the end of the interview, thank the interviewer for the time and consideration. Also, thank the receptionist when you leave.

Illus. 23-8
A successful job applicant knows how to prepare for and how to act during an interview.

The Salary Question. Salary is always important, but don't pass up an interesting position for one that pays a few dollars more a week. If your work is challenging, your performance will soon merit a salary increase.

Your college placement office can obtain information about salaries. The Administrative Management Society publishes an annual survey of office salaries, fringe benefits, and working hours. The Department of Labor also makes an annual occupational wage survey. Survey results may be obtained from a regional office of the Bureau of Labor Statistics. Newspaper advertisements are excellent sources of local salary ranges. Finally, most large businesses have a salary schedule about which you can become informed before applying for a position.

When the salary question comes up in the interview—and it usually does—the best response is, "I am willing to start at your scheduled salary for a person with my background." If, before leaving the interview, you are not told what the starting salary is, it is appropriate to inquire "What is the starting salary for this position?" If an application blank asks about desired salary, supply the standard range for your position.

Asking Questions. An interview is a two-way street. You will be expected to ask questions. In fact, your failure to do so may be interpreted as a lack of genuine interest on your part. What will be the scope of your work? Is there a published job description? With whom will you be working? What opportunities will the position provide for advancement? Does the company promote from within? What is the rate of employee turnover? Is there on-the-job training? These are all thoughtful, intelligent questions that should concern you. Questions about working hours, vacation schedules, coffee breaks, and so forth are appropriate *if* you take care to give the impression that you are more interested in giving than in what you will get.

Concluding the Interview. You will probably know when an interview is coming to an end. Usually the interviewer will rise. If the interviewer has shown interest in your application and in any way encouraged you but has not made a definite commitment about a position, it is permissible to ask directly, "When will your decision be made?" If this does not seem to be a fitting question, you might ask, "May I call you on Friday at two?" If you are offered the job on the spot and you want it, accept the offer. If you need more time, ask for a delay. Do not say that you need time to discuss the job with your spouse or parents. That reply suggests that you are not a decision maker and could give the wrong impression to the interviewer.

When the interview is over, you should rise and thank the interviewer for the opportunity to discuss the position. Make no attempt to prolong the visit. Leave at once, pleasantly and with dignity. Remember to thank the receptionist as you leave.

Personnel Selection Practices

Those who are responsible for hiring employees rely on selection mechanisms in addition to application forms, data sheets, cover letters, and personal interviews. Job-related tests and other considerations are also factors in the decision making process.

Employment Tests. If you made a favorable impression on an interviewer, you may be asked to take some form of an employment test. By law, any test must be job-related. For a secretarial position, a job-related test may ask you to type a letter or to take notes in order to ascertain your shorthand, typewriting, and spelling abilities. You may be asked to operate an electronic typewriter or a word processor. A test to determine your mathematical ability may be given. Some employers give tests to detect a wide variety of abilities. The main thing to remember when taking an employment test is to do what you are asked quietly, confidently, and efficiently.

For some positions, you may be asked to take a psychological test or a lie detector test. You can refuse to take these tests; but, if you do, for all practical purposes you have removed yourself from any consideration for the position. If you submit to a lie detector test, ask to see a list of the questions before taking the test and object to any you feel unfair or inappropriate. Insist upon seeing the test results. Examples of types of employment tests and questions follow:

Type of Test	*Questions*

A personal preference test (also known as an occupational test) has no right or wrong answers. Employers try to establish an occupational preference from answers given to a series of statements.	Of these three activities, indicate which you like the most and which you like least.
	    Work with detail
	    Operate office machines
	    Sell office equipment

A clerical ability test consists of a series of problems that test basic skills, such as spelling, arithmetic, proofreading, vocabulary, and reasoning ability.

Is accomodate or accommodate the correct spelling of this word?

What is 33 1/3% of 0.50?

What do the following words mean: ethics, principles, and etiquette.

Gray is to black as tan is to _____. (green, brown, or red)

A general employment test is very similar to clerical ability tests.

Which number in this series is out of order? 2, 4, 6, 8, 10, 11, 12

If three notebooks cost $2.25, how many can you buy for $10?

What is the opposite of sit?

Other Considerations. Personal habits of job applicants, if known, enter into hiring decisions. Discrimination against hiring smokers has been found not to be in violation of equal employment opportunity statutes, and personnel managers are giving more and more preference to nonsmokers. Companies have found that smokers are twice as likely to be absent from work as nonsmokers. In addition, it is well known that smokers represent a health risk to nonsmokers. It is estimated that alcohol abuse costs American industry $43 billion a year in absenteeism, sick pay, and low productivity. Drug abuse is becoming more prevalent among employees at all classification levels. The personal habits of employees in the form of drug use, smoking, and alcohol use have not only been found to cost industry in terms of productivity but also in terms of plant and office safety and security of information. It is little wonder that personnel directors probe for indications of negative personal habits.

Evaluation of the Interview

After leaving an interview, it is a good practice to evaluate your performance and attitude. Note any changes you will make in the future. Ask yourself the following questions:

Were your answers logical?
Did your conversation ramble?

Were you completely honest?
Were you convincing in your sales approach?
Did you keep your eyes focused on the interviewer?
Were you always courteous and positive in your replies?
What did you learn about the position?
Which questions did you handle well? poorly?
Can you do anything else to increase your chances of obtaining the position sought?

Besides evaluating your own behavior, it is important that you decide whether this is the best job for you. Refer to "Evaluating a Company" on page 679 to assist you in your decision.

Interview Follow-Up

If you decide you are interested in the position, a follow-up letter, arriving within two or three days after the interview, may put your application on top. A good follow-up letter includes an expression of appreciation for the meeting, a statement reaffirming your interest in the position, and additional selling points not completely covered during the visit. If you are offered and accept a position, notify your references and thank them for their help. At the same time, telephone or write other interviewers giving them this information.

You may decide not to accept a position that has been offered. This situation demands a prompt, courteous, and straightforward letter of explanation. The day may come when you need the goodwill of that company or person.

Job Hunting Within the Company

Most companies have internal policies covering promotions. These policies specify the job levels that can be considered for certain positions. In some companies, job vacancies are posted on bulletin boards. Generally when a vacancy occurs, qualified personnel at the required job levels are notified and asked to interview. Other factors, such as education and seniority, are considered. For these reasons, you should make an effort to keep your personnel file up to date. Additional courses you have taken, offices you have held in a professional organization, and other pertinent information should be noted in your personnel file. Keeping a diary of your accomplishments in your current position will provide impressive information to bring to an interview.

If a job that represents a promotion for you becomes available, you should discuss it with your employer first, then make an appointment for the interview. An approach *not* recommended is to go directly to the executive or supervisor with whom the opening exists. When applying for a promotion, follow the procedures set up by the company so that you will not be subject to criticism from either your fellow workers or your present supervisor.

TERMINATION OF EMPLOYMENT

As you grow in your career, if you are like many office workers, you may decide to leave a position. Perhaps you become unhappy with your job, or your salary is not commensurate with your responsibilities or with local salary levels. Another reason may be that fringe benefits are better elsewhere. Never leave a job on impulse or for the wrong reasons.

Once you decide to resign, follow the rules of convention. If the company has a policy manual, you will find the proper procedures for resigning given there. Otherwise give notice first verbally and then in written form (if requested). A resignation letter specifies the date of notice, the last day of employment, and the reason for leaving. It should also include a summary statement about the pleasant associations you have enjoyed with the firm. While still on the job, inquire about any benefits to which you are entitled, such as insurance options or unused vacation. Ask if any benefits, such as health insurance, can continue for a specified time. After the notice period (usually two weeks, unless you have made special arrangements), simply go pleasantly.

In the event that your employer initiates a termination, you should be entitled to advance notice or severance pay. Before you leave, request an exit interview to determine what benefits you have and whether you can expect a good reference from the company. If you suspect discrimination, you can turn to the Equal Employment Opportunity Commission for assistance, but recognize that relatively few firing decisions are reversed even if the employee wins the case. In addition, an employee who sues a former employer may have great difficulty in securing another position.

Regardless of the reason for termination, your exit should be an amicable one. Avoid expressing ill will toward the company or attempting to make fellow workers dissatisfied with the company and their jobs.

FOR THE PART-TIME JOB SEEKER

Sometime in your working career you may decide to seek a part-time position because you have additional personal responsibilities. Perhaps your health does not permit full-time work, you plan to continue your education, your spouse's occupation requires mobility, or you are approaching retirement and do not want the responsibilities of a full-time job. As with other job seekers, an individual looking for part-time employment must be resourceful. Successful part-time job seekers offer this advice:

Visit firms that have part-timers on their payroll
Apply at federal, state, and local government offices
Visit smaller firms, because they are often more flexible and thus more responsive to part-time workers
Do not ask for part-time employment on your application. Talk about this possibility during the interview.
Suggest a trial period to the employer

Job sharing is becoming more accepted in professional ranks (see Chapter 1) and should be explored. If you can identify a potential partner, possibly an employee already on the payroll, both of you should present your plan to management. Many employers who would not normally hire part-timers will accept a job-sharing arrangement to keep a valued employee. In the event that you and your partner are unemployed, together you should plan your strategy by preparing joint data sheets and application letters. Seeking a part-time job is a full-time proposition. It can and is being done, successfully.

FOR THE MATURE JOB SEEKER

None is so old as the person who has outlived enthusiasm.

Henry Thoreau

The Age Discrimination in Employment Act of 1967 protects workers in the 40 to 65 age bracket. Basically, the act states that employers cannot discriminate against workers or applicants because of their age.

The mature job seeker has much to offer a company: work experience, the prospect of a good attendance record, and the ability to learn. An employer's only reservation probably concerns the cost of benefits for mature recruits. Retirement benefits, for instance, begin much sooner than for a young person.

If you are told you are overqualified for the job, the interviewer usually considers you too old or too high priced. You can turn this reaction into an advantage by emphasizing that your experience will lessen the training time required for the job. As for salary, you can stress that the salary designated is acceptable.

The reentry secretary must devote some time to preparation for employment. Dormant office skills must be revitalized by taking a refresher course or an individualized instructional program. The next step is to make a survey of employment opportunities. Temporary service agencies and companies that utilize part-time workers should be included. Finally, the reentry job seeker should prepare a personal data sheet and letters of application. Include all your work experience, both paid and volunteer. An example of a data sheet prepared by a secretary reentering the job market after several years' absence is shown in Illus. 23-9.

Illus. 23-9
This functional data sheet gives no dates of employment. Instead, emphasis is placed on the duties of former positions and the applicant's accomplishments.

```
                              Pat L. Swenson
                            8209 East 13th Street
                         Vancouver, WA  98661-9873
                             (206) 555-2247

        CAREER OBJECTIVE       A secretarial position requiring a high level
                               of stenographic skill and administrative ability

        SUMMARY                Five years of full-time secretarial experience in
                               the paper industry and three years of part-time
                               stenographic experience in the medical field

        EDUCATION              Associate Degree, Secretarial Studies, Santa Rosa
                               Junior College, Santa Rosa, California

        EXPERIENCE
          Secretary to         As secretary to the Administrative Vice-President
          Executive            of St. Regis Paper Company, I coordinated the efforts
                               of the clerical personnel in the section in addition
                               to accomplishing the varied duties of the position.
                               In a typical day it was not unusual for me to type
                               fifty letters from shorthand dictation.  Routine
                               record keeping was necessary to control the volume
                               of mail entering the office each day.  Maintaining
                               confidential files was a responsibility of this
                               position.

          Stenographer         During my college training, I held a part-time
                               stenographic post at the Santa Rosa Medical Clinic.
                               My major responsibilities included transcribing
                               medical records from a dictating machine and
                               assisting with posting charges and credits to
                               patients' accounts.

        SPECIAL QUALIFICATIONS  Ability to handle a wide variety of secretarial
                               responsibilities and supervise clerical workers.
                               Especially capable in the area of human relations.
                               Health and stamina to work under pressure.

        MEMBERSHIPS            Professional Secretaries International
                               Word Processing Society, Inc.
                               President, Parent-Teachers Association, John F.
                                  Kennedy School.

        REFERENCES             Can be provided on request.
```

A last word of advice for all job seekers: Don't be in a hurry to accept your first job offer. Evaluate each company and position in terms of your own goals and interests. Accepting a job you don't really want may prevent you from later accepting the very job that you were seeking. The next interview just might be the right position for you.

SUMMARY

When seeking employment, the qualified secretary has a number of decisions to make in selecting the right position. Among them the secretary must decide whether to work in a small office or a large organization; whether to specialize in a particular area of secretarial work or to work in a general office. The small office offers the advantage of being an excellent training ground for all facets of secretarial work. A large firm offers promotional opportunities, set personnel policies, and fringe benefits.

There are unlimited opportunities for the qualified secretary to specialize in a particular field. This chapter describes the duties of the medical secretary, the legal secretary, and the educational secretary. In addition, their specific professional organizations and certification programs are discussed. The roles of the technical secretary and the public secretaries and their environments are also discussed.

Providing part-time office workers is big business. The opportunities for temporary workers are varied. Employment through a temporary agency is an excellent way to enhance skills after an absence from the job market. Working for the nation's largest employer, the government, is discussed in detail. Requirements for being a secretary in the Foreign Service are given particular attention.

A job search begins with a survey of employment opportunities. College placement offices, free and private employment agencies, newspaper advertisements, friends, relatives, and associates should be contacted to devise a job prospect list. The next step in a job search is to gather information about every prospect on that list. This can be done by doing research at the library and by contacting the local chamber of commerce and the Better Business Bureau. Each prospect should be evaluated in terms of its reputation, fair employment practices, financial standing, and opportunities for training and advancement.

After taking an inventory of interests and capabilities, the job seeker prepares a personal data sheet. The major sections of a personal data sheet include a heading (name, address, telephone number), education, work experience, special interests (abilities and accomplishments), and references. An application letter can be solicited or unsolicited. Its purpose is to expand on the applicant's qualifications in relation to the specific job in question and to gain a personal interview. In both the personal data sheet and an application letter, the use of action verbs is recommended. Specific guidelines for writing an application letter are given.

A company's hiring process generally includes two interviews. One is with the personnel department and the other is with the supervisor who will actually oversee the applicant's work. A pre-interview checklist is provided. Interviewers ask specific job-related questions; some questions may take the applicant off guard. In order to have a successful interview, the applicant must be able to answer questions honestly, with confidence and poise. The salary question is a special one and recommended replies are given. The applicant should go to an interview equipped with questions for the interviewer as well. Finally, when an interview is over, recognize it and leave promptly. The hiring process may also include the administration of employment tests. Be aware that other considerations, such as negative personal habits, enter into a hiring decision. A follow-up letter is recommended, especially if the applicant is interested in the position.

The process of career development will most likely include resigning from a position. Procedures for doing so are discussed in this chapter. Employment strategies for the part-time job seeker and the mature job seeker conclude the chapter.

SUGGESTED READINGS

Bolles, Richard Nelson. *What Color Is Your Parachute?*, 2d ed. Berkeley: Ten Speed Press, 1984.

Camden, Thomas M. *The Job Hunter's Final Exam*. Warminster, PA: Surrey Books, 1984.

Corwen, Leonard. *Résumés for Secretaries*. New York: Arco Publishing, Inc., 1985.

Levering, Robert, Milton Moskowitz, and Michael Katz. *The One Hundred Best Companies to Work for in America*. Reading, MA: Addison-Wesley Publishing Co., Inc., 1984.

Levitt, Julie G. *Your Career*, How to Make It Happen. Cincinnati: South-Western Publishing Co., 1985.

Olmstead, Barney and Suzanne Smith. *The Job Sharing Handbook*. New York: Penguin Books, Inc., 1983.

QUESTIONS FOR DISCUSSION

1. Although there are many fine opportunities for employment in the suburbs of large cities, why is it that most young secretaries prefer to work in offices located downtown?

2. What advantages are there for being a secretary with the federal government?

3. After carefully considering your training, interests, and special aptitudes, would you choose a specialization in the secretarial field (for example, legal, medical, technical, or educational)? If so, which one? Give reasons for your choice.

4. What advantages can you give for working for a temporary employment agency?

5. What circumstances would make it desirable for a secretarial applicant to register with a private employment agency?

6. What factors would influence your selection of references for your personal data sheet?

7. Which data sheet format would you select and what personal information, if any, would you provide if you were
    a. male, 26 years old, married, one son, height 6'1", 170 lbs., willing to relocate
    b. female, 40 years old, divorced, two small children at home, 20 years of office experience
    c. male, 52 years old, divorced, excellent health

8. What questions do you think an interviewer would ask of your former employer?

9. In addition to those questions listed in the textbook on pages 691-692, what other questions could be asked by the *applicant* during an interview?

10. Is it ethical to accept permanent employment without informing your potential employer that you consider the job temporary? Examples include a job for the summer only, one you intend to keep only until another comes along, or one to gain experience to qualify for a position in another company.

11. Assume that you work for a large company. The position of secretary to the vice-president becomes vacant, and you and your colleagues in your job classification are in line. Why would you antagonize your fellow workers and possibly your supervisor if you went directly to the vice-president asking for consideration for the position instead of going through company channels?

12. In terminating employment, why is it good practice to avoid creating ill will toward your employer and the company?

13. It is stated in this chapter that the negative personal habits of employees cost a firm money in terms of absenteeism and lower productivity. Do you agree, therefore, that an interviewer should let information concerning an applicant's habits affect the hiring decision?

14. A compound word may be written as a solid word, joined with a hyphen, or written as individual words. Explain why the follow-

ing groups of words are written as shown. Consult the Reference Guide to verify and correct your answers.

a. forty-four, twenty-six, thirty-five, one-third
b. re-cover, re-form, re-collect, re-creation
c. four-day conference, up-to-date buildings, first-class accommodations
d. ex-Ambassador, pro-British, pre-Christmas, anti-American

PROBLEMS

1. Interview an experienced secretary in your community. Ask specific questions about the position concerning qualifications, duties, and promotional possibilities. Report your findings to the class.

2. Assume that you are seeking a position as a secretary. Prepare a data sheet and an application letter in reply to the following newspaper advertisement:

SECRETARY

Needed: a secretary with better-than-average communication skills; shorthand 100 wpm; typing 60 wpm. Position involves maintaining a large volume of correspondence, telephone work, and customer assistance. Salary commensurate with ability. Reply Box 2100, JOURNAL.

3. When applying for a specific position, you are asked the following questions. Type your replies on a sheet of paper. In preparing your answers, try to analyze the motive behind the question.

a. What are your career plans?
b. How do you spend your spare time?
c. Why do you want to work for this company?
d. Are you willing to relocate?
e. Do you like to work with office machines?
f. Do your interests lie in the area of data processing?
g. What do you consider a good starting salary for this position?
h. Do you think your college grades reflect your true ability?
i. Are you willing to work overtime when the situation warrants?
j. What qualifications do you have that you believe will make you successful in your chosen career?
k. Do you plan to join a professional organization?

4. Just before completing your secretarial training, you decide to survey the secretarial openings in your community by sending out a

number of unsolicited letters of application. Using your own data and the names of local companies, prepare the letter, making sure that it is appropriate for each of the companies.

5. Review the help-wanted advertisements in the newspaper for secretarial positions. Select one for which you are qualified and that appeals to you. On a separate sheet of paper type two headings: *Requirements* and *Qualifications*. List each requirement, then specify your qualifications that meet each requirement.

6. On a sheet of paper make three vertical columns with these headings: *Duties, Evaluation, Improvement*. Describe your perfect job by listing at least ten duties of that position in the *Duties* column. For each task, rate yourself poor, fair, good, or superior. If improvement is needed, specify what action you should take.

Chapter 24

Planning for Your Professional Future

For most secretaries, doing important work for an influential executive is a fundamental career goal. Your study thus far has made you aware of the variety of career opportunities available to you, prepared you to perform various secretarial duties, and briefed you on how to get the position you seek. You should now consider how you will fulfill your long-range ambition of becoming a successful secretary.

This chapter discusses the personal characteristics requisite to success as a secretary, and the means at your disposal for getting off to the right start and growing professionally. It deals with some of the difficulties you will encounter and how you can cope with them to assure the professional future to which you aspire.

USING YOUR PERSONAL ATTRIBUTES

New secretaries enter the job market with varying degrees of competence in the skills necessary to perform the job. The same is true of personal qualities. One secretary may have all the characteristics that contribute to a successful career, while another may be weak in one or more of them.

Successful secretaries, those who are proficient in their work and who enjoy satisfaction and recognition in their careers, suggest certain prerequisites to achievement. Some are innate to the individual, and some can be learned on the job. They are:

1. *Initiative* in performing your work
2. *Flexibility* in your approach to office needs and operations
3. *Awareness* of the business and of your employer
4. *Adeptness* in human relations

Displaying Initiative

A new secretary may be reluctant to do work without being told or to assume new responsibilities not understood as part of the job description. Displaying initiative comes with confidence in one's ability to do the job. It may be difficult, however, to show initiative if you are assigned to an executive who expects no more than performance of habitual, routine tasks; or if you follow a predecessor who undertook only assigned jobs. Also, routinization of many office tasks reduces, if not eliminates, the opportunity to be enterprising or creative or to do anything out of the ordinary. You may have to start slowly, but you can overcome resistance if you demonstrate how much you can increase your effectiveness and that of your employer by extending your activities to include responsible tasks. Taking initiative, unfortunately, means taking risks. Use your judgment in taking action, then review what you have done with your employer. If you acted in error, you can profit from what you learn and apply this new knowledge to a similar situation in the future.

There are many opportunities in the secretarial position to use initiative. In fact, making independent decisions and taking actions soon become a daily exercise. A secretary who composes a reply to a letter without the employer requesting it is displaying initiative. A secretary who obtains information for an employer before being asked to do so is using initiative. You, the college-trained secretary, should feel comfortable in displaying your initiative. You have the background to be successful in making decisions on your own.

Being Flexible

You probably have heard that nothing is more certain than change. For years the functions of the office were accomplished in the same way and with the same equipment. Earlier chapters of this text discussed the ways in which technology has revolutionized the way we communicate, the way we calculate, and the way we send correspondence. Secretaries have to learn to cope with change. The look of the office has also changed. An ambitious person entering the business world must be flexible. That person must be able to adjust to tomorrow's office and tomorrow's duties quickly.

Offices usually have their own routines, their own ways of working with information and getting jobs done. A new secretary must be willing to learn from others. On occasion the employer may request that you work a half hour longer or on a Saturday. Although this is a disruption of your regular schedule, if you are flexible, you will be willing to make alterations in your work schedule and in your personal schedule.

One very sensitive area in an office community is the promotion or shift of personnel. The secretary may be transferred to another department with a new set of co-workers and tasks, may be assigned a new employer or employers, may have to learn to operate new equipment, or to adopt new office procedures. These changes are a way of life in all organizations. Whether you like or dislike, approve or disapprove, you must maintain a positive attitude. A flexible employee makes the most of these changes.

Developing Awareness

Being able to look at the office and its operations is one thing, but seeing what is there is quite another matter. Awareness is the capacity to draw accurate inferences from what is seen, heard, and learned. A secretary must be aware of how each person fits into the work scheme. You must see quickly the part your employer plays in an organization and how your work contributes to the organization. *Listen and watch* would be a good motto for you during your initial weeks on the job.

A college-trained secretary should have little difficulty in developing awareness. In college you studied business principles and organization, you understood office costs, and you learned the meaning of profit. With this background, *see* what you can do to assist the growth of your company, your employer, and yourself. (A word of caution is needed here: Temper any feelings of superiority you may have over your co-workers because of your college training.)

Building Positive Human Relations

To be happy and to grow in your secretarial position, you must feel good about going to the office each day. One reason a secretary may feel content about being in an office is the people in it. Good working relationships with one's supervisor, co-workers, and subordinates will play an extremely important role in your well-being on the job. Although you will like some of your colleagues better than others, assume a positive attitude toward all co-workers. You may have the highest of secretarial skills to offer an employer. Yet without the ability to maintain good working relationships, you could soon become dispensable.

The golden rule approach with co-workers is worth considering. To be successful in establishing friendships throughout your life, you must be sensitive to the needs of others. Play a part in making a new office colleague feel like a member of the group. Cooperate with others. Treat each person courteously.

Your relations with executives, the ones to whom you report and others, are especially important to your success. Showing that you are a good team member enhances your opportunities to *be* a real member of the team. Be cheerful even when you are called on to go beyond the call of duty. Maintain a smiling countenance and a voice with a smile. Avoid emotionality, especially when you are under pressure. Remain calm. Respect confidentiality. Reveal neither organization nor executive secrets. The word "secretary" is derived from the word "secret." Never say anything in the office that you would not want displayed on the office bulletin board. People often repeat what is said in confidence.

Carry your good human relations attitudes over to the public. Every office or telephone visitor is important. Often the secretary is the contact with the outside world that makes the difference in how a company is perceived.

BECOMING ACCLIMATED TO THE JOB

That first week or two on the job can be overwhelming. Everything will be new to you—the people, the office, and the work. This section gives you some clues on how to survive the first week of getting to know the office staff and learning about the company.

Some companies have well-planned programs for inducting new employees. If you obtain a position in such a firm, someone will be assigned to welcome you, introduce you to your colleagues, show you your work area, perhaps take you to lunch, tell you something of the history of the organization, possibly show you a movie about your new company, and provide you with booklets describing company policies and benefits. Many companies, however, have no organized orientation program. If you are fortunate, the secretary whose place you are taking will remain on the job for a few days to train you. In many cases, though, you will report to an employer whose secretary has already left, and you sink or swim alone.

One of the first decisions you will have to make on the job is to determine priorities. You should decide what work must be done immediately, what must be done by the end of the day, and what can be done at some later time. Setting priorities will be especially difficult if you report to more than one executive.

Creating a Good First Impression

Everyone in the office forms first impressions of you, just as you will of them. Because you were hired, you can assume that you made a satisfactory impression on your employer. Now you must make a satisfactory impression on those with whom you work and make this impression a permanent one.

You will be under critical and detailed inspection that first day. Your dress, your grooming, and everything you do and say will be observed. At this point, exercise good judgment by first being an attentive *listener*. It is a human trait to be defensive toward an outsider or a newcomer until that person wins one's goodwill and approval. Don't be disconcerted by this; if you understand it, you will be encouraged to make your associates like and accept you. Remember that their approval is most important to your future welfare and your happiness.

Begin your first day on time, allowing plenty of time for the things that fate seems to have in store for the first day on a new job! Being even a few minutes late will require an explanation to your employer, a situation that you will find uncomfortable.

Learning Names

Certainly one way to create a good first impression is to learn promptly and pronounce correctly the names and titles of those with whom you work. Associate the name with a mental picture of the person when you are introduced. An effective plan is to write the name and practice pronouncing it, then address the person by name at every appropriate occasion. Drawing a floor plan to show the location of desks and the names of their occupants will help you through that first week.

Some of your co-workers and some executives may be sensitive to titles. An office manager may be offended at being referred to as a supervisor. A vice-president may take exception to being called an assistant manager. To help you learn the titles and ranks of those with whom and for whom you work, study your company's organizational chart.

Observing Ground Rules

New employees are expected to learn quickly a company's regulations relative to rest periods, lunch hours, personal telephone calls, coffee breaks, smoking, and other similar activities. Some of these rules may be in writing; others have been established by custom but are nonetheless binding. One of the surest ways to get off to a poor start is to be a rule breaker. Ignorance is a poor excuse. The only safe policy is to find out the rules and customs of the office and observe them. Some organizations even test new employees on the content of company manuals.

Living Up to a Code of Ethics

At its 1980 convention, Professional Secretaries International adopted a code of ethics for the professional secretary. The introduction to the code states:

> The development of a code of ethics demonstrates that the secretarial profession accepts the obligation to engage in self-discipline and accepts the responsibility and trust earned by secretaries throughout past generations.
>
> Each secretary has a personal obligation to support and follow the *Code*, recognizing that the greatest penalty possible for its violation is loss of the respect of professional colleagues and the trust of employers, clients, and society.

Broad principles are embodied in four standards. Each standard is applied to office behavior:

I. The secretary shall act as a trusted agent in professional relations, implementing responsibilities in the most competent manner and exercising knowledge and skill to promote the interests of the immediate and corporate employer.

II. The secretary shall strive to maintain and enhance the dignity, status, competence, and standards of the profession and its practitioners.

III. The secretary shall insist that judgments concerning continued employment, compensation, and promotion be based upon professional knowledge, ability, experience, and performance.

IV. The secretary must consider the promotion and preservation of the safety and welfare of the public to be the paramount duty.

In addition to observing this code and company rules and policies, you should observe an unwritten work code. This code includes an appreciation of what belongs to your employer. For instance, you have agreed to work a certain number of hours a week. You have agreed also to the length of the workday. Any abuse of time which is to be devoted to your work is in violation of your work code. In addition, have respect for the equipment and the supplies that belong to your employer. This means a concerted effort to reduce waste and to maintain the security of these materials in the office.

Developing Office Friendships

Many secretaries make a distinction between their work lives and their personal lives. They try to avoid socializing with members of the office staff outside office hours. They believe this separation makes them immune from office gossip and office cliques.

Of course, these same secretaries recognize that office friendships are beneficial. Certainly the secretary who has friends throughout the company is better able to serve the employer. Through these friendships the secretary gains a better understanding of the company as a whole and the functions of various departments.

Friendliness should extend to all employment levels. The goodwill of office messengers, custodians, and reprographics operators is important to your success.

Coping with Sexual Harassment

Secretaries work in close contact with principals and co-workers. Sometimes employers or co-workers engage in sexual harassment. In 1980 the Equal Employment Opportunity Commission (EEOC) defined sexual harassment and adopted guidelines for employers to deal with the problem. Sexual harassment, according to the EEOC, is "unwelcome sexual advances, requests for sexual favors, and other verbal or physical conduct of a sexual nature" that take place under any of the following circumstances:

1. When submission to the sexual advance is a condition of keeping or getting a job, whether expressed in explicit or implicit terms
2. When a supervisor or employer makes a personnel decision based on an employee's submission to or rejection of sexual advances
3. When sexual conduct unreasonably interferes with a person's work performance or creates an intimidating, hostile, or offensive work environment

Sexual harassment, ranging from suggestive speech to actual physical attack, threats of withholding promotions, and threats of dismissal have been widely exposed in the media. Women's groups have played an important role in alerting the public to these offenses.

Handling sexual harassment is especially perplexing for the young secretary in a new position who is eager to please associates. The problem becomes more difficult because of the informality of today's office contrasted with the office of ten years ago. Cordial but not familiar relationships should be maintained. Ignoring suggestive words and actions often discourages them. Do not make an issue of one isolated incident. However, in case of continued infractions the secretary should speak unemotionally, asking the offender to refrain from such actions. If this does not stop the harassment, you should report the situation to your superior or ask for a transfer.

Learning about the Company

From the first moment on the job, learn as much as you can about everything you can as soon as you can. This is a sizable order for a new employee, but it can be done.

In some companies a job analysis, a job description, or job specifications for your new position are available in a company manual to give you an idea of the scope of your duties. To serve your employer effectively, you need to learn about the organization quickly so that you can interpret any request and carry out directions without asking for elementary information.

Learn as quickly as possible the names of customers, the names of your employer's close associates, frequently used telephone numbers, frequently used terminology in dictation, and the technical language of the company. The more you know and the more ready you are to apply what you know, the quicker you will become valuable to your employer and to the organization.

Company Manuals. Most organizations have one or more company manuals or instruction sheets for office routines. A general office manual usually explains the organization of the company, the relationships of various offices and departments, general rules and regulations, and information that affects all employees, such as methods of distributing paychecks, descriptions of company benefits, and a list of the holidays observed. Some manuals chart the work of all departments; others give directions for initiating and completing specific activities.

Operating manuals are often available for various office machines and other equipment. Most large companies have style manuals or other forms of direction for setting up correspondence and company forms. If your office has such a manual, spend many of your spare moments studying and thoroughly digesting everything that has a bearing on your work to the point of memorizing important facts.

If it is permissible for you to take some of these materials home for study, you should do so. Devoting an hour or so of quiet time at home studying an office manual may reduce considerably the amount of time it takes to learn a new job.

The Office Files. Office files offer a wealth of information to the new secretary. Previous correspondence, incoming and outgoing, indicates the types of correspondence you can expect to execute. Office files are also an excellent source of terminology and technical language. As you look through the files, list the terms with which you are unfamiliar. Note your employer's letter-writing style and proper title. Note where and how to file letters and records. Become familiar with various company forms and types of stationery.

Other Sources of Information. Special types of records are often available to the secretary. Scrapbooks or collections of clippings about the executive, the company, or its products are sources of background information. Many organizations publish a *house organ*, a periodical written by and about its employees. Back issues will tell you a great deal, as will industry journals.

One way to determine the actual scope of your position is to acquaint yourself with the duties of other company employees. Seeing how your job relates to theirs will help you understand not only your own job but also the total functions of the office.

Questions. Of course you must ask questions; but make them few and make them count. There are two kinds of questions. *Learning* questions help you find out things you need to know; they are excellent questions. *Leaning* questions are those about something you really should know or can research yourself; they are the kind that you should avoid.

There is a time and place for questioning. During the first few days on a new job, whenever possible, accumulate your problems and questions and ask them all at a logical time in one session with the employer or with your temporary mentor. As you compile your list, however, be sure that it does not include a problem that you should solve yourself.

The other employees usually help answer questions, but remember that they have full-time work to do themselves. Sometime later you will probably have an opportunity to repay those who helped you by returning the favor when they need extra help.

Developing a Desk Manual

A desk manual is a helpful organizer for the secretary in a new job. If you have inherited one, you will find in this loose-leaf notebook explanations of company procedures, examples of company forms, and instructions for handling the duties peculiar to your job. If one is not available, begin at once to compile information for your desk manual.

You can start some sections, such as correct letter form and mailing procedures, immediately. Accumulating others requires time and experience. You may want to breakdown your duties by time periods: daily, weekly, monthly, and annually. If you are always busy during the day, take the time to prepare the bulk of your desk manual after office hours. The first draft will be the most time-consuming; once written and thoughtfully indexed, the manual can be updated quickly and easily.

Procedures Sections. Undoubtedly one of the first sections you will prepare is the one that explains how to handle various secretarial duties. The topic outline on pages 716-719 suggests a way to organize this part of the manual. If you are an administrative secretary in a company with a word processing center, a topic outline for a word processing center desk manual appears on page 719.

In addition to these procedural sections, include information of a general nature concerning the company and a directory of important employer contacts, customers, or projects. A personal data section about the employer is appropriate for the manual. If a secretary reports to several principals, it is a good idea to have specific information for each in the manual.

Company Information. One section of the manual should consist of pertinent company information, such as an organizational chart showing the lines of authority and the names of persons in each executive and supervisory position. In addition, the following information should be helpful to a secretary in a new job:

1. Addresses and telephone numbers of branch offices and subsidiaries
2. Names and titles of supervisory personnel at branch offices and subsidiaries
3. Company rules and regulations (hours of work, lunch hour, coffee breaks, and the like)
4. Company policies (vacations, sick leave, insurance, and other fringe benefits) in summary form
5. Telephone numbers of specific office services

Who's Who Directory. Another section of the manual will likely be a directory of the persons with whom the employer has frequent contacts. Individual circumstances determine whether to subdivide this directory into *in-company* and *outside* listings. At any rate, the list should include the following:

1. Those with whom the employer frequently corresponds or holds telephone conversations
2. Frequent office visitors
3. The names of the executive's attorney, doctor, broker, automobile service, etc.

To build a list of names for the directory, jot down each one as it comes to your attention. Then prepare a card for each name with the following information: correct spelling, company affiliation and address, telephone number, salutation and complimentary close for correspondence (you must learn when "Dear Charles" is more appropriate than Dear Mr. Jones" as you learn the relationship of the correspondent to the executive). Cross-reference affiliations and identifications. For example, if you have Mr. Ericson's name as advertising manager of Acme Metal Company and Ms. Curry as sales manager of the same company, make a card for Acme and list the names of both executives. Likewise, if Ms. Roberta Nolan is your employer's attorney, make one card for Roberta Nolan, Attorney, and a cross-reference card for Attorney, Roberta Nolan. Copy the cards onto loose-leaf sheets and insert in the manual. (Some secretaries prefer to use a card file.) Update changes by pasting over the original entry.

Clients and Projects Directory. When your employer works with a succession of important clients, customers, projects, or jobs, a special section is necessary. Provide a page for each person or project, listing such information as the title of the job, the work to be performed, pertinent data, terms, and special procedures that the secretary must follow. A list of all persons connected with the job is also helpful. Here, too, cross-referencing should be freely used.

TOPIC OUTLINE FOR PROCEDURES SECTION
OF THE DESK MANUAL

  I. INCOMING MAIL
     A. Mail register
        1. Explanation of posting procedure
        2. Sample form
     B. Distribution of the mail

II. CORRESPONDENCE
    A. Interoffice correspondence
        1. Model interoffice memorandum forms
        2. Number and distribution of copies
    B. Outside correspondence
        1. Model letter forms
        2. Stationery examples
        3. Number and distribution of copies
    C. Mail schedules
    D. Word processing center
        1. Dictation instructions
        2. Forms
            a. Dictated material
            b. Hard copy
            c. Review sheet
            d. Rush work
            e. Form letters
        3. Proofreading/copying responsibilities
        4. File retention procedures

III. COMPANY FORMS
    A. Models of all forms
    B. Instructions for completing
    C. Number and distribution of copies

IV. FILING
    A. Centralized filing system
        1. Materials that go to centralized file
        2. Procedure for release of materials for fil-
           ing
        3. Procedure for obtaining materials from fil-
           ing
    B. Secretary's file (full explanation of filing
       system)
    C. Transfer and storage policies

V. FINANCIAL DUTIES
    A. Bank account
        1. Procedure for making deposits
        2. Procedure for reconciling the bank statement
        3. Disposition of canceled checks and bank
           statements
        4. Location of bankbook and checkbook

B. Payments of recurring expenses (membership dues and miscellaneous fees)
   1. Dates of payments
   2. Procedures for payments
C. Petty cash
   1. Location of fund
   2. Regulations covering expenditures from fund
   3. Filing of receipts
   4. Procedure for replenishing fund

VI. INFORMATION SYSTEMS AND ELECTRONIC EQUIPMENT AVAILABLE WITHIN THE ORGANIZATION
   A. Locations
   B. Instructions for using services
   C. When to use

VII. OFFICE MACHINES
   A. Inventory of machines in office (serial numbers and purchase dates of all machines)
   B. Repair services (service contracts, name and telephone number of each service)

VIII. SUPPLIES
   A. List of supplies to be stocked
      1. Quantities of each to be ordered
      2. Names and addresses (or telephone numbers) of suppliers
   B. Procedure for obtaining supplies
   C. Procedure for controlling supplies

IX. SUBSCRIPTIONS TO PUBLICATIONS
   A. Names, number of copies, renewal dates
   B. Procedure for renewal
   C. Routing of publications in office

X. PUBLIC RELATIONS
   A. News releases
   B. Announcements

XI. TELEPHONE PROCEDURES
   A. Types of services available
   B. Regulations for use of various types
   C. Procedures for reporting toll charges
   D. Special instructions relating to use of equipment

XII. TELECOMMUNICATIONS
    A. Examples of telegrams, Telex, TWX, Fax
    B. Number and distribution of copies
    C. Procedure for sending
        1. Determination of method used
        2. Time restrictions
    D. Procedure for recording charges

XIII. TRAVEL
    A. Employer's travel and hotel preferences
    B. Names and telephone numbers of persons in travel
        agency or airlines office
    C. Locations of timetables
    D. Model itinerary
    E. Method of ticket pickup
    F. Expense report form
        1. Number and distribution of copies
        2. Receipts required

XIV. REFERENCE SECTION
    A. Form letters
    B. Guide letter paragraphs
    C. Vocabulary list

WORD PROCESSING CENTER DESK MANUAL
TOPIC OUTLINE

I. MACHINE OPERATIONS
    A. Machine codes (menus)
    B. Machine capabilities

II. CORRESPONDENCE AND REPORTS
    A. Authorization for rush items and turnaround
        time
    B. Distribution of copies
    C. Filing
    D. Storage
    E. Standard proofreading marks

III. DIRECTORY OF CUSTOMERS, CLIENTS
    A. Names and addresses
    B. Selective salutations and complimentary clos-
        ings

```
IV. COMPANY INFORMATION
    A. Organizational chart
    B. List of administrative secretaries

 V. COMPANY FORMS
    A. Signature authorizations
    B. Distribution of copies

VI. WORD PROCESSING REPORTING PROCEDURES
    A. Production report
    B. Transcription report
```

Personal Data Section. In addition to the major items that comprise the basic desk manual, many secretaries add a personal section. This section contains unusual reminders—dates and events of special significance to the employer or employers—and other personal information including the following:

> Biography of employer or a complete list of educational achievements, employment records, awards, and community services
> Important numbers (social security, passport, and credit cards)
> Insurance policy numbers, amounts, and payment dates (unless already in an insurance register)
> Memberships in professional and civic organizations, offices held, meeting dates, dues, committee assisgnments, and so on
> Wedding anniversary
> Family birthdays
> College or school addresses of executive's children
> Other birthdays the executive should remember
> Expected retirement dates for company officials and other office personnel
> Dates of important sports tournaments

MOVING UP IN YOUR SECRETARIAL POSITION

After you have demonstrated your competence, you can hope for promotion. Advancement depends on your performance and your professional growth while in your present position.

Making Job-Enhancing Efforts

The secretarial profession is exactly what you make it. If you stay in your own little niche, doing only the work that has been assigned to you, you are likely to remain in the same position and at about the same salary indefinitely. Many employees who do not represent the standards set throughout this textbook carry the title of secretary. Some employers do not recognize the potential of their secretaries and limit their activities to routine tasks. Advancement is very much up to you. Each time you find a way to free your employer of some task, you become more valuable. Each time you assume a new responsibility and prove yourself equal to the task, you become better qualified for advancement. This statement does not mean that you should use aggressive tactics or that you should infringe on the work of your co-workers—sure ways to ensure your being thoroughly disliked—but it does mean that if you expect to get ahead, you must be a self-starter, alert to opportunities to prove your value by assuming more responsibility. In your rush to get ahead, don't overlook the fact that there is no substitute for competence. Competence comes at a high price—a price paid in hard work, study, and dedication. A capacity for growth must be coupled with the self-discipline necessary to carry out a sustained effort toward growing with a job.

Build an impressive record of service to your employer and to others. Continue to promote your own individuality by maintaining a wholesome balance between business and social life, by developing interests and hobbies, and by cultivating friendships. Be well informed about business practices and the world around you.

Assertiveness, not Aggressiveness. In today's society, people are encouraged to speak out more forcefully, to express viewpoints more freely, to assume a leadership role instead of blindly following decisions with which they do not agree or that affect them adversely. With the growth of affirmative action programs, interest in assertiveness has extended to the office. Various groups promote assertiveness training to enable employees to express their views when fair employment practices are not followed. Numerous college courses, workshops, and seminars train employees to practice assertiveness effectively. Techniques learned help employees not only reduce employment abuses but also improve job effectiveness in all areas.

If you have a well-documented case concerning unfair employment practices that should be brought to the attention of management, you are completely justified in calling the situation to the attention of appropriate personnel. If, for example, you believe that you have been passed over for a raise or promotion, tell your employer, not your colleagues. A frank discussion of your job evaluation with your employer is usually fruitful.

There is, though, quite a difference between assertivesness and aggressiveness. Assertiveness (desirable) can spill over into excessive aggressiveness (undesirable). Excessive aggressiveness may label you as pushy and work against your moving up in an organization. It may alienate management and other groups that could be useful allies in achieving your goals. In other words, recognize and respect the fine line between assertiveness and aggressiveness.

Job Descriptions. Work for the establishment and utilization of improved personnel practices. Most large organizations have adopted job descriptions that should be updated periodically by the executive and the secretary. Have any expanded responsibilities put into writing; for example, setting up the conference room for a meeting may be your responsibility. But if you also organize the meeting, write the agenda, and prepare the report of the proceedings, make certain that these additional responsibilities are also included in your job description. Upward mobility may be limited if you let a job description limit creativity and initiative. Performance beyond that called for in a job description often results in a salary increase greater than the standard increase given most employees.

Authority for Giving Executive Orders. Employers exercise a great deal of authority. Sometimes they forget that their secretaries do not have the same authority and say, "Tell Ms. Montgomery to give me a report on the bid by Thursday." Unfortunately, your authority to give an order is not always established by your superior. Your request, although tactfully worded, may be resented by Ms. Montgomery. If you have a problem of this kind, ask the executive to establish your authority to make such requests.

Growing Professionally

Your on-the-job activities shape your professional development. You need to learn all that you can on the job, but you can also make out-of-the-office activities contribute to your growth.

Participation in organizations is one way you can grow professionally. Taking part in professional groups is important to all employees. Many advancements are secured because of contacts made in both social and professional groups. *Networking*, the exchange of information among professionals in a social setting, often leads to advancement. Many professional organizations promote personal development by providing information, contacts, and support. They keep members updated on equipment and organizational changes, enabling them to work as part of a larger team and to learn new work styles.

Professional Organizations. The largest professional organization for secretaries is Professional Secretaries International, which has chapters in the United States and foreign countries. Another fast growing organization is the Association of Information Systems Professionals, formerly the International Information/Word Processing Association. Executive Women International, with membership comprised of executive secretaries and administrative assistants, is another organization which provides many opportunities for service and professional growth.

Certification Programs. Several organizations sponsor rigorous certification programs. Anyone passing these examinations demonstrates superior competency in the field. The certification programs of the American Association of Medical Assistants, the National Association of Legal Secretaries (International), and the National Association of Educational Office Personnel are described in Chapter 23.

Professional Secretaries International awards a certified professional secretary certificate (CPS) to those who pass a two-day examination and have the required amount of verified secretarial experience. About 23,000 secretaries have qualified for the certificate since its inception in 1951. The examination is divided into six sections and tests behavioral science in business, business law, economics and management, accounting, office administration and communication, and office technology. It is prepared by the Institute for Certifying Secretaries and is given in May and November at more than 100 testing centers in the United States, Canada, Puerto Rico, and Jamaica.

Students may take the examination near the end of their college program; but if they pass all sections, they will not be certified until they complete the experience requirement. Specific information about qualifying is not included here since it changes from year to year. It is available from Professional Secretaries International, 301 East Armour Boulevard, Kansas City, MO 64111-1299. To prepare for the examination, you may obtain the following materials from PSI for a minimal fee: *CPS Outline and Bibliography; CPS, a Sampling of Questions;* and *University/College Directory of Credits* granted for the CPS rating.

Unfortunately management personnel are not as well informed about the CPS program as secretaries wish they were. There are notable exceptions, however. The governors of Indiana and Illinois have issued policy statements indicating that CPS holders will receive special consideration for promotions. A number of colleges grant college credit to holders of the CPS certificate.

Seminars and Courses for Secretaries. Several professional organizations offer seminars and courses to improve secretarial performance. The local chapters of Professional Secretaries International conduct workshops, seminars, and CPS preparation courses. Private organizations such as the Dartnell Institute of Management sponsor seminars in major cities of the United States. Management organizations offer special seminars for secretaries, the Administrative Management Society and the American Management Association, to name only two. Colleges offer such programs through their adult education programs.

Many companies send their secretaries to these programs. If you are interested in attending any of them, request financial support from your immediate employer. If your request is granted, arrangements for time off from work and payment of registration fees can be made with your employer.

A study of companies with 500 or more employees shows that 75 percent of them offer some in-house courses, with one eighth of all employees participating, mostly during working hours. Many of these courses are designed to improve secretarial performance. It is obvious that educational opportunities are available to those ambitious enough to take advantage of them.

Promoting Your Employer

The more important your employer appears in the eyes of others— company executives, customers, clients, and friends—the more important you appear, too. Here are some suggestions which will help keep you both in the limelight:

1. Keep your employer's personal data sheet up to date. Many employers have a prepared data sheet which they submit when applying for membership in a professional organization or when supplying a biographical sketch prior to a speech or publication. This sheet needs to be updated regularly.
2. Watch the newspaper and magazines for press notices that mention your employer. See that they are clipped, identified, and filed. They can be rubber cemented into a scrapbook. Many people are too modest to handle or supervise such a task; so the secretary should take the initiative. Posting clippings about your employer on the bulletin board is one way of letting everyone in the office know that your employer is important.
3. Keep your employer's committee and project folders in good order and up to date to assure that your employer presents a good image in the eyes of other company personnel.

4. Watch the news for items concerning your employer's business associates and friends. When they are honored or promoted, draft a letter of congratulations for your employer's signature and submit it with the clipping.
5. Look for news reports about new firms or plants that may be potential customers. Your employer will watch for these items also, but it does no harm for you to say, "Did you happen to see this in yesterday's paper?"

There is no better way to promote a good image of your employer than to see that all work going out of the office is flawless and is turned out with dispatch. Mistakes, delays, and sloppiness are not the marks of a professional secretary.

If you have worked with an executive for a period of time, you should be able to assess whether or not that person is on the way up the company ladder. Executive positions are extremely competitive. It is a cruel fact that many bright young executives do not make the grade and are destined for dead-end jobs. People who get ahead in business are usually helped by a mentor (sponsor), someone who pushes for their advancement. If you are assigned to an executive whose promotional opportunities are nonexistent or to one who is not your mentor, you may decide that the best thing for you is to move out since you will probably not move up. Ask for a transfer or change to another organization.

Be aware that beginners are not always willing to wait until a sound assessment of an executive's potential situation can be made before deciding to seek greener pastures. Nothing is more questionable on your employment record than proof that you are a job-hopper. However, an honest appraisal of your employer is valuable in planning your professional future. If you decide on a move after you have been in a position long enough to establish that you were successful in it, leave with poise and dignity and without animosity. Any derogatory remarks could haunt you for a long time after you are gone. A letter of resignation will help to keep a good relationship intact.

Identifying Yourself with Management

Being a secretary to a major official of a business is not a position that you step into or inherit because you have completed a degree or a technical program. These positions must be earned and are usually filled from the inside. Therefore, although you will probably start on a lower level, your goal is eventually to associate yourself with top management.

To work effectively on this level, the secretary must develop the ability to look at problems from the management point of view. This trait requires an orientation toward management thinking. Read the same magazines that management reads, such as *Fortune, Nation's Business, BusinessWeek, The Wall Street Journal, Forbes, The Office, Office Administration and Automation, Today's Office,* and others; become concerned with management problems; study management books, and take management courses.

The emphasis of much of your secretarial training has been on following instructions, observing directives, carrying decisions through and assuming the initiative in a relatively narrow range of operation. Management, however, involves determining courses of action, making decisions, giving directions, and delegating authority and responsibility. To shift to the management outlook, the secretary must view problems basically from the other side of the desk. This transition requires a carefully planned program of self-education, orientation, and discipline.

You need to grow every day of your working life. If the time comes when you cannot keep up with your employer, be assured that you will be replaced by someone who can. If you continue to grow with the job, you will have a position as long as you want it; and possibilities for advancement become limitless.

As you grow into a management role, you will gradually perform more supervisory functions. The higher up the management ladder you climb, the greater your supervisory responsibilities will be. The final chapter in this text will discuss management and supervisory problems.

SUMMARY

As new technology continues to increase office productivity and to eliminate much of the drudgery formerly associated with the secretarial role, new and exciting opportunities emerge for the professional secretary. The future promises increased jobs, advancement opportunities, and recognition.

Once you have decided upon a company which you think will offer you a good starting point for your career, analyze the personal characteristics that will help you get off to the right start and to grow professionally on the job. Competent secretaries who achieve recognition and enjoy a high degree of job satisfaction suggest that initiative, flexibility in dealing with change, awareness of the needs of the business and the employer, and adeptness in human relations are prerequisites for success as a professional secretary.

The first week or two on the job can overwhelm the beginning secretary. There is so much to learn—the people, the environment, and the work. During your first days on the job, everyone in the office forms first impressions of you. You will work under critical inspection. Strive to make a favorable first impression by being a good listener, learning names and titles quickly, observing the ground rules, and living up to the secretarial code of ethics. Develop a network of friends throughout the organization. Goodwill at all levels of an organization is essential to the secretary's effectiveness.

In addition to knowing the prerequisites for getting off on the right foot, you should also be aware of possible obstacles with which you will have to cope. Be aware of your rights in all situations. Learn how to handle problems when they occur.

From the first day on the job, begin learning about the company that employs you—names of customers, your employer's close associates, and company terminology. The more you know about a company, its products, its people, and its customers, the more valuable you will be to your employer. Several sources of information are available to you. These sources include company manuals, office files, company publications, newsletters, trade journals, and the like.

Asking questions is a good way to learn, but they should be *learning questions* that count. Don't ask someone else a question when you can find answers yourself.

A desk manual will help you organize your work. If one is not provided for you, make one. It should contain sections on procedures for handling certain duties, company information, a directory of those with whom your employer frequently interacts, a directory of clients and projects, and a personal data section on your employer.

After you have demonstrated your competence, you can hope for promotion. Advancement depends on your performance and professional growth in your present job. The secretarial profession is exactly what you make it: advancement depends on you. Each time you assume a new responsibility and successfully see it through, you enhance your chances for promotion. There is no substitute for competence. Understand the difference between *assertiveness* and *aggressiveness*. Work for the establishment of improved personnel practices. Update your job description periodically to include expanded responsibilities. Ask your executive to establish your authority for giving executive orders.

You also need to grow professionally by participating in activities outside the office. There are several avenues open for professional growth. One of the most effective is membership in professional organizations, such as Professional Secretaries International and the Association of Information Systems Professionals. Certificate programs, such as the certified professional secretary, also give direction to your professional education. Seminars and special courses are also available from several professional organizations. Attend them. Very often, employers pay fees for their secretaries to attend.

The secretary should keep in mind that the picture the public sees of the employer is one the secretary paints. The more impressive the employer's image, the more impressive the secretary appears. To do an effective job of promoting the employer, the secretary should produce flawless work. In addition, the employer's personal data sheet should be kept up to date. Keep a scrapbook of publicity relating to the employer's activities. Keep committee and project folders in good order. Look for publicity about your employer's customers, associates, and competitors that will help you stay informed of the changes that affect you and your employer.

Keep in mind that your employer can have a great deal of influence on your advancement. After you have worked for an executive for a period of time, you should be able to assess whether or not that person is on the way up the corporate ladder. Realize that people who get ahead in business are often helped by a mentor (someone who takes an interest in their advancement). If you sense that your employer is destined for a dead-end job, you may decide to move out or ask for a transfer. Don't build a reputation as a job-hopper; but should you decide that your opportunities for advancement are limited in your present job and you have established a record of success in it, leave with poise and dignity.

SUGGESTED READINGS

Amburgey, Lillian. "How Companies Develop Employees." *Management World* (May, 1982), p. 14.

Clement, Robert W. "Careers in Corporate Hands." *Management World* (May, 1982), p. 13.

Fusselman, Kay. "Secretaries Wanted." *The Secretary* (January, 1985), p. 3.

Goddard, Robert W. "I Won't Be in Today." *Management World* (November, 1982), p. 17.

Kushell, Elliot, and Dorothy Heide. "Professional Development Starts With You." *The Secretary* (October, 1985), p. 18.

"Salary Outlook for Secretaries and Office Personnel." *The Secretary* (November/December, 1985), p. 3.

QUESTIONS FOR DISCUSSION _____

1. Cite three examples, other than those mentioned in the text, of a new secretary showing initiative that is desirable. Cite three examples in which you think that the secretary exceeded his/her authority.
2. What recommendations would you make to a co-worker who asks your advice on how to grow in the secretarial profession?
3. In what ways can a secretary profit from joining a local chapter of a professional organization?
4. Assume that you are employed to replace the secretary to a department manager in a large company and that the secretary has already left when you report. Where would you obtain the following information?

   a. Your job description
   b. Your employer's proper title
   c. The lines of authority in the office
   d. The letter style preferred by your employer
   e. The name of the company president's secretary
   f. The branch offices of the company
   g. Your employer's professional memberships

5. Do you think a new secretary should be willing to take company manuals and work materials home for study when first learning a new job? Why or why not?
6. As a new employee, you are asked to learn the functions of other closely related jobs in your office. What are the advantages of this practice? Are there any disadvantages?
7. What do you think about the theory of some secretaries that professional work life should remain separate from personal life?
8. In today's office, why should a secretary have a code of ethics, while some other employees may not?
9. Personnel changes in company organization have resulted in your being assigned a second employer. In your own mind you question whether you can handle the work of another person. What attitude should you take with your present employer and the new one?
10. What factors might influence a secretary to leave an organization? Why could this decision be a risky one?
11. Why is it important that the secretary train an understudy?

12. Retype the following sentences choosing the correct word from those in parentheses. Check the Reference Guide to verify and correct your answers.
    a. The luggage is (identical to, identical with) that I took to college.
    b. The (ingenius, ingenuous) use of software has reduced the number of spelling errors.
    c. We must take at least two members (off, off of) the project.
    d. He (lead, led) the company in sales that month.
    e. (Later, Latter) in the year we will take up the (later, latter) of the two proposals.

PROBLEMS

1. Prepare a report on one of the following topics:
   a. What you believe are the personal contributions a secretary makes to the office, to co-workers, and to secretarial work
   b. How you plan to meet the challenge of new office technology in secretarial work
2. Select a professional organization that has a chapter in your area. Make arrangements to attend one of the meetings or interview one of the members. Give an oral report to the class including a description of the organization, its objectives, activities, membership requirements, and services to members.
3. Write to the Institute for Certifying Secretaries or the National Association of Legal Secretaries and request information on requirements for taking the CPS or the PLS examination. Prepare a written report outlining the requirements for after you graduate but before you have had any secretarial experience.

Chapter 25

Fulfilling Your
Administrative Role

At some point in your career you may want to look beyond the secretarial position and explore the possibilities of moving into management. As you grow in experience, in intellectual curiosity, and in your ability to solve problems and make decisions, you will find increased opportunities for jobs that will broaden your business perspective, increase your authority, and permit you to make major decisions. Increased knowledge and experience will strengthen your confidence in your ability to motivate and to lead others in the achievement of common goals.

Your contribution to your employer as a secretary permits you to exhibit your managerial talent; it can also indicate whether you will make an effective manager. Study the job ahead. If you believe you have the ability to attain results through the work of others, start now to direct your professional development toward a management position.

This chapter focuses on the fundamentals of the management process and on the basic qualifications for effective administration and supervision. Throughout this book, some of the secretary's administrative duties were identified as an integral part of the secretarial position. This chapter goes beyond the administrative duties performed by the secretary by outlining the functions of management and the popular styles of leadership. It also gives some suggestions for continuing your professional growth as a manager.

APPRAISING YOUR MANAGEMENT POTENTIAL

In many offices, secretaries perform a dual role; that is, their secretarial duties are combined with the supervision of other employees. Often these employees work for and answer to someone other than the secretary, and the secretary's authority is limited. Therefore, extreme tact and ability are required to keep work flowing smoothly. Because the secretary's lines of authority are hazy under such an arrangement, frustration sometimes results; however, handling the secretary/supervisor role successfully can prove your ability as a potential manager.

As you expand your horizons beyond the support functions associated with your secretarial position, focus on a particular management job and analyze it.

MANAGEMENT POTENTIAL

If you can answer yes to most of these questions, you show promise as a successful executive.

____ Do I have the managerial qualifications that are different from those required in my present job?

____ Am I willing to let go of the technical details of my present job and take on broader responsibilities?

____ Have I trained someone to take my place so that the transition will be a smooth one?

____ Do I want to devote more time and thought to my work than I do now?

____ Could I travel if the job required it?

____ Am I fully aware of the negative aspects of being a manager?

____ Could I make unpopular decisions and deal with criticism?

____ Could I build an effective team?

____ Could I cope with conflict and maintain discipline?

____ Do I have sufficient knowledge of my company, its people, products, and markets?

____ Would I rather move up than remain at the support level, retaining close associations with my secretarial peers?

____ Am I willing to give up most of the close associations with my peers?

UNDERSTANDING MANAGEMENT FUNCTIONS

Management is executive leadership or the ability to obtain desired results through the use of an organization's resources and the efforts of others. The success of every organized activity depends on the managerial skills of its leaders. Although some managers seem to be born with the ability to lead, others must acquire management skills through reading, specialized courses and seminars, experience, and observation of successful executives.

The functions of management at all levels involve planning, organizing, controlling, and directing. To become an effective manager, you must understand each of these functions and how it contributes to the total organization.

Planning

Planning is the primary management function. It gives an organization a course of action. Before anything worthwhile can happen in an organization, goals must be set, objectives established, and checkpoints and target dates defined. This is the essence of planning.

Plans may be made for the long term (more than one year) or for the short term (one year or less). Long-range plans are general in nature. They must anticipate changes in social, economic, and political climates that can affect outcomes over a five-year or ten-year period. Short-range plans are spelled out in detail, and in some cases are devised to guide a specific, nonrecurring project. For example, a manager might make a short-range plan to conduct a feasibility study for installing a word processing unit in a company. Once the decision is made and the equipment is installed, there is no further need for the plan.

Good plans are not too rigid. Some flexibility is built in to allow for the uncertainties of the future. It should be possible to make slight adjustments without major deviation from the requirements of the plan.

Organizing

Once plans have been formulated, a structure must be developed within which the plans can be carried out. Tasks must be divided among personnel. Each worker and supervisor must know who is to perform each task as well as when and how the work is to be done. The organizational function defines duties, assigns responsibilities (the obligation to perform a task), delegates authority (the power to make decisions related to the work), and establishes staff relationships (who reports to whom).

In an effective organization, employees answer to one supervisor. This is called *unity of command*. Imagine your dilemma, for example, in working as secretary to four executives, each of whom feels that his or her work should be given priority. Violation of the unity of command principle, although not uncommon in many offices, is a cause of frustration, low morale, and high turnover.

Good organizational structure adheres to the principle of *span of control*. Span of control refers to the number of employees who report to a single supervisor. A manager who supervises too many employees will not be able to perform all supervisory duties effectively. On the other hand, supervision of too few employees is a waste of executive time. As a general rule, the lower the level of management, the larger the span of control can be. For example, a supervisor of a word processing center might supervise 12 word processing specialists effectively, but it would be difficult for an administrative manager to be responsible for more than five supervisors of such operations as word processing, mail room, reprographics, records, and credit and collections because of the complex nature of these operations.

Business responsibilities may be organized in a number of ways. Two major types of organizational structures used in business are *line* and *line and staff*, but others are also in use.

Line Organization. *Line organization* means that authority flows in a straight line from the top official in the company to the lowest administrative segment of the organization. A popular device for illustrating the line form of organization is an organizational chart, which shows relationships among members of an organization and their areas of responsibility. An example of a line organizational chart appears in Chapter 2 on page 27.

Line and Staff Organization. The line and staff concept of organization originated in the military. Business adopted it as a means of coping with expanding relationships that accompany growing organizations. Most large companies today use line and staff organization because the structure permits the use of staff specialists for advice and assistance. The term *staff* refers to support activities of two kinds: specialist and personal. Staff specialists serve in an advisory capacity only; that is, they have no authority over line personnel. Their relationships to line personnel are indicated in Illus. 25-1 by broken lines.

Functional Authority. The concept of *functional authority* is closely related to line and staff organization but it violates the principle of unity of command. Functional authority delegates power to individuals or to departments over departments other than their own. For

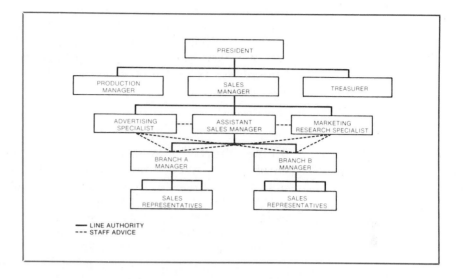

Illus. 25-1
A line and staff
organization
defines
relationships
between managers
and staff.

example, the president of your company decides to install microcomputers for payroll preparation and gives authority to a specialist from the data processing department to supervise the accounting department in purchasing software, establishing procedures, and the like. The president assigned *functional authority* to the data processing specialist.

Functional authority is usually concerned with when and how something is done rather than with what is to be done and who is to do it. Functional authority should only be used when specialists are needed; otherwise, it undermines the line manager's authority to organize, plan, staff, direct, and control. Functional authority does, however, save time and expedite the flow of information in complex situations.

Committee Organization. A committee is a group of people responsible for a specific project or situation. This form of organization is common to all types of institutions—religious, educational, governmental, and commercial. Committees are used to obtain the best judgment and thinking of a group. Those who advocate the use of this type of organization believe that groups are more capable of solving problems and guiding projects than individuals. Because of the combined education, experience, and personal influence of a committee's members, better solutions to problems are possible. Committees are also used to avoid centering too much authority in one person. Because a committee involves several people, it has certain weaknesses: committee work is time-consuming and decisions are sometimes difficult to reach; meetings sometimes result in compromise rather than a solid solution; and some managers use committees to avoid making unpleasant decisions themselves. Employees who serve on committees, however, have an opportunity to get involved in large projects. Committees provide high visibility and an opportunity to influence decisions.

Matrix (Project) Management. *Matrix management* is a form of organization that pools the skills and knowledge of teams of personnel from various departments throughout a company to complete major company projects. Employees from various departments may be assigned to a special project on a part-time or on a full-time basis until it is completed. Matrix management allows an organization to make the most effective use of its personnel.

Because many firms face complex problems brought on by increased government regulation and rapidly growing technology, expertise that crosses departmental lines is often needed. Because word processing and telecommunications touch every aspect of a firm—personnel, production, marketing, and finance—they are good candidates for matrix management.

A company planning to introduce a new brand of cake mix illustrates matrix management. Introducing a new cake mix would involve specialists from production, marketing, and finance working together as a team until the cake mix is on grocers' shelves. Because of the need for administrative support for the project, a word processing specialist might be assigned to the project on a temporary basis to support the project team. When the project is completed, the specialist would return to the word processing center.

Members of a project team work in a climate unlike the traditional line and staff organization. As with any other management structure, matrix management has both advantages and disadvantages. On the positive side, there is the ability on the part of the firm to make more efficient use of skilled personnel. Because employees from different functional areas are required to work together for a common goal, the organization can quickly respond to special demands. On the negative side, matrix management violates the unity of command principle. Employees are responsible to home department managers as well as to the manager of the special project. Project managers find that employees borrowed from functional departments are extremely loyal to those departments. Therefore, it is frequently difficult to coordinate the efforts of employees on temporary assignments.

Controlling

Control is the monitoring function that ensures that work meets specifications. Control must be exercised to ensure that work is of the proper quality and produced in expected quantities at the most economical cost according to predetermined schedules, policies, and procedures.

Cost Control and Work Measurement. Two major types of control exist in every type of organized activity: cost control and production control. Effectiveness in cutting costs—the ability to reduce the cost of supplies, overtime, absenteeism, etc.—is one of the best measures of competence as a manager.

The other area of control in which the supervisor must be especially skillful is the area of production. Measurement techniques of several kinds are employed by supervisors as a basis on which to set production standards and to arrive at pay scales for employees. Measuring the production of factory workers engaged in routine assembly line operations has been practiced for many years. Until recently, however, measuring office work has not been practiced on a large scale.

In evaluating your work and that of your subordinates, you need a set of criteria on which to base your judgments. Output in highly repetitive office operations has been successfully measured, and realistic quantitative standards have been established. In word processing centers, line and page counts are commonly used to measure worker productivity and the success of the center concept itself. In management literature you can find standards for straight copy, letter typing, addressing envelopes, or filling in form letters. Determining qualitative standards is not as easy; just remember that the quality of all work from your department is your responsibility.

Corrective Action. In spite of adequate planning, efficient organization, and proper control, something will occasionally go wrong. A subordinate may not perform up to the expected standard or external delays and errors may prevent the completion of a project on time. When this happens the supervisor must take corrective action. Corrective action, when taken promptly, can prevent more serious problems later on and help keep morale and productivity high. Problems, such as computer down time, failure of a printer to deliver forms, careless employees who make serious errors, and the like, must be dealt with by the supervisor decisively, calmly, and as soon as possible.

Quality Circles. *Quality circles*, originally known as *quality control circles*, are a proven technique for controlling quality. This management concept was borrowed from the Japanese in the early 1980s. A quality circle consists of a voluntary group of workers who share an area of responsibility. The group meets frequently on company time and on company premises to discuss, analyze, and propose solutions to problems relating to quality.

A quality circle is usually composed of a normal crew that works together to produce a product or service. The leader of the circle, usually the group supervisor, is trained to function as a group leader rather than as an authority figure. Circle leaders go through leadership training which includes adult learning techniques, group motivation, and communications. Members of the circle are trained in work measurement and in other strategies for controlling quality—data collection and sampling techniques, for example. A quality circle usually includes five to ten members, but more than one circle may be formed within a department. These circles call upon company experts to help solve problems and to advise the group on effective procedures.

Many companies have found that quality circles are an effective way to reduce errors, cut costs, reduce waste, and enhance morale and team spirit among employees. As members of a quality circle, employees gain visibility and enhance their opportunities for advancement.

Directing

An effective manager leads employees in such a way that organizational goals are achieved. This is the function of directing. Expanding government regulations, new technology, and increased costs have magnified the importance of this management function. Employee turnover is expensive, and top management in every organization is aware that the key to managing through people is to have the best possible people through whom to manage. Leaders must motivate employees to work efficiently and attempt to boost morale by providing an environment conducive to job satisfaction.

SUPERVISING OTHERS

Effective supervision is the ability to get people to do *what* you want done, *when* you want it done, the *way* you want it done because they *want* to do it. Supervision is the first level of management. As you move up professionally, you will probably find yourself in a supervisory position. As a supervisor, you will be a member of the management team that is responsible for getting work done. What's more, you will be the communication link between top and middle management and those you supervise. Your job will be a multifaceted one. You will report to top and middle management, interpret management policies to those you supervise, and coordinate with other supervisors to facilitate the flow of work throughout the organization. You will be promoting teamwork.

The amount of supervision needed depends on the quality of the orientation process and subsequent training on the job. If an employee receives in-depth orientation and adequate training, the need for supervison is considerably lessened. After the initial training period, the right amount of supervision becomes important. Too much supervision gives the employee the feeling of being policed; too little leads to confusion. A supervisor's duties consist of all or some of the following tasks:

Helping select the right people for the job
Controlling absences and tardiness
Inspecting and proofing work
Keeping workers informed
Carrying out objectives and instructions of management
Keeping track of hours worked
Maintaining office discipline
Planning, assigning, and scheduling work
Controlling office costs
Promoting teamwork and cooperation
Listening to employees' problems
Providing and caring for equipment and supplies
Training employees
Handling employee discipline problems
Keeping records and making reports to management
Maintaining high quality and quantity of production
Maintaining high morale among workers
Improving work methods
Maintaining safe, clean working conditions
Evaluating employees for raises and promotions
Orienting new employees to the job
Handling matters of compensation
Delegating work to others
Interpreting employees' needs to management
Interpreting management's needs to employees

Fulfilling the role of a successful supervisor requires more than job competence and hard work. It also requires the ability to recognize and select outstanding employees and to develop their potential for making a contribution to the company and the department to which they are assigned.

Recruiting

Recruitment of employees is usually the responsibility of the personnel department. Before any recruiting begins, however, a study of the complete job description and the educational, work experience, and skill requirements for the position is made. Later, potential employees who meet screening standards are sent to the immediate supervisor for final approval or rejection. (Note the word "rejection." The supervisor, being close to the job, may recognize valid reasons why a proposed candidate would not be effective. It is best to say no now and avoid trouble later.)

An objective of every company is promotion from within. An effective supervisor or administrator makes the development of replacements and personnel for new jobs an important objective. In fact, without a well-trained replacement, you may not be considered for a promotion.

Assisting employees in reaching their potential begins with the orientation to the job. The better the orientation process, the less supervision required, and the more time supervisors have to accomplish their work.

Orienting

Large organizations have formal orientation programs for new employees. Films, slides, and lectures acquaint new employees with the history, products, and fringe benefits of the company. Information related to the specific job, however, is left to the immediate supervisor. It is the supervisor's responsibility to explain and demonstrate the tasks of the job.

If you are a supervisor, discuss how and when the employee will be evaluated and how this evaluation is tied to salary increments. The supervisor also introduces new employees to the office workers and conducts a tour of the office facilities. In a small organization, the secretary/supervisor provides the entire orientation program including general information about the company and specific information about the job.

Many supervisors develop an induction checklist to follow in orienting a new employee to the company and to the position. This list may include 50 to 100 items, whatever it takes to explain the job. Supplementary materials, such as an organizational chart and an office telephone directory, are useful in outlining the office hierarchy and office procedures.

Training

Before employees can perform effectively as team members, a basic understanding of procedures, policies, and technology is essential. Rarely can an employee learn a complex job merely by observing. One of your supervisory duties will be to provide sufficient training to make employees fully productive as soon after induction as possible. Too little training is expensive when it leads to errors, employee insecurity, and low productivity. On the other hand, training programs that prolong the time before an employee takes full responsibility for a job are also costly. To determine the types and length of training that an employee needs, a list of specific duties and responsibilities is helpful. It is also suggested that the supervisor follow these guidelines:

1. Focus attention on what the employee is to do. First, have the employee observe as you complete a task. Then check the employee's understanding by having the trainee work through the process step by step. Allow more time for difficult tasks.
2. Discuss the purposes behind each task and encourage questions. Explain the *who, what, where, when, why,* and *how* of each task. Suggest that the employee compile a list of instructions. For more complicated tasks, it is a good practice for the supervisor to provide a written set of instructions. Use materials and office forms that are part of the job in your explanations.
3. Allow the employee some quiet time to digest information.
4. Assist the employee in seeing what tasks are important and those which are not so important. Emphasize the key steps in each job task.
5. Provide feedback to the employee on work that has been done. You may have to reteach certain points which may have been misunderstood by the employee or overlooked in your explanation.

After an employee has been in the office long enough to learn an assigned job, continue your teaching responsibility by training the employee to do other jobs in the department. This technique is called *cross training*. Cross training has merit for the supervisor and for the employee. When an employee is absent because of sickness or vacation, another employee can assume the duties of the position. Cross training makes the employee more valuable to the department and increases the employee's job skills.

An example of cross training can be found in the administrative support/word processing center concept. Many companies train administrative secretaries on word processing equipment to provide for better understanding of the center's functions as well as to provide greater flexibility of personnel. Although word processing specialists are usually assigned to one specific piece of equipment, they might be trained on all equipment in the center for the same reason—staff flexibility.

Delegating

Supervisors must delegate to survive the avalanche of paperwork that characterizes the modern office and to get jobs done accurately and on time. As your supervisory responsibilities expand, you must let go of details and assign them to others. Working frantically from one crisis to another, attempting to do everything yourself, leads to fatigue and inefficiency and does little to develop the potential of those you supervise. As a supervisor you will be judged by your ability to develop productive employees. By delegating some of your duties, you can give those you supervise added experience. Start your task of delegation simply. Delegate routine tasks, such as filling out reports and forms, checking materials and supplies, and composing routine correspondence.

As you begin your supervisory duties, you may find that you are not very skillful in delegating work to others. Many supervisors admit that early in their careers they labored under the false notion that it was easier to do a job than to explain it to someone else, or that they were afraid to risk employee error on an important job. These are common misgivings; but, if you are to become an effective supervisor, you must become effective at delegating work. Don't make the mistake of keeping busy with lots of routine details. Delegate routine jobs that can free you to perform major management functions—planning, organizing, controlling, and directing.

Motivating

A supervisor has the obligation to obtain the best results from employees. The ability to inspire people to undertake a job enthusiastically, to work as productive team members, and to exercise initiative is the hallmark of successful management. It is essential that you understand why some people do superior work while others do as little as possible. Hundreds of books have been written on the subject of motivation, and behavioral scientists are still seeking answers on how to motivate people effectively.

Closely allied to job motivation is the need for job satisfaction. Each individual has a set of needs that must be satisfied. In the past, money was used as the major motivation in the workplace. The assumption that people worked only for money has been debunked by recent motivational research. Studies reveal that, after a certain level of income, money ceases to be a significant motivator for many employees. Research studies by behavioral scientists Abraham Maslow and Frederick Herzberg have helped management personnel to determine the needs of employees. Maslow identified a *hierarchy* of human needs: physiological (food, clothing, shelter), safety, belonging, esteem, and self-actualization (see Illus. 25-2). He indicated that once a lower need is fairly well satisifed, a worker can be motivated only by a desire to satisfy the next higher need. His work suggests that managers must help employees realize their upper level needs (belonging, esteem, self-actualization) before complete job satisfaction—and higher productivty—can be obtained. In the office, *belonging*, the third level of needs, refers to acceptance and achievement of status with one's peers. The fourth level, *esteem*, is the need for prestige, recognition, and achievement. *Self-actualization*, the highest level, emphasizes becoming whatever a person can be, reaching one's full potential. The supervisor can assist subordinates in achieving a higher level in the following ways:

> Give each employee complete responsibility for the preparation of one section of a report or one unit of work
> Grant increased authority in the accomplishment of office tasks
> Allow employees to participate in making decisions that affect their work

Frederick Herzberg took another approach to understanding employee morale. His research of factors which result in employee satisfaction and dissatisfaction has helped managers in their attempts to reduce employee turnover and increase productivity.

Herzberg's major findings revealed that task-related experiences (achievement, recognition, interesting work, growth, advancement, and responsibility) led to job satisfaction. He called these experiences *satisfiers*. On the other hand, he found that experiences that caused employees to be unhappy were related to the job environment (working conditions, company policies and administration, supervision, money, status, job security, and interpersonal relationships). Herzberg classified these as *dissatisfiers*.

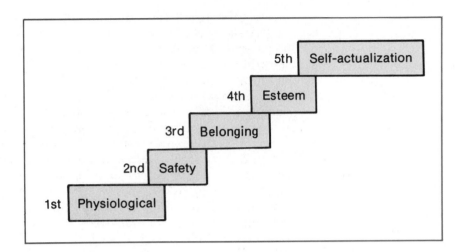

Illus. 25-2
Maslow's needs
hierarchy contains
five levels.

Supervisors face the problems of tardiness, absenteeism, careless-ness, and errors. These are barriers to productivity. As a supervisor, you are the catalyst who motivates and inspires employees to over-come these barriers. Some ways in which you can help your subordi-nates become successful in their work are given here:

1. Set specific objections for each major undertaking. Set a rea-sonable standard and give clear instructions.
2. Make employees feel that every job is important.
3. Make employees feel that they are important contributors to your team.
4. Ask employees for assistance, advice, and suggestions.
5. Let employees express their own ideas.
6. Train your employees and then trust them by giving them the freedom to work on their own.
7. Judge your employees' actions by results obtained.
8. Suggest and request rather than demand.
9. Praise employees publicly when praise is deserved, but repri-mand privately.
10. Give credit where credit is due.
11. Listen to learn what is important to your employees.
12. Reward those who achieve and use their accomplishments to inspire others.
13. Look in on employees occasionally to check progress, offer help, answer questions, or boost confidence.
14. Don't assign a job that you don't know how to do.
15. Find out why employees do poor work.
16. Don't do the work yourself if subordinates get into deep water; let them learn from the experience.

17. Remember that employees focus their best efforts where the supervisor places emphasis. Don't be a stickler for just one aspect of the job.
18. Put your critics to work. When you detect a complainer, delegate an important task to that person.

Evaluating

Periodically the secretary/supervisor must evaluate subordinates' work. In addition to being a job requirement, evaluation is wanted and needed by the employee. Your evaluation can be either formal or informal. In order to assess an employee's job performance you must observe the following:

Be thoroughly familiar with the work involved.
Have a set of job performance criteria.
Be aware of individual differences in performing tasks required by the position.
Consider such factors as accuracy, neatness, and quantity of the employee's production.
Be able to communicate your evaluation.
Praise the work, not the person who performed it.

FOURTEEN IMPORTANT WORDS: *That was a good job; What is your opinion; Will you please; Thank you.* ONE UNIMPORTANT WORD: *I*

The importance of evaluations cannot be overstated. Assume that you are responsible for the yearly evaluation of a subordinate. It is time for the first year evaluation, and you know that, in general, the person has done a good job. In the past few weeks, however, you noticed a change in performance and in attitude. The person is cooperative but sullen; the work is not up to former standards. Reluctant to make negative statements on record, you decide to disregard the last few weeks' performance and complete the form on the basis of the previous record. You are confident that something personal is bothering the person and that it will work out in time. Also, you decide not to mention these points in your conference with the person.

Is this the best course of action? Surprisingly, many supervisors in this situation react in exactly the same way. They tend to avoid possible unpleasant incidents and, in general, do not want to become involved in the personal problems of employees. Yet it is the supervisor's responsibility to maintain quality and to assist the employee in every way to be a happy and effective worker. Unpleasant situations should be faced and an attempt should be made to resolve any problems as soon as possible.

A supplement to a formal yearly evaluation would be to determine an employee's cooperativeness at specific points during the year. Such a checkup may point out problem areas for you to investigate. The result of such an approach might be to commend high performers, encourage the average group, and work more closely with those who appear to need help. Here are some activities you can review:

Does the employee accept instructions and assignments willingly?
Does the employee perform as directed?
Does the employee assume responsibility for work, inform the supervisor if something goes wrong, and call relevant matters to the supervisor's attention?
Does the employee volunteer for special assignments?
Does the employee give the job better than average attention?

Enriching the Job

Increased automation, the lack of diversity in many office jobs, and the monotony of some office tasks have brought a new challenge to the supervisor. More managers are beginning to give attention to the concept of *job enrichment*. Job enrichment attempts to bridge the gap between an employee's capabilities and job responsibilities. This is done by providing greater challenge, more of a sense of accomplishment, and wider latitudes for decision making. Flexible hours, job rotation, cross training, assigning full responsibility for an entire project, and establishing a pleasant working environment also provide job enrichment. In many companies, jobs are being redesigned to fill this need.

After all is said and done, unless actual benefits accrue to the worker, job enrichment techniques will become ineffective. Artificial measures cannot replace the need for training and promotions that move employees through the hierarchy of an organization.

MAKING DECISIONS

One of the best gauges of your potential as a manager is the ability to make effective decisions. Decisions are a part of every manager's job. Your survival as a supervisor depends on your ability to weigh facts, consider alternate courses of action, foresee outcomes, and decide what to do. Deciding on day-to-day activities can be done quickly and without much thought. Major decisions, however, require

My advice to managers is try leadership. Take one step forward. Think, and say what you think. Be out front. You may fall flat on your face. You may be wrong. You may take some outrageous slings and arrows, but you will never know the job of leading until you have stopped following.

H. Justin Davidson
Cornell University

much thought, time, and effort. Deciding what to do in a crisis can be a traumatic experience for a worker who has always referred problems to a superior. As you grow in your knowledge of your job, learn which decisions you can make on your own and which ones to refer to your superior. To arrive at the proper course of action, successful decision makers do the following:

Determine exactly what the problem is and write it down.
Develop a list of alternative solutions to the problem.
Examine the advantages and disadvantages of each possible solution.
Select the best solution and review all the ramifications of this choice.
Implement (and later evaluate) the chosen course of action.

Further evidence of your management potential is your reluctance to dump your problems in the lap of your superior for solution. In the army, all problems are handled on a "staff-work-accomplished" basis. The person with the problem is required to present all data and a recommendation for at least one solution to a superior . Preferably several alternate ones should be provided. After a problem is identified, the person closest to it should be in the best position to work out a solution and to recommend action.

MAINTAINING A COMMUNICATION NETWORK

A chief executive who did an amazing job of transforming a rundown company into an outstanding success instructed each department head to submit every Monday morning a report of all the *good* things that happened in the department during the preceding week.

It is estimated that 85 percent of a successful manager's job lies in the area of interpersonal communication skills. The ability to communicate effectively with employees is essential to the productivity of the office and to the well-being of its staff. Communication skills are also important for the secretary/supervisor. The secretary must develop and maintain open channels of communication between and among subordinates, other supervisors, and company executives. A communication network allows instructions, problem solving, work, and information to flow. Understanding how communications are generated in the office is basic to the establishment of this network.

Organizational Communications

Very little work can be accomplished in an office without communication. All office employees have an obligation to speak, write, and listen so that messages are understood. Through communication, information is furnished to management for use in decision making and control. Communication also serves to motivate and influence employees to achieve higher productivity and meet the goals of the company.

Organizational communication takes many forms. It can be oral—on a one-to-one basis—or in a group. It can be written. Reports, forms, company magazines, newsletters, an employee suggestion system, and bulletin boards are all forms of written communication.

Organizational communication can take several different directions. It can flow upward through the company hierarchy; it can flow horizontally to those on the same managerial level; and it can flow downward to supervisees.

Barriers to Communication

No two people enter the office with exactly the same educational, economic, and ethnic background. Yet, many office managers assume that if an individual has the skills to do the job, adaptation to the work, people, procedures, and equipment will come in due time. The fallacy in this assumption is that it assumes all people communicate successfully with each other.

There are several reasons why communication between two people in the office can fail. Perhaps the most important reason is *semantics*, the meanings of words and changes in the meanings of words. *Lack of common knowledge* is another. A secretary who uses words that can be easily misinterpreted or uses a technical vocabulary with a new employee is essentially wasting training time. Miscommunication can also occur because of the mere fact that the employee is new and the secretary represents rank in the company.

Other barriers to effective communication are the physical distances between desks and offices, noise levels, and other distractions. The supervisor must recognize these as potential barriers and attempt to make changes to overcome them.

Communicating Effectively

In order to be successful in a supervisory role, you must communicate honestly, sincerely, and directly with your subordinates. Employees tend to be more responsive to managers who create an atmosphere of understanding and trust.

Effective communication is a two-way street. The sender and receiver must understand what was related. In a supervisory capacity you will learn quickly the advantages of listening to employees. By doing so, you can establish a common ground on which to base further communications. You can also learn to know your subordinates so that a climate of mutual respect is possible. Two areas in which the secretary can demonstrate interpersonal communication skill are the explanation of work instructions and the interpretation of personnel policies to subordinates.

Work Instructions. Work instructions can be given orally or in writing. Oral instructions have certain advantages over written ones. With oral instructions, the secretary knows immediately whether a subordinate understands the instructions. An employee's facial expression and questions asked provide clues. If the instructions are complicated, give them orally and in writing.

Often the supervisor needs to write job instructions in order to update a procedures manual or to see that instructions are available, understood, and followed. Two important points to remember when giving job instructions are how to perform a certain procedure and why that specific type of procedure is desirable and important.

Personnel Policies. Supervisors are responsible for interpreting management policy to workers in such a way that whatever conformity is needed is obtained. Usually this means explaining the reasons behind a policy and the benefits that will accrue from its enactment. Whether you are in sympathy with the policy or not, you have an unavoidable obligation to support all company personnel policies. Conversely, you have an equal obligation to communicate suggestions for change— either your own or those under your supervision—to management.

DEVELOPING A LEADERSHIP STYLE

In every business organization men and women rise to positions of leadership and responsibility only to find that their previous experience has not prepared them to deal comfortably with their new managerial roles. A significant number of these managers develop an effective leadership style by imitating those who supervised them. Because managers use different leadership styles to get the job done, you should be aware of various styles and the disadvantages of each. A leadership style that works for one manager may be totally ineffective for another. Much has been done to make managers aware of various leadership styles. Study them to discover one that will help you exercise leadership in a manner that is compatible with your personality and temperament.

Theory X and Theory Y

One classic philosophy of human behavior is Douglas McGregor's *Theory X* and *Theory Y*. McGregor maintains that most managers base their leadership on the mistaken concept that employees work only for reward. Theory X assumes that the average worker is lazy, self-centered, lacks ambition, resists change, and is indifferent to company objectives. Theory X managers also believe that the average worker does as little as possible to get by, is not very bright, and prefers to be told what to do rather than to think independently. Theory Y managers take the opposite view. They believe that all people have the potential for development, that they are not naturally lazy, and that most workers have the capacity to focus their behavior to achieve company goals. Theory Y managers believe that the primary task of management is to provide an environment that allows workers to achieve personal goals while working to achieve the goals of the organization that employs them.

Management by Objectives (MBO)

A popular leadership style that uses the participative approach (Theory Y) is *management by objectives (MBO)*. Using this approach, the manager and the subordinate agree on the objectives they wish to accomplish in a specified time and the standards that will be used to measure performance. Once these are agreed on, the objectives are put in writing. Under MBO leadership, the employee has complete freedom to accomplish objectives. The manager checks progress at regular intervals and evaluates the employee's progress relative to predetermined goals. MBO, when properly administered, involves the entire organization by integrating goals, plans, and evaluations from the top echelon of management to the lowest work unit. MBO is the purest form of participative leadership because objectives, and how they are measured, are determined with the subordinate. To implement MBO, at least three steps should be followed:

1. A superior meets with a subordinate. Together they work out realistic performance objectives concerning the subordinate's work.

2.   They agree on the means by which the employee is to reach the specified results.

3.   At the end of a given time period, the superior and the employee compare actual results with expected results and then make appropriate decisions concerning future action.

If you are working in an MBO environment, you will establish goals with your employer concerning your area of responsibility. The goals agreed upon will be specific, measurable, and time-bound. Once the goals are identified, you will make plans to achieve them. As a supervisor, you will meet with your subordinates to determine their objectives. After a specified length of time, you may be evaluated in terms of the results you and your subordinates achieve.

The Managerial Grid

In the late 1960s, Robert R. Blake and Jane S. Mouton developed the managerial grid, which identified two basic concerns of managers: the concern for production and the concern for people. This leadership theory provided a technique for managers to identify their managerial styles by plotting their behavioral patterns on a set of coordinate axes. One axis represents the concern for people and the other represents the concern for production. These concerns were rated from 1 to 9 with 9 being the highest score. By ranking managers in this way, Blake and Mouton classified leaders in five categories. The intent was to draw managers' attention to the need to integrate their concerns for production with the concern for people. (Refer to the Suggested Readings at the end of this chapter.)

Situational Leadership

Although a number of behavioral theories of management exist, there is a growing tendency among management experts to believe that situational leadership is more practical than the behavioral approaches. *Situational leadership* is based upon the theory that the amount of leadership exercised by a supervisor varies from situation to situation. Some situations require careful supervision while others require little, if any. As the amount of authority exercised by the supervisor increases, autocratic leadership emerges. On the other hand, as the amount of participation by those supervised increases, democratic leadership is the focus. Any given situation determines how much supervisory authority is necessary and how much subordinate freedom is appropriate. The test of an effective supervisor is in knowing when and how much supervision is appropriate.

CONTINUING YOUR PROFESSIONAL GROWTH

Whether or not you seek a management position, you should continue your professional growth to ensure your job satisfaction and to increase your value to your employer. As a conclusion to this book, some additional suggestions are offered for improving your managerial skills and for growing professionally.

Nurturing Creativity

Many people think that only a chosen few, those in artistic fields, are creative. They believe that creativity is a talent that one must be born with. Everyday in the business world these people are proved wrong.

Creativity can take many forms. Anyone who has an idea and develops it is being creative. Successful business people have to be creative to be successful. You can be creative, too. You can become a contributor in the business office, a creator of ideas and actions.

Where to begin? Start by having an open mind. Ideas are born in imagination. Nonconformist alternatives to office problems are often creative solutions. Build a kit of ideas and experiment with them. A little idea can be expanded into a bigger or better idea.

Be an active observer of management functions. Look for *questions* but also seek *answers*. Look for ways to improve work and information flow. Be a sounding board for your superior, and let ideas happen.

Most people have a certain time of the day when they operate at their best level. For some people it may be the early morning hours; for others, it may be at twilight. Determine when you operate best, then set your mind to action. A mind can be alert only if it is well rested. Adequate leisure time and proper eating habits are stimulants to creative brain activity.

Welcome new office experiences. In themselves, they enlarge visionary powers from which ideas and actions come. A person who wants to can be creative; therefore, it is up to you.

Improving Your Communication Skills

As you grow in your job, try to improve your communication skills. Even presidents of companies and countries continue to search for clearer and more persuasive ways of telling their stories. You may find yourself on a committee where you want to influence the actions of others. Keep in mind the staff-work-accomplished approach. Make sure that when you speak you are making a constructive suggestion.

Plan what you say before you put it in writing. A well-presented communication reduces your superior's reading time. Write and rewrite to reduce verbiage. Abstract material and present it graphically. Arrange material to highlight salient points. Become a master at presenting the heart of a matter in one succinct paragraph.

Consider the possibility of expressing your ideas in articles and talks. Too many people are afraid to attempt public speaking or to write for publication; yet, these are tremendous aids to personal development and creativity. Public speaking teaches you to think on your feet. It makes you clarify and organize your thoughts effectively. Learn to judge the reactions of your listeners and emphasize or rephrase a point according to your listeners' reactions.

Developing Personal Specialties

Work to develop one or more specialties for which you are known throughout the organization. For instance, become an expert in personnel work, state tax laws, or company pricing policies. Through your training of subordinates in your office, your reputation as a superior teacher may be known. Recognition creates opportunities. You may be asked to develop and teach a company sponsored secretarial training course. Your desk manual may lead to the development of an office procedures manual. You may be considered a resource person, the person who knows the answers to questions frequently asked in the office. If you have become acquainted with word processing, you may be asked to participate in a feasibility study for your office. Whatever your inclination, your specialty or specialties can work to the company's advantage and to your own.

Meeting the Challenge of Technology

As a professional in your field, you must keep up with technological developments that affect you and your office. You must think positively and see applications that can be put into effect. No other behavior is acceptable for the professional. Read these magazines religiously: *Office Administration and Automation*, *Today's Office*, *The Secretary*, and *Modern Office Technology*. Attend office equipment exhibits and put your creative mind to work. This is the way to meet the challenge of the future.

Taking Advantage of Professional Growth Opportunities

As you look at the management opportunities in the firm where you work, you may feel the need for additional education. Most colleges and universities offer a variety of evening courses that lead to advanced degrees in management, marketing, accounting, information systems, and economics. Should you want to specialize in an area that you feel promises a bright future, make your employer aware of your interest in additional education. In many cases, financial support for your efforts is available.

Special seminars sponsored by universities, consulting firms, equipment vendors, publishing houses, and your own company's training department also offer excellent opportunities for self-improvement. Many of these seminars feature outstanding consultants in every major area of administration and management, and are helpful in keeping your management skills up to date.

Membership in a professional organization can provide valuable contact with those who share your business problems and professional interests. Through your association with other professionals you enhance your management skills and strengthen your influence in the business community.

The spectrum of useful professional organizations broadens as you move up. Every major segment of business activity (accounting, sales, personnel, records, etc.) has a professional organization structured to bring people together periodically to share new ideas and opportunities. The Administrative Management Society (AMS), the Association of Information Systems Professionals (AISP), the Data Processing Management Association (DPMA) , and Executive Women International are just a few of the many organizations that offer opportunities for leadership, creativity, and professional growth. (Investigate the advantages of membership in a local chapter of an appropriate organization.)

Professional certification is another way to improve your upward mobility as a manager and to upgrade your management skills. In much the same way that the CPS rating represents the capstone of your secretarial preparation, other certification programs are also available to managers. The certified administrative manager (CAM) program sponsored by the AMS is one. It consists of a series of five examinations in personnel, finance, administrative services, information systems, and management concepts. A sixth examination, a management case study, is given to measure a candidate's ability to integrate and apply material covered in the first five examinations. Candidates must also meet experience, leadership, communications, and character qualifications.

Only a few of the many opportunities for professional growth have been presented in this chapter. As you gain experience and improve your management skills, your opportunities for promotions will become more frequent and more attractive. Your professional growth, therefore, will be a continuing part of your work life.

SUMMARY

At some point in a secretary's career, the opportunity to move into a management position may arise. Experience, intellectual curiosity, and the ability to solve problems and make decisons increases a secretary's opportunities for jobs with greater authority and broader decision-making power.

In many offices, secretaries perform a dual role. Supervision of other employees is combined with their normal secretarial duties. Under such an arrangement, the secretary's lines of authority can be hazy and frustration sometimes results.

To move up in an organization it is necessary to focus on a particular job and to analyze the requirements needed to attain it. It is also necessary for the secretary to understand the managerial functions of planning, organizing, controlling, and directing. Concepts of line and staff organization, functional authority, committee organization, matrix management, and quality circles should also be familiar.

Since supervision is the first level of management, the secretary must be aware of the duties of the supervisor including recruiting, orienting, and training employees. A supervisor also has the responsibility to enrich the jobs of subordinates.

Decision making is a primary management skill. To make effective decisions, it is necessary to maintain a communication network that provides essential information to all levels of the organization. Since 85 percent of a manager's time is spent communicating, an awareness of the many forms of organizational communication and knowledge of the barriers to and the techniques for effective communication are vital.

A study of various management styles will help a secretary select and develop a management style that will be compatible with personality and temperament. A wide variety of management styles and philosophies have been researched and practiced with good results through the years. Some of these are Theory X and Theory Y, management by objectives, and situational leadership.

Once a management position has been attained, it is necessary to continue to grow professionally. To do this, a new manager must nurture creativity, improve communication to ensure understanding, and develop a personal specialty to enhance visibility in the organization. New technology presents an exceptional opportunity for professional growth in all types of businesses, and technical literacy is vital to success in today's office. Many opportunities for professional growth are available to managers. Membership in professional organizations, college courses, seminars, workshops, and professional certification programs can improve the upward mobility of new managers.

SUGGESTED READINGS

Blake, Robert R., Jane Srygley Mouton, and Artie Stockton. *The Secretarial Grid.* New York: AMACOM, 1983.

Chruden, Herbert J., and Arthur W. Sherman, Jr. *Managing Human Resources*, 7th ed. Cincinnati: South-Western Publishing Co., 1984.

Haimann, Theo, and Raymond Hilgert. *Supervision*, Concepts and Practices of Management, 3d ed. Cincinnati: South-Western Publishing Co., 1982.

Keeling, B. Lewis, and Norman F. Kallaus. *Administrative Office Management*, 8th ed. Cincinnati: South-Western Publishing Co., 1983.

Koontz, Harold, Cyril O'Donnell, and Heinz Weihrich. *Management*, 8th ed. New York: McGraw-Hill Book Company, 1984.

Williams, J. Clifton, Andrew J. DuBrin, and Henry Sisk. *Management and Organization*, 5th ed. Cincinnati: South-Western Publishing Co., 1985.

QUESTIONS FOR DISCUSSION

1. A manager must sometimes make decisions that are unpopular with subordinates. Give some examples of unpopular decisions that an office supervisor might have to make.

2. Why is supervision considered the first level of management, and why is it so important in the organizational structure?

3. Is a Theory X or a Theory Y manager more effective? Why?

4. You believe that your experience and education as a secretary have prepared you for a particular management position. What evidence could you give management to support your claim?

5. As a secretary, you have had many tasks delegated to you, but when you move into a management position you need to delegate to others. How would you do this without causing resentment among your subordinates?

6. Why might a secretary without a well-trained replacement not be considered for a promotion?

7. Why is the orientation process for new employees so important?

8. Your company usually follows the policy of promoting from within. As the office manager, you find it necessary on one occasion to recruit a replacement from outside the company. What is your responsibility to the employees in your office?

9. What is meant by the term *cross training*? How does it benefit the employer? the employee?

10. As a supervisor, what contributions could you make to assist subordinates in reaching their full potential?

11. What qualifications must a person have in order to evaluate the job performance of another employee?

12. Why is job enrichment so important in today's business office?

13. Assume that you are working as a secretary in an organization which follows the MBO leadership style. How would this affect your position?

14. Why is creativity so important to the secretary who seeks promotion and advancement?

15. What specialty do you have that might be developed into a plus factor in your job?

16. Why do some companies use the matrix form of management although it violates the principle of unity of command?

17. Why should a secretary willingly serve on company committees?

18. What function do quality circles have in the modern office?

19. Situational leadership advocates state that some situations require more supervison than others. Give some examples of office tasks that require more supervision than others.

20. Retype the following sentences. Capitalize the appropriate words in each line. Refer to the Reference Guide to verify and correct your answers.

    a. This is the space age—an era of Amazing Communication technology.

    b. Every successful executive has studied accounting, marketing, finance, and economics.

    c. A biblical reference is often used to begin a speech.

    d. If you understand latin or other languages, you will probably excel in english and spelling.

    e. Washingtonians, who live in the district, are very helpful to tourists.

PROBLEMS

1. Your firm has decided to automate its order processing department. This means a complete reorganization of the department as it presently operates. Your employer, vice-president for administration, has asked you to work with a consultant to determine the number of personnel needed to staff the department. The consultant, Mr. Wynn, is employed by the manufacturer of the equipment your company is considering purchasing. He has assured your employer that by automating the order processing department, 20 percent fewer people will be required.

    Fifty-eight people now staff the department, and although some backlogs occur, they have been infrequent. The staff of the order processing department now consists of the following:

> 50 typists
> 5 record specialists
> 1 proofreader
> 1 messenger/mail clerk
> 1 supervisor

Working with Mr. Wynn, you determine that 1,700 orders are processed daily. Each order averages ten minutes to process; ten thousand documents are filed each day. Each document requires 0.5 minutes to file. Office hours are from 8:30 a.m. to 4:30 p.m., with one hour for lunch and two 15-minute breaks.

    Using the above data, and assuming that Mr. Wynn is correct in his estimate that 20 percent fewer employees will be needed, determine the number of people necessary to staff the order processing department. Prepare a memorandum to your employer, Mr. Blanks, showing your calculations. Keep in mind that this reorganization could provide an opportunity for you to move into management because the present supervisor will retire if the department is automated.

2. Your employer is concerned about losses caused by employee absenteeism. He gives you the following chart and asks you to compute cost figures. Further, he requests that you include in your report (for his investigation) general categories for some possible causes of excessive absenteeism (such as inadequate recruitment procedures).

    > Total sick days paid previous 12 months   _____
    > Average daily pay multiplied by total sick days   _____
    > Annual cost five year   _____
    > Total accrued expense   _____

    You learn from the accounting department that in the last year 2,450 sick days have been paid and that the average daily pay is $40.

3. Assume that in your current secretarial position you have learned all that you can about the job and you see little possibility for advancement. You decide to seek another position. Before you begin, develop a career plan by compiling the following data and type your analysis in memorandum form:
    a. A description of the next job you wish to hold
    b. Status of the job market
    c. The size of the organization that will best assist you in your professional development now, three years from now, and six years from now
    d. The working conditions of those organizations listed in *c*

Part Seven   Case Problems _____

Case 7-1
LIVING WITH A
PROMOTION

Sylvia Murphy was promoted to secretary to Paul Whitman, President of the Conners Manufacturing Company. Sylvia had expected that her co-worker, Elizabeth Morgan, would get the promotion because of Elizabeth's excellent performance ratings. Elizabeth had also been with the company three years longer than Sylvia. The promotion came as a complete surprise to Sylvia. The only explanation that she could think of for her promotion was that she had been taking night courses for two years and had successfully completed the CPS examination. She had also worked on a special assignment for Mr. Whitman.

Sylvia decided that the best way to prevent hard feelings would be to discuss the situation with Elizabeth before Elizabeth had time to brood and build up resentment. Sylvia felt that by winning Elizabeth's support, she would allay any resentment on the part of other members of the office staff.

If you were Sylvia, would you discuss your promotion with Elizabeth?

Case 7-2
ASSUMING A
NEW POSITION

For 12 years, Marcie Gray served as secretary to the personnel director at State University. Marcie was a hard worker, always punctual, seldom complained about her work load, and had something nice to say to those who contacted her in person or by telephone. Last year she was selected as Secretary of the Year by her chapter of PSI. She also received an outstanding employee award two years in a row at the university.

When the president's secretary retired last year, Marcie was appointed to the position. Marcie was honored to receive the promotion because the job represented the highest secretarial job on campus. She also thought that the job would be much easier than her job in personnel. She thought that she would do little besides act as the president's receptionist.

During her first week on the job, Marcie was astounded to find that the president's schedule required early arrival and late departure three times a week. The president's appointment calender was a constant series of cancellations, substitutions, and rearrangements. Marcie's telephone contacts, her correspondence, and her relationships with office visitors were extremely important. The job required her to make many decisions that she had relied upon her former boss to make. During her first week, she made several errors in judgment. Some technical foul-ups also left her feeling inadequate.

Although Marcie likes the prestige and power that goes with her new job, she misses the orderly, organized, regular work of her previous job. What should Marcie do?

**Case 7-3
SEXUAL
INNUENDOS**

Helen Fisher was attending the annual out-of-town sales meeting with her employer, George Crane, Vice-President, Sales. At Mr. Crane's request, she went to lunch with three regional sales representatives and her employer so that she could summarize the conversation. One of the sale representatives was a woman.

As the luncheon progressed, two of the sales representatives began to tell off-color stories, each topping the other in crudity. Helen became more and more uncomfortable.

Was she in a position to do anything about the situation? What?

**Case 7-4
DEVELOPING
POSITIVE
ATTITUDES**

Apartment Furniture, Inc., has a buddy system under which selected experienced employees are assigned on a one-to-one basis to help new workers adjust to their jobs. This assignment is considered a compliment to experienced employees.

Blanche Woods, secretary to J. W. Mills, was delighted when Mr. Mills said to her, "Blanche, will you help me out? Ben Falk, who is buddy to Martica Joyer, wants to give up his assignment. Martica is a griper. She takes a negative attitude toward other employees and toward work assignments. Her supervisor and she are almost at swords' points, and she is becoming a misfit among her colleagues. Yet she does the best work that we have had from a beginner in months. She *could* become a real asset and is definitely worth saving. Personally, I like her.

"Ordinarily this situation would be handled by her supervisor, but you know as well as I do how rigid and inflexible Ms. Cruz is. I remember that you told me that you are interested in psychology, so why not give this assignment a fling?"

Blanche decides to accept the challenge, but needs help in developing a plan. What recommendations would you make to her?

Case 7-5
SECRETARIAL
ETHICS

Janet Ying is secretary to Carl Bachman, Vice-President of Sales for the Morris Company, a manufacturer of office supplies. Mr. Bachman is well known locally, regionally, and nationally because of his position as president of the National Association of Sales Managers and his long service to the organization at local and regional levels. His work with the association requires considerable travel. Janet has worked with Mr. Bachman for seven years. When he is out of town, he leaves her in charge of the office.

Recently, while Mr. Bachman was out of town on an extended trip, Janet received a call from a sales manager in Detroit indicating that Mr. Bachman had agreed to send him the customer mailing list of all the companies holding membership in the National Association of Sales Managers. The caller indicated that he had paid $500 for the list and that he needed it immediately. Janet recognized the Detroit firm as a leading competitor and was surprised to receive such a request, since her employer's customers would be on that mailing list. In Janet's opinion releasing such a list could be potentially damaging to the Morris Company.

If you were Janet's co-worker, what would you advise her to do?

PART EIGHT

REFERENCE GUIDE

The English language continually adapts to advances in technology, science, business, and all aspects of our complex society. The study of this multifaceted language is fascinating and challenging. No part of this text should be of more help to the secretary than this Reference Guide, particularly those sections devoted to English usage and punctuation.

Handbooks and dictionaries *report* usage at different levels; they are not definitive authorities, nor does this guide purport to be the final authority. It, too, *reports* current, acceptable business usage. When more than one usage is reported in this guide, it is because opinion is *divided*—dictionaries and handbooks do not agree. A secretary, therefore, cannot presume that one reference book stands alone as the supreme authority on usage. But once a selection of form has been made, that form should be used consistently.

Formal English is usually found in reports, important letters, papers for publication, and the like. Colloquial English is for the most part customary in business letters. (A designated *colloquial* term means that it occurs in English conversation at an educated level.)

Business correspondence often is direct and to the point; economy in the use of words saves time for the writer and the reader. Frequently, however, the purpose of a business letter is to obtain a favorable result or to create a friendly reaction. Purposes such as these can often best be served by using informal conversational English. Thus, colloquial English can be appropriate and at times even desirable in business writing.

Industry and science often provide new and colorful terms and expressions to the language. *Power your engine* and *all systems go* are two examples. Business people often coin needed words. *Flowchart, reprography, software* are three terms that have been accepted by industry and by the publishers of *Webster's New Collegiate Dictionary*. When confronted with a coined word or expression, the secretary must recognize it and know how to call attention to it in a letter or report.

The trend in punctuation is toward less punctuation at the informal level; however, complete and accurate punctuation is still required at the formal level. The purpose of punctuation is to help make the meaning of the written word clear to the reader. Using standard punctuation will attain this objective.

The purpose of this guide is to help you acquire expertise and confidence as you fulfill your secretarial responsibilities. It should provide a handy and easy-to-use reference when transferring your employer's thoughts from shorthand notebook or word processing equipment to final form or when you do any original writing.

CONTENTS

Punctuation

Effective writing expresses precisely the author's intended meaning. Punctuation helps the reader understand the meaning of a sentence through the use of a system of familiar symbols. While punctuation usage may vary in some instances, many fundamental rules are accepted and are generally adhered to in a precise yet simple manner.

THE APOSTROPHE

1. Use an apostrophe to designate the possessive of nouns and indefinite pronouns.

   a. To form the possessive of a singular or plural noun or an indefinite pronoun which does not end in a sibilant sound (*s*, *x*, *z*), add an apostrophe and an *s*.

dog's leash	William's coat
horse's bridle	children's coats
man's coat	Marivaux's plays (silent *x*)
men's coats	one's coat

   b. To form the possessive of a plural noun or an indefinite pronoun ending in a sibilant sound, add only an apostrophe.

dogs' leashes	three years' work
girls' coats	the Thomases' house
others' ills	ten dollars' worth

   c. To form the possessive of a singular noun ending in a sibilant sound, add an apostrophe and an *s*.

Burns's poems	the fox's tail
Jones's store	Liz's idea

   Exception: *If the singular noun has two or more syllables and if the last syllable is not accented and is preceded by a sibilant sound, add only the apostrophe for ease of pronunciation.*

Moses' law	Jesus' nativity
Ulysses' voyage	Demosthenes' oration
conscience' sake	

   d. To denote joint ownership, add the apostrophe or the apostrophe and *s* after the second noun only. Individual ownership is shown by making both elements possessive.

      John and Amy's store (one store, owned by John and Amy)
      John's and Amy's stores (two stores, one John's and one Amy's)
      Waterfords and Tuckers' annual picnic

   e.   To form the possessive of compound nouns and indefinite pronouns, add the apostrophe or apostrophe and *s* after the last element of the compound.

daughter-in-law's   daughters-in-law's
father-in-law's   fathers-in-law's
everyone else's

2.   Use an apostrophe to denote the omission of letters or figures.

It's too far to go.
They haven't been here today.
The class of '75 had its reunion this year.
Who's going?

3.   Use an apostrophe to designate plurals of figures, letters, signs, and words to which special allusion is made.

If there are no 6's left in this type, use 9's turned upside down.
Your *T*'s and *F*'s are too much alike, and so are your *u*'s and *v*'s.
Use +'s and −'s to denote whether the sentences are correct or not.
When *and*'s and *the*'s are used in titles, they should not be capitalized, unless they are the first word.

BRACKETS

The use of brackets is generally confined to writing of a technical or scholarly nature.

1.   Use brackets to enclose information—an editorial interpolation, correction, explanation, or comment—which the writer wishes to include in quoted material.

"These [the free silver Democrats] asserted that the artificial ratio could be maintained indefinitely."
"In 1630 [a typographical error for 1603] James came to the throne."
In applying for the job, he wrote, "I am very good in atheletics [*sic*], and I can teach mathmatics [*sic*]."

Note: *The term* sic, *Latin for* thus, *is inserted to show that a misspelling or other error appeared in the original and is not an error by the person quoting.*

2.   Use brackets when it is necessary to place parenthetical material

within parentheses; however, such complicated usage should be avoided.

> At 10:30 a.m. (the time agreed upon to have the meeting [see the correspondence of Ms. Blair and Mr. Williams]) only five of the ten committee members were present.

Note: *In the use of other punctuation marks with brackets, the same rules apply as for parentheses.*

THE COLON

The colon is a mark of introduction or anticipation. In general it denotes formality. The colon indicates a break in continuity that is greater than that requiring a semicolon and less than that requiring a period. It may be used to expand or emphasize a thought or to amplify in a second clause an idea contained in the first clause.

1. Use a colon to introduce a long or formal quotation.

    > Winston Churchill, in his opening statement as Prime Minister, declared to the House of Commons: "Victory at all costs, victory in spite of all terror, victory however long and hard the road may be; for without victory there is no survival."

    > John F. Kennedy, on conferring honorary citizenship on Sir Winston Churchill, said: "He mobilized the English language and sent it into battle."

2. Use a colon to introduce an example or a formal list; that is, a list preceded by a summarizing term.

    > A check payable to a married woman should include her given name, not her husband's: *Joan Ritson* rather than *Mrs. Harry Ritson.*

    > The following items are put on the check stub: the amount of the check, the date, the person or business to whom the check is payable, and the purpose of the check.

    Exception: *Do not use a colon to introduce a brief, informal list when the colon would immediately follow a verb or a preposition.*

    > The only major types of coverage which cannot be written on an SMP policy are automobile, workers' compensation, surety bonds, and life or health insurance.

3. Use a colon between independent clauses or independent sentences when the second clause amplifies the first or when the

second gives a concrete illustration of a general statement in the first. (Notice that the first word of an independent clause after a colon is capitalized.)

> In time, however, one of her favorite contentions was justified: In the long run people who are conscientious, set goals, and work diligently will achieve the position for which they are best qualified.

> George Washington, in a letter to the captains of the Virginia Regiment, said that discipline is the soul of an army: It makes small numbers formidable and procures success to the weak and esteem to all.

4. Use a colon after terms such as *the following* or *as follows* when these terms precede a list of enumerated items, a tabulation, a computation, etc.

> You will need the following:
> 1. Typewriter
> 2. Transcription equipment
> 3. Stationery

> Their actions were as follows: They went to the supermarket, purchased a number of items, returned to their car, and drove away.

> Each category of liability should be listed and the total amount of liabilities presented in the following manner:

> Notes payable $1,500
> Accounts payable 1,100
> Salaries payable   300
> Total liabilities $2,900

5. By common acceptance, a colon is used in the following instances:

    a. After the salutation in certain styles of formal or business letters

    > Ladies and Gentlemen: Dear Ms. McDaniel:
    > Dear Sir: Dear Professor Gordon:

    b. Between the hour and the minute when time is expressed in figures

    > 12:15 a.m.   2:30 p.m.

    c. Between chapter and verse in references to the Bible and between volume and page reference

    > *Genesis* 9:10   *Papers of James Madison* 1:16

THE COMMA

Since studies have indicated that three-fourths of all punctuation errors involve the use of the comma, knowledge and correct use of the comma are necessary in order to convey ideas in a concise and clear manner.

1. Use a comma to separate independent clauses that are linked by a coordinating conjunction (*and, but, for, or,* and *nor*).

    It was a beautiful June day, and the fragrance of the roses permeated the air.

    The man was not afraid, nor was he upset by the news.

    Exception: *When the clauses are short and closely related, no comma is required.*

    The chairperson called for order and everyone sat down.

2. Use a comma to separate each item when three or more elements form a series without linking words between the elements.

    They brought sandwiches, potato salad, baked beans, and soft drinks to the picnic.

    The new secretary is aggressive but not offensive, efficient but not officious, and friendly but not servile.

    The woman was either 21, 22, or 23 years old.

    Note: *Although the use of* etc. *is discouraged, this abbreviation should be set off by commas when used.*

    The store sold clothing, housewares, furniture, food, pharmaceuticals, linens, etc., at its Seventh Street location.

    Exception: *When the elements in a series are simple and are joined by conjunctions, omit the commas.*

    I cannot remember if that symphony was composed by Bach or Beethoven or Brahms.

3. Use a comma to separate coordinate adjectives which modify a noun. (Adjectives are coordinate if *and* can be used between them.)

    The gaudy, tasteless decorations detracted from the appearance of the room. (the gaudy *and* tasteless decorations)
    An old straw hat was lying in the street. (NOT an old *and* straw hat)
    The late Senator Humphrey was a prominent public official. (NOT a prominent *and* public official)

4. Use a comma to separate elements which might be misread if the comma were omitted.

> Abruptly the car stopped, throwing her forward.
> As I approached, Mary held out her hand.
> To John, Smith was an enigma.

5. Use commas to set off *nonrestrictive* clauses, phrases, and appositives (clauses, phrases, and appositives not essential to the meaning of a sentence).

> Dr. Mary Towne, the eminent surgeon, was the principal speaker.
> Effective listening, a major ingredient of empathetic communication, is a skill in which people differ greatly.

Restrictive clauses, phrases, and appositives are necessary to the meaning of a sentence and are not set off by commas.

> The place *to be blunt* is at the meeting.
> Those executives *planning to attend the conference* must register in advance.
> John Wayne *the actor* starred in many movies; John Wayne *the doctor* is my neighbor.

Note: *The conjunction* or *may appear with an appositive.*

> The instructions, or information for correct use, were printed on the warranty card.

Note: *In some cases, only the writer knows if a clause is restrictive or nonrestrictive.*

> My brother, who is on the team this year, is a senior. (The writer has only one brother.)
> My brother who is on the team this year is a senior. (The writer has more than one brother.)

6. Use commas to set off complementary or antithetical (contrasting or opposing) elements.

> The unjust, though at the same time necessary, restriction was placed on all members of the class.

     a. Commas should set off an antithetical clause or phrase introduced by *not* if the modified element is complete without it.

> The dignitaries hoped that the president herself, not the vice-president, would attend the ceremony.
> Betty went to the concert, not to hear the orchestra, but to observe the soloist.

b.   Commas should separate interdependent antithetical clauses.

> The more Maria read about Greece, the deeper became her resolve to visit that historic land.

Exception: *Short antithetical phrases should not be separated by commas.*

> The bigger the better.
> The more the merrier.

7.   Use a comma to separate an introductory adverbial clause or phrase from the rest of the sentence.

> Where the opportunities are available, first line supervisors should be encouraged to move into higher management.
> Because of the unusual circumstances, the president of the company addressed the assembled employees.

8.   Commas set off an adverbial phrase or clause located between a subject and a predicate.

> Olga, after receiving the award, left immediately for home.

Exception: *If a dependent adverbial clause follows a main clause and is restrictive, it should not be set off by a comma.*

> Annette was surprised *when she heard the news.*

Exception: *A comma is not used after a short introductory adverbial phrase if the clarity of the sentence does not suffer.*

> *On Wednesday* the group attended the meeting.

Exception: *A comma is not used following an introductory adverbial phrase that immediately precedes the verb it modifies.*

> *On the beach* stood a man, a woman, and a child.

9.   Use commas to set off introductory absolute, participial, infinitive, and gerund phrases.

> That being true, Paul had nothing more to say.
> After winning the election, the president addressed the students.
> In order to succeed, one must work hard.
> Driving as fast as traffic would allow, he arrived just in time.

10. An omitted word or omitted words are replaced by a comma.

> The Imbus Corporation has long had a reputation for integrity and social responsibility; Hall and Hall, for questionable methods. (The comma takes the place of the words *has long had a reputation.*)

11. Use commas with the following parenthetical elements:
   a. To separate items of address and geographical names

> Margaret stopped at 1673 Cedar Avenue, Cincinnati, Ohio, to see a friend. Princeton, New Jersey, is now her home.

   b. To separate dates

> Stephen Foster was born on July 4, 1826, in Pittsburgh.

   c. To separate items in a reference

> In *Hamlet,* II, ii, 255, you will find the reference under discussion.

   d. To set off words used in direct address

> Is it true, Ann, that you are going to Switzerland?

   e. To set off introductory expressions and those used to mark transitions

> To tell the truth, the employer was very generous.
> The restrictive clause, on the other hand, limits the main clause.

   f. To set off parenthetical words, phrases, and clauses

> The secretary, it was believed, turned the problem over to the sales department.

12. Use a comma to separate a short direct quotation from the statement that precedes or follows it. (A long or formal quotation is introduced by a colon.)

> He shouted as he ran toward the house, "No one on the peninsula has a boat."

Note: *Do not use a comma to set off a quotation that is an integral part of the sentence.*

> He said that his racing car would "do 200 m.p.h." and he was "going to let it out."

13. A comma may be used to separate two identical words or phrases, even though the grammatical construction does not require the separation.

> They marched in, in pairs.
> What is done, is done.

14.   Use a comma to separate unrelated adjacent numbers.

In 1987, 175 new books were published.

Note: *It is preferable to rewrite the sentence to avoid the foregoing construction.*

The company published 175 new books in 1987.

15.   Use commas with numerals in the following instances:
a.   With figures of 1,000 or more, between every group of three digits, counting from the right

1,456
11,420
117,560,000

Note: *The comma is frequently omitted in writing four-digit numbers not included in a set containing numbers of five or more digits. If a text contains a great quantity of numerical matter, it is advisable to choose a consistent use for that text.*

b.   With time divisions

November, 1989
New Year's Day, 1960

Exception: *Do not use commas with historical references, page numbers, dimensions, weights, measures, time, policy numbers, room numbers, telephone numbers, and most serial numbers.*

2200 B.C.   3 feet 6 inches
page 1463   4 pounds 2 ounces
806423518   2 hours 4 minutes

16.   Use a comma after *that is, i.e.,* and *namely.* The punctuation mark preceding such expressions is determined by the importance or length of the interruption. If the interruption is minor, use a comma. If the interruption is important or lengthy, use a semicolon. Always use a semicolon if the expression is followed by an independent clause.

He came up through the ranks, that is, through hard work.
The editor persuaded the author to change the direction of his manuscript; i.e., she convinced him that his book should appeal to management's interest in current ideas and practices rather than in historical methods of operating business firms.
She submitted the problem to three of her friends, namely, Carlos, Evelyn, and Rosemary.

He said that he was going to give consideration to the three options the company presented to him; namely, to transfer to Duluth, to accept the production management position at the home office in Chicago, or to expand the branch office in Louisville.

THE DASH

The dash should not be confused with the hyphen. For purposes of typewriting manuscript, the dash consists of two hyphens (--) placed together with no space preceding or following them.

1.   Use a dash when a sentence is interrupted abruptly and an entirely different sentence or thought is added.

The game will be—by the way, are you going to the game?
Robert's lawyer—she had spent most of the night working on the case—looked tired and pale when she entered the courtroom.

2.   Use a dash to indicate the omission of words or letters.

Little acorns—great oaks, you know.
Mary J—, of C—Street, was the witness.

3.   Use a dash before a word or statement which summarizes a preceding series or which is an emphatic repetition of the preceding statement.

Verdi, Puccini, Rossini—these were the most popular operatic composers at that time.
The editor stated that the author's work was original and scholarly—original and scholarly in the sense that it presented new information that had been well researched.

4.   Use a dash to set off appositives that have internal punctuation or that are used for emphasis.

All friends of the fine arts—civic leaders, professional and business people, concerned citizens—cooperate to make the annual Fine Arts Fund drive a success.

5.   When strong emphasis is desired, the dash may be used in place of the comma, the colon, the semicolon, or parentheses.

Consultants rely heavily upon their authority of competence—the right of a person to influence others by virtue of recognized ability and expertise. (replaces a comma)

The most realistic view of supervisors is that to varying degrees they are a special class of managers—they are strategically placed management representatives. (replaces a semicolon)

THE ELLIPSIS MARK

The ellipsis mark—three periods with a space before, after, and between each period (. . .)—is used to show the omission of a passage that is being quoted. If the omitted passage comes at the end of the sentence a period is added, making four periods.

In Illus. 13-3, if the calculations have been made correctly, the materials and parts needed . . . will be ready at the same time. Adequate time for delivery and production will be allowed, and in most cases . . . spare time must be allowed so that there will be no costly delay in assembling the final product simply because one part was not ordered early enough . . . . The problems outlined here are particularly true of certain types of products made on special orders for special purposes.

THE EXCLAMATION POINT

The exclamation point has two basic uses: after an exclamatory sentence and after words that express strong emotion or feeling. Exclamation points should be used sparingly; they should not be used in parentheses to express humor or irony.

Then the captain shouted, "Cast off!"
Look out! You'll fall!

THE HYPHEN

The hyphen has two chief uses: to mark the division of a word that appears at the end of a line and to designate certain compound words. As to the first use, words should be divided between syllables according to *Webster's New Collegiate Dictionary*. Never divide words of one syllable.

In typewriting manuscript, in order to avoid confusion for the typesetter, do not hyphenate words at the end of a line; let long words run into the right margin.

In forming compound words, it is always wise to consult *Webster's New Collegiate Dictionary*, since there are wide variations in styling compounds and numerous exceptions to the rules. For example, *vice-chancellor* is hyphenated, but *vice admiral* is two words; *vice-chancellorship* is hyphenated, but *viceroyalty* is one word. A few general rules apply to the use of hyphens in forming compounds.

1. Use a hyphen between a prefix and a root word under these circumstances:

    a. When the combination is a prefix and a proper name

        un-American
        pro-Canadian

    b. When the combination of the prefix and root word constitutes a homonym[1]

        recover, re-cover
        recreation, re-creation
        reform, re-form

    c. When the combination is a prefix ending in a vowel and a root word beginning with a vowel, if the omission of the hyphen will cause misreading

        re-ink
        co-op

    Note: *The prefixes* ex-, self-, half-, *and* all- *are often used with a hyphen.*

        ex-manager
        self-control
        half-baked
        all-around

    d. When figures, letters, or numbers are compounded with words to form a single idea

        two-year period
        25-foot stick
        T-shaped rod
        U-turn

2. Use a hyphen between two or more words that precede a noun and act as a compound adjective.

        long-established custom
        coarse-grained wood

---

[1]One of two or more words that are pronounced alike but are different in meaning: *right, write; piece, peace; sail, sale; stationary, stationery.*

well-known speaker
up-to-date method
up-to-the-minute technology

Exception: *This usage does not apply when one of the words is an adverb ending in* ly, *when the words form a comparative or superlative compound adjective, or when the words follow the noun.*

highly paid executive
better known speaker

3. Some phrases used as adjectives are hyphenated in any position.

The equipment is up-to-date.
Up-to-date equipment has been installed.

4. Use a hyphen between the spelled-out **numbers twenty-one through ninety-nine.**

5. Use a hyphen in compounds formed from **a noun or a verb and a** preposition.

set-to
head-on
house-to-house
give-and-take

6. Use a hyphen in writing fractions which **are single adjectives** before a noun.

a one-fourth share
a two-thirds majority vote

Exception: *Do not use a hyphen when the fraction consists of an adjective plus a noun or when the numerator or denominator already contains a hyphen.*

three fourths of the population
two thirds of a mile
twenty-one hundredths (21/100)
twenty one-hundredths (20/100)

7. Use a hyphen after each word or number in a **series that modifies** the same noun (suspended hyphenation). **Notice the use of the** space following the hyphen.

six- or eight-cylinder engine
first-, second-, or third-class mail

8.   Use a hyphen in compounding capitalized words.

the New York-Chicago flight

9.   Use a hyphen to indicate continuing or inclusive numbers—dates, times, or reference numbers.

1981-1985
May-June, 1982
10:00 a.m.-5:00 p.m.
See pages 451-455.

PARENTHESES

1.   Use parentheses to enclose nonessential information which interrupts the flow of a sentence or is incidental to the topic of a paragraph. Parentheses usually de-emphasize information rather than emphasize it, as is the case with dashes.

At 10:30 a.m. (the time agreed upon to have the meeting) only five of the ten committee members were present.
By using a captive insurer, the parent may be able to deduct such premiums paid to a captive and thus handle the loss reserve need with funds that are tax deductible. (The Internal Revenue Service has ruled that certain conditions must be met before premiums paid to a captive are tax deductible.)

2.   Use parentheses to enclose letters or numbers in an enumeration that is not shown in list format.

The professor issued these instructions: (1) smoking is allowed only in designated areas, (2) punctuality in attending classes is expected of all students, and (3) completed assignments are to be submitted on time.

3.   Use parentheses to enclose signs, numbers, and words when accuracy is essential.

Make out the check for the exact amount ($45.50).
The cash drawer was over by $200 (two hundred dollars).
An asterisk (*) was placed at the end of the sentence to indicate the footnote.

4.   Parentheses are frequently used in text to enclose references to other parts of the text.

The current worth of this loss is $79,995 (see Table 31-1).
See Chapter 10 (pages 64-75) for complete coverage.

Note: Before *a parenthesis within a sentence, no punctuation mark is used.* After *parentheses within a sentence, no punctuation mark is used unless it would be required if the parenthetical material were removed; then whatever mark required follows the closing parenthesis.*

Within *parentheses inside a sentence, the punctuation is the same as if the material were a separate sentence. However, when it is a complete sentence, no capital is used at the beginning and no period at the end—although a question mark or exclamation point is used if one is required.*

Parentheses may enclose a separate sentence, in which case the ordinary rules for using the capital and period apply.

THE PERIOD

A period is used to mark the end of a declarative or imperative sentence, a legitimate fragmentary sentence, or a run-in heading. It is also used to mark an abbreviation.

1. When a period is used after an abbreviation, it is followed (except at the end of a sentence) by whatever punctuation mark would normally be used there.

    Breakfast is served at 8 a.m., lunch at 12:30 p.m., and dinner at 6:30 p.m.

2. Examples of legitimate fragmentary sentences include the following:
    a. A transition sentence

        Now for the second cause.

    b. Questions and answers

        Who says this? The man who only four years ago said exactly the opposite.

    c. Sentences reporting direct discourse where there is no chance of mistaking the speaker.

        "Ramona was at the meeting."
        "No!"
        "With her partner."
        "Not Pedro?"
        "No one else."
        "What a surprise!"

3.   A period may be used after a rhetorical question.

Will the audience please rise.
May I take this opportunity to express my thanks.

4.   A run-in heading is one which is followed on the same line by text material. A period or other appropriate end-of-sentence punctuation ends the run-in heading.

The Authority of Organized Labor. The National Labor Relations Act of 1935 for the first time clearly legitimized at the national level the authority of organized labor. . . .

Note: *The design of a publication may call for the period to be omitted in typeset copy, but the author should always include the period in typewritten manuscript.*

5.   Use a period in enumerated lists if the individual items are complete sentences. If the items are single words, short phrases, or incomplete sentences, use no period.

The main arguments for decentralized filing are:
1.   The confidential nature of the material suggests that it be kept from the majority of employees.
2.   Unnecessary delay in getting papers from the centralized department is avoided.
3.   The papers filed will not be required by any other department.

The office manager should have available information about each of the following:
1.   Principal types of furniture and equipment and reputable suppliers for each
2.   Reliable statistics for comparing the effectiveness of competing brands of equipment and furniture
3.   Suppliers' catalogs and current prices
4.   Possibilities for standardizing equipment throughout the firm

THE QUESTION MARK

1.   Use a question mark after a direct question.

What are you doing?
Where are you going?
When will you return?

Note: *Do not use a question mark after an indirect question.*
She asked what you are doing.
He asked where you are going.

Note: *Placing a question mark at the end of a declarative or imperative sentence transposes the sentence into an interrogative remark.*
This is where you are going to stay?

2. In a series of questions within an interrogative sentence, a question mark may follow each question. When used in this way, the question mark substitutes for a comma; the second and subsequent elements are preceded by one space and begin with a lower-case letter.

> Where is my shorthand book? my pencil? my paper?
> Can you find your hat? your coat? your scarf?

3. Use a question mark in parentheses (?) to express doubt or uncertainty.

> Nathaniel Bacon, the Virginia patriot, was born in 1642(?).

Note: *Do not use a question mark to make a joke or to be ironical, since such usage questions the reader's intelligence.*

> Jack, you know, is the most studious(?) member of the family.

QUOTATION MARKS

The main function of quotation marks is to enclose matter quoted from any source, either spoken or written. Other functions are to enclose words used in a special manner and to enclose certain titles.

1. Use quotation marks to enclose direct quotations.

> The manufacturing superintendent, in a heated discussion with the director of personnel, said, "I've had it with your job enrichment propaganda. It has taken me years to set up an assembly line that works smoothly and efficiently. Productivity is high, quality is on standard, and nobody is complaining. So why rock the boat?"

2. Use quotation marks to enclose the title of (a) a chapter in a book; (b) an individual poem, essay, or story in a volume; and (c) any item from a book or magazine. (Titles of books and magazines are italicized.)

> The poems "Emerson" and "Lands End" appear in the volume *More People* by Edgar Lee Masters.
> For information about how the actions of the Federal Reserve Board affect you personally, read "ABC's of How Federal Reserve Works" in *U.S. News & World Report*, January 9, 1978.

3. Use quotation marks to enclose words used in a special manner or words coined for special, limited use. Discretion should be practiced in using quotation marks in these instances. Only if readers

are unfamiliar with the term should quotation marks be used to suggest that its status in the language is tentative.

The Federal Reserve Board controls the amount of reserves by use of a tool known as the "open market operation."
The speaker described his opponent's principal problem as the "ineptitude of innocence."

Note: *Quotation marks should be used sparingly for coined words, words used in a special manner, colloquialisms, irony, and slang, and then only if the word is foreign to the reader.*

4.   The following general rules should be observed relative to the use of quotation marks:

a.   When several different speakers are quoted, each person's remarks are enclosed in quotation marks.

When Mark returned from the football game, everyone shouted questions at once: "Who won?" "What was the score?" "What did Jim do?" "Was there much passing?"

b.   When quoting a fragment of a sentence, do not begin the quotation with a capital letter unless the quoted passage began with a capital.

Senator Margaret Hall said that "the machinations of a corrupt political machine would have to stop."

c.   Quotations within quotations use single quotation marks. Quotations within single quotations use double quotation marks.

In a letter the new student wrote: "I have been following the advice of my instructor who said, 'When I decide to write something, I first read Pope's "An Essay on Criticism" to inspire me to do my best'; but I find that it doesn't help me at all."

Exception: *Do not use quotation marks for proverbs, phrases, or figures of speech that are known to everyone.*

He was honest, not because he believed that honesty was the best policy, but because honesty was inherent in his character.
Absence makes the heart grow fonder, but out of sight out of mind was her usual experience.
Silence is golden when one has much studying to do.

Exception: *Do not use quotation marks to label your own humor or irony.*

Exception: *Do not use quotation marks for statements which are not quoted from someone else but are quotations in form only.*

She thought, Shall I wear gloves to go on my interview?
He said to himself, I think I'm going to make manager this year.

Exception: *Do not use quotation marks with the term* so-called. *The term* so-called *is sufficient to mark off the usage as a special one.*

The so-called easy way sometimes turns out to be the most difficult and longest way to get results.

Exception: *Do not quote the words* yes *and* no *except in direct discourse.*

Many persons have difficulty saying no, so they frequently answer yes against their better judgment.

Exception: *Do not use quotation marks where the name of a speaker introduces the speech.*

JEAN GROBE: It appears to me that we should give this experiment a chance before discarding the whole idea.

MARK WHITE: A good suggestion, except that we have spent entirely too much time and money already on trying to solve this problem.

Exception: *Do not use quotation marks to enclose material that is set off as a block quotation. Block quotations of one long paragraph or several short paragraphs are usually set in smaller type than the text and are indented—usually on both right and left sides. Any quoted matter within a block quotation should be enclosed in double quotation marks, even if the source quoted uses single quotation marks.*

Exception: *Do not use quotation marks to enclose an indirect quotation.*

Cynthia said that she was leaving because she wanted to arrive home before dark.

Other Punctuation with Quotation Marks

The rules for punctuating sentences containing direct quotations are illustrated below:

1.   Introductory expression preceding the quotation

She called, "Where are you going?"

2.   Explanatory expression interrupting the quotation

"It is not," she interrupted, "my habit to change my mind so quickly."
"This is my idea," Bob declared; "therefore, I won't have you stealing it."

3. Explanatory expression after the quotation

"What are you going to do about it?" she inquired.

Note: *Commas and periods precede closing quotation marks, including single quotation marks. Semicolons and colons follow closing quotation marks. The position of question marks or exclamation points depends on the content of the sentence: place them before inside closing quotation marks if they apply only to the quotation; or place them after closing quotation marks if they apply to the entire sentence.*

"Are you coming to the dance?" he asked.
Have you ever heard her say, "I don't play bridge"?
"What a wonderful day!" he exclaimed.
How generous of her to say, "You may take my new car"!
The professor was not shocked when the young instructor said, "I was dismayed at having one of my students define *salutary* as 'one who salutes.' "

Recording Telephone Conversations

Word-for-word personal or business telephone conversations are typed in any quickly typed, easily read style. All speakers must be fully identified.

Telephone call, 6/10/82, 2:50 p.m., Mr. Alan King to Mr. Willis Burt.

K   Hello, Willis, how are you?
B   Fine, Alan. What can I do for you?

Note: *It is not necessary to use quotation marks when typing a word-for-word telephone conversation since the identification of the speaker precedes each comment.*

THE SEMICOLON

If a comma indicates the smallest interruption in continuity of thought, the semicolon then stands midway between the functions of the comma and the period. The semicolon substitutes at times for the comma and at times for the period. But when it replaces either, there must be a logical basis for the substitution.

1. Use a semicolon to separate independent clauses of a compound sentence that have a close, logical relationship when they are not connected by a coordinate conjunction.

The plane was overdue; it arrived three hours behind schedule.
She did not let her emotions sway her; she considered the various alternatives objectively.

2. Use a semicolon between independent clauses when a conjunctive adverb joins the clauses. The semicolon precedes the conjunctive adverb. The most common conjunctive adverbs are *therefore, nevertheless, however, moreover, consequently, so, also, thus, hence, then, still, accordingly, besides, furthermore, likewise,* and *otherwise.* These connecting words are generally followed by a comma.

> The farmer used a new method of cultivation; therefore, the yield was larger.
> The roads were impassable; consequently, the schools were closed.

3. A semicolon precedes a coordinate conjunction (*and, but, for, or,* and *nor*) between two independent clauses when either or both contain internal punctuation.

> On their trip they went to Rome, which they found awesome; and then they went to Florence, Venice, and Assisi, which they considered the pearls of the Italian peninsula.
> The office manager ordered pencils, shorthand notebooks, dictating tapes, and typewriter ribbons for the staff; but the order was lost in the mail.

4. A semicolon separates items in a series which are long and complex or which involve internal punctuation. (A comma is used between items in a series if a word or words are omitted.)

> The defendant, in justification of his act, pleaded that (1) he was despondent over the death of his wife; (2) he was without employment, a place to live, and warm clothing; (3) he was rejected by his only son, who had moved to Alabama; and (4) he was under the influence of potent medication that had impaired his judgment.
> When the vote was tabulated, Alvarez won first place; O'Connor, second place; and Schmidt, third place.
> The speaker holds that democracy, although slow moving and inefficient, is the best form of government; that the freedom we possess, although bought with war and death, is worth the cost; and that our form of government is worth living for, fighting for, and if need be dying for.

5. A semicolon is used before such expressions as *for example (e.g.), for instance, that is (i.e.),* and *namely (viz.),* depending upon the importance and length of the interruption.

> Some pairs of words are bothersome to students; for example, *affect* and *effect, loose* and *lose, sit* and *set.*
> Every puncuation rule suggests three acts on your part; namely, learn it, use it, and check your writing to see if you have used it correctly.
> The professor spoke with authority; i.e., she set down the rules and stated that she expected them to be observed.

6. A semicolon follows a closing quotation mark if it would be used normally at the place the interruption comes.

    The president shouted, "The motion is carried!"; nevertheless, pandemonium erupted in the crowded hall.

Accepted Usage in Writing

Rules concerning capitalization, italics, abbreviations, and numbers have evolved from writing practices found to be economical and effective, rather than from fundamental laws of language. Although all rules covering writing mechanics do not have the same degree of acceptance, those presented here are basically accepted and should be followed.

CAPITALIZATION

The tendency today is to capitalize as little as possible; hence a good practice is not to capitalize unless a rule exists for its use.

1. Capitalize the first word of a sentence.

2. Capitalize the first word of a direct quotation.

3. Capitalize all proper nouns and adjectives.
    a. Names and initials of individuals (When a name includes particles such as *de, du, la, l', della, von, van, van der,* and *ten,* observe carefully the way the name is written and extend the courtesy of spelling the individual's name accurately.)

        Mary Van Reck
        John von Bruckner
        Charles de Gaulle
        Lee De Forest

b.   Epithets, nicknames, and titles used as part of the name

> Honest Abe
> Blondy Gordon
> Stonewall Jackson
> Catherine the Great

c.   All words referring to the deity, the Bible, the books of the Bible, and other sacred books

> the Trinity
> Talmud
> the Supreme Being
> the Koran

d.   Names of months, days of the week, holidays, holy days, and periods of history

> October   Epiphany
> Tuesday   Yom Kippur
> Fourth of July   the Ice Age

e.   Names of organizations, political parties, and religious bodies

> Boy Scouts
> the Democrats
> the Republican party
> the Methodist Church

f.   Names of geographic sections and places: continents, countries, states, cities, rivers, mountains, lakes, and islands

> Africa   Rocky Mountains
> Carson City   Missouri River
> Portage Lake   Long Island
> Lakes Michigan and Huron the South

Exceptions: *Directions are not capitalized, nor are generic terms preceding a proper noun.*

> He drove south on I-75.
> city of Dallas

g.   Names of divisions of a college or university

> Department of Chemistry
> the College of Medicine
> the School of Business Administration

h.   Names of specific historical events, specific laws, treaties, and departments of government

> World War II   Treaty of Versailles
> the Bill of Rights   Department of Justice

i.   Titles that precede the names of individuals and abbreviations after a name

General MacArthur
Professor Robinson, A.B., A.M., Ph.D.
the Reverend William Hammerstein
Father O'Toole
J.A. Hempstead, D.D.S.

j.   Names of streets, avenues, buildings, churches, hotels, parks, and theaters

the DuBois Tower
First Avenue
St. Thomas Church
the Astor Hotel

k.   Derivatives of proper nouns which are used as adjectives

Elizabethan play
Mexican music

l.   Personifications

Spring's warm touch

4.   Capitalize the first word and all other words—except articles, conjunctions, and prepositions—in titles of books, magazines, newspaper articles, stories, poems, musical compositions, theatrical productions, and chapters or subdivisions of books and periodicals.

Book Review Section of the *New York Times* (newspaper)
The Enjoyment of Drama (book)

5.   Capitalize the words *Where as* and *Resolved* in formal resolutions, and the first word following either of these.

6.   Capitalize words before figures (except *page, line,* and *note*).

Chapter 12
Figure 14
Check 213
Invoice 92A

7.   Capitalize registered trademarks and trade names.

Coca-Cola
Orlon
Laundromat

8.   When two independent clauses are separated by a colon and the second amplifies an idea presented in the first, capitalize the first word of the second independent clause.

> Thomas Carlyle has said that he who first shortened the labor of copyists by devising movable type was disbanding hired armies, and cashiering most kings and senates, and creating a whole new democratic world: He had invented the art of printing.

Exception: *Do not capitalize for emphasis.*

Exception: *Do not capitalize the names of the seasons of the year unless personified.*

Exception: *Do not capitalize prefixes to proper names.*

> pre-Revolutionary colony
> non-European country

Exception: *Do not capitalize the names of college classes (freshman, sophomore, etc.) unless the class is referred to as a specific organization.*

Exception: *Do not capitalize words which were once proper nouns but which through common usage have become common nouns.*

> macadam
> boycott
> venetian blind
> turkish towel
> panama hat
> manila envelope

ITALICS

Discretion should be exercised in the use of italics for emphasis. The trend among good writers is to attain emphasis through sentence structure rather than through the use of italics.

In typewriting manuscript, indicate material that should be typeset in italics by underlining once.

1.   Italicize to designate a key term in a discussion, a term with a special meaning, a technical term, or a term that is accompanied by a definition.

> In expectancy theory, *valence* refers to the value a person places on a particular *outcome* (consequence of an action).

2. Italicize titles of books, pamphlets, newspapers, magazines, plays, lengthy poems, musical compositions, motion pictures, paintings, drawings, and statues.

Note: *Parts of complete works, such as chapters of a book or articles in a magazine, are placed in quotation marks.*

The information is found in "The Management of Conflict and Stress" on page 346 of *Human Behavior in Organizations.*

3. Italicize letters used as letters and words used as words.

Always dot your *i*'s and cross your *t*'s.
The word *thane* refers to one of superior rank.
Do not write *and* and *the* slantwise across the line.

4. Italicize foreign words or phrases that have not yet been adapted to everyday English usage.

Most businesses realize that a permanent clientele cannot be built upon the principle of *caveat emptor.*
If demand rises *ceteris paribus*, it is hypothesized that price will rise.

Exception: *Many abbreviaitons that in the past were italicized are now used so frequently that it is customary to use roman type in printing and to omit the underline in typing.*

c.	e.g.	i.e.	q.v.
et al.	ibid.	loc. cit.	viz.
etc.	idem	op. cit.	passim

Exception: *However, because of its unique use with quoted matter,* sic *is still italicized and enclosed in brackets.*

5. Italicize the names of ships, trains, aircraft, and spacecraft.

S.S. *Stella Solaris* (S.S. is not italicized.)
Lindbergh's *Spirit of St. Louis*
Gemini VI

6. Italicize the names of legal cases (plaintiff and defendant) but not *v.* (versus) when cited in text. Do not italicize the names of legal cases in footnote citations.

Labor leaders were disappointed when in 1921 the Supreme Court held in *Duplex Printing Press Company* v. *Deering* that the Sherman Act applied to unions under certain conditions.

---

[1]Ertel v. Radio Corporation of America (IndApp) 297 NE2d 446.

7.   Italicize the word *Resolved* in formal resolutions.

8.   Italicize the words *See* and *See also* in index cross-references.

9.   Italicize such phrases as *Continued on page 321, Continued from page 321,* and *To be continued.*

ABBREVIATIONS

Although abbreviations are used infrequently in formal and general writing, advancing technology has resulted in an increased use of abbreviations and symbols in scientific and technical writing. This section treats only the general use of abbreviations.

1.   Personal titles *Mr., Mrs., Ms., Messrs., Dr.,* and *St.* (Saint) are abbreviated with proper names, whether initials or first names are included.

Mr. Brainard	Messrs. Whitney and Fleming
Mrs. Alice Meyer	Dr. A. E. Kraus
Ms. Jones	St. Francis of Assisi

2.   Other personal titles such as *Rev., Hon., Prof., Gen., Col., Capt.,* and *Lieut.* are abbreviated when they precede the full name—surname and given name. When only the surname is used, these titles should be spelled out.

Prof. John McDaniels, A.B., Ph.D.
Professor McDaniels
General MacArthur

Note: *The titles* Reverend *and* Honorable *are spelled out if preceded by* the.

the Reverend Martha Graham
Rev. Martha Graham
Hon. Charles H. Percy

3.   Abbreviate titles and academic degrees used after a person's name.

Abner Thorp, Jr.
Ralph A. Phillips, Sr.

Francis Mixter III, LL.D.
Rev. Josephus Martin II

Notice that Jr. *and* Sr. *are preceded by a comma,* II *and* III *are not.* (Personal preference as to the use of the comma between the name and the abbreviation should be respected.)

4.   The abbreviations B.C., A.D., *a.m., p.m., No.* (for *number*), and the dollar sign ($) may be used with numerals.

> 559 B.C. (before Christ) (B.C. follows the year cited.)
> A.D. 33 (in the year of the Lord) (A.D. precedes the year cited.)

5.   The abbreviations *Bro., Bros., Co., Corp., Inc., Ltd.,* and & are sometimes used as part of a company name; however, it is recommended that the official spelling of a company name be determined and that usage followed.

6.   Names of government agencies, network broadcasting companies, associations, fraternal and service organizations, unions, and other groups are often abbreviated. The first time the name of the organization is used in a manuscript or text it is spelled out with the abbreviation in parentheses—Federal Bureau of Investigation (FBI). Subsequently, use the abbreviation in all capitals with no periods and no space between the letters.

FTC	UNESCO	NATO
WAKW	AFL-CIO	USMC
FOE	NBC	YWCA

Note: *Avoid abbreviating the following categories of words within text, except in tabulations or enumerations:*

1.   *Names of territories and possessions of the United States, countries, states, and cities*
2.   *Names of months*
3.   *Days of the week*
4.   *Given names, such as* Chas. *for Charles,* Jas. *for* James
5.   *Words such as* avenue, boulevard, court, street, drive, lane, parkway, place, road, square, terrace, building
6.   *Parts of geographic names, such as* Ft. (Fort), Pt. (Port), Mt. (Mountain)
7.   *Parts of company names, such as* Bro., Bros., Co., *and* Corp., *unless they are abbreviated in the official company name.*

8.   *Compass directions when they are part of an address—* North, South, East, West *(Exceptions are* NW, NE, SE, *and* SW *after a street name.)*

NUMBERS

Since there is no simple, uniform style for the use of numbers, the decision to use a figure rather than a word can sometimes be perplexing. This section presents general guidelines covering current usage and should answer most puzzling questions that may arise.

Exact Numbers

1.   Generally numbers from one through ten are spelled out unless the sentence contains a series of numbers that are over ten.

> Since only eight people gathered for the meeting, it was canceled.
> The employees of that department include a manager, two supervisors, and seven clerks.
> The team won 17 games in 1979, 14 games in 1980, 10 games in 1981, and only 8 games in 1982.

Exception: *If the numbers contained in a sentence or paragraph are in different categories, use consistency in treating them in context.*

> In the past ten years, the company acquired three subsidiaries employing 212 people—one, 103; another, 99; and a third, 10—of whom 150 have at least eight years of service.

2.   Spell out any number that begins a sentence; however, in most instances restructuring the sentence to avoid starting with a number is preferred.

Round Numbers

Spell out round numbers that can be expressed in one or two words. Round numbers over one million may be expressed as a combination of words and numerals.

about two thousand employees
a population of three million
3.2 billion items of merchandise
$170 million

Note: *A round number such as 1,500 is expressed in hundreds rather than in thousands.*

fifteen hundred members (not one thousand five hundred members)

Adjacent Numbers

1.   When one of two adjacent numbers is part of a compound adjective, spell out the smaller number.

> 25 twenty-two cent stamps
> ten 22-cent stamps
> twelve 25-inch pipes

2.   Separate unrelated adjacent numbers by a comma.

> In 1979, 2,560,479 fans attended the baseball games in the new stadium.

Ordinal Numbers

Spell out isolated ordinal numbers of less than one hundred. Ordinals of one hundred or more should be written in figures. (See Fig. 1 on page 834.)

The company is marking the twenty-fifth anniversary of its founding.
For the 120th time, an employee is retiring under the company's pension plan.
The 200th customer will receive a prize.

Addresses

1.   Express federal, state, and interstate highways in figures.

> U.S. Route 41 (U.S. 41)
> Ohio 50
> Interstate 64 (I-64)

2.   Spell out numbered street names from one through ten. When figures are used for numbered street names, a hyphen with a space on both sides should separate the house number from the numbered street name. Use *d, st,* or *th* where necessary with a numbered street name.

> 345 Fifth Street
> 345 West Fifth Street
> 345 - 21st Street
> 345 West 21st Street

3.   Express house numbers in figures, except *One*, which is spelled out.

One Fourth Avenue

Dates

1.   Use figures to designate the day and year after a month.

November 22, 1983

2.   Use a figure to express the day of the month plus *d*, *st*, or *th* when it stands alone or precedes the month. It is also acceptable, although more formal, to spell out the day of the month.

On the 22d of July we will fly to Athens.
Her letter dated the 14th did not arrive until last Monday.
The events of the twenty-second of November, 1963, are still a source of controversy.

3.   Spell out, in lowercase letters, references to particular centuries and decades.

twentieth century
during the sixties and seventies

BUT the 1980s (Plurals of figures are formed by adding an *s* alone, unless used in a special context. See page 768.)

Money

1.   Except in legal documents, sums of money (whether in dollars or foreign denominations) should be typed in figures. Whole dollar amounts are set with ciphers after the deciminal point when they appear in the same context with fractional amounts. Even sums of money do not require the decimal point and ciphers.

The book was $20.50, but the store offered a discount of $2.00.
The discount of $2 was a temptation the customer could not resist.

2.   In legal documents use capitalized words to express sums of money followed by figures in parentheses.

I agree to pay the sum of Seven Hundred Fifty-Five Dollars ($755).
I agree to pay the sum of Seven Hundred Fifty-Five (755) Dollars.

3.   Amounts of money less than one dollar are typed or set in figures with the word *cents* spelled out.

The bottle of lotion was on sale for 89 cents.

4.   A sum of money used as an adjective should be spelled out and hyphenated.

She bought a ten-dollar purse.

Time

1.   To designate time, use a number with *a.m.* or *p.m.* When using *o'clock*, spell out the number.

8:00 p.m.
10:45 in the morning (Do not use *a.m.* or *p.m.* with *morning* or *evening.*)
nine o'clock
12:00 M (noon)
12:00 p.m. (midnight)

2.   The time of day may be spelled out in textual matter.

The Senator left the office at five.
The Senate hearing was expected to last until half-past six.

Fractions, Decimals, and Percentages

1.   Spell out isolated simple fractions in words. Write mixed fractions and decimals in figures. When a decimal fraction is not preceded by a whole number, a cipher is often used before the decimal point.

The bakery held one-half dozen doughnuts for us.
She was only 7 1/2 years old when she made her debut with the Dallas Symphony Orchestra.
Almost all the students arrived at 0.611 as the answer.

2.   A percentage is written as a number with the word *percent* spelled out, except in statistical copy where the symbol % is used.

Only 3 percent of the loans were paid off.

Quantities, Measures, Weights, and Dimensions

1. In mathematical, statistical, technical, or scientific text, express physical quantities such as distances, lengths, areas, volumes, pressures, and so on in figures.

    55 miles
    3 cubic feet
    250 volts
    6 meters

2. Designate measures, weights, and dimensions in figures without commas.

    6 ft. 4 in.
    7 lbs. 4 oz.
    The editor specified 8½-by 11-inch paper. (In technical matter, *x* is used instead of *by* to express dimensions.)

Governmental Designations

The name of a governing body, political division, military unit, and the like is designated by a spelled-out ordinal number preceding the noun. Ordinals that require more than two words (ordinals over 100) are expressed in numbers.

Ninetieth Congress
Court of Appeals for the Tenth Circuit
Fifth Ward
Second Naval District
Fifth Army
Third Battalion, 122d Artillery

Glossary of English Usage

This glossary is intended as a guide to acceptable usage. It is also a reference to which the reader may turn when a question of diction arises. For the most part this glossary provides information that is not found in standard dictionaries but which is sometimes needed by those involved in spoken and written communication.

A or an before h. Use *a* if the *h* is sounded; *an* if the word begins with a vowel sound: a historic novel, a humorous story, a hotel, a hysterical person; an hour drive, an heir, an herb, an honest opinion.

Ability. Use *to* with ability plus a verb: *ability to* influence not *ability of* influencing.

Above. Avoid using *above* as an adjective to mean foregoing or preceding (except in legal writing).

Access, excess. *Access* means *permission, liberty*, or *the ability to enter, approach, communicate with, or pass to and from. Excess* means *more than enough.*

Accept, except. *Accept* is always a verb meaning *to receive; except* is a verb meaning *to exclude,* but is usually a preposition meaning *with the exception of.*

Acquiesce in (not to). He acquiesced in the matter of the bonus.

Adapt, adopt, adept. *To adapt* means *to change* or *make suitable. To adopt* means *to accept* or *put into practice. To be adept* means *to be expert.* They adapted to the harsh change in weather. They adopted the proposal. He is adept at training beginners. (*Adept* may be used with *at* or *in.*)

Adhere, adherent. *Adhere* (hold fast) *to: adhere to* our policy; An adherent *of:* an *adherent of* that policy.

Advice, advise. *Advice* is a noun meaning a *recommendation; advise* is a verb meaning *to counsel.* I can advise you, but will you follow my advice?

Adverse, averse. *Adverse* means *antagonistic, hostile; averse* means *having a dislike* or *distaste for.* Use *to* with both words. She was adverse to racism. Joseph is averse to manual labor.

Affect, effect. *Affect* is a verb meaning *to influence. Effect* is a noun meaning *result* or *consequence. Effect* is also a verb meaning *to accomplish or produce.* The weather affected our sales. The weather had an adverse effect on our sales. The delegates effected a compromise.

Aggravate, irritate. *To aggravate* means *to make worse; to irritate* means *to annoy.* The thunder irritated me, but it aggravated my headache.

All, any, none, some, more, most. These words may be either singular or plural, depending on intended meaning. None of the money has been collected. None of the bills have been paid.

All of. Use *all; of* is redundant. If a pronoun follows *all,* reword the sentence. Check all the reports. They are all going, not all of them are going.

All right. This is the only correct usage. *Alright* is incorrect.

All together, altogether. *All together* means *in a group; altogether* is an adverb meaning *entirely.* The correspondence is all together in one folder. He is altogether too casual in his manner.

Allude, elude. *Allude* means to *refer indirectly; elude* means to *avoid.* They alluded to a possible wage increase, but a real settlement eluded them.

Allusion, illusion. *Allusion* means *an indirect reference to; illusion* means *a false impression.*

Already, all ready. *Already* is an adverb meaning *previously; all ready* is an adverb-adjective compound meaning *completely ready.* Ms. Adams has already left. Are you all ready to go?

Altar, alter. An *altar* is a *raised structure which serves as a center of worship or ritual. Alter* is a verb meaning to *change.* They decorated the altar. The tailor altered Mr. Davis's suit.

Alumna, alumnae, alumnus, alumni. An *alumna* is *a woman graduate* or *a former female student* (plural, *alumnae).* An *alumnus* is a *man graduate* or *a former male student* (plural, *alumni). Graduate, graduates* are good substitutes.

Among, between. *Between* implies two, whereas *among* implies more than two. There is quite a bit of feeling between my brother and sister. There is a great deal of rivalry among the women at the club.

Amount, number. *Amount* is usually used when referring to money and to that which cannot be counted; *number* generally refers to things that can be counted. The unusually large number of speculators accounted for the large amount of speculation.

Angry. One is *angry at* an action or *with a* person. She is sure to be angry at having to wait. He is sure to be angry with Mr. Lane about the oversight.

Anxious, eager. *Anxious* connotes *distress, fear, uneasiness, worry. Eager* connotes *enthusiasm, anticipation, impatient desire or interest.* We are anxious to meet your requirements (but worried that we may fail). We are eager to start on our trip.

Any. Use singular or plural verbs and pronouns according to the intended meaning. Was any of the dessert left? Are any of the students eligible for the prize?

Any place, every place, no place, some place. These are illiterate expressions. Use *anywhere, everywhere, nowhere,* and *somewhere.*

Appraise, apprise. *Appraise* means to *set a value on; apprise* means to *inform.* The adjuster will appraise the damage and will apprise you of the estimate.

Apt, likely, liable. *Apt* means *unusually suitable* or *qualified*; *likely* emphasizes the idea of probability; *liable* means *susceptible to something unpleasant* or *responsible*. A short-sighted person is apt to make mistakes in financial planning. It is likely that it will rain tomorrow. She was liable for damages according to the contract.

As. *As* should not be used for *that* or *whether*. Never say: I don't know *as* I can go today (use *that*).

As . . . as, not so . . . as. In making comparisons, use *as . . . as*. She is not so tall as me may pass colloquially but should not be used in writing.

Awful, awfully. As a synonym for *extreme, extremely,* or *very* these words are overused. Incorrect: She was *awfully* confused. Correct: She was *very* confused.

Back of, in back of. Colloquial for *behind* or *at the back of.* The garden is *behind* the house, not *in back of* the house.

Bad, badly. *Bad* is a predicate adjective and should be used after verbs of sensing when used as linking verbs. *Badly* is an adverb. He feels bad about losing. She looks bad. The news sounds bad. He played badly in the tournament. He was injured badly in the accident. The home team played the game badly; the loss made them feel bad.

Balance, remainder. *Balance* is usually used as an accounting or banking term. *Remainder* connotes something that is left over. The balance in her account was substantial. Ship the remainder of the order.

Bases, basis. *Bases* is the plural of *base* and *basis*.

Between. See *Among*.

Biannual, biennial, semiannual. *Biannual* means *twice a year*; *biennial, once in two years*; *semiannual, every half year*.

Bimonthly, semimonthly. *Bimonthly* means *every two months*; *semimonthly, twice a month*.

Blond, blonde. Blond is masculine; blonde is feminine.

Brunet, brunette. Brunet is masculine; brunette is feminine.

Can, may. *Can* means *to be able to*; *may* means *to have permission*. This model can be used for heating and air conditioning. Tell him that he may leave when he is finished.

Canvas, canvass. When *canvas* is used as a noun to mean *a firm closely woven fabric*, it is usually spelled with one *s*, though canvass is also acceptable. When *canvass* is used as a verb, meaning *to survey or solicit*, it is usually spelled with two *s*'s though canvas is also acceptable. The cartons were covered with canvas. Mr. Lindsay will canvass the employees for their reactions.

Capital, capitol. Use *capital* unless you are talking about the building that houses a government. Capitalize *capitol* only when it is part of a proper name. The United States Capitol is located on Capitol Hill.

Cite, sight, site. *Cite* means *to quote; sight* means *vision; site* means *location*. She cited some good examples in her lecture. They sighted another ship on the horizon. We chose the site for our new branch plant.

Claim. *Claim* is not a synonym for *maintain. Claim* means *to demand something that is due.* She maintained that she was correct. He intends to claim his inheritance.

Comedian, comedienne. *Comedian* is masculine; *comedienne* is feminine.

Complected, complexioned. *Complected* is a provincialism for *complexioned:* a dark-complexioned person.

Complement, compliment. *Complement* means *to complete, fill,* or *make perfect; compliment* means *to praise.* Her attention to detail complements his energetic professionalism. He complimented Miss Shelley on her good work.

Confidant, confidante. Confidant is usually masculine; confidante is usually feminine.

Consensus of opinion. Although there has been much discussion about the redundancy of this phrase, most dictionaries remain silent about it.

Considerable. Although *Webster's New Collegiate Dictionary* recognizes this term as a noun, it is considered a colloquialism by most writers. We lost *much* in the hurricane (rather than *considerable).*

Consist of, consist in. *Consist of* means *composed of; consist in* means *to lie, reside.* The mixture consists of four kinds of herbs. Liberty consists in the absence of obstruction.

Consul, council, counsel. A *consul* is a representative. A *council* is an assembly. *Counsel* is advice. When used as a verb *counsel* means *to advise.*

Consult. *Consult about* something or merely *consult (consult with* is redundant). The heirs consulted the lawyer about the will.

Contact. Although business communicators use this term as a verb, its preferred usage is as a noun. Please contact the dealer's office. Preferred: We wish to establish a business contact in Brazil.

Continual, continuous. *Continual* means *occurring in rapid succession; continuous* means *without break.* There were continual interruptions. The machine has been in continuous use for the past three hours.

Credible, credulous. *Credible* means *believable; creditable, praise-worthy; credulous* means *ready to believe on weak evidence.*

Data. *Data* is the plural form of the Latin *datum. Data* should be used with a plural verb. Data are processed electronically at incredible speeds.

Descendant, descendent. *Descendant* and *descendent* can be either *nouns or adjectives.*

Desert, desert, dessert. *Desert* (Dezert) is an arid region lacking moisture; *desert* (dizert) means to abandon; *dessert* is a fruit or sweets served at the close of a meal.

Differ. One thing *differs from* another; persons *differ with* each other. One author's style differs from that of another in many ways. He differs with us on that point.

Different from. This usage is correct. *Different than* is incorrect. The circumstances were different from those he recalled.

Discreet, discrete. *Discreet* means *showing good judgment in conduct; discrete* means *separate; individually distinct.*

Disinterested, uninterested. *Disinterested* means *an impersonal, unbiased,* or *unprejudiced interest; uninterested* means *lacking in* or *an absence of any interest.* Professional ethics requires accountants to be disinterested in the success of their clients. She is uninterested in fiction.

Doubt. To express doubt, use *if* or *whether.* To express lack of doubt, use a negative and *that.* I doubt if there is time. He doubts whether she will attend. I do not doubt that there is time. I have no doubt that there is time.

Due to. An adjective construction that should not be used as an adverb to introduce prepositional phrases. Use *because of.* Incorrect: Due to faulty brakes, we drove slowly. Correct: Because of faulty brakes, we drove slowly.

Each other, one another. *Each other* refers to two persons; *one another* to more than two. George and Mary are very fond of each other. All the men on the team like one another.

Eager. See *Anxious, eager.*

Effect. See *Affect, effect.*

Either, neither. Used as adjectives or as pronouns these words usually take singular verbs. Either day is correct. Neither has replied to my letter.

Either . . . or, neither . . . nor. When these connectives join compound subjects, the subject that is nearer the verb determines whether a singular or plural verb is used. Usually place the plural subject near the verb. Either Mr. Lance or his associates are going. Neither the reports nor the book is here.

Else. Add apostrophe *s* to form the possessive. I saw no one else's grade. Matthew took someone else's coat inadvertently.

Eminent, imminent. *Eminent* means *high, lofty, distinguished; imminent* means *impending* or *threatening.*

Ensure, insure. *Ensure* means *to make certain* or *safe; insure* means *to give, take,* or *procure insurance* (used in a financial sense). Snow tires will ensure safe driving in the snow. Every automobile owner should insure his or her vehicle in case of accident.

Enthuse. This verb is a back-formation of *enthusiasm.* It is generally considered colloquial and/or informal. *Enthuse* should not be used in formal writing; *to be enthusiastic* is better usage even in conversation. She was enthusiastic about the plan.

Etc. *Etc.* is an abbreviation for *et cetera,* which means *and other things.* If *et cetera* is dictated, the secretary usually transcribes it as *and so forth.* To avoid using either *and so forth* or *etc.,* substitute *and the like. Etc.* should never be used when referring to persons. We must have all sales reports, expense reports, budgets, and the like, by the tenth of the month.

Ethics. *Ethics* is a plural noun but may be used in both plural and singular constructions. Professional ethics (singular) prohibits our advertising. His ethics (plural) have been questionable.

Except. See *Accept.*

Excess. See *Access.*

Farther, further. *Farther* refers to distance or space; *further* refers to time, quantity, or degree. The airport is a mile farther on this road. We can go into the matter further tomorrow.

Female. *Female* is used in records and statistics but is not acceptable as a synonym for *woman, lady,* or *feminine.*

Fewer, less. *Fewer* refers to number; *less* to degree or quantity. There are fewer people living in single homes than formerly. She has less money this year.

Fiancé, fiancée. A *fiancé* (masculine) or a *fiancée* (feminine) is a person engaged to be married. Both words are pronounced fē-än-'sā.

Fine, well. *Fine* is used too often and too carelessly. It is a dubious colloquialism. Use *well.* The motor works well (not *fine*).

Flaunt, flout. *Flaunt* means *to wave; to display boastfully. Flout* means *to treat with contempt or to insult.*

Formally, formerly. *Formally* means *rigidly ceremonious* or *respectful of form. Formerly* means *previously.*

Good, well. To *feel good* and to *feel well* are not synonymous. Both *good* and *well* are adjectives; well is also an adverb. Used as adjectives, I *feel good* and I *feel well* have different meanings. I feel good implies an actual bodily sensation; I feel well simply means I am not ill.

Got, gotten. *Got* is preferred to *gotten* as the past participle of *get*. It is colloquial when used for *must* or *ought:* I've got to leave at once. Improved: I must leave at once.

Graduated. Use either *graduated from* or *was graduated from*. In letters of application, use the latter form—in case your reader is a purist. Formal: He was graduated from Indiana University. Informal: He graduated from Indiana University.

Hopefully. *Hopefully* is often misused. It is an adverb and should be used as such. It is not a synonym for *it is hoped* or *I hope/we hope*. Use: We hope Miss James will do a good job. Avoid: Hopefully, Miss James will do a good job.

Hope phrases. Do not use *in hopes* of and *no hopes* of. Use the singular form. We sent the letter to Fairbanks, Alaska, in the hope of reaching Ms. Hanna.

However. Avoid starting a sentence with *however* when it is used as a transitional word. Used as an adverb, *however* can start a sentence. Transitional: We waited for hours; however, he . . . Adverb: However you advised him, he did not . . . .

Identical with. To compare likeness, use *identical with,* not *identical to.*

Illusion, allusion. *Illusion* means *a deceptive appearance; allusion* means something *referred to.*

Imply, infer. To *imply* means to *give a certain impression;* to *infer* means to *receive a certain impression.* Your question implies that you don't understand. I infer from your question that you don't understand.

In, into. *Into* is a preposition implying *motion. In* is a preposition implying *place in which*. She was diving into the pool (but was not yet in the pool). She was swimming in the pool (she is already in the pool).

Inconsistent. Use with *in* or *with*. He is inconsistent in his arguments. Her statements were inconsistent with her record.

Incredible, incredulous. *Incredible* means *unbelievable; incredulous* means *unbelieving*. The story is incredible; and, frankly, I'm incredulous.

Inferior to. Use *inferior to,* not *inferior than.*

Ingenious, ingenuous. *Ingenious* means *inventive; ingenuous* means *candid* or *artless.*

Inside of. Colloquial for within.

Irregardless. Illiterate. Use *regardless.*

Its, it's. The possessive case takes no apostrophe. *It's* is a contraction of *it is.*

Job, position. Both words mean a post of employment, but with this distinction: A laborer who uses physical effort has a *job* and is paid *wages* at an hourly rate. A worker with special training or ability has a *position* and is paid a weekly or monthly *salary.* In personnel terminology, *job* is used for both because it is short; for example, a *clerical job. (Job* is also used to describe a unit of work.)

Junior, Senior, Jr., Sr. *Junior* is usually dropped after the death of the father of the same name. *Senior* or *Sr.* is unnecessary and is almost never used unless the two identical names are closely associated (such as business partners) or unless each is so well known that a distinction is needed.

Kind, kinds. Use singular verbs and pronouns with *kind;* plural verbs and pronouns with *kinds.* This applies also to *type, types; class, classes;* etc. That kind of machine performs well. The two types of machines used were suitable. Avoid: That kind of a machine performs well.

Later, latter. *Later* means *after a time; latter* means the *second of two things.* I shall reply later. I prefer the latter.

Latest, last. Although these words can be synonymous, a common distinction is to use *last* to mean *at the end in time or place; latest* is used to mean *following all others in time only, but not necessarily being the end.* This is the latest edition of the book. It is not the last edition, because we have started to work on the next edition.

Lay, lie. *Lay* means *to put something in place; lie* means *to recline or to rest on.* Principal parts of *lay* are *lay, laid, laid.* Principal parts of *lie* are *lie, lay, lain.* Lay the mail down. He laid the mail down. The mail lies on the table. It lay there yesterday.

Lead, led. The past tense of *lead* is *led.* He led the opposition.

Leave, let. *Leave* means *to depart; let, to permit or allow.*

Less. See *Fewer, less.*

Like. *Like* should not be used for *as, as if,* or *as though.* Incorrect: The report looks like he took pains with it. Correct: The report looks as though he took pains with it.

Loan, lend. Although some writers use *loan* as a noun only, some dictionaries show both *loan* and *lend* as verbs. The principal parts are *loan, loaned, loaned; lend, lent, lent.*

Loose, lose. These words are frequently confused. *Loose* means *to be free of restraint; lose* means *forget* or *misplace; to suffer a loss.* It is easy to lose a loose button.

Lots of. Colloquial for *many, much, a great many, a considerable number.*

Marital, martial, marshall. *Marital* means *pertaining to marriage; martial* means *warlike* or *military.* *Marshall* can be either a noun or a verb. As a verb, *marshall* means *to rally;* as a noun, marshall means *an official.*

May. See *Can.*

Might of. Misused for *might have.*

Neither . . . nor. See *Either . . . or.*

None. See *All, any, none, some, more, most.*

Not, and not. When either of these two introduces a phrase in contrast to the subject, the subject determines whether the verb is singular or plural. Results, not wishful thinking, count.

Not only . . . but also. In this construction, the noun closest to the verb determines whether the latter is singular or plural. When used with independent clauses, this construction is separated by commas. Not only the reports but also his report was due. Not only was it their first visit here, but also it was their first trip by air.

Off, off of. Use *off* only, not *off of.* The part fell off the machine. The girl jumped off the wall.

On, onto, on to. She drove *on* the expressway berm (implies position and movement over). He stepped *onto* the porch (implies motion). They went on to the next town. (*On* is an adverb in the verb phrase *went on; to* is a preposition.)

Oneself. Preferred to *one's self.* Taking oneself too seriously is a foolish practice.

Only. *Only* should be placed as close as possible to the word or clause that it modifies. Alan types only form letters. Alan types form letters only when he has spare time. Do not substitute *only* for *except* or *but.* Incorrect: No one is interested only Mr. Lane.

Oral, verbal. *Oral* means *spoken; verbal* means *relating to* or *consisting of words.* Although both are commonly used for *spoken,* use the dictionary meaning cited here in formal writing: an oral agreement; a verbal contract.

Out loud. Colloquial for *aloud*.

Other. Use *than* after *no other*. Incorrect: It was no other but Jane. Correct: It was no other than Jane.

Outside of. Ungrammatical for *except* or *besides*.

Pair. The preferred plural of *pair* is *pairs*, although *Webster's New Collegiate Dictionary* shows *pair* as a second usage for the plural of this word.

Passed, past, pastime. *Passed* is the past tense and past participle of the verb *to pass*. *Past* is a noun or an adjective meaning *a time gone by* or *bygone*. It is also a preposition and an adverb. A *pastime* (often misspelled *passtime* or *pasttime)* is a *diversion*. They passed the time by reading. Go two blocks past Elm Street. In the past my favorite pastime was reading.

Percent, percentage. *Percent* is one word. *Percentage* is also one word and should not be used with a number. *Percentage* is a dubious colloquialism when used for *proportion*. A large proportion (rather than *percentage*) of the fish were cod.

Person, individual, personage, party, people. A *person* is a human being; an *individual* is one apart from a group; a *personage* is a person of importance; a *party* is a legal term for person. Use *persons* for small numbers and *people* for large masses.

Personal, personnel. *Personal* means *private*; *personnel* means *a body of persons, usually employed in a factory, office, or organization*.

Personally, in person. These terms intensify meaning. Avoid using them in formal writing. I personally guarantee each one. Mr. Lane made the award in person.

Politics. This term is commonly used with singular verbs.

Position. See *Job, position*.

Practical, practicable. *Practical* means *sensible, efficient,* or *useful*. *Practicable* implies something that can be put into practice. My practical secretary suggested a practicable method for handling follow-ups.

Precedence, precedents, precedent. *Precedence* means *priority* or *preference*; *precedents* is the plural of the noun *precedent* and means *an earlier occurrence*; *precedent* (preSEEdent) is an adjective and means *earlier in order*. Completing the school year took precedence over her desire to take the trip. There are several precedents for that decision. The precedent decisions that apply to this case must be considered.

Preferable. Follow by *to*, not by *than*. I find ice cream preferable to cake.

Prerequisite. As a noun, prerequisite is used with *for*; as an adjective, it is used with *to* (to be prerequisite to).

Principal, principle. *Principal* may be a noun or an adjective. As a noun it means *a person who has controlling authority* or *is in a leading position*. It also means *a capital sum of money*. As an adjective, *principal* means *chief*. *Principle* is a noun meaning *a law, a doctrine, a rule* or *code of conduct*. The principals in the legal case are present. The principal actor was outstanding in his part. Mrs. Palmer invested the principal of the trust fund and used the interest for living expenses. Mr. Palmer was always a man of principle, but he was principal of the school.

Proposition. Correctly used as a noun, *proposition* means an *assertion* or *dignified proposal*. Do not use this word as a verb.

Proved, proven. Although either word may be used as the past participle of *prove, proved* is preferred. *Proven* is better confined to use as an adjective. You have proved your point. It was a proven fact.

Raise, increase, increment. In business, *raise* and *increase* may be used interchangeably when referring to wage or salary. *Raise* is the popular term, but *increase* is a more dignified term. *Increment* is generally used in personnel offices.

Real. *Real* should not be used for the adverb *very*. She had a very professional appearance (not real professional).

Remainder. See *balance*.

Respectfully, respectively, respectable. *Respectfully* means *in a courteous manner*; *respectively* refers to *being considered singly in a particular order*; *respectable* means *being of good name* or *fairly numerous*.

Retroactive. *Retroactive* is always used with the preposition *to* not *from*. The price increase is retroactive to July 1.

Salary. See *Job, position*.

Set, sit. *Set* means *to put or place something*. *Sit* means *to place yourself*. She set the cup and saucer on the table. She sits on the porch every evening.

Species. *Species* means *a class of individuals having common attributes and designated by a common name*. It is spelled the same in the singular and plural. *Specie* is money in the form of coins.

Stationary, stationery. *Stationary* means *stable* or *fixed; stationery* is writing paper.

Statistics. Use the plural form except when referring to the science of statistics.

Statue, stature, statute. *Statue* is a *sculptured or molded figure; stature* refers to height (as applied to people); *statute* refers to written law.

Stimulus, stimulant. *Stimulus* means *a mental goad; stimulant* means *a physical goad.* (In medicine, these two words are used synonymously.)

Superior. Use *superior to,* not *superior than.*

Sure, surely. *Sure* is an adjective; *surely* is a modifying adverb. Are you sure? That was surely record time.

Tantamount. Use with *to.* His actions were tantamount (equivalent) to betrayal.

These kind, those kind. Ungrammatical. Use *this kind* or *these kinds.*

Till, until. *Until* is preferred at the beginning of a sentence; although as prepositions and conjunctions, *until* and *til* are interchangeable.

Try and. This usage should be avoided. Use *to* with the infinitive: try to listen.

Type. *Type* is a noun or verb; do not use it as an adjective. This type of process is new. Incorrect: This type process is new.

Uninterested. See *Disinterested, uninterested.*

Unique. *Unique* means *the only one of its kind.* It does not mean *rare* or *odd.* It is incorrect to say, "She is the most unique person I know."

United States. Use *the* before *United States,* rephrasing if necessary to avoid an awkward construction. (If necessary, substitute *American.*) Poor: According to United States laws . . .; preferred: According to the laws of the United States . . .

Unkempt, unkept. *Unkempt* means *unrefined, unpolished,* or *rough. Unkept* means *not maintained or preserved.*

Until. See *Till.*

Up. Avoid the use of *up* with verbs such as *connect, divide, end, open, rest, settle, finish.*

Verbal. See *Oral, verbal.*

Very. *Very* should not be used to modify a past participle. It may modify an adjective directly. Incorrect: She was very interested in the position. Correct: She was very much interested in the position.

View. As a verb, use *to view* with *with;* as a noun, use *in view of* or *with a view to.* We view it with indifference. In view of the time, we will adjourn.

Vulnerable. To be vulnerable (assailable) *to* something *in* some way or place. He was vulnerable to criticism in his business practices.

Wages. See *Job, position.*

Well. See *Good, well.*

Where compounds. *Anywhere, everywhere, nowhere,* and *somewhere* are adverbs and are written as one word.

Whether. In indirect questions, *whether* is preferred to *if.* They asked whether he had come. Not: They asked if he had come.

Whether . . . or, whether or not. For alternatives, use *whether . . . or* or *whether or not.* State whether you will go or stay. State whether or not you will go. Not: State whether you will go or not.

While, awhile. Use *while* as a connective for time or as a noun. *Awhile,* an adverb, is written as one word. While Mrs. Lambert was out, her caller arrived. Once in a while, we find that. . . . He left awhile ago. *While* can be used for *although,* but it should not be used for *and.* While we see your point, we do not agree. Not: We order nails from the H & P Company, while we order hammers from Black and Burns.

Conversions

A *conversion* is the unconventional use of a word. Enclose the word in quotation marks only if the reader may think it is a grammatical error. Some typical conversions include the following:

1.   A noun or noun phrase converted to an adjective

     He is a meat-and-potatoes man.

2.   An adjective or adverb converted to a verb

     We nonstopped to Miami. He low-keyed the presentation.

3.   A noun converted to a verb

     We *jetted* to Europe for the summer.
     He *sugar-coated* the complaint.

Quick Grammar Reminders

These quick grammar reminders are not intended to be a substitute for a comprehensive grammar book. They are meant to be quick references to jog a reader's memory or to quickly clarify a point of confusion that may arise when composing letters, preparing reports, drafting speeches, or performing any of the multitudinous writing tasks that beset an executive or secretary.

ACRONYMS

Acronyms are words from the initial letters or syllable of two or more words. They are neither enclosed in quotes nor underlined. Plurals, possessives, and tenses are formed regularly.

WAC, snafu, NATO

ACTION VERBS

See "Transitive (Action) Verbs."

AND IN COMPOUND SUBJECTS

Compound subjects of two or more words joined by *and* take plural verbs and pronouns unless the words together comprise a single element.

Our sales manager and our advertising director have sent in their reports.
Our sales manager and advertising director has sent in his report.
A pen and a pencil were found after the meeting.
A matching pen and pencil makes a welcome gift.

COMPOUND WORDS

Compound words fall into three groups: hyphenated compounds, one-word compounds, and two-word compounds. Information about the two latter groups can generally be found in any standard dictionary. Compounds formed with prefixes and suffixes are treated under "Prefixes, Joined" and under "Suffixes." For information about hyphenated compounds *see* "The Hyphen."

EUPHEMISMS

Euphemisms are softened, tactful phrases for blunt or harsh facts. Some common euphemisms are:

For *buried*: laid to rest.
For *discharged*: left our employ.
For *died*: passed away
For *claim*: think or believe

EUPHONY

Euphony (pleasing speech sounds) can be achieved by

1.   Avoiding harsh or ugly sounds (*f*'s, *b*'s, *ch*'s, *t*'s, *ug*'s, *og*'s)

2.   Repeating pleasant sounds

3.   Using rhythmically accented syllables

> *Choppy:* We are glad indeed to be able to advise you.
> *Euphonious:* We are pleased that we can tell you . . . . The record of all receipts and expenses . . . .

GERUND

1.   A *gerund* is a verbal (ending in *ing*) used as a noun. Gerunds can be used in all noun usages.

> *Subject:* You learn that editing takes time.
> *Object:* She learned editing from the senior editor.

2.   In formal writing a possessive is used with a gerund.

> His editing included Chapter 10.
> The team's winning made the crowd happy.

> **Exception:** *The possessive form is not necessary with a compound or inanimate modifier.*

> The No. 2 mill breaking down caused a delay.
> The mill (or mill's) breaking down caused a delay.

IDIOMS

1. An *idiom* is an expression or phrase that is somehow peculiar—an arbitrary grouping of words that is often illogical in construction or meaning but which is acceptable. Some common American idioms are *to make ends meet, to take pains, laid up with a virus, by and large,* and *to catch a cold.*

2. A prepositional idiom is one in which the combination of words has a special meaning; for example, *to live up to, to live down* something, *to put up with* something, *to set up, to set about* something, *to hand over, to bring up* a point.

INFINITIVES

An *infinitive* is the principal part of any verb. It is usually introduced by *to* and is used as a noun, adjective, or adverb.

Noun, subject: To go will be a privilege.
Noun, object: He wants *to talk* with you.
Adjective: The place *to go* is Spain.
Adverb: He saved his graduation checks *to go* to Spain.

The *to* is usually omitted after the following verbs: *hear, feel, watch, let, dare, help, see, make, please, bid, need,* and *do.*

Help me (to) carry the luggage.
They bid us (to) leave immediately.
There was nothing to do but (to) read.

A *split infinitive* occurs when a word or phrase separates *to* and the verb. Use a split infinitive only when necessary for clarity or emphasis. Notice in the examples below how the meaning changes subtly with a shift of the infinitive.

The attorney invited them to *first* consider . . .
The attorney invited them to consider first . . .

INTRANSITIVE VERBS

See "Transitive (Action) Verbs."

LINKING VERBS

Linking verbs *connect* a subject with a predicate noun or adjective. *See also* "Transitive (Action) Verbs."

to be (am, is, was, has been, etc.), act, appear, become, feel, get, grow, look, seem, sound, taste, turn

NUMBER OF (USE OF)

The meaning intended determines whether *number of* takes a singular or plural verb.

The number of replies that we received is gratifying.
A number of the replies were critical of our policy.

OR (USE OF)

When *or* joins two subject words, the verb agrees with the word that is nearest to it.

Only one or two are needed.
No pencils or paper was furnished.

PARALLEL CONSTRUCTION

If two or more sentence parts are joined by one or more conjunctions, the parts should be of like kinds; that is, all single words of the same part of speech, all phrases, or all clauses.

The shipment was returned not only because it was late but also because two items were incorrect. *(connecting two clauses)*

NOT

The shipment was returned not only for being late but also because two items were incorrect. *(connecting a phrase and a clause)*

A good secretary not only is prompt but also shows initiative. *(connecting two verb phrases)*

NOT

A good secretary is both prompt and shows initiative. *(connecting an adjective and a verb phrase)*

Our plan is to decide on the type of building, to choose an architect, and to let the contracts. *(connecting infinitives)*

NOT

Our plan is to decide on the type of building, choosing an architect, and letting the contracts. *(connecting an infinitive and participles)*

PARTICIPLES, DANGLING

A participial construction should modify a related, logical word except when the construction is absolute (modifying nothing).

Dangling: Leaving the office, the letter was dropped.
Logical: Leaving the office, I dropped the letter.
Absolute: The situation having developed, let's accept the changes it necessitates.

PLURALS

Since standard dictionaries give irregularly formed plurals of words, this section provides only that information pertaining to common problems that confront writers in day-to-day business usage. Refer also to "The Apostrophe."

Abbreviations

1.   For most, add *s*: gals, yds, Drs., bbls
2.   For abbreviations in all caps, add *s*: CPSs, CPAs, R.N.s, RNs
3.   For abbreviations consisting of single lowercase letters, add *'s*: btu's, cc's

Compound Nouns

1.   The plurals of compound nouns are generally formed by adding *s* to the principal word in the compound: attorneys general, judge advocates, notaries public, trade unions, assistant postmasters general.
2.   Compound nouns that contain prepositions form the plural by adding *s* to the principal word: chambers of commerce, attorneys-at-law, powers of attorney, points of view, bills of lading.
3.   Hyphenated compounds form the plural by adding *s* to the noun: lookers-on, passers-by, hangers-on, runners-up, goings-on.
4.   If there is no important word in the hyphenated compound noun, add an *s* to the end of the compound to form the plural: forget-me-nots, Jack-in-the-pulpits. If neither word in a compound is a noun, add *s* to the last word: also-rans, come-ons, follow-ups, go-betweens, higher-ups, trade-ins.

5. Some compounds form their plurals by making both parts plural: manservant, menservants; woman doctor, women doctors; Knight Templar, Knights Templars or Knights Templar.

6. Compounds ending in *ful* form their plurals by adding *s* to the end of the compound: spoonfuls, cupfuls, handfuls, bucketfuls.

Foreign Words

Given a choice between a foreign and an English plural, use the English, or use the plural that is most familiar for the subject.

English Plural	Foreign Plural
appendixes	appendices
criterions	criteria
curriculums	curricula
indexes	indices
mediums	media
memorandums	memoranda
ultimatums	ultimata

Numbers

See "Numbers" under the "Accepted Usage in Writing" section.

Proper Names

To form the plurals of proper names add *s* or *es:* the Smiths, the Joneses, the Foxes, the Americas, the Eskimos, the Lillys, the Murrays, the Randolphs.

PREFIXES, JOINED

Compounds with the following prefixes are usually written as one word. When the second element is capitalized or is a figure, use a hyphen: anti-American, pre-Raphaelite, pre-1914, post-1945. Use a hyphen to distinguish homonyms: re-cover, re-form.

anti	antifreeze	*over*	overanxious
bi	bimonthly	*post*	postdate
co	coplanner	*pre*	prearrange

dis	disaffect	*pro*	procreate
extra	extracurricular	*pseudo*	pseudointellectual
fore	foreknown	*re*	restyle
hydro	hydrochloride	*semi*	semicircular
hyper	hypertension	*sub*	substandard
in	incapable	*super*	superstructure
infra	infrastructure	*supra*	supranational
inter	international	*trans*	transcontinental
intra	intramural	*tri*	tricity
mis	misread	*ultra*	ultrasound
non	noncombatant	*un*	unsuitable
out	outdistance	*under*	underestimate

PREPOSITIONS

Prepositions should end a construction only to avoid awkward phrasing or when used in a prepositional idiom.

A collective noun takes a singular verb when the *group* is thought of.
He left his car to be worked on.

REDUNDANCY

Redundancy is the needless repetition of words. In each redundant phrase below, the italicized word is sufficient for clarity.

both *alike*	*depreciate* in value
close *proximity*	month of *April*
continue on	*repeat* again
customary *practice*	two *twin sisters*

SPLIT INFINITIVES

See "Infinitives."

SUBJUNCTIVE MOOD

In formal writing, the subjunctive mood is commonly used in contrary-to-fact clauses; clauses expressing doubt; clauses expressing wishes, regrets, demands, recommendations, and the like.

Subjunctive mood

If he were here, he would agree with me.
If time were available, I would come.
If that be true, we must act now.
I wish I were confident of the outcome.
We recommend that it be tried.

Conventional (indicative) usage

I know he was here because he left a note.
If he was (*not* were) here earlier, he didn't leave a note.
If she was planning to go, she didn't tell me.

SUFFIXES

Suffixes, such as -fold, -hood, -like, -proof, and -wide, are usually joined to the base word. But, compounds formed from proper names, words that end in *ll*, and word combinations are hyphenated.

threefold, multifold
childhood, motherhood
catlike, childlike
burglarproof, fireproof
nationwide, worldwide

BUT

Indian-like
bell-like
vacuum-bottle-like

THAT, WHICH, WHO (USE OF)

1. *That* and *which* are not always interchangeable. *That* is preferred for introducing a restrictive clause.

    The phrasing that you suggest is good.
    The book that you recommend is excellent.

2. *Which* is preferred for introducing a nonrestrictive clause.

    The new phrasing, which seems clearer, is better.
    Your help, which we need badly, will save the day.

3. *Who* refers to persons and sometimes to animals. *Who* can introduce either restrictive or nonrestrictive clauses.

> The members who favored the amendment voted yes.
> Mr. Jones, who was out of town, voted by proxy.
> Native Dancer, who won many important races, was a famous racehorse.

4. In formal writing, do not omit *that* as a conjunction.

> *Formal:* We think that this proposal is fair.
> *Informal:* We think this idea is a good one.

TRANSITIVE (ACTION) VERBS

Dictionaries designate verbs as *transitive (action)* or *intransitive (linking)* verbs.

1. Transitive verbs take objects. Intransitive verbs do not.

> *Transitive:* Send the letter today.
> *Intransitive:* She arrived this morning.

2. Some verbs are transitive *and* intransitive.

> *Transitive:* I wrote a full report.
>   She left her luggage at the hotel.
> *Intransitive:* I wrote yesterday.
>   She left yesterday.

VERBAL PHRASES

See "Infinitives" and "Participles, Dangling."

WHO, WHOM (USE OF)

Use *who* as the subject of a verb; *whom* as the object of a verb or a preposition or as the subject of an infinitive.

> Send it only to those *who asked* for it.
> *Who* do you think *will be made* chairman?
> Everyone *upon whom* I called accepted.
> *Whom shall* I *ask* first?
> *Whom* did they ask *to be* chairman?

WHOSE (USE OF)

Use *whose* as a possessive conjunction if *of which* is awkward. Most writers prefer to use *whose* because it is less cumbersome than *of which*.

A large box, whose contents were unknown, stood on the loading dock.
   NOT
A large box, the contents of which were unknown, stood on the loading dock.

Word Division

Typewriters without proportional spacing cannot and need not maintain even right margins. But because a reader will be distracted by an unduly ragged margin and by excessive end-of-line word divisions, follow these word division rules.

1. Divide words
   a. After an internal one-letter syllable

      criti-cism   tele-vision   sepa-rate

      Exception: *Do not divide* able, ible, icle, ical, cial, *or* sion: *biolog-ical, change-able, deduct-ible, spe-cial.*

   b. Between two vowels separately pronounced

      radi-ator   sci-ence   cli-ents   situ-ation

   c. Preferably at a prefix or suffix

      mis-spelled   driv-ing   depart-ment   exten-sion

   d. Between double consonants unless the base word ends in a double consonant

      neces-sary   capil-lary   excel-lent   car-rier
      will-ing   tell-ing   staff-ing   careless-ness

      Exception: *discus-sion, impres-sive, impres-sion.*

    e. By putting as much of a word on a line as is practical, even though the word has several acceptable points of division

       considera-tion (*not* consid-eration)
       documenta-tion (*not* docu-mentation)

2.   Divide hyphenated words only at the hyphen.

    self-criticism   high-sounding

3.   Do not divide
    a. One-syllable words
    b. Words of five or fewer letters (preferably six or fewer)
    c. Abbreviations, numbers, dates, or names of persons (Avoid separating titles, initials, and professional or scholastic degrees from a name. If necessary divide at a logical point: May 14,/1987; Mr. James A./Hanover.)
    d. Two-letter first or last syllables
    e. Contractions
    f. The last word in over two successive lines of typing
    g. The last word in a paragraph or on a page

Alphabetic Filing

Because of the many documents that are processed, stored, and retrieved in an office, it is essential that well-organized files be maintained. Generally accepted rules of alphabetic filing are presented in this section. All files are to some degree based on an alphabetic system. Minor variations from these alphabetic rules are occasionally found in different organizations. Be sure to follow the established rules of your organization.

RULE 1: ORDER OF INDEXING UNITS

A personal name is indexed in this manner: (1) the surname (last name) is the key unit, (2) the given name or initial is the second unit, and (3) the middle name or initial is the third unit. Unusual or obscure names (frequently foreign names) are indexed in the same manner. If it is not possible to determine the surname, consider the last name as the surname. Cross-reference unusual or obscure names using the first name written as the key unit.

Index Order of Units in Personal Names

Name	Unit 1	Unit 2	Unit 3
Joan Ander	Ander	Joan	
Joan E. Ander	Ander	Joan	E
Louise Ander	Ander	Louise	
Adam Anders	Anders	Adam	
Anna Andersson	Andersson	Anna	
Alma Lee Andrews	Andrews	Alma	Lee
E. Bennett Andrews	Andrews	E	Bennett
Soo On Bee	Bee	Soo	On

RULE 2: ARTICLES AND PARTICLES

A foreign language article or a particle in a business or personal name is combined with the part of the name following it to form a single indexing unit. The indexing order is not affected by a space between a prefix and the rest of the name, and the space is disregarded when indexing. Examples of articles and particles are: a la, D', Da, De, Del, De la, Della, Den, Des, Di, Dos, Du, El, Fitz, Il, L', La, Las, Le, Les, Lo, Los, M', Mac, Mc, O', Per, Saint, St., Ste., San, Santa, Santo, Te, Ten, Ter, Van, Van de, Van der, Von, Von der.

Index Order of Units in Names

Name	Unit 1	Unit 2
Catherine Lemate	Lemate	Catherine
Francis LeMate	LeMate	Francis
Joan MacDowell	MacDowell	Joan
James McDaniel	McDaniel	James
Karen O'Bonner	OBonner	Karen
Edith St. Marner	StMarner	Edith

RULE 3: INITIALS AND ABBREVIATIONS

Initials in personal names are considered separate indexing units. Abbreviations of personal names (Wm., Jos., Thos.) and brief personal names or nicknames (Liz, Bill) are indexed as they are written. Examples of Rule 3 are given here.

Index Order of Units in Names

Name	Unit 1	Unit 2	Unit 3
Paula Cameron	Cameron	Paula	
D.D. Crawford	Crawford	D	D
Dale Crawford	Crawford	Dale	
Jane Dackman	Dackman	Jane	
Jas. E. Dackman	Dackman	Jas	E
Bob L. Davirro	Davirro	Bob	L
Robert Davirro	Davirro	Robert	

RULE 4: TITLES

A personal title (Miss, Mr., Mrs. and Ms.) is considered as the last indexing unit when it appears. If a seniority title is required for identification, it is considered the last indexing unit in abbreviated form, with numeric titles (II, III, etc.) filed before alphabetic titles (Jr. and Sr.). When professional titles (D.D.S., M.D., CRM., Dr., Mayor) are required for identification, they are considered the last units and are filed alphabetically as written. Royal and religious titles followed by either a given name or a surname only (Father Leo) are indexed and filed as written. When all units of identical names, *including titles*, have been compared and there are no differences, filing order is determined by addresses.

Index Order of Units in Names

Name	Unit 1	Unit 2	Unit 3	Unit 4
Miss Mary J. Fatam	Fatam	Mary	J	Miss
Father Delbert	Father	Delbert		
Rev. A. O. Hanson	Hanson	A	O	Rev
Ralph Hanson, D.D.S.	Hanson	Ralph	DDS	
Father Robert O. Hanson	Hanson	Robert	O	Father
A. Michael Henderson II	Henderson	A	Michael	II
A. Michael Henderson III	Henderson	A	Michael	III
A. Michael Henderson, Jr.	Henderson	A	Michael	Jr
A. Michael Henderson, Sr.	Henderson	A	Michael	Sr
Mrs. Ann Jones Milton	Milton	Ann	Jones	Mrs
Dr. Diana Miltson	Miltson	Diana	Dr	

RULE 5: HYPHENATED NAMES

Hyphenated surnames are considered as one indexing unit and the hyphen is ignored. This rule also applies to given names, such as Jo-Mar.

Index Order of Unit in Names

Name	Unit 1	Unit 2
Ruth Martin-Ames	MartinAmes	Ruth
Jo-Mar Odell	Odell	JoMar

RULE 6: NAMES OF MARRIED WOMEN

A married woman's name is filed as she writes it. It is indexed according to Rule 1. If more than one form of a name is known, the alternate name may be cross-referenced. A married woman's name in a business name is indexed as written.

Index Order of Units of Names

Name	Unit 1	Unit 2	Unit 3	Unit 4
Ms. Becky Jones Fritts	Fritts	Becky	Jones	Mrs
Mrs. Becky Mae Fritts	Fritts	Becky	Mae	Mrs
Mrs. Lucien Fritts	Fritts	Lucien	Mrs	
Miss Becky Mae Jones	Jones	Becky	Mae	Miss
Mrs. Gerald V. Kingston	Kingston	Gerald	V	Mrs

RULE 7: IDENTICAL NAMES

When the names of individuals are identical, their alphabetic order is determined by their addresses, starting with the city. Names of states are considered when the names of the cities are also alike. When the city names and the state names as well as the full names of the individuals are alike, the alphabetic order is determined by street names; next house and building numbers, with the lowest number filed first.

Index Order of Units of Names

Name	Unit 1	Unit 2	Unit 3	Unit 4
Janice Hess 314 Elm Street Toledo, Ohio	Hess	Janice	Toledo	Elm
Janice Hess 92 Plum Avenue Toledo, Ohio	Hess	Janice	Toledo	Plum
Edward Iglecia Akron, Ohio	Iglecia	Edward	Akron	
Edward Iglecia Columbus, Ohio	Iglecia	Edward	Columbus	
Edward Iglecia Dayton, Ohio	Iglecia	Edward	Dayton	
Edward B. Iglecia	Iglecia	Edward	B	

RULE 8: ORDER OF INDEXING UNITS

Business names are filed *as written* using letterheads or trademarks as guides. Business names containing personal names are indexed as written. Newspapers and periodicals are indexed as written. For newspapers and periodicals having identical names that do not include the city name, consider the city name as the last indexing unit. If necessary, the state name may follow the city name.

Index Order of Units in Names

Name	Unit 1	Unit 2	Unit 3	Unit 4
Jill Nobee News Corner	Jill	Nobee	News	Corner
Nelson Lumber Company	Nelson	Lumber	Company	
Newsweek	Newsweek			
S. Martin Hats	S	Martin	Hats	
Sam Martin Garage	Sam	Martin	Garage	
Times Dispatch (Danville)	Times	Dispatch	Danville	
Times Dispatch (Winchester)	Times	Dispatch	Winchester	

RULE 9: ARTICLES, CONJUNCTIONS, AND PREPOSITIONS

Each complete English word in a business name is considered as a separate indexing unit. Prepositions and conjunctions are separate units. When the word "The" is used as the first word of a business name, it is considered the last unit.

Index Order of Units in Names

Name	Unit 1	Unit 2	Unit 3	Unit 4
By the Lane Inn	By	the	Lane	Inn
Charles of the Ritz	Charles	of	the	Ritz
The Mill End Shop	Mill	End	Shop	The

RULE 10: INITIALS, ABBREVIATIONS, AND TITLES

Initials and abbreviations in business names are indexed as written. If there is a space between single letters, index each letter as a separate unit; however, an acronym (a word formed from the first, or first few, letters of several words) is indexed as one unit regardless of punctuation or spacing, such as AAA, Y M C A, or Y.W.C.A. Cross-reference spelled-out names to their acronyms if necessary. For example: American Automobile Association SEE *AAA*. Titles in business names are filed as written.

Index Order of Units in Names

Name	Unit 1	Unit 2	Unit 3	Unit 4	Unit 5
Ball Crank Co.	Ball	Crank	Co		
BB Brakes	BB	Brakes			
C and C Dress Shoppe	C	and	C	Dress	Shoppe
Donahue, Ltd.	Donahue	Ltd			
Dr. Footeze	Dr	Footeze			
Miss Della Knits	Miss	Della	Knits		
Mr. Jim's Steak House	Mr	Jims	Steak	House	

RULE 11: SYMBOLS

Symbols (&, ¢, $, #, %) are considered as spelled in full (and, Cent, Dollar, Number, Percent).

Index Order of Units in Names

Name	Unit 1	Unit 2	Unit 3	Unit 4
$5 Bargain Store	5	Dollar	Bargain	Store
Flowers & Foliage	Flowers	and	Foliage	

RULE 12: NUMBERS

Numbers spelled out in a business name are considered as written and filed alphabetically. Numbers written in digit form are considered as one unit. Names with numbers written in digit form as the first unit are filed in ascending order before alphabetic names. Arabic numerals are filed before Roman numerals (2, 3; II, III). Names with inclusive numbers (33-37) are arranged by the first number only (33). Names with numbers appearing in other than the first position (Pier 36 Cafe) are filed alphabetically within the appropriate section and immediately before a similar name without a number (Pier and Port Cafe). In indexing numbers written in digit form which contain *st*, *d*, or *th* (1st, 2d, 3d, 4th), ignore the letter endings and consider only the digits (1, 2, 3, 4).

Index Order of Units in Names

Name	Unit 1	Unit 2	Unit 3	Unit 4
8th & Walnut Cafe	8	and	Walnut	Cafe
8th Street Bldg.	8	Street	Bldg	
8th Street Garage	8	Street	Garage	
The 800 Club	800	Club	The	
5100 Condominiums	5100	Condominiums		
A 1 Garage	A	1	Garage	
Fortilla Flats	Fortilla	Flats		
Route 250 Market	Route	250	Market	
Route 250 Motel	Route	250	Motel	

RULE 13: HYPHENATED NAMES

Hyphenated business names are considered as one indexing unit and the hyphen is ignored.

Index Order of Units in Names

Name	Unit 1	Unit 2	Unit 3
A-1 Retail Markets	A1	Retail	Markets
Read-N-Sew Studio	ReadNSew	Studio	
Ready-Built Shelf Shop	ReadyBuilt	Shelf	Shop
Self-Service Laundry	SelfService	Laundry	
Self-Study Society	SelfStudy	Society	
South-East Plaza Cafe	SouthEast	Plaza	Cafe

RULE 14: SEPARATED SINGLE WORDS

When a compound word is separated into two or more parts in a business name, the parts are considered separate indexing units. If a name contains two compass directions separated by a space (South East Car Rental), each compass direction is a separate indexing unit. *Southeast* and *south-east* are considered as single indexing units. Cross-reference compound words if necessary. For example: South East SEE ALSO Southeast, South-East.

Index Order of Units in Names

Name	Unit 1	Unit 2	Unit 3	Unit 4
Semi Weekly Cleaning Service	Semi	Weekly	Cleaning	Service
Semi-Trailer Rentals Inc.	SemiTrailer	Rentals	Inc	
South Western Office Supplies	South	Western	Office	Supplies
Southwestern Machines	Southwestern	Machines		
South-Western Publishing Co.	SouthWestern	Publishing	Co	

RULE 15: COMPOUND GEOGRAPHIC NAMES

Compound business or geographic names with spaces between the parts of the name follow Rule 14 and the parts are considered separate units. In the example which follows, Le, Los, San, and St., are considered as articles; therefore, they are not treated as separate units.

Index Order of Units in Names

Name	Unit 1	Unit 2	Unit 3
Le Mont Food Products	LeMont	Food	Products
Los Angeles Actors' Guild	LosAngeles	Actors	Guild
North Dakota Curios	North	Dakota	Curios
Northumberland Fisheries	Northumberland	Fisheries	
San Diego Playhouse	SanDiego	Playhouse	
St. Thomas Island Home	StThomas	Island	Home

RULE 16: POSSESSIVES

All punctuation is disregarded when indexing names. Commas, periods, hyphens, and apostrophes are disregarded.

Index Order of Units in Names

Name	Unit 1	Unit 2	Unit 3	Unit 4
Girl Scouts of America	Girl	Scouts	of	America
Girl's Sporting Goods	Girls	Sporting	Goods	

Name	Unit 1	Unit 2	Unit 3	Unit 4
Harpers'	Harpers			
Harper's Restaurant	Harpers	Restaurant		
Jones's Electric Co.	Joness	Electric	Co	

RULE 17: IDENTICAL BUSINESS NAMES

When identical names of businesses, organizations, and institutions occur, filing order is determined by the address with address parts treated as identifying elements. If the names of cities are alike, filing arrangement depends upon names of states or provinces, followed by street names and house or building numbers in that order.

When street names are written as figures (14th Street), the street name is considered in ascending numeric order and is filed before alphabetic street names.

Street names with compass directions are indexed as written. Numbers after compass directions are considered before alphabetic names (East 8th would precede East Main).

House and building numbers, written as figures, are considered in ascending numeric order and placed together before spelled-out building names. If a street address and a building name are included in an address, disregard the building name. ZIP Codes are not considered in determining filing order.

Seniority titles are indexed according to Rule 4 and are considered *before* addresses.

Index Order of Units in Names

Name	Unit 1	Unit 2	Address
Janicki Stationers Decatur, Illinois	Janicki	Stationers	Decatur, Illinois
Janicki Stationers Decatur, Indiana	Janicki	Stationers	Decatur, Indiana
Janicki Stationers Topeka, Illinois	Janicki	Stationers	Topeka, Illinois
Janicki Stationers Topeka, Kansas	Janicki	Stationers	Topeka, Kansas
Kastner's 531 East Main	Kastners		531 East Main
Kastner's 2910 West Main	Kastners		2910 West Main
Lovington Lamps 55 - 14th Street Ames, Iowa	Lovington	Lamps	55 - 14th Street, Ames, Iowa

Name	Unit 1	Unit 2	Address
Lovington Lamps 35 - 25th Street Ames, Iowa	Lovington	Lamps	35 - 25th Street, Ames, Iowa
Lovington Lamps 2789 Beacon Street Ames, Iowa	Lovington	Lamps	2789 Beacon Street, Ames Iowa

RULE 18: ORGANIZATIONS AND INSTITUTIONS

The names of banks and other financial institutions, clubs, colleges, hospitals, hotels, motels, museums, religious institutions, schools, unions, universities, and other organizations and institutions are indexed and filed according to the names on their letterheads. If "The" is used as the first word in these names, it is considered as the last unit. Radio and television station call letters are indexed as one unit.

Index Order of Units in Names

Name	Unit 1	Unit 2	Unit 3	Address
Bank of Atlanta	Bank	Of	Atlanta	
Bloomington Trust Co. Bloomington, Illinois	Bloomington	Trust	Co	Bloomington, Illinois
Bloomington Trust Co. Bloomington, Indiana	Bloomington	Trust	Co	Bloomington, Indiana
First Federal Savings Fairfield, California	First	Federal	Savings	Fairfield, California
First Federal Savings Fairfield, Illinois	First	Federal	Savings	Fairfield, Illinois
Newport High School Newport, Rhode Island	Newport	High	School	Newport, Rhode Island
Newport High School Newport, Washington	Newport	High	School	Newport, Washington
Petersburg Kiwanis Club	Petersburg	Kiwanis	Club	
United Methodist Church	United	Methodist	Church	
University of Idaho	University	of	Idaho	
Virginia State College	Virginia	State	College	
WLBC Radio Station	WLBC	Radio	Station	
Yancey Motel	Yancey	Motel		
York Medical Center	York	Medical	Center	
The York Museum	York	Museum	The	

RULE 19: FEDERAL GOVERNMENT OFFICES

The name of a federal government office is indexed by the name of the government unit (United States Government) followed by the most distinctive name of the office, bureau, department, etc., as written. Such words as "Office of," "Department of," "Bureau of," etc., if needed in the official name are added and considered separate indexing units. If "of" is not a part of the official name as written, it is not added.

Name	*Index Form of the Name*

Bureau of the Census
    U.S. Department of Commerce
	United States Government
	    Commerce Department of
	    Census Bureau of

Bureau of Indian Affairs
    U.S. Department of the Interior
	United States Government
	    Interior Department of
	    Indian Affairs Bureau of

RULE 20: OTHER GOVERNMENT OFFICES

The names of state, county, parish, city, town, township, and village governments/political divisions are indexed by their distinctive names. The words "State of," "County of," "City of," "Department of," etc., are added only if needed for clarity and if in the official name. They are considered separate indexing units.

Name	*Index Form of the Name*

Department of Public Safety
    State of California
	California State of
	    Public Safety Department of

Board of Health
    Cincinnati, Ohio
	Cincinnati
	    Health Board of

Cook County
    Tax Collector
	Cook County
	    Tax Collector

RULE 21: FOREIGN GOVERNMENTS

Foreign language names are translated into English for indexing, and the distinctive English name of the foreign country is considered first. This is followed by the balance of the formal name of the government, if needed and if in the official name. Branches, divisions, and departments follow in order by their distinctive names. Cross-reference the written foreign name to the English name, if necessary.

Index Order of Units in Names

Name	Unit 1	Unit 2	Unit 3	Unit 4	Unit 5
Republique Francaise Armee de l'Air	France	Air	Force		
Estados Unidos Mexicanos Secretaria de Industrio y Commercia	Mexico	Industry	and	Commerce	Secretary

Numerals—Cardinal (Arabic, Roman), Ordinal

Two types of numerals are used in business—cardinal and ordinal. Cardinal numerals are used in simple counting: one (1), two (2), three (3). They may be used as nouns (a count of ten), as adjectives (ten persons), or as pronouns (ten were lost). Ordinal numerals are used to show the order or succession in which such items as names, objects, and periods of time are considered (the seventh month, the fifth row of seats, the twentieth century). Arabic and Roman symbols distinguish cardinal numerals. Below, in Fig. 1, a table of numerals shows the usual range of numbers that an executive or secretary will need in business.

Fig. 1
Business communicators use cardinal and ordinal numbers.

TABLE OF NUMERALS

Cardinal Numbers

Name	Symbol Arabic	Roman*
zero *or* naught *or* cipher	0	
one	1	I
two	2	II
three	3	III
four	4	IV
five	5	V
six	6	VI
seven	7	VII

Ordinal Numbers

Name	Symbol
first	1st
second	2d *or* 2nd
third	3d *or* 3rd
fourth	4th
fifth	5th
sixth	6th
seventh	7th

eight	8	VIII	eighth		8th
nine	9	IX	ninth		9th
ten	10	X	tenth		10th
eleven	11	XI	eleventh		11th
twelve	12	XII	twelfth		12th
thirteen	13	XIII	thirteenth		13th
fourteen	14	XIV	fourteenth		14th
fifteen	15	XV	fifteenth		15th
sixteen	16	XVI	sixteenth		16th
seventeen	17	XVII	seventeenth		17th
eighteen	18	XVIII	eighteenth		18th
nineteen	19	XIX	nineteenth		19th
twenty	20	XX	twentieth		20th
twenty-one	21	XXI	twenty-first		21st
twenty-two	22	XXII	twenty-second		22d or 22nd
twenty-three	23	XXIII	twenty-third		23d or 23rd
twenty-four	24	XXIV	twenty-fourth		24th
twenty-five	25	XXV	twenty-fifth		25th
twenty-six	26	XXVI	twenty-sixth		26th
twenty-seven	27	XXVII	twenty-seventh		27th
twenty-eight	28	XXVIII	twenty-eighth		28th
twenty-nine	29	XXIX	twenty-ninth		29th
thirty	30	XXX	thirtieth		30th
thirty-one	31	XXXI	thirty-first		31st
thirty-two, *etc.*	32	XXXII	thirty-second, *etc.*		32d or 32nd
forty	40	XL	fortieth		40th
forty-one, *etc.*	41	XLI	forty-first		41st
fifty	50	L	fiftieth		50th
sixty	60	LX	sixtieth		60th
seventy	70	LXX	seventieth		70th
eighty	80	LXXX	eightieth		80th
ninety	90	XC	ninetieth		90th
one hundred	100	C	hundredth *or* one hundredth		100th
one hundred and one *or* one hundred one	101	CI	hundred and first *or* one hundred and first		101st
one hundred and two, *etc.*	102	CII	hundred and second, *etc.*		102d or 102nd
two hundred	200	CC	two hundredth		200th
three hundred	300	CCC	three hundredth		300th
four hundred	400	CD	four hundredth		400th
five hundred	500	D	five hundredth		500th
six hundred	600	DC	six hundredth		600th
seven hundred	700	DCC	seven hundredth		700th
eight hundred	800	DCCC	eight hundredth		800th
nine hundred	900	CM	nine hundredth		900th
one thousand *or* ten hundred, *etc.*	1,000	M	thousandth *or* one thousandth		1,000th
two thousand, *etc.*	2,000	MM	two thousandth, *etc.*		2,000th
five thousand	5,000	$\overline{V}$	ten thousandth		10,000th
ten thousand	10,000	$\overline{X}$	hundred thousandth *or* one hundred thousandth		100,000th
one hundred thousand	100,000	$\overline{C}$			
one million	1,000,000	$\overline{M}$	millionth *or* one millionth		1,000,000th

Repeating a Roman numeral increases its value. This is done up to three times.
Placing a numeral of lesser value before another decreases its value.

$$IX = 9 \quad (10 - 1)$$
$$XX = 20 \quad (10 + 10)$$
$$XXX = 30 \quad (10 + 10 + 10)$$
$$XL = 40 \quad (50 - 10)$$
$$CM = 900 \ (1,000 - 100)$$

Placing a numeral of lesser value after one of greater value increases the value.

$$XIII = 13 \qquad XIV = 14 \qquad XVI = 16$$

A dash over a numeral multiplies it by 1,000:

$$\overline{V} = 5,000 \qquad \overline{M} = 1,000,000$$

Communications Guide

This section contains a condensed guide for preparing business communications. Samples of letters typed in block style with open punctuation, modified block style with blocked paragraphs and open punctuation, modified block style with indented paragraphs and mixed punctuation, and simplified style are shown in Fig. 2. An example of a personal letter typed on personal letterhead appears in Fig. 3. Fig. 4 is

Fig. 2
Choosing the appropriate letter style can enhance the effectiveness of a business communication.

BLOCK STYLE, OPEN PUNCTUATION

MODIFIED BLOCK STYLE, BLOCKED PARAGRAPHS, OPEN PUNCTUATION

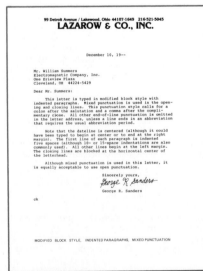

MODIFIED BLOCK STYLE, INDENTED PARAGRAPHS, MIXED PUNCTUATION

SIMPLIFIED STYLE

an interoffice memo. Fig. 5 describes the form and placement of envelope address parts. Fig. 6 summarizes the form and arrangement of business letter parts. A summary of forms of address appears in Fig. 7.

JWR

5902 AUDUBON ROAD
INDIANAPOLIS, IN 46220-8213

December 10, 19--

Dear Henry,

The letter address typed at the end of a letter removes
the business touch and tone and makes it more personal.

This letter style is also used for very formal letters,
such as letters to public officials and honored persons.
In addition, letters of appreciation or sympathy or
congratulations are typed in this form.

The reference initials are omitted. If the recipient
knows the writer well, it is not necessary that the
writer's name be typed as part of the signature.

Cordially,

John

Mr. Henry D. Ransom
302 Peachtree Street
Atlanta, CA 30308-4848

PERSONAL AND FORMAL STYLE
TYPED ON PERSONAL LETTERHEAD

Fig. 3
Some writers
personalize their
communications by
using personal
letterhead and by
omitting the letter
address.

INTEROFFICE MEMORANDUM   Donaldson enterprises, inc.

TO: New Members of the Stenographic Pool

FROM: Judith L. Reese, Correspondence Supervisor

DATE: December 10, 19--

SUBJECT: Interoffice Correspondence

An interoffice or interdepartment letterhead is used for messages
between offices or departments within a company. One advantage of
this form is that it can be set up quickly. This letter requires
settings only for margins. Titles (Mr., Mrs., Dr., etc.) the salutation, the complimentary close, and the formal signature are
usually omitted.

Triple-space between the last line of the heading and the first line
of the message. Short messages of no more than five lines may be
double-spaced. Longer messages should be single-spaced.

Reference initials should be included. When enclosures are sent,
the enclosure notation should appear below the reference initials.

sva

Fig. 4
Interoffice memos
are an important
form of written
communication
within a company.

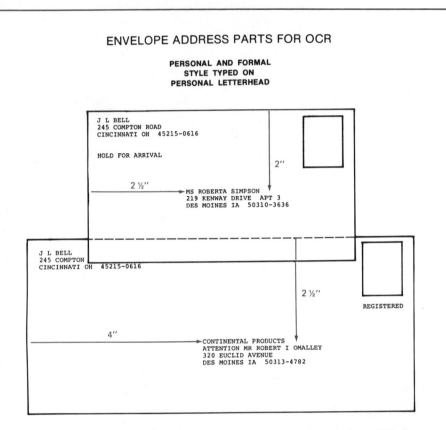

Post office optical character readers are programmed to scan a specific area; so the address must be completely within the read zone, blocked and single-spaced. Two-letter state abbreviations must be used. Apartment and room numbers should follow the street address on the same line. Acceptable placements for No. 10 and No. 6 3/4 envelopes are shown above. The U.S. Postal Service prefers the use of uppercase letters and no punctuation in envelope addresses.

Notations to Post Office

Type below the stamp at least three lines above the address in all caps. Underline if desired. Such notations include *HAND STAMP*, *REGISTERED*, and *SPECIAL DELIVERY*.

On-Receipt Notations

Type in all caps a triple space below the return address in three spaces from the envelope's left edge. Such notations include *HOLD FOR ARRIVAL, PLEASE FORWARD*, and *CONFIDENTIAL*.

Foreign Addresses

The last word in the address block should be the country name in all caps. If an address code is used, it should be placed on the left side of the last line or on the next to the last line.

Fig. 5
The form and placement of envelope parts must meet the specifications of optical character readers.

Fig. 6

FORM AND ARRANGEMENT OF BUSINESS LETTER PARTS

	Line Position	Horizontal Placement	Points to be Observed	Acceptable Forms
DATE	*Floating Dateline:* Typed from 12 to 20 lines from the top, depending on the letter's length. *Fixed Dateline:* Typed a double space below the last line in the letterhead.	*Block and Simplified Styles:* Even with the left margin. *Modified Block Style:* At center; to end flush with the right margin; or according to the letterhead.	1. Do not abbreviate names of months. 2. Unusual 2- or 3-line datelines are not commonly used. 3. Do not use st, d, nd, rd, or th following the day of the month. 4. Dates for government and military correspondence are often typed in this manner: 2 May 19--.	December 14, 19-- 2 May 19--
ADDRESS	*With Floating Dateline:* Typed on the fourth line below the date. *With Fixed Dateline:* Typed 3 to 9 lines below the date, depending on the letter's length. *Personal Letter:* Typed at the left margin 5 or 6 lines below the letter's closing line.	Single-spaced at the left margin. Use at least three lines for an address. Place business titles at the end of 1st line or at the beginning of the 2d line, whichever gives better balance. Break long company names at a logical point and indent the overrun 2 or 3 spaces.	1. Observe the addressee's letterhead style. 2. Do not abbreviate *Street* or *Avenue* unless it improves appearance. 3. Include the ZIP Code. 4. Spell out *In Care of;* do not use c/o. (This follows the name line.)	Miss Rose Bannaian Manager, Rupp Steel Co. 2913 Drexmore Avenue Dallas, TX 75206-8215 Mr. Russell H. Rupp 68 Devoe Avenue Dallas, TX 75206-8116
ATTENTION LINE	The preferred placement is a double space below the address and a double above the salutation.	Even with the left margin; centered; or indented at the paragraph point.	1. Do not abbreviate *Attention.* 2. Do not use the expression *Attention of.*	Attention Mr. R. H. Rupp Attention Purchasing Agent Attention Mr. L. Cox, Agent
SALUTATION	Typed a double space below the address or a double space below an attention line. (Interoffice correspondence and letters typed in the simplified style omit the salutation.)		1. Use *Gentlemen* for a company, a committee, a post office box, or organization made up entirely of men. 2. In addressing women, use *Ladies* or *Mesdames; Madam; or Miss, Mrs.,* or *Ms.* 3. Use *Ladies and Gentlemen* for a company, a committee, a post office box, or an organization made up of women and men. 4. The salute opening is growing in popularity. It omits the traditional salutation and uses the reader's name in the first sentence: Thank you, Mrs. Williams, for your recent film order.	Dear Mr. Rupp Gentlemen Dear Sir Dear Russell Dear Miss Mason Dear Ms. Willis Dear Mrs. Cox Ladies and Gentlemen

FORM AND ARRANGEMENT OF BUSINESS LETTER PARTS
(continued)

	Line Position	Horizontal Placement	Points to be Observed	Acceptable Forms
SUBJECT (OR REFERENCE) LINE	Typed a double space below the salutation. (Some letterheads indicate a position for the subject or a file number. Usually it is near the top of the letterhead.)	*Block Style:* Typed at the left margin. *Simplified Style:* Typed at the left margin in all caps a triple space below the last line in the address. The word "Subject" is omitted. *Modified Block Style:* Typed at the left margin, at paragraph point, or centered.	1. The word "Subject" is typed in all caps, with an initial cap only, or it may be omitted. If used, the word "Subject" is followed by a colon. 2. Do not abbreviate the word "Subject." Capitalize important words in the subject.	Subject: Pension Plan SUBJECT: Pension Plan Pension Plan Pension Plan PENSION PLAN Your File 987 Reference: File #586 Re: File 586
BODY	Typed a double space below the salutation or the subject line. *Simplified Style:* Typed a triple space below the subject line.	*Block Style:* 1st line of each paragraph typed at the left margin. *Modified Block Style:* 1st line of each paragraph typed at the left margin or indented (commonly 5 or 10 spaces.)	1. Keep right margin as even as possible. Avoid end-of-line hyphens. 2. Indent enumerations 5 spaces from both margins; double-space between items. (Do not indent enumerations if using simplified. If indented material is not enumerated, it may be indented 5 spaces.)	
SECONDARY HEADING	*Heading:* Begin approximately 1" from the top (about line 6). Type the addressee's name, the page no., and the date in a 3-line block at the left margin; or use a 1-line arrangement and type the addressee's name at the left margin, center the page no., and position the date to end at the right margin. *Body:* Begin a triple space below the heading, using the same margins used for the preceding page.		1. Type second and succeeding pages on plain paper. Do not use letterhead. 2. Do not begin a page with the last part of a hyphenated word. The last paragraph on a page should include at least 2 lines.	Mr. Jerry W. Robinson Page 2 (Current Date) Mr. Jerry W. Robinson 2 (Current Date)

FORM AND ARRANGEMENT OF
BUSINESS LETTER PARTS
(continued)

	Line Position	Horizontal Placement	Points to be Observed	Acceptable Forms
COMPLI-MENTARY CLOSE	Typed a double space below the last line of the body. (The complimentary close is omitted in the Simplified style and in interoffice correspondence.)	Typed at center. If a block style is used, the complimentary close may be typed at the left margin.	1. Longest closing line should not extend noticeably beyond the right margin. 2. Cap first word only. 3. Avoid contractions.	Very truly yours, Sincerely yours, Cordially, Cordially yours, Respectfully yours,
COM-PANY NAME	Typed flush with the complimentary close.	If used, typed a double space below the complimentary close.	1. Cap all letters. 2. Use addressee's letterhead as a guide for correct spelling and punctuation.	RAND CLOTHING, INC. JOHNSON SHOE CO.
SIGNA-TURE (NAME AND TITLE OF SIGNEE)	Typed 3 blank lines below complimentary close (or company name, if used.) If both the name and title are used, type them on the same line, or type the title on the next line, whichever gives better balance. *Simplified Style:* Typed in all caps at least 4 lines below body.	Typed flush with the complimentary close (or company name, if used.) *Simplified Style:* Typed at the left margin.	1. Cap important words in title. 2. If dictator's name appears in the letterhead, use only the title. 3. Do not use a courtesy title (Mr.) when typing a man's name unless the name can be masculine and feminine: Chris, Dana, Lynn. 4. If using AMS Simplified, the name and title of the signer are typed in all caps.	Harold A. Wenchstern Director of Personnel Brenda Ryan, Manager Purchasing Department Mr. Lynn B. Carter Mrs. Beverly Compton LOUIS K. COX-AGENT
I.D. NOTA-TION	Typed a double space below or on the last closing line.	Typed at the left margin.	1. Omit dictator's initials if his or her name appears in the closing lines.	jc jwr/jc JWRobinson/jc JWR/jc JWR:jc

FORM AND ARRANGEMENT OF BUSINESS LETTER PARTS
(continued)

	Line Position	Horizontal Placement	Points to be Observed	Acceptable Forms
ENC.	Typed a double space below the identification notation.	Typed at the left margin.	1. Although *Enc.* and *Encl.* are not preferred forms, they are commonly used to save time.	Enclosures 3 Encs. 2 Enclosures: Check Contract
POST-SCRIPT	Typed a double space below the identification notation or below last typed line.	Indent or block according to paragraph style used in body.	1. Initials of the writer may be typed below the postscript in place of a 2d signature. 2. The *P.S.* may be omitted, and the postscript may be written in the same form as paragraphs.	
PHOTO-COPY OR CARBON COPY NOTATION	Typed a double space below the identification notation or below the last typed line. (If this notation is not to appear on the original, type at the top of the carbon or photo copies.)	Typed at the left margin. (If typed on a copy, it may be centered or flush left.)	1. For carbon copy to, type *cc* or *Copy.* 2. For blind copy to, type *bc,* if notation is typed on copies only. 3. For photocopy to, type *pc.*	cc: pc: bc: copy: cc: Mr. H. R. King Miss K. Neilen Copy to Mr. H. R. King
MAILING NOTA-TION	Typed midway between date and first line of the address or 2 lines below the last typed line.	Typed at the left margin.	1. Type in all caps. 2. May be typed on copies only.	SPECIAL DELIVERY REGISTERED MAIL CERTIFIED MAIL
SEP. MAILING NOTATION	Typed a double space below the last typed line.	Typed at the left margin.	1. Used to indicate the method of transportation and the no. of envelopes or packages sent.	Separate Mail-Express Separate Mail-2

Fig. 7

CORRECT FORMS OF ADDRESS AND REFERENCE

Person and Address (Envelope and Letter)	Salutation	Complimentary Close	In Referring to the Person: Informal Introduction	In Speaking to the Person
U.S. PRESIDENT The President The White House Washington, D.C. 20500	Dear President (Surname) Mr. President Dear Mr. President Dear Madam President	Respectfully yours Very truly yours	The President Mr. (Surname) Mrs. (Surname)	Mr. President Sir Madam President Madam
SPOUSE, U.S. PRESIDENT Mrs., Ms., or Mr. (Last name only) The White House Washington, D.C. 20500	Dear Mrs. (Last name only) Dear Mr. (Last name only) Dear Ms. (Last name only)	Respectfully yours	Mrs. (Last name only) Mr. (Last name only) Ms. (Last name only)	Mrs. or Ms. (Last name only) Mr. (Last name only)
U.S. VICE-PRESIDENT The Vice-President United States Senate Washington, D.C. 20510	Dear Vice-President (Surname) Dear Mr. or Madam Vice-President Mr. or Madam Vice-President	Respectfully yours Very truly yours	The Vice-President Mr. or Madam (Surname)	Mr. or Madam Vice-President Mr. (Surname)
U.S. CHIEF JUSTICE The Chief Justice The Supreme Court Washington, D.C. 20543	Mr. Chief Justice Dear Mr. Chief Justice	Respectfully yours Very truly yours	The Chief Justice	Mr. Chief Justice
U.S. ASSOCIATE JUSTICE Justice (Full Name) The Supreme Court Washington, D.C. 20543	Mr. Justice Madam Justice Dear Mr. Justice Dear Madam Justice Dear Justice (Surname)	Very truly yours Sincerely yours	Mr. or Madam Justice (Surname)	Mr. or Madam Justice Mr. or Madam Justice (Surname)
CABINET OFFICER The Honorable (Full Name) Secretary of (Office) Washington, D.C. 20520 The Secretary of (Office) Washington, D.C. 20520	Dear Mr. Secretary Dear Madam Secretary Dear Secretary (Surname)	Very truly yours Sincerely yours	The Secretary of . . ., Mr., Mrs., Miss, or Ms. (Surname) The Secretary Mr., Mrs., Miss, or Ms. (Surname)	Mr. Secretary Madam Secretary Mr., Mrs., Miss, or Ms. (Surname)

CORRECT FORMS OF ADDRESS AND REFERENCE
(continued)

Person and Address (Envelope and Letter)	Salutation	Complimentary Close	In Referring to the Person: Informal Introduction	In Speaking to the Person
SPEAKER OF THE HOUSE OF REPRESENTATIVES				
The Honorable (Full Name) Speaker of the House of Representatives Washington, DC 20515	Dear Mr. or Madam (Surname) Mr. Speaker Madam Speaker Dear Madam Speaker	Very truly yours Sincerely yours	The Speaker, Mr., Mrs., Miss, or Ms. (Surname) Mr., Mrs., Miss or Ms. (Surname)	Mr. Speaker Madam Speaker Mr., Mrs., Miss, or Ms. (Surname)
U.S. SENATOR, SENATOR-ELECT				
The Honorable (Full name) United States Senate Washington, DC 20510	Dear Senator (Surname) Dear Mr., Mrs., Miss, or Ms. (Surname)	Very truly yours Sincerely yours	Senator (Surname)	Senator (Surname) Mr., Mrs., Miss, or Ms. (Surname)
The Honorable (Full name), Senator-elect				
U.S. REPRESENTATIVE				
The Honorable (Full name) House of Representatives Washington, DC 20515	Dear Representative (Surname) Dear Mr., Mrs., Miss, or Ms. (Surname)	Very truly yours Sincerely yours	Representative (Surname) Mr., Mrs., Miss, or Ms. (Surname)	Mr., Mrs., Miss, or Ms. (Surname)
Representative (Full name) House of Representatives Washington, DC 20515				
U.S. GOVERNMENT OFFICIAL				
The Honorable (Full name) Director of Bureau of the Budget Washington, DC 20503	Dear Mr., Mrs., Miss, or Ms. (Surname)	Very truly yours Sincerely yours	Mr., Mrs., Miss, or Ms. (Surname)	Mr., Mrs., Miss, or Ms. (Surname)
Librarian of Congress Washington, DC 20540				

CORRECT FORMS OF ADDRESS AND REFERENCE
(continued)

Person and Address (Envelope and Letter)	Salutation	Complimentary Close	In Referring to the Person: Informal Introduction	In Speaking to the Person
AMERICAN AMBASSADOR The Honorable (Full name) American Ambassador Paris, France	Dear Mr. Ambassador Dear Madam Ambassador Dear Ambassador (Surname)	Very truly yours Sincerely yours	The American Ambassador The Ambassador Mr., Mrs., Miss, or Ms. (Surname) Madam Ambassador	Mr., Mrs., Miss, or Ms. Ambassador Madam Ambassador Mr., Mrs., Miss, or Ms. (Surname)
AMERICAN MINISTER TO ANOTHER COUNTRY The Honorable (Full name) American Minister Ottawa, Canada	Dear Mr., Mrs., Miss, or Ms. Minister Dear Minister (Surname) Dear Madam Minister	Very truly yours Sincerely yours	The American Minister, Mr., Mrs., Miss, or Ms. (Surname)† The Minister; Mr., Mrs., Miss, or Ms. (Surname)	Mr., Mrs., Miss, or Ms. Minister Mr., Mrs., Miss, or Ms. (Surname) Madam Minister
U.S. REPRESENTATIVE TO THE UNITED NATIONS The Honorable (Full name) United States Representative to the United Nations New York, New York 10017	Dear Mr., Mrs., Miss, or Ms. (Surname) **With Ambassadorial Rank:** Dear Ambassador (Surname)	Very truly yours Sincerely yours	Mr., Mrs., Miss, or Ms. (Surname) Madam Ambassador Mr. Ambassador	Mr., Mrs., Miss, or Ms. (Surname) Madam Ambassador Mr. Ambassador
FOREIGN AMBASSADOR IN U.S. His/Her Excellency (Full name) The Ambassador of France Washington, DC 20516	Excellency Dear Mr. Ambassador Dear Madam Ambassador Dear Ambassador (Surname)	Respectfully yours Sincerely yours Very truly yours	The Ambassador of . . ., Mr., or Madam (Surname) The Ambassador Mr., or Madam (Surname)	Mr. Ambassador Madam Ambassador Mr., Mrs., Miss, or Ms. (Surname)
FOREIGN MINISTER IN U.S. The Honorable (Full name) Minister of Italy Washington, DC 20516	Dear Mr. Minister Dear Madam Minister Dear Minister (Surname)	Respectfully yours Sincerely yours Very truly yours	The Minister of . . ., Mr. or Madam (Surname) The Minister	Mr. Minister Madam Minister Mr., Mrs., Miss, or Ms. (Surname)

†In presenting or referring to American Ambassadors and Ministers in any Latin American country, say "Ambassador of the United States" or "Minister of the United States."

CORRECT FORMS OF ADDRESS AND REFERENCE
(continued)

Person and Address (Envelope and Letter)	Salutation	Complimentary Close	In Referring to the Person: Informal Introduction	In Speaking to the Person
AMERICAN CONSUL (Full name), Esq. The American Consul United States Embassy (Foreign City, Country)	Dear Mr., Mrs., Miss, or Ms. (Surname)	Very truly yours Sincerely yours	Mr., Mrs., or Ms. (Surname)	Mr., Mrs., Miss, or Ms. (Surname)
FOREIGN CONSUL (Full name), Esq. The French Consul (American City, State)	Dear Mr. (Surname) Dear Madam (Surname)	Very truly yours Sincerely yours	Mr. (Surname) Madam (Surname)	Mr. (Surname) Madam (Surname)
GOVERNOR OF A STATE His/Her Excellency, the Governor of (State) or The Honorable (Full name), Governor of (State) (Capital City, State)	Dear Governor Dear Governor (Surname)	Respectfully yours Very truly yours Sincerely yours	Governor (Surname) The Governor The Governor of (State)	Governor (Surname) Governor
MEMBER, STATE LEGISLATURE The Honorable (Full name) The State Senate or The House of Representatives (Capital City, State)	Dear Senator or Representative (Surname) Dear Mr., Mrs., Miss, or Ms. (Surname)	Very truly yours Sincerely yours	Mr., Mrs., Miss, or Ms. (Surname) Senator (Surname) Representative (Surname)	Mr., Mrs., Miss, or Ms. (Surname) Senator (Surname) Representative (Surname)
MAYOR OF A CITY The Honorable (Full name) Mayor of the City of . . . (City, State)	Dear Mayor (Surname)	Very truly yours Sincerely yours	Mayor (Surname) The Mayor	Mayor (Surname) Mr. Mayor Madam Mayor
JUDGE OF A COURT The Honorable (Full name) Judge of the . . . Court (Local Address)	Dear Judge (Surname)	Very truly yours Sincerely yours	Judge (Surname)	Judge (Surname)

CORRECT FORMS OF ADDRESS AND REFERENCE
(continued)

Person and Address (Envelope and Letter)	Salutation	Complimentary Close	In Referring to the Person: Informal Introduction	In Speaking to the Person
MILITARY PERSONNEL (Rank) (Full name) Post or Name of Ship City, State	Dear (Rank) (Surname)	Very truly yours Sincerely yours	(Rank) (Surname)	(Rank) (Surname)
CLERGY (PROTESTANT) The Reverend (Full name), D.D. or The Reverend (Full name) Parsonage Address City, State	Dear Mr., Mrs., Miss, or Ms. (Surname) Dear Dr. (Surname) Dear Reverend (Surname)	Respectfully yours Sincerely yours Yours faithfully	The Reverend Doctor (Surname) Doctor (Surname) The Reverend (Surname) Mr., Mrs., Miss, or Ms. (Surname)	Dr. (Surname) Sir Mr., Mrs., Miss, or Ms. (Surname)
RABBI (JEWISH FAITH) Rabbi (Full name) or Rabbi (Full name), D.D. Local Address	Sir My dear Rabbi (Surname) My dear Rabbi	Respectfully yours Sincerely yours Yours faithfully	Dr. (Surname) Rabbi (Surname)	Dr. (Surname) Rabbi (Surname)
PRIEST (ROMAN CATHOLIC) The Reverend (Full name) (followed by comma and initials of order) Local Address	Reverend Father Dear Father (Surname)	Sincerely yours Respectfully yours Yours faithfully	Dr. (Surname) Father (Surname)	Dr. (Surname) Father (Surname)
SISTER (ROMAN CATHOLIC) Sister (Full name) (followed by comma and initials of order) Local Address	Dear Sister Dear Sister (Religious name)	Sincerely yours Respectfully yours Yours faithfully	Sister (Religious name) Sister	Sister (Religious name) Sister
PRESIDENT (COLLEGE OR UNIVERSITY) Dr. (Surname) or President (Surname), (Degree) Name of University City, State	Dear President (Surname) Dear Dr. (Surname)	Very truly yours Sincerely yours	Dr. (Surname)	Dr. (Surname)

Secretarial Typing Aids

Sometimes it is necessary for secretaries to use standard typewriters. The typing techniques that are discussed in the following paragraphs are proven time savers for secretaries who use standard typewriters.

CORRECTIONS

Corrections that defy detection are evidence of a top-notch secretary. Good corrections are an absolute necessity for quality final documents. In fact, if any correction is evident in an otherwise excellent document, the typescript is not quality level.

Careful Erasing

A neat erasure results from the skillful use of erasing tools. Erasing tools are easily obtained, but erasing skill is acquired by patience and practice. *Erasers and shields* are available in a variety of sizes, forms, textures, and materials. For corrections, you need two kinds of erasers—a soft eraser to remove surface ink and carbon smears and a more abrasive eraser to remove imbedded ink. Try various brands and shapes of erasers until you find those that you can use most effectively.

Unless you use an electric eraser, use a flat metal or plastic shield with letter height open spaces to confine the erasing. Such a shield can be used for erasures on papers in or out of the typewriter. The shield permits erasing to the extreme edge of the error without eradicating correctly typed adjacent letters.

A pressure proof shield of metal or card stock is used to protect the carbon copies under the page being erased. A curved metal shield that hugs the cylinder gives the best protection and is easy to find among papers on the desk.

To fade out an erasure, rub a whitening agent into the paper before typing the correction. A piece of chalk, an aspirin, or a commercial *cover-up stick* can be used.

Another cover-up method is to put a chalk or chemically coated strip of paper, coated side down, over the error and retype the *error* so that some of the chalk transfers and covers it. Then go back and type the correction. A special type of cover-up paper is available for use on carbon copies.

Instead of erasing, a white correction fluid marketed under such trade names as Snopake and Liquid Paper may be painted over the error.[2] If this is done carefully and if the fluid matches the paper in whiteness, acceptable results can be achieved.

White, self-adhesive correction tape is available in one-line, two-line, and three-line widths. The required length of tape is torn off and placed over the error. Corrections are typed on top of the tape. Since the correction is obvious, use this method only on copy where appearance is not important, such as interoffice communications, dummy layouts, and material that is to be reproduced by the photographic or offset process. (See Chapter 10 for a description of these processes.)

Self-correcting devices consist of a separate correction ribbon attached to the typewriter or provided in a separate ribbon cartridge. When an error is made, the secretary shifts to the correction mode. Errors are removed by typing over the error with the second ribbon. This ribbon contains a chemical that interacts with the ink on the paper and literally fades or lifts off the error. On some machines this is done by depressing a special key; on others, it involves shifting the ribbon control or inserting a special correction cartridge. The secretary then backspaces, strikes over the error, and types the correction.

Perfect Positioning for Corrections

It is easy to reposition the element for an immediate correction, unless the error occurs at the very bottom of the page. In that case, do not try to correct it at once, for the sheets almost always slip out of line during erasing and repositioning. Instead finish typing the page, remove the pack from the typewriter, and make the correction on each copy separately.

To save time in repositioning, learn the exact relationship of your typing line to your aligning scale. To acquire speed in realigning, watch intently as you type a line of words and notice the exact distance *at the typing point* between the bottom of the typed line and the aligning scale. It is the barest fraction of an inch, but memorizing it visually helps you to realign more quickly and accurately.

You can find the approximate letter position more quickly by keeping the paper guide set at one spot and using it squarely each time

---

[2]Send a sample of your office stationery to the manufacturer of the correction fluid, and the manufacturer will prepare fluid that matches your letterhead.

you insert sheets in the typewriter. On a reinserted sheet move the carriage or element to the first letter of the correction. The typing point will be in almost exact position. A quick position test can be made by shifting the ribbon mode to stencil and striking the correct letter.

Tests for Exact Positioning. To position a reinserted page for a correction, use the paper release lever to move the page sideways and the variable line spacer to roll it up or down. Test the exactness of position by the following procedure:

1. Cover the document with a transparent second sheet. Roll the two sheets into the typewriter to the correction line.
2. Test for exactness of position by typing over a letter near the erased error. Adjust the sheets and type over another letter until the copy is in exact position.
3. Roll the sheets forward a couple of inches. Fold back the transparent sheet, crease it all the way across, and tear it off. Roll the page into line position, set the carriage or element at the typing point, and type the correction.

    This method wastes paper but assures exact positioning of corrections and is the cleanest way of correcting reinserted carbon copies. Proofreading a document before it is removed from the typewriter, however, usually makes repositioning unnecessary.

Squeezing and Spreading. To insert a word containing one letter more than the error on a typewriter, proceed as follows after an erasure has been made:

1. Move the print-point indicator to the first space where the correction begins.
2. Manually push the element carrier back one half-space and hold while striking the correct key.
3. Repeat the process until the correction is completed.

This procedure will leave one half-space before and after the corrected word.

To insert a word containing one letter fewer than the error:

1. Move the print-point indicator to the space occupied (before the erasure) by the second letter of the error.
2. Manually push the element carrier back one half-space and hold while striking the correct key.

3. Repeat the process until the correction is completed.
    This procedure will leave 1½ spaces before and after the corrected word.

Inserting a Space or Hyphen. To insert a space or a hyphen between two words, erase the two letters that must be separated. Retype the first letter by moving the print-point indicator to the space where the first letter was erased. Manually push the element carrier back one half-space and hold while striking the first letter. Retype the second letter by moving the print-point indicator to the space beyond the second erasure. Manually push the element carrier back one half-space and hold while striking the second letter. Center a hyphen in the space available by manually pushing the element carrier to the correct position and holding it while striking the hyphen. In this manner you can make a near perfect correction.

Inserting a Thin Letter in a Word. In some cases you can insert an *l*, an *i*, or a *t* within a typed word by fractional spacing. Experiment with your typewriter to determine when you can use this method of correcting. Keep in mind that the correction will be discernible.

Making an Insertion between Lines. When time is of the essence, you may have to make a neat insertion between lines. Use the underline and diagonal keys to indicate the point of insertion. Find the midpoint between the lines for the line of typing. In single-spaced copy type the correction to the right of the diagonal; in double-spaced copy center it over the upper end of the diagonal.

Applying Printed Letters over Errors

Sheets of letters, like the one shown in Fig. 8, are available in pica, elite, and letter gothic style. They can be positioned over an error after the page has been removed from the typewriter. To correct an error, place the sheet of letters over the document, aligning the desired or correct letter over the error. Press the sheet with a pencil or pen so that the correct letter covers the error without retyping. Sheets should be ordered in a type style matching that of your typewriter. They are available three sheets to the package (5½″ × 8″) for office use.

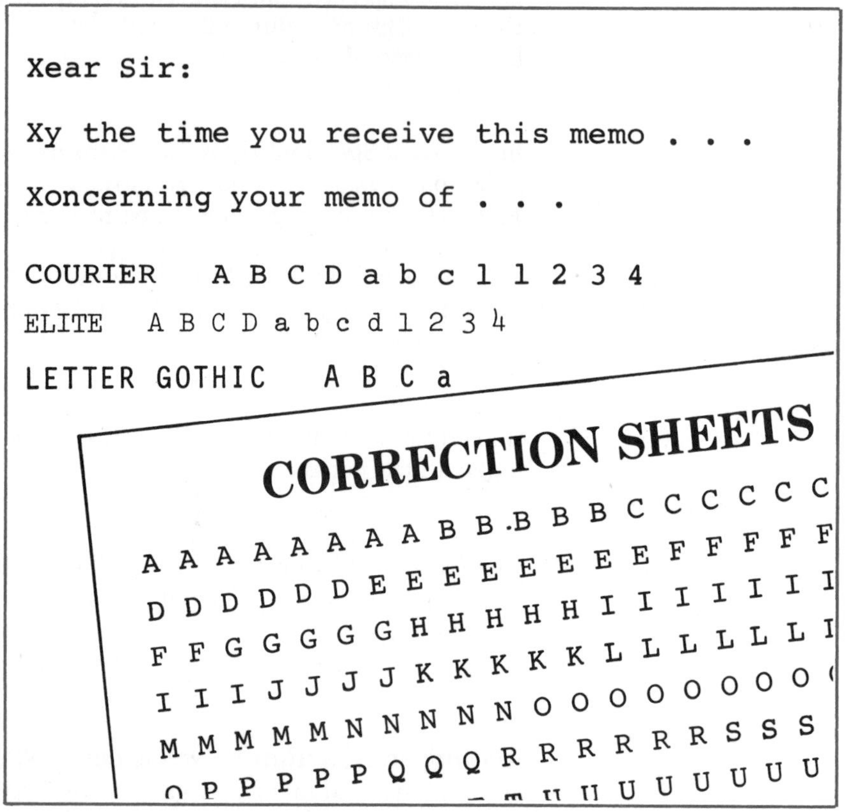

Xear Sir:

Xy the time you receive this memo . . .

Xoncerning your memo of . . .

COURIER   A B C D a b c l l 2 3 4

ELITE   A B C D a b c d l 2 3 4

LETTER GOTHIC   A B C a

CORRECTION SHEETS

A A A A A A A B B B B B B C C C C C
D D D D D E E E E E E E F F F F F
F F G G G G G H H H H I I I I I I I
I I I J J J K K K K K L L L L L L
M M M M M N N N N O O O O O O O O
O P P P P P Q Q Q R R R R R R S S S
O P P P P P Q Q Q   T U U U U U U U U

Fig. 8
Correction sheets
are available in
pica, elite, and
letter gothic styles
to match your
typewriter type.

Correcting a Topbound Document

Topbound documents can be corrected without unbinding. Feed a blank sheet of paper into the machine in the usual way until the paper shows about a two-inch top margin. Insert the bottom of the sheet to be corrected between the top edge of the blank paper and the cylinder. Roll the cylinder back to the line to be corrected, position the element for the correction, and type the correction.

To reinforce paper
to go into a loose-
leaf notebook,
attach a strip of
tape along the back
edge of the paper
where the holes
will be. Punch
holes through both
tape and paper.

Matched Typing

To make a correction in carbon on a reinserted page of carbon copy, staple together several slips of paper and a small piece of carbon paper, carbon side out. A good size is 1 by $2\frac{1}{2}$ inches. After positioning the carriage or element for the first letter of the correction, put this pad behind the ribbon with the carbon side against the paper. Type in the correction lightly.

Certain strikeovers in certain typewriter type styles are likely to be almost imperceptible. Experiment in order to learn which letters match and blend. They may include: *d* over *c; h* over *n; o* over *c; E* over *F;* and semicolons, colons, or question marks over periods.

SPECIAL TYPEWRITER CHARACTERS

A number of special characters can be constructed on standard typewriters. Fig. 9 shows a partial list of these characters.

Fig. 9
Special typewriter characters can be constructed on a standard typewriter.

SPECIAL TYPEWRITER CHARACTERS

Brackets	[ ]	*Left Bracket.* Type underline, backspace, strike diagonal, turn platen back one line space, and type underline. *Right Bracket.* Type underline, diagonal, backspace, turn platen back one line space, and type underline.
Degree sign	12°	Turn platen back slightly; strike lowercase *o.*
Ditto mark	"	Turn platen forward slightly; strike the quotation mark.
Division sign	÷	Type hyphen, backspace, and strike the colon.
Equal sign	=	Type hyphen, backspace, turn platen forward a bit and strike the hyphen.
Paragraph mark	¶	Type capital *P,* backspace, and strike 1.
Plus sign	+	Type hyphen, backspace, and strike diagonal.
Pound sterling	£	Type *f,* backspace, strike *t.*

State Abbreviations

Name	Standard Abbreviation	Two-Letter Abbreviation	Capital
Alabama	Ala.	AL	Montgomery
Alaska	Alaska	AK	Juneau
Arizona	Ariz.	AZ	Phoenix
Arkansas	Ark.	AR	Little Rock
California	Calif.	CA	Sacramento
Colorado	Colo.	CO	Denver
Connecticut	Conn.	CT	Hartford
Delaware	Del.	DE	Dover
District of Columbia	D.C.	DC	Washington
Florida	Fla.	FL	Tallahassee
Georgia	Ga.	GA	Atlanta
Hawaii	Hawaii	HI	Honolulu
Idaho	Idaho	ID	Boise
Illinois	Ill.	IL	Springfield
Indiana	Ind.	IN	Indianapolis
Iowa	Iowa	IA	Des Moines
Kansas	Kans.	KS	Topeka
Kentucky	Ky.	KY	Frankfort
Louisiana	La.	LA	Baton Rouge
Maine	Maine	ME	Augusta
Maryland	Md.	MD	Annapolis
Massachusetts	Mass.	MA	Boston
Michigan	Mich.	MI	Lansing
Minnesota	Minn.	MN	St. Paul
Mississippi	Miss.	MS	Jackson
Missouri	Mo.	MO	Jefferson City
Montana	Mont.	MT	Helena
Nebraska	Nebr.	NE	Lincoln
Nevada	Nev.	NV	Carson City
New Hampshire	N.H.	NH	Concord
New Jersey	N.J.	NJ	Trenton
New Mexico	N.Mex.	NM	Santa Fe
New York	N.Y.	NY	Albany
North Carolina	N.C.	NC	Raleigh
North Dakota	N.Dak.	ND	Bismarck
Ohio	Ohio	OH	Columbus
Oklahoma	Okla.	OK	Oklahoma City
Oregon	Oreg.	OR	Salem
Pennsylvania	Pa.	PA	Harrisburg
Rhode Island	R.I.	RI	Providence

South Carolina	S.C.	SC	Columbia
South Dakota	S.Dak.	SD	Pierre
Tennessee	Tenn.	TN	Nashville
Texas	Tex.	TX	Austin
Utah	Utah	UT	Salt Lake City
Vermont	Vt.	VT	Montpelier
Virginia	Va.	VA	Richmond
Washington	Wash.	WA	Olympia
West Virginia	W. Va.	WV	Charleston
Wisconsin	Wis.	WI	Madison
Wyoming	Wyo.	WY	Cheyenne

Footnote and Bibliography Entries

Footnote entries are illustrated below. Notice that Footnote 3, *Ibid. (ibidem, the same)*, is used to refer to a single work cited in the note immediately preceding. It may or may not be italicized. *Op. cit. (opere citato, in the work cited)* and *loc. cit. (loco citato, in the place cited)* have, for convenience, been replaced by a short form. For example:

Op. cit (different page)

[12]Heinze, *Managerial Statistics*, p. 15.

Loc. cit (same page)

[13]Heinze, *Managerial Statistics*, p. 9.

One author ⟶   [1]David G. Heinze, *Fundamentals of Managerial Statistics* (Cincinnati: South-Western Publishing Co., 1980), p. 9.

Two authors ⟶   [2]James L. Pappas and Mark Hirshey, *Fundamentals of Managerial Economics* (Hinsdale, Illinois: The Dryden Press, 1984), p. 116.

Ibid. ⟶   [3]*Ibid.*, pp. 158-160.

Three authors ⟶   [4]Robert T. Davis, Harper W. Boyd, Jr., and Frederick E. Webster, Jr., *Marketing Management Casebook* (4th ed.; Homewood, Illinois: Irwin, 1984), p. 306.

Four or more authors ➤   [5]Dale Keiger *et al.*, *A Guide to International Trade* (4th ed.; New York: Macauley Publishing Co., 1982), pp. 115-117.

Author and editor ⟶   [6]Douglas S. Sherwin, "The Meaning of Control," *Readings in Management*, edited by Max D. Richards (6th ed.; Cincinnati: South-Western Publishing Co., 1982), p. 255.

Editor ⟶   [7]Max D. Richards (ed.), *Readings in Management* (6th ed.; Cincinnati: South-Western Publishing Co., 1982), p. 255.

Magazine article
No author ⟶   [8]"CPA Firms Use Business Graphics," *InfoSystems* (November, 1981), p. 71.

Newspaper article ⟶   [9]Alan L. Otten, "Japanese Firms Press European Ventures to Help Profits and Deter Protectionism," *The Wall Street Journal*, April 16, 1982, p. 44.

Unpublished material ➤   [10]From the report by the County of Henrico, Virginia Schools on career decisions, Richmond, February 3, 1982.

Government
publication ⟶   [11]U.S. Department of Commerce, Bureau of Economic Affairs, *Economic Indicators*, (Washington: U.S. Government Printing Office, December, 1985), p. 15.

Bibliography entries are alphabetized as illustrated below. Notice the difference between footnote construction and bibliography construction. Periods rather than commas are used between items in a bibliography. Footnotes use paragraph indentations; bibliographies use hanging indentations. Footnotes are listed by number; bibliographies are listed alphabetically.

Unpublished material ➤ County of Henrico, Virginia Schools. A report on career decisions, Richmond, February 3, 1982.

Magazine article ➤ "CPA Firms Use Business Graphics." *Info-Systems* (November, 1981), p. 71.

Three authors ➤ Davis, Robert T., Harper W. Boyd, Jr., and Frederick E. Webster, Jr. *Marketing Management Casebook*, 4th ed. Homewood Illinois: Irwin, 1984.

One author ➤ Heinze, David G. *Fundamentals of Managerial Statistics*. Cincinnati: South-Western Publishing Co., 1980.

Four or more authors ➤ Keiger, Dale, *et al. A Guide to International Trade*, 4th ed. New York: Macauley Publishing Co., 1982.

Newspaper article ➤ Otten, Alan L. "Japanese Firms Press European Ventures to Help Profits and Deter Protectionism." *The Wall Street Journal*, April 16, 1982, p. 44.

Two authors ➤ Pappas, James L. and Mark Hirshey. *Fundamentals of Managerial Economics*. Hinsdale, Illinois: The Dryden Press, 1984.

Editor ➤ Richards, Max D. (ed.). *Readings in Management*, 6th ed. Cincinnati: South-Western Publishing Co., 1982.

Author and editor ➤ Sherwin, Douglas S. "The Meaning of Control." *Readings in Management*, 6th ed., edited by Max D. Richards. Cincinnati: South-Western Publishing Co., 1982.

Government agency ➤ U. S. Department of Commerce, Bureau of Economic Affairs. *Economic Indicators*. Washington: U.S. Government Printing Office, December, 1985.

Proofreaders' Marks

INSERT MARKS FOR PUNCTUATION

⩗	Apostrophe
[/]	Brackets
: ⊙	Colon
⌃ ˀ/	Comma
˟˟˟/	Ellipsis
!/	Exclamation point
-/	Hyphen
⌃ ⌃	Inferior figure
· · ·/	Leaders
(/)	Parentheses
⊙	Period
?/	Question mark
⩍ ⩍	Quotation mark
; ⑤	Semicolon
⩔ ⩔	Superior figure

OTHER MARKS

‖	Align type; set flush
bf	<u>Boldface</u> type
× ⓧ	Broken letter
≡ Cap	Capitalize
C+sc	Capitals and small capitals
ℐ	Delete
ℐ	Delete and close up
⌃	Insert (caret)
ital	<u>Italic</u>, change to
Bf ital	<u>Italic boldface</u>
stet	Let type stand
lc	Lower ¢ase type

⊔	Move down; lower
⊓	Move up; raise
⊏	Move to left
⊐	Move to right
¶	Paragraph
no ¶ ⊏	No new paragraph
out s.c.	Out; omit; see copy
⟲	Reverse; upside down
rom	Roman, change to
⟳	Run in material
run in	Run <u>in material</u> on same line
#	Space, add (horizontal)
>	Space, add (vertical)
◡	Space, close up (horizontal)
<	Space, close up (vertical)
(sp)	Spell out
tr ∩	Transpose
(?) (?)	Verify or supply information
wf	Wrong font

All marks should be made in⌃the margin on the line in which the error occurs; if more⌃ than one correction occurs in one line, they should appear in their ⌃order separated by a slanting line.

Errors should not be blotted out.

Weights and Measures with Metric Equivalents

There are two commonly used methods of measurement. One, the *English*, or *imperial*, system, is used in the United States; the other is the *metric* system, which is used in most parts of the world. In the English system, units used for measuring lengths are inches, feet, yards, and miles. The basic unit in the metric system for these measurements is the meter. The metric system is a decimal system, which means that you change from one measurement to another by merely moving a decimal point. For example: 10 decimeters = 1 meter. By moving the decimal point one place to the left, you have converted decimeters into meters.

LENGTHS

English System	*Metric System*	*Equivalencies*
12 inches = 1 foot	10 millimeters = 1 centimeter	1 inch = 2.54 centimeters
3 feet = 1 yard	10 centimeters = 1 decimeter	1 foot = 30.48 centimeters
5,280 feet = 1 mile	10 decimeters = 1 meter	39.37 inches = 1 meter
	10 meters = 1 dekameter	1 mile = 1.609 kilometers
	10 dekameters = 1 hectometer	
	10 hectometers = 1 kilometer	

WEIGHTS

English System	*Metric System*	*Equivalencies*
16 ounces = 1 pound	10 milligrams = 1 centigram	1 ounce = 28.35 grams
100 pounds = 1 hundredweight	10 centigrams = 1 decigram	1 pound = 453.6 grams
2,000 pounds = 1 ton	10 decigrams = 1 gram	1 ton = 907.2 kilograms
	10 grams = 1 dekagram	
	10 dekagrams = 1 hectogram	
	10 hectograms = 1 kilogram	

DRY AND LIQUID MEASURES

English System

Dry Measure
2 pints = 1 quart
8 quarts = 1 peck
4 pecks = 1 bushel

Liquid Measure
2 pints = 1 quart
4 quarts = 1 gallon

Metric System

Dry and Liquid Measure
10 milliliters = 1 centiliter
10 centiliters = 1 deciliter
10 deciliters = 1 liter
10 liters = 1 dekaliter
10 dekaliters = 1 hectoliter
10 hectoliters = 1 kiloliter

Equivalencies

Dry Measure
1 pint = 0.550 liters
1 quart = 1.101 liters
1 peck = 8.809 liters
1 bushel = 35.238 liters

Liquid Measure
1 pint = 0.473 liters
1 quart = 0.946 liters
1 gallon = 3.785 liters

TEMPERATURE CONVERSION

From Celsius to Fahrenheit
$F = 9/5 \; C + 32$

From Fahrenheit to Celsius
$C = 5/5 \; (F - 32)$

Practical Business Mathematics

Every business person uses percentages in one form or other for calculating interest, costs, commissions, discounts, taxes, and the like. The following pages contain the principles of determining percentages and should be helpful to the executive or secretary who needs a quick memory refresher.

PERCENTAGE

Percent is an abbreviation for the Latin term *per centum*, meaning for each hundred. Six percent (6%) means 6 parts of 100 or 6/100. The symbol (%) is also used to denote percent. Since *percent* means a part of 100, any fraction whose denominator is 100 may be written as a percentage or as a fraction. For example:

$$25\% = {}^{25}/_{100} = {}^1/_4 \qquad 50\% = {}^{50}/_{100} = {}^1/_2$$

$$75\% = {}^{75}/_{100} = {}^3/_4 \qquad 33{}^1/_3\% = \frac{33\,1/3}{100} = {}^1/_3$$

$$66{}^2/_3\% = \frac{66\,2/3}{100} = {}^2/_3 \qquad 5\% = {}^5/_{100} = {}^1/_{20}$$

$$2{}^1/_2\% = \frac{2\,1/2}{100} = {}^1/_{40} \qquad 12{}^1/_2\% = \frac{12\,1/2}{100} = {}^1/_8$$

EXPRESSING DECIMALS AS PERCENTAGES

Write the decimal as hundredths (two places) and the number of hundredths is the percent. For example:

$$.4 = .40 = {}^{40}/_{100} = 40\% \qquad .33{}^1/_3 = \frac{33\,1/3}{100} = 33{}^1/_3\%$$

$$.8 = .80 = {}^{80}/_{100} = 80\% \qquad .50 = {}^{50}/_{100} = 50\%$$

$$.25 = {}^{25}/_{100} = 25\% \qquad .87{}^1/_2 = \frac{87\,1/2}{100} = 87{}^1/_2\%$$

If the decimal has more than two decimal places, the figures after the second one are written as a fraction of a percent. For example:

$$.255 = \frac{25\,1/2}{100} = 25{}^1/_2\%$$

$$.163 = \frac{16\,3/10}{100} = 16{}^3/_{10}\%$$

To change a fraction to a percent: (1) change the fraction to a decimal, and (2) express the decimal as hundredths. The result is the percent desired.

$$\begin{array}{llll}
{}^1/_2 = .5 & = .50 = 50\% & \quad {}^9/_{10} = .90 & = 90\% \\
{}^3/_4 = .75 & = 75\% & \quad {}^8/_9 = .88{}^8/_9 & = 88{}^8/_9\% \\
{}^2/_3 = .66{}^2/_3 & = 66{}^2/_3\% & \quad {}^7/_8 = .87{}^1/_2 & = 87{}^1/_2\%
\end{array}$$

OR

$$\begin{array}{ll}
{}^3/_4 = {}^3/_4 \text{ of } {}^{100}/_{100} = {}^{75}/_{100} = 75\% & \quad {}^1/_2 = {}^1/_2 \text{ of } {}^{100}/_{100} = {}^{50}/_{100} = 50\% \\
{}^2/_3 = {}^2/_3 \text{ of } {}^{100}/_{100} = \frac{66\,2/3}{100} = 66{}^2/_3\% & \quad {}^9/_{10} = {}^9/_{10} \text{ of } {}^{100}/_{100} = {}^{90}/_{100} = 90\%
\end{array}$$

TERMS USED IN CALCULATING PERCENTAGES

There are three major terms or quantities to consider in working with percentage: *base (principal), percentage rate,* and *amount.* When any two are given, the third can be calculated.

1.   The rule for *finding amount* if the base and rate are given is base

× rate = amount. If the down payment on a car costing $5,000 is 6%, how much is the down payment?

$5,000.00 = Base
$\underline{\times .06}$ = Percentage rate expressed as a decimal
$300.00 = Amount

2. The rule for *finding base* if the amount and rate are given is amount ÷ rate = base. Marie received interest of $16 on a savings account earning 4%. What was the base or principal on which the interest was calculated?

$\dfrac{\$16.00}{.04}$ $\dfrac{\text{Amount}}{\text{Rate}}$ = $400.00 Base

Betty bought a bracelet for $186; this amount included 4% sales tax. What was the net cost of the bracelet (the cost before the sales tax)?

$\dfrac{\text{Amount}}{1.00 \text{ plus rate}}$ $\dfrac{\$186.00}{1.04}$ = $178.85 (net cost)

3. The rule for *finding rate* if the amount and base are given is $\dfrac{\text{Amount}}{\text{Base}}$ = Rate. Andrew paid $120 interest on a loan of $1,000 for one year. What was the rate of interest paid by Andrew?

$\dfrac{\$120}{\$1,000} = \dfrac{\text{Amount}}{\text{Base}} = \dfrac{\$120}{\$1,000} = 0.12 = 12\%$ Rate

PROFIT AND LOSS

When an item is sold for more than it cost the seller, it is sold at a profit. If it is sold for less than the cost, it is sold at a loss. Therefore,

Profit = Selling Price − Cost Price
Loss = Cost Price − Selling Price

A profit or loss is generally figured as a percentage. It is always understood that the percentage is calculated on the cost price.

Example   You buy wheat at 60 cents and sell it for 75 cents. What is the percentage of gain?

Solution   The gain is the difference between 75 cents and 60 cents, or 15 cents; 15 cents is 25% of the cost. Therefore, you gain 25%.

That is   75 cents − 60 cents = 15 cents
15 cents ÷ 60 cents = .25 or 25%

Example   You bought flour at $3.50 a barrel. At what price must you sell it to gain 20%?

Solution   You must sell it for 100% of the cost plus 20% of the cost, or 120% of the cost.

120% of $3.50 = $4.20

Example   You sold your camera for 80% of its cost and received $90.00 for it. What was the cost?

Solution   1% of the cost is 1/80 of $90.00 or $1.125.

100% of the cost = 100 × $1.125 or $112.50

$$\frac{\$90.00}{.80} = \$112.50$$

INTEREST

When money is borrowed, interest is charged for the loan. The amount borrowed is called the *principal*. The amount paid for use of the money is called *interest*. Interest is calculated at a percentage rate per year.

Example   If you borrow $400.00 at 12% for one year, you will pay the lender $48.00 at the end of one year. One of the simplest ways of calculating interest uses 360 days as a business year. The formula is: principal × rate × time = interest.

Example   If you borrow $1,200.00 for 96 days at 12% interest, how much interest will you pay the bank at maturity?

$1,200.00 × $^{12}/_{100}$ × $^{96}/_{360}$ = $38.40

Index